INVENTION AND CRAFT

A Guide to College Writing

MLA Updated Edition

Ronda Leathers Dively

Southern Illinois University Carbondale

Mc
Graw
Hill
Education

INVENTION AND CRAFT: A GUIDE TO COLLEGE WRITING, MLA UPDATED EDITION

Published by McGraw-Hill Education, 2 Penn Plaza, New York, NY 10121. Copyright © 2016 by McGraw-Hill Education. All rights reserved. Printed in the United States of America. No part of this publication may be reproduced or distributed in any form or by any means, or stored in a database or retrieval system, without the prior written consent of McGraw-Hill Education, including, but not limited to, in any network or other electronic storage or transmission, or broadcast for distance learning.

Some ancillaries, including electronic and print components, may not be available to customers outside the United States.

This book is printed on acid-free paper.

1 2 3 4 5 6 7 8 9 LCR 21 20 19 18 17

ISBN 978-1-259-98866-0
MHID 1-259-98866-X

Senior Vice President, Products & Markets: *Kurt L. Strand*
Vice President, General Manager, Products & Markets: *Michael Ryan*
Vice President, Content Design & Delivery: *Kimberly Meriwether David*
Managing Director: *David S. Patterson*
Director: *Susan Gouijnstook*
Executive Brand Manager: *Claire Brantley*
Director, Product Development: *Meghan Campbell*
Senior Marketing Manager: *Brigeth Rivera*
Lead Product Developer: *Lisa Pinto*
Coordinator: *Lindsey Varghese*
Lead Digital Product Analyst: *Janet Smith*
Director, Content Design & Delivery: *Terri Schiesl*
Program Manager: *Jennifer Gehl*

Content Project Managers: *Diane L. Nowaczyk, Samantha Donisi-Hamm, Judi David*
Buyer: *Michael McCormick*
Design: *Debra Kubiak*
Content Licensing Specialist: *Lori Hancock*
Cover Image: *franckreporter/Getty Images*
Compositor: *Laserwords Private Limited*
Printer: *LSC Communications*

All credits appearing on page or at the end of the book are considered to be an extension of the copyright page.

Library of Congress Cataloging-in-Publication Data

Dively, Ronda Leathers.
   Invention and craft : a guide to college writing / Ronda Leathers Dively, Southern Illinois University-Carbondale.
   pages cm
   ISBN 978-0-07-340603-9 (alk. paper)
   1. English language—Rhetoric.   2. Report writing.   3. College readers.   I. Title.
   PE1408.D585 2015
   808'.042—dc23

                    2014038968

The Internet addresses listed in the text were accurate at the time of publication. The inclusion of a website does not indicate an endorsement by the authors or McGraw-Hill Education, and McGraw-Hill Education does not guarantee the accuracy of the information presented at these sites.

www.mhhe.com

DEDICATION

To my family

Brief Contents

Contents •

List of Readings, Myths, and Genre Diagrams

Readings by Chapter

Myth and Reality Boxes by Chapter

Genre Diagrams by Chapter

Flexible Text Format

- McGraw-Hill Education's CREATE allows instructors to build their own course material to perfectly match their course by selecting specific chapters from *Invention and Craft*. Instructors may also add readings from a wide range of collections or include their own content, such as syllabi, assignments, and course information. Finally, instructors may choose to offer their students a print or electronic version of their customized version of *Invention and Craft*.

Connect Composition

McGraw-Hill Education's *Connect Composition*® offers a wide array of tools for students and instructors:

- **SmartBook**®. SmartBook is the first and only adaptive reading experience designed to change the way students read and learn. Dively's *Invention and Craft* will be offered in the SmartBook format.
- **Writing Assignments.** Instructors can choose from a wide variety of customizable writing assignments, with intuitive instructor commenting and annotating capabilities.
- **LearnSmart Achieve**®. McGraw-Hill Education's newest adaptive learning environment offers modules on writing topics across the curriculum: Writing Processes, Critical Reading, the Research Process, Reasoning and Argument, Grammar and Common Sentence Problems, Punctuation and Mechanics, and Style and Word Choice, as well as a module for Multilingual Writers.
- **Power of Process.** This brand-new *Connect Composition* tool guides students through performance-based assessment activities that require them to apply active reading and writing strategies.
- **Simple LMS Integration.** *Connect Composition* seamlessly integrates with any learning management system. Instructors can quickly access registration, attendance, assignments, grades, and course resources in real time in one location.
- **Mobile Access.** Students can now access powerful *Connect Composition* study resources directly from their tablets and phones.

- **Tegrity.** Students can replay recordings of instructor lectures with this lecture-capture tool.
- **Connect Insight.** This analytics tool provides a series of visual data displays—each framed by an intuitive question—to provide instructors with at-a-glance information regarding how their classes are doing.
- **Outcomes-Based Assessment for Writing Assignments.** Instructors and administrators can incorporate their own custom learning outcomes into *Connect Composition*, creating a grading rubric for specific course outcomes and generating detailed reports for students, sections, or departments.
- **Four Years of Student Access.** Students benefit from this dependable writing and research resource throughout college, at a fraction of the cost of traditional textbooks.

Why *Invention and Craft?*

Invention and Craft: A Guide to College Writing offers a new approach to teaching and learning in the first-year writing classroom. *Invention and Craft* draws on the relationship between writing processes and the creative process model and teaches a problem-solving, insight-driven approach to writing clearly and effectively in all genres. Its emphasis on knowledge transfer instructs students to recognize the patterns that occur within and across genres and to apply what they know to each new writing assignment. *Invention and Craft* offers special promise for casting students in the role of meaning-makers by pinpointing strategies for transforming knowledge—the hallmark of successful expository prose.

The *Invention and Craft* Structural Framework

Building on her own scholarship about knowledge transfer, Ronda Leathers Dively has designed a leading-edge instructional framework that guides students through each step of their writing processes, from exercises that spur invention and insight to strategies for transferring their knowledge to new writing situations. Dively explicitly maps the similarities between expository writing and creative activity in other venues and invites students to write about their own creative and composing processes. Dively's creative approach demystifies the complexities of composition, thereby building students' confidence and energizing them to write.

Features of *Invention and Craft*

Invention and Craft offers innovation and flexibility with customizable content and a learning support system that reinforces the author's focus on creativity, reflection, and metacognition.

Together with the tools available in *Connect Composition, Invention and Craft* addresses the specific needs of the composition course:

■ **A flexible solution for the writing course.** In contrast to viewing all acts of writing as disparate, with no familiar points of departure, *Invention and Craft* acknowledges differences in both process and product, as well as applicability across multiple contexts. SmartBook provides students with an adaptive reading experience, assists them in long-term knowledge retention, and prepares them for active in-class participation and writing assignments that tap into students' creative impulses.

- **Multiple features that promote metacognitive skills.** *Invention and Craft* promotes reflection through writing activities at the end of each assignment chapter that invite students to write about their own creative and composing processes. By focusing on writing as a creative act, *Invention and Craft* promotes metacognitive skills and helps students understand that expository composition isn't as unfamiliar or intimidating as it may seem. LearnSmart Achieve prepares students to write in any situation by teaching the core topics in composition in an adaptive environment that promotes knowledge transfer.

- **A methodical approach that deconstructs common barriers to writing.** Students often arrive with a host of preconceptions about writers and writing that undermine their capacity for mastering college-level writing challenges. *Invention and Craft* identifies and dispels common misconceptions in *Myth and Reality* boxes placed at strategic points throughout the text.
  Each assignment chapter features *A Look Inside,* a carefully annotated sample reading exemplifying the genre in focus. *A Look Inside* walks students through each genre, identifying rhetorical patterns and strategies that students can transfer to their own reading and writing activities.

MYTH

"I don't need a composition course. My career plans won't require me to write."

The first problem with this statement is that most every career involves some sort of writing, even if only in the form of data charts or business-related communications with employers or colleagues. The second problem is that it implies that your goals won't change. At some point you'll likely consider switching careers or specific jobs within a given profession. If that different path is more dependent on writing skills and you have failed to transfer what your writing course had to offer, you may be restricted in following your dreams or advancing your career.

REALITY

A LOOK INSIDE: ANALYZING A DREAM

From *The Interpretation of Dreams*

by Sigmund Freud

It often happens that matter appears in the dream content which one cannot recognise later in the waking state as belonging to one's knowledge and experience. One remembers well enough having dreamed about the subject in question, but cannot recall the fact or time of the experience. The dreamer is therefore in the dark as to the source from which the dream has been drawing, and is even tempted to believe an independently productive activity on the part of the dream, until, often long afterwards, a new episode brings back to recollection a former experience given up as lost, and thus reveals the sou

Freud introduces his analysis by indicating his interpretive lens: a pattern he's noticed in the way dreams pull "forgotten" experiences from the subconscious.

- **A fresh approach to writing processes.** *Invention and Craft* takes a fresh approach to writing processes. Chapter 2 focuses on the interplay between writing process and creative process models. By gaining an understanding of the recursive nature of writing processes, students begin to see that all writing is creative. Chapters 3, 4, and 5 cover the foundational concepts students need to approach any writing assignment, from employing rhetorical strategies to engaging in invention and research. Twelve assignment chapters feature illustrations of genres that inform, analyze, and argue. These illustrations engage visual learners with the abstract concepts that support writing in every genre.

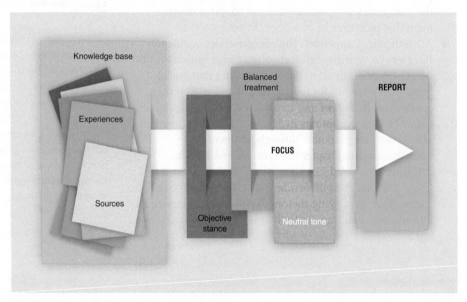

Figure 9.2 Some key features of a report. Reports focus on explaining some aspect of the current knowledge base on a topic. As this figure illustrates, an objective stance, balanced treatment, and neutral tone are key features of this genre.

Each assignment chapter closes with a focused discussion of how students can transfer their knowledge of key elements of that genre to other writing situations. With *Invention and Craft,* students learn to approach each new writing assignment equipped with the skills and strategies acquired from previous writing tasks, effectively transferring their knowledge from one assignment to the next.

- **An abundance of opportunities to practice skills.** *Invention and Craft* provides students with extensive practice of reading and writing skills through invention exercises and strategies for drafting, as well as more comprehensive activities at the end of each chapter. Built off the proven *LearnSmart* engine that identifies what a student does or does not know and adapts in real time to maximize each minute of time spent learning the material, the SmartBook for *Invention and Craft* contains four stages: Preview, Read, Practice, and Recharge. Starting with an initial preview of each chapter and key learning objectives, students read the material and are guided to topics that need the most practice on the basis of their responses. In this way, students engage with the text as it prepares them to respond to various writing situations.

ACTIVITY

Considering the Rhetoric of Fashion Human beings communicate through various media, many of them visual in nature, such as clothing. Locate a picture (like the one of Lady Gaga in Figure 14.5) that depicts someone who is clearly sending a message through his or her fashion choices. Using whatever rhetorical elements or appeals seem most applicable, analyze this person's fashion statement.

IDEA FOR EXTENDED WRITING

Rhetorically Analyzing a Published Essay Think of a document you recently read that really frustrated you, angered you, made you want to cry, excited you, motivated you to take action, made you proud to be a part of something, caused you to admire somebody or some institution, or caused you to view something differently than you viewed it before. (If you can't remember an article that had a strong impact on you, search for one relevant to an issue that really interests you.) Once you have a copy of that article in hand, read it again (and again), paying attention not only to what the author said about the topic but also to the way he or she said it. Apply the tools of rhetorical analysis to help you understand how the author appears to use rhetorical elements and appeals to influence his or her intended audience. Share your conclusions in a formal rhetorical analysis targeted for members of that audience.

Figure 14.5 **Lady Gaga using fashion to make a "statement"**

Why a Digital Solution for Writing Courses?

Connect Composition and *LearnSmart Achieve* ensure that students learn the core topics of composition in a personalized system that identifies what they already know while providing direct instruction on unfamiliar concepts. This integrated system constantly adapts and changes as it learns more about each student—the student's strengths as well as knowledge gaps. McGraw-Hill Education's digital tools provide the kind of support instructors need to focus class time on the highest course expectations while helping students establish themselves as critical thinkers, communicate their ideas effectively, and transfer these skills to different courses and assignments throughout their college experience.

Connect Composition offers **four years of access** to comprehensive, reliable writing and research instruction. The following tools and services are available as part of *Connect Composition*.

Feature	Description	Instructional Value
Simple LMS Integration	• Seamlessly integrates with every learning management system.	• Students have automatic single sign-on. • *Connect* assignment results sync to the LMS gradebook.
LearnSmart Achieve	• Continuously adapts to a student's strengths and weaknesses to create personalized learning moments. • Covers Writing Processes, Critical Reading, the Research Process, Reasoning and Argument, Multilingual Writers, Grammar and Common Sentence Problems, Punctuation and Mechanics, and Style and Word Choice. • Provides reports for instructors, with data on student and class performance.	• Students independently study the fundamental topics across Composition 1 and 2 in an adaptive environment. • Metacognitive component supports knowledge transfer. • Students track their own understanding and mastery and know where their gaps are.
SmartBook	• *Available for rhetorics*, the first and only continuously adaptive reading experience that identifies and highlights the topics a student has not mastered. • Provides reports for instructors, with data on student and class performance.	• The text adapts to the student on the basis of what he or she knows and doesn't know and focuses study time on critical material. • Metacognitive component supports knowledge transfer. • Students track their own understanding and mastery and know where their gaps are.
Power of Process	Guides students through the critical reading and writing process step-by-step.	• Students demonstrate understanding and develop critical-thinking skills for reading, writing, and evaluating sources by responding to short-answer and annotation questions. Students are also prompted to reflect on their own processes. • This tool guides students to consider a source carefully.
Insight	Provides a quick view of student and class performance with a series of visual data displays that provide analysis on the following: 1. How are my students doing? 2. How is this student doing? 3. How is my section doing? 4. How is this assignment doing? 5. How are my assignments doing?	Instructors can quickly check on student and class performance.
Writing Assignments with Peer Review	• Allows instructors to assign and grade writing assignments online. • Enables instructors to easily and efficiently set up and manage peer review assignments for the entire class. • Allows students to highlight and comment on their classmates' writing submissions in response to peer review questions assigned by their instructor.	• This feature makes grading writing assignments more efficient, saving time for instructors. • Students import their Word document(s), and instructors can comment and annotate submissions. • Frequently used comments are automatically saved, so instructors do not have to type the same thing over and over. • Students can download all comments made by their peers to use as a reference when rewriting their assignment.
Outcomes-Based Assessment Tool	• Allows instructors or course administrators to assess student writing on the basis of specific learning outcomes. • Generates easy-to-read reports on program-specific learning outcomes. • Includes the Writing Program Administrators learning outcomes or allows you to create your own.	• This tool provides assessment transparency to students. They can see why a "B" is a "B" and what it will take to improve to an "A." • Reports allow a program or instructor to demonstrate progress against section, course, or program goals.
Connect eReader	Provides access to additional readings that are assignable via *Connect Composition*.	Sample essays provide models for students on writing.

Feature	Description	Instructional Value
Instructor Reports	• Enables review of the performance of an individual student or an entire section. • Enables review of multiple sections to gauge progress toward course, department, or institutional goals.	• Instructors can identify struggling students early and intervene to ensure retention. • Instructors can identify challenging topics and adjust instruction accordingly. • Reports can be generated for an accreditation process or program evaluation.
Pretests and Posttests	Provides precreated nonadaptive assessments for pre- and posttesting.	Pretest provides a static benchmark for student knowledge at the beginning of the program. Posttest offers a concluding assessment of student progress.

Spotlight on Three Tools in *Connect*

LearnSmart Achieve   *LearnSmart Achieve* helps learners establish a baseline understanding of the language and concepts that make up the critical processes of composition—writing, critical reading, research, reasoning and argument, grammar, mechanics, and style, as well as issues surrounding multilingual writers.

UNIT	TOPIC	
THE WRITING PROCESS	The Writing Process Generating Ideas Planning and Organizing	Drafting Revising Proofreading, Formatting, and Producing Texts
CRITICAL READING	Reading to Understand Literal Meaning Evaluating Truth and Accuracy in a Text	Evaluating the Effectiveness and Appropriateness of a Text
THE RESEARCH PROCESS	Developing and Implementing a Research Plan Evaluating Information and Sources	Integrating Source Material into a Text Using Information Ethically and Legally
REASONING AND ARGUMENT	Developing an Effective Thesis or Claim Using Evidence and Reasoning to Support a Thesis or Claim	Using Ethos (Ethics) to Persuade Readers Using Pathos (Emotion) to Persuade Readers Using Logos (Logic) to Persuade Readers
GRAMMAR AND COMMON SENTENCE PROBLEMS	Parts of Speech Phrases, Clauses, and Fragments Sentence Types Fused (Run-on) Sentences and Comma Splices Pronouns Pronoun-Antecedent Agreement	Pronoun Reference Subject-Verb Agreement Verbs and Verbals Adjectives and Adverbs Dangling and Misplaced Modifiers Mixed Constructions Verb Tense and Voice Shifts
PUNCTUATION AND MECHANICS	Commas Semicolons Colons End Punctuation Apostrophes Quotation Marks Dashes	Parentheses Hyphens Abbreviations Capitalization Italics Numbers Spelling
STYLE AND WORD CHOICE	Wordiness Eliminating Redundancies and Sentence Variety Coordination and Subordination	Faulty Comparisons Word Choice Clichés, Slang, and Jargon Parallelism
MULTILINGUAL WRITERS	Helping Verbs, Gerunds and Infinitives, and Phrasal Verbs Nouns, Verbs, and Objects Articles	Count and Noncount Nouns Sentence Structure and Word Order Verb Agreement Participles and Adverb Placement

LearnSmart Achieve is one of the adaptive learning tools offered in *Connect Composition.*

Outcomes-Based Assessment of Writing Writing assignments with Outcomes-Based Assessment provide a way for any instructor to grade a writing assignment using a rubric of outcomes and proficiency levels. The Writing Program Administrators (WPA) outcomes are preloaded; however, instructors may adapt any of these outcomes or use their own. Instructors or administrators may choose to share specific outcomes with other instructors or the whole department. Writing Assignments with Outcomes-Based Assessment offer a range of clear, simple reports that allow instructors or course administrators to view progress and achievement in a variety of ways. These reports may also satisfy department or college-level requests for data relating to program goals or for accreditation purposes.

The *Outcomes-Based Assessment* tool offers a range of clear, simple reports that allow instructors to view progress and achievement in a variety of ways.

Power of Process   *Power of Process* is the newest tool in *Connect Composition*. *Power of Process* provides strategies that guide students through how to critically read a piece of writing or consider it as a possible source for incorporation into their own work. After they work through the strategies, which include highlighting and

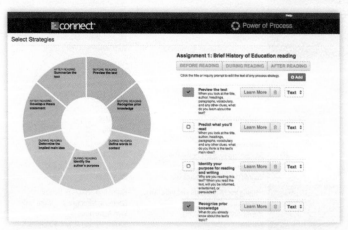

Power of Process provides strategies that guide students in reading critically.

annotating a piece of writing, students are encouraged to reflect on their interaction with the reading. Students can print out a summary of their work to use with other projects or to submit alongside their own assignment for grading.

Connect Composition Reports

Connect Composition generates a number of powerful reports and charts that allow instructors to quickly review the performance of a specific student, an entire section, or various sections. Students have their own set of reports (which include only their individual performance) that can demonstrate at a glance where they are doing well and where they are struggling. Here are a few of the reports that are available:

- *Assignment Results Report*—shows an entire section's performance across all assignments.
- *Assignment Statistics Report*—provides quick data on each assignment, including mean score as well as high and low scores.
- *Student Performance Report*—focuses on a specific student's progress across all assignments.
- *Learning Outcomes Assessment Report*—for instructors who use the Outcomes-Based Assessment tool to grade a writing assignment, this report provides data on student performance for specific outcomes.
- *At-Risk Report*—provides instructors a dashboard of information that can help identify at-risk students on the basis of low engagement levels.
- *LearnSmart Achieve Reports*—focus on student usage, progress, and mastery of the modules contained within *LearnSmart Achieve*.

Support for Digital Success

McGraw-Hill Education provides a variety of ways for instructors to get the help and support they need when incorporating new technology into a writing program. The digital tools in *Connect* were developed by experts to create a teaching and learning environment that engages learners with a wide variety of course assignments, suited for online as well as hybrid or face-to-face courses. New users of *Connect* have several options for assistance in setting up courses initially as well as throughout the first term:

- **Digital Faculty Consultants.** Instructors currently using *Connect Composition* are available to offer suggestions, advice, and training for new adopters. To request a Digital Faculty Consultant's assistance, simply e-mail your local McGraw-Hill representative.
- **Learning Technology Consultants.** Local McGraw-Hill Education representatives can provide face-to-face training and support. Find your local rep at **mhhe .com/rep.**
- **Digital Learning Consultants.** These specialists in the field are available to support instructors with initial setup and training as well as answer questions that may arise throughout the term. DLCs may be contacted directly or by simply asking your local McGraw-Hill Education representative.

- **Digital Success Team.** Team members offer one-on-one training to instructors to demonstrate how *Connect* works while also providing information and guidance on how to incorporate *Connect* into a specific course design and syllabus. Ask for a session with a Team Member by writing to your local McGraw-Hill Education representative.
- **National Training Webinars.** McGraw-Hill Education offers an ongoing series of webinars for instructors to learn and master the *Connect* platform as well as its course-specific tools and features. New webinars are being scheduled all the time, so be sure to check the online catalog of courses at **webinars.mhhe.com/**.

In general, instructors are encouraged to contact us anytime they need help. Our Customer Support Team is available at 800-331-5094 or online at **mhhe.com/ contact.php.**

Need a *Connect* Account?

Request access to *Connect Composition* from your local McGraw-Hill Education representative (**www.mhhe.com/rep**) or write to **english@mheducation.com**. If you have an account already, log in at **http://connect.mheducation.com/**.

Professor Ronda Leathers Dively received her Bachelor of Arts degree in English (with teacher certification) and her Master of Arts degree in English (literature) from Eastern Illinois University. After gaining a few years of teaching experience in the secondary English classroom, she pursued her Doctor of Arts degree in English (Rhetoric and Composition) at Illinois State University, completing her degree in 1994 and accepting an assistant professorship in the English Department at Southern Illinois University Carbondale that same year. Currently an associate professor at SIUC, Dr. Dively serves as the Director of Writing Studies for the Department of English and teaches in the Rhetoric and Composition program. Her areas of teaching specialization include composition pedagogy, empirical research methods, intermediate and advanced composition, and classical rhetoric. She has also enjoyed teaching special topics courses that explore intersections between creativity theory and composition theory. Professor Dively's scholarship investigates how intersections of creativity and composition theory may illuminate how individuals negotiate transitions between various academic composing contexts—from high school to college classrooms, from general education to discipline-specific writing courses, from status as undergraduate student to graduate student, from status as graduate student to professional. Such interests generated a book-length empirical study entitled *Preludes to Insight: Creativity, Incubation and Expository Writing* (Hampton Press, 2006), as well as various articles and conference presentations. She has also published in the areas of knowledge transfer and religious expression.

A Letter from the Author

As writers and as teachers of writing, we share many goals for our composition students. We want them to establish themselves as critical thinkers, we want them to be able to communicate their ideas as effectively as possible, and we want them to learn how they can transfer these skills across assignments and into subsequent courses. Additionally, although it might seem too much to hope for, we want them to own and enjoy their writing—to view it as the fulfilling, creative activity that we know it is. With these objectives in mind, I decided to write a textbook that would bring together concepts and materials at the foundation of various undergraduate composition courses I've taught over the past 20-some years. In its pages, I hope novice instructors will find guidance for engaging their first-year students, I hope master teachers will find fresh inspiration, and I hope students will find motivation for further developing their writing abilities.

Invention and Craft: A Guide to College Writing is, in part, a response to teachers and students who question the long-standing divide between types of writing completed for composition courses and types of writing more commonly referred to as "creative" (i.e., poetry and fiction). While acknowledging that genres constituting both categories differ in certain ways, this textbook also works to underscore similarities, emphasizing that, anytime someone is preoccupied with writing, he or she is being creative. To be more specific, neither expository nor creative writing is necessarily more rigid or more free—nor are the respective genres associated with each. Rather, all genres are subject to constraints and opportunities that require active minds to grapple with the processes involved in generating text, the elements of the rhetorical situation, and the status of formal conventions. Ultimately, by emphasizing features that all kinds of writing have in common, alongside the distinctions between genres that enable access to diverse communities, acts of composing can be demystified and pathways for confidence building and knowledge transfer can be opened.

Commonalities between acts of composing—in fact, between composing and a multitude of other activities—are elucidated in this textbook through the lens of creativity theory, which clarifies various practices and habits of mind that result in contributions to a given field. Such contributions may come in the form of new discoveries, novel perspectives, or unique combinations of existing information. It is this goal of making a contribution through writing that leads to the focus on invention indicated in the title. As this textbook asserts, extended time on and attention to invention are crucial to successful writing, perhaps more crucial than many composition classrooms and textbooks demonstrate. Through a chapter devoted to intersections between composing processes and creative processes, as well as through discussions of process within its 12 genre chapters, *Invention and Craft* elaborates the paradigmatic composing model by juxtaposing it with the paradigmatic creative process model, the latter revealing how to break invention into a number of subprocesses so as to render it more manageable for developing writers.

Also crucial to successful writing, as it emphasizes commonalities between acts of composing, is attention to knowledge transfer. The call to help students transfer what they are learning requires anticipating which processes, strategies, and skills that they are applying in one context will be applicable in other contexts that they are likely to encounter. *Invention and Craft* alerts students to the need for transfer through an extended discussion in Chapter 2 and, then, by explaining—with regard to each of the 12 genres addressed in later chapters—which processes, strategies, and skills they can readily carry to other academic and professional contexts.

For all of the boundary breaking, demystifying, and commonality marking that *Invention and Craft* aspires to, it does not take for granted that students will be easily dazzled by what may strike them as a more amenable approach to writing than they've grown accustomed to. In fact, this textbook begins from the premise that many students resist composition courses for one reason or another. Relevant to this premise, it adopts a tone of "straight talk" about the frustrations that many students associate with school-sponsored writing, as well as the (sometimes) institutionally imposed sources of those frustrations. Contributing to this tone is one of the textbook's most notable features: A series of Myth and Reality boxes, which tackle some of the "rules" for writing that students have picked up along the way to their first-year composition classrooms but have later found (or needed to be told) do not hold true across all times or circumstances. Each box succinctly articulates a given myth and then provides a more accurate way of viewing (i.e., articulates the reality surrounding) the myth in question.

As a long-time teacher of college composition, a writing program administrator responsible for preparing other composition teachers, and an individual who loves writing, I've grown ever-more committed to meeting students where they are (not where I think they should be) as I challenge them toward greater achievements. This is the case not only in terms of writing ability but with regard to their attitudes toward and assumptions about writing. Of course, some students entering our classrooms love writing, but even they may hold some erroneous views about it. I believe that by addressing students' attitudes and assumptions up front and head on, teachers establish an ethos that stands a good chance of undermining anxiety, frustration, and resistance, thereby helping students to become more self-assured, successful writers.

Ronda Leathers Dively
Southern Illinois University Carbondale
rldively@siu.edu

Acknowledgments

When I began writing this book, I couldn't imagine how much effort and support it would require from so many people. I'd written a book before, but not a textbook. Naively, I didn't anticipate the extent and layers of collaboration that would be required to carry out such a project. I'm indebted to so many people that it's difficult to know where to begin my list of acknowledgments. Following the lead, then, of other textbook authors, I will begin with the project's origins—the classrooms in which I generated and refined my pedagogical approach. Without the first-year composition students I've had the joy of working with across the past 20-plus years and the graduate students who have listened and responded to my ideas about teaching, this textbook would not exist. Along these lines, I would like to thank my Composition and Rhetoric colleagues at SIUC, Dr. Lisa J. McClure and Dr. Jane Cogie, for their wise counsel and for assisting me in all the ways that great colleagues do when another is involved in a strenuous project.

I'd also like to thank my McGraw-Hill team— Lisa Pinto, Claire Brantley, and Elizabeth Murphy— who were instrumental in refining the initial vision for this textbook. Their sage advice and the resources they provided helped ease my load, keeping the pace of this project on track. Special appreciation goes to Elizabeth Murphy, my development editor, who is a wonderful person to work with. Smart, kind, conscientious, hardworking, humorous, calming, and generous with her time—all authors should be so fortunate to work with an editor like Elizabeth. Of course, there are many other individuals who have contributed to this textbook, including research, design, and marketing experts at McGraw-Hill Education and numerous writing instructors across the country who have reviewed my work.

The remaining paragraphs of acknowledgment are reserved for those I've always turned to first for guidance and support—my family. I can always depend on them for everything I need and more. First, I want to thank my late mother-in-law, Joyce Dively, a former high school English teacher whose genuine interest in and enthusiasm for my scholarship was displayed every time we were able to visit. Her excitement kept me excited. I want to thank my brother, Lee Leathers, his wife, Jackie, and their children, Luke and Ben, not only for their interest in my work but for being such all-around positive influences in my life. My mother, Mary Sue Leathers, one of the most selfless, uplifting people I know—as well as a former successful businesswoman—was always available for a pep talk whenever the weight of this project became a bit overwhelming. My father, Ronald M. Leathers, a former English professor and long-time Higher Education administrator, provided not only constant moral support but also helpful discipline-specific advice in response to early drafts of many chapters constituting this textbook.

On a final note, research reveals that an essential condition for creativity is a supportive life partner, one who willingly gives the time, space, and practical assistance essential for someone involved in intense and demanding artistic/intellectual work. My husband, John A. Dively, Jr., an attorney and professor of Educational Leadership, is the model for that kind of partner. His generosity, patience, emotional support, and assistance with my invention processes were more significant to the completion of this project than could possibly be articulated in a brief acknowledgment. He even did most of the cooking for the past three years and proofread turnover drafts of every chapter! Thank you for everything, John.

Content Consultants and Reviewers

We are indebted to the reviewers who devoted time to reading drafts of chapters, responding to design samples, and participating in live reviews. Their honest reactions have proved invaluable as we shaped every detail of the plans for this first edition. I wish to thank the following instructors:

Alabama Southern Community College Melinda Byrd-Murphy, Samantha Frye

Alamance Community College Susan Dalton, Anne Helms

Alvin Community College Ann Guess

Arapahoe Community College Lindsey Lewan, Josie Mills, Jamey Trotter

Arizona Western College–Yuma Jana Moore, Steve Moore

Arkansas State University–Beebe Sheila Chase, Vivian Walters

Brigham Young University–Idaho Glenn Dayley

Brookdale Community College Nancy Noe

Broward Community College Jason Vinson

Campbellsville University Sarah Stafford

Cedar Valley College Rebekah Rios-Harris

Charleston Southern University Craig Barto

Chesapeake College Eleanor Welsh

Cisco College Kimberly Wombles

College of Coastal Georgia Stephanie Conner, Anna Dewart, Jennifer Gray, David Mulry

Community College of Baltimore County–Catonsville Brooke Bognanni, Evan Balkan, Monica Walker

Community College of Denver Kristi Strother

Davidson County Community College Jennifer Boyle, Mark Branson

Dixie State University Randy Jasmine

Eastern Washington University–Cheney Polly Buckingham, Timothy Roe

El Centro College Devarani Arumugam

El Paso Community College Gloria Estrada

El Paso Community College–Valle Verde Campus Margie Nelson Rodriguez, Roberto Santos

Frederick University Kenneth Kerr

Georgia Southwestern State University Elizabeth Kuipers

Greenville Technical College Andrew Block

Guilford Tech Community College–Jamestown Jo Ann Buck

Hampton University Paula Barnes

High Point University William Carpenter

Hocking College Susan Fletcher

Horry-Georgetown Technical College Kimberly Britt, Michael Hedges, Rebecca Hubbard, Alyssa Johnson

Ivy Tech Community College–Northwest Jared Riddle

Joliet Junior College Tamara Brattoli, Adam Heidenreich, Stacey Murphy

Kankakee Community College Linsey Cuti

Lake Superior College Kelli Hallsten Erickson

Macomb Community College–Center Campus Linda Brender, Ludger Brinker

Monroe Community College Lloyd Milburn

North Central Texas College Kristen Weinzapfel

Northeast Lakeview College Anetia Port

Ohio University–Athens Albert Rouzie, David Sharpe

Oklahoma State University–Stillwater Campus Ron Brooks

Old Dominion University Matt Oliver

Saddleback College Marina Aminy

Salt Lake Community College Ron Christiansen, Brittany Stephenson

Samford University Kathy Flowers, Lynette M. Sandley

San Jose State University Kelly Harrison

Southern Illinois University–Edwardsville Matthew Johnson, Anushiya Ramaswamy

Southwestern Assemblies of God University D'Juana Montgomery

St. Philip's College John Moran

Triton College Alexandra Dragin, Lesa Hildebrand, Bill Nedrow

Truckee Meadows Community College Bridgett Blaque

University of Arkansas Community College–Hope Ashli Dykes

University of Cincinnati Clermont College Kim Jacobs-Beck

University of Idaho–Moscow Diane Kelly-Riley

University of Montana Amy Ratto-Parks

University of Nevada–Reno Mark Bousquet, Chris Field, Candace Hull Taylor

University of North Alabama Anissa Graham, Christa Raney

University of Rhode Island–Kingston Jeremiah Dyehouse

University of Toledo Anthony Edgington

University of Wisconsin–La Crosse Susan Crutchfield

Washburn University Melanie Burdick

Wayne State University Jeff Pruchnic

Weatherford College Diann Ainsworth

Western Iowa Technical Community College Helen Lewis

WPA Outcomes Statement for First-Year Composition

Introduction

This Statement identifies outcomes for first-year composition programs in U.S. postsecondary education. It describes the writing knowledge, practices, and attitudes that undergraduate students develop in first-year composition, which at most schools is a required general education course or sequence of courses. This Statement therefore attempts to both represent and regularize writing programs' priorities for first-year composition, which often takes the form of one or more required general education courses. To this end it is not merely a compilation or summary of what currently takes place. Rather, this Statement articulates what composition teachers nationwide have learned from practice, research, and theory.[*] It intentionally defines only "outcomes," or types of results, and not "standards," or precise levels of achievement. The setting of standards to measure students' achievement of these outcomes has deliberately been left to local writing programs and their institutions.

In this Statement "composing" refers broadly to complex writing processes that are increasingly reliant on the use of digital technologies. Writers also attend to elements of design, incorporating images and graphical elements into texts intended for screens as well as printed pages. Writers' composing activities have always been shaped by the technologies available to them, and digital technologies are changing writers' relationships to their texts and audiences in evolving ways.

These outcomes are supported by a large body of research demonstrating that the process of learning to write in any medium is complex: It is both individual and social and demands continued practice and informed guidance. Programmatic decisions about helping students demonstrate these outcomes should be informed by an understanding of this research.

As students move beyond first-year composition, their writing abilities do not merely improve. Rather, their abilities will diversify along disciplinary, professional, and civic lines as these writers move into new settings where expected outcomes expand, multiply, and diverge. Therefore, this document advises faculty in all disciplines about how to help students build on what they learn in introductory writing courses.

---

[*] This Statement was amended by the Council of Writing Program Administrators (WPA) in July 2014. For further information on its development, please see http://wpacouncil.org/positions/outcomes.html. This Statement is aligned with the *Framework for Success in Postsecondary Writing,* an articulation of the skills and habits of mind essential for success in college, and is intended to help establish a continuum of valued practice from high school through to the college major.

Rhetorical Knowledge

Rhetorical knowledge is the ability to analyze contexts and audiences and then to act on that analysis in comprehending and creating texts. Rhetorical knowledge is the basis of composing. Writers develop rhetorical knowledge by negotiating purpose, audience, context, and conventions as they compose a variety of texts for different situations.

By the end of first-year composition, students should:

■ Learn and use key rhetorical concepts through analyzing and composing a variety of texts
■ Gain experience reading and composing in several genres to understand how genre conventions shape and are shaped by readers' and writers' practices and purposes
■ Develop facility in responding to a variety of situations and contexts calling for purposeful shifts in voice, tone, level of formality, design, medium, and/or structure
■ Understand and use a variety of technologies to address a range of audiences
■ Match the capacities of different environments (e.g., print and electronic) to varying rhetorical situations

Faculty in all programs and departments can build on this preparation by helping students learn:

■ The expectations of readers in their fields
■ The main features of genres in their fields
■ The main purposes of composing in their fields

Critical Thinking, Reading, and Composing

Critical thinking is the ability to analyze, synthesize, interpret, and evaluate ideas, information, situations, and texts. When writers think critically about the materials they use—whether print texts, photographs, data sets, videos, or other materials—they separate assertion from evidence, evaluate sources and evidence, recognize and evaluate underlying assumptions, read across texts for connections and patterns, identify and evaluate chains of reasoning, and compose appropriately qualified and developed claims and generalizations. These practices are foundational for advanced academic writing.

By the end of first-year composition, students should:

■ Use composing and reading for inquiry, learning, critical thinking, and communicating in various rhetorical contexts
■ Read a diverse range of texts, attending especially to relationships between assertion and evidence, to patterns of organization, to the interplay between

verbal and nonverbal elements, and to how these features function for different audiences and situations
- Locate and evaluate (for credibility, sufficiency, accuracy, timeliness, bias, and so on) primary and secondary research materials, including journal articles and essays, books, scholarly and professionally established and maintained databases or archives, and informal electronic networks and Internet sources
- Use strategies—such as interpretation, synthesis, response, critique, and design/redesign—to compose texts that integrate the writer's ideas with those from appropriate sources

Faculty in all programs and departments can build on this preparation by helping students learn:

- The kinds of critical thinking important in their disciplines
- The kinds of questions, problems, and evidence that define their disciplines
- Strategies for reading a range of texts in their fields

Processes

Writers use multiple strategies, or *composing processes,* to conceptualize, develop, and finalize projects. Composing processes are seldom linear: A writer may research a topic before drafting and then conduct additional research while revising or after consulting a colleague. Composing processes are also flexible: Successful writers can adapt their composing processes to different contexts and occasions.

By the end of first-year composition, students should:

- Develop a writing project through multiple drafts
- Develop flexible strategies for reading, drafting, reviewing, collaborating, revising, rewriting, rereading, and editing
- Use composing processes and tools as a means to discover and reconsider ideas
- Experience the collaborative and social aspects of writing processes
- Learn to give and to act on productive feedback to works in progress
- Adapt composing processes for a variety of technologies and modalities
- Reflect on the development of composing practices and how those practices influence their work

Faculty in all programs and departments can build on this preparation by helping students learn:

- To employ the methods and technologies commonly used for research and communication within their fields
- To develop projects using the characteristic processes of their fields
- To review work in progress for the purpose of developing ideas before surface-level editing
- To participate effectively in collaborative processes typical of their field

Knowledge of Conventions

Conventions are the formal rules and informal guidelines that define genres, and in so doing, shape readers' and writers' perceptions of correctness or appropriateness. Most obviously, conventions govern such things as mechanics, usage, spelling, and citation practices. But they also influence content, style, organization, graphics, and document design.

Conventions arise from a history of use and facilitate reading by invoking common expectations between writers and readers. These expectations are not universal; they vary by genre (conventions for lab notebooks and discussion-board exchanges differ), by discipline (conventional moves in literature reviews in Psychology differ from those in English), and by occasion (meeting minutes and executive summaries use different registers). A writer's grasp of conventions in one context does not mean a firm grasp in another. Successful writers understand, analyze, and negotiate conventions for purpose, audience, and genre, understanding that genres evolve in response to changes in material conditions and composing technologies and attending carefully to emergent conventions.

By the end of first-year composition, students should:

- Develop knowledge of linguistic structures, including grammar, punctuation, and spelling, through practice in composing and revising
- Understand why genre conventions for structure, paragraphing, tone, and mechanics vary
- Gain experience negotiating variations in genre conventions
- Learn common formats and/or design features for different kinds of texts
- Explore the concepts of intellectual property (such as fair use and copyright) that motivate documentation conventions
- Practice applying citation conventions systematically in their own work

Faculty in all programs and departments can build on this preparation by helping students learn:

- The reasons behind conventions of usage, specialized vocabulary, format, and citation systems in their fields or disciplines
- Strategies for controlling conventions in their fields or disciplines
- Factors that influence the ways work is designed, documented, and disseminated in their fields
- Ways to make informed decisions about intellectual property issues connected to common genres and modalities in their fields

Composition and Creativity

Which of these activities is the most creative? Your immediate reaction is to say "painting," right? If so, why? Is it the colors? Is it the freedom of expression? Maybe it's the simple fact that common usage associates creativity with the fine arts. Regardless, many psychologists and educators—those who study human thought processes—operate by a broader definition of the concept, one that views painting, scientific research, and even academic and professional writing as creative processes. They do so on the grounds that all of these activities involve problem solving with the goal of making meaning or some contribution to a given field. This chapter elaborates on that perspective, suggesting how and why viewing all writing as creative can assist you in negotiating the challenges it presents and in applying or transferring your knowledge about writing to various composing situations.

Some students entering college love to write, and they approach any course that involves writing with a sense of excitement. If this description fits you, it may be that you've already realized how writing supports your personal and academic goals. If it doesn't, you may be hesitant about taking a required first-year composition

1

course—and you would not be alone. In fact, even students who like to write may harbor a reservation or two about composition courses. Understanding the sources of these reservations can help you overcome them, which is a significant step in learning to express yourself effectively in writing.

Some Straight Talk about Composition Courses

Reservations about composition courses stem from a variety of sources. One possibility is the belief that your future plans won't require you to write very often and, when they do, the products will be short and require little effort. Although this belief may be dispelled only with time and experience, some of the following observations about the four realms of writing depicted in Figure 1.1 may ring true, even as you are just beginning your college career. Related to these four realms, college composition courses seek to increase your understanding of how writing well can help you succeed in all areas of your life, and that understanding will grow as you progress through college, search for a job, and become part of a work community.

Relevant to these goals, improving your writing ability will require time and effort. To be sure, most college composition courses will present you with new and complex assignments intended to challenge your abilities and thereby strengthen them. These assignments will call upon you to devote several hours each week outside class to various reading and writing activities. This is all part of the sustained study and practice that composition courses are designed to promote as they introduce you to the productive routines of experienced writers, such as researching, revising, and editing.

Committing time and effort to your composition course, as well as assuming its relevance to your future success, can ease the transition to college-level writing; but these mindsets won't necessarily erase the anxieties that writing sometimes provokes, even in those who write for a living. In fact, **writing anxiety** is more

Personal Realm

Writing enriches and supports your daily life and prepares you for much of the writing that you do for more public purposes.

Civic Realm

Writing is crucial to rectifying wrongs in your community and to participating in the political life of your country.

Academic Realm

Writing offers the practical benefit of helping you earn a degree, along with the more charitable benefit of contributing knowledge to the world.

Professional Realm

Writing is essential in helping you secure and maintain a job and in achieving the mission of your institution or company.

Figure 1.1 **Four realms of writing and their significance**

common than you probably imagine, and it takes various forms: a general nervousness regarding any kind of writing, frustration with certain types of assignments, or isolated tension relevant to a specific problem within a text. Whatever its form, the causes of writing anxiety may include:

- A lack of experience with a particular kind of writing or writing challenge
- A past writing course in which you felt you didn't or couldn't learn anything
- Past criticism that bred insecurity about your writing abilities
- A fear of sharing your writing with others
- The impression that your peers find writing easy while you have to labor over it

If you do experience writing anxiety, whether periodic or ongoing, sharing your concerns will reveal common points of struggle with other writers and will help your instructor and your peers learn how to best support your composing processes.

Another source of resistance to composition courses is the opinion that writing is just plain boring. There is little doubt that everyone has felt bored by a writing assignment at one time or another, but for some individuals, the lack of excitement is chronic. If you have ever felt this way, the impression could have resulted from any number of factors. Maybe your past experiences led you to view writing as a confining exercise in which there is a "right" way of responding to every composing situation. Maybe you find nit-picking over surface concerns such as spelling and punctuation to be tedious. Regardless of the causes for low motivation, a principal challenge for writers in any composing situation is to find an angle that stimulates them. When the subject matter or nature of the exercise is not stimulating enough, you will have to search for or generate motivation. One productive strategy for doing so involves viewing all writing as a creative activity.

The Search for Creativity in Expository Writing

Creativity relevant to writing has been associated almost exclusively with fiction and poetry. Consequently, it seems that many students (and even some teachers) believe that whatever fun is to be had in a writing course can happen only in fiction and poetry workshops. Many other teachers and scholars, however, regret the separation between creative writing and **expository writing**—that is, writing that straightforwardly communicates ideas and information, as in essays, lab reports, business memos, and so forth. These individuals suggest that, as a developing writer, you can benefit from learning about what expository writing and creative writing—as well as other creative activities—have in common (Bishop; Cain et al.; Freisinger; Karnezis). Thinking in these terms involves viewing all creative activities, including writing assignments completed for your composition course, as opportunities for **meaning-making** (Berthoff)—or, in other words, as occasions for sharing insights in forms that fit your goals and satisfy your readers' expectations. This vantage point casts you in an active role. Not only does it require you to identify purposes for writing that will hold your interest and appeal to your readers, but it also invites you to experiment with ideas and ways of expressing them.

Expository Writing and Other Creative Activities

The discipline of psychology encourages comparisons between writing and many other creative activities—perhaps those that you more readily enjoy. In fact, psychologists who study creativity and creative individuals have demonstrated that all creative products come into being through similar processes. These processes include:

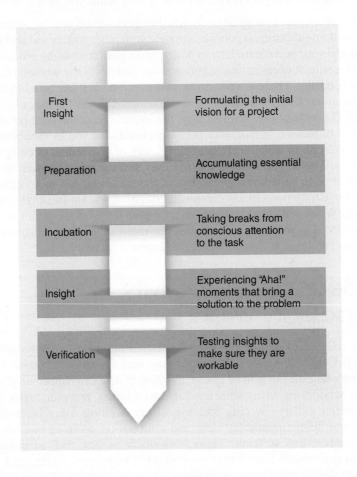

First Insight	Formulating the initial vision for a project
Preparation	Accumulating essential knowledge
Incubation	Taking breaks from conscious attention to the task
Insight	Experiencing "Aha!" moments that bring a solution to the problem
Verification	Testing insights to make sure they are workable

If you think about these processes (Kneller; Wallas) relevant to a hobby or pastime that you frequently engage in, you'll likely find that they closely characterize your journey toward achievement or innovation. For some examples, see Figure 1.2, which illustrates how these processes might play out in the context of two distinct activities: photography and basketball.

Any intellectual, artistic, or recreational activity might have served just as effectively as photography or basketball in portraying the creative process model in action. Take a few minutes and imagine applying it to an activity that you especially enjoy. If that activity happens to be expository writing, your model could look something like the one shown in Figure 1.3.

Comparing Figure 1.2 with Figure 1.3, you can see that working through a creative problem in the context of three very different activities involves many of the same practices and maneuvers. If you don't enjoy writing or if it seems especially difficult for you, connecting it through the creative process model with activities you take pleasure in can render it more inspiring and familiar. In addition, through the lens of this model, reflecting on strategies that lead to success or failure in areas *other than* writing can help you manage various activities that are involved *in* writing, such as generating ideas, organizing your plans, dealing with writer's block, and polishing your work.

MYTH

"Good writers are born."

This myth could mislead you into believing that "you've either got it or you don't."

There are many factors and conditions besides genetics (such as personality traits, focus, and diligence) that contribute to achievement, and you can consciously cultivate them in your own life. What's more, attributes that appear to be natural talents in someone you know might actually be the result of, for example, economic privilege or exposure to a field of study throughout childhood (maybe as a result of a parent's profession or hobbies).

REALITY

Creative Process	Example
Photography	
First insight	A friend tells you about a new business that she's started, and you realize you could help her by taking photos to advertise that business.
Preparation	You talk to your friend about the business, read her business plan, study the website she's developed, etc.
Incubation	When an exciting idea for the ad campaign doesn't immediately strike, you decide to leave these materials (i.e., your photos, her business plan and website) behind for a while, giving yourself time to reflect on them.
Insight	While you are making a sandwich a few days later, an ideal visual pops into your head; you run out to take the photos.
Verification	You show the images to your friend, who approves, and then you seek reactions from members of the target market, who offer positive feedback.
Basketball	
First insight	An arrogant rival team talks trash about an upcoming game, and you have a vision of scoring the final basket, sealing the victory.
Preparation	You work harder than usual during practice and even spend some extra hours at the gym shooting baskets.
Incubation	On the bus ride to the game, you close your eyes, falling into a state of relaxation; images of yourself driving to the hoop float in and out of your mind.
Insight	Though you've been successfully blocked by the quick, 6-foot-7 player who has been guarding you all night, suddenly, with the score tied and seconds left in the game, you spot a pathway around him and put up a shot.
Verification	The ball passes through the basket; the buzzer sounds; 2 points are recorded on the scoreboard; the crowd roars.

Figure 1.2 **The creative process model applied to two different activities**

Expository Writing	
Creative Process	Example
First insight	A job ad in the university newspaper catches your eye, and you begin imagining yourself applying for the position.
Preparation	With the intent of revising your résumé and writing a letter of application, you visit the business to observe, and you talk with some friends who used to work there.
Incubation	Trying to think of an angle on your application letter that will set you apart, you become blocked and decide to work on some course assignments.
Insight	Suddenly, as you are toiling with a math problem, you realize how you can frame your letter to help you stand out from the crowd of applicants.
Verification	After drafting the letter to your satisfaction, you show it to friends who are currently employed by the business. After making a couple of small changes in response to their suggestions, you drop your letter and résumé in the mail. A few days later, you are called for an interview.

Figure 1.3 **An expository writing situation mapped onto the creative process model**

Creativity and Self-Awareness

Often, when students are asked to explain how they go about composing a paper, they react with a touch of embarrassment. They hesitantly describe their habits and sometimes even apologize for them, claiming they know they "do it wrong." Actually, it's more productive to think about writing practices as "more or less effective" as opposed to "right" or "wrong." Many writers adopt ineffective strategies by default, latching on to certain methods simply because they have not been exposed to possible alternatives or encouraged to experiment with them. Whether or not you or other writers are content with given practices in contrast to other possibilities could be linked to specific personality traits or special areas of intelligence.

Studies focused on the nature of creativity and on creative personalities reveal much about attitudes and intellectual qualities that tend to spark achievement in all disciplines, including expository writing. The findings of these studies aren't perfectly in sync, but they demonstrate considerable overlap, particularly in relation to the following qualities (Davis 78-79):

- Tolerant of ambiguity
- Aware of creativity
- Energetic
- Thorough
- Artistic
- Imaginative
- Open-minded
- Curious
- Independent
- Willing to take risks
- Appreciative of alone time
- Appreciative of humor

Thinking about such qualities can help you identify strategies for overcoming your limitations and for making the most of your strengths. Regarding your *limitations,* if you don't consider yourself artistic, for example, you could take a class in graphic design. That experience might broaden your perspective on writing, encouraging you to experiment with the way you communicate, especially through surface features of a text. Regarding your *strengths,* you'll want to become more specifically aware of how you can capitalize on them.

Some influential research that can help you build on your strengths is referred to as **multiple intelligence theory** (Gardner). Basically, multiple intelligence theory suggests that intelligence isn't a singular entity that can be accurately measured by an IQ test. Rather, it is multifaceted—a combination of many different capabilities, some that are more pronounced than others in any given individual. The different intelligences and concepts associated with each are listed below:

Linguistic	• Language, words, speaking, reading, writing
Logical-Mathematical	• Numbers, calculations, relationships between entities
Spatial	• Pictures, visual layout, imagery, multidimensional thought
Bodily-Kinesthetic	• Physical movement and coordination, sports, dancing
Musical	• Voice, instruments, components of musical composition
Interpersonal	• Friendship, service to others, empathy, leadership
Intrapersonal	• Self-knowledge, self-regulation, memories, future goals
Naturalistic	• Sensitivity to the environment, ecology, plants, animals

Multiple intelligence research suggests that every individual enjoys a proclivity for certain areas of study or performance. This doesn't mean that if you possess special ability in a given area, you cannot perform well in other areas; on the contrary, the presumption is that all people exhibit at least some ability with regard to every type of intelligence. What it does mean, however, is that certain areas of study or performance probably come more easily for you. It also means that in disciplines that don't come as easily, it is wise to seek out strategies for taking advantage of your special areas of ability.

If you aren't sure about where your special abilities lie, you should know that there are numerous websites available to help you determine your primary intelligences and learn more about them. Whatever such tests reveal, Figure 1.4 suggests at least a couple of ways that your strongest areas of intelligence can serve you when writing.

Again, it is important to stress that all individuals possess some degree of intelligence in all of these areas. Even if linguistic intelligence doesn't rank high in your own profile, rest assured that you *do* possess linguistic intelligence, as evidenced by your capacity to read, speak, and write. In addition, remember that you can build on your strongest intelligences to make the act of writing increasingly comfortable and to support your problem-solving efforts as you work through a text.

Intelligence	Specific Applications to Writing
Linguistic	• You typically have plenty to say. • You easily grasp spelling, grammar, and punctuation guidelines.
Logical-mathematical	• You express clear relationships between ideas through sound reasoning. • You can fit ideas together in ways that make sense to readers.
Spatial	• You are comfortable experimenting with form. • You respond to visual representations of ideas when planning (i.e., in flowcharts or other diagrams).
Bodily-kinesthetic	• You benefit from incorporating physical movement of some sort into your writing processes (e.g., jogging your way through a bout of writer's block). • Changing environments and positions when composing typically gets your creative juices flowing.
Musical	• You find that music playing in the background stimulates your writing processes. • You are tuned into rhythms of language, with a good sense of when syllables, words, sentences, and paragraphs are flowing in ways that are pleasing.
Interpersonal	• You enjoy collaborative writing assignments. • You enjoy receiving feedback on your writing by participating in conferences with teachers or peers.
Intrapersonal	• You excel on assignments that ask you to explore personal feelings or experiences. • You are adept at reflecting on writing processes and products.
Naturalistic	• You draw inspiration from nature in preparation for or while writing (e.g., walking in the woods or gazing at a sunset). • You tend to be a close observer of your surroundings and, therefore, are effective at description.

Figure 1.4 **Multiple intelligence theory applied specifically to writing**

The Transfer of Composing Knowledge

As previous sections of this chapter suggest, you are primed to be creative simply by virtue of being human. When you acknowledge your creative potential in various areas of your life and understand that expository writing is a creative act, you will hopefully feel encouraged to explore connections between those other areas of achievement and the writing you complete for your college composition course. Exploring such relationships can also reveal similarities between writing tasks you will complete in first-year composition and those you will face in other contexts—whether academic or professional.

Of course, there's no denying that the documents you'll compose for college and the workplace will display some different features. But these features can't hide the reality that all acts of writing depend to a large extent on many of the same processes, strategies, and skills. If you focus only on the differences and fail to identify the similarities, you will perceive every composing task you encounter as unlike all those that came before it. This perspective may cause you to feel confused and overwhelmed by each new assignment, and it can undermine growth and achievement by preventing you from taking advantage of what you've already learned.

One key to successful writing, then, is the ability to consciously seek out and apply appropriate composing principles and practices *across* assignments—that is, to engage in **knowledge transfer.** Although knowledge transfer may occur naturally, or through direct instruction, you need to supplement what your courses and teachers provide by locating possible routes for knowledge transfer on your own. After all, your unique perspectives and experiences present connection-making possibilities that no curriculum or instructor could possibly anticipate.

Conditions for Knowledge Transfer

The ease with which knowledge will transfer across situations depends to some degree on the nature of the concepts or experiences you're associating. Consider the example of driving a car (Perkins and Salomon). Even if you've driven only a couple of different models, there's no doubt that the act of driving one prepared you for driving the other. Looking at the dashboard of a vintage car next to that of a modern hybrid (see Figure 1.5), you'll recognize that, despite some differences in the ways these cars operate, they share similarities that would enable you to transfer between them what you know about driving. These similarities include turning a steering wheel, determining speed and fuel levels, announcing your presence by honking the horn, and so on. Because the acts of driving two different cars are so similar in nature, applying knowledge about one to the other would be referred to as an instance of **near transfer** (Perkins and Salomon). In such situations, the connections will likely be fairly obvious and the transfer relatively easy.

Figure 1.5 **Car dashboards from two different eras**

Of course, many situations conducive to productive transfer require more diligence and a greater level of consciousness on your part. Suppose you want to learn to drive a boat. Although boats are like cars in a few respects (e.g., they have similar steering mechanisms, windshields, and rearview mirrors), they simultaneously pose some stark contrasts, including size, maneuverability, suspension, and so on. Applying knowledge across dissimilar situations—for example, from car to boat— is referred to as **far transfer.** While far transfer can be more challenging than near transfer, it stands to produce the most innovative or creative results since the connections tend to be unique to some degree (Perkins and Salomon).

In the context of writing, an example of near transfer is applying what you know about composing a letter of recommendation for a friend to composing a cover letter for your own résumé, as both would employ the same form and share the purpose of endorsing someone for a position. An example of far transfer is applying what you know about writing a letter of recommendation to writing a research proposal. Although these two documents diverge in many ways, they both call on process and grammatical knowledge, and they both require you to "sell a product"—respectively, the promise of an individual to perform a job effectively and the promise of a research study to produce valuable findings. The point is that even when constructs don't seem obviously relatable on the surface, if you actively try associating them, you can often unearth helpful connections.

Routes for Knowledge Transfer in Composition

Knowledge transfer is vital in all learning situations but especially in writing, as a result of its cross-disciplinary relevance. To be more specific, writing provides a primary tool for learning and communicating in *all* academic disciplines and professions (in contrast, for instance, to a mathematical equation or a painting technique). Given the wide-ranging applications of writing, composition assignments will allow you to pull strategies and content from courses across the curriculum, such as those that might have introduced you to thinking processes, specialized writing practices, or even subject matter. Moreover, because writing also mediates your personal life and job performance, you might even draw from experiences outside school to support your writing. Of course, it would be impossible to imagine all potential resources or routes for transferring composition knowledge, but Figure 1.6 identifies those that are fairly common (including some concepts this chapter has already introduced).

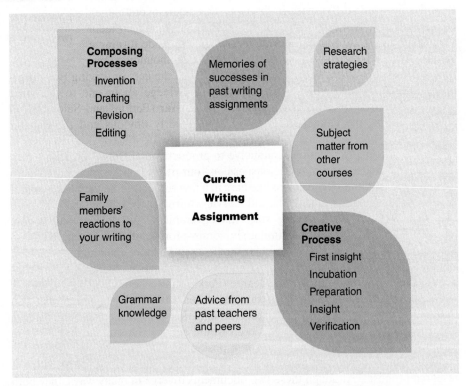

Figure 1.6 Common resources for knowledge transfer in composition. The pools of knowledge depicted here have served your writing processes in some form or fashion throughout your years in school. These resources will continue to serve you, and with greater impact, as you develop further as a writer and consciously work to relate them to the new composing challenges that await you.

Processes Involved in Knowledge Transfer

When a writing assignment places you in unfamiliar territory—that is, when simply mapping the new assignment onto one that you've already mastered is impossible—it is time to reflect. Despite popular usage of the term, **reflection** relevant to knowledge transfer should not be regarded as a casual trip down memory lane. Rather, it's a penetrating, systematic exploration of knowledge that you've accumulated with the specific purposes of (1) searching for points of overlap between a new challenge and what you've already learned and (2) ascertaining specific ways of applying what you've learned when approaching the new challenge (Georghiades). As such, reflection requires you to become more expansive and flexible in your thinking and to be on the lookout for possibly less-than-obvious relationships. For an illustration of how reflection might play out in a specific writing situation, read the paragraphs in Figure 1.7 about a student in a first-year composition course who is facing an assignment unlike any she has ever written before.

The reflection in Figure 1.7 reveals a student who is at first somewhat intimidated by a new assignment but who, by actively searching for connections with past personal and educational experiences, comes to understand that she has already

When she first heard that she and her classmates would be writing a memoir, Maggie felt a jolt of nerves. She had seen the term *memoir* before, above a shelf in the local bookstore, so she gathered that it is a popular medium. In addition, she had overheard members of her mother's book club excitedly discussing memoirs, so she thought they must be pretty engaging. However, she wasn't exactly sure about their content or shape.

Once her teacher, Mr. Jenkins, explained that a memoir is a type of life writing, in which the author tells the story of some personally significant set of experiences while also offering an analysis of their impact, Maggie began feeling a little more comfortable. Thinking on past experiences, she focused in on the fact that she had written several short stories and had read even more. She understood, therefore, that, when writing a memoir, she would be narrating some events, as well as describing people and places and possibly even employing some dialogue. All of these were strategies at which she excelled. Then,

suddenly, her mind flashed on the portraits she had recently painted; perhaps the detail she brought to the canvas provided a model for the detail she could bring to a memoir.

Although she hadn't spent much time analyzing life experiences, she remembered that she had analyzed literature in her high school English class, and she predicted that the analytical strategies she applied to literature might also apply to real-life stories. But had she ever read actual life writing before?

Mr. Jenkins's examples of memoirs and other types of life writing sparked memories of her great grandmother's journal, which held verbal snapshots of a childhood very different from her own, a time well before smartphones and other technologies that she and her friends now took for granted. Even though that journal had not been published and wasn't as polished as she knew Mr. Jenkins would expect a finished memoir to be, she figured that those snapshots could help her grasp some of the expectations for a memoir.

Figure 1.7 **Reflection in preparation for a writing assignment**

absorbed plenty of information that is applicable to the task before her. Aided by her teacher's definitions and examples, this student finds several points of overlap with what she already knows and, therefore, places herself in a far better position to complete the assignment successfully than would be the case if she had rested on her initial impressions regarding the unfamiliarity or difficulty of the assignment. If she had rested on those early impressions, passively walking her way through the assignment with nothing familiar to ground her or help her capitalize on skills she had already mastered, she might have doubted her ability to handle the load or, even worse, struggled unnecessarily with the assignment.

Once you've reflected on the potential applicability of past learning situations, you need to carefully **evaluate** the seemingly relevant information that you've retrieved from memory (Georghiades). In other words, you will want to think more critically about *if* and *how* that information might be applicable to your project. For an example of how these processes might play out, consider Figure 1.8, which comments on the scenario depicted in Figure 1.7. The left column recounts information produced by the student's reflections that might be pertinent to writing a memoir; the column on the right shares her evaluation of each.

After evaluating the knowledge you believe may transfer as demonstrated in Figure 1.8, you're ready to apply that which seems usable (Georghiades). Of course, this doesn't mean that your evaluations will necessarily be accurate, or have to be,

Knowledge Recalled through Reflection	Evaluation of the Knowledge Produced
Memoir is a popular genre that appears to be targeted for the general public.	The fact that it has its own section in the local bookstore is an indicator that the general public appreciates the genre. Given that the general public is a potential target audience, I know that I don't have to worry about sounding academic. I can write in a conversational style.
It seems that memoirs are generally engaging and provocative.	My mother's book club could be considered representative of the general public, or the audience for a memoir. The nature of the club members' reactions suggests that my own memoir should center on an intriguing or provocative issue—one that would hold significance for many people and get them talking.
A memoir is a type of life writing.	Mr. Jenkins said a memoir is a type of life writing. Obviously, then, my memoir needs to focus on my life. I wonder if it might also focus on the lives of others. That's a question I will want to ask during class.
A memoir tells a story.	Mr. Jenkins also said that a memoir tells a story. That makes sense since life writing seems to involve recounting personal experiences, much like recounting the plot of a movie or short story. Consequently, I should be able to invoke other elements of fiction, like character, setting, theme, and style, when drafting my memoir.
Given that a memoir tells a story, it will likely involve narration, description, and dialogue—as well as lots of visual detail.	I have read and written many stories, so I am comfortable with narrating and describing. And the portraits I paint are studies in detail—I need to capture that level of detail in words. These strategies will help readers visualize what I write. In addition, I know that dialogue helps bring characters to life. My former teachers told me that I have an ear for authentic dialogue, so I want to make sure I demonstrate that skill in my memoir.
A memoir offers some analysis of the life events portrayed.	I imagine that the author of a memoir would try to show the significance of the events in his or her own life and suggest their relevance to readers. I need to find out how I should do this. Should I explain the significance at the end, or should I try to imply it subtly through my portrayal of the experience and the people involved?

Figure 1.8 **Evaluation of potentially transferable knowledge**

before you can begin composing. However, if you spend time reflecting on what you already know that may be pertinent to the assignment at hand and evaluate that knowledge as part of your prewriting or invention activities, the application process will proceed more smoothly, as you will have already rejected obviously weak associations and arrived at a more fully developed plan for writing.

Negative Transfer and Composing Myths

Becoming a successful student and an insightful writer involves reconsidering, from time to time, what you have learned. In other words, when something contradicts what you have come to believe, you need to question the discrepancy, try to uncover the reason for it, and then adjust your understanding if the new information seems more fitting, accurate, or workable. Approaching knowledge in this manner can help you avoid **negative transfer,** or the continued reliance on knowledge that is false, constraining, or otherwise detrimental. For some concrete examples, consult the Myth and Reality boxes in this chapter (and elsewhere in this textbook). Some of these myths surface through teachers' well-meaning attempts to simplify writing for beginners; others very likely functioned as rules at some distant point in time and have since been revised.

But the fact is that the knowledge base in composition is always evolving, and there are numerous examples of this phenomenon in Standard Written English. One such example has to do with pronoun usage. For instance, it used to be acceptable to employ masculine forms, such as *he* or *his,* when referring to nouns that could stand for either gender, as in the following sentence: "The business college awards one student a semester's paid tuition at the end of his junior year." However, it is now considered unconventional to use only masculine forms in such cases; instead, you would write, "The business college awards one student a semester's paid tuition at the end of his or her junior year." To keep up with such changes in usage and to address the seeming contradictions between what you may have been told about writing in the past and what you are discovering now, you'll need to be a conscientious reader and listener regarding current communication practices. You'll also need to collaborate with your teachers and peers to determine appropriate usage and to understand the reasons behind conflicting information. Confronting the inconsistency and rooting out its origins are preferable to ignoring it in favor of misunderstandings or misguided maxims.

An Invitation to Create in Your Composition Course

Some students enter college suspecting that, somewhere, there exists a correct formula for writing—a simple recipe that guarantees success. But writing is just too complex an act to lend itself to ready-made prescriptions. In the face of this complexity, you will need to analyze each writing situation to determine what

"I don't need a composition course. My career plans won't require me to write."

The first problem with this statement is that most every career involves some sort of writing, even if only in the form of data charts or business-related communications with employers or colleagues. The second problem is that it implies that your goals won't change. At some point you'll likely consider switching careers or specific jobs within a given profession. If that different path is more dependent on writing skills and you have failed to transfer what your writing course had to offer, you may be restricted in following your dreams or advancing your career.

skills from previous experiences you might transfer to it, as well as what features make it unique. From there, you can apply the composing knowledge and strategies most appropriate to that specific situation. Viewing expository writing as a creative activity supplies a fresh lens through which you can build on previous composing knowledge and strategies. As a result, you'll be more able to respond to an array of composing scenarios, to raise your motivation level, to generate insightful prose, and to become more confident in your writing abilities.

No matter what your background, previous educational experiences, or predispositions, your prospects for improving as a writer this semester will be tremendous. At no other time in your college career will you have the luxury of concentrating so exclusively and intently on your writing processes and products, which are so essential to your success in the academy and beyond. And you'll be doing so with the assistance of an expert devoted to the teaching of writing—your instructor. So with a boost that comes from knowing that inborn talent is not a requirement for success and with the excitement that comes from tapping your own creativity, you hopefully will seize the opportunities that your composition course provides.

ACTIVITY

Thinking about Writing Rules versus Writing Myths   What myths about writing (or "rules" that you suspect may be myths) might you add to those introduced in this chapter? What myths or rules have influenced your own writing? What has been the impact of those myths or rules on your writing processes and/or products? What, if any, myths or rules have been violated in the chapter you just read? What was their impact on you as a reader? Record your answers to these questions, and be prepared to share them with the rest of your class.

IDEA FOR EXTENDED WRITING

Exploring an Instance of Knowledge Transfer   Think of an incident in your daily life or in school that illustrates knowledge transfer—a time when you had to accomplish something that challenged you, and you did so by drawing on information from another area of expertise. This incident might have involved a skill you had to learn for school, or it might have involved something as personal as figuring out how to solve a relationship problem with someone you are close to.

Once you've settled on an instance of knowledge transfer to explore, your ultimate task will be to compose an essay in which you:

- Characterize the challenge.
- Explain how you approached it.
- Point out specific resources and routes for transfer.
- Acknowledge specific difficulties in working through the challenge.
- Portray how the challenge was resolved.

Be reminded that, although you will want to touch on all of these areas to produce a well-developed essay in keeping with the goals of this assignment, the above list is not meant to prescribe an organization for your essay. On the contrary, you should feel free to be creative in portraying these events while being sure to assist readers in following your line of development.

WORKS CITED

Berthoff, Ann E. *The Making of Meaning: Metaphors, Models and Maxims for Writing Teachers.* Boynton, 1981.

Bishop, Wendy. "Crossing the Lines: On Creative Composition and Composing Creative Writing." *Writing on the Edge*, vol. 4, no. 2, 1993, pp. 117–33.

Cain, Mary Ann, et al. "Letters/Interchanges: Inquiring into the Nexus of Composition Studies and Creative Writing." *College Composition and Communication*, vol. 51, no. 1, 1999, pp. 70+.

Davis, Gary A. *Creativity Is Forever.* 4th ed., Kendall, 1999.

Freisinger, Randall R. "Creative Writing and Creative Composition." *College English*, vol. 40, no. 3, 1978, pp. 283–87.

Gardner, Howard. *Frames of Mind: The Theory of Multiple Intelligences.* Basic, 1993.

Georghiades, Pedro. "Beyond Conceptual Change Learning in Science Education: Focusing on Transfer, Durability and Metacognition." *Educational Research*, vol. 42, no. 2, 2000, pp. 119–39.

Karnezis, George T. *Teaching Writing Creatively.* Edited by David Starkey, Boynton, 1998, pp. 29–42.

Kneller, George. *The Art and Science of Creativity.* Holt, 1965.

Perkins, David N., and Gavriel Salomon. "Teaching for Transfer." *Educational Leadership*, vol. 46, no. 1, 1998, pp. 22–32.

Wallas, Graham. *The Art of Thought.* Harcourt, 1926.

Composing Processes and Creative Processes 2

Imagine that you are spending the weekend at a friend's home when, after she leaves to run some errands, a storm knocks out all the power. With evening quickly turning into night, you realize that you need to find a way of lighting this unfamiliar space, but all you can find are the items lying on the table in this photo—matches, a candle, and a box of thumbtacks. So you are faced with a problem: How are you going to illuminate the place from above (so you can see as much of the room as possible) without candle wax dripping on and ruining your friend's table? [To check the solution, perform a Google search for "candle problem" (Duncker).]

This problem challenges what psychologists refer to as "functional fixedness," or what might be described as falling into a rut when thinking about a problem. A complex problem-solving process itself, writing is subject to recurring episodes of functional fixedness. This chapter approaches writing processes in ways that can help you avoid the ruts often associated with them—or climb out of those ruts more quickly if you do fall in.

Because effective writing processes are known to vary across individuals and writing situations, composition scholars concluded some time ago that there can be no single, correct definition of "the writing process." That being said, you're sure to discover plenty of overlapping activity between your composing processes and those of others in your class, as well as between the various composing challenges you will face in college and in the workplace. Writing teachers often represent that overlapping activity in a model involving four interrelated activities, defined in Figure 2.1.

It's important to note, however, that the act of composing is not as neat and orderly as the model in Figure 2.1 suggests. In fact, most writers don't proceed through the composing process model in linear fashion; rather, they move freely among various activities as their individual composing needs dictate (see Figure 2.2). This back-and-forth movement is referred to as **recursivity.** For example, during revision you might discover that a section of your composition needs to be further developed with secondary source material, so you return to activities typically linked with invention. Or you might find yourself editing as you draft—that is, correcting misspellings or punctuation errors *while* you are putting your ideas into words.

Of course, no single depiction of recursivity could account for all the possible variations in composing processes across individuals or writing situations. However, realizing that back-and-forth movement between composing processes is natural, you shouldn't feel alarmed if you deviate from the order portrayed in the standard model. Instead, you should view deviations as signals that some previous effort was insufficient to your purposes.

A Composing Model

Even though it tends to oversimplify, the standard composing model can assist you in managing your writing processes by breaking the larger act of composing into more manageable parts. This section provides additional detail about components

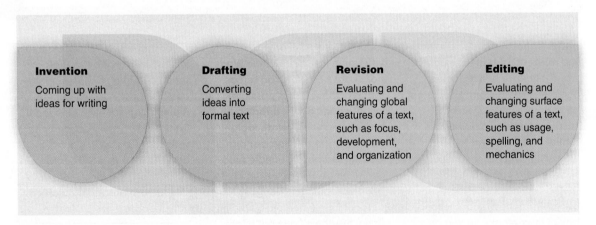

Invention

Coming up with ideas for writing

Drafting

Converting ideas into formal text

Revision

Evaluating and changing global features of a text, such as focus, development, and organization

Editing

Evaluating and changing surface features of a text, such as usage, spelling, and mechanics

Figure 2.1 **The standard composing model.** The four activities involved in this process model—invention, drafting, revision, and editing—overlap; that is, writers will often move back and forth between them.

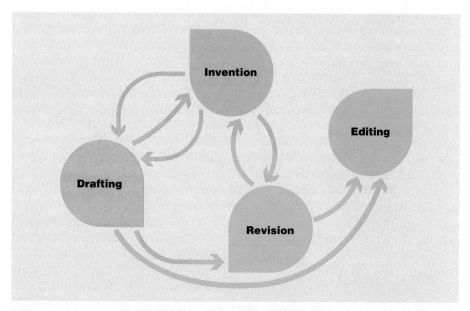

Figure 2.2 An illustration of writing's recursive nature. Although the standard composing model portrays writing as following a straight line, an application of its various processes might actually look more like the activity diagrammed here.

of the model, which serves as a template for jump-starting, generating, and polishing responses to most any writing assignment. Without such a template, the prospect of addressing an unfamiliar or intimidating challenge can seem daunting, causing you to avoid it—perhaps until only a few hours before a deadline. This one-shot, night-before-it's-due approach to producing a paper often results in weakly developed texts, by-products of spending too little time thinking about an assignment or of thinking about it in ways that are unproductive. You can sidestep such hazards by learning to apply the specific composing strategies addressed in the following paragraphs.

Invention

Invention refers to the work involved in generating ideas, researching them, questioning them, playing around with them, combining them in different ways, and refining them. Although it seems pretty obvious that invention would drive your early composing activities, you should know that it may occur at virtually any time while you are writing. In other words, whenever you are producing new material or new strategies for responding to a given task, you are engaged in invention.

Some invention activities will take longer than others. The time such activities may take depends largely on the extent of your knowledge about a topic, your audience, and so forth. Fortunately, there exist numerous strategies for increasing your knowledge and for confronting information in ways that will stimulate your thinking. These strategies include various forms of research and prewriting.

Research as an Invention Strategy   Perhaps the most obvious means of increasing knowledge is to conduct research. For most students, this means sitting in front of the computer and browsing the Internet—an attractive option, given that it is probably the quickest and most convenient way to locate information. Nevertheless, you'd be well advised to reach beyond the Internet and take advantage of resources available through your school's library. For example, you might consult specialized databases, which provide countless articles (many in full-text form) that are not accessible through the Internet. And, of course, the library provides free and immediate access to many potentially helpful books and reference texts. Time in the library is time well spent since disregarding what it has to offer might cause you to miss resources that are vital to your project, particularly scholarly articles or materials that can't be accessed without paying a subscription. Other research options you might want to consider include searching your memory, systematically observing phenomena around you, and talking with others—especially those who have some level of expertise regarding the issues at hand. (To learn more about research strategies, see Chapter 5.)

Prewriting as an Invention Strategy   In addition to conducting library and Internet research, you can support invention by experimenting with prewriting techniques. When you are struggling to find constructive approaches to your work, prewriting can limber up your mind and help you view materials from various perspectives, nudging you through episodes of writer's block or beyond desolate pathways in your thinking. Prewriting strategies that you may be familiar with include **brainstorming** and **freewriting,** both of which call on you to (quickly and without judgment) dump every idea that crosses your mind onto a notepad or computer screen. The primary benefit of both activities is that they can unleash your thoughts and/or silence your internal editor—that persnickety little being inside your head that sneers, "This idea stinks!" Once you've spilled all your initial thoughts onto paper or screen, you can return to them at a later time to more carefully weigh their potential.

There exist numerous prewriting strategies from which you can choose—too many to cover in this brief overview of invention. (Several additional techniques are detailed in Chapter 4.) Regardless of which prewriting techniques or research strategies you use, the old cliché rings true: "You only get out of them what you put into them." In other words, the more you're willing to experiment with different invention strategies and the more time and effort you're willing to invest in them, the more likely they are to yield positive results.

Loose Plans for Organizing Ideas   When pursued seriously, invention techniques will produce an abundance of raw material for your writing. Once you've generated the raw material, you'll want to consider organizing it in some sort of flexible arrangement. Typically, this means identifying a main point for the document and then implementing a loose plan for how the text might unfold. This plan could be expressed as a list, a flowchart, a rough outline, or any sort of framework that shows how your thoughts relate to one another. Unlike formal outlines, less rigid organizing strategies encourage experimentation with order.

Additionally, flexible arrangements may enable your work to grow organically—that is, to allow the nature of what you've just written to suggest where you should go next.

Drafting

Drafting generally refers to the act of producing prose that is more polished than that typically produced in response to invention exercises. In the context of drafting, differences in individual writing habits and preferences become especially noticeable. For example, some writers must spend time preparing their writing spaces before they feel comfortable drafting. Doing so might involve turning on a certain kind of music, adjusting the lights, brewing a pot of coffee, surrounding the computer with source materials to be consulted, and so on. Some writers need to be sitting in a stiff chair staring at a computer screen while others prefer lounging on the couch with a laptop computer or sitting on the deck with a notepad, gazing at some trees.

Beyond the physical environment, another factor that can influence your writing processes is your **cognitive style.** Your cognitive style indicates the way your mind tends to work. Relevant to drafting, your cognitive style may become apparent in the speed with which you write and in the order of your words, sentences, or paragraphs. For example, some writers plow systematically along, needing one sentence to seem nearly perfect in content, word choice, and rhythm before they can move on to the next. As a result of their linear, step-by-step approach, they may be referred to as **methodical writers.** Such writers typically begin drafting with the text's introduction. They then proceed in lockstep order through the body of the document toward the conclusion—at least until they encounter a hurdle that can be overcome only with further invention activities. In contrast, **nonmethodical writers** move through their prose much more quickly and haphazardly, knowing they can always return to it later to make adjustments. They tend to jump around, maybe writing body paragraphs before the introduction or maybe writing the conclusion before anything else (Harris).

All sorts of variations exist between the extremes of methodical and nonmethodical drafting, but, regardless of your personal habits or preferences, it is a relief when you feel ready to draft—really ready, not forced to draft because of some deadline. However, drafting rarely proceeds as smoothly as you imagine or hope that it will. Even under the best circumstances (feeling motivated, having completed essential research, having arrived at some sense of how the document might be organized), this part of the process ordinarily ebbs and flows, waxes and wanes, and, sometimes, stops moving altogether. Although glitches will likely arise during every subprocess of composing, you are particularly

MYTH

"There is a right way to draft."

One approach to drafting isn't necessarily better than any other. For example, orderly, plodding writers spend less time revising, since effort devoted up front reduces the rigor of reworking the text later. In contrast, fast, free-flowing writers spend more time revising since their main goal in drafting is to get ideas out quickly, even if they aren't fully formed. In short, no specific combination of habits or preferences can protect against obstacles you may face when writing. The key to improving your writing processes is to experiment, with the intent of identifying those strategies—or combinations of them—that work best for you.

REALITY

vulnerable to writer's block while drafting, given the many variables you must simultaneously attend to:

> Searching for the best words to convey thoughts and intentions
>
> Weaving ideas together through language that establishes their relationships
>
> Tightening organization so that readers can process the line of narration, analysis, or argument
>
> Integrating material from external sources so that it supports or illustrates claims and leaves no doubt as to the origin of cited material
>
> Keeping in mind conventions of the document type as well as the common beliefs and values of the audience
>
> Figuring out how to begin and conclude the document, etc.

Considering all these concurrent challenges, it's a small wonder that writer's block frequently occurs during drafting. The good news is that, in recursive fashion, you can always seek out additional invention strategies to prompt you through these frustrating moments.

Revision

Revision consists of taking another look at what you've written to ensure that you are fulfilling your intentions as a writer, as well as the expectations of your readers. Revision is distinct from editing, which focuses on correcting surface errors. During revision, you should devote attention to major issues as opposed to minor mistakes like misspelled words, missing commas, and so on. After all, revision—which sometimes involves deleting large chunks of text—often removes some of these smaller problems. Revision in the standard model, then, foregrounds issues that are relevant to the substance of a piece. These issues might include:

- Focus (scope of your topic relevant to page limits)
- Development (amount and nature of support for your claims)
- Organization (logic and coherence in the order of your ideas)
- Introductions and conclusions
- Practices for effectively integrating sources and appropriately citing them

As you turn your attention toward revising these aspects of your texts, remember that you can increase your chances for improving a draft if you set it aside for a while since, in a refreshed state of mind, you'll be less inclined to overlook any problems. You might also want to seek feedback from others because additional sets of eyes will notice issues that you may not have flagged on your own (see Chapter 24 on peer and instructor response). They can also help determine how accurately you are communicating your ideas and purposes to your target audience, as well as offer varied possibilities for reworking your text at the global level. (You can read more about strategies for revising your documents in Chapter 23.)

Editing

The significance assigned to revision is not intended to undermine the importance of **editing** for surface errors. In fact, editing is crucial to your credibility as a writer and to a reader's ability to access your ideas. Complicating the editing process is the fact that expectations for grammar and punctuation will vary depending on the situation in which you're communicating. For example, when you write to friends (especially via text or e-mail), your approach will be more relaxed than when you write a paper for a class or when you respond to questions on a job application. More specifically, when you write for friends, you might disregard punctuation to some degree, and you might employ slang and/or abbreviations for certain terms, such as *'sup?* and *LOL,* since these practices will fit their expectations.

In contrast, many of the readers you'll be targeting in your college coursework will expect you to follow conventions associated with Standard Written English (SWE)—that is, the more formal rules of usage associated with academic or business-oriented writing. Figure 2.3 lists some informal expressions you might use when interacting with friends, as well as SWE versions of those expressions.

Unfortunately, errors in SWE such as those listed in the left column of Figure 2.3 (as well as errors in spelling and punctuation) can distract readers from the content of your work, regardless of how compelling your ideas might be. Not only do they render the document difficult to understand, but also they may suggest that you are a less-than-conscientious writer. No matter the type of oversight, readers typically feel justified in casting aside a document that contains surface errors.

In certain contexts a minor error or two might be excused; however, the problem is that you often won't know the leanings of your readers in this respect. A single missing apostrophe on a résumé or cover letter, for example, might seem minor to you, but to a prospective employer, it can be perceived as a sign of laziness or lack of knowledge. In the end, though, you can be certain of at least one reality: A clean, well-edited document will shield you from some potentially damaging criticism. (See Chapter 23 for specific editing advice.)

Informal Expressions	Alternate Versions in SWE
Me and her attended the concert.	She and I attended the concert.
The ending of that movie upset him and I.	The ending of that movie upset him and me.
There's some interesting facts in that book.	There are some interesting facts in that book.
They might have went too early.	They might have gone too early.

Figure 2.3 **Sentences contrasting informal expressions and Standard Written English**

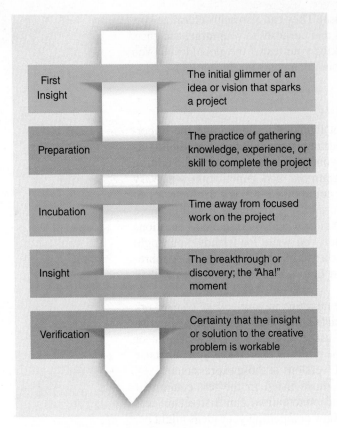

Figure 2.4 **The creative process model**

Source: Adapted from George F. Kneller, *The Art and Science of Creativity.* Holt, 1965; Graham Wallas, *The Art of Thought.* Harcourt, 1926.

Expository Writing as a Creative Act

The standard composing model discussed earlier often surfaces in discussions of expository writing, which aspires to straight-forwardly inform, analyze, or persuade a reader. At times, you may feel uninspired or even confined by this type of writing. But you can alleviate such feelings if you view expository writing processes alongside processes commonly associated with a *creative* activity, whether it be writing poetry, painting, designing video games, and so on. The creative process model (see Figure 2.4) defines several activities associated with creative production.

The promise of the creative process model for expository writers lies in its potential for productively elaborating the standard composing model (Figure 2.1). This benefit is most evident with regard to invention, which the creative process model divides into several additional components (see Figure 2.5). Juxtaposing the creativity and composing models clarifies that invention is shortchanged to some degree in the composing model, since the bulk of activity that model represents centers on expressing ideas, as opposed to generating them. To be more specific, as Figure 2.5 makes clear, invention in the context of composing involves four of the five components characterizing the creative process model: first insight, preparation, incubation, and insight.

The Creative Process Model

Like the standard composing model, the creative process model should not be regarded as rigid and orderly. It, too, is subject to back-and-forth movement between stages—that is, to recursivity. Following is a more thorough discussion of the specific components of the creative process model and how they mesh with components of the standard composing model.

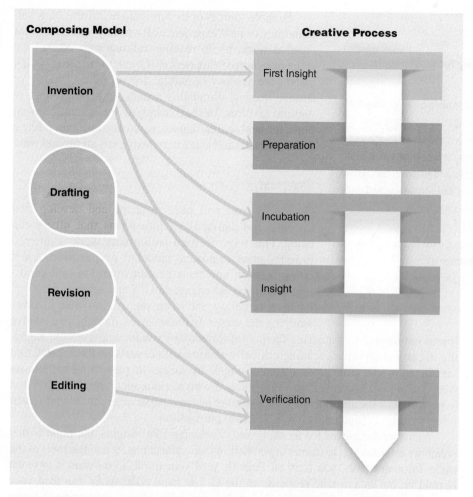

Figure 2.5 Juxtaposition of the composing model and the creative process model. A comparison of the two models reveals the significance of invention in the context of composing. Invention involves four of the five components of the creative process.

First Insight

Every artistic pursuit or intellectual challenge, including writing, begins with **first insight,** which is the initial glimmer of an idea or vision for a project. Although in most cases it will need to be honed, first insight will provide you at least some sense of direction in what can seem like a stagnant pond of uncertainty or a raging sea of possibility. At times, first insight visits on its own, even when you aren't actively seeking to create anything. At other times, it is stimulated when someone else poses a question or task for you to address, such as an essay assignment in a writing course.

MYTH

"Writing comes easily for most people."

Although writing may come more easily for some than for others in certain situations, to say that writing comes *easily* for anyone perpetuates a damaging fiction. The truth is that even the best writers must work diligently to create effective and engaging texts. In fact, famous writers across history have revealed the self-doubt, countless false starts, and hours of intense effort they endured while pursuing their goals. In short, the complexity characterizing most composing tasks prevents writing from ever being easy.

REALITY

Possible sources of first insight are infinite. New surroundings or new experiences frequently spark ideas for creative work, as do reading, talking with others, and reflecting on past experiences. Often, the sources of first insight are sensory in nature, arising from beautiful or strange images, stimulating sounds, fragrant aromas, or unusual textures. In short, catalysts for scientific inventions, musical scores, dances, paintings, fashions, athletic moves, novels, and expository texts exist all around you.

Preparation

Ordinarily, you will need to shape and develop first insights, translating them into forms that others can enjoy. This more focused preliminary work is referred to in the creative process model as **preparation,** and it constitutes yet another aspect of invention in composing. When you are engaged in the arts, such as painting, dancing, sculpting, and so on, preparation often involves applying the senses. In the sciences, it might also involve (but is not limited to) gathering factual information by conducting research, engaging in close observation, reading critically, talking with experts on the subject, and viewing subject matter from different angles by means of prewriting techniques (see Chapter 4). Moreover, gaining practice with various mediums of expression (e.g., brushes, oils, and canvas when painting; pen and paper or keyboard and screen when writing) is fundamental to successful preparation.

Whatever the means for focusing and developing first insights, the point is that creativity requires you to immerse yourself in your subject matter and the tools of the trade. In other words, you must sufficiently feed your mind if you want it to reach beyond an obvious or trite response to the task at hand (Gates). As you feed your mind, the creative problem itself is becoming more refined—reconfiguring in a way that more effectively captures the nuances and intricacies of the ideas you want to express. In addition, as your knowledge base about your subject matter expands, confidence in your ideas and in your capacity for communicating them grows. But a high level of preparation (on the heels of an exciting first insight) is sometimes not enough to elicit the kind of breakthrough that leads to an impressive final product. Ordinarily, such a breakthrough requires incubation, or the opportunity for ideas to percolate.

Incubation

Incubation, yet another aspect of invention in composing, can be characterized as a break from the problem or challenge you are working to address. Productive breaks might involve forgetting your project entirely while you focus on other activities or thinking about it only intermittently. Some of the most productive breaks occur while you are asleep, when your subconscious can work on the problem in the form of dreams. Whatever form the break assumes, the key to successful incubation is to relax your concentration on the task at hand for some period of time.

To illustrate, think of a time when you became stymied while trying to solve a puzzle only to have the solution pop into your head once you turned your attention to something else. Maybe you decided to make a snack or hop in the shower. Then, suddenly, the answer that eluded you—perhaps for a long period of intense labor—became accessible. That answer is termed a *breakthrough* or *insight.* One classic example of incubation surfaces in the musings of poet A. E. Housman, who scheduled lengthy daily walks, during which he made a point of clearing his mind, focusing only on sensory perceptions of his surroundings. Housman reported that this downtime consistently produced fully formed lines of poetry, accompanied by larger impressions of the completed works of which those lines would become a part (90-91).

As such incidents suggest, when you've tried everything you can think of to forge ahead with your writing projects but still find that you're stopped in your tracks, chances are your mind is telling you that you need to rest. Go ahead and take the break; allow your subconscious to carry the load for a while. Just be careful not to confuse a productive break with **procrastination,** or the willful avoidance of a task.

Insight

Insight is the "Aha!" moment—the moment when you realize that you have arrived at a solution to a composing or other creative challenge. When you achieve insight, you overcome **cognitive dissonance,** or that feeling of uneasiness you experience when you encounter a phenomenon that doesn't make sense to you or when you are faced with a question that you can't immediately answer. Because insights are the cure for dissonance, they are frequently accompanied by a profound sense of relief: At last, all elements of the solution to the problem you've been struggling with have fallen into place (M. Murray 24-32).

Insights assume many different forms. In scientific inquiry, for example, ideas can arise from dream images. Eighteenth-century chemist Kekule figured out the structure of the ring-shaped benzene molecule (a problem he'd been grappling with for some time) when a vision of a snake swallowing its own tail entered his mind while he was dozing by the fire (Harman and Rheingold 40-41). Insights might also arise from unusual connections, such as the one that spawned Stephen King's horror tale *Carrie,* which resulted from the sudden merging of two originally separate story lines about topics he initially viewed as unrelated—telekinesis and teenage cruelty (75).

Depending on the nature of the challenge, insights sometimes come relatively quickly. At other times they emerge only after long periods of feeling blocked. Insights differ from *first insights* in that the former are significantly more developed. Put another way, while first insights offer initial direction, insights suggest that the final destination is in view, at least if the insights are genuine. An insight tends to be genuine if it results in a state of **flow**—"an almost automatic, effortless, yet highly focused state of consciousness," when your work progresses in fast and furious fashion (Csikszentmihalyi 110). Regardless of the discipline or medium in which you are working, flow will result in similar sensations and states of mind.

Once you achieve flow, creative activity moves along quickly and in a satisfying rhythm. Typically, the vagueness surrounding earlier phases of your work is replaced by a clear sense of purpose and an understanding of the means for fulfilling it. In addition, you may feel so consumed by the activity at hand that you lose all sense of time, with several hours of work seeming like minutes.

Verification

In fact, flow can be viewed as connecting insight and **verification,** or assessment of the solution. But, of course, you can't verify the worth of a solution to your composing problem before that solution, or insight, has occurred. Verification in the creative process model—which encompasses drafting, revision, and editing in the composing model—consists of two activities: **elaboration** and **evaluation.** Elaboration involves representing the solution you've conceived in the medium in which you're creating (e.g., words, sentences, and paragraphs in writing). Evaluation involves judging that proposed solution as you are crafting it (Wallas 80-81).

Elaboration and evaluation tend to occur simultaneously. In other words, as you work to *elaborate* or express an insight, the extent to which that activity flows often predicts whether or not your *evaluation* of the insight will be positive—that is, whether or not you'll find that it actually solves your problem. For example, if you're painting, and the elaboration is succeeding, the brush may seem almost to be moving itself; similarly, if you're writing, your fingers will fly across the keyboard in perfect continuity with your thoughts. On the other hand, if a presumed insight stops flowing (i.e., the brush stops moving or the fingers stop flying), there's a distinct possibility that the solution you're elaborating is not workable after all.

The Creative Process Model and Expository Writing

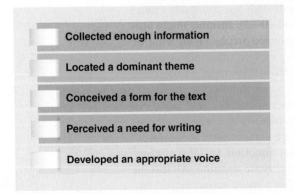

Collected enough information

Located a dominant theme

Conceived a form for the text

Perceived a need for writing

Developed an appropriate voice

The emphasis placed on invention in composing as viewed through the lens of the creative process model is significant since many novice writers tend to rush invention and proceed almost immediately to formal drafting. This tendency is potentially so limiting that composition scholar Donald Murray encourages writers to delay drafting until they have realized the goals listed to the left.

If you do shortchange invention in a hurry to begin formal drafting, you deny yourself the opportunity to capitalize on aspects of process that are at the heart of creative production. To be sure, invention processes are crucial in moving you beyond mundane or clichéd approaches to the writing challenges you will face throughout your college and professional careers.

Another benefit of viewing composing processes alongside creative processes is that doing so allows you to connect writing to all sorts of activities in which you might more eagerly engage. For example, reviewing strategies you use for percolating information (incubation) or achieving flow in the context of an art, sport, math problem, and so on, can stimulate your thinking about how you might conquer certain challenges you face when you are writing. In fact, many of the practices that help you achieve your goals in other creative realms might be effectively applied when you are generating ideas for writing, working through blocks, and improving upon early versions of the product. By making such positive and instructive connections, you will find that writing processes seem less foreign. As a result, you'll likely discover that writing will become more manageable and, therefore, more enjoyable.

Taking what you learn from those associations and carrying them into future contexts is vital for your continued success. In subsequent college courses, you will encounter many different types of writing assignments that, collectively, will require knowledge of various issues, audiences, and conventions for communicating. Thinking about creative and composing processes can provide a sense of continuity across these diverse assignments. While the composing process model offers you a definite place to start addressing virtually any writing assignment, the creative process model holds additional promise for transferring knowledge between writing situations because of its broad applicability to all disciplines.

Reflection and Your Development as a Writer

As noted in Chapter 1, knowledge transfer occurs through careful **reflection.** The primary goal of reflection, which involves recollecting, analyzing, and evaluating, is to learn from your former experiences. In the context of writing, in particular, the potential benefits of reflection include:

- Increased understanding of your composing tendencies and strategies
- Rejection of strategies that are not working
- Experimentation with strategies that are possibly more helpful
- More effective management of the overall composing enterprise
- Transfer of composing knowledge and skills to various contexts

Reflection can happen naturally at any time, but formalizing the activity can help you deepen and retain the sort of self-knowledge indicated in the above list. Toward such ends, your teacher will most likely assign exercises that ask you to think specifically about your writing processes and to record your observations about them. These might include, for example, keeping a journal that characterizes your composing strategies or engaging in "postwrites" that describe successes and challenges you experienced relevant to a given assignment. Over time, such exercises can help you identify productive and inefficient patterns in your composing practices and, therefore, support your development as a writer.

ACTIVITY

Considering Your Drafting Style The following sets of questions (one pair per bullet point) are intended to help you figure out your preferences or tendencies when it comes to drafting. If the description before the "or" in each case seems to fit you best, you tend to be methodical in your approach. If the one following the "or" fits you best, you tend to be less methodical. Once you determine where your tendencies lie, consider how you might capitalize on them, listing as many specific strategies as you can.

What Is Your Drafting Style?

To explore whether you tend to gravitate toward a nonmethodical or methodical drafting style, answer the following questions:

- Do you like to have a very clear and specific sense of where your text is going before you start drafting, **or** do you usually begin drafting without a plan to see where the writing takes you?
- Do you write a lot of your text in your head, **or** do you craft it entirely on paper or screen?
- Do you begin a project with readers' expectations clearly in mind, **or** do you begin your projects writing mainly for yourself, content to revise later as you consider readers' needs?
- When questions about your text arise as you are drafting, do you make decisions quickly, **or** do you like to play around or experiment with various possibilities?
- When you near completion of a draft, are you ready to be finished with it, **or** do you like returning to it several times, rereading it for more possibilities?
- Do you find that when you have a complete first draft it is in really good shape, **or** do you find that your first drafts require extensive reworking?

Source: Based on Muriel Harris, "Composing Behaviors of One- and Multi-Draft Writers," *College English*, vol. 51, no. 2, 1989, pp. 174–91.

IDEA FOR EXTENDED WRITING

Reflecting on a Creative Activity Think of a creative activity that you enjoy and/or excel in that doesn't involve writing (e.g., some form of visual artistry, dancing, music, a particular sport, fashion, interior design). For an audience of your classmates, write an essay in which you describe contexts, processes, and emotions involved in this activity, as well as particular aspects of it that you find engaging. (Feel free to interject anecdotes of specific creative moments to illustrate your more general observations.) This essay should eventually move toward a discussion of any lessons, processes, skills, or attitudes that might be transferred from the creative activity just described to the act of expository writing.

WORKS CITED

Csikszentmihalyi, Mihaly. *Creativity: Flow and the Psychology of Discovery and Invention.* Harper, 1996.

Duncker, Karl. "Reasoning in Humans II: The Solution of a Problem and its Appearance in Consciousness." *Journal of Comparative Psychology*, vol. 12, 1931, pp. 181–94.

Gates, Rosemary. "Applying Martin Greenman's Concept of Insight to Composition Theory." *Journal of Advanced Composition*, vol. 9, 1989, pp. 59–68.

Harman, Willis, and Howard Rheingold. *Higher Creativity: Liberating the Unconscious for Breakthrough Insights.* Tarcher, 1984.

Harris, Muriel. "Composing Behaviors of One- and Multi-Draft Writers." *College English,* vol. 51, no. 2, 1989, pp. 174–91.

Housman. A. E. "The Name and Nature of Poetry." *The Creative Process: Reflections on Invention in the Arts and Sciences.* Edited by Brewster Ghiselen. U of California P, 1985, pp. 85–91.

King, Stephen. *On Writing: A Memoir of the Craft.* Scribner, 2000.

Kneller, George F. *The Art and Science of Creativity.* Holt, 1965.

Murray, Donald. "The Essential Delay." *When a Writer Can't Write*, edited by Mike Rose. Guilford, 1985, pp. 219–26.

Murray, Mary. "The 16 Features of Insight." *Artwork of the Mind: An Interdisciplinary Description of Insight and the Search for It in Student Writing,* Hampton, 1995, pp. 23–40.

Wallas, Graham. *The Art of Thought.* Harcourt, 1926.

Rhetorical Situations

3

Study the restaurant sign above. Even if you don't like drive-in food, think for a moment about how this sign attempts to attract customers. What specific strategies does it employ? How might those strategies influence passersby looking for a place to eat? In answering these questions, you are considering the rhetoric of that sign—the specific appeals it makes to convince people like yourself to support that business. To be an effective writer, you must understand and be able to apply rhetorical concepts for purposes of encouraging readers to accept your ideas. This chapter will introduce you to the rhetorical concepts that are central to effective communication.

When associating the words *writing* and *creativity*, many people would immediately think of fiction and poetry. Maybe that's because the characters and events in these works are often "made up." Or maybe it's because fiction writers and poets tend to experiment with form and like to employ a lot of descriptive language to paint verbal pictures in the minds of their readers. At first consideration, these features do seem to place creative writing in a category different from **expository writing** (i.e., most school and workplace writing). On closer examination, however, you'll find that the contrast between the two is actually less pronounced and that expository writing offers abundant opportunity for creativity in content, form, and style.

33

Overlap between Creative and Expository Writing

Although one defining quality of fiction is that it portrays imaginary events, it is commonly "based on a true story." Even when it isn't, it often portrays shared human experience and, in that sense, upholds a version of reality. Although expository writing is held to a more stringent standard regarding facts and the nature of research, you can consider the reality it presents as also a version since it is filtered through the author's unique perspective (as well as the perspectives of any sources consulted).

Regarding the forms of creative and expository writing, most short fiction and novels fulfill widely held expectations for how a story should be ordered: A conflict will arise; the conflict will progress toward a climax; the conflict will be resolved; and all loose ends will be neatly tied together. Poetry doesn't always relate a story, but when it does, the structure is similar to that of a short story or a novel (think especially of lengthy, action-based epic poems). "Free verse," as suggested by its label, is subject to few constraints on form, but many other types of poems (e.g., sonnet, haiku) must adhere to some rigid structural constraints. These constraints might dictate number and length of stanzas (i.e., individual sections), number of syllables per line, rhyme patterns, and so on. Similarly to poetry, expository writing can assume many forms (e.g., essay, résumé, lab report), some of which allow significant freedom while others present a number of constraints.

As for language choices, poems and short stories are filled with words intended to help readers see, hear, smell, taste, and feel what their characters are experiencing. In contrast, expository writing is typically presumed to communicate meaning in a plain or straightforward manner. Generally speaking, it is more direct in stating its aims and conclusions. Still, expository writers frequently use vivid description or imagery to enliven their prose and express their ideas in ways that readers can readily grasp. For an illustration of how different genres of writing may violate preconceived notions, such as those addressed in the previous few paragraphs, consider Figure 3.1, which contrasts a résumé with a Shakespearean sonnet.

Most people would not label the résumé presented in Figure 3.1 as creative, but it did require its author to make many choices about content, document design, and the like. On the other hand, the Shakespearean sonnet beside that résumé would readily be categorized as "creative writing," but it has a pre-set form: 14 lines with 10 syllables each; a meter or rhythm known as iambic pentameter; a rhyme scheme of abab, cdcd, efef, gg.

The point of these comparisons between creative and expository texts is to illustrate that all writing invites you to be creative with content, form, and language. Put another way, all writing is an act of "meaning-making" (Berthoff) during which you confront many choices in achieving your goals. These choices involve applying composing strategies and tools that are appropriate to the task at hand. Of course, appropriateness is crucial to all writing, but—as the opening sections of this chapter suggest, it should not be guided by some rigidly perceived divide between creative and expository texts. On the contrary, it should be guided by the nature of the **rhetorical situation,** as specifically defined in the next paragraph.

Matthew Trujillo
MATTHEW.TRUJILLO@TOPCANDIDATE.COM
31 EUREKA WAY • BUENA VISTA, CA • (555) 555-5555

Career Objective
Apply production and communication skills gained through study and first-hand experience to help launch, produce, and market local news programming.

Education

2010–2014   Emerson College, B.A., Film & Television Production, Marketing
magna cum laude

Skills Summary
- Extensive experience in media production and design
- Tech savvy and well-versed in a range of post-production software programs
- Skilled in project management and leadership
- Outstanding communication skills, written and spoken

Professional Experience

2011–present, Part-Time Administrative Assistant, Department of Communication Studies: Assisting faculty in a variety of tasks related to office-related logistics, budgeting, supply purchasing, and hiring and supervising of interns.

2010–2011, Tech Assistant, Equipment Distribution Center, Emerson College: Assisting in the loaning and maintenance of state-of-the art equipment and facilities to faculty and students.

2007-2009–Intern, ITRAF Media: Network trouble-shooting; preventative maintenance and repair; monitored and responded to network problems; assisted in event planning and marketing.

Grants and Awards

2013, Long Beach Arts Council Project Grant Recipient for short film on a growing local news organization.

WILLIAM SHAKESPEARE

Sonnet 116

Let me not to the marriage of true minds

Admit impediments. Love is not love

Which alters when it alteration finds,

Or bends with the remover to remove:

O, no! it is an ever-fixed mark,

That looks on tempests and is never shaken;

It is the star to every wandering bark,

Whose worth's unknown, although his height be taken.

Love's not Time's fool, though rosy lips and cheeks

Within his bending sickle's compass come;

Love alters not with his brief hours and weeks,

But bears it out even to the edge of doom.

  If this be error, and upon me prov'd,

  I never writ, nor no man ever lov'd.

Figure 3.1 A résumé and a Shakespearean sonnet. Contrary to popular assumptions, the acts of writing a sonnet and writing a résumé are both subject to freedoms and constraints.

Most contemporary definitions of **rhetoric** draw from Aristotle's view on the subject: "Let rhetoric be [defined as] an ability, in each [particular] case, to see the available means of persuasion" (*On Rhetoric* 37). The goal of rhetoric, then, is to persuade your readers—whether to convince them of your position on a given issue, the accuracy of facts and figures you're citing, the credibility of your interpretation, and so on. The set of circumstances in which you exercise your rhetorical or persuasive know-how is the rhetorical situation, and it encompasses the following elements:

- **Audience**—your intended readers
- **Forum**—a place for publishing or sharing your writing
- **Topic**—your focused subject matter
- **Genre**—the type of document you're composing
- **Author's purpose**—your reason for writing
- **Author's role**—your stance toward your readers and topic

Understanding these rhetorical elements is crucial to effective communication, as is understanding the **rhetorical appeals,** or aids to persuasion, listed below:

- **Ethos**—features of your text that establish your credibility as an author
- **Pathos**—features of your text that impact the emotions of your readers
- **Logos**—features of your text that clarify your reasoning or establish the logic of your position

The remainder of this chapter elaborates on the rhetorical elements and rhetorical appeals, offering strategies for helping you make effective choices relevant to the rhetorical situations that you will be entering.

Creativity and the Rhetorical Situation

Every rhetorical situation—whether in academic, workplace, or more public contexts—poses a problem: How can you communicate your ideas in a way that will be instructive and convincing for your audience? Some of these situations will be defined entirely *for* you, and others will be defined entirely *by* you. Between the extremes exist composing problems characterized by all varieties of limitations and freedoms.

In your college composition courses, you will respond to many different writing assignments, some that outline very specific expectations and others that establish expectations only very loosely. Of course, the latter type leaves greater room for creativity. But even in highly structured assignments, you will have opportunities to exercise your creative potential—that is, to critically address the elements of the rhetorical situation for purposes of expressing meaning in ways that will engage your audience.

The starting point for any composing challenge is to identify the elements of the rhetorical situation through questions like these: What is the topic or subject matter? What is my purpose for writing? Who are my intended readers? What role or stance will I assume in presenting my ideas? The answers to these questions will guide you as you work to fulfill your overall composing objective. As you dig more deeply into your project—that is, thinking more critically about it, talking with others, conducting research—your understanding of the rhetorical situation will continue to evolve. Not only will it become more focused and detailed, but it may even suggest a direction for your writing other than what you originally planned. Of course, when you are *assigned* a writing task, you will be determining fewer components of the rhetorical situation than when your writing is self-directed. But even when you are limited in this sense, you will have to make at least some decisions about the rhetorical situation.

In illustration of this point, consider the following two assignments:

ASSIGNMENT 1	ASSIGNMENT 2
Write a letter to the editor of your university newspaper about a problem on campus for which you'd like to propose a solution.	Write an article on a topic of special interest to you for a magazine whose readers share your interest.

Clearly, Assignment 1 is more structured, as it stipulates several components of the rhetorical situation: genre (a letter), forum (the university newspaper), and audience (the institution's students and employees). In addition, the assignment implies a role for the author (concerned citizen) and a purpose (improving the university community in some way). Although the author will enjoy some freedom with regard to topic, the letter must focus on a campus concern. In contrast, Assignment 2 leaves more responsibility for defining the task up to the writer. Virtually any subject matter is fair game, and the only requirement placed on the forum is that its readers are interested in the same subject matter. While a genre (article) is designated, it is a less precise category than a letter.

Although Assignment 1 is more restrictive than Assignment 2, it still requires your active engagement in representing the rhetorical situation. To complete the assignment, you would have to single out a campus problem, offer solutions to the problem, find ways of expressing ideas, determine how to best order information, and so on. These decisions are invitations for meaning-making—that is, for taking on the role of creative thinker and creative user of language and form. Of course, this is not to suggest that "anything goes." Effective writing balances creative drive with an understanding of the rhetorical situation and the conventions—identifying features and practices—that are implicit in it. Remember, however, that even though assigned elements of the rhetorical situation may initially feel confining, they could ultimately prove helpful or *constructive* since they offer many vantage points for responding to the writing challenge before you and evaluating your approach.

Rhetoric and Constructive Constraints

Think for a moment about how many times you've been asked to accept some statement about writing as a rule, only to see or hear that statement violated in a later context. To be sure, as you continue to develop as a writer, you'll discover that very few observations about composing will stand as hard-and-fast rules. Of course, some students may appreciate advice about writing presented in the form of rules because it simplifies their role as author and eliminates the need for trial and error. But keep in mind that reducing the complexity inherent in writing to a set of rules can undermine your success since engaging approaches to expository writing are most likely to occur when you work through that complexity—when you engage in trial and error while pushing against perceived boundaries.

On the other hand, it's important to note that a complete absence of boundaries or constraints can be just as problematic as too many rules. Despite associations of creativity with freedom, the reality is that creativity occurs in an existing **conceptual space.** A conceptual space can be understood as a recognized activity or field of inquiry (e.g., an academic discipline or major). Some examples are ballet, rock music, poetry, biochemistry, football, and nature writing, to name just a few. The defining characteristics of a conceptual space include the features and tools that its products and processes have in common. For example, ballet is defined by certain features and tools that distinguish it from modern dance or hip-hop. Football is defined by particular features and tools that distinguish it from baseball or soccer (Boden 79). Figure 3.2 depicts the conceptual spaces of ballet and football and the features and tools that distinguish one from the other.

The content of the conceptual spaces for ballet and football is too vast to fully represent in the small diagrams constituting Figure 3.2. However, this snapshot is sufficient to demonstrate that both activities (and many others you could think of) are identified with special uniforms, physical moves, and performance sites. However, the *types* of uniforms, physical moves, and performances are what distinguish ballet and football from each other and from other activities.

The features and tools characterizing a conceptual space, then, impose certain constraints. For example, football players would find it difficult to run in pointe shoes; they need cleats to grab the sod or turf. Though ballerinas might appreciate some protection during a fall, they would sag under the weight of shoulder pads and helmets; they need lightweight leotards that allow for a range of fine movement. Without such constraints, the dancer or athlete would lack a viable point of entry into the activity, as well as strategies for managing a performance. For these

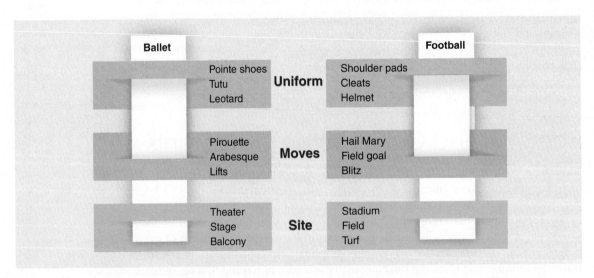

Figure 3.2 Conceptual spaces. Ballet and football share certain defining characteristics: Both require uniforms, an ability to move in particular ways, and a specifically designed site at which to perform those moves for the enjoyment of an audience. Their distinguishing features and tools are listed toward the center of this figure, in the colored boxes.

reasons, constraints imposed by features of the conceptual space or field of inquiry can be viewed as useful and productive—even essential (Boden 79; Sharples 129).

The conceptual space emphasized in the composition course you are taking is, of course, expository writing. Figure 3.3 partially diagrams this conceptual space, which is defined by its own categories of features and tools, including elements of the rhetorical situation and the rhetorical appeals introduced earlier in this chapter.

The conceptual space in Figure 3.3 could be expanded by adding items to the boxes labeled "Content" and "Physical Tools"; it also could be expanded by adding boxes to represent various composing activities, such as researching and correcting mistakes. Because the conceptual space of expository writing has more in common with academic activities than with physical activities such as ballet or football, the categories of distinguishing features differ. For instance, while you may wear certain clothes (e.g., sweatpants and T-shirt) when you write, or you may always write in a certain place (e.g., your bedroom or the library), these are not the most significant features in defining the act of expository writing—at least they are not as significant as they are in defining the acts of ballet dancing or playing football.

While all the contents of the conceptual space illustrated in Figure 3.3 are potentially relevant to any expository writing task, experts agree that the most useful and efficient point of entry is the rhetorical situation itself. The specific elements of the rhetorical situation (i.e., audience, topic, forum, genre, purpose, role), as well as the rhetorical appeals (ethos, pathos, and logos) can be viewed as **constructive constraints.** They are constructive in the sense that they serve as catalysts for generating and managing your text; if you engage them thoughtfully, they can assist you in making meaning. At the same time, they constrain the writing in ways that make it appropriate in the eyes of your readers.

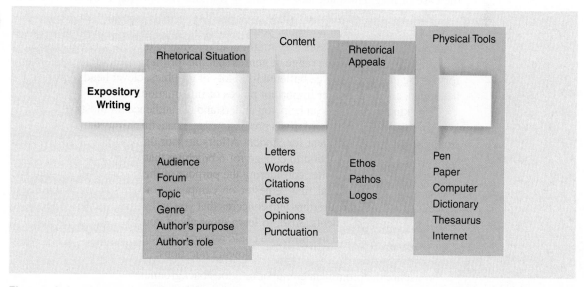

Figure 3.3 Conceptual space of expository writing. The conceptual space of expository writing includes features that pertain to the rhetorical situation, the content of the piece, the appeals the author makes, and the physical tools he or she employs.

Elements of the Rhetorical Situation

As the previous paragraphs explain, each rhetorical situation has its constraints and its creative potential. One way to explore the creative potential of any writing assignment is to consider the following questions:

- How might you place a "fresh spin" on an overworked topic?
- What knowledge about your readers might help you create a surprising hook to draw them in?
- How might you play with the typical organization of a document so that it will more effectively convey your ideas but still "fit" the genre you are pursuing?
- How might you experiment with the conventions of language to most effectively communicate your meaning?

Keep these questions in mind as you read about each element of the rhetorical situation.

Audience and Forum

Composition teacher and scholar Peter Elbow has suggested that if you think too early and too much about audience and forum you can bring on a case of writer's block. If you sense this is happening to you, by all means let your ideas flow freely onto the page or screen without worrying about potential readers. Then, once your thoughts are unlocked and you have a substantial draft, you can return to what you have written and apply your knowledge of readers' expectations.

In contrast to Elbow, other teachers and scholars argue that considering audience and forum at the beginning of a new writing challenge can help you focus your efforts by locking down certain variables of the rhetorical situation. For example, in the case of magazines and newspapers, if you analyze specific features of several issues (the nature of the articles, advertisements, etc.), you can construct a portrait of the typical reader. In addition, you can identify topics that tend to attract such readers, as well as any biases they might hold relevant to those topics. Further, such analysis brings to light the range of genres that the forum publishes, its stylistic and formatting preferences (e.g., bulleted lists, lots of graphics, clever headings and sub-headings), and many other important pieces of information.

This kind of analysis can help you understand the audience for most of your writing projects, whether personal, civic, professional, or academic. Consider the following example: The Vice President for Student Affairs at your university has asked you to write about your introduction to college for a brochure that will be distributed to the next class of freshmen. After considering the purpose of the brochure—to provide an insider's view of a typical first semester on campus—you might spend some time reflecting on common questions and concerns that you and your friends had when you were first-semester students. Also, to learn more about your target readers and what they might want or need to know, you could research demographics of the last several freshman classes, perhaps asking the following questions:

- What are the prominent ethnic or religious backgrounds?
- Do students come from a particular region of the state or country?
- Are there any majors that attract especially large groups of students?
- What activities and services does the school offer that attract the most interest?

The list of potential questions about audience relevant to this rhetorical situation goes on and on.

Your expanding knowledge about your target audience might also suggest ways of presenting the ideas you generate. For example, if you predict that your readers will be overwhelmed by information during their first days on campus, you might employ bulleted lists (like the one above), which are easy to process at a glance. Or, if you believe your readers may need reassurance that they are not alone in their confusion and anxiety, you might include a "Frequently Asked Questions" (FAQs) section in your brochure. This list of questions would suggest to your readers that most new students have experienced the same uncertainties they are experiencing.

Of course, as previously noted, aspects of audience and forum will affect and be affected by other elements of the rhetorical situation. Figure 3.4 indicates some

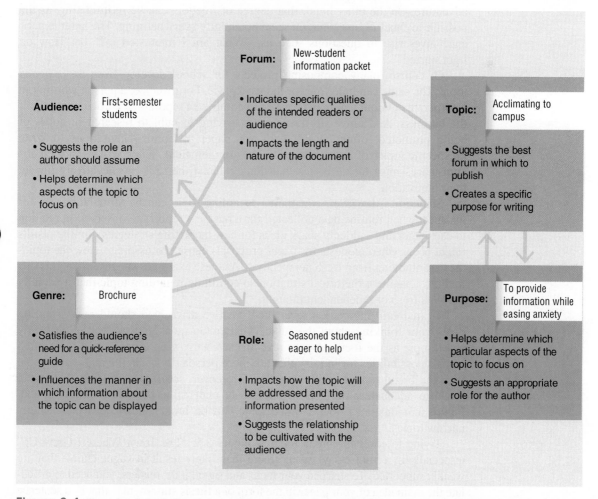

Figure 3.4 Flowchart depicting interactions among elements of the rhetorical situation. Each box represents a different element of the rhetorical situation. The bullet points offer insight as to how each element can guide or inform a writer's choices.

ways in which these various elements might impact each other in the brochure-writing scenario detailed above.

Interactions like those depicted in Figure 3.4 occur within every rhetorical scenario. When reading about sample rhetorical situations in the sections that follow, try to project how the elements that are not explicitly addressed might influence those that are and vice versa.

Topic

When a given rhetorical situation invites you to choose your own topic for writing, you may feel motivated, frustrated, or maybe a little of both. On the one hand, thoughts of searching the library stacks or cruising the Internet—free to learn about any issue that sparks your curiosity and enthusiasm—may excite a sense of adventure. On the other hand, that degree of freedom can be intimidating, as the possible avenues of investigation seem potentially overwhelming. The latter experience gives rise to questions such as, "What am I interested in?" or "How do I get started?"

Of course, many composing projects for school develop from an *assigned* topic. The same can hold true for the workplace. For instance, a person working in a corporate environment may be asked to compose a report on a particular aspect of the business. And university professors, striving to publish research in hopes of being promoted, often consult calls for paper proposals—invitations to write on specific topics of interest to colleagues in their field. When writers in such circumstances must tackle issues that don't interest them, it can negatively impact their motivation.

Sometimes, however, constraints regarding topic can be stimulating, as, for instance, when routine data collected for a business report are observed in relation to each other and suddenly spark ideas for new marketing strategies. Similar results might occur when requests for paper proposals cause professors to view the topics they are studying from fresh perspectives. As these examples suggest, then, it is difficult to imagine a rhetorical situation so confining regarding topic that it actually prevents fresh or independent thought.

To maintain motivation levels and creative drive, you should resist shutting down your thinking about the subject matter too quickly or accepting an overly broad topic as the focus of your text. In fact, narrowing a prescribed topic often reveals possibilities for inquiry that are more personally engaging and manageable than the broad topic initially suggests. Moreover, settling for a topic that is too broad to adequately develop will seriously undermine the quality of your text. Figure 3.5 illustrates how a broad topic can be broken down into increasingly narrow topics.

Trying to cover the broad topic in Figure 3.5, "The Town Where I Grew Up" (especially in a brief essay), would more than likely result in vague claims that are weakly supported. To sharpen your focus and signal it for readers, you need to articulate the main idea of your paper in the form of a **thesis statement**—that is, a sentence (sometimes a few sentences) that forecasts the specific topic of the paper. Depending on the proposed length of your document, an effective thesis might grow from any

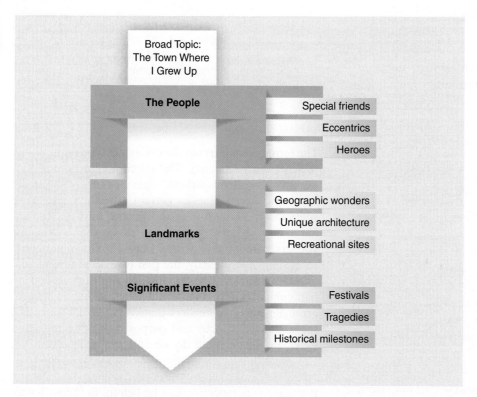

Figure 3.5 **Possibilities for narrowing a broad topic.** Note that the nine relatively specific topics on the far right could be refined into even more tightly focused topics—for example, a specific hero or a particular tragedy that impacted you personally.

of the nine focuses indicated at the far right of Figure 3.5. With regard to any of them, the next step would be to ask yourself what specific insight or point you want to communicate about the focus you've settled on. That insight or point will evolve into your thesis.

For some examples, consult Figure 3.6, which provides possible thesis statements for three of the narrowly focused topics in Figure 3.5—the topics of a hero, a festival, and a tragedy, respectively. Notice the specificity in each of these thesis

- The statue commemorating Captain Franklin in the Frankfort town square is well deserved for the many contributions he made in founding and developing the community.

- Summer in Waterville, Maine, brings with it the long celebrated blueberry festival, a weekend of eclectic musical performances, displays by local artisans, delicious food, and, of course, the crowning of the Blueberry Queen.

- Although five years have passed since the derecho hit Carbondale, Illinois, the impact of that devastating storm still lingers.

Figure 3.6 **Thesis statements about focused topics**

MYTH

"All essays should contain five paragraphs—an introduction, three body paragraphs, and a conclusion."

This myth extends even further by suggesting that (1) the introduction should be only one paragraph long and should contain a thesis statement that announces the topics of the body paragraphs and (2) the conclusion should briefly summarize the body paragraphs, using repetitive language.

While this ready-made form might help you arrange your ideas, it can blind you to organizational tools that would better serve your intentions, such as:

- Taking more than one paragraph to introduce your topic or to discuss a given subtopic
- Using transitions that articulate specific relationships between ideas—as opposed to "point 1, point 2, point 3"
- Fashioning conclusions that don't merely repeat what has already been said but that inspire readers to take action

REALITY

statements. Even though they are narrowly focused, they encompass topics that can easily sustain a multi-page essay. With such a focused statement of your topic, you would be well prepared to compose a detailed, thoroughly developed paper.

Genre

The term **genre** refers to the document type required by the rhetorical situation. The specific genre label—for example, "academic article," "personal essay," "letter," "memorandum"—implies certain expectations or conventions with regard to form, content, and style. **Form** has to do with how you arrange ideas in your text or how you structure it on the whole. Consider a memorandum, for instance. Ordinarily, the first paragraph of a memo presents an overview of the main topic, with subsequent paragraphs offering more detailed information. This arrangement helps readers quickly and easily identify the document's focus and purpose. After reading the overview, readers can decide if they need or want to wade into the details provided.

Such conventions of form, rooted in efficiency from the reader's perspective, can be helpful to the writer as well, supplying clear guidelines for various parts of the document. Within those guidelines, however, the writer must think critically about generating and presenting information appropriate to that rhetorical situation. Moreover, the writer must prepare readers for what is to come by providing effective transitions between parts of the memo. Of course, not all genre conventions are as obvious as those characterizing a memo, but you'll want to become more vigilant in locating conventions since doing so can facilitate your reading and writing processes.

In addition to arousing certain expectations for form, genre may also arouse certain expectations for **content.** Of course, some genre labels, such as "editorial" and "essay," apply to compositions spanning a wide range of issues. Pushing the label "essay" a bit further, the subcategory "personal essay" arouses more exact expectations, causing readers to anticipate an author's reflection on significant moments from his or her past. Personal essays rely heavily on narrative passages as the author shares stories from his or her experience that help illustrate certain life lessons. Another genre that foregrounds clear expectations for content is that referred to as "nature writing." Though it might involve personal reflection, it also incorporates thick description of the outdoors and possibly even scientific facts and figures. Ultimately, though, the defining quality of nature writing is that it focuses attention on specific aspects of the natural world, with the objective of awakening appreciation.

Less Formal Style:

A Textbook Written for Students
Ancient Greek poets, composers and others credited their ideas to inspiration from the Muses, nine sister goddesses, daughters of Zeus and Mnemosyne, who presided over the arts (which curiously included astronomy). Plato suggested that a state of "divine madness" helps the inspiration. Chalking up creativity to inspiration from gods seems an unscientific idea with remarkable endurance. A few ancient and contemporary people, with more imagination than objectivity, attribute creativity to somehow tapping a *universal mind* or *universal consciousness*—a mysterious information source said to float throughout the universe.

Source: Gary Davis, *Creativity Is Forever.* Kendall/Hunt, 2010.

More Formal Style:

A Scholarly Book Written for Professors
Clark resists any mystifying notion of "inspiration" as something that just "happens," and re-inscribes the concept within critical discourses that require a sense of cause or agency, whether internal or external.

The key concept here is that of dictation by an other: the sense of the individual moved by a force larger than her- or himself. Clark's use of the phrase is prompted by Derrida, especially his "Psyche: invention of the other" (Derrida 1992: 3-11-43), but as he argues throughout the book, the concept resonates in various ways with both archaic notions of "the Muse" and modern constructions of "the Unconscious."

Source: Rob Pope, *Creativity: Theory, History, Practice.* Routledge, 2005.

Figure 3.7 **Contrasting styles for a textbook and a scholarly book**

A final category of expectations relevant to genre involves issues of **style** or, more specifically, word- and sentence-level concerns. Contrasting an academic research paper with a textbook excerpt provides a good example of stylistic differences. To be more specific, academic research articles are relatively formal, employing jargon familiar to experts in the field and sophisticated sentence structures helpful in communicating complex ideas. The tone is often detached, as the author tries to project an unbiased stance toward the subject matter.

In contrast, although textbooks are also academic in nature, they aspire to be less formal, with simpler sentence structures and full definitions of specialized terms intended to clarify complex ideas to nonexperts. The excerpts in Figure 3.7 illustrate this contrast in style. Both passages address the nature of creative inspiration, but one comes from a textbook and the other from a scholarly work. Note how the scope of each discussion, the vocabulary, the sentence structures, and the treatment of secondary sources differ. Note, too, how these distinctions suggest very different target audiences.

Author's Purpose

Regardless of the rhetorical situation you've entered, you should have a clear purpose, or reason for writing, in mind. That purpose might be to increase readers' knowledge, raise their awareness, convince them to accept a position, or move them toward action. In your college courses, your instructor may occasionally assign a purpose to give you practice at navigating unfamiliar rhetorical scenarios. At other times, teachers will urge you to locate your own purposes for writing. Assigned or not, your purpose will guide your approach to a given writing situation. As is the case with all rhetorical elements, pushing yourself to think carefully and critically about purpose will suggest a multitude of possibilities for addressing the challenge at hand.

To illustrate, assume that your purpose is to raise readers' awareness about some issue—global warming, for example. The easy route toward fulfilling this purpose would be to simply provide a summary of facts and figures about global warming. If that tactic seems a bit routine, you might be moved to think about what is at stake if society ignores the threat of this phenomenon. After adopting this perspective, you might decide that, rather than straightforwardly reporting facts and figures, you could begin your essay with a dramatic description of a weather disaster theorized to result from global warming. With this approach, you not only raise awareness but also incite people to consider what could happen if this threat is ignored, thus jolting them from their apathy. Further, you might reinforce your message by gently scolding those whose actions may have contributed to global warming (e.g., by using aerosol sprays or driving big cars) so that they not only become intellectually committed to the issue but also live their lives in ways that are more mindful of the consequences of global warming. This example demonstrates how an overarching purpose, such as raising awareness, can be refined by searching for possible subpurposes, such as changing behavior or promoting action, thus encouraging different outcomes in response to the issue under consideration.

Author's Role

The final rhetorical element to be addressed—author's role—can be characterized as a writer's attitude in relation to the topic and/or intended reader(s). Extending the global warming example, the author might adopt the role of "concerned citizen." As such, he or she projects a certain attitude toward global warming—that it is a menace, posing danger for the world's population. In contrast, an author who is not convinced by research arguing for the reality of global warming might cast him- or herself in the role of "informed skeptic."

Clearly, these contrasting roles will guide a writer's composing strategies in divergent directions. Most obviously, conflicting stances on the issue of global warming will result in different treatments of the published scholarship about it. A concerned citizen will work to portray it as legitimate, while an informed skeptic might charge that it is irrational or based on faulty research. Additionally, the concerned citizen and the informed skeptic will probably address readers in distinct ways. The concerned citizen may scold readers as a strategy for making them feel guilty about their carefree attitude toward the environment. The informed skeptic, on the other hand, might appeal to readers' egos by portraying believers in global warming as gullible and panicky and by regarding those who question this theory about climate change as more stable and reasonable.

The possible roles you might adopt as a writer become more limited when addressing audiences whose readers share similar, deeply held beliefs, such as those who subscribe to certain political publications. For example, the more "liberal" or "conservative" a publication is, the less flexible its readers will be in considering the ideas of outsiders. The same is likely true for certain religious publications. Their readers' systems of belief are so personal and fundamental to the ways they make sense of the world that they may resist exposure to ideas that conflict with their core values.

In addition to the nature of the forum and the beliefs of its readers, your own values and beliefs will affect the role you adopt, but there will always be options for positioning yourself. To be more specific, even a firm believer in global warming—the concerned citizen—might just as likely assume other roles, such as the "exasperated environmentalist" or the "objective scientist." Although representing the same general position on the controversy, each of these specific roles suggests a different approach to communicating that position and can help you effectively manage other elements of the rhetorical situation.

Rhetorical Appeals

In the previous section, you learned that thinking critically about elements of the rhetorical situation can help you manage any composing challenge you might face. Building on this knowledge, the paragraphs that follow will introduce you to **rhetorical appeals,** or what Aristotle characterized as the specific means of persuasion. These appeals—ethos, pathos, and logos—will suggest additional strategies for convincing your readers to accept your ideas.

Ethos

Ethos relates to the author's character or credibility—in other words, how trustworthy or respectable she or he is. To be sure, readers are more willing to consider the ideas of authors they trust, but remember that criteria for trust vary to some degree between audiences. For certain audiences, such criteria for trust might include evidence of an author's knowledge base or extensive experience in a given field. For other audiences, the criteria might include particular accomplishments, such as climbing Mt. Everest or being designated a master chess player. Still other audiences might be impressed by good deeds, such as volunteering to assist in war-torn regions or in a community literacy program. In some situations, trust might be granted in accordance with labels indicating that an author's system of values matches that of his or her readers. Depending on the audience, political candidates, for example, attain a certain amount of

spare me
the guilt chip.

Katy Perry

Figure 3.8 Scene from a Popchips commercial featuring the performer Katy Perry

credibility simply by wearing the label "Democrat" or "Republican"—associations that suggest they will think and act in certain ways on key issues.

Simply being a celebrity carries significant ethos for some audiences. For instance, employing young pop stars to advertise products or ideas is a prevalent marketing strategy, as they can influence an especially impressionable group of consumers (see Figure 3.8). The fact that these stars have achieved incredible levels of fame and monetary success at a young age may cause teens, who admire those celebrities' grand lifestyles, to buy what they are selling or to follow their causes.

In your own writing, you can establish ethos or credibility through various means. First and foremost, you can do so by showing that your knowledge base is adequate for discussing your topic intelligently. Doing so won't be too difficult if you are writing about personal experience, but this won't always be possible in school and the workplace. In that event, you can enhance your ethos by invoking the ethos of others—that is, citing experts or scholars with reputations in a pertinent field who have published material on your subject. Of course, all credibility that you gain by referencing these sources will be lost if you don't carefully document them (see Chapter 21 for guidelines).

Ethos will also derive from the sense that you are treating your subject matter in a balanced and fair manner. This doesn't mean that you can't establish a firm position, but it does mean that you should make an effort to seek out opinions or interpretations that counter your own, acknowledge them in your text, and respond to them in keeping with your thesis statement. In fact, conceding certain points may be necessary to making the strongest case, and doing so is much more supportive of an appealing ethos than trying to act as if opposing opinions don't exist. (For more on addressing counterarguments, see Chapter 16.)

Pathos

The appeal referred to as **pathos** denotes an attempt to arouse emotions. For example, a doctor advocating for the Food and Drug Administration's approval of a controversial medical treatment might recount the story of a sick child whose life it saved. A politician arguing for a change in national leadership might infuse his campaign brochure with references to specific injustices that citizens have endured under current policies. An athletic director raising money for university sports programs might fill her department's newsletter with tales of victory on the court and in the field, reminding readers of the excitement and institutional pride that many associate with winning teams. Advertisers in popular magazines liberally employ emotional appeals, both visual and verbal, to sell their products or services. Adorable infants, cuddly animals, grandparents walking on the beach with grandchildren—all are images used to make potential consumers feel good about the products being sold or the messages being promoted.

As an author, you may want to similarly tap emotions in moving readers to accept your ideas. But keep in mind that the effect of emotional appeals depends to large degree on the universality and power of the emotion projected for a given audience. To be sure, few people would not be upset by the suffering of a child, so arguing for a course of action by establishing its relevance to children's well-being would be a fitting approach for even a highly diverse audience. Comparatively more individualized appeals—for example, those that speak to a person's religious or political leanings—would be more risky in the context of a diverse audience. Because emotional appeals are some of the most powerful you have to offer, you must be familiar with readers' values so as to avoid unintentionally offending their sensibilities. While some authors will purposefully offend readers as a means of shocking them into attention (e.g., provoking them at the beginning of a paper on a human rights issue by quoting the offensive words of a despot), you should enact such strategies with caution since a failure to anticipate and moderate the ill effects of offending readers usually results in a rhetorical disaster.

While readers' values must guide pathos, within those parameters you have ample space to experiment with creative approaches to emotional appeals. After all, emotional appeals often carry a sense of drama, presented in verbal snapshots that are narrative in form and rich with description. Of course, as already noted in this chapter, there is room for creative maneuvering in your approach to all rhetorical elements and appeals. Pathos, though, is particularly promising in this regard.

Logos

Logos (root of the word *logic*) is an appeal attached to the viability of an author's assertions, the quality of information presented to support those assertions, and the processes of reasoning that sustain them. If you're thinking that logos seems closely related to ethos, you're correct. But, whereas ethos is, generally speaking, impacted by logos, the study and application of logos shine a more focused light on the building blocks of reasoning behind an author's central claim. Essential to effective logos are thoroughness and accuracy. As you develop logos in your own texts, you'll want to make certain that all claims have appropriate and sufficient evidence to back them and that readers can understand why that evidence should be considered convincing. In its most impressive state, logos leads to insight—an actual contribution to the current knowledge base.

Potential constraints on logos have to do with whether or not the content of your message will set well with intended readers (yet another testament to the interconnectedness of rhetorical elements). For example, imagine a rhetorical situation in which an author holding strong fundamentalist Christian values wishes to argue for capital punishment in a forum aimed at a diverse audience, such as faculty members at a state university. In doing so, she cites a passage from the Bible as evidence in support of her position. Although this might be an appropriate rhetorical gesture in forums targeting individuals who share the author's belief system, for audiences that are mixed with regard to religious belief systems—such as the faculty at a public university—invoking the Bible in this manner would be a risky, if not rhetorically self-defeating, move.

Does this mean that Christians and other religious individuals can't access an academic audience? Of course not—but it does suggest that they must consider the extent to which that audience will accept the validity of cited sources. In short, they might want to stick with sources that would be more widely influential in that context than a given sacred text. Indeed, all writers must consider the perceived validity of their sources relevant to the readers they are hoping to influence, in addition to other contributing factors associated with logos.

Rhetoric and Creative Drive

This chapter challenges views of expository writing that portray it as dry and formulaic. In doing so, it introduces you to elements of the rhetorical situation as openings for active, critical, creative thought and expression. Such modes of thought and expression may include strategies and textual features associated with fiction and poetry. Most definitely, they will include the writer's purposeful attempts at meaning-making. Such efforts stand in sharp contrast to searching out recipes for good writing (as if they exist), dumping ideas into preexisting forms, or simply patching together the ideas of others.

In the end, thinking critically about the elements of a rhetorical situation will help you harness your creative drive with the intent of gaining confidence in the power of your ideas, asserting your presence in the texts you write, and engaging your readers with fresh ideas and perspectives. What's more, the rhetorical elements and appeals lie at the heart of every composing activity; therefore, you can carry them with you as a template of sorts for exploring how you might craft communications in other classes, on the job, and in your personal life.

ACTIVITY

Characterizing the Target Audience   In any situation that requires you to evaluate rhetorical strategies or appeals, you will need to consider the nature of the target audience. This is because audiences differ in terms of values, beliefs, interests, levels of expertise, and so on, and, consequently, strategies that will have a significant impact on one set of readers might not be the most effective choices for another. Using a magazine that you have access to (or that your instructor provides), characterize the target audience by answering the following questions:

- What is the magazine's title?
- Is it affiliated with a particular organization?
- Is it associated with a specific philosophy or political ideology?
- Does it have a particular disciplinary orientation?
- What stated or evident purpose(s) does it serve?
- What kind of people write for this forum (i.e., if revealed, what are their credentials, professional backgrounds, etc.)?
- What are key experiences that readers of the forum might have in common, and/or what sources might they all be familiar with?
- What kinds of topics or issues does this magazine typically address?
- What types of documents does it publish (e.g., articles, reviews, speeches, poems)?
- How long do the documents tend to be?
- What organizational pattern(s) do the documents typically follow?
- What formatting conventions do the documents reveal (e.g., subheadings, graphics, abstracts)?
- Do the authors cite any sources for their ideas; if so, how?
- How complex are the sentence structures?
- Do the authors employ jargon or technical language?
- What stance do the authors typically take in addressing their audience?

Source: Adapted from James Porter's forum analysis worksheet, published in the appendix to his article "Intertextuality and the Discourse Community."

Once you've answered all or most of these questions, compose a portrait of the magazine's target audience and consider what this portrait suggests about rhetorical strategies that likely would or would not impress the intended readers.

IDEA FOR EXTENDED WRITING

Evaluating Rhetorical Strategies   Locate two articles that argue different sides of a given issue. (Film reviews and political discourse are examples of publications that invite opposing stances.) Study these articles to identify the rhetorical strategies the authors use in making their respective cases—including each element of the rhetorical situation and all three appeals defined and illustrated in this chapter. Once you've finished, compose an essay (with your writing class as an audience) in which you compare and contrast the articles' treatment of the topic at hand. Remember that any evaluation of rhetorical strategies needs to be grounded in discussion about the presumed values, beliefs, and levels of expertise of readers targeted by the publications in which these articles appear (see the Activity above, "Characterizing the Target Audience").

WORKS CITED

Aristotle. *On Rhetoric.* Translated by George Kennedy, Oxford UP, 2007.

Berthoff, Ann E. *The Making of Meaning: Metaphors, Models and Maxims for Writing Teachers.* Boynton, 1981.

Boden, Margaret. "What Is Creativity?" *Dimensions of Creativity,* MIT P, 1994, pp. 75–117.

Davis, Gary A. *Creativity Is Forever.* Kendall, 1999.

Elbow, Peter. "Closing My Eyes as I Speak: An Argument for Ignoring Audience." *College English*, vol. 49, 1987, pp. 50–69.

Pope, Rob. *Creativity: Theory, History, Practice.* Routledge, 2005.

Porter, James. "Intertextuality and the Discourse Community." *Rhetoric Review*, vol. 5, no. 1, 1986, pp. 34–47.

Sharples, Mike. "An Account of Writing as Creative Design." *The Science of Writing: Theories, Methods, Individual Differences and Applications*, edited by Michael Levy and Sarah Ransdell, Erlbaum, 1996, pp. 127–48.

Invention Strategies

4

Grab a piece of paper, take five minutes, and list as many uses as you can think of for the tin can pictured here.

How many uses did you think of? 15? 25? 45? How many "types" of uses did you come up with? (Any use that assumes the role of a container counts as one type.)

You have just engaged in a renowned creativity test by psychologist J. P. Guilford. The number of ideas you generated counts as your fluency score; the number of different types as your flexibility score; the uniqueness of your ideas as your originality score; and the amount of detail you provide as your elaboration score. This test involves a technique called *brainstorming,* which encourages you to record your thoughts as quickly as possible, without editing, as a way of encouraging you to "think outside the box." Such creative thinking is crucial to invention—the act of generating and focusing ideas for writing. This chapter discusses brainstorming and many other activities that will support your invention processes.

Writing is always challenging, even for those who excel at it. To some extent, your capacity for meeting the challenge will be proportionate to the degree of excitement you feel for your subject matter. Put another way, you will best be prepared to tackle composing problems you face in

MYTH

"The best writers are those who immediately know what they want to say."

While some writers in some situations may be immediately inspired with ideas for writing, most—depending on the nature of the task—will take days, months, or even years to formulate and refine the concepts they want to address. Even when you are facing strict deadlines for a project, it's crucial that you reserve some time for invention. The more fully formed ideas that typically result from such efforts can facilitate drafting and can save you the disappointment of submitting products that are less insightful or well developed.

REALITY

college and the workplace if you are genuinely engaged with the topic you're writing about or if you can locate some angle on it that particularly interests you. This is why **invention**—the act of generating and focusing ideas—is so crucial to composing.

Productive invention depends on your willingness to spend time playing around with your subject matter so as to consider it from different vantage points and to explore its potential connections with issues that may seem unrelated. Invention activities stretch your thinking and can, therefore, help you find unique approaches to writing projects that will motivate you to take up the challenges they pose. Challenges associated with writing (or any creative activity, for that matter) are marked by a sense of unease or dissonance that occurs when you discover that your composing objectives and the strategies by which you plan to achieve those objectives don't match.

When facing such challenges at the beginning of a project, your immediate inclination may be to alleviate the discomfort as quickly as possible. Doing so might involve latching on to the first idea for a topic that pops into your head (even if you aren't very enthused about it) or pursuing the least strenuous methods for preparing to write (even if they don't seem to be very promising). Although tactics like these might make you feel better in the moment, the calm will pass when you realize that the end product falls short of your expectations. Maybe the topic was clichéd or mundane. Maybe it wasn't effectively focused. Or maybe the supporting material was weak, insufficient, or lackluster. To stand the best chance of sidestepping these pitfalls, you'll want to devote plenty of attention up front to invention—attention that is concentrated on figuring out what you would really enjoy writing about and what your audience would really enjoy reading. Furthermore, remember that invention activities can assist you *at any point* in completing a writing project. In other words, you should return to invention *whenever* you feel yourself becoming blocked and in need of some fresh ideas—for example, if you realize while putting the finishing touches on your introduction that you need to narrow the scope of your thesis, or if you determine as you approach the end of your piece that you need more evidence to support your primary argument.

Prewriting Techniques

Prewriting techniques can facilitate your writing by helping you focus initial ideas, provide information to illustrate or support them, and reveal patterns of organization. These techniques are designed to help you power through writer's block and escape ruts in your thinking. Generally speaking, they fall into two categories: **unstructured** and **structured.** The difference between these two types of strategies hinges on the extent to which they direct idea-generating processes—with unstructured techniques providing very little direction and structured techniques offering more specific instruction.

Unstructured Prewriting Techniques

Unstructured prewriting techniques encourage your thought processes to flow in free-form fashion. Although they are applicable to any composing project and can be applied at any point when you feel your momentum begin to wane, they are particularly helpful when you first begin an assignment and attempt to formulate an approach.

Brainstorming   Perhaps the most well-known prewriting technique, **brainstorming** is an exercise in which you allow your ideas to rain down on the page or screen without interruption. When you engage in a brainstorming session, you'll want to designate beforehand how many minutes it will last (3? 5? 10?) as a way of stimulating quick thinking. When your time is up, you can evaluate the resulting list of ideas to determine which items hold the most promise for further development.

The point of brainstorming exercises is to generate as many ideas as you can—as quickly as you can—without judging them. Doing so should loosen up your mind in ways that will produce more and potentially better ideas than if you stop to weigh the quality of each one as it comes to you. Judging as you go not only slows your invention processes but also can undermine them by causing you to prematurely discard a fruitful idea.

The partial brainstorming exercise in Figure 4.1 lists potential topics for a personal narrative relating the story of an embarrassing moment. For such an assignment, any of these ideas would suffice; however, the question of how you might effectively develop them remains. Brainstorming can also assist in that process, as is demonstrated in Figure 4.2, which lists details the author deems relevant to depicting the embarrassing moment of failing to perform during a class debate.

Embarrassing Moments

- Blowing my part in a class debate
- Listening to my roommate grill my dates
- Fainting in health class during a movie on heart surgery
- Tripping up the stairs when receiving my high school diploma

Figure 4.1 Brainstorm for a broad paper topic

Blowing My Part in a Debate

- Belonged to the debate team in high school
- Bragged to my team about the preparations I had made
- Worked my team really hard during practice
- Knew a large chunk of our grade depended on a successful debate
- Forgot crucial facts and statistics on three different occasions

Figure 4.2 Focused brainstorm

Clustering   The prewriting technique known as **clustering** is similar to brainstorming in that it challenges you to generate as many ideas as you can about a topic. However, it differs in that, instead of inviting a simple list, it calls on you to group ideas in clusters that represent relationships between the ideas. For an illustration, consider the contents of Figure 4.3, the results of a clustering exercise for a paper characterizing an influential person in the author's life.

Figure 4.3 demonstrates how clustering can help you develop subtopics *and* support for a broad topic by systematically pushing you toward increasing levels of specificity. In this cluster diagram, the broad topic is "Uncle Pete," which the

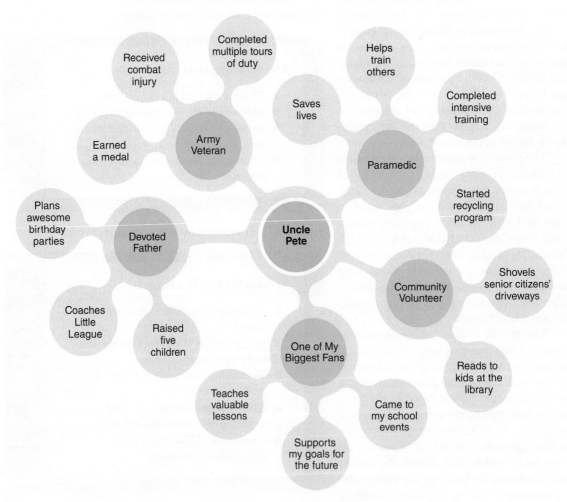

Figure 4.3 **A cluster diagram**

author placed in a circle in the middle of the page. From there, in the gold circles, the writer generated five possible subtopics or supporting ideas in the form of influential roles that Uncle Pete fulfills. Pushing to a greater level of detail, the writer comments in the light gray circles on activities that Uncle Pete participates in relevant to each of those roles.

Of course, if you decided to take up the challenge of writing about an influential person in your life, you might want to create several cluster diagrams, one for every individual who might become the topic of your essay. These diagrams would allow you to visualize the nature and level of detail that you could provide for each person, helping you decide which would lead to the most engaging and richly textured essay. Moreover, each of those diagrams would help you envision a structure for your paper, with every branch emanating from the central circle (or main topic) representing a paragraph or larger unified section of the final product.

Freewriting   Similar to brainstorming, **freewriting** is a prewriting technique intended to unlock your ideas by encouraging you to express them without any form of judgment—at least initially. It involves sitting down with a pen and paper (or a keyboard and computer) and letting your ideas flow onto the page without any attention to "correctness." The primary difference from brainstorming is that freewriting is more fluid; that is, whereas brainstorming usually results in lists of words or phrases, freewriting usually results in larger chunks of prose.

The key to engaging in productive freewriting is to never stop writing. In other words, your pen or keyboard should be active during the entire time you have designated for the activity. For example, if you decide you will conduct a 10-minute freewriting session, your pen should be gliding across the paper, or your fingers flying across the keyboard, for that entire period. But "What," you might ask, "if no ideas are coming to mind?" The answer is that you should record that fact—the fact that you can't think of anything to write at the moment. Then, as soon as something you believe might be relevant comes to mind, you start writing about *that*. See Figure 4.4 for a minute's worth of results from a freewriting session on a

Topic: Campus Issue

O.K. I have to write about an issue on campus that bothers me . . . actually I can think of a few things like parking, computer access, the fact that you can only demonstrate or protest in certain designated areas—that doesn't seem fair. Why shouldn't we be able to express our opinions in the area that makes the most sense? Parking, that's the real beast. All the lots for students are far from the buildings where we take most of our classes. What else, what else, I can't think, I can't think arrrrrrggghhh . . . oh yeah the computers. There aren't many open labs for studying or research and when you can find an open station it's usually been left because there is something wrong, the computer is locked up or something. . . .

Figure 4.4 **Response to a freewriting exercise**

Topic: Parking on Campus

I get really frustrated with the parking situation on our campus. There aren't enough lots, and the lots provided for students are a good walking distance from buildings in which most of my classes are held. Even in those lots, you have to search and search to find a space. And what about the cost? So much money just to be able to hunt for a space? In addition they're not in good shape. They need to be resurfaced, especially that one on Adams Ave. . . .

Figure 4.5 **Response to a looping exercise**

controversial campus issue. Imagine how much material might have been produced in 5 minutes . . . or 10.

Again, like brainstorming, this technique derives its benefits from the refusal to prejudge the information you're generating. By forcing yourself to keep going—even if what you're coming up with is off-topic or gibberish—you can overcome bouts of writer's block that are common during invention. Once your freewriting session is over, you'll have several lines of text that you can scan for a focused paper topic and possibly some support for your claims about that topic.

Looping   Also referred to as *focused freewriting,* **looping** involves composing quickly and informally about an idea from a previous freewriting session. For example, Figure 4.5 displays the results of a looping session on a topic that surfaced during the freewriting exercise on a campus issue excerpted in Figure 4.4. The looping session should adhere to the same guidelines as those for a freewriting session, but instead of exploring a broad topic, you need to pinpoint an observation from the related freewriting session and write for a given amount of time about that more specific concept.

Looping is a strategy for further focusing your initial thoughts about a subject. As such, it often leads directly to viable thesis statements. Of course, to the extent that ideas produced while you are looping need to be refined, you might consider looping the results of your looping exercises.

Journaling   Many people keep **journals** for the pure joy or catharsis of it—that is, to preserve memories of rewarding experiences they've had or to work through problems or emotions. While writers in particular may keep journals for similar reasons, they also enjoy the practical advantage of having a convenient storehouse of ideas for writing. Although journals are similar to diaries in that they serve as an informal record of one's thoughts, they differ in the respect that they are not simply a run-down of daily occurrences, as diaries tend to be. On the contrary, journals are associated with deeper reflection on matters that may excite, intrigue, or confound you. (You can read more about reflection in Chapters 1 and 2.)

In some writing courses, teachers will ask you to keep journals to record insights for your writing projects or to ruminate on your composing processes (see Figure 4.6). These insights often become the subject matter for end-of-semester reflective essays or introductions to portfolios of your best work (see Chapter 25). Teachers who assign journals may ask you to keep one for the entire semester, adding entries as you're moved to do so about whatever issues capture your interest. Others may require entries on assigned topics to be submitted at regular times

When I came to class Tuesday I was very worried. It seemed like I had just scratched the surface of research for my project. . . . I wasn't ready to put my ideas together in a formal text. The research I had was changing my original focus, and I knew there was much more research to be done before I could write a decent first draft that had some direction. So I decided to freewrite, hoping that I could clarify some thoughts that had been running around in my mind. Usually, I'm not much for prewriting techniques. I like to jump right into the fray. But this time it felt necessary because of the vast nature of my topic. . . .

Figure 4.6 Journal entry

throughout the semester. Whatever the case, the expectation is that you will challenge yourself to reflect in depth and in detail on the subject of inquiry so as to compile a rich pool of information from which to draw.

Double-Entry Notebook   A **double-entry notebook** is especially helpful when you are asked to intertwine objective feedback with interpretation or personal commentary on whatever you happen to be writing about, whether a text composed by another author or an event you are observing. This type of notebook involves drawing a line down the middle of a blank page, with the left column labeled "Observations" and the right column labeled "Reactions." In the left column, you will list words or sentences that record "the facts," summarizing what an author has said or describing colors, actions, and sounds representing what you see or hear. In the right column, you will provide opinions or reactions directly beside each item in the left column.

Figure 4.7 illustrates how you might effectively use a double-entry notebook. This set of responses recalls impressions of a botanical garden that might lead to a reflective essay, like those that appear in travel guides. Note that in the left column, the author simply records sense impressions, while reserving the right column for the feelings aroused by those impressions. Distinguishing objective analysis from emotions and opinions can help organize your prewriting or invention efforts, keeping what is apparent about your subject on the surface separate from your

Observations	Reactions
It's 3 miles from Kuhio Shores and other hotels.	Wow. This is really convenient for tourists—close enough to walk to for some.
The tour starts at gift shop—reservations required.	There's a great selection of souvenirs—some artwork from local artisans. Tickets are reasonably priced.
The guide asks everyone to board a tram to travel up a winding dirt road overlooking some deep valleys.	The views are breathtaking—the ocean, lush greenery, rocky cliffs, all in one glance.
The walking tour passed trees that were filmed in _Jurassic Park_.	Standing next to these trees I felt soooooo small. And they brought back memories of how scary that movie was when I saw it the first time.
Lilies were creamy white with shocking pink centers. They were about three feet tall and swayed in the wind.	This was my favorite part of the garden. Beautiful flowers were what I came to see.

Figure 4.7 Record in a double-entry notebook

feelings and attitudes about it. This is especially crucial when the focus of analysis is a document, the content of which—as opposed to your *reaction* to it—may need to be cited or credited to the author. In addition, the presence of the right-hand column compels you to personally engage the topic under consideration, to formulate commentary about it that will help establish your authorial presence in a formal paper.

Structured Prewriting Techniques

More directive than unstructured prewriting techniques, **structured** prewriting techniques (sometimes referred to as **heuristics**) typically move you through prescribed tasks or questions that encourage certain types of interaction with your subject matter. Although initially more confining than unstructured techniques, structured techniques are also intended to unleash the free flow of ideas that their less stringent counterparts encourage. As with unstructured prewriting techniques, you can use structured techniques at any point in a project when you sense the need for additional information. Nevertheless, the level of specificity they inspire makes them particularly useful for constructing thesis statements and for eliciting supporting material for the body paragraphs of your papers.

Cubing   The most apparent relationship between the technique known as **cubing** and a physical cube is that both are six-sided. Just as a cube has six sides, a cubing exercise involves six steps; moreover, just as a cube's six sides constitute a multidimensional shape, the six steps in a cubing exercise constitute a multidimensional perspective on the subject under consideration (see Figure 4.8). Cubing prompts you to view a topic from diverse angles and, therefore, pushes your thinking beyond predictable pathways. Although some of the perspectives it imposes may not seem to fit certain topics, you should try to force a fit in order to capitalize on unanticipated connections that such intellectual activity tends to produce.

For each step in a cubing session, your goal should be to list as many ideas as you're able to (as if you were brainstorming). From the resulting assortment of

Cubing Step	Definition
Describe	Using your senses, characterize the person, place, or object you are observing.
Compare or contrast	Consider how the person, place, or object you are studying is similar to or different from others of his, her, or its kind.
Associate	Explore connections between the person, place, or object and any other entity he, she, or it brings to mind.
Analyze	Study how the parts of the person, place, or object relate to each other or to the whole they are part of.
Apply	Think about how, or for what, the person, place, or object is used.
Argue for or against	Advocate for or criticize the person, place, or object.

Figure 4.8 **Steps in a cubing exercise and their definitions**

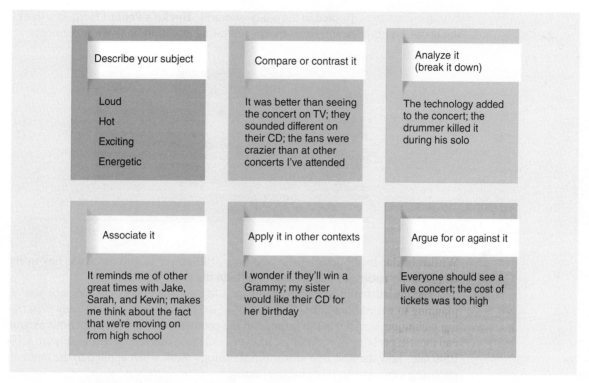

Figure 4.9 Cubing exercise about a rock concert

ideas, you might select a focus for your piece, or you might locate the most promising observation and run it through additional prewriting techniques. Figure 4.9 illustrates a cubing exercise about the experience of attending a rock concert. The ideas in this figure point to possible focuses for a variety of papers—a concert review, an analysis of the band's sound in the live show versus on the recordings, a discussion of how technology is changing the music business, a commentary on special friendships, and so on.

Journalistic Questions   Who? What? When? Where? Why? These are the five **journalistic questions** commonly employed by newspaper reporters and others who are writing about significant events. Often, this list is supplemented with a sixth question: How? The processes for employing this heuristic are rather obvious: You answer the questions. But you should remember that reporters can't adequately represent events by means of single or one-word responses. On the contrary, any of these questions, in and of themselves, should lead to multiple responses and considerable detail. The power of this structured prewriting technique is that it points to specific areas of inquiry that you would need to probe whenever you are describing events or narrating experiences—composing strategies you will use in various types of documents.

Burke's Pentad   Rooted in the study of drama, **Burke's Pentad** facilitates thinking about events or occurrences by concentrating attention on five key elements:

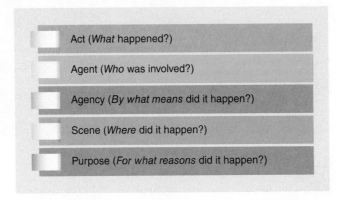

While similar to the journalistic questions, the power of this heuristic lies in its emphasis on **ratios,** or relationships between the five elements.

The initial step in a pentadic analysis is to view the event or occurrence you're planning to write about through the lenses of the five elements. As with any prewriting technique, you'll want to respond to the prompts with as many reactions as you can muster, pressing beyond single answers and those that seem obvious. Figure 4.10 illustrates how the first step of this process might work when applied to the topic of choosing a career—in this example, acting.

Once you have supplied several ideas for each of the five questions as in Figure 4.10, you conjoin the items in each category according to ratios between the five elements. More specifically, you might ask questions like these: How does the act relate to the scene? How does the scene relate to the purpose? The answers you come up with suggest possible thesis statements for your paper, as Figure 4.11 demonstrates.

The unique quality of Burke's Pentad, in contrast to other prewriting techniques, is that it will carry you further into the processes of narrowing your focus, which is

Element	Response
Act What happened?	Decided what I want to do with my life; accepted challenge of a highly competitive profession; realized I'd have to live in a large city
Agent Who was involved?	Me; relatives; career counselor; teachers; drama coach; audience for my plays
Agency By what means did it happen?	Talking to mentors; talking to local actors; participating in community theater; reading biographies of famous actors; convincing loved ones that this is what I want; uniting passion with work
Scene Where did it happen?	On the stage; in drama classes; in career counselor's office; over the dinner table; in classes I didn't enjoy; in my imagination
Purpose For what reasons did it happen?	Heading to college and needing to choose a major; pursuing what I always knew I wanted to be; following my dreams; figuring out how I was going to support myself

Figure 4.10 **First step in applying Burke's Pentad—answering questions**

Source: Kenneth Burke. *A Grammar of Motives.* U of California P, 1945.

Ratios between Elements of Burke's Pentad	Possible Theses Based on Ratios from Ideas Generated in Figure 4.10
Agency and purpose	The experience of participating in community theater taught me that I want to be in front of an audience and that I need to be performing to be content.
Scene and agency	More than any other experience, the frustration of sitting through classes I didn't enjoy impressed upon me the importance of uniting my life's work with my passions.
Purpose and act	Anyone who is hoping to sustain a career as an actor would be well advised to know not only which cities provide the most opportunities for actors in general but also which cities offer opportunities for particular types of acting jobs.

Figure 4.11 **Second step in applying Burke's Pentad—exploring ratios**

a special challenge associated with invention. Since this benefit rests in formulating ratios between elements of the Pentad, it makes sense to generate as many ideas as you can up front so that you will have more relationships to consider.

Invention beyond the Composition Classroom

Hopefully, after reading this chapter, you understand that you don't need to feel helpless or resign yourself to frustration when faced with a writing assignment that doesn't immediately spark an idea that appeals to you. Using unstructured and structured prewriting techniques, you can chip away at writer's block, either by unlocking thought processes when you are searching for a topic or by suggesting avenues for probing a topic to locate theses and supporting material. These techniques will be applicable to almost any paper you write in your college courses and in the workplace.

Given their potential for use across a variety of writing assignments, it would be worth your while to learn and experiment with all of these techniques. As you do so, you'll discover which are most attuned to your own writing processes and to particular types of assignments. You'll also find that their benefits extend beyond coming up with viable ideas; in fact, if regarded seriously, they often lead to *creative* ideas.

ACTIVITY

Penetrating a Topic with Burke's Pentad   Apply Burke's Pentad to the topic of banning junk food or fast food in public school settings. Conduct at least a five-minute brainstorming session for each element of the Pentad, and then, playing out various ratios, generate at least 10 possible thesis statements that could serve as the focus of a paper on some issue related to monitoring children's nutrition. Think about which thesis holds the most promise and why (even if you don't actually write the paper it points to).

IDEA FOR EXTENDED WRITING

Exploring the Impact of a Fresh Perspective   You may recognize the style of painting in Figure 4.12 as belonging to the cubist movement. Cubism is recognizable for the distinct manner in which it represents familiar objects, challenging conventional perception. Cubist artists like Louis Casimir Marcoussis helped the world view ordinary forms in a new way that highlights elements that routine vision might not prioritize. This sort of fresh perspective or insight is the objective of invention—the subject of the chapter you've been reading. The insight embodied in this painting represents a significant influence on the world of modern art. But insights don't need to occur on such a grand scale to be considered significant. You undoubtedly can recall several moments in your life when you adopted a fresh perspective that significantly altered your thinking about some issue or person. For this assignment, narrate the story of a time when you escaped a rut in your thinking and, by viewing something from a new or different angle, experienced an insight that profoundly affected you.

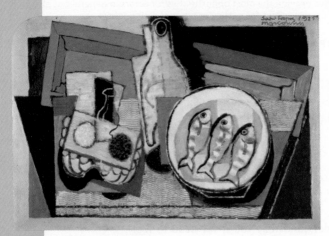

Figure 4.12 *Still Life with Three Fish 1925* **by Louis Casimir Marcoussis**

Research Strategies

5

Look at the simple threads pictured here. Take a minute to imagine something they might become—create an image of it in your mind.

What did you come up with? A colorful sweater? An intricately patterned rug? (Flip to Figure 5.5 at the end of this chapter to find one artist's vision of how these threads could be combined.)

Whether the product is a sweater, rug, or tapestry, a weaver of these threads would assume an active role in carefully placing them to realize a creative insight. Much like the weaver, when you are writing, you will need to assume an active role in determining how the sources you consult (the threads) can serve the insight that you wish to communicate (the woven artifact). In other words, your insight or vision for a text, not the sources, should drive your work. This chapter offers advice for conducting research and using sources to support your goals for writing.

All writing requires research. This may sound like an overstatement to you, especially if you equate research with a hunt for published sources to cite in one of your own papers. Certainly, combing the library or Internet for books and articles to support your own composing projects is a common and often effective mode of research, but it is by no means the only one. If you consider "research" in its broader sense—as any act of gathering material to inform your writing—you can expect that the term covers a variety of activities beyond collecting and citing sources and, moreover, that it is associated with a diversity of genres.

This broader conception of research serves you as a writer in two significant ways. First, it underscores the reality that research is not a specialized activity that you engage in only for lengthy, formal, academic exercises. Second, it encourages you to think creatively about strategies for carrying out your writing assignments. Although successful writers understand methods for conducting library and Internet research and for accurately crediting the materials they cite, they also understand that books, journal articles, and reports are not always the most fitting or fertile resources for realizing their vision of a text. As you broaden your own experiences as a writer, you'll want to experiment with a variety of research strategies, including surveys, interviews, and observations. Doing so can increase your flexibility in answering the questions that drive your composing projects. It can also boost your potential for arriving at workable and profound answers to those questions.

Research Methods

Whether the composing problem you are facing involves sharing a life lesson through a personal essay, arguing against proposed legislation for an article in your hometown newspaper, or formulating a letter of complaint to a local supermarket that seems to be overcharging its customers, you will need to engage in research. More specifically, in solving the problem of how to vividly convey a life lesson, for instance, you would concentrate on recollecting past experiences that best illustrate it. In solving the problem of how to argue convincingly against a newly proposed law, you would scour library databases and the Internet, marshaling facts and figures from the work of published scholars in support of your cause. In solving the problem of how to articulate customers' displeasure to a supermarket manager, you might start comparing charges recorded on receipts from that store with advertised prices at other stores in the area.

All of these are forms of research, but they mine different reserves of information—memory, published documents, personal documents, and records of business transactions. These examples point to merely a few of the sources you might consult, through just a few of the research methods available to you. Your credibility as a writer (or ethos, as discussed in Chapter 3) rests largely on your ability to pin-point the kind of information that is best suited to your purposes and to skillfully employ the most appropriate strategies available for gathering that information.

Early deliberations about appropriateness might center on whether your focus or research questions call for primary or secondary research. **Primary research** is that which involves your direct interaction with the people, places, or texts you are studying. Examples would include reflecting on your own memories, interviewing others, or even analyzing texts for some feature that interests you, like use of slang. **Secondary research** involves a more distanced approach in the sense that—instead of directly accessing the subject of investigation—you depend on the work of others to increase your understanding. For example, although you might not have the resources to travel to Egypt and view the Sphinx in person, or to compile the amount of data necessary for tracking national trends in spending on specialty coffee drinks, you could learn more about these phenomena by consulting books or articles written about them. The next several pages of this chapter will introduce, or re-familiarize you with, a number of primary and secondary research strategies that you can employ in and outside your composition course.

Primary Research

Memory Search   Whenever you are embarking on a new writing project, you will want to start with what you already know—with what you can pull from your memory. Doing so makes the most obvious sense when you are composing a personal narrative (the story of a significant occurrence in your life) or an essay that would benefit from anecdotes about your personal experience. But even when you aren't writing about personal experience, beginning with what you know can help you take charge of the subject matter and assert your own views about it.

To stimulate effective memory searches, you'll probably want to employ some of the unstructured and structured prewriting techniques introduced in Chapter 4. The former invite a sort of free-form reflection, while the latter guide your memory in ways that can unearth information you otherwise might not recall. Once you take stock of what you know or remember about the topic or issue at hand, you'll be in a better position to determine the extent and nature of the research you have left to do.

Interviews   Often, the most effective way of gathering the information you need is to talk with people who are familiar with your subject matter or whose response to certain research questions will help provide insights essential to completing your project. For example, if you wish to re-create an important event in the history of your hometown for a human interest story in your local newspaper, you might want to talk with a few longtime residents—preferably those who directly experienced the event. Their memories will help you bring the details of that event to life. In contrast, if you are writing a report on the influence of the print version of your hometown newspaper versus its online version, you would want to talk with a larger number of individuals to gauge which medium is preferred and why. After all, you can't form a sense of widespread tendencies by interviewing only a few subjects.

Preplanning is important for all methods of research, but it is especially important when interviewing since you are dependent on the goodwill of other people and, therefore, need to demonstrate consideration for their time and trouble. If your

MYTH

"As long as they are willing, I am free to conduct research on other people."

Your college will have a policy for conducting research with human subjects. In most cases, this involves submitting a proposal for approval by an institutional review board prior to soliciting participation of the individuals who will be interviewed or observed. Some institutions will have exceptions for research that is to remain "in-house." In other words, if you plan to share your findings only with your teacher and classmates, you may not need to seek formal approval for the study. If you do plan to publish it in any spoken, print, or electronic form to any other audience, you will need to seek the board's approval. Your teacher can help you figure out the requirements and procedures for conducting human-subjects research at your school.

REALITY

research questions require that you talk with a few experts on your topic, you'll want to contact them as soon as possible after identifying them to determine if they are willing to participate and to allow some leeway in scheduling the interviews at times and places that are convenient for them. If your research questions call for a larger pool of interview subjects, you might, instead, situate yourself in a location (e.g., a mall, coffee shop, or post office) where you can spontaneously request the assistance of passersby who would offer you a reasonable sample of the population you want to study—such as newspaper readers in your hometown.

With either approach, a crucial part of the preplanning process is constructing effective interview questions. You need to keep several factors in mind:

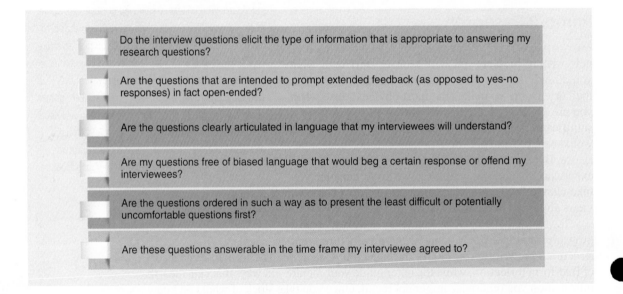

Do the interview questions elicit the type of information that is appropriate to answering my research questions?

Are the questions that are intended to prompt extended feedback (as opposed to yes-no responses) in fact open-ended?

Are the questions clearly articulated in language that my interviewees will understand?

Are my questions free of biased language that would beg a certain response or offend my interviewees?

Are the questions ordered in such a way as to present the least difficult or potentially uncomfortable questions first?

Are these questions answerable in the time frame my interviewee agreed to?

If you answered no to any of these queries, you'll need to revise your interview questions to address whatever weaknesses undermine them, whether that involves being more accurate in labeling the constructs you are studying, reducing the number or complexity of questions to accommodate your subjects' schedules, and so forth. If you don't revise them, you may fail to collect the kind and quantity of information you need or may risk alienating the people who've agreed to help you.

After you have refined your questions, solicited volunteers, and scheduled the conversations, you can help ensure that the interview process will proceed smoothly by attending to some additional advice:

- *Remember that you may need to ask follow-up questions to clarify your interviewees' responses.* You might ask such questions on the spot or during a mutually agreed-on second interview.
- *Know that you'll want to take careful notes during your interview.* You might even arrange beforehand for audio or video recordings of your subjects, if they are agreeable.

■ *Show appreciation for those who've agreed to participate in your study.* Being punctual is key, as is being conscious of your interviewees' physical comfort. In addition, you'll want to thank them at the end of the interview, as well as send a thank-you note.

■ *Share your paper with interviewees before it's due, if possible.* This will allow them to correct any inaccuracies or misinterpretations of their responses to your questions.

Surveys   Many skills relevant to conducting interviews can also be applied to administering surveys. Both methods involve asking questions of people who are in some way qualified to shed light on your research questions. In addition, the success of both methods depends on well-conceived and well-constructed questions. Despite these similarities, however, survey and interview methodologies are not necessarily interchangeable. Surveys are the better choice when you need to consult a large number of subjects (in classes, clubs, political organizations, etc.) in a compressed amount of time or when you don't have an opportunity to sit down with every individual you'd like to hear from. If you don't have direct access to the target population, you might be able to send your surveys through e-mail. Collecting responses in this manner will take longer than administering them in person, and, in fact, you may need to send reminders to procrastinating subjects, some of whom may still fail to contact you. Even in these circumstances, however, the ease with which you can reach large numbers of people through surveys is greater than it is with interviews.

Regardless of the population, or sample of the population, that you consult, you need to remember that, when administering print surveys or e-mail surveys, you typically won't have as much opportunity to clarify points of confusion for your research participants as you might during an interview. Therefore, it's vital that the form itself is user-friendly. To help make your own print surveys user-friendly, take note of the criteria listed in Figure 5.1.

While considering these criteria can help you avoid common hazards, the best strategy for ensuring that a survey is user-friendly is to **pilot** it—that is, take it for a test run on some individuals who are similar to your research subjects but not part of the actual population you will draw from for your study. After they have filled out the survey, they can help you troubleshoot the form by sharing reactions about the clarity of the questions and the amount of time it took to answer them.

After collecting the completed surveys, you can concentrate on compiling the results. If the survey questions elicit quantitative data, you will be counting numbers and calculating percentages. For example, regarding questions focused on demographics, such as gender, you might want to record the number or percentage of female versus male respondents. If the survey questions are more open-ended, you'll be searching for themes that speak to the issues covered in your study's overarching research questions. For example, if you asked a sample of students attending your school to state their primary reasons for enrolling, each line of reasoning (e.g., cost, location, reputation, programs offered, support services available) might represent a different theme. Of course, depending on the nature of the phenomenon you're investigating, your survey might seek both quantitative and qualitative data.

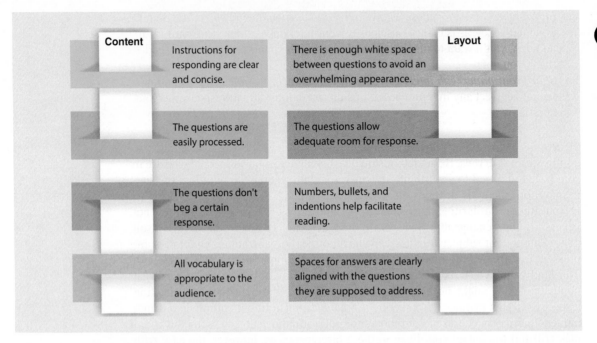

Content

Instructions for responding are clear and concise.

The questions are easily processed.

The questions don't beg a certain response.

All vocabulary is appropriate to the audience.

Layout

There is enough white space between questions to avoid an overwhelming appearance.

The questions allow adequate room for response.

Numbers, bullets, and indentions help facilitate reading.

Spaces for answers are clearly aligned with the questions they are supposed to address.

Figure 5.1 **Criteria for evaluating a survey tool.** Use this figure to create your own user-friendly surveys.

Observation   For a more detached perspective on people than interviews and surveys elicit, or for insights about places and events, you may want to engage in **observation.** This research strategy requires careful attention to detail in designing and executing a research plan and in analyzing the findings or data that the plan produces. The data that you ultimately focus on will be determined by your purpose for conducting the study and the specific research questions that arise from that purpose. To see how these components interact, refer to Figure 5.2, which sketches a modest study investigating how the dining options available on a given college campus might be improved.

In addition to determining your research questions and methods for answering them, you'll need to give some thought to the best means for recording data. Recording your observations in some concrete manner (as opposed to relying on memory) is crucial since you will be trying to manage so many stimuli and since distance from the observational context can, over time, distort your recollections. Once you have completed your observations, you can turn to analyzing the data. Considering the research questions driving the study outlined in Figure 5.2, you would focus your analysis on what the numbers suggest are the most and least popular restaurants overall and, perhaps, over lunch as opposed to dinner hours.

To be more specific, with a total of 189 visitors for the time allotted, you can see that China Express is the most popular restaurant and Taco Trio is the least popular, with 104 visitors. However, even though Taco Trio is the least popular

Purpose	Research Questions	Observational Focus	Data		
			Restaurant	Time	Number of Students
To learn how to improve the appeal of the student center's food court	What *type* of cuisine (not specific food items) is the most popular choice during lunch and dinner hours at the food court? What type of cuisine is the least popular?	On the first two days of a regular week of classes, for every restaurant in the food court, record the number of students who walk out with food in hand between the hours of 11 a.m. and 1 p.m. and the hours of 5 and 7 p.m.	Taco Trio	11–1	87
				5–7	17
			Subway	11–1	85
				5–7	30
			Pizza Hut	11–1	38
				5–7	111
			McDonald's	11–1	79
				5–7	43
			China Express	11–1	62
				5–7	127

Figure 5.2 **Brief sketch of an observational study**

overall, it draws the highest number of patrons over the lunch hours. Pushing your analysis further, you might additionally infer from the data that the restaurants serving heavier fare (i.e., pizza; meat and vegetables in sauce over rice) have more concentrated dinnertime business than those that serve lighter fare (sandwiches). Of course, to increase your level of certainty about all these conclusions, you might repeat the study across an entire week or two.

Another issue you'll want to consider when reporting findings from observational studies and other forms of primary research is whether, and to what extent, you should describe your methods for collecting and analyzing data. Generally speaking, that decision would depend on the nature of the document you are preparing. If, as a student center employee, you were asked to conduct a formal study about students' food preferences and to submit a report to be used in making important business decisions, your readers would likely be expecting a specific rundown of the procedures you followed. On the other hand, if you decided to conduct such a study as a means of introducing a larger issue you wanted to explore—for instance, in the opening paragraphs of an exposé on college student nutrition—detailing the procedures would not be necessary. As these examples indicate, the bottom line is that genre and purpose significantly influence decisions about gathering and presenting primary research.

Secondary Research

Internet Searches   The Internet offers quick and convenient access to a mind-boggling variety of resources—including books, reference works (dictionaries and encyclopedias), articles from popular magazines and academic journals, blog posts, and government documents. Before initiating a web search, you'll want to spend some time thinking about key terms that accurately and specifically represent your area of interest. Even after identifying such terms, you'll need to expend some effort sifting through the inevitably diverse collection of hits that every web search produces. You will be sifting based on relevance to your topic, but also on the credibility of the source.

The credibility of your sources can seriously impact your credibility as an author. If any of those sources is found to be inaccurate, outdated, or somehow negligent in its treatment of the subject at hand, your own ideas, observations, and capabilities may become suspect. Guidelines for evaluating sources, both on the Internet and in print form, arise from several important considerations, summarized in Figure 5.3. Of course, the relative credibility of certain sources is readily apparent in contrast to others. For example, an article on migraines published in the *Journal of the American Medical Association* garners more trust than does an online discussion forum where laypersons share their experiences with home treatments for chronic migraine symptoms.

One commonly consulted Internet resource whose credibility might prove to be problematic in the context of formal college-level writing assignments is *Wikipedia*, which relies on software that allows any user to contribute, edit, and/or arrange content. Since virtually anyone can add to a "wiki," the information provided at any given point in time might be brought into question. In other words, the entries in their entirety may or may not have been edited by qualified individuals. Therefore, you must be judicious in using *Wikipedia*, first of all determining if your teacher will allow it as a resource. If you can and wish to use it, double-checking its content against other sources would be a good idea.

Question	Helpful Hints
When was the source published?	In some cases, date of publication may not be that significant. For instance, an insight published years ago about love in one of Shakespeare's sonnets may still have relevance today, whereas scientific research tends to become outdated rather quickly. Regarding websites, you'll want to check how recently they've been updated.
Who is the author?	Not only do you want to consider the author's credentials (e.g., degrees, employment), but also you'll want to determine if he or she has any well-known political leanings or affiliations that might induce bias. To find this information, you may need to conduct additional research focused specifically on the author. On certain websites, this might require searching various links. *Wikipedia* is one resource that might be questioned on this count since anyone, regardless of credentials, can contribute to it.
What press or Internet venue published the work?	Works published by university and other education-oriented presses tend to invoke greater trust than popular presses or presses that promote self-publishing. As for Internet venues, some indication of credibility lies in the ending of the URL (or web address). Those ending in *.edu* are educational venues, those ending in *.gov* are sponsored by the government, and those ending in *.mil* are associated with the military, for example.
Does the publication itself project a strong bias?	Certain print and online magazines, as well as various websites, exist for purposes of communicating political and religious viewpoints. While you may determine that citing from such sources will serve your purposes (e.g., you want to characterize opposing positions in the debate on a given issue), you must be cautious about treating such sources as if they are objective.
Is the subject matter treated in a fair and balanced manner?	If your purpose for citing a source is to represent the current, widely accepted knowledge base on a subject, you should examine the extent to which it integrates various sides or multiple perspectives in establishing that knowledge base. A good indication of its doing so is that it cites a wide range of sources.

Figure 5.3 **Some criteria for evaluating source credibility**

Library Searches   Despite the convenience of Internet searches for contextualizing and supporting your own writing projects, you should remember that many potentially enlightening and useful resources are simply not available on the web. Given this reality, familiarity with your campus library is crucial in conducting successful research. Not only should you learn your way around the physical site, but also you should familiarize yourself with your library's website, which offers an array of online databases. Using these databases, you can identify potentially helpful resources with the same ease that you can surf the Internet.

Some databases are generalized in nature, covering a vast array of resources, while others are specialized by disciplines of study. Figure 5.4 lists some widely used databases and the fields they are associated with. Once you identify potential resources using databases like those listed in this figure, you'll need to study the entries for information about where those sources are located—that is, whether your library has stored them in digital form or on library shelves.

Occasionally, you'll discover that your library doesn't own a copy of a book or article that you need. In that case, you should know that most libraries have agreements with one another that would enable you to secure that source through an interlibrary loan. More than likely, you'll be able to find instructions for obtaining such a loan on your library's website; if not, you'll need to ask a librarian for assistance. But, of course, several categories of resources from all disciplines of study will be available in your campus library. In addition to shelves of books, journals, and government documents, these resources also include specialized dictionaries and encyclopedias.

Be mindful, though, that a source isn't necessarily credible relevant to a writing project you're working on simply because it resides in a library. As in the case of web resources, you will need to develop strategies for considering the appropriateness of library sources given your purpose for writing, your intended readers, and so on. Whenever you are in doubt, you should return to the criteria listed in Figure 5.3 since they can help you gauge the extent to which the sources you are consulting or wish to cite are trustworthy and specifically suited to your purposes.

Database	Disciplines
EBSCO Host	Multidisciplinary
JSTOR	Multidisciplinary
ERIC	Education
LexisNexis	Legal, business, government
MLA	Modern languages, literature
PSYCInfo	Behavioral sciences, mental health
SocINDEX	Sociology
Web of Knowledge	Sciences, social sciences, arts, humanities

Figure 5.4 **Commonly consulted research databases**

"There is a correct way to manage sources."

To help beginners navigate this complex process, some teachers require specific procedures for conducting research. The following list presents a commonly taught set of procedures:

1. Record bibliographic information on a set of notecards.
2. Color-code those cards to other cards that contain notes from their respective sources (a separate card for each cited passage).
3. Arrange these cards in the order of a formal outline you've prepared.
4. Connect the ideas on these cards with transitional phrases as a means of drafting your paper.

To be sure, some writers find such procedures confining. If you feel this way, you should experiment with strategies that seem more in sync with your own preferences for processing and organizing information—perhaps some of those discussed later in this chapter.

Strategies for Managing Secondary Research

After collecting pertinent digital or print sources for your writing projects, you'll need to study them closely to determine how each might be used to the greatest advantage. As is the case with writing processes in general, there exists no single or proper way of managing your sources. But if you don't take some time to think through such matters, you can end up with a jumbled mess of material that is difficult to make sense of or correctly cite. When you procrastinate with regard to organizing and citing your sources, you risk having to repeat your effort, hunting down key passages again, double-checking sources' identifying information, and verifying the accuracy of your notes. Incomplete or inaccurate notes can lead to **plagiarism,** which is a type of academic dishonesty. Plagiarism results from using someone's ideas or words as if they are your own without properly crediting them. (Chapter 21 addresses strategies for avoiding plagiarism in considerable detail.)

Viable strategies for taking notes range widely. Some writers like to annotate texts they are studying, making comments in the margins and marking important pages or paragraphs with sticky notes for quick reference. Others like to make copies of the sources that they can mark with colored highlighters, perhaps with different colors connecting a given section of the source to a given section of the paper they plan to write. Still others prefer to paraphrase or transfer key passages verbatim into a notebook or computer file. Whatever methods you gravitate toward, you need some way of ensuring that you can later connect the notes you take with the sources they came from.

Depending on the source, if you are taking notes on it or highlighting copies of it, remember that much of the bibliographic information (e.g., article title, author, journal title, page numbers) appears on the original. Any required information that doesn't can be recorded somewhere in the margins of the piece so you don't have to look it up later. If you are copying or paraphrasing passages into notebooks or word processing files, you might want to begin the section devoted to that source with all of its identifying information.

When you move on to the drafting phase of the writing project, you'll be able to proceed most efficiently if you have a plan for quickly recovering the information you need at the moment you need it. Ordinarily, being able to do so rests on some system of organizing by subtopic or by the projected sections of the document you're composing. Having memorized what types of information their sources have to offer, some writers will simply lay out all their sources on their desk so that they can quickly grab and scan them as necessary. Other writers might keep track of their sources' substance by attaching sticky notes that briefly outline those sources' respective content or by maintaining a separate hard copy or digital list of key ideas contained in each.

Research, Invention, and Knowledge Transfer

Effective inquiry through internal and external research methods is crucial to the early stages of composing. To be sure, research methods might be thought of as prewriting strategies in and of themselves since many writers stimulate and refine their ideas *through* research—not necessarily *before* they conduct it. Whatever the case, the interplay of prewriting strategies and research methods in the context of writing is typically recursive. For example, sometimes even after you have begun drafting and have integrated some external research into a text, you may realize that you need to narrow your thesis. Consequently, you might engage in a looping exercise or call on Burke's Pentad to help refine your focus (see examples in Chapter 4). In turn, that new focus may require additional research, prompting you to return to the library, Internet, interview subjects, or observation site for additional information. That extra research effort on your part just might make the difference between an ordinary paper and one that will sustain attention and increase your readers' understanding.

Such goals for research are consistent across the college curriculum, as well as in civic and professional realms of composing. While different majors and the jobs they prepare you for will introduce you to additional, specialized research strategies that are frequently employed in those specific disciplines, the methodologies characterized in this chapter (interviews, surveys, library searches, etc.) are applicable across many fields of study. In addition to transferring knowledge from this chapter about these particular methodologies, you should also be able to transfer knowledge about locating, evaluating, and managing sources as you prepare to integrate them into your writing projects. (Chapter 21 offers advice for integrating and citing sources.) Although your subsequent courses will build on and refine your repertoire and understanding of research strategies, the information in this chapter establishes a foundation for developing research skills essential to college-level writing.

ACTIVITY

Taking and Analyzing Field Notes   Form a group with four or five of your classmates. With each group member using his or her own notebook or laptop, visit a location on campus that's typically filled with activity. With the goal of representing the nature of the activity, find a comfortable place to sit, and, for 15 minutes, record your impressions. Whom do you see? What are they doing? How are they doing it? What are they wearing? What's going on around them? Once the 15 minutes have passed, return with your group to your classroom and compare your individual field notes. What similarities do you notice in what you observed? What differences? What might account for those differences? What do these discoveries suggest about guidelines for conducting and presenting observational research?

IDEA FOR EXTENDED WRITING

Exploring the Role of Research in Your Future Career All careers involve research. Some, like those associated with scientific disciplines or medicine, rely heavily on formal laboratory research. Business-oriented professions study economic trends that predict impending monetary success or failure and suggest ways of evading the latter. Fiction writers and poets spend hours observing human behavior to realistically capture it in their characters; likewise, visual artists observe their subjects to capture specific nuances of shape, color, and shadow. What kind of research methods are associated with the profession you are considering? What kinds of questions guide the scholarship in that field? What special background or skills do individuals in that field need to have in the interest of conducting effective research? With attention to such questions, compose an essay that characterizes the kinds of research typical in your chosen profession or one you are considering. Of course, to complete this assignment, you'll need to engage in certain research strategies discussed in this chapter. Target your essay for an audience of individuals who may be imagining a similar career path.

Figure 5.5 Tapestry created from colorful threads like those pictured at the beginning of this chapter. Much like this tapestry, your finished written work should reveal your vision or insight into your topic.

Introduction to Texts That Inform

6

Are you familiar with the icons in this photograph? At the very least, you probably recognize them as icons for apps that can help you locate certain kinds of information. The yellow icon represents the Internet Movie Database, which might assist you in selecting a classic horror film to watch this weekend. The green icon represents MapQuest, which could help you determine

the best route for a summer road trip. You are, no doubt, quite capable of using apps like these (as well as other digital resources) to *search* for information. But what happens when you want to *share* information with others, acquainting them with topics that you know well? This chapter discusses the nature and goals of genres that inform. Particular genres are

explored more specifically in Chapters 7 through 10.

The primary purpose of writing that **informs** is to bring readers up to speed regarding some concept, issue, or experience. In doing so, it strives to be *objective*— that is, to convey knowledge impartially, without attempting to sway readers in any given direction regarding their beliefs or opinions about the subject matter. Of course, objectivity in any absolute sense is a questionable goal when you consider that an author's perspective is inevitably influenced by his or her education, background, experiences, and so on.

In fact, some language experts argue that all writing is persuasive, and, if you think about it, you can imagine how they might draw this conclusion. For example, consider a travel log. Although its primary purpose may be to record sensory impressions about new places, the beauty and excitement expressed in the log's descriptions could have a persuasive impact as they entice readers to visit that destination. Regardless of the impact on readers, when your main goal as a writer is simply to share your account of an event or experience, present facts and figures, or instruct your readers about a topic they may need or want to know about, you are engaging in writing that is informative.

Purposes and Strategies for Informing

Informative genres cast you in the role of expert—or, at least, someone who knows more about the topic than your intended readers do. This role requires that your knowledge of the topic be deep, accurate, and current. Projecting this level of knowledge will be easier in some genres than in others. For instance, in a **memoir** (a form of autobiography), self-knowledge is your primary source, and it's safe to assume that you know more about yourself than others do. In contrast, if you are writing a **research report,** you will probably need to rely on library and Internet sources to help you explain how research you've performed or clarified builds on that which came before it. Referencing sources lends credibility to your work, demonstrating that you are familiar with the larger context in which your own research project is set. Regardless of the informative genre that you are composing, explicitly establishing that you know what you are talking about is fundamental.

For an example of informative writing, consider the passages in the Look Inside box, excerpted from an article on sibling rivalry published in *The Wall Street Journal*. In this article, author Elizabeth Bernstein sets out to explain the nature and causes of the sometimes subtle, sometimes overt conflicts that commonly define relationships between children living in the same family.

In this excerpt, you can see that the author foregrounds an explicitly stated need for the information she provides—a need that would appeal to a large portion of *The Wall Street Journal*'s readership (i.e., readers who have brothers or sisters). To establish her credibility as a writer who is knowledgeable on this issue, she recaps relevant research findings, attaching them to experts in the field, and she specifically cites a well-credentialed scholar on sibling rivalry.

While creating a need for the content of your piece and asserting its reliability are strategies common to informative writing, perhaps the quality that most obviously distinguishes it from other types of writing is its **tone,** or the author's attitude toward the topic. Connected tightly to its purpose—which is simply to share knowledge—an informative text adopts an impartial tone, one that suggests the only agenda is to increase readers' understanding of the subject matter. Although

From "Sibling Rivalry Grows Up"

by Elizabeth Bernstein

A LOOK INSIDE:
SHARING INFORMATION ABOUT SIBLING RIVALRY

Adult sibling rivalry. Experts say it remains one of the most harmful and least addressed issues in a family. We know it when we see it. Often, we deeply regret it. But we have no idea what to do about it.

> Early in the piece, the author refers to experts on the topic to establish its significance and to point to a lack of understanding about it, thus creating a need for information.

Ms. Walsh and Ms. Putman have been competitive since childhood—about clothes, about boyfriends, about grades. Ms. Walsh remembers how in grammar school her sister wrote an essay about their grandfather and won a writing award. She recited it at a school assembly with her grandpa standing nearby, beaming. Ms. Walsh, seething, vowed to win the award the next year and did.

Ms. Putman married first. Ms. Walsh, single at the time, clearly recalls the phone call when her sister told her she was pregnant. "I was excited because this was the first grandchild. Then I got off the phone and cried for two hours," says Ms. Walsh.

Ms. Putman, 39 and a stay-at-home-mom in Bolingbrook, Ill., remembers that she too felt jealous—of her sister's frequent travel and promotions in her marketing career. "The way my parents would go on and on about her really made me feel 'less than,'" Ms. Putman says. . . .

> Specific examples of sibling rivalry reveal that the author has done her homework, extending her expertise by conducting interviews with siblings.

Sibling rivalry is a normal aspect of childhood, experts say. Our siblings are our first rivals. They competed with us for the love and attention of the people we needed most, our parents, and it is understandable that we occasionally felt threatened. Much of what is written about sibling rivalry focuses on its effects during childhood.

But our sibling relationships are often the longest of our lives, lasting 80 years or more. Several research studies indicate that up to 45% of adults have a rivalrous or distant relationship with a sibling. . . .

> Referencing experts again, the author provides some facts and figures gained through published research on the topic.

The rivalry often persists into adulthood because in many families it goes unaddressed. "Most people who have been through years of therapy have worked out a lot of guilt with their parents. But when it comes to their siblings, they can't articulate what is wrong," says Jeanne Safer, a psychologist in Manhattan and author of "Cain's Legacy: Liberating Siblings from a Lifetime of Rage, Shame, Secrecy and Regret."

Dr. Safer believes sibling rivals speak in a kind of dialect (she calls it "sib speak"). It sounds like this: "You were

> Here the author actually cites an expert whose background clearly qualifies her to disseminate reliable information on the subject matter.

always Mom's favorite." "Mom and Dad are always at your house but they never visit me." "You never call me."

"It's not the loving language that good friends have," Dr. Safer says. "It's the language of grievance collection."

It's hard to know what to say in response. "You are afraid that what you say will be catastrophic or will reveal awful truths," Dr. Safer says. "It's a lifelong walk on eggshells."

Sibling discord has been around since the Bible. Cain killed Abel. Leah stole Rachel's intended husband, Jacob. Joseph fought bitterly with his 10 older half brothers. Parents often have a hand in fostering it. They may choose favorites, love unevenly and compare one child with the other.

> This reference to the Bible (used here as a lens on an ancient culture) provides readers a sense of just how long this issue has seriously impacted peoples' lives.

Dr. Safer draws a distinction between sibling rivalry and sibling strife. Rivalry encompasses a normal range of disagreements and competition between siblings. Sibling strife, which is less common, is rivalry gone ballistic—siblings who, because of personality clashes or hatred, can't enjoy each other's company.

Dr. Safer says brothers' rivalries often are overt, typically focusing on things like Dad's love, athletic prowess, career success, money. Women are less comfortable with competition, she says, so sister rivalries tend to be passive-aggressive and less direct. Whom did Mom love best, who is a better mother now.

Brothers often repair their rivalries with actions. When women reconcile, it's often through talking. Ms. Putman and Ms. Walsh have learned to stop arguments using a trick from childhood. When a discussion gets heated, one sister will call out "star," a code word they devised as kids to mean the conversation is over. The sister who ends it gets the last word. "You may still be mad, but you adhere to the rules of childhood," Ms. Walsh says.

> The author elaborates on information about sibling rivalry provided by the expert she cites, summarizing the researcher's findings on the relevance of gender.

that increased understanding might cause them to take action, the author is not overtly encouraging them to do so. For example, Elizabeth Bernstein, in the article excerpted above, maintains an objective tone throughout her piece, ending with suggestions from Dr. Jeanne Safer about how to reduce or diffuse sibling rivalry.

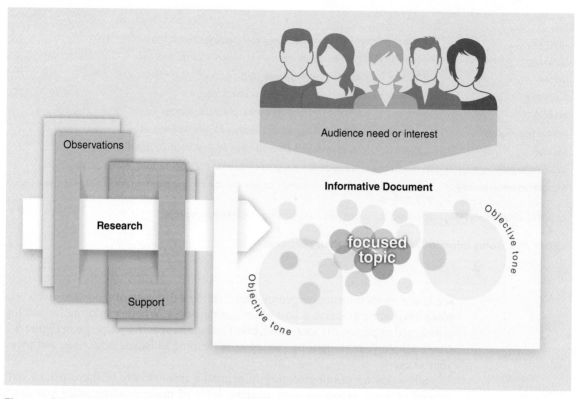

Figure 6.1 Elements of an informative text. Research, observations, and support reinforce the impartial presentation of a focused topic in informative texts.

While providing suggestions might be construed as a mode of subtle persuasion, note that the author does not incite readers to implement them; she merely offers them as options for those who might want to improve relationships with their brothers or sisters. Figure 6.1 illustrates the role of an impartial or objective tone in informative documents. As you can see, an objective tone encompasses all elements of an informative document, including the observations and other support applied to the topic. An author meets the audience's interest in receiving unbiased information by presenting research in an evenhanded manner.

Application in College and the Workplace

There are many genres, or categories of documents, that are used to inform—and nothing more. The distinct nature of these genres suggests how the broad aim of informing can be broken down into more specific purposes. In Figure 6.2, you can

Informative Genre	Focused Purpose
Journal	To record happenings in your life and your feelings about them
Newspaper article	To record events by reporting who, what, when, where, and why
Memo	To update employers or colleagues regarding meetings, projects, etc.
Brochure	To provide a brief overview of a service, institution, etc.
Profile	To introduce readers to intriguing people, places, or events
Instruction manual	To offer directions for setting up and using a particular product
Memoir	To share particular memories from your past and relate their significance
Business report	To record the findings of some aspect of a company's operations, earnings, etc.
Annotated bibliography	To catalog and summarize sources on a given topic in preparation for additional research and writing
Research or lab report	To record the procedures and findings for a research project

Figure 6.2 **Some informative genres and their purposes**

see how various informative genres, representing a diversity of academic and workplace environments, serve a host of unique purposes. Whether informative writing is assigned or personally motivated, considering the specific purposes in Figure 6.2 can facilitate your composing processes by helping to isolate objectives and focus your work.

Strategies for communicating information through any of these genres will depend to some extent on your readers' level of understanding since you don't want to talk down to them or over their heads. To be sure, informative genres cover a wide spectrum of general and specialized audiences, as illustrated in Figure 6.3. Although many of the genres in Figure 6.3 can slide along the spectrum from general to specialized, their positions in this diagram represent common applications. However, it's crucial to note that these positions reflect tendencies. For example, while an instruction manual for a personal computer may be targeted for a large portion of the public, the instruction manual for a new computer-aided design (CAD) system would be targeted especially to engineers. Sometimes memos are targeted to colleagues in the same office who are responsible for a particular aspect of a business; at other times they are addressed to the entire company.

As a general rule of thumb, you can predict that the more specialized a given audience is, the more field-specific knowledge its members have. However, when the audience is as diverse as the general public, you will likely need to begin with the basics. Whatever the case, you'll have plenty of opportunities in the next four chapters to consider how readers' needs and expectations will influence your informative writing.

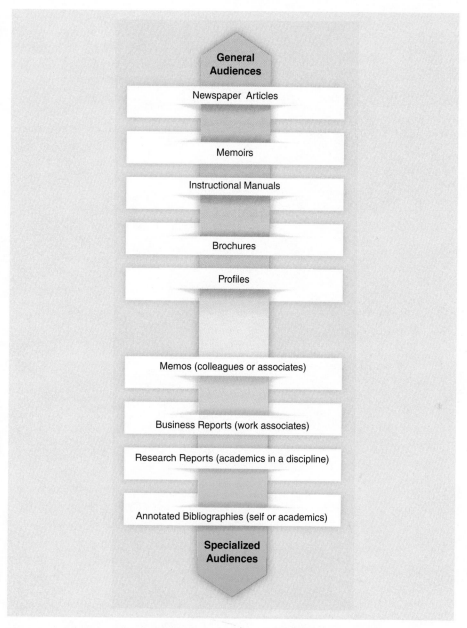

Figure 6.3 Spectrum of audiences for informative genres

Memoir

Reflect for a moment on the woman in this photograph. What is her story? Where is she going? Where has she been? What emotions are behind the expression on her face? What might you learn from reading about her experiences? What might she learn from reading about yours? Such questions drive the genre introduced in this chapter, a genre referred to as *memoir*.

People are storytellers by nature. From the earliest civilizations, stories have served to entertain, to instruct, and to explain what is otherwise inexplicable. The mythologies of ancient cultures stand as testaments to these long-standing influences of the story. Although from your vantage point in time, you know that the myths you've read are fictional, original audiences regarded these tales as true accounts of their heroes' personal lives, death-defying adventures, and quests to make sense of the world around them.

Stories about others' personal lives, adventures, and quests for understanding maintain tremendous appeal even today, whether fictional or nonfictional. For example, novels, short fiction, journals, biographies, and autobiographies enjoy extensive readerships in both print and digital formats. The subject matter of these genres is often profound as they relate traumatic events, unique happenings, or remarkable triumphs over intimidating odds. At other times the subject matter is mundane but treated in a way that helps readers view it from a fresh perspective. This chapter will introduce you to strategies for putting the subject matter of your own life—or at least a snapshot from it—into story form as the focus of a memoir.

Distinguishing Features of a Memoir

A memoir is a kind of life writing that has much in common with an autobiography, except for the fact that a memoir typically covers less ground. More specifically, instead of chronicling your entire life or much of it, as an autobiography would do, a memoir will represent a particular time period or event within your life, spanning hours, days, weeks, or possibly a few years. Typically, the focus of a memoir derives from a given **theme**—that is, the message or central concept you'll communicate through the experiences you wish to portray. For example, you might decide to write about a special friendship with an elderly relative or neighbor. Wishing to show that you have gained as much from the relationship as he or she has (this being your theme), you craft your memoir to emphasize the moments you shared that are most effective in illustrating a mutual give-and-take.

This is not to suggest that you must identify a theme *before* you decide to compose a memoir. In many cases, the unique or widely relevant nature of a life event begs that it be told. The theme then arises from deeply reflecting on that event, its precursors, its aftermath, and even the experiences of others involved, so you can pull meaning from it that will resonate with others.

Memoirs invite attention for various reasons. In some instances, they attract readers simply because they are written by some famous (or infamous) individual. Examples might include *Grace, Gold, and Glory: My Leap of Faith* by Olympic gymnast Gabrielle Douglas and *Life* by rock legend and lead guitarist of The Rolling Stones, Keith Richards.

In other cases, however, a memoir will cultivate interest not by the reputation of its author but by the very nature of the story he or she is telling. Maybe it relates experiences that are similar to the reader's and therefore promises to increase self-knowledge or to provide comfort through identification with another human being. Maybe it relates experiences that are so different from the reader's that it arouses his or her curiosity. The point is that—even if you aren't yet famous—your memoir could prove significant to others as it sheds light on their own experiences or helps them live and learn vicariously through yours.

When writing a memoir, you will be depicting actual occurrences. Nevertheless, because you will be viewing them from a distance, your portrayal of them will be subject to the relative strength of isolated memories, your changing perspectives on those memories, and your shifting sense of their importance in contrast to each other. The memoir will capture your up-to-the-moment sense of these occurrences in writing, as you re-create them in a form that helps readers grasp their significance as you understand it.

In telling the story of these experiences, your memoir will capitalize on many of the qualities you probably associate with good fiction. Beyond **theme** (discussed earlier), these include:

- A stirring **plot**—the action constituting the story
- Intriguing **characters**—the people involved in the action
- A vividly portrayed **setting**—the time and place in which the action occurs
- A pleasing **style**—the author's vocabulary, sentence structures, voice, and form

Figure 7.1 depicts relationships between these elements as they function within a memoir.

As Figure 7.1 suggests, the elements of fiction carry the meaning you hope readers will draw from the life event(s) that you've decided to embody in your memoir.

"Memoirs focus strictly on the author's self."

If you research the label, you'll find that the term *memoir* is sometimes used to refer to writing about the lives of others. But with regard to its more common application, which denotes writing about the self (the definition applied in this chapter), be advised that *relationships* between the author and other people may become the focus.

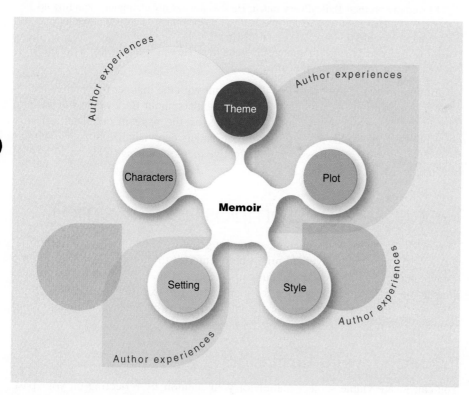

Figure 7.1 Key elements in a memoir. A memoir relies on certain key elements also applied to fiction, including plot, characters, setting, style, and theme. However, unlike a fictional story, a memoir's details depict the author's actual experiences.

Because fictional stories and memoirs resemble each other, readers will expect the latter to progress much like short stories, demonstrating chronological development, plenty of rich description, dialogue authentic to the characters, and so on. Such features are rich with creative possibility, so be encouraged to experiment while bringing the people and scenes in your memoir to life.

The fiction-like feel of a memoir is beautifully displayed in author Maya Angelou's widely praised autobiographical work, *I Know Why the Caged Bird Sings*. This book-length project recounts numerous episodes from Angelou's life growing up as an African-American woman in the southern United States during the late 1930s and early 1940s, and many of these episodes can stand as brief memoirs in and of themselves. A particularly poignant moment from Chapter 4 of *Caged Bird* focuses on Angelou's love and admiration for her brother. In an excerpt from that chapter displayed in the Look Inside box that follows, you can see how Angelou harnesses the elements of fiction to draw readers into her experience.

The direct contrast of the ladies' insensitive behavior with Bailey's compassionate loyalty makes a strong impression, not only for its substance but for the manner in which Angelou renders it. Of course, the content of this episode from *Caged Bird* could be accurately communicated in a more straightforward manner:

> I loved my brother, Bailey, very much. He was always my champion, standing up for me whenever others treated me badly. For example, when people called me names, he would find a way of embarrassing them.
>
> He also had many other interesting qualities. He was handsome, smart, hardworking and sometimes a little ornery. . . .

But compare the impact of this dry account with the manner in which Angelou portrays the relationship. Rather than telling readers about Bailey, she *shows* them who he was by re-creating certain behaviors on the page in detail and vividly describing aspects of his appearance so that readers can visualize him. *Showing* as opposed to *telling* is a skill essential to effective memoir writing (it is also addressed in Chapter 12).

Processes for Composing a Memoir

As clarified earlier in this chapter, memoirs grow from authors' recognition that the life experiences they've had might be of interest to others, whether providing enjoyment or teaching readers about some aspect of their own lives. The following sections offer specific advice for identifying life experiences through which you might educate others and for depicting those experiences through the elements of fiction.

Invention toward First Insight

You can locate viable subject matter for your memoir by reflecting on your past, recalling events that remain at the forefront of your memory as a result of their significance. Moments of great joy, sorrow, fear, or excitement; catalysts for personal growth; important milestones; incidents that changed you or the way you view the

From *I Know Why the Caged Bird Sings*

by Maya Angelou

A LOOK INSIDE:
MEMOIR

Bailey was the greatest person in my world. And the fact that he was my brother, my only brother, and I had no sisters to share him with, was such good fortune that it made me want to live a Christian life just to show God that I was grateful. Where I was big, elbowy and grating, he was small, graceful and smooth. When I was described by our playmates as being shit color, he was lauded for his velvet-black skin. His hair fell down in black curls, and my head was covered with black steel wool. And yet he loved me.

Angelou uses vibrant language to depict the visible differences between her and her brother. In addition, instead of simply stating her profound love, she communicates the extent of her emotion by deeming it worthy of sacrifice. (Angelou wrestles with religion throughout *Caged Bird*.)

When our elders said unkind things about my features (my family was handsome to a point of pain for me), Bailey would wink at me from across the room, and I knew that it was a matter of time before he would take revenge. He would allow the old ladies to finish wondering how on earth I came about, then he would ask, in a voice like cooling bacon grease, "Oh Mizeriz Coleman, how is your son? I saw him the other day, and he looked sick enough to die."

Aghast, the ladies would ask, "Die? From what? He ain't sick."

And in a voice oilier than the one before, he'd answer with a straight face, "From the Uglies."

Launching into a narrative illustrating qualities that inspired her love for her brother, she attributes the people involved with dialect appropriate to the time period and locale, maintaining an air of authenticity.

I would hold my laugh, bite my tongue, grit my teeth and very seriously erase even the touch of a smile from my face. Later, behind the house by the black-walnut tree, we'd laugh and laugh and howl.

Bailey could count on very few punishments for his consistently outrageous behavior, for he was the pride of the Henderson/Johnson family.

His movements, as he was later to describe those of an acquaintance, were activated with oiled precision. He was able to find more hours in the day than I thought existed. He finished chores, homework, read more books than I and played the group games on the side of the hill with the best of them. He could even pray out loud in church, and was apt at stealing pickles from the barrel that sat under the fruit counter and Uncle Willie's nose. . . .

Here, instead of relying on vague adjectives to label her brother's gifts, she implies them through a list of specific activities.

> Of all the needs (there are none imaginary) a lonely child has, the one that must be satisfied, if there is going to be hope and a hope of wholeness, is the unshaking need for an unshakable God. My pretty black brother was my Kingdom Come.

Source: Excerpts from I KNOW WHY THE CAGED BIRD SINGS by Maya Angelou. Copyright © 1969 and renewed 1997 by Maya Angelou. Used by permission of Random House, an imprint and division of Random House, LLC. All rights reserved.

Angelou ends this reflection about the depth of her brother's influence on her life through a powerfully expressed religious metaphor.

world—these are just a few points of entry for coming up with topics. For some topics broached in recent memoirs, see Figure 7.2.

Once you've brainstormed a list of experiences that fit the genre and assignment expectations, you might want to spend a few minutes freewriting about those that seem most thought-provoking. As you reflect on each experience, consider which one sustains your motivation level, which elicits the most material, and which carries a theme that will be interesting or valuable to your audience. For example, think about the widely relevant theme characterizing the Look Inside excerpt from *Caged Bird*—that is, the power of a sibling's love and loyalty in coping with the pains of childhood. Once you settle on an experience that motivates you and suggests a theme that you feel you can effectively develop, you'll probably want to conduct a little research to help focus, support, and illustrate your ideas.

Preparation through Research

Obviously, the most productive method for preparing to compose a memoir is a memory search. Although you were searching your memory as you were brainstorming or

Title and Author	Topic
Teacher Man by Frank McCourt	The author's experiences as a teacher in New York secondary and postsecondary schools
Dreams from My Father by Barack Obama	President Obama's distant relationship with his father as a result of his residence in another country and untimely death
Sickened: The Memoir of a Munchausen by Proxy Childhood by Julie Gregory	The author's experiences as a child purposely made ill by her mother, who was satisfying her need to be a martyr
The Know-It-All: One Man's Humble Quest to Become the Smartest Person in the World by A. J. Jacobs	A year the author spent reading all volumes of the *Encyclopedia Britannica* from cover to cover
She's Not There: A Life in Two Genders by Jennifer Finney Boylan	The author's experience of changing genders from a man to a woman
Dream Catcher by Margaret Salinger	The author's childhood as the daughter of extremely private and reportedly eccentric author J. D. Salinger

Figure 7.2 Various memoirs and their subject matter

freewriting during your initial stabs at invention, now is the time to double your efforts, using prewriting strategies such as clustering or cubing (see Chapter 4) that push you to greater levels of specificity in exploring your subject matter. Whatever you do to jog your memory, at this point in planning your memoir, you should be producing material relevant to each element of fiction (see Figure 7.1). More specifically, relevant to the larger experience you're exploring, you'll want to think of particular episodes that seem important to establishing your theme, compile information about the characters who are central to those events, and record actions of those characters as they become crucial in driving the plot.

As an example, think again about the Look Inside excerpt from *Caged Bird*. Maya Angelou might have chosen any number of episodes to illustrate the support and loyalty of her brother, as well as her admiration and love for him. But the one she portrays levels a strong impact because it sharply contrasts the meanness of some of her relatives with Bailey's admirably mischievous way of calling them out for their bad behavior. This episode demonstrates his fiercely protective spirit and the good humor he and his sister enjoy, clearly establishing their genuine affection.

In addition to searching your memory for such episodes and noteworthy details about them, you may want to mine some external resources that are well suited for memoir writing, such as those listed in Figure 7.3. Although much of what you discover through these resources will enhance your memoir by enabling more accurate and textured depictions of people, places, and situations, you will not directly cite your sources as you would in an academic paper. Put another way, you might consider this use of resources as background research—a type of fact-checking that is crucial to shaping your memoir but that won't be overtly acknowledged within it. Any direct citations that become necessary—for example, from a document that you directly quote as part of the story—can be credited at the end of the piece. (For more on documentation practices, see Chapter 21.)

Invention toward More Focused Insight

The details you generate while researching your proposed topic should help narrow the scope of your memoir. You may discover, for example, that the life event or time period that surfaced at first insight is too vast and you'll need to select a smaller episode within it. Maybe by reflecting more on the particulars of the event or the relationships

Resource	Purpose
Personal diaries or journals	To accurately recall your reactions to an event at the time it occurred
Life artifacts or keepsakes	To stimulate your memory and help you visualize special or critical moments in your life
Others' diaries or journals	To gain alternate perspectives on happenings depicted in your memoir
Interviews	To gain alternate perspectives on happenings depicted in your memoir or to seek elaboration on information you already have
Photographs	To generate details that can add depth to your characterizations of people and settings
Historical records	To gather information about the past that will add credibility to your portrayal
Published documents	To gather all sorts of facts about people, places, events, etc., that will bring integrity to your treatment of them

Figure 7.3 **Resources commonly consulted when writing memoirs**

of the people involved, you'll determine how to refine the theme in ways that will grab and hold your readers' attention. Or maybe you'll find that individuals you originally pegged as central to your story are actually marginal, or less important to your purposes. Whatever the case, your focus should be tight enough to avoid gratuitous detail and to allow thorough treatment of all the essential components of your memoir. Reining in your focus helps ensure that readers will not miss or mistake your theme.

A strategy specific to narrative writing that can assist you in focusing and structuring your memoir is **storyboarding.** This technique results in a graphic representing scenes in the plot that are key to developing the theme. Storyboards might take the shape of simple flowcharts with short descriptions of these scenes, or they might employ images, as in Figure 7.4. The more elaborate a storyboard is, the more guidance it will offer when you're composing a memoir. On the other hand, a storyboard that is overly elaborate may prove confining and discourage productive avenues of thought that arise while you're drafting.

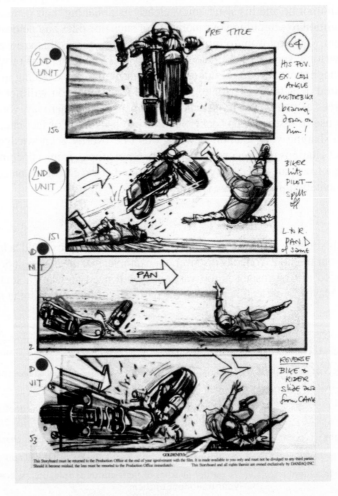

Figure 7.4 **Storyboard from the motorcycle chase scene in** *James Bond: Goldeneye*

Strategies for Drafting

Your own composing preferences—whether you need to have everything mapped out or whether you like to leave plenty of room for ideas to emerge organically—will point to the optimum level of detail to include in your storyboard or other tools for planning your memoir. If you fall into the former category, remember that tying yourself too rigidly to any plan may cause you to overlook opportunities for profitable experimentation. In fact, it might be worth taking a little time to explore such opportunities, while being careful to avoid tangents that could interrupt the flow of events and derail your readers.

Whatever the interplay between your planning and drafting strategies, you'll need to take care in weaving together scenes from the plot so that you can effectively indicate the passage of time and help readers follow the order of occurrences. This is especially important with regard to **flashbacks,** which involve taking readers momentarily to a period preceding that of the central narrative (e.g., a past experience that taught you a lesson crucial to overcoming a more current challenge). Casting back in time to relate an event that is vital for understanding the central action requires special attention to transitional elements that will help readers follow your movement into the past and then back again.

Beyond attending to plot considerations in crafting your memoir, you will also want to think carefully about developing characters, including yourself. These individuals should engage readers and help them understand the significance of the experiences you have chosen to share. One way they can do so is through dialogue—either **inner dialogue** in the form of reflections, dreams, and so on, or **external dialogue** in the form of conversation with others. The words people utter and how they utter them offer insight into their personalities, in some cases much more effectively than what the author says about them. For example, in the Look Inside excerpt from *Caged Bird,* Bailey's endearing impudence is skillfully portrayed in his exchange with the rude ladies who insulted his sister. That dialogue appears in Figure 7.5. In contrast to the impact of witnessing this conversation on the page, imagine how lackluster Bailey would seem if Angelou had simply stated that her brother "answered the ladies' insults with insults of his own."

If you do incorporate dialogue into your memoir, you'll want to take particular note of how it should be presented. In Figure 7.5, you can see that whenever the speaker changes, the line is indented to indicate a new paragraph. You can also see that introductions to direct quotes are followed by commas and that the quoted lines, as well as punctuation marks at the end of those lines, are encompassed in quotation marks.

Of course, dialogue is only part of the portrait you might create for your characters; in addition, you will need to describe them—their appearances, personalities, mannerisms, and so on. Features ripe for

"Oh Mizeriz Coleman, how is your son? I saw him the other day, and he looked sick enough to die."

Aghast, the ladies would ask, "Die? From what? He ain't sick."

And in a voice oilier than the one before, he'd answer with a straight face, "From the Uglies."

Figure 7.5 **Effective use of dialogue**

description are potentially overwhelming, but you can manage the numbers and kinds of details by thinking about their importance in defining an individual's role in the context of the message you want to communicate. For example, you don't need to spend much time discussing your friend's love of sports if the point of his or her involvement in your memoir has to do with generosity of spirit. However, love of sports may become relevant if a particular sports-related incident effectively demonstrates that spirit. (To learn more about describing as a composing strategy, see Chapter 8.)

The same approach to managing detail generally holds true for settings. In fact, setting can be a powerful indicator of a story's theme—this becomes clear when you imagine the different feelings evoked by a location suggesting poverty as opposed to wealth, fear as opposed to contentment, fantasy as opposed to reality, and so on. Of course, a memoir's reliance on actual occurrences rules out fabricating a setting that might better suit your imagination than the real one, but you can highlight features that best convey your meaning. Regardless, you need to be aware that while vivid descriptions help readers visualize setting and other components of a story—helping them relate to the action, people, and surroundings—unnecessary or overly tedious detail can bog a text down, making it difficult to process.

The vocabulary you gravitate toward in describing elements of your memoir contributes to its style. But style also rests in voice, sentence structure, and form. Memoirs are typically geared toward the general public and, therefore, adopt a conversational voice in contrast to the more formal voice of an academic article, for example. As a result, you'll want to avoid specialized terminology and long, winding sentences.

Furthermore, in depicting the events of your memoir, you will want to liberally employ **action verbs,** or verbs that show the characters or subject of the sentence dynamically interacting with people, engaging the environment, or portraying emotions. In contrast to passive verb constructions (in which the subject is being acted on by an object) or state-of-being verbs (*is, are, was, were,* etc.), action verbs are generally considered superior choices for their energy. Figure 7.6 clarifies the differences between active, passive, and state-of-being verbs. Although you might express any of the examples in Figure 7.6 more eloquently while still maintaining the features of their respective categories, you'll want to opt for action verbs whenever possible because they bring greater vibrancy and precision to your writing.

Relevant to the form or structure of your memoir, its beginning and ending deserve careful attention. To understand their importance, think about stories with introductory paragraphs that immediately grab your attention and pull you in, as opposed to those that simply announce their topics in offhand fashion—or think about stories with conclusions that provide a satisfying sense of closure, as opposed to those that leave compelling issues unresolved. Of course, the beginnings and

Action Verb	Passive Verb	State-of-Being Verb
Norman **grimaced** at the clock as he **hurried** into class, late as usual.	Norman **was reminded** by the clock of his chronic lateness to class.	Norman **was** late to class as usual; the minute hand was way past the 12.

Figure 7.6 **Verb constructions**

endings of memoirs do not mimic the introductions and conclusions of essays. Instead, a memoir's opening paragraphs tend to immediately familiarize readers with an element of fiction, maybe jumping directly into an exciting or unsettling exchange between characters or into a dramatic portrayal of the locale.

Conclusions should leave readers with a sense of how you've come to terms with the events or experiences you've portrayed. This might involve answering questions that, as a means of building suspense, you left unanswered earlier in the text; for another example, it might involve delivering a final scene that demonstrates how you addressed any conflicts at the center of your memoir. You should keep in mind, though, that the conclusion of a memoir should not pronounce a set of lessons you want your readers to learn from it. Rather, you should strive for an ending that conveys your theme in a subtle but unique way, leaving an impression readers won't soon forget. For example, compare the passages in Figure 7.7. The one on the left ends the episode presented earlier from *Caged Bird;* the one on the right is a paraphrase of that ending. While these passages communicate nearly identical sentiments, Angelou's version couches them in unexpected phrasing and religious references that are much more striking and memorable.

Revision and Editing

Questions for Revising

- Does the event or theme hold potential significance or interest for others?
- Do the elements of the memoir effectively carry the theme?
- Does the introduction grab readers' attention and entice them to enter the story?
- Are the plot, characters, and setting thoroughly described?
- Is the dialogue, if any, authentic to the individuals portrayed, as well as to the setting?

Original Conclusion

Of all the needs (there are none imaginary) a lonely child has, the one that must be satisfied, if there is going to be hope and a hope of wholeness, is the unshaking need for an unshakable God. My pretty black brother was my Kingdom Come.

Paraphrase of Original Conclusion

I was lonely as a child, and I had a lot of needs. The only way I could feel better about myself was through remembering that my wonderful brother loved me. His friendship gave me hope for a better future.

Source: Excerpt from I KNOW WHY THE CAGED BIRD SINGS by Maya Angelou. Copyright © 1969 and renewed 1997 by Maya Angelou. Used by permission of Random House, an imprint and division of Random House, LLC. All rights reserved.

Figure 7.7 Contrast between conclusions for a memoir

- Is the plot effectively paced, with rising action, climax, and falling action?
- Does the plot progress by *showing* the action instead of telling about it?
- Does the narrative follow a logical sequence aided by transitions that effectively signal movement through time and connections between ideas or reflections?
- Does the conclusion impress upon readers the significance of the subject matter and offer a sense of closure?

Questions for Editing

- Are the details essential to the memoir's objective?
- Is the style conversational, enabling a general readership to readily process it?
- Are sources properly credited at the end of the piece?
- Is the memoir free of spelling, punctuation, and usage errors?

Transfer to Other Writing Situations

Memoirs are valuable in their own right as they preserve personal histories and share experiences that hold interest or significance for others. But their value for study in composition courses extends beyond these benefits. To be specific, many genres benefit from **personal anecdotes,** or what might be called "mini-memoirs," which depict authors' experiences for their relevance in illustrating key points.

Personal anecdotes are fairly common in the discourse of the humanities and social sciences, which value authors' unique insights about their subject matter as *part of* the scholarly conversation (in contrast to the hard sciences, for instance, which strive to downplay individual perception). For a concrete example, consider teachers who, in writing about their profession, share stories from their classrooms to illustrate the promise of an instructional strategy they've developed. Or consider anthropologists or social workers who reflect on relationships with their subjects as a way to provide background for a study and to explore the impact of the researchers' presence within the communities they are representing.

As for the skills of description and narration associated with memoir writing, they serve numerous academic and workplace genres. In fact, all writing depends on precise description to accurately and notably depict its subject matter and on thoughtful narration to sequence situations in ways that are essential to understanding their nature and relationships. Figure 7.8 cites just a few genres in various disciplines that rely on description and narration.

The list of genres that depend on effective description and narration goes on and on. Whatever the motivation for writing your memoir, or for describing or narrating in other contexts, you should recognize that these strategies are potential outlets for creative energy, allowing you to portray the world around you in a manner that helps others see it in deeper, richer, and more illuminating ways than they have seen it before.

Discipline	Genre	Key Strategies
Chemistry	Lab report	*Describing* elements and their properties *Narrating* the sequence of activities in an experiment
Advertising	Marketing proposal	*Describing* the visual appeals of the ad campaign *Narrating* a plan for testing it with the target demographic
Nursing	Medical record	*Describing* the nature of a wound *Narrating* procedures for treating it
Law	Case brief	*Describing* the parties involved in the dispute *Narrating* the event that led to it
Aviation	Maintenance report	*Describing* problems that might affect the plane's performance *Narrating* the steps taken to fix them
English	Literary analysis	*Describing* the characters of the literary work *Narrating* segments of its plot in abbreviated form

Figure 7.8 Description and narration in genres from various disciplines

ACTIVITY

Storyboarding a Family Tale or Legend   All families tell stories that characterize or define them. These stories might elicit laughter, sadness, embarrassment, fear, or, more probably, multiple emotions. They may be the kinds of stories that are told time and again at holiday gatherings or that, although painful to recall, are important for their role in preserving a sense of family history. As practice for planning a memoir, select a family story with a narrative that is intimately familiar to you, one that you wouldn't mind sharing with classmates or your teacher. Then, create a storyboard capturing key moments that suggest the story's significance.

IDEA FOR EXTENDED WRITING

Writing a Literacy Memoir   In composition courses like the one you're taking now, your teacher and classmates (the target audience for this assignment and a subset of the general public) benefit from learning about your literacy practices (i.e., reading and writing), not only so they can better assist you in improving them but also so they can learn something about their own literacy practices in comparison to yours. For this assignment, you are invited to compose a memoir about some life event or specific experience that is significant for what it reveals about your literacy development—that is, your development as a reader or a writer. Maybe you have memories of a special someone reading to you when you were a child, and he or she instilled in you a love for literature. Maybe you won an essay contest in grade school or high school, having written about an issue that really mattered to you, and you realized the impact of your own rhetoric. Or maybe the experiences you recall are not so positive. Reflecting on disappointments and struggles can be as instructive as (sometimes more so than) reflecting on joys and achievements, and they tend to make for especially powerful memoirs. Regardless of the event you choose, the genre calls on you to re-create it in story form, in a way that portrays its significance for you and its potential significance for your audience.

One Writer's Beginnings

by Eudora Welty

I learned from the age of two or three that any room in our house, at any time of day, was there to read in, or to be read to. My mother read to me. She'd read to me in the big bedroom in the mornings, when we were in her rocker together, which ticked in rhythm as we rocked, as though we had a cricket accompanying the story. She'd read to me in the diningroom on winter afternoons in front of the coal fire, with our cuckoo clock ending the story with "Cuckoo," and at night when I'd got in my own bed. I must have given her no peace. Sometimes she read to me in the kitchen while she sat churning, and the churning sobbed along with *any* story. It was my ambition to have her read to me while *I* churned; once she granted my wish, but she read off my story before I brought her butter. She was an expressive reader. When she was reading *Puss in Boots,* for instance, it was impossible not to know that she distrusted *all* cats.

It had been startling and disappointing to me to find out that story books had been written by *people,* that books were not natural wonders, coming up of themselves like grass. Yet regardless of where they came from, I cannot remember a time when I was not in love with them—with the books themselves, cover and binding and the paper they were printed on, with their smell and their weight and with their possession in my arms, captured and carried off to myself. Still illiterate, I was ready for them, committed to all the reading I could give them.

Neither of my parents had come from homes that could afford to buy many books, but though it must have been something of a strain on his salary, as the youngest officer in a young insurance company, my father was all the while carefully selecting and ordering away for what he and Mother thought we children should grow up with. They bought first for the future.

Besides the bookcase in the livingroom, which was always called "the library," there were the encyclopedia tables and dictionary stand under windows in our diningroom. Here to help us grow up arguing around the diningroom table were the Unabridged Webster, the Columbia Encyclopedia, Compton's Pictured Encyclopedia, the Lincoln Library of Information, and later the Book of Knowledge. And the year we moved into our new house, there was room to celebrate it with the new 1925 edition of the Britannica, which my father, his face always deliberately turned toward the future, was of course disposed to think better than any previous edition.

In "the library," inside the mission-style bookcase with its three diamond-latticed glass doors, with my father's Morris chair and the glass-shaded lamp on its table beside it, were books I could soon begin on—and I did, reading them all alike and as they came, straight down their rows, top shelf to bottom. There was the set of Stoddard's Lectures, in all its late nineteenth-century vocabulary and vignettes of peasant life and quaint beliefs and customs, with matching halftone illustrations: Vesuvius erupting, Venice by moonlight, gypsies glimpsed by their campfires. I didn't know then the clue they were to my father's longing to see the rest of the world. I read straight through his other love-from-afar: the Victrola Book of the Opera, with opera after opera in synopsis, with portraits in costume of Melba, Caruso, Galli-Curci, and Geraldine Farrar, some of whose voices we could listen to on our Red Seal records.

My mother read secondarily for information; she sank as a hedonist into novels. She read Dickens in the spirit in which she would have eloped with him. The novels of her girlhood that had stayed on in her imagination, besides those of Dickens and Scott and Robert Louis Stevenson, were *Jane Eyre, Trilby, The Woman in White, Green Mansions, King Solomon's Mines.* Marie Corelli's name would crop up but I understood she had gone out of favor with my mother, who had only kept *Ardath* out of loyalty. In time she absorbed herself in Galsworthy, Edith Wharton, above all in Thomas Mann of the *Joseph* volumes.

St. Elmo was not in our house; I saw it often in other houses. This wildly popular Southern novel is where all the Edna Earles in our population started coming from. They're all named for the heroine, who succeeded in bringing a dissolute, sinning roué and atheist of a lover (St. Elmo) to his knees. My mother was able to forgo it. But she remembered the classic advice given to rose growers on how to water their bushes long enough: "Take a chair and *St. Elmo*."

To both my parents I owe my early acquaintance with a beloved Mark Twain. There was a full set of Mark Twain and a short set of Ring Lardner in our bookcase, and those were the volumes that in time united us all, parents and children.

Reading everything that stood before me was how I came upon a worn old book without a back that had belonged to my father as a child. It was called *Sanford and Merton.* Is there anyone left who recognizes it, I wonder? It is the famous moral tale written by Thomas Day in the 1780s, but of him no mention is made on the title page of *this* book; here it is *Sanford and Merton in Words of One Syllable* by Mary Godolphin. Here are the rich boy and the poor boy and Mr. Barlow, their teacher and interlocutor, in long discourses alternating with dramatic scenes—anger and rescue allotted to the rich and the poor respectively. It may have only words of one syllable, but one of them is "quoth." It ends with not one but two morals, both engraved on rings: "Do what you ought, come what may," and "If we would be great, we must first learn to be good."

This book was lacking its front cover, the back held on by strips of pasted paper, now turned golden, in several layers, and the pages stained, flecked, and tattered around the edges; its garish illustrations had come unattached but were preserved, laid in. I had the feeling even in my heedless childhood that this was the only book my father as a little boy had had of his own. He had held onto it, and might have gone to sleep on its coverless face: he had lost his mother when he was seven. My father had never made any mention to his own children of the book, but he had brought it along with him from Ohio to our house and shelved it in our bookcase.

My mother had brought from West Virginia that set of Dickens; those books looked sad, too—they had been through fire and water before I was born, she told me, and there they were, lined up—as I later realized, waiting for *me*.

I was presented, from as early as I can remember, with books of my own, which appeared on my birthday and Christmas morning. Indeed, my parents could not give me books enough. They must have sacrificed to give me on my sixth or seventh birthday—it was after I became a reader for myself—the ten-volume set of Our Wonder World. These were beautifully made, heavy books I would lie down with on the floor in front of the diningroom hearth, and more often than the rest volume 5, *Every Child's Story Book,* was under my eyes. There were the fairy tales—Grimm, Andersen, the English, the French, "Ali Baba and the Forty Thieves"; and there was Aesop and Reynard the Fox; there were the myths and legends, Robin Hood, King Arthur, and St. George and the Dragon, even the history of Joan of Arc; a whack of *Pilgrim's Progress* and a long piece of *Gulliver.* They all carried their classic illustrations. I located myself in these pages and could go straight to the stories and pictures I loved; very often "The Yellow Dwarf" was first choice, with Walter Crane's Yellow Dwarf in full color making his terrifying appearance flanked by turkeys. Now that volume is as worn and backless and hanging apart as my father's poor *Sanford and Merton.* The precious page with Edward Lear's "Jumblies" on it has been in danger of slipping out for all these years. One measure of my love for Our Wonder World was that for a long time I wondered if I would go through fire and water for it as my mother had done for Charles Dickens; and the only comfort was to think I could ask my mother to do it for me.

I believe I'm the only child I know of who grew up with this treasure in the house. I used to ask others, "Did you have Our Wonder World?" I'd have to tell them The Book of Knowledge could not hold a candle to it.

I live in gratitude to my parents for initiating me—as early as I begged for it, without keeping me waiting—into knowledge of the word, into reading and spelling, by way of the alphabet. They taught it to me at home in time for me to begin to read before starting to school. I believe the alphabet is no longer considered an essential piece of equipment for traveling through life. In my day it was the keystone to knowledge. You learned the alphabet as you learned to count to ten, as you learned "Now I lay me" and the Lord's Prayer and your father's and mother's name and address and telephone number, all in case you were lost.

My love for the alphabet, which endures, grew out of reciting it but, before that, out of seeing the letters on the page. In my own story books, before I could read them for myself, I fell in love with various winding, enchanted-looking initials drawn by Walter Crane at the heads of fairy tales. In "Once upon a time," an "O" had a rabbit running it as a treadmill, his feet upon flowers. When the day came, years later, for me to see the Book of Kells, all the wizardry of letter, initial, and word swept over me a thousand times over, and the illumination, the gold, seemed a part of the word's beauty and holiness that had been there from the start.

Learning stamps you with its moments. Childhood's learning is made up of moments. It isn't steady. It's a pulse.

In a children's art class, we sat in a ring on kindergarten chairs and drew three daffodils that had just been picked out of the yard; and while I was drawing, my sharpened yellow pencil and the cup of the yellow daffodil gave off whiffs just alike. That the pencil doing the drawing should give off the same smell as the flower it drew seemed part of the art lesson—as shouldn't it be? Children, like animals, use all their senses to discover the world. Then artists come along and discover it the same way, all over again. Here and there, it's the same world. Or now and then we'll hear from an artist who's never lost it.

In my sensory education I include my physical awareness of the *word*. Of a certain word, that is; the connection it has with what it stands for. At around age six, perhaps, I was standing by myself in our front yard waiting for supper, just at that hour in a late summer day when the sun is already below the horizon and the risen full moon in the visible sky stops being chalky and begins to take on light. There comes the moment, and I saw it then, when the moon goes from flat to round. For the first time it met my eyes as a globe. The word "moon" came into my mouth as though fed to me out of a silver spoon. Held in my mouth the moon became a word. It had the roundness of a Concord grape Grandpa took off his vine and gave me to suck out of its skin and swallow whole, in Ohio.

This love did not prevent me from living for years in foolish error about the moon. The new moon just appearing in the west was the rising moon to me. The new should be rising. And in early childhood the sun and moon, those opposite reigning powers, I just as easily assumed rose in east and west respectively in their opposite sides of the sky, and like partners in a reel they advanced, sun from the east, moon from the west, crossed over (when I wasn't looking) and went down on the other side. My father couldn't have known I believed that when, bending behind me and guiding my shoulder, he positioned me at our telescope in the front yard and, with careful adjustment of the focus, brought the moon close to me.

The night sky over my childhood Jackson was velvety black. I could see the full constellations in it and call their names; when I could read, I knew their myths. Though I was always waked for eclipses, and indeed carried to the window as an infant in arms and shown Halley's Comet in my sleep; and though I'd been taught at our diningroom table about the solar system and knew the earth revolved around the sun, and our moon around us, I never found out the moon didn't come up in the west until I was a writer and Herschel Brickell, the literary critic, told me after I misplaced it in a story. He said valuable words to me about my new profession: "Always be sure you get your moon in the right part of the sky."

Source: Reprinted by permission of the publisher from "Listening" in ONE WRITER'S BEGINNINGS by Eudora Welty, pp. 5–11, Cambridge, Mass.: Harvard University Press. Copyright © 1983, 1984 by Eudora Welty.

The Workers

by Richard Rodriguez

It was at Stanford, one day near the end of my senior year, that a friend told me about a summer construction job he knew was available. I was quickly alert. Desire uncoiled within me. My friend said that he knew I had been looking for summer employment. He knew I needed some money. Almost apologetically he explained: It was something I probably wouldn't be interested in, but a friend of his, a contractor, needed someone for the summer to do menial jobs. There would be lots of shoveling and raking and sweeping. Nothing too hard. But nothing more interesting either. Still, the pay would be good. Did I want it? Or did I know someone who did? I did. Yes, I said, surprised to hear myself say it.

In the weeks following, friends cautioned that I had no idea how hard physical labor really is. ("You only *think* you know what it is like to shovel for eight hours straight.") Their objections seemed to me challenges. They resolved the issue. I became happy with my plan. I decided, however, not to tell my parents. I wouldn't tell my mother because I could guess her worried reaction. I would tell my father only after the summer was over, when I could announce that, after all, I did know what "real work" is like.

The day I met the contractor (a Princeton graduate, it turned out), he asked me whether I had done any physical labor before. "In high school, during the summer," I lied. And although he seemed to regard me with skepticism, he decided to give me a try. Several days later, expectant, I arrived at my first construction site. I would take off my shirt to the sun. And at last grasp desired sensation. No longer afraid. At last become like a *bracero*. "We need those tree stumps out of here by tomorrow," the contractor said. I started to work.

I labored with excitement that first morning—and all the days after. The work was harder than I could have expected. But it was never as tedious as my friends had warned me it would be. There was too much physical pleasure in the labor. Especially early in the day, I would be most alert to the sensations of movement and straining. Beginning around seven each morning (when the air was still damp but the scent of weeds and dry earth anticipated the heat of the sun), I would feel my body resist the first thrusts of the shovel. My arms, tightened by sleep, would gradually loosen; after only several minutes sweat would gather in beads on my forehead and then—a short while later—I would feel my chest silky with sweat in the breeze. I would return to my work. A nervous spark of pain would fly up to my arm and settle to burn like an ember in the thick of my shoulder. An hour, two passed. Three. My whole body would assume regular movements; my shoveling would be described by identical, even movements. Even later in the day, my enthusiasm for primitive sensation would survive the heat and the dust and the insects pricking my back. I would strain wildly for sensation as the day came to a close. At three-thirty, quitting time, I would stand upright and slowly let my head fall back, luxuriating in the feeling of tightness relieved.

Some of the men working nearby would watch me and laugh. Two or three of the older men took the trouble to teach me the right way to use a pick, the correct way to shovel. "You're doing it wrong, too fucking hard," one man scolded. Then proceeded to show me— what persons who work with their bodies all their lives quickly learn—the most economical way to use one's body in labor.

"Don't make your back do so much work," he instructed. I stood impatiently listening, half listening, vaguely watching, then noticed his work-thickened fingers clutching the shovel. I was annoyed. I wanted to tell him that I enjoyed shoveling the wrong way. And I didn't want to learn the right way. I wasn't afraid of back pain. I liked the way my body felt sore at the end of the day.

I was about to, but, as it turned out, I didn't say a thing. Rather it was at that moment I realized that I was fooling myself if I expected a few weeks of labor to gain me admission to the world of the laborer. I would not learn in three months what my father had meant by "real work." I was not bound to this job; I could imagine its rapid conclusion. For me the sensations of exertion and fatigue could be savored. For my father or uncle, working at comparable jobs when they were my age, such sensations were to be feared. Fatigue took a different toll on their bodies—and minds.

It was, I know, a simple insight. But it was with this realization that I took my first step that summer toward realizing something even more important about the "worker." In the company of carpenters, electricians, plumbers, and painters at lunch, I would often sit quietly, observant. I was not shy in such company. I felt easy, pleased by the knowledge that I was casually accepted, my presence taken for granted by men (exotics) who worked with their hands. Some days the younger men would talk and talk about sex, and they would howl at women who drove by in cars. Other days the talk at lunchtime was subdued; men gathered in separate groups. It depended on who was around. There were rough, good-natured workers. Others were quiet. The more I remember that summer, the more I realize that there was no single *type* of worker. I am embarrassed to say, I had not expected such diversity. I certainly had not expected to meet, for example, a plumber who was an abstract painter in his off hours and admired the work of Mark Rothko. Nor did I expect to meet so many workers with college diplomas. (They were the ones who were not surprised that I intended to enter graduate school in the fall.) I suppose what I really want to say here is painfully obvious, but I must say it nevertheless: The men of that summer were middle-class Americans. They certainly didn't constitute an oppressed society. Carefully completing their work sheets; talking about the fortunes of local football teams; planning Las Vegas vacations; comparing the gas mileage of various makes of campers—they were not *los pobres* my mother had spoken about.

On two occasions, the contractor hired a group of Mexican aliens. They were employed to cut down some trees and haul off debris. In all, there were six men of varying age. The youngest in his late twenties; the oldest (his father?) perhaps sixty years old. They came and they left in a single old truck. Anonymous men. They were never introduced to the other men at the site. Immediately upon their arrival, they would follow the contractor's directions, start working—rarely resting—seemingly driven by a fatalistic sense that work which had to be done was best done as quickly as possible.

I watched them sometimes. Perhaps they watched me. The only time I saw them pay me much notice was one day at lunchtime when I was laughing with the other men. The Mexicans sat apart when they ate, just as they worked by themselves. Quiet. I rarely heard them say much to each other. All I could hear were their voices calling out sharply to one another, giving directions. Otherwise, when they stood briefly resting, they talked among themselves in voices too hard to overhear.

The contractor knew enough Spanish, and the Mexicans—or at least the oldest of them, their spokesman—seemed to know enough English to communicate. But because I was around, the contractor decided one day to make me his translator. (He assumed I could speak Spanish.) I did what I was told. Shyly I went over to tell the Mexicans that the *patrón* wanted them to do something else before they left for the day. As I started to speak, I was afraid with my old fear that I would be unable to pronounce the Spanish words. But it was a simple instruction I had to convey. I could say it in phrases.

The dark sweating faces turned toward me as I spoke. They stopped their work to hear me. Each nodded in response. I stood there. I wanted to say something more. But what could I say in Spanish, even if I could have pronounced the words right? Perhaps I just wanted to engage them in small talk, to be assured of their confidence, our familiarity. I thought for a moment to ask them where in Mexico they were from. Something like that. And maybe I wanted to tell them (a lie, if need be) that my parents were from the same part of Mexico.

I stood there.

Their faces watched me. The eyes of the man directly in front of me moved slowly over my shoulder, and I turned to follow his glance toward *el patrón* some distance away. For a moment I felt swept up by that glance into the Mexican's company. But then I heard one of them returning to work. And then the others went back to work. I left them without saying anything more.

When they had finished, the contractor went over to pay them in cash. (He later told me that he paid them collectively—"for the job," though he wouldn't tell me their wages. He said something quickly about the good rate of exchange "in their own country." I can still hear the loudly confident voice he used with the Mexicans. It was the sound of the *gringo* I had heard as a very young boy. And I can still hear the quiet, indistinct sounds of the Mexican, the oldest who replied. At hearing that voice I was sad for the Mexicans. Depressed by their vulnerability. Angry at myself. The adventure of the summer seemed suddenly ludicrous. I would not shorten the distance I felt from *los pobres* with a few weeks of physical labor. I would not become like them. They were different from me.

After that summer, a great deal—and not very much really—changed in my life. The curse of physical shame was broken by the sun: I was no longer ashamed of my body. No longer would I deny myself the pleasing sensations of my maleness. During those years when middle-class black Americans began to assert with pride, "Black is beautiful," I was able to regard my complexion without shame. I am today darker than I ever was as a boy. I have taken up the middle-class sport of long-distance running. Nearly every day now I run ten or fifteen miles, barely clothed, my skin exposed to the California winter rain and wind or the summer sun of late afternoon. The torso, the soccer player's calves and thighs, the arms of the twenty-year-old I never was, I possess now in my thirties. I study the youthful parody shape in the mirror, the stomach lipped tight by muscle; the shoulders rounded by chin-ups; the arms veined strong. This man. A man. I meet him. He laughs to see me, what I have become.

The dandy. I wear double-breasted Italian suits and custom made English shoes. I resemble no one so much as my father—the man pictured in those honeymoon photos. At that point in life when he abandoned the dandy's posture, I assume it. At the point when my parents would not consider going on a vacation, I register at the Hotel Carlyle in New York and the Plaza Athenée in Paris. I am as taken by the symbols of leisure and wealth as they were. For my parents, however, those symbols became taunts, reminders of all they could not achieve in one lifetime. For me those same symbols are reassuring reminders of public success. I tempt vulgarity to be reassured. I am filled with the gaudy delight, the monstrous grace of the nouveau riche.

In recent years I have had occasion to lecture in ghetto high schools. There I see students of remarkable style and physical grace. (One can see more dandies in such schools than one ever will find in middle-class high schools.) There is not the look of casual assurance I saw students at Stanford display. Ghetto girls mimic high-fashion models. Their dresses are of bold, forceful color; their figures elegant, long; the stance theatrical. Boys wear shirts that grip at their overdeveloped muscular bodies. (Against a powerless future, they engage images of strength.) Bad nutrition does not yet tell. Great disappointment, fatal to youth, awaits them still. For the moment, movements in school hallways are dancelike, a procession of postures in a sexual masque. Watching them, I feel a kind of envy. I wonder how different my adolescence would have been had I been free. . . . But no, it is my parents I see—their optimism during those years when they were entertained by Italian grand opera.

The registration clerk in London wonders if I have just been to Switzerland. And the man who carries my luggage in New York guesses the Caribbean. My complexion becomes a mark of my leisure. Yet no one would regard my complexion the same way if I entered such hotels through the service entrance. That is only to say that my complexion assumes its significance from the context of my life. My skin in itself, means nothing. I stress the point because I know there are people who would label me "disadvantaged" because of my color. They make the same mistake I made as a boy, when I thought a disadvantaged life was circumscribed by particular occupations. That summer I worked in the sun may have made me physically indistinguishable from the Mexicans working nearby. (My skin was actually darker because, unlike them, I worked without wearing a shirt. By late August my hands were probably as tough as theirs.) But I was not one of *los pobres*. What made me different from them was an attitude of *mind,* my imagination of myself.

I do not blame my mother for warning me away from the sun when I was young. In a world where her brother had become an old man in his twenties because he was dark, my complexion was something to worry about. "Don't run in the sun," she warns me today. I run. In the end, my father was right—though perhaps he did not know how right or why—to say that I would never know what real work is. I will never know what he felt at his last factory job. If tomorrow I worked at some kind of factory, it would go differently for me. My long education would favor me. I could act as a public person—able to defend my interests, to unionize, to petition, to speak up—to challenge and demand. (I will never know what real work is.) I will never know what the Mexicans knew, gathering their shovels and ladders and saws.

Their silence stays with me now. The wages those Mexicans received for their labor were only a measure of their disadvantaged condition. Their silence is more telling. They lack a public identity. They remain profoundly alien. Persons apart. People lacking a union obviously, people without grounds. They depend upon the relative good will or fairness of their employers each day. For such people, lacking a better alternative, it is not such an unreasonable risk.

Their silence stays with me. I have taken these many words to describe its impact. Only: the quiet. Something uncanny about it. Its compliance. Vulnerability. Pathos. As I heard their truck rumbling away, I shuddered, my face mirrored with sweat. I had finally come face to face with *los pobres*.

Source: From HUNGER OF MEMORY: THE EDUCATION OF RICHARD RODRIGUEZ by Richard Rodriguez. Reprinted by permission of David R. Godine, Publisher, Inc. Copyright © 1982 by Richard Rodriguez.

FOR DISCUSSION

1. To what extent or in what ways are the experiences portrayed in these memoirs relevant to a potentially broad or general audience?
2. How would you express the theme of each memoir in your own words?
3. How do the other elements of fiction support these memoirs' respective themes?
4. How do the opening strategies work to draw in readers?
5. Which passages strike you as being especially powerful in terms of description—engaging you through appeals to your senses?

Profile

Gordon Freeman was ranked number one in a list of the 50 best video game characters of all time by *Empire* magazine online. The website hosting this list features brief profiles including pictures of the characters along with explanations of their distinctive qualities. Read the following profile of Freeman to get a sense of how this genre focuses on key traits that identify the subject as unique in some way.

"Ginger hair, thick-rimmed glasses, a tidy goatee and a Ph.D. degree in Theoretical Physics—Gordon Freeman was never your average gun-toting FPS hero. However . . . Freeman has become a gaming icon, synonymous with the apotheosis of first-person action. The character is the quintessential geek fantasy: a first class, card-carrying uber nerd who's thrust into the breach and forced to fend off an inter-dimensional invasion as well as

squads of well-armed govern-ment goons—not something the average MIT graduate expects on his first day at work. He's a far cry from the muscular machismo and implausibly proportioned heroes who traditionally make up the genre: [Freeman is] one of the most unlikely heroes in gam-ing, while simultaneously one of the most believable. . . . It would be a disservice to Freeman's laconic charm to say he's void of personality due to never uttering

a word—or being directly seen. . . . In keeping Freeman mute and unseen, Valve can-
nily laid the groundwork for a character that players can fully embody, enabling each
would-be Freeman to shape Gordon's persona themselves. . . ."

Profiles are essays or articles that characterize persons, places, or events by concentrating attention on their unique or compelling features. Although they often highlight attributes—for example, the noteworthy achievements of an individual, the
physical beauty of a place, the fund-raising potential of an event—profiles are not
limited to emphasizing the positive. In fact, many profiles strive for a balanced
approach, acknowledging the complexity or contradictory nature of their subjects,
while still others may accentuate negative or troubling qualities.

Although most profiles assume an informative posture, their authors may have
additional purposes in mind. For example, an article in *Time* magazine that introduces readers to the contributions of a famous humanitarian might also be intended
to inspire others toward good deeds. Or a *National Geographic* article depicting a
third-world village suffering from a disease caused by a tainted water supply might
also be intended to incite action toward improving others' safety or quality of life.
As these examples illustrate, an overtly informative text, such as a profile, may
wield subtly persuasive impact.

Distinguishing Features of a Profile

Whatever the subject of a profile, its goal is to create an engaging portrait of that
person, place, or event as viewed from a particular vantage point or angle. In other
words, the objective is to characterize some especially compelling aspect of the
subject—not every aspect of it. Figure 8.1 portrays ele-
ments of a profile in relation to one another.

As Figure 8.1 suggests, one quality that unites all
profiles is their use of details to tap readers' senses,
helping them see, hear, smell, feel (and possibly even
taste!) the object of investigation. Take a look at
the passages in Figure 8.2 drawn from profiles of a
place (a pond) and an event (a woodworking class).
As you read, pay attention to how the authors help
you experience these respective scenes through rich
description.

Despite its rhetorical power, keep in mind that
engaging in rich description is not a call to bombard
readers with random observations. On the contrary, you
should be selective regarding the information you provide, limiting yourself to specifics that clearly relate to
your focus or thesis. In addition to rich description,
a profile might include direct quotes about the subject,
as well as **anecdotes** or brief narratives. Whatever
the case, your profile should leave readers with the

MYTH

**"Composing a profile is the same
as profiling."**

Profiling is a term that carries disturbing connotations
as it is often associated with overgeneralizing or ste-
reotyping people. Such acts can invite prejudicial treatment of entire populations based on the behavior of a
few individuals. The act of *composing a profile* does
not involve leaps from single entities to groups. Rather,
it seeks to represent some aspect of a given person,
place, or event, with the intention of underscoring its
individuality.

REALITY

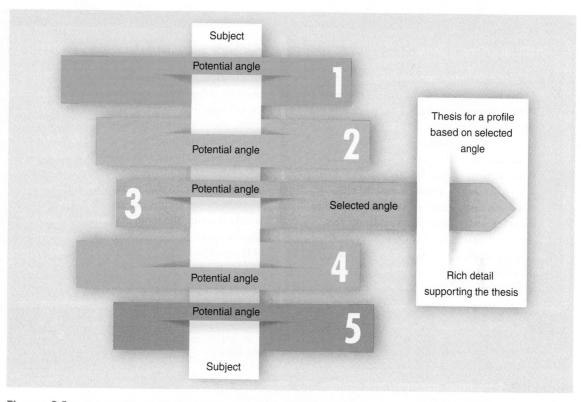

Figure 8.1 **Relationships between elements of a profile.** The author of a profile aims to present a portrait of his or her subject—often a person, place, or event—from a particular angle. Rich detail supports a thesis based on that angle.

impression that they have met the person, visited the place, or witnessed the event about which you are writing. To achieve this, you'll want to be creative in marshaling details to serve your focus.

You can see how details help to establish focus in the Look Inside excerpt later in this chapter, taken from a profile about Steven Spielberg, legendary director of films like *E.T. the Extraterrestrial, Jurassic Park,* and *Lincoln.* Writing for *BusinessWeek* magazine, the author of this profile ultimately zeroes in on Spielberg's financial prowess, but, in doing so, he establishes how Spielberg's success is rooted in an intense drive for movie-making that surfaced in his early childhood.

Processes for Composing a Profile

If you have ever written a memoir, a short story, or another genre that depends heavily on description and narration, you'll find yourself on familiar ground regarding many processes associated with composing a profile. Despite these

Profile of a Place: A Pond

Every winter the liquid and trembling surface of the pond, which was so sensitive to every breath, and reflected every light and shadow, becomes solid to the depth of a foot or a foot and a half. . . . Like the marmots in the surrounding hills, it closes its eye-lids and becomes dormant for three months or more. Standing on the snow-covered plain, as if in a pasture amid the hills, I cut my way first through a foot of snow, and then a foot of ice, and open a window under my feet, where, kneeling to drink, I look down into the quiet parlor of the fishes, pervaded by a softened light as through a window of ground glass, with its bright sanded floor the same as in summer.

Source: Henry David Thoreau, "The Pond in Winter," *Walden,* 1854.

Profile of an Event: A Woodworking Class

Mr. Devries finishes up, closes his roll book, and with rising voice says, "OK, let's get to *work.*" And, in movement that is fluid, almost gentle, the students slide out of repose, up and out of their seats, and stream across the floor to stations around the room: to the worktable by the radial arm saw, to the tool cabinet, to the panel router, to wall racks in the far corner where they don aprons and safety glasses. Within minutes, the room is vibrant with the slam of boards laid out to measure, the screech of the circular saw, the acrid smell of blade on wood.

Source: Mike Rose, "A Vocabulary of Carpentry." *The Mind at Work: Valuing the Intelligence of the American Worker,* Viking, 2004.

Figure 8.2 **Descriptive passages from profiles of a place and an event**

similarities to other genres, however, profiles do exhibit distinct qualities, as reviewed earlier in this chapter. The following discussion will guide you in moving between some widely applicable composing strategies and those that are unique to writing profiles.

Invention toward First Insight

Sometimes when you are asked to write a profile for school or work, your teacher or employer will assign a particular person, place, or event. At other times, you'll be free to write about any subject. When the choice rests entirely with you, it makes sense to begin by searching your memory for an exceptional person you know, a unique place you've visited, or an event you've attended that made a lasting impression on you. If a viable idea doesn't jump immediately to mind, you might consult Figure 8.3, which presents a range of possibilities to jump-start your thinking.

Preparation through Research

A profile's sense of authenticity grows from its author's firsthand experience with his or her subject matter. Therefore, when composing in this genre, you'll probably want to perform some **primary research**—that is, to venture out from the library

From "Steven Spielberg: The Storyteller"

by Sam Jaffe

A LOOK INSIDE:
PROFILE

Spielberg has done all this in pursuit of one overriding goal: to tell as many great stories to as many people as will listen. And that's what he has always been about. The son of a computer scientist and a gifted pianist, Spielberg spent his early childhood in New Jersey and, later, Arizona. From the very beginning, his fertile imagination went into overdrive, filling his young mind with images that would later inspire his filmmaking.

The pronoun "this" in the first line refers to the act of building his business empire.

Even decades later, Spielberg says he has vivid memories of his earliest years, which are the origins of some of his biggest hits. He attributes *E.T.* to the unsettling years leading up to his parents' 1966 divorce, saying: "It is really about a young boy who was in search of some stability in his life." *Close Encounters of the Third Kind* was inspired by early morning meteor-gazing with his father, a sci-fi fanatic, when he was four years old. "He was scared of just about everything," recalls his mother, Leah Adler. "When trees brushed against the house, he would head into my bed. And that's just the kind of scary stuff he would put in films like *Poltergeist*." To this day, Spielberg's wife, actress Kate Capshaw, says her husband remains terrified of airplane and elevator rides and closed-in places.

Facts about Spielberg's life lead to a focus for this part of the profile that asserts the relevance of childhood experiences to his career.

Support for the author's focus in this paragraph includes direct quotes from Spielberg and those who know him well.

In high school, Spielberg experienced another kind of terror, which would one day help him understand the subject of his film *Schindler's List.* It was his senior year, and the family had just moved from Phoenix to Saratoga, Calif., an affluent San Francisco suburb. There, Spielberg says, he was tormented by anti-Semitic remarks from his classmates, who would sneeze "Hah-Jew" when he passed in the halls. After school, jocks often beat him up. With his parents' divorce looming, Spielberg's grades sank. He barely graduated from high school and was rejected from both UCLA and USC film schools. Settling for California State University at Long Beach because it was close to Hollywood, Spielberg got a C in his television production course. He dropped out in his senior year.

In this paragraph, the author employs an anecdote that sheds light on how childhood experience offered perspective on one of Spielberg's most memorable films.

It was all very sobering, especially since Spielberg had long since made up his mind to be a director. The home-made movies he started making as a young boy gave Spielberg a powerful escape from his fears. He was 11 when he first got his hands on his dad's 8-millimeter Bell & Howell wind-up camera and began shooting short flicks about flying saucers and World War II battles. Before long, the entire family was selling tickets and making lemonade for living-room showings. "It cost me about $50 to make the movie, and I would charge a quarter a ticket, and at the end of the summer I might have $55," he recalls today. "That's kind of the way Hollywood works today, small margins."

This paragraph offers additional details that work together to establish that the roots of Spielberg's movie empire stretch back to his childhood.

or your computer station to conduct observations or interviews (learn about strategies for primary research in Chapter 5). This is not to suggest that consulting library or Internet documents (**secondary research**) would be inappropriate. In fact, if

Category	Profile Topics
People	• A mentor who made a difference in your life • A neighbor who volunteers in your community • A classmate who is gifted in a particular discipline • A parent who has an unusual career • A friend who is creative and quirky • A relative who has overcome hardship • A teacher who helped you pass a difficult class
Places	• A vacation spot • The campus pond • A building with historical significance • The site of an environmental disaster • A museum • A national forest preserve • The scene of an accident
Events	• A concert • An arts festival • An end-of-season sale • A professional ball game • A political rally • Your best friend's surprise birthday party • A younger sibling's first day at a new school

Figure 8.3 Various topics for open-ended profile assignments

your subject has been written about before, you would be wise to consult published sources for background information.

When conducting observations or interviews—even if you do not yet have a tight focus for your project—you will need to have at least some idea of the qualities or features characterizing your subject that you want to learn more about. For example, if you know you want to pursue some angle on an individual's triumph over a personal challenge, you don't want to waste time during an interview rehashing life events that have nothing to do with that achievement. In short, you need to have a plan for concentrating your research energy. Without such a plan, you might be overwhelmed by the data you collect and walk away from your research site without having recorded enough data on the matters that most intrigue you.

Invention toward More Focused Insight

Once you've completed primary research and collected published information about your subject, you are ready to mine the data for a specific thesis. Returning to the example of a person who triumphed over a personal challenge, perhaps you discover in your interview notes that this individual holds an unusual outlook on life that enabled him or her to adjust to the situation in ways that individuals with a different outlook might not have been able to manage. As a result, you decide to compose a thesis that foregrounds that outlook, providing a lens through which to filter the challenge and its aftermath.

Strategies for Drafting

As with most essays, you will want to craft an introduction for your profile that **hooks** readers, or grabs their attention in some way. In keeping with the objectives of the genre, a profile's hook should suggest that the subject is worthy of special attention. Often, it will do so through a descriptive snapshot or a brief anecdote. More specifically, you'll want to develop openings that set a tone of excitement, drama, or surprise. Certainly, this is a composing strategy that encourages authors to be creative, as the hooks cited in Figure 8.4 illustrate.

Both hooks in Figure 8.4 draw readers in through verbal snapshots that raise questions about their subjects. The hook on the aspiring novelist fuels curiosity by delaying confirmation about exactly what this person is doing. And the hook on Rio establishes tension through starkly contrasting images—that is, how can a city be simultaneously disturbing and beautiful?

Whether you compose your hook before or after you've generated the body of your profile, at some point while drafting you may realize that you need to perform some additional research. If you find yourself in that situation, you should contact the person you're writing about for a follow-up interview or return to the place you visited to absorb more of its distinctive identity. Conducting additional research may prove difficult in the case of one-time events or those that occur on an annual basis. Still, you might supplement your initial findings in those circumstances by talking with others who shared the experience.

Profile of a Person: An Aspiring Novelist

Sitting alone at her computer, the girl pounds away at the keyboard, typing furiously. All around her images and notes are pinned to the walls at odd angles. There are hastily scribbled notes on napkins and scraps of paper, glossy photographs of scenery, and pencil sketches of medieval clothing. Though at first glance the collage seems random and chaotic, the girl has carefully chosen each piece in her collection along one common thread: her novel.

Source: Erin Anderson, a first-year composition student, "From a Dream to Reality," unpublished.

Profile of a Place: Rio de Janeiro

When it comes to Rio de Janeiro there is no avoiding the obvious. The city may be as famous for its *Carnaval,* soccer, flesh and fun as it is infamous for its hillside slums and organized crime. Yet its defining feature remains its breathtaking setting. No visitor can ever forget viewing the city from on high for the first time. Even natives—the Cariocas—stand in awe of its grandeur. How could I feel different? I, too, was born there. As a writer friend, Eric Nepomuceno, put it, "only Paris comes close to matching Rio in self-love."

Source: Alan Riding, "Reinventing Rio: The dazzling but tarnished Brazilian city gets a makeover as it prepares for the 2014 World Cup and 2016 Olympic Games," *Smithsonian,* September 2010. © 2010. Reprinted by permission of the author.

Figure 8.4 Hooks from profiles

Revision and Editing

Questions for Revising

- Is the profile appropriately geared toward the audience of the target publication?
- Does the introduction create a hook that hints at the unique and compelling nature of the subject?
- Does the thesis focus on some aspect of a person, place, or event that the target audience will find intriguing?
- Are the thesis and its subclaims illustrated through details that appeal to the senses?
- Does the organization follow some seemingly logical sequence and employ transitions to effectively connect ideas?
- Does the conclusion impress upon readers the significance of the subject and why they should know about it?

Questions for Editing

- Are the descriptive elements of the profile controlled—specific and vivid, yet not superfluous or overdone?
- Are all sources properly cited, including any interviews conducted with the subject?
- Is the profile free of spelling, punctuation, and usage errors?

Transfer to Other Writing Situations

Profiles commonly appear in publications targeted for a general audience, but you can also find them in specialized resources, some of which you may encounter in your college courses or on the job. To be more specific, interoffice newsletters sometimes highlight the work of productive employees, and business magazines may feature profiles of successful entrepreneurs. From time to time, academic journals will publish profiles of individuals who have contributed significantly to their respective fields.

Key strategies you'll practice in composing your own profile—specifically, interviewing or observing and then drawing conclusions from the data—are vital to various professional and scholarly endeavors. Consider a psychologist, for instance, whose work depends on talking at length with patients and carefully evaluating their personalities and problems before prescribing treatment. Or consider a police detective who must interact intimately with witnesses and suspects to piece together a criminal's methods and motives. Focusing on places and events, architects conduct intensive observations of potential building sites when estimating their viability, and newspaper reporters routinely cover in detail a variety of happenings that are significant to their communities, the nation, and the world.

Practice at writing profiles not only will enable you to transfer research and critical-thinking strategies associated with the genre but also will help you hone the finer skill of incorporating detail. In fact, writing with judiciously chosen details about a person, place, or event in ways that appeal to the senses is crucial to documents as diverse as poetry and scientific lab reports, both of which rely on precise and vivid description to communicate their authors' discoveries.

ACTIVITY

Drafting a Profile from a Set of Given Facts   With a couple of your peers, draft a brief profile that uses the information in Figure 8.5. You don't need to incorporate every fact, but those you choose should converge around a thesis. As time

Has red hair	Is a vegetarian	Fears deep water	Collects antique cars
Has a raspy voice	Sings country music	Won a Grammy	Plays guitar
Born in Oklahoma	Just completed a lengthy U.S. tour	Has a child on the way	Wrote his hit singles about lost love
Known for unusual onstage antics	Married for a few years	Wears a brown cowboy hat	Raised in a family that struggled financially
Always wanted to be a performer	Married his high school girlfriend	Currently resides in Nashville	Writes most of his own music and lyrics
Goes by the name "Jasper Hyde"	Recognized for charity work	Has several hit singles	Rescued an Irish Setter from the pound
Wears a brown leather belt with a turquoise buckle	Focuses most of his charity work on helping children	Tours with two of his siblings who are backup singers	Bought his parents a new home with part of his first million dollars

Figure 8.5 **Details for a profile**

allows, feel free to expand your initial draft with additional details. Once you've finished, compare your profile with those of other groups to determine which is the most engaging or creative and why.

IDEA FOR EXTENDED WRITING

Composing a Profile of a Creative Person   Think of an individual you know who is creative in some way. This person could be a friend, relative, teacher, or anyone you have access to who has demonstrated some level of ability or achievement relevant to a particular creative activity (visual arts, crafts of various kinds, writing, sports, sciences, etc.). After interviewing this person, write an essay, targeted for the "arts" section of your local newspaper, in which you characterize him or her as a "creator." To generate specific content for your profile, you might want to consult the following list of questions:

- What is the nature of this individual's creative activity?
- What has been the impact of this activity on others?
- How did this person become interested in his or her specific area of creative achievement?
- What in particular drives the individual to continue participating in this activity?
- What information about this person's childhood, home environment, and/or educational background seems relevant to his or her creative ability?
- What sources of support did and/or does this person enjoy?
- What special difficulties has he or she encountered?
- How have those challenges been met and overcome?
- What can you find out about his or her typical creative processes?

Of course, there are other questions you might ask in learning about this individual as a creator. (Remember, when presenting the findings of your interview, that simply reporting answers to questions in the form of a list seldom makes for an effective organizing strategy.)

From a Dream to Reality

by Erin Anderson, a First-Year Composition Student*

Sitting alone at her computer, the girl pounds away at the keyboard, typing furiously. All around her images and notes are pinned to the walls at odd angles. There are hastily scribbled notes on napkins and scraps of paper, glossy photographs of scenery, and pencil sketches of medieval clothing. Though at first glance the collage seems random and chaotic, the girl has carefully chosen each piece in her collection along one common thread: her novel. In middle school, Catelyn Connor decided that she wanted to be a writer, but as she moved on to high school and was tracked in the lowest level of English classes, her dream began to fade. "I always just thought I was dumb when I was in class," she recalls. The older she got, the harder she had to work for her grades and she began to struggle to keep up with the other students. It wasn't until her senior year that Catelyn discovered why she was falling behind: she has dyslexia.

Dyslexia is a learning disorder that makes it difficult to read and interpret symbols such as letters or numbers. Had Catelyn's dyslexia been diagnosed earlier, she might have been able to address some of her learning problems, but instead, she has had to adapt and find creative solutions to move through life. "I thought [my dyslexia] was a bit of a curse," she recalls. In coping with her situation in life, Catelyn not only has created the worlds that she writes about, but also has actively changed the world around her to suit her needs.

During high school, Catelyn's teachers often disregarded her writing simply because of her low standing in the classes overall and, as such, Catelyn's views of her own writing were rarely positive. But after she left high school behind, Catelyn's dream began to resurface, and she decided to start writing as a hobby. At first, Catelyn says, she started writing as a way to improve her reading and writing skills in spite of the dyslexia. Simple improvement wasn't the only reason, however: "There was also an element of wanting to show people that I could do it, because I'd had a lot of negativity [in high school]." Catelyn felt like she had to prove to the world that she wasn't dumb, that she could be a writer after all.

With time, her writing became more practiced and she moved from simply cultivating ideas in her notebook to actually writing short stories. Then one day, Catelyn took the next big leap: a novel. "I was just sitting in my room and I was trying to think about something to do. And the first scene with Ariel at age eight . . . came to my head and so I started writing . . . and I just couldn't put the book

---

*The author has replaced all proper names in this reading with pseudonyms.

down from there," she admits. Catelyn knew her dyslexia would make writing difficult, but she had her mind set on proving to the world that she could overcome her learning disorder. It didn't take long for Catelyn to realize that if she really wanted to write, she was going to have to ignore the words themselves for a while. Instead, Catelyn now finds it much more helpful to visualize the scene she wants to write and type as the scene unfolds like a movie in her head. "If I don't visualize it, then others won't, but if I visualize it, everyone else will." For her, the words have no significance unless they can conjure up images in the reader's mind. This is why she surrounds herself with photographs and drawings while she's writing; she relies not only on her mind and her imagination but also on reality to make her scenery and characters as realistic as possible. When she's thinking about the magical world of Lymestria she created for her novel, she can ignore the dyslexia and the words for a little while and focus on images and emotions instead.

Catelyn also spends a lot of time free-writing and training herself to not worry about the spelling or grammar that causes her so many problems, but rather to work on putting the movie down on the page as accurately as possible. She's also learned that if she stops to bother with correcting the spelling errors she still inevitably makes, she will become upset and suffer from writer's block, so she often uses free-writing to move past those feelings of frustration. "Don't force anything anywhere, just see where it takes you," she advises. By ignoring the spelling as much as possible while she writes, Catelyn moves beyond her dyslexia by eliminating the source of the problem: dwelling on her own issues and mistakes.

Because of all the negativity she faced in high school, Catelyn was hesitant to tell anyone about her writing at first; she was nearly two-thirds of the way finished with her novel when she finally did let someone in on what she'd been doing on her computer for nearly two years. "When my friends found out," she says, "they were really encouraging, so that helped me to sort of keep going. . . ." Her friends eventually became Catelyn's next creative solution to writing in spite of her dyslexia. Catelyn knew that avoiding the issue of spelling and grammar forever wasn't going to work, but every time she started to edit, she would become upset and discouraged because of her perceived inadequacy. Friends kept asking her for copies of her story so they could read it, but Catelyn wanted to give them an edited version of the story to read; she didn't want them reading it with so many spelling mistakes because she didn't want them to judge her. It was slow going, but eventually she had edited four or five chapters and sent them out to friends and family members to read.

It didn't take long before the feedback came pouring in. People were loving the story! They had completely fallen in love with Ariel and the magical world of Lymestria. Not only did people have plenty of helpful and supportive feedback to offer, but one friend in particular had an offer that Catelyn could not refuse: She offered to edit the entire novel! Catelyn readily accepted the offer, grateful that she would no longer have to tackle the anger and frustration of confronting the errors her dyslexia caused, but she took the offer one step further. Once she had told everyone about her novel, several other friends had casually commented that they, too, were writing stories, and Catelyn saw this as an opportunity. She invited her friends to be part of a writing group of sorts: a group to work together to improve each other's skills, to edit each other's stories, and to give everyone experience with critiquing, writing, and editing so they would have an edge when it came time to submit a work to a publisher. "So I'm kind of using them to help me a little bit. They're all really happy to do it because they want the experience, so we're all helping each other out. It's quite nice!" Her contribution to the group comes largely in the form of offering feedback on the content and coherency of others' texts, and in exchange she has her friends edit her manuscripts. It's a win-win situation for everyone; everyone gets experience, and Catelyn has found another way to move past her dyslexia and not let it prevent her from writing.

These days, Catelyn can still be found in her bedroom, surrounded by images, typing away furiously at her computer—seeing the words but not really stopping to look at them; she knows what they say after all. She no longer feels like she needs to prove anything to anyone, not even herself. "I'm feeling better about [my writing] than I used to. More confident, that's for sure!" she comments. Those days in the lowest English classes are over, and she knows that even though she might still read and write more slowly than other people, she is improving every day because she writes. Being a writer takes creativity, but not just an initial idea for a story. Rather it takes the belief that one's situation can be improved, if only one can invent a way around his or her own obstacles. In order to totally understand the effort and skill that it has taken Catelyn to make such significant changes in her life, it is important to realize that creativity is not simply the ability to create something "new" from nothing, but rather the unique manipulation of one's existing environment to create something distinctive; simply put, to use what one already has or knows in an original way to make something "new." Catelyn's dyslexia doesn't stop her from doing what she loves, and the strategies she's developed have helped her with more than her hobby. Right now, she's only a few months away from obtaining her bachelor's degree with honors in psychology.

As for the dyslexia? Catelyn doesn't like to dwell on it; she accepts that she has it, but just like she refused to let her teachers tell her whether or not she could be a writer, she refuses to let her disorder dictate what she is and is not capable of. "If you think of all the bad things that are stopping you, you're just gonna be stopped yourself and you're not gonna enjoy things as much," she says. When asked what advice she could give to aspiring authors, Catelyn simply urges for persistence. The road to becoming a writer has been a long and hard one for Catelyn, but with a few creative solutions and the will to set her own boundaries, she's finally fulfilled her childhood goal to become a writer.

Reinventing Rio

by Alan Riding

When it comes to Rio de Janeiro there is no avoiding the obvious. The city may be as famous for its *Carnaval,* soccer, flesh and fun as it is infamous for its hillside slums and organized crime. Yet its defining feature remains its breathtaking setting. No visitor can ever forget viewing the city from on high for the first time. Even natives—the Cariocas—stand in awe of its grandeur. How could I feel different? I, too, was born there. As a writer friend, Eric Nepomuceno, put it, "only Paris comes close to matching Rio in self-love."

Mountains rise to the east and west and protrude like giant knuckles from inside the city itself. Stretching to the north is a vast bay, which Portuguese navigators evidently thought was a river when they first sighted it in January 1502. Hence the name Rio de Janeiro (River of January). For centuries, ferries carried people and cargo to and from the city of Niterói on the bay's eastern shore; today a seven-mile-long bridge crosses the bay. And standing guard at its entrance is the 1,300-foot-high granite mound known as the Pão de Açúcar—the Sugar Loaf.

To the west, two long curving beaches—Copacabana and Ipanema-Leblon—run along the city's Atlantic shoreline, only to be interrupted by twin mountains, the Dois Irmãos, or the Two Brothers. Behind the beaches lies a glistening lagoon, Lagoa Rodrigo de Freitas, and the Botanical Gardens. From there, thick tropical forest reaches up into the Tijuca National Park, "every square inch filling in with foliage," as the American poet Elizabeth Bishop put it a half-century ago. And rising 2,300 feet out of this vegetation is still another peak, the Corcovado, or the Hunchback, crowned by the 125-foot-tall—including the pedestal—statue of Christ the Redeemer.

Then there are the less sublime areas. Rio's North Zone, which begins at the city center and sprawls for miles inland, resembles many cities in developing countries, with crowded highways, run-down factories, crumbling housing projects and many of Rio's more than 1,000 shantytowns, or *favelas,* as they're known. Anyone landing at Antônio Carlos Jobim International Airport (named after the late bossa nova composer) is confronted with this unexpected, dismaying sight as they go to their likely destinations in the South Zone of the city.

Then suddenly another Rio comes into view. The bayside highway curves around the city center before dipping into the majestic Aterro do Flamengo park and sweeping past the Sugar Loaf. It then enters the tunnel leading to Copacabana and the broad Avenida Atlántica, which stretches nearly three miles along the beach. A different route south passes under the Corcovado and reappears beside the Lagoa Rodrigo de Freitas, following its shores to Ipanema-Leblon. (That was my way home when I lived in Rio in the 1980s.)

The Atlantic beaches are the city's playgrounds, with sunbathers crowding near the waves and soccer and volleyball occupying much of the rest. The beaches are also strikingly heterogeneous: people of all income levels and colors mix comfortably, while women and men of every shape feel free to wear the skimpiest of swimsuits. Actors, journalists, lawyers and the like have their favorite meeting places at beachside cafés selling beer, sodas, coconut milk and snacks. There is even a corridor for cyclists and joggers.

Away from the sea, though, the Copacabana neighborhood looks run-down and its streets are often clogged with traffic. Even the more elegant Ipanema and Leblon, one beach but two neighborhoods, coexist with those hillside favelas, highlighting the gulf between Rio's rich and poor. During violent storms in April this year it was mainly residents of the favelas who died—251 in greater Rio—as a result of landslides. Favelas are also routinely blamed for drug-related violence and all-too-frequent muggings. With the pleasures of living in the beauteous South Zone, then, comes the need for security.

Farther west, beyond Leblon and a smaller beach called São Conrado, is a third Rio, Barra da Tijuca, with 11 miles of sand and no encroaching mountains. Forty years ago, it seemed an obvious place to accommodate Rio's growing middle class. But what was intended as a model urban development has become a soulless expanse of apartment blocks, highways, supermarkets and, yes, more favelas, including the one, Cidade de Deus, that gave its name to Fernando Meirelles' award-winning 2002 movie, *City of God.*

So, for all their devotion to "the marvelous city," as they call Rio, Cariocas know full well that their hometown has been in decline. The slide began 50 years ago when Brazil's capital moved to Brasília. For two centuries before then, Rio was the capital of finance and culture as well as politics. To the rest of the world, Rio was Brazil. But once politicians, civil servants and foreign diplomats moved to the new capital in 1960, São Paulo increasingly dominated the nation's economy. Even important oil fields off the coast of Rio brought little solace. The state government received a share of royalties, but no oil boom touched the city. Rio was stripped of its political identity but found no substitute. Many Brazilians no longer took it seriously: they went there to party, not to work.

"I'd call Rio a ship adrift," says Nélida Piñón, a Brazilian novelist. "We lost the capital and got nothing in return. Rio's narcissism was once a sign of its self-sufficiency. Now it's a sign of its insecurity."

Lately, Rio has even fallen behind the rest of Brazil. For the first time in its history, Brazil has enjoyed 16 years of good government, first under President Fernando Henrique Cardoso and now under President Luiz Inácio Lula da Silva, who is to leave office on January 1, 2011. And the result has been political stability, economic growth and new international prestige. But during much of this time, Rio—both the city and the state that carries its name—has been plagued by political infighting, incompetence and corruption. And it has paid the price in poor public services and mounting crime.

Yet, for all that, when I recently returned to Rio, I found many Cariocas full of optimism. The city looked much as it did a decade ago, but the future looked different. And with good reason. Last October, Rio was chosen to host the 2016 Summer Olympics, the first to be held in South America and, after Mexico City in 1968, only the second in Latin America. As if in one fell swoop, Cariocas recovered their self-esteem. Further, Lula's strong support for Rio's Olympic bid represented a vote of confidence from Brazil as a whole. And this commitment looks secure with either of the main candidates to succeed Lula in general elections on October 3—Dilma Rousseff, Lula's hand-picked nominee, and José Serra, the opposition challenger. Now, with federal and state governments pledging $11.6 billion in extra aid to prepare the city for the Olympics, Rio has a unique chance to repair itself.

"Barcelona is my inspiring muse," Eduardo Paes, the city's energetic young mayor, told me in his downtown office, referring to how the Catalan capital used the 1992 Summer Olympics to modernize its urban structures. "For us, the Olympics are not a panacea, but they will be a turning point, a beginning of the transformation." And he listed some upcoming events that will measure the city's progress: the Earth Summit in 2012, known as Rio+20, two decades after the city hosted the first Earth Summit; the soccer World Cup in 2014, which will take place across Brazil, with the final to be held in Rio's Maracanã stadium; and the city's 450th anniversary in 2015.

For the Olympics, at least, Rio need not start from scratch. Around 60 percent of the required sports installations were built for the 2007 Pan American Games, including the João Havelange Stadium for athletics; a swimming arena; and facilities for gymnastics, cycling, shooting and equestrian events. The Lagoa Rodrigo de Freitas will again be used for the rowing competitions and Copacabana for beach volleyball, while the marathon will have numerous scenic routes to choose from. The Rio Olympics Organizing Committee will have a budget of $2.8 billion to ensure every site is in good shape.

But because many competition venues will be a dozen or more miles from the new Olympic Village in Barra da Tijuca, transportation could become an Olympic-size headache. Barra today is linked to the city only by highways, one of which goes through a tunnel, the other over the Tijuca Mountains. While about half the athletes will compete in Barra itself, the rest must be transported to three other Olympic "zones," including the João Havelange Stadium. And the public has to get to Barra and the other key areas.

To pave the way, the organizing committee is counting on a $5 billion state and municipal investment in new highways, improvements to the railroad system and an extension of the subway. The federal government has also committed to modernize the airport by 2014, a long overdue upgrade.

Yet even if the Olympics are a triumph for Rio, and Brazil does unusually well in medals, there is always the morning after. What will happen to all those splendid sports installations after the closing ceremony on August 21, 2016? The experience of numerous Olympic cities, most recently Beijing, is hardly encouraging.

"We're very worried about having a legacy of white elephants," said Carlos Roberto Osório, the secretary general of the Brazilian Olympic Committee. "With the Pan American Games, there was no plan for their use after the games. The focus was on delivering the installations on time. Now we want to use everything that is built and we're also building lots of temporary installations."

Rio already has one embarrassing white elephant. Before leaving office in late 2008, César Maia, then the mayor, inaugurated a $220 million City of Music in Barra, designed by French architect Christian de Portzamparc. It is still not finished; work on its three concert halls has been held up by allegations of corruption in construction contracts. Now the new mayor has the unhappy task of completing his predecessor's prestige project.

At the same time, Paes is looking to finance his own pet project. As part of a plan to regenerate the shabby port area on the Baía de Guanabara, he commissioned Spanish architect Santiago Calatrava, renowned for his sculptural forms, to design a Museum of Tomorrow, which would focus on the environment and, hopefully, be ready for the 2012 Earth Summit. His initial designs were unveiled this past June.

New museums with bold architecture have long been an easy way of raising a city's profile. Rio's Modern Art Museum on the Aterro do Flamengo did that in the 1960s. Since the 1990s, Oscar Niemeyer's UFO-like Contemporary Art Museum in Niterói has been the main reason for tourists to cross the bay. And construction will soon begin on a new Museum of Image and Sound, designed by the New York–based firm Diller Scofidio + Renfro, on Copacabana's Avenida Atlántica.

Culture is the one area where Rio holds its own in its decades-old rivalry with São Paulo, its larger and far richer neighbor. São Paulo boasts the country's most important universities, newspapers, publishing houses, recording companies, theaters and concert halls. But Rio remains the cradle of creativity; Brazil's dominant television network, Globo, is headquartered in the city and employs a small army of writers, directors and actors for its ever-popular soap operas. Also, Globo's nightly news is beamed across Brazil from its studios in Rio. But more importantly, as "a city that releases extravagant freedoms," in Piñón's words, Rio inspires artists and writers.

And musicians, who play not only samba, choro and now funk, but also bossa nova, the sensual jazz-influenced rhythm that gained international fame with such hits as Antônio Carlos Jobim's "Girl from Ipanema." One evening, I joined a crowd celebrating the reopening of the three cramped nightspots in Copacabana—Little Club, Bottle and Baccarat—where the bossa nova was born in the late 1950s.

"Rio remains the creative heart of Brazilian music," said Chico Buarque, who has been one of the country's most admired singer-composers for over 40 years and is now also a best-selling novelist. São Paulo may have a wealthier audience, he says, "but Rio exports its music to São Paulo. The producers, writers and performers are here. Rio also imports music from the United States, from the Northeast, then makes it its own. Funk, for instance, becomes Brazilian when it is mixed with samba."

Popular music can be heard across the city, but the downtown neighborhood of Lapa is the new hot spot. In the 19th century, it was an elegant residential district reminiscent of New Orleans and, while its terraced houses have known better days, many have been converted into bars and dance halls where bands play samba and choro and the forró rhythms of northeastern Brazil. In the weeks before the pre-Lenten Carnaval, attention turns to Rio's *escolas de samba,* or samba "schools," which are, in fact, large

neighborhood organizations. During Carnaval, the groups compete for the title of champion, taking turns to parade their dancers
and colorful floats through a noisy and crowded stadium known
as the Sambódromo.

Rio is also a magnet for writers. As a legacy of its years as the
country's capital, the city is still home to the Brazilian Academy of
Letters, which was founded in 1897 and modeled on the Académie
Française. Among its 40 *immortels* today are Piñón, the novelists
Lygia Fagundes Telles, Rubem Fonseca and Paulo Coelho and the
author of popular children's books, Ana Maria Machado. But even
Fonseca's novels, which are set in Rio's underworld, rely on São
Paulo for their readership.

Except for music, Cariocas are not great consumers of culture.
Alcione Araújo, a playwright and lecturer, thinks he knows why.
"In a city with these skies, beaches and mountains, it is a crime to
lock people inside a theater," he said. And he might have added
movie theaters and art galleries. Walter Moreira Salles Jr., who
directed the award-winning movies *Central Station* and *The
Motorcycle Diaries,* lives in Rio, but looks beyond the city for his
audience. A painter friend of mine, Rubens Gerchman, who died in
2008, moved to São Paulo to be close to his market.

But Silvia Cintra, who has just opened a new gallery in Rio
with her daughter Juliana, prefers to be close to her artists. "São
Paulo has more money, but I think that 80 percent of Brazil's most
important artists live and work in Rio," she said. "São Paulo treats
art as a commodity, while the Carioca buys art because he loves it,
because he has passion. Rio has space, oxygen, energy, everything
vibrates. The artist can work, then go for a swim. You know, I have
never felt as happy about Rio as now."

Cariocas have long accepted the hillside favelas as part of the
landscape. Writing in *Tristes Tropiques,* French anthropologist Claude
Lévi-Strauss described what he saw in 1935: "The poverty-stricken
lived perched on hills in favelas where a population of blacks, dressed
in tired rags, invented lively melodies on the guitar which, during
carnaval, came down from the heights and invaded the city with them."

Today, although many of Rio's favelas still lack running water
and other basic necessities, many have improved. Brick and concrete houses have replaced wooden shacks, and most communities
have shops; many have schools. Until around 20 years ago, the
favelas were relatively tranquil, thanks to the power of the *bicheiros,*
godfather-like figures who run an illegal gambling racket known as
the "animal game." Then the drug gangs moved in.

In the late 1980s, Colombian cocaine traffickers opened new
routes to Europe through Brazil. Homegrown gangsters stepped in
to supply the local market, much of it found among the young and

wealthy of the South Zone. Soon, protected by heavy weapons, they set up their bases inside the favelas.

The response of the state government, which is in charge of security, was largely ineffective. Police would carry out raids, engage in furious gun battles with traffickers—kill some, arrest others—then leave. With most drug gangs linked to one of three organized crime groups, Comando Vermelho (Red Command), Amigos dos Amigos (Friends of Friends) and Terceiro Comando Puro (Pure Third Command), favela residents were routinely terrorized by bloody turf wars.

The reputation of Rio's police was little better. Many were thought to be on the traffickers' payroll. A December 2009 report by the New York City–based Human Rights Watch accused police officers of routinely executing detainees they claimed had been killed resisting arrest. In some favelas, police have driven out the traffickers—only to set up their own protection rackets.

Fernando Gabeira is one politician with direct experience of urban warfare. In the late 1960s, having joined leftist guerrillas fighting Brazil's military dictatorship, he participated in kidnapping the American ambassador, Charles Burke Elbrick. Elbrick was released after he was swapped for political prisoners, while Gabeira was himself arrested and then freed in exchange for another kidnapped foreign diplomat. When Gabeira returned to Brazil after a decade in exile, he was no longer a militant revolutionary and soon won a seat in Congress representing the Green Party. Having narrowly lost in Rio's mayoral elections in 2008, he plans to challenge Sérgio Cabral's bid for re-election as state governor in October.

"The principal characteristic of the violence is not drugs, but the occupation of territory by armed gangs," Gabeira said over lunch, still dressed in beach clothes. "You have 600,000 to 1 million people living in favelas outside the control of the government. And this is the state government's responsibility." Like many experts, he rejects the automatic link between poverty and violence. "My view is that we should combine social action and technology," he said. "I suggested we use drones to keep an eye on the traffickers. I was laughed at until they shot down a police helicopter."

The downing of the helicopter last October took place just two weeks after the city was chosen to host the 2016 Olympics, following Governor Cabral's assurances to the International Olympic Committee that army and police reinforcements would guarantee the security of athletes and the public. After the helicopter was shot down, Cabral threw his weight behind a new strategy designed by the state's security secretary, José Beltrame.

Starting in the South Zone, Cabral ordered the state government to establish a permanent police presence—so-called Police Pacification Units—in some favelas. After police were met by gunfire, they began a policy of leaking to the media which favela they would next target, giving traffickers time to leave and, it soon transpired, to invade favelas farther inland.

One morning I visited Pavão, Pavãozinho and Cantagalo, a three-community favela overlooking Copacabana and Ipanema, which has been peaceful since this past December. First settled a century ago, the favela has a population estimated at 10,000 to 15,000. A cable car built in the 1980s takes residents up the slope and returns with garbage in cans. It has a primary school, running water and some drainage. For years, it was also a drug stronghold. "There were constant gun battles," recalled Kátia Loureiro, an urban planner and financial director of a community organization called Museu de Favela. "There were times when we all had to lie on the floor."

Today, heavily armed police stand at the favela's entrance, while others patrol its narrow alleys and steep steps. After visiting the local school and a boxing club, I came across the Museu de Favela, which was founded two years ago to empower favela residents to develop their community and improve living conditions. Even during the bad times, it organized courses to train cooks, waiters, seamstresses, craftsmen and artists. Now it offers tours of its "museum," which is what it calls the entire favela. Says the group's executive director, Márcia Souza: "The idea is, 'My house is in the favela, so I am part of the museum.'"

My visit began with a rooftop performance by Acme, the stage name of a local rapper and Museu founder. "We don't need more cops," he told me, "we need more culture, more rap, more graffiti, more dance." The Museu sees social exclusion, not violence, as the problem in the favelas.

I took the cable car up to the home of Antônia Ferreira Santos, who was selling local handicrafts. She showed me her rooftop garden of herbs and medicinal plants. My final stop was at a little square where 11 boys and 5 girls of the local samba school were practicing drumming. With Carnaval only two weeks away, there was no time to waste.

Just how many of the city's roughly 1,000 favelas can be "pacified" by 2016 is unclear. Of course if Rio is to fully exploit its potential as a tourist destination, it must do more. It needs an up-to-date airport, better transportation and greater overall security, as well as new hotels and easier access to popular sites like the Corcovado.

One man who believes in getting things done is the city's new cheerleader, Eike Batista, an oil and mining magnate and reputedly Brazil's wealthiest man. After working mainly abroad for years, he returned home in 2000 and, unusually for a Brazilian industrialist, chose to live in Rio rather than São Paulo. "I said at the time, 'I'm going to spend my millions to fix this city,'" he recounted when I called on him at his home overlooking the Botanical Gardens. In a city with little tradition of individual philanthropy, he started by spending $15 million to help clean the lagoon.

In 2008, Batista bought the once-elegant Hotel Glória, which is now undergoing a $100 million makeover. He then acquired the nearby Marina da Glória, a port for leisure boats, and is modernizing it at a cost of $75 million. He is putting up two-thirds of the estimated $60 million it will take to build a branch of a top-flight São Paulo hospital and has invested $20 million in movie productions in Rio. Over a dinner with Madonna last November, he committed $7 million for her children's charity. He even built his own Chinese restaurant a mile from his home. "It's difficult to fly to New York once a week to eat well," he said with a laugh.

So, yes, things are stirring in Rio. Plans and promises are in the air, objectives are being defined and, thanks to the Olympics, a deadline looms to focus the mind. True, not all Cariocas support the Rio Olympics: they fear that massive public works will bring massive corruption. But the countdown has begun and Cariocas have six years to prove they can change their city for the better. When the Olympic flame is lit in Maracanã on August 5, 2016, a verdict will be returned. Only then will they know if the entire exercise was worthwhile.

Source: Alan Riding, "Reinventing Rio: The dazzling but tarnished Brazilian city gets a makeover as it prepares for the 2014 World Cup and 2016 Olympic Games," *Smithsonian,* Sept. 2010. © 2010. Reprinted by permission of the author.

FOR DISCUSSION

1. How would you articulate the specific angles that the authors take on their respective subjects?
2. Which descriptive passages in these profiles carry the most impact? Why?
3. Considering the hooks of these profiles, what specific assumptions do the authors seem to be making about textual features that draw readers in?
4. What purpose, if any, does either author seem to have beyond merely familiarizing readers with the subject of the profile?
5. How do you imagine the art of composing profiles might become important in the context of your chosen major or future career?

Report

9

You may have seen the activity depicted in this photo only in movies about the old West, particularly the Gold Rush. Panning for minerals like gold involves pulling hard substances from the water and sediment flowing around them. But what does this have to do with writing a paper? Well, if the paper is a report, you can imagine the minerals as facts you must separate from your own attitudes (the sediment and water) toward the subject

you're writing about. Of course, just as you probably can't remove every molecule of residue from those minerals, it's unlikely that you can strip all traces of personal perspective from your discussion of a topic. Nevertheless, when your goal is to report—as opposed to interpret or defend—you need to filter out as much of the personal bias as you can and focus on straightforwardly communicating established knowledge about a given

subject. Strategies for doing so are addressed in this chapter.

People tend to apply the term *report* rather loosely, attaching it to a variety of documents with different audiences and purposes. This chapter, however, limits the definition to what is arguably the most common association with this genre. More specifically, this chapter defines **report** as a document whose *dominant* aim is to communicate information

MYTH

"A report *never* expresses the author's opinion or interpretation."

Most reports *do* limit their scope to a straightforward presentation of facts or data. But you will find, for example, that certain types of business reports will tack on recommendations for solving a problem. And lab reports often end with an interpretation of data relevant to the hypothesis that spawned the experiment. This chapter, however, will not attempt to account for all such possible permutations; instead, it will focus on fundamental properties that distinguish reports as a genre from other types of documents.

REALITY

in an unbiased manner with the goal of educating readers about the current status of knowledge on a topic. Ordinarily, then, you can identify a report by its detached, evenhanded treatment of factual content, or that which can be corroborated by other resources. Keeping this definition in mind—while also remembering that reports come in many shapes and sizes—will help you understand and apply the concepts addressed in the remainder of this chapter.

You can access reports through a variety of resources, including blogs, newspapers, magazines, and even scholarly journals. More than likely, you have encountered numerous examples in your lifetime. For example, if you volunteer time and effort to a nonprofit organization, you may read reports about the results of its work. If you or a family member struggles with an illness, you probably stay informed about the latest treatment options as characterized in medical research reports. And, of course, if you've ever read a print or online newspaper, you've come across numerous accounts of current events that are intended to communicate "just the facts" about them.

In addition to regularly reading reports, you've probably written a few throughout your years in school. Teachers across the curriculum engage students in reporting the findings of library or Internet research they've conducted, leading to documents often referred to as *term papers.* Science instructors, in particular, are apt to assign *lab reports,* which record the procedures and results of laboratory experiments. And your previous English teachers may have assigned *book reports,* which provide biographical information about the author, historical facts about the era in which the work was published or set, a summary of the plot, and so on. In all these cases, again, the dominant aim is to present established or verifiable knowledge without interjecting personal opinion.

Distinguishing Features of a Report

Reflecting their dominant aim of conveying "the facts," reports typically adopt a neutral stance and tone. Although writing can never be 100 percent objective (as the product is inescapably filtered through an author's point of view), most reports downplay the writer's personal biases and impressions in favor of an impartial treatment of the subject matter. This matter-of-fact attitude supports the intention of simply explaining the topic, of helping readers to better understand it. Reports typically refer to other sources, citing the work of authors who have also studied the subject matter. Often a report will share findings of multiple sources (identifying and accounting for their biases) to ensure a balanced and reliable approach. In some cases, a report will focus on or be supplemented with primary research, including interviews and observations. (See Chapter 5 for a discussion of primary research.)

As indicated earlier, reports are diverse in nature, invoked for many different types of rhetorical situations. Consequently, their audiences vary widely—from the general public, to laypersons with similar interests, to specialists in a given field. Of course, the nature of the target readership will influence a report's style. For example, when intended for readers of a popular newspaper or magazine, a report would employ words and sentence structures that a broad range of people could easily comprehend. On the other hand, reports intended for readers of an academic journal might require specialized terminology to communicate ideas efficiently, as well as complex sentences to accommodate a given topic's intricate nature.

The rhetorical situation will also influence the components of a report and the order in which they appear. Figure 9.1 outlines the typical content of several different kinds of reports, illustrating ways in which they diverge in substance and structure. Of course, these examples align with very specific rhetorical situations and, as a result, conform to detailed expectations for substance and structure. The reports you compose for your college courses, however, will often assume a less rigid essay form.

Given a report's primary purpose of explaining established knowledge, clarity in organization is a high priority. Frequently, reports demonstrate this priority through **subheadings.** This feature involves assigning each main section of the document its own title and setting it off from the rest of the text on its own line and

Type of Report	Typical Content
Police report	• Explanation of the nature of the investigation • Summary of action taken based on the investigation • Explanation of the status of the case following police action
Business report	• Executive summary (a brief overview of the report's contents) • Problem statement (a description of the issue that is causing difficulties for the business) • Explanation of methods for studying the problem • Identification of decision-making criteria • Overview of possible solutions • Conclusion (a review of what the report revealed)
Lab report	• Introduction (an overview of the research problem, related scholarship, and research questions) • Methodology (an explanation of the strategies and procedures for answering the research questions) • Results (a presentation of the data gathered through research methods) • Discussion (the significance of the data relevant to the research questions)
Committee minutes	• Name of the organization • Date and time of the meeting • Location of the meeting • List of members who attended the meeting • List of members who were absent • Approval or revision of previous minutes • Agenda items and discussion of each • Old business (agenda items left unresolved from the previous meeting) • New business (agenda items raised for the first time) • Announcements • Date and time of the next meeting

Figure 9.1 **Substance and structure of various types of reports**

in bold print (for examples, look at the subheadings in this chapter). In addition to helping readers quickly locate information, subheadings display a report's large-scale development (imagine putting them together in an outline), and they visually signal a change in topic.

Beyond subheadings, reports frequently depend on other visual aids—including tables, graphs, flowcharts, diagrams, illustrations, and photographs—to reinforce or illuminate certain concepts. (Consult Chapter 22 to learn more about document design elements.) After all, especially for individuals who are visually oriented, an image can clarify complex material at a glance. For some examples, consider how an author might enhance a business report with graphs that show growth in sales for various products over a number of years—or might improve a police report with a diagram that records the exact positions of vehicles involved in an accident.

To experience how visuals can clarify certain concepts, consider Figure 9.2, which is intended to enhance your understanding of the relationships between key features of a report. This figure emphasizes the objective, balanced, neutral approach of a report in keeping with its aim of explaining some aspect of the current knowledge base on a given topic or issue. In the Look Inside box, you can observe several criteria associated with effective report writing. In this piece, a first-year composition

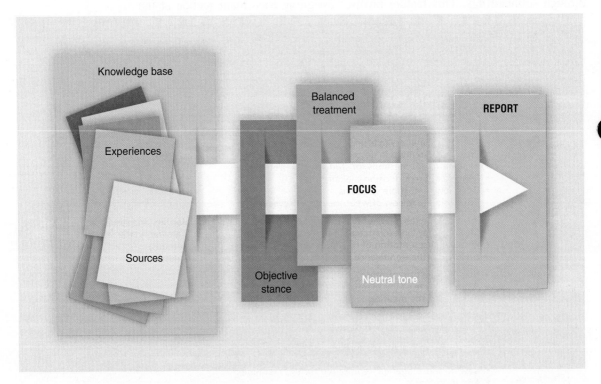

Figure 9.2 Some key features of a report. Reports focus on explaining some aspect of the current knowledge base on a topic. As this figure illustrates, an objective stance, balanced treatment, and neutral tone are key features of this genre.

From "The Wizard's Influence"

by Mandi Jourdan, a First-Year Composition Student

A LOOK INSIDE:
REPORTS

The date is July 15, 2011, and the time is nearly midnight. People who have been standing in line for hours, most of them in costume, have finally settled into their seats to watch a film they've been waiting too long to see. Four years after the release of the book *Harry Potter and the Deathly Hallows,* the readers who have turned the series into a phenomenon are about to watch the second half of the adaptation of the final book; the saga of a boy wizard that began in 1997 comes to an end. The movie begins, and over the course of the next few hours, most of the costumed fans shed tears for the characters they watch die, as they did while watching previous films and while reading the books on which they are based. One cannot mention the deaths of Sirius Black, Albus Dumbledore, Severus Snape, or even Bellatrix Lestrange without receiving a strong emotional reaction from Harry Potter fans, be it devastation or triumph. J. K. Rowling has managed to reach a worldwide fan base across generations. . . .

> The opening paragraph shares an anecdote describing fans waiting for the final *Harry Potter* movie to begin.

> The author moves here to her thesis about the influence of the *Potter* series—a factual observation that nobody of reading age from the late nineties onward could deny.

Joanne Rowling was born in Chipping Sodbury. . . . She attended Wydean Comprehensive after high school, followed by the University of Exeter. Rowling wanted to study English, but her parents encouraged her to study French instead, which she did. Her studies allowed her to spend a year in Paris, and after she completed her degree in French and Classics, she went to London, where she worked for Amnesty International and other similar organizations. Eventually, Rowling moved to Portugal, where she taught English (Pettinger; Rowling). While living there, Rowling married Portuguese journalist Jorge Arantes (Dunbar) and gave birth to her eldest daughter, Jessica. After she and her husband divorced, Rowling returned to the United Kingdom. In 1990, Rowling was returning to London from Manchester when she was first struck by the idea of a young boy named Harry Potter and his world of magic and adventure. She didn't have a pencil or pen with which to write her ideas down, and she was too shy to ask to borrow one. When she reached London, however, she began her work on the book through which she would begin to tell Harry's story (Pettinger).

> At this point, the author starts integrating biographical information about Rowling from a variety of resources.

> The biographical information continues here, moving into established facts about the first installment of the *Potter* series.

Rowling raised her daughter as a single mother living in poverty in Scotland. She wrote *Harry Potter and the Philosopher's Stone* "in Edinburgh cafes while she and her daughter survived on state benefits—and her emergence from [poverty] is now the stuff of literary legend" (Crown). In 1997, the book was published. The publishers advised Rowling that her book would not sell if it was clear that it had been written by a woman, and they encouraged her to use initials, instead. Though Rowling was not given a middle name at birth, she adopted "Kathleen" after her grandmother, and *Harry Potter and the Philosopher's Stone* was published under the name J. K. Rowling. Rowling went on to write six more novels in the Harry Potter series, as well as *Fantastic Beasts and Where to Find Them, Quidditch through the Ages* (which are considerably shorter than the novels and are based on textbooks Harry studied at Hogwarts School of Witchcraft and Wizardry), and *The Tales of Beedle the Bard,* based on fairytales told to Wizarding children within the Potter universe (Rowling).

> Here, a direct quote succinctly summarizes the backstory of Rowling and her rise to fame—a fact well-known among those who've paid even modest attention to the *Potter* phenomenon.

Harry Potter has come a long way from an idea birthed on a train ride and written in cafes. Today, it has developed into a full-blown phenomenon with a worldwide fan base. It has influenced countless works of fan art and fan-fiction, or stories written by fans based on an existing work. It has inspired clothing, toys, collectibles, video games, a card game, and even parody series, including several available on YouTube. While all of these products have sold worldwide and helped the franchise to become successful, they are not the most recognizable feature of Potter's fan base.

> At this point, the author transitions from biographical facts about Rowling to a reminder of the report's thesis, coupled with specifics that begin to illustrate it.

One facet of the fandom (the word itself was popularized by Harry Potter's fans) that is the most well-known is its tendency to hold costumed gatherings for recreation or for book releases and film premieres. At the midnight releases of the books and films, fans have waited in line for hours to make sure they were among the first to read or watch. At these events, there are costume contests and themed activities, and lovers of Harry Potter come out in full force to show their support and devotion to the series. . . .

Another perfect example of a group of fans celebrating their love for Rowling's series is the annual "Harry Potter Night" held in the library at Lycoming College, a small liberal arts college in Pennsylvania. The idea of a Potter-themed evening was put forth by a student worker, and the College's

> These two paragraphs offer more illustration for the thesis, describing two events that demonstrate the popularity of Rowling's novels.

first attempt was rather small, consisting predominantly of a game of Harry Potter Scene-It and a bit of Potter-themed food. The night became an annual fixture at Lycoming's library, and the following year, their efforts were much more in-depth. Staff members dressed as characters from the Harry Potter books, and the library's entrance was converted to resemble Platform 9¾, the terminal through which students of Hogwarts School of Witchcraft and Wizardry travel to the school. The library itself was decorated to resemble Hogwarts, and visitors were sorted into houses upon entry as are the students in the books. Even the food and drinks offered were themed and more elaborate than they were in the first attempt. In the years since, many new ideas have been implemented to keep the annual event interesting. The sorting ceremonies, a potions table, sock competitions reminiscent of Dobby the House Elf (who was freed from servitude through the presentation of clothes from Harry in the form of a sock), and costume and trivia contests take place each year. The trivia contests take several forms, from Jeopardy! to questions asked in the style of a Potter-esque wizard duel. Students are sorted into houses upon entering the library, and there is a House Cup competition inspired by those that take place in the books and films among the attendees. The winning house is featured on a READ poster (Broussard). . . .

> This paragraph offers an especially detailed summary of a Potter event as described in one of the several sources consulted for this report.

Works Cited*

Broussard, Mary J. Snyder. "No Muggles in the Library Tonight! Harry Potter Night at an Academic Library." *Library Trends*, vol. 61, no. 4, Spring 2013, pp. 814–24. *Project MUSE*, doi:10.1353/lib.2013.0017.

Crown, Sarah. "JK Rowling's First Novel for Adults Draws on Her Struggles with Poverty." *The Guardian*, 21 Sept. 2012, www.theguardian.com/books/2012/sep/22/jk-rowling-first-novel-casual-vacancy.

Dunbar, Polly. "I Hit Rock Bottom over Harry Potter: J K Rowling Reveals How Instant Fame and a 'Tsunami' of Begging Letters Drove Her to Therapy." *Daily Mail*, Newspapers Ltd, 22 Sept. 2012, www.dailymail.co.uk/news/article-2207319/J-K-Rowling-reveals-hit-rock-Harry-Potter-fame.html.

"Biography." *J. K. Rowling*, 2012, www.jkrowling.com/en_US/#/about-jk-rowling.

Pettinger, Tejvan R. "J. K. Rowling Biography." *Biography*, www.biography.com/people/jk-rowling-40998.

*The Works Cited list has been abbreviated to reflect the excerpt's content.

student discusses the impact of J. K. Rowling's *Harry Potter* series in a piece targeted for a popular audience. After providing some biographical information about Rowling, the author of this report explains several ways—as asserted in a diversity of publications—that the books are presumed to have affected generations of fans.

The remainder of this report surveys additional ways in which Rowling and her boy wizard have made their mark. These include sparking a rise in children's love for reading, encouraging interest in etymology (word history), providing a vehicle for psychological therapy relevant to problem solving, and making plenty of people (not just Rowling) a whole lot of money. The report ends with an overview of the awards Rowling has received in connection with the *Potter* series. This information, as shown in the Look Inside excerpt, is presented as factual and is linked to one or more sources that originally recorded it. In addition, the author maintains her matter-of-fact tone, presenting the information in a straightforward fashion as opposed to promoting or criticizing the books (as in a review) or interpreting the books (as in a literary analysis). (Reviews and literary analyses are discussed, respectively, in Chapters 18 and 15.)

Processes for Composing a Report

Because reports tend to present straightforward accounts of established knowledge or data, you might assume they are less demanding than genres that interpret phenomena or argue a position. Whether or not your experience ultimately supports that assumption, the reality is that all writing poses problems to be solved—in the form of determining the most promising research methods, formulating a thesis, devising a compelling conclusion, and so on. The following sections explain some strategies that can help you address many of the challenges involved in developing a report.

Invention toward First Insight

Motivation for writing a report usually arises from one of two objectives: (1) You want to educate an audience about a topic you know quite well, or (2) you want to find out more about a topic that is especially interesting to you. Either possibility is exciting—the former for the satisfaction that comes from sharing an area of your own expertise with others, and the latter from the luxury of being able to spend time answering questions about issues that intrigue you.

Regarding the first source of motivation, in many work environments, composing reports on set topics that you fully understand will be a part of your job description. Your first insight in such instances will likely be tied to the nature of those tasks. Hopefully, though, you have pursued a career that genuinely engages you, and your interest level will be high. As for your composition course, you will probably have considerable freedom to write about any topic that you can comment on with some authority. In this situation, you might stimulate first insights by surveying your achievements, hobbies, and unique experiences and then determining which of those inspires the most excitement for writing. After settling on those you find most inspiring, you might ask yourself which one your intended audience would find most useful or interesting.

Regarding the second source of motivation for writing a report—to study something you're curious about—you should take time to recall and reflect on all those moments in the past when you wished you had time to read particular works, observe certain events, or talk to experienced people, whether for increased understanding or for pure enjoyment. To keep motivation high, you should delay closure regarding topic selection. After all, this is your opportunity to meld coursework and your own special interests in ways that are impossible in many school-sponsored assignments.

Preparation through Research

Presenting the status of current knowledge on a topic requires researching widely, in a variety of places. As alluded to earlier in this chapter, to make certain that your coverage is adequate and accurate, you'll want to conduct Internet or library database searches to gather a range of perspectives on your topic. Even if you're writing a report on a hobby or an experience you've had, you'll need to engage in research to help update or elaborate your understanding. Doing so will ensure that you're offering the most accurate and thorough account possible.

Because your purpose is to forward a neutral presentation of current knowledge, you should collect multiple sources embodying a variety of approaches and viewpoints. (Research strategies are addressed at length in Chapter 5.) Next, you'll want to study those sources for any common ground that exists between them and for any controversy or disagreement they may exhibit. As a result, you'll be able to represent your topic in all its complexity. This act of thinking about sources in relation to each other, often referred to as **synthesis,** is discussed further in Chapter 21.

Invention toward More Focused Insight

Depending on how broad your initial insight was, you may need to narrow your scope by focusing on a single *sub*topic. Indeed, as is the case with many other genres, one of the most significant moves you'll make is figuring out how to limit your subject matter so that you have time and space to thoroughly develop it. Chances are that the research you've conducted so far will reveal many possibilities for reining in your scope. If not, or if you are feeling overwhelmed by the possibilities, you might call on the structured prewriting activities discussed in Chapter 4 to assist you. Thinking about the background and special interests of your intended audience should also help, as should considering your capacity for building on prior knowledge about the subtopic or addressing it in a fresh way.

Strategies for Drafting

Because the rather broad category of "report" encompasses a diversity of forms, it makes good sense to begin drafting with some reflection on the structure. If the type of report you're writing must follow a rigid format with many specified parts

Strategy	What the Strategy Involves	What the Strategy Looks Like
Defining concepts formally	Elaborating the concept in question by placing it in a category and then identifying features that distinguish it from other items in that category	1. A dalmatian (is) (a) dog with a white coat and black spots. 2. A dachshund (is) (a) dog with a long body and short legs. 3. A shar-pei (is) (a) dog with a black tongue and wrinkled skin.
Defining through example	Illustrating the concept by *depicting* its unique characteristics—by *showing* them through a specific instance	Alliteration is a figure of speech in which several words in consecutive order begin with the same consonant, such as in the childhood tongue twister "Peter Piper picked a peck of pickled peppers." (As is evident in this illustration, definition by example can enhance a formal definition.)
Defining through description	Capitalizing on readers' capacity for seeing, hearing, smelling, tasting, and touching by offering sensory detail that clarifies distinguishing features of the concept	Hydrangeas are voluminous flowers—actually large flowers consisting of many smaller flowers—that grow on bushes or trees characterized by vivid green foliage. Although they typically appear in shades of off-white or light pink, they may assume a dark blue color if the soil in which they are planted is sufficiently acidic. They are exceptionally fragrant, with a light, fruity aroma. Fragile to the touch, the blooms bruise easily and will brown and crisp around the edges without regular and plentiful watering.

Figure 9.3 **Strategies for defining terms**

(refer again to Figure 9.1), you can think about each section as a "mini-essay"—a mindset that will guide you in placing content. Of course, within and between these sections (which may be signaled by subheadings), you will have to figure out how to connect your ideas to each other and to pertinent sources. If, on the other hand, the type of report you are writing allows for a looser arrangement, you might start thinking about organization simply in terms of introduction, body, and conclusion.

The introductory paragraphs of a report typically establish the significance of the topic; that is, they apprise readers of the needs satisfied or benefits earned from expanding their knowledge about your subject matter. In addition, these early paragraphs provide context necessary for understanding information in the following sections. Often, this context requires that you define key terms. Of course, in certain situations, you might be able to define a term simply by offering another word that shares its definition—also known as a **synonym.** This is usually the case when the concept that the synonym stands for is fairly clear-cut. In other situations, however, you're going to need to provide your readers more assistance. Figure 9.3 characterizes a few common strategies for defining terms in the reports that you compose (as well as in other genres).

Beyond establishing the significance of your topic and defining key terms, the early paragraphs of your report will also include a thesis statement. In generating a thesis, however, you need to remember that a report is not a simple cut-and-paste summary of your source material; rather, it is a focused presentation of factual information that you've pulled together in meaningful relationships and explained in a way that readers can understand. Whatever the nature of your thesis, as with other genres, it may evolve as you continue drafting (so, at this point, it's actually a "working thesis"). Even so, having some general direction at the outset of composing will help you resist the temptation to pursue random tangents suggested by the many sources you've gathered. In fact, the working thesis will help you identify which sources promise to be most useful in illustrating concepts that are crucial to your presentation of the subject matter.

If you are writing primarily from experience, projecting a voice of authority in the midst of your sources probably won't be that much of a challenge. But if you are writing about a topic that you're less sure of, sources can easily overtake the text if you don't consciously confine them to a supporting role. One strategy that might help in this regard is to draft first without referencing sources. Then you can go back and carefully cite the sources you drew from, being careful to credit any and all information that extends beyond the realm of common knowledge, or that which is documented in several different sources. (For more specific guidelines on citing sources, see Chapter 21.)

When concluding your report, you'll likely want to reemphasize the significance of the topic, leaving readers with a sense of why learning about it was worth their time. One strategy for doing so is to consider the implications of the information you addressed. Additionally, if you've been reporting on some sort of problem (i.e., explaining it without arguing for a solution), you might provide a run-down of solutions that have been tried or recommended.

Revision and Editing

Questions for Revising

- Have I appropriately geared the report toward my target audience?
- Have I clearly defined potentially unfamiliar or imprecise terms essential to understanding subsequent information?
- Do my introductory paragraphs establish essential context?
- Does my thesis clearly articulate my focus?
- Does the thesis denote a detached or neutral approach to the subject matter?
- Would any of the concepts I've addressed be enhanced by providing a visual?
- Does the organization follow conventions for formatting a specific type of report or some other logical sequence?
- Does the report employ transitions to effectively connect ideas?
- Is my voice prevalent in relation to the sources I cite?
- Does the conclusion leave readers with a sense of the topic's significance?

Questions for Editing

- Are my language choices clear and sentence structures easily processed?
- Are the sources cited in the report properly cited?
- Is the finished report free of spelling, punctuation, and usage errors?

Transfer to Other Writing Situations

Figure 9.1 (near the beginning of this chapter) briefly profiles different types of reports from a range of disciplines. Of course, that sample highlights only a few documents that might be categorized under this genre label. As you proceed through your college major and into your profession, you'll be introduced to many other types of reports that reflect the unique research practices and writing conventions of that field. Despite differences in content and format, however, you'll find that, across the board, reports tend to share many of the features addressed in this chapter, including a neutral stance toward the subject matter, a presentational tone, reference to diverse sources, and so on. Moreover, you'll find that these features—and the strategies employed to create them—can be applied across various other genres wherein you need to establish accepted knowledge about a given issue or topic before you can analyze or argue a position in response to it.

Figure 9.4 Scene of an event

ACTIVITY

Reporting Events   Imagine the story behind the photograph in Figure 9.4. Along with the rest of your class, brainstorm possible settings, characters, and occurrences leading up to the scene it depicts. Based on these notes, collaborate with a couple of your classmates in composing a one-page report about this scene, modeled after a newspaper article. Compare your report with those written by other groups, and evaluate it based on criteria introduced in this chapter.

IDEA FOR EXTENDED WRITING

Reporting on a Hobby or Pastime   Reflect on a hobby or pastime that you participate in regularly—one about which you've developed considerable knowledge. Compose a report about this activity for an audience that is unfamiliar with it but interested in learning more about it. Remember that your purpose is to characterize the activity, not to sell it. Although some of the information for this report will arise from what you've learned as a participant in this activity, you should elaborate on that information with reference to additional resources—perhaps by researching the history of the activity, its contributions to society, accomplished individuals associated with it, and so on. You might also explain how readers can become involved in this activity.

Mirror, Mirror on My Facebook Wall: Effects of Exposure to Facebook on Self-Esteem

by Amy L. Gonzales, M.A., and Jeffrey T. Hancock, Ph.D.

ABSTRACT

Contrasting hypotheses were posed to test the effect of Facebook exposure on self-esteem. Objective Self-Awareness (OSA) from social psychology and the Hyperpersonal Model from computer-mediated communication were used to argue that Facebook would either diminish or enhance self-esteem respectively. The results revealed that, in contrast to previous work on OSA, becoming self-aware by viewing one's own Facebook profile enhances self-esteem rather than diminishes it. Participants that updated their profiles and viewed their own profiles during the experiment also reported greater self-esteem, which lends additional support to the Hyperpersonal Model. These findings suggest that *selective self-presentation* in digital media, which leads to intensified relationship formation, also influences impressions of the self.

INTRODUCTION

Over a decade ago, Internet use was thought to promote negative psychosocial well-being, including depression and loneliness.[1] Having attracted attention in and out of the research community, these findings prompted researchers to take a more nuanced look at the relationship between Internet use and psychosocial health,[2,3] at times finding evidence that Internet use could be beneficial.[3,4] The present study extends this research by examining the effects of the social-networking site Facebook (http://facebook.com), which represents a popular new form of Internet communication, on self-esteem.

Previous work has addressed the role of Facebook and the ability to socialize, and the role that socializing online plays in supporting self-esteem and various forms of social capital.[5,6] For example, one recent study found that Facebook can enhance "social self-esteem," measured as perceptions of one's physical appearance, close relationships, and romantic appeal, especially when users received positive feedback from Facebook friends.[5] Also, individuals with low self-esteem may see particularly positive benefits from the social opportunities provided by Facebook.[6]

The effect of Facebook exposure on general self-esteem has not been explored. Yet Facebook, and other social-network sites, have the potential to affect temporary states of self-esteem. Social-network sites are designed to share information about the self with others, including likes/dislikes, hobbies, and personal musings via "wall posts," and "status updates." This information could make people aware of their own limitations and shortcomings, which would lower self-esteem,[7] or it could be that this information represents selective and therefore positively biased aspects of the self, which might raise self-esteem.[8] Does Facebook operate on self-esteem in the same way non-digital information does, by decreasing self-esteem? Or does the opportunity to present more positive information about the self while filtering negative information mean that reviewing one's own Facebook site enhances self-esteem? The following piece examines these questions, by exploring the theoretical predictions of Objective Self-Awareness (OSA) theory[9] and the Hyperpersonal Model.[8]

Objective Self-Awareness

One theoretical approach relevant to the effects of social-networking sites on self-esteem is OSA theory, one of the first experimentally tested psychological theories of the self. The theory assumes that humans experience the self as both subject and object.[9] For example, the self as subject is found in daily experiences of life (e.g., waiting for the bus, eating lunch, watching TV[10]). In those experiences the self is an active participant in life and is not self-conscious. However, people become the "object of [their] own consciousness" when they focus attention on the self,[9(p2)] which can have both positive and negative effects.

In a state of objective self-awareness, Duval and Wicklund[9] claim that people are prone to self-evaluations based on broader social standards and norms. This usually results in a greater sense of humility, or downgraded ratings of self, and increased pro-social behavior. For example, people report feeling greater responsibility for social injustice,[11] or are less likely to take an extra helping of candy without being observed.[12] On the other hand, because most people often fall short of social standards when self-awareness is heightened, positive affect and self-esteem typically decrease when people are exposed to objective self-awareness stimuli.[13]

The stimuli used to evoke objective self-awareness is most commonly a mirror,[13] although other stimuli include images of the self,[14] audio feedback,[15] having a video camera pointed at participants,[16] or having participants write autobiographical information.[11] These stimuli cause people to view themselves as they believe others do, even if they are not immediately under observation. Exposure to these stimuli is what leads to pro-social behavior and decreases in self-esteem.

Given that social-networking profiles include information about the self similar to the type of information that is used to prompt objective self-awareness (e.g., photos, autobiographical information), viewing one's profile should prompt a downgrading of self-esteem according to OSA theory. That is, viewing one's Facebook profile should negatively affect one's self-esteem. Furthermore, research in computer-mediated communication has found that information online is often over-interpreted relative to the same information provided offline,[17] leading to exaggerated or stereotyped impressions.[18] Is it possible that this same process could occur for impressions of the self? If Facebook acts on self-esteem in the same way as previous OSA stimuli, only to a more extreme degree, one prediction is:

> **H1: Exposure to one's Facebook site will have a more negative effect on self-esteem than traditional objective self-awareness stimuli (e.g., mirror).**

Selective Self-Presentation

A second relevant theoretical approach to understanding effects of Facebook use is the Hyperpersonal Model.[8] Walther posits that affordances of the Internet allow users to *selectively self-present* themselves in asynchronous media. People can take their time when posting information about themselves, carefully selecting what aspects they would like to emphasize. Evidence of selective self-presentation is found in a variety of Internet spaces, including e-mails,[19] discussion boards,[20] and online dating Web sites.[21,22]

In addition to evidence that online self-presentations are especially positive presentations, recent research in computer-mediated communication (CMC) suggests that online self-presentations can become integrated into how we view ourselves, especially when the presentations take place in a public, digital space.[23] This phenomenon, known as *identity shift,* demonstrates that self-presentations enacted in online space can impact users' self-concepts.

Self-presentations online can be optimized through selective self-presentation, and online self-presentation affects attitudes about the self. Facebook profiles may provide sufficiently positively biased stimuli to counter the traditional effects of objective self-awareness, and instead prompt a positive change in self-esteem. From this perspective, the hyperpersonal prediction of exposure to Facebook is:

> **H2: Exposure to one's Facebook site will have a more positive effect on self-esteem than a control condition or traditional self-awareness stimuli (e.g., mirror).**

Furthermore, if exposure to one's own Facebook profile increases self-esteem due to selective self-presentation, then behaviors associated with selective self-presentation should correlate with changes in self-esteem. For example, because self-stimuli are most likely to be on one's own profile page, we would expect that participants who only view their own profile page would report higher self-esteem than participants who view other profiles within Facebook. Thus:

> **H3: Participants who exclusively examine only their own profile will report higher self-esteem than participants who view other profiles in addition to their own profiles.**

Finally, selective self-presentation should be reflected primarily in editing of one's online self-presentation, according to Walther.[8] That is, the ability to edit one's self-presentation after the fact is a unique attribute of asynchronous, text-based communication. Thus, according to the Hyperpersonal Model, we predict that:

> **H4: Participants who make changes to their profile during the experiment will report higher self-esteem than participants who do not.**

Each of these predictions is tested in the following study, comparing the effect of viewing one's Facebook site, viewing one's own image in a mirror, and being in a control condition on self-reported self-esteem.

METHODS

Participants

A total of 63 students (16 males, 47 females) from a large, Northeastern university participated in this study for extra credit. The study consisted of three conditions: exposure to a mirror, exposure to one's own Facebook site, and a control condition in which participants used the same room without any treatment. Participants were randomly assigned to one of the three conditions, with a total of 21 participants taking part in each of the three conditions.

Procedure

Each participant was told that the study was designed to examine "people's attitudes about themselves after exploring different Internet sites." People in both offline conditions were told that they were in a control condition, and thus would not be online. In the online condition, participants were asked to examine their own Facebook site.

In the Facebook stimulus condition, after logging on to Facebook, participants were instructed to click on the "Profile" tab after the experimenter left the room. The profile page contains the primary source of information on an individual user. Participants were told to look through any of the tabs on that page (Wall posts, Photos, Info, Boxes). Participants were given no specific instructions about making changes to their profile during the study. In addition to the main profile photo, the profile page has information on recent activity on Facebook sent to and from the site owner, personal demographic information, photos, and quizzes completed by the site owner. After being on Facebook for 3 minutes, the experimenter returned with a survey. Participants were instructed to keep the profile page open while completing the questionnaire.

Participants in the offline conditions were taken to the same small computer cubicle used in the online condition. In the objective self-awareness stimulus condition, a mirror was placed against the computer screen. To reduce suspicion of the mirror, they were also told that the cubicle was being used for another experiment and that they should not move anything. Other items were laid about the room in all conditions (e.g., intercoms, a television) in order to enhance the perception that the room was being used for another experiment. Participants were given a survey of questions, which were answered while being exposed to their own reflection in the mirror.

In the offline control condition, participants sat in the same room as participants in the previously mentioned two conditions, but without the mirror present and without the computer screen turned on. Participants were left with the survey and given instructions to buzz the experimenter when they had finished completing the survey. In all conditions, experimenters returned to collect the survey, and participants were then debriefed and probed for suspicion or failure to comply with instruction.

Measures

Self-Esteem. Self-esteem was measured using the Rosenburg Self-Esteem scale,[24] in which 10 items were used to assess self-esteem ($\alpha = 0.82$). Half of the items were reverse coded. Responses were scored on a 4-point scale, ranging from "strongly agree" to "strongly disagree." Although this scale is generally used to measure trait self-esteem, as mentioned above, previous studies of objective self-awareness have used this measure to capture temporary changes in self-esteem due to awareness-enhancing stimuli.[7]

Selective Self-Presentation. In order to examine behaviors predicted by the Hyperpersonal Model, we asked participants in the Facebook condition about their behavior while they were on Facebook. Questions included, "Did you leave your profile at any time during the study?" (1 = "yes," 2 = "no"), and "Did you change your profile while you were on the Web site?" (1 = "yes," 2 = "no").

RESULTS

To establish that the objective self-awareness stimuli had an effect on self-esteem, an analysis of variance (ANOVA) was first performed. Gender was also included in the model as a covariate, given previous research suggesting that gender may predict differences in self-esteem.[25] The following analyses all reflect significant differences using two-tailed tests of significance, unless otherwise noted. Indeed, the stimuli did have an effect on self-esteem, $F(1, 59) = 4.47, p = 0.02, \eta^2 = 0.13$. However, gender was not a significant predictor of self-esteem, $F(1, 60) = 0.94, p = 0.34$. This finding reveals that self-reported self-esteem did vary by condition.

To test the hypothesis that Facebook had a more negative effect on self-esteem than traditional objective self-awareness stimulus (H1), a linear contrast analysis was performed with a weight 0 assigned to the traditional objective self-awareness stimulus condition (i.e., mirror, $M = 2.97, SD = 0.51$), a weight of -1 assigned to the Facebook condition ($M = 3.35, SD = 0.37$), and a weight of 1 assigned to the control condition ($M = 3.23, SD = 0.40$). The results of this test were not significant, $F(1, 60) = 0.95, p = 0.33$.

To test the opposing hypothesis that Facebook has a positive impact on self-esteem (H2), a different linear contrast analysis was performed. A contrast weight of -1 was assigned to the traditional objective self-awareness stimuli condition, 0 was assigned to the control condition, and $+1$ was assigned to the Facebook condition. This contrast analysis was significant, $F(1, 59) = 8.60, p < 0.01$, $\eta^2 = 0.13$, demonstrating support for H2 and suggesting that Facebook has a positive effect on self-esteem relative to a traditional objective self-awareness stimulus.

Given that viewing Facebook enhanced self-esteem, is there additional evidence that the process of selective self-presentation was responsible for influencing self-esteem? Our first method of testing this question included examining whether participants who exclusively viewed their own profile reported having higher self-esteem than participants who also viewed the profiles of others. An ordinary least squares (OLS) regression of self-esteem on viewing behavior (self-only profile vs. self and other profiles) and gender revealed a significant effect on viewing behavior, $b = 0.40, p = 0.03$ (one-tailed, 1 = "yes," 2 = "no"), indicating that participants who left their profile during the study reported lower self-esteem than those participants who exclusively viewed their own profile site, supporting H3. The relationship between gender and self-esteem was not significant, $b = 0.33, p = 0.12$ (1 = female, 2 = male).

Finally, we expected that changes to any part of the profile (i.e., status, photo, etc.) during the study would increase participant self-esteem (H4), as editing is a primary means of optimizing self-presentation, according to the Hyperpersonal Model.[8] We tested this hypothesis using OLS regression, and once again included gender in the analysis. In support of this hypothesis, participants who changed their profile during the study reported higher self-esteem than those who did not change their profile, $b = -0.53$, $p = 0.01$ (1 = "yes," 2 = "no"). These data suggest that, because asynchronous social-network profiles allow for added time and energy to construct positive self-presentations, profiles contain information that prompts positive, rather than negative, effects on self-esteem. Men reported having greater self-esteem than women after controlling for the likelihood that participants changed their profile, $b = 0.45$, $p = 0.03$. However, this result cannot be fairly interpreted due to the very small number of men (17 women, 4 men).

DISCUSSION

This study was designed to test the effects of exposure to Facebook on self-esteem relative to traditional self-awareness enhancing stimuli, such as a mirror or photo of oneself. The study suggests that selective self-presentation, afforded by digitally mediated environments, can have a positive influence on self-esteem.

These findings are in contrast to predictions from OSA theory, which posits that stimuli that prompt self-awareness (e.g., mirror, photo, autobiographical information) activate discrepancies between oneself and social standards,[9] and consequently lower self-esteem.[13,15] Instead, the results demonstrate that exposure to information presented on one's Facebook profile enhances self-esteem, especially when a person edits information about the self, or *selectively self-presents*. These findings are consistent with Walther's Hyperpersonal Model[8] and suggest that the process of selective self-presentation, which takes place in mediated spaces due to increased time for creating a self-presentation, makes Facebook a unique awareness-enhancing stimuli.

This study is a preliminary step toward understanding how selective self-presentation processes, which have been previously discussed in the context of interpersonal impression formation,[19,20,22] may also influence impressions of the self. Whereas a non-edited view of the self (i.e., mirror) is likely to decrease self-esteem, these findings suggest that the extra care involved in digital self-presentations may actually improve self-esteem. By allowing people to present preferred or positive information about the self, Facebook is a unique source of self-awareness stimuli in

READINGS

that it enhances awareness of the optimal self. This finding is consistent with previous work that has found that digital self-presentations can shape self-assessments.[23] In this case, however, the findings are striking because they contradict previous work on the negative effect of self-awareness enhancing information on self-assessments.

Previous work examining self-esteem suggests that consistency between the actual and the ideal self is an important factor in understanding how information can affect self-esteem.[26] Although participant perceptions between the actual and ideal self were not measured, it is possible that Facebook activates the ideal self. Future research on implications of self-evaluations on self-esteem is needed to test this possibility.

Facebook may also be unique in that the public nature of the site may contribute to objective self-awareness. In previous work, autobiographical information or photos have prompted objective self-awareness.[11,14,15] We tested OSA in Facebook because these features are present there. However, Facebook is a public site, which should also remind users of self-evaluation. In this case, the same information that is prompting OSA is *actually* viewed and evaluated by others as well. Further work is necessary to determine whether public Internet audiences alone may stimulate OSA. In this case, we can only speculate that the high visibility of one's Facebook profile further adds to a sense of objective self-awareness. The difference is that while Facebook may prime awareness of an audience and self-evaluation, it is a more optimal self that is being evaluated. Thus the effect of self-esteem is positive rather than negative.

Limitations

An important limitation of this study was our failure to account for the effect of the number of Facebook friends on self-esteem. As previous research has demonstrated, the social opportunities in Facebook contribute to an enhanced feeling of social competence.[5,6] We cannot rule out the possibility that reminders of one's social connections are partially responsible for the increase in self-esteem. On the other hand, social connection does not seem to be completely responsible for this effect. Changes to one's profile and attention to one's profile (vs. others' profiles) have a positive effect on self-esteem, which suggests that selective self-presentation is a factor in shaping the resultant self-reports of self-esteem.

Another limitation is that we cannot know the long-term implications of using Facebook on self-esteem from a single study. The measure of self-esteem used in this study is generally used as a measure of stable self-esteem, but has been used on other occasions to measure temporary shifts in self-esteem.[7,13,15] Though difficult to perform in an experimental setting, research that examines long-term effects of social-network sites, such as Facebook, would be valuable. Also, incorporating pre- and post-test measures of self-esteem and other relevant psychological measures would be useful in future work.

The focus in the present study is on Facebook, although we make arguments about social-network sites in general regarding their effect on self-esteem. While future research will be required to extend these findings beyond Facebook, the Facebook interface has several advantages over other sites, such as MySpace (http:// myspace.com), including a more uniform layout and the sheer popularity of the site. Given that every person must view their own site, the increased uniformity and popularity of Facebook made it a useful starting point for examining digital self-awareness stimuli and self-esteem.

Finally, participants in the offline conditions did not have the same 3-minute lapse between coming into the room and completing the questionnaire as participants in the Facebook condition. We were concerned, however, that including a filler task would potentially introduce an additional and unintended manipulation into the study. It seems unlikely that the time lapse alone was part of the reason for the different ratings of self-esteem, but to be sure, future research will need to account for this effect by providing an appropriate filler task for participants in the non-digital environments.

CONCLUSION

The Internet has not created new motivation for self-presentation, but provides new tools to implement such motives. The negative effects of objective self-awareness on self-esteem originated from work in the early 1970s.[9,13-15] Social-networking sites, a product of the 21st century, provide new access to the self as an object. By providing multiple opportunities for selective self-presentation—through photos, personal details, and witty comments—social-networking sites exemplify how modern technology sometimes forces us to reconsider previously understood psychological processes. Theoretical development can benefit from expanding on previous "offline" theories by incorporating an understanding of how media may alter social processes.

ACKNOWLEDGMENTS

We would like to thank Angela Falisi, Allison Fishler, and Regine Mechulan for their assistance in collecting the data for this experiment.

READINGS

READINGS

DISCLOSURE STATEMENT
No competing financial interests exist.

REFERENCES

1. Kraut R, Patterson M, Lundmark V, et al. Internet paradox: A social technology that reduces social involvement and psychological well-being? American Psychologist 1998; 53: 1017–31.
2. Bessière K, Kiesler S, Kraut R, et al. Effects of Internet use and social resources on changes in depression. Information, Communication & Society 2008; 11:47–70.
3. McKenna KYA, Bargh JA. Plan 9 from cyberspace: The implications of the Internet for personality and social psychology. Personality & Social Psychology Review 2000; 4:57–75.
4. Shaw LH, Gant LM. In defense of the Internet: The relationship between Internet communication and depression, loneliness, self-esteem, and perceived social support. CyberPsychology & Behavior 2002; 5:157–71.
5. Valkenburg PM, Peter J, Schouten AP. Friend networking sites and their relationship to adolescents' well-being and social self-esteem. CyberPsychology & Behavior 2006; 9:484–590.
6. Ellison NB, Steinfield C, Lampe C. The benefits of Facebook "friends": Social capital and college students' use of online social network sites. Journal of Computer-Mediated Communication 2007; 12:1. jcmc.indiana.edu/vol12/issue4/ellison.html (Accessed Jan. 27, 2009).
7. Heine SJ, Takemoto T, Moskalenko S, et al. Mirrors in the head: Cultural variation in objective self-awareness. Personality & Social Psychology Bulletin 2008; 34:879–87.
8. Walther JB. Computer-mediated communication: Impersonal, interpersonal, and hyperpersonal interaction. Communication Research 1996; 23:3–43.
9. Duval S, Wicklund RA. (1972) A theory of objective self awareness. New York: Academic Press.
10. Moskalenko S, Heine SJ. Watching your troubles away: Television viewing as a stimulus for a subjective self-awareness. Personality & Social Psychology Bulletin 2003; 29:76–85.
11. Duval S, Duval VH, Neely R. Self-focus, felt responsibility, and helping behavior. Journal of Personality & Social Psychology 1979; 37:1769–78.
12. Beaman AL, Klentz B, Diener E, et al. Self-awareness and transgression in children: Two field studies. Journal of Personality & Social Psychology 1979; 37:1835–46.
13. Fejfar MC, Hoyle RH. Effect of private self-awareness on negative affect and self-referent attribution: A quantitative review. Personality & Social Psychology Review 2000; 4:132–42.
14. Storms MD. Videotape and the attribution process: Reversing actors' and observers' points of view. Journal of Personality & Social Psychology 1973; 27:165–75.
15. Ickes WJ, Wicklund RA, Ferris CB. Objective self-awareness and self-esteem. Journal of Experimental Social Psychology 1973; 9:202–19.
16. Duval T, Duval V, Mulilis J. Effects of self-focus, discrepancy between self and standard, and outcome expectancy favorability on the tendency to match self to standard and withdraw. Journal of Personality & Social Psychology 1992; 62:340–8.
17. Hancock JT, Dunham PJ. Impression formation in computer-mediated communication. Communication Research 2001; 28:325–47.

18. Epley N, Kruger J. When what you type isn't what they read: The perseverance of stereotypes and expectancies over e-mail. Journal of Experimental Social Psychology 2005; 41:414–22.

19. Duthler KW. The politeness of requests made via email and voicemail: Support for the hyperpersonal model. Journal of Computer-Mediated Communication 2006; 11. jcmc.indiana.edu/vol11/issue2/duthler.html (accessed Jan. 13, 2009).

20. Walther JB. Selective self-presentation in computer-mediated communication: Hyperpersonal dimensions of technology, language, and cognition. Computers in Human Behavior 2007; 23:2538–57.

21. Ellison N, Heino R, Gibbs J. Managing impressions online: Self-presentation processes in the online dating environment. Journal of Computer-Mediated Communication 2006; 11. //jcmc.indiana.edu/vol11/issue2/ellison.html (Accessed Sept. 12, 2007).

22. Toma CL, Hancock JT, Ellison NB. Separating fact from fiction: An examination of deceptive self-presentation in online dating profiles. Personality & Social Psychology Bulletin 2008; 4:1023–36.

23. Gonzales AL, Hancock JT. Identity shift in computer-mediated environments. Media Psychology 2008; 11:167–85.

24. Rosenberg M. (1965) Society and the adolescent self-image. Princeton, NJ: Princeton University Press.

25. Josephs RA, Markus HR, Tafarodi RW. Gender and self-esteem. Journal of Personality & Social Psychology 1992; 63:391–402.

The History and Psychology of Clowns Being Scary

by Linda Rodriguez McRobbie

There's a word—albeit one not recognized by the *Oxford English Dictionary* or any psychology manual—for the excessive fear of clowns: *Coulrophobia*.

Not a lot of people actually suffer from a debilitating phobia of clowns; a lot more people, however, just don't like them. Do a Google search for "I hate clowns" and the first hit is ihateclowns.com, a forum for clown-haters that also offers vanity @ihate-clowns.com emails. One "I Hate Clowns" Facebook page has just under 480,000 likes. Some circuses have held workshops to help visitors get over their fear of clowns by letting them watch performers transform into their clown persona. In Sarasota, Florida, in 2006, communal loathing for clowns took a criminal turn when dozens of fiberglass clown statues—part of a public art exhibition called "Clowning Around Town" and a nod to the city's history as a winter haven for traveling circuses—were defaced, their limbs

READINGS

broken, heads lopped off, spray-painted; two were abducted and we can only guess at their sad fates.

Even the people who are supposed to like clowns—children—supposedly don't. In 2008, a widely reported University of Sheffield, England, survey of 250 children between the ages of four and 16 found that most of the children disliked and even feared images of clowns. The BBC's report on the study featured a child psychologist who broadly declared, "Very few children like clowns. They are unfamiliar and come from a different era. They don't look funny, they just look odd."

But most clowns aren't trying to be odd. They're trying to be silly and sweet, fun personified. So the question is, when did the clown, supposedly a jolly figure of innocuous, kid-friendly entertainment, become so weighed down by fear and sadness? When did clowns become so dark?

Maybe they always have been.

Clowns—as pranksters, jesters, jokers, harlequins, and mythologized tricksters—have been around for ages. They appear in most cultures—Pygmy clowns made Egyptian pharaohs laugh in 2500 BCE; in ancient imperial China, a court clown called YuSze was, according to the lore, the only guy who could poke holes in Emperor Qin Shih Huang's plan to paint the Great Wall of China; Hopi Native Americans had a tradition of clown-like characters who interrupted serious dance rituals with ludicrous antics. Ancient Rome's clown was a stock fool called the *stupidus;* the court jesters of medieval Europe were a sanctioned way for people under the feudal thumb to laugh at the guys in charge; and well into the 18th and 19th century, the prevailing clown figure of Western Europe and Britain was the pantomime clown, who was a sort of bumbling buffoon.

But clowns have always had a dark side, says David Kiser, director of talent for Ringling Bros. and Barnum & Bailey Circus. After all, these were characters who reflected a funhouse mirror back on society; academics note that their comedy was often derived from their voracious appetites for food, sex, and drink, and their manic behavior. "So in one way, the clown has always been an impish spirit . . . as he's kind of grown up, he's always been about fun, but part of that fun has been a bit of mischief," says Kiser.

"Mischief" is one thing; homicidal urges is certainly another. What's changed about clowns is how that darkness is manifest, argued Andrew McConnell Stott, Dean of Undergraduate Education and an English professor at the University of Buffalo, SUNY.

Stott is the author of several articles on scary clowns and comedy, as well as *The Pantomime Life of Joseph Grimaldi,* a much-lauded 2009 biography of the famous comic pantomime player on the Regency London stage. Grimaldi was the first recognizable ancestor of the modern clown, sort of the *Homo erectus* of clown evolution. He's the reason why clowns are still sometimes called "Joeys"; though his clowning was of a theatrical and not circus tradition, Grimaldi is so identified with modern clowns that a church in east London has conducted a Sunday service in his honor every year since 1959, with congregants all dressed in full clown regalia.

In his day, he was hugely visible: It was claimed that a full eighth of London's population had seen Grimaldi on stage. Grimaldi made the clown the leading character of the pantomime, changing the way he looked and acted. Before him, a clown may have worn make-up, but it was usually just a bit of rouge on the cheeks to heighten the sense of them being florid, funny drunks or rustic yokels. Grimaldi, however, suited up in bizarre, colorful costumes, stark white face paint punctuated by spots of bright red on his cheeks and topped with a blue mohawk. He was a master of physical comedy—he leapt in the air, stood on his head, fought himself in hilarious fisticuffs that had audiences rolling in the aisles—as well as of satire lampooning the absurd fashions of the day, comic impressions, and ribald songs.

But because Grimaldi was such a star, the character he'd invented became closely associated with him. And Grimaldi's real life was anything but comedy—he'd grown up with a tyrant of a stage father; he was prone to bouts of depression; his first wife died during childbirth; his son was an alcoholic clown who'd drank himself to death by age 31; and Grimaldi's physical gyrations, the leaps and tumbles and violent slapstick that had made him famous, left him in constant pain and prematurely disabled. As Grimaldi himself joked, "I am GRIM ALL DAY, but I make you laugh at night." That Grimaldi could make a joke about it highlights how well known his tragic real life was to his audiences.

Enter the young Charles Dickens. After Grimaldi died penniless and an alcoholic in 1837 (the coroner's verdict: "Died by the visitation of God"), Dickens was charged with editing Grimaldi's memoirs. Dickens had already hit upon the dissipated, drunken clown theme in his 1836 *The Pickwick Papers*. In the serialized novel, he describes an off-duty clown—reportedly inspired by Grimaldi's son—whose inebriation and ghastly, wasted body contrasted with his white face paint and clown costume. Unsurprisingly, Dickens' version of Grimaldi's life was, well, Dickensian, and, Stott says, imposed a "strict economy": For every laugh he wrought from his audiences, Grimaldi suffered commensurate pain.

Stott credits Dickens with watering the seeds in popular imagination of the scary clown—he'd even go so far as to say Dickens *invented* the scary clown—by creating a figure who is literally destroying himself to make his audiences laugh. What Dickens did was to make it difficult to look at a clown without wondering what was going on underneath the make-up: Says Stott, "It becomes impossible to disassociate the character from the actor." That Dickens' version of Grimaldi's memoirs was massively popular meant that this perception, of something dark and troubled masked by humor, would stick.

Meanwhile, on the heels of Grimaldi's fame in Britain, the major clown figure on the Continent was Jean-Gaspard Deburau's Pierrot, a clown with white face paint punctuated by red lips and black eyebrows whose silent gesticulations delighted French audiences. Deburau was as well known on the streets of Paris as Grimaldi was in London, recognized even without his make-up. But where Grimaldi was tragic, Deburau was sinister: In 1836, Deburau killed a boy with a blow from his walking stick after the youth shouted insults at him on the street (he was ultimately acquitted of the murder). So the two biggest clowns of the early modern clowning era were troubled men underneath that face-paint.

After Grimaldi and Deburau's heyday, pantomime and theatrical traditions changed; clowning largely left the theater for the relatively new arena of the circus. The circus got its start in the mid-1760s with British entrepreneur Philip Astley's equestrian shows, exhibitions of "feats of horsemanship" in a circular arena. These trick riding shows soon began attracting other performers; along with the jugglers, trapeze artists, and acrobats, came clowns. By the mid-19th century, clowns had become a sort of "hybrid Grimaldian personality [that] fit in much more with the sort of general, overall less-nuanced style of clowning in the big top," explains Stott.

Clowns were comic relief from the thrills and chills of the daring circus acts, an anarchic presence that complemented the precision of the acrobats or horse riders. At the same time, their humor necessarily became broader—the clowns had more space to fill, so their movements and actions needed to be more obvious. But clowning was still very much tinged with dark hilarity: French literary critic Edmond de Goncourt, writing in 1876, says, "[T]he clown's art is now rather terrifying and full of anxiety and apprehension, their suicidal feats, their monstrous gesticulations and frenzied mimicry reminding one of the courtyard of a lunatic asylum." Then there's the 1892 Italian opera, *Pagliacci (Clowns),* in which the cuckolded main character, an actor of the Grimaldian clown mold, murders his cheating wife on stage during a performance. Clowns were unsettling—and a great source for drama.

England exported the circus and its clowns to America, where the genre blossomed; in late 19th century America, the circus went from a one-ring horse act to a three-ring extravaganza that trav-elled the country on the railways. Venues and humor changed, but images of troubled, sad, tragic clowns remained—Emmett Kelly, for example, was the most famous of the American "hobo" clowns, the sad-faced men with five o'clock shadows and tattered clothes who never smiled, but who were nonetheless hilarious. Kelly's "Weary Willie" was born of actual tragedy: The break-up of his marriage and America's sinking financial situation in the 1930s.

Clowns had a sort of heyday in America with the television age and children's entertainers like Clarabell the Clown, Howdy Doody's silent partner, and Bozo the Clown. Bozo, by the mid-1960s, was the beloved host of a hugely popular, internationally syn-dicated children's show—there was a 10-year wait for tickets to his show. In 1963, McDonald's brought out Ronald McDonald, the Hamburger-Happy Clown, who's been a brand ambassador ever since (although heavy is the head that wears the red wig—in 2011, health activists claimed that he, like Joe Camel did for smoking, was promoting an unhealthy lifestyle for children; McDonald's didn't ditch Ronald, but he has been seen playing a lot more soccer).

But this heyday also heralded a real change in what a clown was. Before the early 20th century, there was little expectation that clowns had to be an entirely unadulterated symbol of fun, frivolity, and happiness; pantomime clowns, for example, were characters who had more adult-oriented story lines. But clowns were now almost solely children's entertainment. Once their made-up persona became more associated with children, and therefore an expectation of innocence, it made whatever the make-up might conceal all the more frightening—creating a tremendous mine for artists, filmmak-ers, writers and creators of popular culture to gleefully exploit to terrifying effect. Says Stott, "Where there is mystery, it's supposed there must be evil, so we think, 'What are you hiding?'"

Most clowns aren't hiding anything, except maybe a bunch of fake flowers or a balloon animal. But again, just as in Grimaldi and Deburau's day, it was what a real-life clown was concealing that tipped the public perception of clowns. Because this time, rather than a tragic or even troubled figure under the slap and motley, there was something much darker lurking.

Even as Bozo was cavorting on sets across America, a more sinister clown was plying his craft across the Midwest. John Wayne Gacy's public face was a friendly, hard-working guy; he was also a registered clown who entertained at community events under the name Pogo. But between 1972 and 1978, he sexually assaulted and killed more than 35 young men in the Chicago area. "You know . . . clowns can get away with murder," he told investigating officers, before his arrest.

Gacy didn't get away with it—he was found guilty of 33 counts of murder and was executed in 1994. But he'd become identified as the "Killer Clown," a handy sobriquet for newspaper reports that hinged on the unexpectedness of his killing. And bizarrely, Gacy seemed to revel in his clown persona: While in prison, he began painting; many of his paintings were of clowns, some self-portraits of him as Pogo. What was particularly terrifying was that Gacy, a man who'd already been convicted of a sexual assault on a teenage boy in 1968, was given access to children in his guise as an innocuous clown. This fueled America's already growing fears of "stranger danger" and sexual predation on children, and made clowns a real object of suspicion.

After a real life killer clown shocked America, representations of clowns took a decidedly terrifying turn. Before, films like Cecil B. DeMille's 1952 Oscar-winning *The Greatest Show on Earth* could toy with the notion of the clown with a tragic past—Jimmy Stewart played Buttons, a circus clown who never removed his make-up and who is later revealed to be a doctor on the lam after "mercy killing" his wife—but now, clowns were really scary.

In 1982, *Poltergeist* relied on transforming familiar banality— the Californian suburb, a piece of fried chicken, the television— into real terror; but the big moment was when the little boy's clown doll comes to life and tries to drag him under the bed. In 1986, Stephen King wrote *It,* in which a terrifying demon attacks children in the guise of Pennywise the Clown; in 1990, the book was made into a TV mini-series. In 1988, B-movie hit *Killer Klowns from Outer Space* featured alien clowns harboring sharp-toothed grins and murderous intentions. The next year saw *Clownhouse,* a cult horror film about escaped mental patients masquerading as circus clowns who terrorize a rural town. Between the late 1980s and now—when the *Saw* franchise's mascot is a creepy clown-faced puppet—dozens of films featuring vicious clowns appeared in movie theatres (or, more often, went straight to video), making the clown as reliable a boogeyman as Freddy Kreuger.

Kiser, Ringling's talent spotter and a former clown himself, acknowledged the damage that scary clown images have done to clowning, though he was inclined to downplay the effect. "It's like, 'Oh man, we're going to have to work hard to overcome that one,'" he says.

But anecdotally at least, negative images of clowns are harming clowning as a profession. Though the Bureau of Labor Statistics doesn't keep track of professional clowns specifically (they're lumped in with comedians, magicians, and other miscellaneous performers), in the mid-2000s, articles began popping up in newspapers across the country lamenting the decline of attendees at clown conventions or at clowning workshop courses. Stott believes that the clown has been "evacuated as a figure of fun" (notably, Stott is personally uncomfortable with clowns and says he finds them "strange"); psychologists suggest that negative clown images are replacing positive clown images.

"You don't really see clowns in those kinds of safe, fun contexts anymore. You see them in movies and they're scary," says Dr. Martin Antony, a professor of psychology at Ryerson University in Toronto and author of the *Anti-Anxiety Work Book.* "Kids are not exposed in that kind of safe fun context as much as they used to be and the images in the media, the negative images, are still there."

That's creating a vicious circle of clown fear: More scary images means diminished opportunities to create good associations with clowns, which creates more fear. More fear gives more credence to scary clown images, and more scary clown images end up in circulation. Of course, it's difficult to say whether there has been a real rise in the number of people who have clown phobias since Gacy and *It.* A phobia is a fear or anxiety that inhibits a person's life and clown fears rarely rate as phobias, psychologists say, because one simply isn't confronted by clowns all that often. But clown fear is, Antony says, exacerbated by clowns' representation in the media. "We also develop fears from what we read and see in the media. . . . There's certainly lots of examples of nasty clowns in movies that potentially put feet on that kind of fear," he says.

From a psychologist's perspective, a fear of clowns often starts in childhood; there's even an entry in the psychologists' bible, the *Diagnostic and Statistical Manual of Mental Disorders* or *DSM,* for a fear of clowns, although it's under the umbrella category of a pediatric phobia of costumed characters (sports mascots, Mickey Mouse). "It starts normally in children about the age of two, when they get anxiety about being around strangers, too. At that age, children's minds are still developing, there's a little bit of a blend and they're not always able to separate fantasy from reality," explains Dr. Brenda Wiederhold, a veteran psychologist who runs a phobia and anxiety treatment center in San Diego that uses virtual reality to treat clients.

Most people, she says, grow out of the fear, but not everyone—perhaps as much as 2 percent of the adult population will have a fear of clowns. Adult clown phobics are unsettled by the clown's face paint and the inability to read genuine emotion on a clown's face, as well as the perception that clowns are able to engage in manic behavior, often without consequences.

But really, what a clown fear comes down to, what it's always come down to, is the person under the make-up. Ringling's Kiser agreed.

"I think we have all experienced wonderful clowns, but we've also all experienced clowns who in their youth or lack of training, they don't realize it, but they go on the attack," Kiser says, explaining that they can become too aggressive in trying to make someone laugh. "One of the things that we stress is that you have to know how to judge and respect people's space." Clowning, he says, is about communicating, not concealing; good clown make-up is reflective of the individual's emotions, not a mask to hide behind—making them actually innocent and not scary.

But have bad, sad, troubled clowns done too much damage? There are two different, conflicting visions of the clown's future.

Stott, for one, sees clowning continuing on its dark path. "I think we'll find that the kind of dark carnival, scary clown will be the dominant mode, that that figure will continue to persist in many different ways," he says, pointing to characters like Krusty the Clown on *The Simpsons,* who's jaded but funny, or Heath Ledger's version of The Joker in the *Batman* reboot, who is a terrifying force of unpredictable anarchy. "In many respects, it's not an inversion of what we're used to seeing, it's just teasing out and amplifying those traits we've been seeing for a very long time." Other writers have suggested that the scary clown as a dependable monster under the bed is almost "nostalgically fearful," already bankrupted by overuse.

But there's evidence that, despite the claims of the University of Sheffield study, kids actually *do* like clowns: Some studies have shown that real clowns have a beneficial effect on the health outcomes of sick children. The January 2013 issue of the *Journal of Health Psychology* published an Italian study that found that, in a randomized controlled trial, the presence of a therapy clown reduced pre-operative anxiety in children booked for minor surgery. Another Italian study, carried out in 2008 and published in the December 2011 issue of the *Natural Medicine Journal* found that children hospitalized for respiratory illnesses got better faster after playing with therapeutic clowns.

And Kiser, of course, doesn't see clowning diminishing in the slightest. But good clowns are always in shortage, and it's good clowns who keep the art alive. "If the clown is truly a warm and sympathetic and funny heart, inside of a person who is working hard to let that clown out . . . I think those battles [with clown fears] are so winnable," he says. "It's not about attacking, it's about loving. It's about approaching from a place of loving and joy and that when you really look at it, you see, that's it really genuine, it's not fake."

FOR DISCUSSION

1. Locate the thesis for each of the model reports. On what, specifically, do they intend to educate readers?
2. Think about the support that the authors provide to clarify their subject matter. Is this support illuminating? Why or why not?
3. What other kinds of support might have been helpful in clarifying the topics of these reports?
4. Where do you see the authors obviously striving for unbiased treatment of their subject matter? What specific strategies do they employ to demonstrate their neutral stance?
5. Study the introductions and conclusions of these reports. How do they establish the significance of their respective topics?

Annotated Bibliography

10

This photo depicts a visual representation of the term *chaos*. Note the apparent lack of order. For many writers, chaos can be a wellspring of creativity when working with sources they want to cite in their own writing. Disorder allows sources to mingle and connect in various and unexpected ways, expanding possibilities for insight. If you've experienced these advantages of chaos, you probably also realize that—once you've finally located a focus for writing—you need to impose some order on your sources so you can efficiently manage them in pursuit of your specific goals. An annotated bibliography, the subject of this chapter, provides one avenue for organizing sources, as well as for keeping track of their contents.

If you've ever written a paper that incorporated sources of information beyond your own thoughts or observations, you've probably compiled what is referred to as a "Works Cited" or "References" page, such as the examples in Figure 10.1. Such documents, which typically appear at the end of a research-based text, serve two important purposes: (1) to acknowledge that you have used the ideas or research of others, and (2) to provide publication details for the sources you've mentioned in case readers would like to consult them.

Works Cited

Barron, Frank, et al., editors. *Creators on Creating: Awakening and Cultivating the Imaginative Mind*. Penguin, 1997.

Dively, Ronda Leathers. *Preludes to Insight: Creativity, Incubation, and Expository Writing*. Hampton, 2006.

Ghiselin, Brewster, editor *The Creative Process: Reflections on Invention in the Arts and Sciences*. U of California P, 1985.

Gourevitch, Phillip. *The Paris Review Interviews*. Picador, 2009. 4 vols.

References

Barron, F., Montuori, A., & Barron, A. (Eds.). (1997). *Creators on creating: Awakening and cultivating the imaginative mind*. New York, NY: Penguin.

Dively, R. L. (2006). *Preludes to insight: Creativity, incubation, and expository writing*. Cresskill, NJ: Hampton Press.

Ghiselin, B. (Ed.). (1985). *The creative process: Reflections on invention in the arts and sciences*. Berkeley: University of California Press.

Gourevitch, P. (Ed.). (2009). *The Paris review interviews* (Vol. 1-4). New York: Picador.

Figure 10.1 *Left:* **A Works Cited page for a paper written in Modern Language Association (MLA) format.** *Right:* **A References page with the same source information in American Psychological Association (APA) format**

Like a Works Cited or References page, an **annotated bibliography** catalogs—typically in alphabetical order and in the appropriate format—a number of sources that are relevant to your own writing project. The similarities stop there, however, as an annotated bibliography expands on the structure of a Works Cited or References page in significant ways—most notably, by supplying annotations (or brief summaries) for each source. In certain circumstances, the annotations will also include evaluations of the sources, and the entire bibliography may be prefaced by an introduction that previews its scope and substance.

As an annotated bibliography is a record of the sources you consult for a given research project, you will be its primary audience. A common secondary audience for an annotated bibliography is the teacher who may have assigned it, perhaps to jump-start your research processes or to provide a means to help monitor them. A third potential audience for an annotated bibliography is a particular community of academics. In fact, scholars often publish annotated bibliographies in their areas of expertise to serve colleagues interested in the same topics of study. Annotated bibliographies are valuable because they represent substantial legwork in locating sources and because they condense those sources' content so that readers can quickly determine if they deserve closer attention.

Distinguishing Features of an Annotated Bibliography

Annotated bibliographies assume a form that is distinct from other genres you may have written for school, such as essays or reports. As opposed to a seamless flow of tightly connected paragraphs supporting an appropriately narrow thesis, an annotated bibliography is a collection of several separate entries or self-contained commentaries on sources of information that may relate only generally to each other around a focused topic of inquiry. Figure 10.2 illustrates the annotated bibliography's status as a catalog of sorts, representing the sources you've studied in learning about your topic.

When you're composing a basic annotated bibliography, such as the one presented in Figure 10.2, you'll need to include a **citation** (publication information) and an annotation for each source you wish to include. The citation should be formatted in the documentation style appropriate to the discipline or publication for which you are composing, and each annotation will include a summary of the source in question. The summary should capture the source's thesis or controlling idea and provide an overview of the claims that support it.

In some writing situations, you may be asked to supplement these basic components with **evaluations,** or judgments of the sources' quality. Evaluations should comment on the strengths and weaknesses of your sources, as well as on their

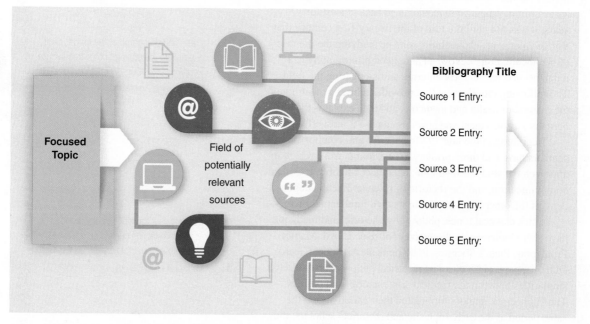

Figure 10.2 **Path of development for an annotated bibliography**

specific value for your project. In other situations, you may be asked to preface the entries in your bibliography with an introduction. The introduction should address the bibliography's focus, the nature of the sources cited, and the status of knowledge about your topic as demonstrated through the cited sources.

All potential components of an annotated bibliography are illustrated in the Look Inside excerpt from a 2012 contribution to *Present Tense: A Journal of Rhetoric in*

A LOOK INSIDE:
ANNOTATED BIBLIOGRAPHY

From "An Annotated Bibliography of Literature on the Rhetoric of Health and Medicine"

by Jessica Masri Eberhard

Introduction

Ten years ago, compiling a bibliographic review of medical rhetoric would have seemed a manageable task. Although studies examining language in medicine go back at least forty years, it was not until the turn of the twenty-first century that a large amount of scholarship sprung up studying the rhetoric of healthcare, proper. Now, an annotated bibliography is a much needed resource for entering and navigating the field. The following introduction first provides a brief genealogy of the rhetoric of health and medicine, and then explains the bibliography's arrangement and how one can use it most effectively.

Beginning in the late 1970s, rhetoric and composition scholars have had three primary access points from which to approach the study of medicine: canonical rhetoric, technical communication, and the rhetoric of science. Each is dependent on the other but is rooted in its own intellectual history.

Since classical times, philosophy, rhetoric, and medicine have shared interwoven discursive roots (see Lloyd, Magic). Protagoras, Plato's Socrates, Plato himself, Aristotle, Cicero, Quintilian—all of the classical rhetorical philosophers—discuss similarities between the medical arts, rhetoric, and politics. The Hippocratic authors formulated their canon during the same period as the early sophistic and rhetorical scholars; thus, they engaged in many of the same epistemological, ethical, and ontological debates (see Lloyd, "Epistemology" and Magic). Judy Z. Segal identifies practitioners of "canonical rhetoric" as

The title contains the genre label as well as the content focus.

The first paragraph of the introduction points to the bibliography's significance, as well as its layout.

Context for the bibliography provided by the introduction centers on the evolution of health-related rhetorics throughout history.

those who employ classical rhetoric as well as major rhetorical scholarship of the twentieth century to study contemporary health-related discourse (Segal, "Rhetoric" 229). Studies in this annotated bibliography address topics such as epideictic rhetoric, the erotema, the jeremiad, and identification; as a result, these studies exemplify the canonical branch of health rhetorics.

Anderson, Charles. *Richard Selzer and the Rhetoric of Surgery.* Southern Illinois UP, 1989.

> Anderson's work illustrates the strong and rich relationship that has always existed between rhetoric, medicine, and magic. His book considers surgeon and author Richard Selzer's literary work, which deals mainly with his experiences as a physician. Anderson focuses on the "convergence of historical presence, artistic perception, and factual constraint" in Selzer's writing that poetically weaves together strands of discourse usually segregated in the modernist mindset (xvi). Anderson also displays this capacity in his own analysis. As much concerned with the philosophy of writing as it is with rhetoric, the study is a beautiful model of how literary, composition, rhetorical, and historical scholarship can operate as a harmonious, theoretical whole.

In addition to providing a summary of the source, this entry also includes a positive evaluation of it.

Condit, Celeste. *Decoding Abortion Rhetoric: Communicating Social Change.* University of Illinois P, 1990.

> In this book, Condit, a speech professor, takes a neutral stance to analyze the history of abortion discourse through a rhetorical lens. She begins in the 1950s, considering rhetorical devices physicians used to petition for a change in abortion laws. She argues that in Roe v. Wade the ruling centered on competing narratives about women and their identities. Because the ruling depended upon the new characterization of women, which expanded their control of choices, and not upon the definition of "life" directly, the court decision has left open to the public debate the fetus's right to life. Condit traces the expansion of the conversation, rhetorically analyzing a variety of media including pamphlets, billboards, slogans, television and magazine advertisements, as well as narrative tropes that have defined either side of the debate. Condit observes that polarized or "over-weigh[ted]" rhetorics have brought discursive closure between activists, leaving the majority of the public in the middle with mixed views about the subject. Condit also suggests, with well-documented textual support, that the pro-choice movement has not found a strong enough ground, rhetorically, from which to make its appeals.

Note that there's a line separating the citation information and the summary. Note also that the summary is indented as are all lines of the citation following the first line.

Although she does so more subtly than she did for the previous source, the author also evaluates this source, complimenting the evidence it supplies to back certain claims.

Source: Jessica Masri Eberhard, "An Annotated Bibliography of Literature on the Rhetoric of Health and Medicine," *Present Tense: A Journal of Rhetoric in Society.* Copyright © 2012. Reprinted by permission of the author.

Society. In this annotated bibliography, using MLA format, author Jessica Masri Eberhard provides scholars in her discipline (rhetoric and composition) with an overview of published works in the growing subfield of health-based rhetoric. Although the originally published bibliography presents sources in chronological order as a means of stressing the historical arc of research on this topic, the brief Look Inside excerpt reflects the alphabetical arrangement typifying the majority of annotated bibliographies.

Processes for Composing an Annotated Bibliography

Annotated bibliographies are more rigid with regard to structure than most other documents you'll be writing for your composition course. At the same time, their quality is tied to the author's critical engagement with his or her sources. The sections below explain strategies that can help you achieve a balance between the constraints of the genre's form and the need for meaning-making in response to your research materials.

Invention toward First Insight

Inspiration for annotated bibliographies is usually not as hard as it is for other genres you'll encounter in your college courses. This is because an annotated bibliography is usually written after you have chosen a research topic or an instructor has assigned you one. In other words, an annotated bibliography—which is a record of your research—almost always occurs in support of another project, and plans for that project usually supply the first insight for your early work on the bibliography.

Preparation through Research

When preparing to compose an annotated bibliography, you will need to conduct a broad search of library databases and the Internet for sources relevant to your topic. You will also need to consider their credibility. (Learn more about both of these processes in Chapter 5.) The amount of time you spend combing through and sorting materials will depend on a couple of factors: the number of sources assigned by your teacher and/or your sense of thoroughness in representing the published scholarship on your topic.

Some sources you come across will immediately strike you as timely and closely linked to your topic. Others may seem outdated or only tangentially connected—in this case, you may have a difficult time deciding whether to save or abandon a source. Remember, though, that when you first begin researching, you can't predict exactly how a source might become useful since you've only just begun to build your knowledge base;

MYTH

"When researching print sources, it's more efficient to skim than to read them."

This strategy can backfire since recalling the specifics of sources you locate early on often becomes difficult as you consider the viability of subsequent sources. In most cases, then, the effort you devote to taking notes up front will be well spent.

REALITY

indeed, your knowledge about a subject will deepen over time, and this may cause your plans to evolve. For this reason, you may want to err on the side of caution, keeping the remotely related sources around until you have a better sense of what your ultimate focus will be.

Since you will be working with many diverse sources that you may later need to synthesize in an introduction or a formal paper, it makes sense to devise a system for keeping track of their relationships—perhaps grouping them by subtopics, genres, or the disciplines in which they were published (on occasion, published annotated bibliographies will reflect such groupings, alphabetized *within* them). To aid your memory, you'll also want to take notes about the sources' general content and about your initial judgments regarding their potential contributions to your project. In addition, you may want to place each source's identifying information in the format required by the documentation style that you will be using. As a result, your attention will not be diverted by surface details when you are striving for "flow" while drafting. (See sample citations of commonly cited sources in Chapter 21.)

Invention toward More Focused Insight

Reading is a productive method of invention; therefore, reading a variety of sources related to your topic should lead to a unique angle on your first insight and a tighter focus for the project. As this tighter focus emerges, your sense of relevance regarding the sources you've collected so far may change, causing you to reconsider some and to fully reject others.

Whatever the case, unlike Works Cited or References lists, annotated bibliographies are not confined to presenting only those sources that *will* be cited in a future essay. Rather, they can include any sources that are *potentially* relevant to your project. As you move closer to drafting your annotated bibliography, however, the ultimate goal is to make sure that the sources you do include adequately reflect the focus of the work that the bibliography will inform. Being able to articulate this focus is crucial for the introduction to your annotated bibliography (if one is required).

As you reread the sources that you collected in anticipation of drafting the bibliography, you'll want to elaborate on the general notes you initially took on them. These elaborated notes will assist you in summarizing the sources—that is, reducing them to their essential components and highlighting the main points that the authors make—particularly as they connect with the focus of your project.

Strategies for Drafting

Your annotated bibliography will include up to four components, as listed below—the first two are mandatory; the third and fourth may or may not be required:

1. A Works Cited *or* References list
2. A summary of each source
3. An evaluation of each source's worth or relevance to your paper
4. An introduction to the bibliography

MLA Documentation Style

Perry, Susan K. *Writing in Flow: Keys to Enhanced Creativity.* Writer's Digest, 1999.

APA Documentation Style

Perry, S. (1999). *Writing in flow: Keys to enhanced creativity.* Cincinnati: Writer's Digest.

Figure 10.3 **Works Cited (MLA) and References (APA) entries**

Whether or not your annotated bibliography includes components 3 and 4 will depend on the preferences of your teacher or the conventions of a given publication.

Works Cited or References Ideally, as you took notes for your annotated bibliography, you placed the publication information for each source in the appropriate citation format. If you did not, now is the time to consult Chapter 21, or a reliable online resource, for guidelines about documenting the different types of sources you plan to incorporate in your bibliography. Even if you are the only audience for the bibliography, it makes sense to ensure that information for the citation is accurate. Doing so will simplify the process of compiling a Works Cited or References page for a document based on your bibliography.

When you begin drafting, you'll want to confirm that you are attending to all details of the appropriate documentation style. As Figure 10.3 illustrates, the type and order of information provided at the beginning of a bibliographic entry differ between MLA and APA, for example. In closely studying Figure 10.3, you'll note that even though MLA and APA citations contain virtually the same information, they are marked by some key distinctions in formatting, as listed in Figure 10.4. Also keep in mind that expectations for indenting lines and for spacing within and between entries on the bibliography can vary.

Paying attention to the details that characterize a given documentation style is crucial to building an accurate annotated bibliography. Because formatting guidelines are somewhat intricate and because they seem to change every few years, you must be cautious about relying on memory to craft your citations. If you did tackle citation details during your initial research efforts, you'll want to double-check the formatting while drafting to ensure that you did not misuse a punctuation mark here and there, inadvertently omit a certain element, and so

MLA Style Distinctions	APA Style Distinctions
• Spells out the author's last and then his or her first name	• Spells out the author's last name but records only the initial of his or her first name
• Places the publication year after the publisher's name, near the end of the citation	• Places the publication year after the author's name, near the beginning of the citation
• Capitalizes all nouns and verbs in the title	• Capitalizes only the first word of the title and the first word of the subtitle

Figure 10.4 **Differences between MLA and APA citations**

forth. Of course, you'll be able to look again for errors in the context of your editing processes; nevertheless, it's wise to pace yourself through these numerous details because the more you leave for the final stages of composing as you are working to meet a deadline, the more likely you are to become overwhelmed and miss any mistakes you've made.

Summaries   The summary you draft for each source should recount its thesis and its primary support. Beyond these elements, the summary will be driven by your own purposes for writing. In other words, you will inevitably highlight aspects of the source that best serve your intentions for writing the bibliography and, ultimately, the writing project it may support. The length of each summary (and, by extension, the entire bibliography) will differ in accordance with the length of the sources cited. Length will also differ in accordance with a teacher's or a publication's requirements, and so you may want to explore such expectations as you begin drafting. (Chapter 21 offers additional information about summarizing.)

MYTH

"Annotated bibliographies stifle creativity since their primary purpose is to represent what others have said."

This genre invites creativity in the context of many strategies it calls on: selecting sources, imagining how you'll apply those sources to complete your own project, crafting summaries and introductions that establish the sources' relevance to your research focus, reflecting critically on your sources to evaluate them, and making decisions about organization and style.

REALITY

Evaluations   When the composing situation requires you to follow each summary with an evaluation, you will be expected to communicate your judgment about the quality of the source, possibly in contrast to others. For example, you might note that the author's method for researching the issue is faulty in some respect and/or is not as convincing as the study performed by another author. If you are compiling the bibliography in support of a formal academic paper, your evaluation might also explain the promise of the source in bolstering that larger project. For example, you might note that you plan to quote a line or two from the source to back a particular argument you want to make in the paper you will be writing. Regardless, you should keep in mind while drafting your evaluations that their purpose is to assist you in the following ways:

- By helping you keep track of the sources you find especially valuable
- By clarifying the role of certain sources within your larger composing plan
- By recording relationships between sources
- By pinpointing areas that need further investigation

Introduction   In drafting an introduction for your annotated bibliography, you'll want to familiarize readers with the topic and offer an overview of the range and types of sources the bibliography covers. Most importantly, you'll want to preview your sources' commentary on the current state of knowledge about your topic—for example, any known or commonly accepted premises about it, as well as issues that remain debatable or controversial. To some extent, this will require you to compare and contrast the sources' messages, noting issues on which they agree or disagree, the extent to which they build on each other, and any revelations about the topic they bring to light. Readers will need this assistance in gaining a comprehensive picture of your research results and their relevance in supporting your ultimate composing agenda since the summaries for each entry may seem to be only superficially connected.

Revision and Editing

Questions for Revising

- Is the scope of my bibliography adequate; does it include enough sources to sufficiently represent my topic and support a subsequent writing project?
- Do the summaries accurately and comprehensively reflect the sources' content—do they capture the sources' theses and primary support?
- Do the summaries internally cohere with apparent beginnings, middles, and endings?
- Do the evaluations offer a sense of the sources' value in supporting a subsequent project and explain the manner in which they will do so?
- Does the introduction forward a thesis that reflects the collective subject matter and relationships between the cited sources?
- Does the introduction provide readers a comprehensive overview of the bibliography's contents?
- Do the observations in the introduction cohere at the sentence and paragraph level?

Questions for Editing

- Is the citation information accurate and arranged in accordance with the guidelines established by the designated documentation style?
- Are all parts of the bibliography free of spelling, punctuation, and usage errors?

Transfer to Other Writing Situations

The act of compiling an annotated bibliography calls upon various widely applicable composing strategies. First, it immerses you in sustained research, requiring you to locate numerous sources relevant to your topic and compelling a deep level of familiarity with those sources. In short, putting together an annotated bibliography introduces a way of systematizing your research processes, cultivating a sense of thoroughness that will serve you well in courses across the college curriculum.

Second, in selecting materials you will include in the finished version of your annotated bibliography, this genre causes you to think about how sources relate to each other and how you might articulate those relationships relevant to a given focus. These considerations are crucial when you are composing any document that incorporates library or Internet research. Such skills are further exercised when you are crafting the bibliography's introduction, which will clarify your focus and provide readers with a preview of the entries to come.

Third, in regard to its individual entries, an annotated bibliography depends heavily on summarizing and documenting sources. The former strategy is common to many genres of writing. Although summarizing library or Internet sources may not be required for certain essay assignments, it's hard to imagine a text that does not include a summary of at least some phenomenon (e.g., a process, a personal experience, an event you observed). As such, the necessity of learning to summarize effectively cannot be overstated—and neither can the necessity of learning to correctly document essential publication information, as you will do in the citations preceding your bibliography's summaries. Certain guidelines for documenting sources, as well as the general logic of citation practices, will readily transfer to many academic and professional writing situations.

ACTIVITY

Comparing and Contrasting Source Summaries

Write a summary of the brief *New York Times* article below. After you are finished, form a small group with at least two of your peers who have finished writing their own summaries. Share your individual summaries, and take note of how they compare or contrast with each other. How, specifically, are they similar or different? What might explain the differences between them? Do any of the summaries seem better than the others? Why or why not? Remember to apply what you learned when composing your annotated bibliography.

A Poverty Solution That Starts with a Hug
by Nicholas Kristof

Perhaps the most widespread peril children face isn't guns, swimming pools or speeding cars. Rather, scientists are suggesting that it may be "toxic stress" early in life, or even before birth.

This month, the American Academy of Pediatrics is issuing a landmark warning that this toxic stress can harm children for life. I'm as skeptical as anyone of headlines from new medical studies (Coffee is good for you! Coffee is bad for you!), but that's not what this is.

Rather, this is a "policy statement" from the premier association of pediatricians, based on two decades of scientific research. This has revolutionary implications for medicine and for how we can more effectively chip away at poverty and crime.

Toxic stress might arise from parental abuse of alcohol or drugs. It could occur in a home where children are threatened and beaten. It might derive from chronic neglect—a child cries without being cuddled. Affection seems to defuse toxic stress—keep those hugs and lullabies coming!—suggesting that the stress emerges when a child senses persistent threats but no protector.

Cues of a hostile or indifferent environment flood an infant, or even a fetus, with stress hormones like cortisol in ways that can disrupt the body's metabolism or the architecture of the brain.

The upshot is that children are sometimes permanently undermined. Even many years later, as adults, they are more likely to suffer heart disease, obesity, diabetes and other physical ailments. They are also more likely to struggle in school, have short tempers and tangle with the law.

The crucial period seems to be from conception through early childhood. After that, the brain is less pliable and has trouble being remolded.

"You can modify behavior later, but you can't rewire disrupted brain circuits," notes Jack P. Shonkoff, a Harvard pediatrician who has been a leader in this field. "We're beginning to get a pretty compelling biological model of why kids who have experienced adversity have trouble learning."

This new research addresses an uncomfortable truth: Poverty is difficult to overcome partly because of self-destructive behaviors. Children from poor homes often shine, but others may skip school, abuse narcotics, break the law, and have trouble settling down in a marriage and a job. Then their children may replicate this pattern.

Liberals sometimes ignore these self-destructive pathologies. Conservatives sometimes rely on them to blame poverty on the poor.

The research suggests that the roots of impairment and underachievement are biologically embedded, but preventable. "This is the biology of social class disparities," Dr. Shonkoff said. "Early experiences are literally built into our bodies."

The implication is that the most cost-effective window to bring about change isn't high school or even kindergarten—although much greater efforts are needed in schools as well—but in the early years of life, or even before birth.

"Protecting young children from adversity is a promising, science-based strategy to address many of the most persistent and costly problems facing contemporary society, including limited educational achievement, diminished economic productivity, criminality, and disparities in health," the pediatrics academy said in its policy statement.

One successful example of early intervention is home visitation by childcare experts, like those from the Nurse-Family Partnership. This organization sends nurses to visit poor, vulnerable women who are pregnant for the first time. The nurse warns against smoking and alcohol and drug abuse, and later encourages breast-feeding and good nutrition, while coaxing mothers to cuddle their children and read to them. This program continues until the child is 2.

At age 6, studies have found, these children are only one-third as likely to have behavioral or intellectual problems as others who weren't enrolled. At age 15, the children are less than half as likely to have been arrested.

Evidence of the importance of early experiences has been mounting like snowflakes in a blizzard. For example, several studies examined Dutch men and women who had been in utero during a brief famine at the end of World War II. Decades later, those "famine babies" had more trouble concentrating and more heart disease than those born before or after.

Other scholars examined children who had been badly neglected in Romanian orphanages. Those who spent more time in the orphanages had shorter telomeres, a change in chromosomes that's a marker of accelerated aging. Their brain scans also looked different.

The science is still accumulating. But a compelling message from biology is that if we want to chip away at poverty and improve educational and health outcomes, we have to start earlier. For many children, damage has been suffered before the first day of school.

As Frederick Douglass noted, "It is easier to build strong children than to repair broken men."

IDEA FOR EXTENDED WRITING

Sharing Knowledge through an Annotated Bibliography   Although many writers compose annotated bibliographies simply in the interest of facilitating their own writing processes, sometimes they choose to publish them in hopes of helping others gain a head start on their research. Thinking about students in your major (or a major that interests you), compose an annotated bibliography that will familiarize them with an issue that is central to that field. The issue could be one that especially intrigues you or one that you just want to know more about as you consider pursuing a given major.

Teen Dating Violence: A Literature Review and Annotated Bibliography

A report prepared by the Federal Research Division, Library of Congress under an interagency agreement with the Violence and Victimization Research Division, National Institute of Justice, April 2011. Researcher: Priscilla Offenhauer; Project Manager: Alice Buchalter

INTRODUCTION

Abuse in dating relationships is common among adolescents. In the United States, according to commonly cited figures, 10 to 12 percent of teens report physical abuse, and 33 percent report some kind of abuse.[1] Other sources cite different figures, often higher. This dating abuse has a plethora of negative associated conditions or consequences. Despite the high prevalence rates and deleterious effects, however, teen dating abuse has been slow to gain recognition as a critical public-health and policy concern. Adult intimate-partner violence and marital abuse more generally have gained such recognition, as seen, especially in the past three decades, in policy, program, and legal responses, and in an extensive research literature base devoted to the problem. Adolescents, by comparison, were long overlooked as a population that suffers from relationship abuse. The research literature on this age-group, particularly, pre-college-age teens, has been sparse, notwithstanding indications that dating violence among teens is not only serious, but also exhibits unique features as compared with its manifestation at other life periods. Only recently, especially in the decade 2000 to 2010, has this neglect shifted, with teen dating violence moving higher on the policy and research agenda.

This recent emergence of teen dating violence as a societal concern was confirmed and advanced by a recent gesture in the U.S. Congress. In January 2010, the Senate passed a resolution (S. Res. 373) to designate the month of February 2010 as National Teen Dating Violence Awareness and Prevention Month. In March 2010, the House passed a companion resolution (H. Res. 1081).[2] Along with expanding the previously designated Teen Dating Violence Awareness and Prevention Week to a month, this legislation calls for prioritizing efforts to stop teen dating violence. The Senate resolution "calls upon the people of the United States, including youth and parents, schools, law enforcement, state and local officials, and interested groups to observe . . . [the month] with appropriate programs and activities that promote awareness and prevention of the crime of teen dating violence in their communities."

. . .

In addition to this recent action by the Congress to elevate teen dating violence on the policy agenda, more and more states have brought increased recognition to the issue. In particular, state legislatures have acted to improve legal provisions pertinent to dating abuse among teens, e.g., laws governing access to orders of protection, requirements for parental consent to such access, and mandates requiring schools to provide education for violence prevention.[3] As of March 2011, 14 states reportedly had laws mandating education on teen dating violence: Connecticut, Florida, Georgia, Illinois, Massachusetts, Nebraska, New Jersey, Ohio, Pennsylvania, Rhode Island, Tennessee, Texas, Virginia, and Washington. Another five had similar pending legislation: California, Georgia, Maryland, Oregon, and Texas.[4] Accompanying and spurring legislative responses at the state level as well as the federal level has been a growing body of empirical research on adolescent dating violence. The current decade has seen belated stepped-up efforts to examine the nature and extent of teen dating abuse, to illuminate various forms of abuse, to investigate age, gender, racial, and other demographic differences, and to understand correlates, predictors, and outcomes with which the abuse is associated. A limited but growing quantity of evaluation research has also emerged with the aim of assessing the effectiveness of an array of prevention and intervention initiatives that seek to combat teen relationship abuse. The stepped-up research efforts of this decade are the focus of this summary of research and annotated bibliography. The summary and bibliography cover the following topics as they pertain to this decade's literature on dating violence: how adolescent dating violence is defined and measured, the prevalence of such violence, what factors influence dating violence for teens, and what types of programs might be effective means of prevention or intervention.

[Note: The summary (i.e., literature review) and several bibliography entries have been omitted in the interest of space. Additionally, bibliography entries have been edited to reflect the most recent MLA guidelines.]

1. NOTE: The footnotes in this summary of research generally consist of abbreviated citations that are cross-references to relevant items in the annotated bibliography. A full citation is provided only in the case of quoted material and other specific debts.
2. S.Res 373, 111th Cong. (2010); H. Res 1081, 111th Cong. (2010), thomas.loc.gov/cgibin/query/D?c111:2:./temp/~c111BhpNXK.
3. Break the Cycle, 2010 State Law Report Cards: A National Survey of Teen Dating Violence Laws, April 12, 2010, www.breakthecycle.org/system/files/pdf/2010-Dating-Violence-State-Law-Report-Card-Full-Report.pdf.
4. National Conference of State Legislatures, "Teen Dating Violence," March 22, 2011, www.ncsl.org/default.aspx?tabid=17582.

READINGS

BIBLIOGRAPHY

Adelman, Madelaine, and Sang Hea Kil. "Dating Conflicts: Rethinking Dating Violence and Youth Conflict." *Violence Against Women*, vol. 13, no. 12, 2007, pp. 1296–1318.

This research examined the role of friends in conflicts and violence associated with heterosexual teen dating. The study explored the implication of friends as confidants and participants in teen dating/violence. The research investigated the ways in which friends influence who constitutes an acceptable date, as well as attitudes that tend to conserve or challenge gender stereotypes and sexual conformity that may fuel abuse. The study provides evidence that peer attitudes are critical influences on teen behaviors and attitudes.

Adler-Baeder, Francesca, et al. "The Impact of Relationship Education on Adolescents of Diverse Backgrounds." *Family Relations*, vol. 56, no. 3, 2007, pp. 291–304. *ProQuest*, search.proquest.com/openview/139b53fd3f0fb1b3f670bf3b8da1212a/1?pq-origsite=gscholar&cbl=41641.

This study examined the effectiveness of an adolescent-focused marriage education program, an adapted version of the curriculum entitled Love U2: Increasing Your Relationship Smarts. The evaluation studied the program's use with an economically, geographically, and racially diverse sample of 340 high school students. The evaluators found that students improved in multiple dimensions of their relationship knowledge, including their ability to identify unhealthy relationship patterns. The program also increased the participants' realistic beliefs about relationships and marriage, and decreased their use of verbally aggressive conflict tactics at post-program compared to controls. These findings held across race, household income, and family structure type, with all participating students benefiting in similar ways.

Arriaga, Ximena B., and Vangie A. Foshee. "Adolescent Dating Violence: Do Adolescents Follow Their Friends' or Their Parents' Footsteps?" *Journal of Interpersonal Violence*, vol.19, no. 2, 2004, pp. 162–84.

This study examined two possible antecedents of adolescent dating violence—having friends in violent relationships and having parents who are violent toward one another. It sought to establish which, if either, is more strongly predictive of a young person's dating violence perpetration and victimization. A group of 526 eighth- and ninth-grade students completed self-report questionnaires on two occasions over a six-month period. Consistent with hypotheses, interparental violence and friend dating violence each exhibited cross-sectional associations with a youth's perpetration and victimization. However, only friend violence consistently predicted later dating violence. That is, this peer variable was more influential than the effects of witnessing interparental violence. In the author's longitudinal analysis (one of the few studies that used a longitudinal design), friend violence statistically predicted later perpetration of dating violence for both males and females, but statistically predicted becoming the victim only for females.

Bailey, Clarice Machette. "Teenage Intimate Partner Violence: An Exploratory Study." Diss. Portland State U, 2000. *ProQuest*,

This dissertation surveyed a sample of ninth- to twelfth-graders in Portland, Oregon, to explore their experiences with teenage partner violence. Five findings emerged from this exploratory study. First, 91 percent of the respondents were not involved in teenage partner violence. Second, there was no statistically significant difference between males and females as either victims or offenders. Instead, the statistics indicated reciprocity and mutuality. Third, teens identified as victims/abusers were more likely to come from families of origin where there had been partner abuse. However, living with one's biological parents seemed to reduce the likelihood of students demonstrating partner abuse. Fourth, race, previous partner abuse, parental risk behaviors, sexual involvement, and other teen risk behaviors were statistically significant predictors of teenage partner violence for this sample. Fifth, there was very little to no legal or school-based protection in the form of policy or practice for students who found themselves involved in teen partner violence. The study supports social learning theories and theories of the intergenerational transmission of violence.

Banyard, Victoria L., and Charlotte Cross. "Consequences of Teen Dating Violence: Understanding Intervening Variables in Ecological Context." *Violence Against Women*, vol. 14, no. 9, 2008, pp. 998–1013.

This study examined the educational and mental-health problems associated with adolescent dating violence victimization. The research included attention to mediating and moderating factors in the link between victimization and negative consequences. As hypothesized, being a survivor of dating violence was associated with higher levels of depression and suicidal thoughts, as well as poorer educational outcomes and attitudes. Mental-health symptoms in part mediated the relationship between victimization and school outcomes. The use of alcohol and depression complicated the relationship between victimization and outcomes. In addition, gender and social support both affected the relationship between victimization and outcomes. Perceived social support as a moderator had more significant effects for girls.

Cantrell, Lorrie, and Sarah Buel. "Changing Texas Law to Include Minors in Protective Order Legislation." *American Bar Association*, 13 Nov. 2008, www.americanbar.org/minors_in_protective_legislation.

This article details the provisions of the Texas Family Code that, as of November 2008, posed barriers to the protection of minor victims of dating violence. Among these barriers are obstacles for minors attempting to obtain protective orders. The Texas Family Code currently differs from the pertinent laws of many other states, which allow teens to file for a protective order without parental consent or an adult to file on behalf of the teen. The article calls upon the Texas legislature to amend the Texas Family Code to allow minors to file for protective orders. Further, it advocates that school officials, judges, prosecutors, and law enforcement be educated on the dangers of teen dating violence and on what steps can be taken to ensure the victim is protected and the batterer is held accountable.

Source: Priscilla Offenhauer and Alice Buchalter, "Teen Dating Violence: A Literature Review and Annotated Bibliography." U.S. Department of Justice, 2011.

Design and the Social Sector: An Annotated Bibliography

by Courtney Drake and Deirdre Cerminaro with William Drenttel

INTRODUCTION

Design thinking, user-centered design, service design, transformation design. These practices are not identical but their origin is similar: a definition of design that extends the profession beyond products. The rise of service economies in the developed world contributed to this movement toward design experiences, services and interactions between users and products. The literature about design thinking and contemporary ideas reveals common elements and themes, many of which are borrowed from product design processes. . . .

The implications of the rise of design thinking are twofold. First, corporate and organizational leaders concerned with innovative prowess are recognizing design thinking as a tool for developing new competitive advantages. Design thinking considers consumers' latent desires and thus has the potential to change markets rather than simply make incremental improvements in the status quo. Second, many organizations have encountered significant barriers to practicing design thinking internally. In some ways, design thinking runs counter to the very structure of a corporation—it is intended to break paradigms, which may mean questioning power relationships, traditions and incentive structure, and it may require a corporation to overhaul its business model and cannibalize its success. Additionally, many corporate leaders treat design thinking in a linear manner, a process that compromises the critical elements of conflict and circularity. In many instances, designers have failed to sufficiently translate and articulate their process, and businesses tend to favor past trends over the promise of new discovery. . . .

The value of co-creation is a predominant theme in the literature surveyed here, particularly for Western designers contributing to foreign communities. Another critical factor is continual presence within projects, or better, a longer-term, sustained involvement. . . . Because the process is founded on a deep understanding of a particular user group's needs, the solution for one community likely does not translate directly to another. However, authors suggest that it is the design *process* that is scalable and should be taught to local leaders. Failed projects support this assertion; benefits flow through the process of a project as well as the end-product, which further advocates for co-creation. Finally, the literature leaves us with an unsettling question: Is breakthrough innovation possible in the social sector? Most veterans in this field suggest the answer is no—they recommend that designers start small and introduce incremental change because the complexity of the systems and problems they face will demand it. However, this finding does not negate the potential value of the designer. The social sector needs designers to identify problems, imagine possibilities for a better future and facilitate problem-solving processes. —*Courtney Drake*

[Note: The summary (i.e., literature review) and several bibliography entries have been omitted in the interest of space. Additionally, bibliography entries have been edited to reflect the most recent MLA guidelines.]

PART ONE: BEYOND PRODUCT DESIGN

Andrews, Kate. "Social Design: Delivering Positive Social Impact." *This Is Service Design Thinking*, edited by Marc Stickdorn and Jakob Schneiders. BIS, 2010, pp. 88–93.

Designer and writer Kate Andrews explores the role of service design in social design, which she defines as "employing the design process to tackle a social issue or with an intent to improve human lives." Andrews points out that while design is all around us, designers and the design process have long been invisible and misunderstood. She traces the recent popularization of design thinking, which was followed by an emergence of socially-motivated designers. Andrews claims that service design is helping to reveal the broader social applications of design and shift the understanding of design to that of process, not just product. The article ends with a case study of Colalife, in which designers harnessed social media and web technology to develop a plan to deliver medical equipment in Africa via Coca-Cola's distribution channels. According to Andrews, service design is contributing to a better understanding of design's social value while simultaneously bringing designers out from behind the curtain. [DC]

Beckman, Sara L., and Michael Barry. "Innovation as a Learning Process: Embedding Design Thinking." *California Management Review*, vol. 51, no. 1, 2007, pp. 25–56.

Sara Beckman, faculty director of Haas Management of Technology Program, and Michael Barry, consulting assistant professor of Stanford Design Program, integrate the second generation of design theory with experiential learning theory to derive an innovation process and insights for leaders of innovation. They overlay diverging, converging, assimilating, and accommodating learning styles with a design process that moves fluidly between analysis and synthesis and abstract and concrete conceptualization. The design process itself closely mirrors that used extensively at IDEO, but Beckman and Barry introduce learning styles to relate the process to constructing an innovation team. For each carefully detailed phase in the innovation process, they identify the most adept learning style along with Myers-Briggs type indicators, college majors, and career choices. Beckman and Barry encourage corporations to institute leaders who understand the innovation process, can recognize when to transition between phases, and can integrate a diverse team. Such a leader considers both professional expertise and learning styles while composing innovation teams, selects roles based on learning styles, and incorporates a high level of diversity in teams. [CD]

Chapman, Jonathan, and Nick Gant, editors. *Designers, Visionaries + Other Stories: A Collection of Sustainable Design Essays*. Earthscan, 2007.

Most of the environmental impacts of products, services and infrastructure are not a result of purchase or use, but design. Each of the authors, Ezio Manzini, Kate Fletcher, Alastair Fuad-Luke, Stuart Walker, and John Wood, present different practical and theoretical understandings of sustainable design in order to engage design professionals, students, and academics in a meaningful debate. The essays cover topics ranging from building a new wave of sustainable fashion; restoring value to still-functioning products displaced by newer versions; using principles of physics to express the mutually beneficial advantages of sustainable design; the concept of designing with, for, and by society; and envisioning a sustainable society as a network of interconnected communities. The purpose of presenting these varying viewpoints is to further the discourse on sustainable design beyond popular strategies such as solar, wind and recycling to include a broader set of principles, philosophies and methodologies. [DC]

Clark, Kevin, and Ron Smith. "Unleashing the Power of Design Thinking." *Design Management Review*, vol. 19, no. 3, 2008, pp. 8–15.

Kevin Clark, program director, and Ron Smith, designer and brand experience strategist of IBM Corporate Marketing and Communications, implore business executives to take up design thinking as a business strategy, particularly in a business environment focused on innovation. Clark and Smith view design methods as vehicles that can take intentions to reality and they attribute the divide between designers and business executives on designers' inability to translate design issues into the business language. Alternatively, they translate design thinking through three types of intelligence: emotional, integral, and experiential. Emotional intelligence is necessary to understand the emotions that drive customers to act, integral intelligence is used to reconcile customer needs and an organization as a system, and experiential intelligence helps businesses understand how customers interact with products. Clark and Smith exemplify each category with initiatives at IBM and culminate with a brief case study of IBM's Client Briefing Experience Initiative. [CD]

Clune, Stephen. "Design and Behavioral Change." *Journal of Design Strategies*, vol. 4, no. 1, 2001, pp. 68–76.

Clune, whose research at the University of Western Sydney explores design as a facilitator of social change, reasons that the shift to a more sustainable society will require not just new products and materials, but significant behavior change from individuals and communities. Clune proposes that industrial designers utilize their skills to encourage sustainable behaviors. Community-Based Social Marketing (CBSM) is presented as a potential process for designers to follow, which involves: (1) identifying the benefits of and barriers to desired behaviors, (2) designing effective strategies to accentuate benefits and eliminate the barriers, (3) piloting strategies before implementing at full scale, and (4) evaluating strategies over time. This methodology is illustrated with examples of a programmable stove, a community garden, and a modular home. Clune envisions how design informed by the behavioral change methods of CBSM may provide viable future vocations for designers as specialized product designers, entrepreneurs, and consultants. Sustainable design education should go beyond teaching students to design green "things" to include design for large-scale behavior change. [DC]

Davis, Meredith, et al., *Design as a Catalyst for Learning*. Association for Supervision and Curriculum Development, 1998.

This book is the outcome of a research project conducted by National Endowment for the Arts and The OMG Center for Collaborative Learning. The book is directed at educators, not just arts educators, but all educators, to better understand the value that design brings to students in early development and as a precursor to life-long learning. Design is a problem-solving method; a mode of inquiry. In the context of history, science, mathematics, or language arts, the design process teaches students to identify needs and define problems; reflect individually and collaborate with a group; test ideas and evaluate alternatives; make abstract concepts tangible; communicate verbally and visually; and see meaningful connections across disciplines. The authors argue that these skills are at the heart of engaged citizenship because learners come to understand a variety of perspectives and recognize their own agency in shaping their environments and communities. The book reviews the history of design in the international classrooms; poses opportunities and challenges for schools and education reform; and makes recommendations for teacher education and classroom learning. [DC]

Doorley, Scott, and Scott Witthoft. *Make Space: How to Set the Stage for Creative Collaboration.* Wiley, 2012.

Appropriately for the subject matter, this book is a collaborative effort between Scott Doorley and Scott Witthoft, directors of the Environments Collaborative at Stanford University's Hasso Plattner Institute of Design, better known as the "d.school." The d.school is best known for innovation via collaboration and prototyping, and in this book the lens turns inward to analyze and illustrate the spaces that make this possible. The basic premise is that space has a real impact on behavior and attitudes and can be intentionally manipulated to foster creativity and collaboration. While intended to be used as a tool to shape culture and habits, the book is not a typical "how to" guide. Mini-entries are categorized by five content areas (tools, situations, design template, space studies, and insights) and scattered throughout the book. Entries range from case studies of a restaurant to insights from the ancient Greeks to measured drawings and instructions. The book is not meant to be read sequentially, but rather turned to again and again. In between, the goal is to move the reader from inspiration to action: to build something new, reconfigure an existing space, or design a new environment from scratch. [DC]

CREDITS FOR CONTRIBUTIONS

[DC] Deirdre Cerminaro is a graduate student, Yale School of Management.

[CD] Courtney Drake is a graduate student, Yale School of Management.

Courtney Drake, Deirdre Cerminaro, and William Drenttel, "Design and the Social Sector: An Annotated Bibliography," *The Design Observer Group,* October 27, 2011. designobserver.com/feature/design-and-the-social-sector-an-annotated-bibliography/30158/.

FOR DISCUSSION

1. Study the annotated bibliographies above. What seems to be the focus for each?
2. How does the target audience or publication appear to impact the format and style of each piece?

3. What deviations from MLA or APA formatting guidelines do you detect in these bibliographies?
4. On what grounds do you think the editors of the forums publishing these bibliographies might justify any deviations?
5. How well does the collection of entries match the bibliography's purpose as stated in the introduction? How, specifically, might you support your critique?

Introduction to Texts That Analyze

11

Scan this picture. What do you see? Obviously, it portrays a landscape. But when most people look at this well-known illusion, they see more than a landscape—they see faces in the rocks, trees, and other elements that constitute it. To find all of the faces, you'll need to engage in analysis, a strategy you'll employ for many writing assignments in school and the workplace. This chapter introduces general strategies associated with analysis, while the following chapters will characterize specific analytical genres.

Human beings are cognitively wired to perceive and recognize faces—this explains why several immediately jump out at you from the picture at the beginning of this chapter. However, if you are going to find all of the faces (10 total), chances are you'll need to study the picture carefully, searching for proper configurations of two eyes, a nose, and a mouth, as formed by the natural scenery. In doing so, you are **analyzing;** that is, you are applying an interpretive lens (in this instance, the schema of a face) to make sense of relationships between parts of an entity, as well as between the parts and the whole.

Purposes and Strategies for Analyzing

As a composing strategy, analysis is commonly associated with academic and professional writing, which may lead you to view it as somewhat specialized and even intimidating. But consider for a moment just how often you analyze in the course of your everyday life. In fact, it's difficult to make it through a single hour of any day without engaging in analysis. For example, if your computer crashes, you evaluate its behavior—along with any error messages—to identify the problem and decide on the best course of action to fix it. If you are nutritionally conscious, you analyze food labels to determine the relative percentages of the listed ingredients so that you can make crucial dietary decisions. If you enjoy music, you might draw meaning from songs by thinking about how the lyrics relate to the melody, harmony, rhythm, and so on. All of these activities require that you consider relationships between individual parts in order to better understand the whole. In other words, they require you to analyze.

It's important to note that analyses are seldom objective or disinterested. On the contrary, they are derived from an **interpretive lens,** or a way of viewing the world that is rooted in a belief system, school of thought, or specific theory. Consider Figure 11.1, which identifies various interpretive lenses common to the discipline of psychology. Each of these lenses—even when applied in the same

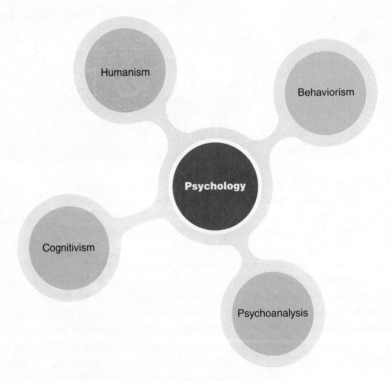

Figure 11.1 **Possible interpretive lenses from psychology**

situation—focuses a psychologist's attentions differently, highlighting certain issues over others. These various focuses lead in diverse analytical directions toward the goal of better understanding people's thoughts and emotions.

Behavioral psychologists, for example, study people's actions as clues to how they are impacted by their environment, whereas cognitive psychologists concentrate on the brain's information-processing functions. Humanistic psychologists analyze people in terms of self-actualization (or progress in reaching their full potential), while psychologists who adopt a psychoanalytical perspective are particularly interested in the influence of the subconscious. Although these different lenses will result in different findings, none of them will necessarily be incorrect. They simply represent contrasting beliefs about the best way of accounting for the inner workings (the parts) of the human mind (the whole).

Remembering that analyses are interpretive, when you present an analysis in a formal document for your college coursework or future job, you'll need to provide substantial support for your "reading" so that others will grasp the basis of your interpretation and possibly be convinced by it. This support might include information from published sources that help clarify your interpretive lens, and it would certainly include examples and illustrations from the text you are analyzing, whether an interview transcript, a work of literature, a film, and so forth. The Look Inside excerpt on pages 189–190, from Sigmund Freud's *The Interpretation of Dreams,* demonstrates the use of evidence to support interpretive claims in a psychoanalytical approach to understanding how memory (the part) operates in the subconscious (the whole). The text he is analyzing in this case is an individual's detailed account of a dream and some related experiences.

Elsewhere in this piece, Freud discusses additional cases to support his claim that dreams often summon memories that have lain dormant, sometimes for many years, in a person's subconscious. Without these examples, readers would simply have to take Freud's word that his analysis is viable. With them, readers have access to the foundation of his reasoning and are better prepared to judge whether the analysis is sound. You might think further about the role of examples or other kinds of support by studying the relationships between elements of an analysis, illustrated in Figure 11.2.

Application in College and the Workplace

Whatever your major, you will soon find yourself analyzing phenomena of special interest in that field. In preparing you to do so, your professors will familiarize you with the most fitting intellectual tools (e.g., theories, research methodologies, logic) and physical tools (e.g., video cameras, petri dishes, computer software). These tools will help you apply the broad strategy of analysis for particular purposes.

Figure 11.3 provides several examples of how analysis is specifically employed across disciplines in a variety of genres. As the examples in that figure

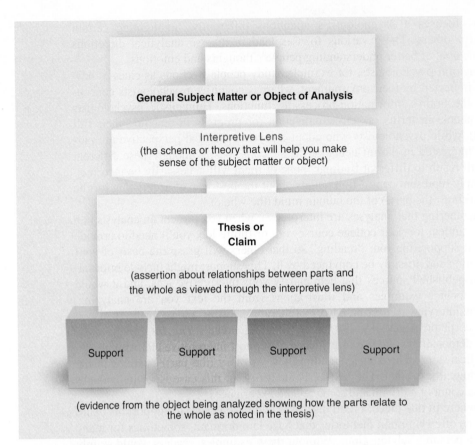

Figure 11.2 Elements of an analysis. Filtering an object of analysis through an interpretive lens will help generate a focused thesis. In analytical genres, the thesis asserts the relationships between the parts of that object and the whole while detailed support shows how the parts and the whole relate.

Discipline	Purpose	Genre
Psychology	Psychologists analyze people's thoughts and actions to gauge their mental health and/or to speculate about the causes of certain behaviors.	Case studies
Marketing	Marketing specialists analyze economic trends to determine consumer behavior and thus project effective sales strategies.	Advertising campaign proposal
Education	Teachers often analyze previous lesson plans in hopes of improving instruction.	Reflective-process journal
English	Literature professors analyze poetry and fiction to figure out how plot, theme, symbolism, etc., might contribute to a work's meaning.	Literary analysis
Political science	Campaign managers analyze the speeches of their candidates' opponents to determine the best way for their candidates to respond.	Rhetorical analysis
Meteorology	Meteorologists analyze atmospheric conditions to predict weather patterns, including those that might be dangerous.	Weather forecast

Figure 11.3 Analytical genres from various academic disciplines

From *The Interpretation of Dreams*

by Sigmund Freud

It often happens that matter appears in the dream content which one cannot recognise later in the waking state as belonging to one's knowledge and experience. One remembers well enough having dreamed about the subject in question, but cannot recall the fact or time of the experience. The dreamer is therefore in the dark as to the source from which the dream has been drawing, and is even tempted to believe an independently productive activity on the part of the dream, until, often long afterwards, a new episode brings back to recollection a former experience given up as lost, and thus reveals the source of the dream. One is thus forced to admit that something has been known and remembered in the dream that has been withdrawn from memory during the waking state.

Delboeuf narrates from his own experience an especially impressive example of this kind. He saw in his dream the courtyard of his house covered with snow, and found two little lizards half-frozen and buried in the snow. Being a lover of animals, he picked them up, warmed them, and put them back into a crevice in the wall which was reserved for them. He also gave them some small fern leaves that had been growing on the wall, which he knew they were fond of. In the dream he knew the name of the plant: Asplenium ruta muralis. The dream then continued, returning after a digression to the lizards, and to his astonishment Delboeuf saw two other little animals falling upon what was left of the ferns. On turning his eyes to the open field he saw a fifth and a sixth lizard running into the hole in the wall, and finally the street was covered with a procession of lizards, all wandering in the same direction, etc.

In his waking state Delboeuf knew only a few Latin names of plants, and nothing of the Asplenium. To his great surprise he became convinced that a fern of this name really existed and that the correct name was Asplenium ruta muraria, which the dream had slightly disfigured. An accidental coincidence could hardly be considered, but it remained a mystery for Delboeuf whence he got his knowledge of the name Asplenium in the dream.

The dream occurred in 1862. Sixteen years later, while at the house of one of his friends, the philosopher noticed a small album containing dried plants resembling the albums that are sold as souvenirs to visitors in many parts of Switzerland.

A LOOK INSIDE: ANALYZING A DREAM

Freud introduces his analysis by indicating his interpretive lens: a pattern he's noticed in the way dreams pull "forgotten" experiences from the subconscious.

Freud describes the dream in detail, including specific elements (the Latin name of the plant and a procession of lizards) that he will later show to be memories that his subject had apparently forgotten but stored in the subconscious.

Here Freud asserts a direct correspondence between the dream and the past experience—that is, the dream's capacity for recalling traces of the experience for consideration in a conscious state.

A sudden recollection occurred to him; he opened the herbarium, and discovered therein the Asplenium of his dream, and recognised his own handwriting in the accompanying Latin name. The connection could now be traced. While on her wedding trip, a sister of this friend visited Delboeuf in 1800—two years prior to the lizard dream. She had with her at the time this album, which was intended for her brother, and Delboeuf took the trouble to write, at the dictation of a botanist, under each of the dried plants the Latin name.

The favourable accident which made possible the report of this valuable example also permitted Delboeuf to trace another portion of this dream to its forgotten source. One day in 1877 he came upon an old volume of an illustrated journal, in which he found pictured the whole procession of lizards just as he had dreamed it in 1862. The volume bore the date of 1861, and Delboeuf could recall that he had subscribed to the journal from its first appearance.

That the dream has at its disposal recollections which are inaccessible to the waking state is such a remarkable and theoretically important fact that I should like to urge more attention to it by reporting several other "Hypermnesic Dreams."

Source: Sigmund Freud, *The Interpretation of Dreams,* 1899.

> In this paragraph and the next, Freud reveals the source of the knowledge about plants that surfaced in the subject's dream, showing relationships between the forgotten experience and knowledge that had surfaced in the dream.

demonstrate, you'll rarely engage in analysis merely for its own sake. Rather, your efforts will support some larger purpose, whether it be understanding why someone acted a certain way (analyzing behavior), protecting others (analyzing weather patterns), or selling a product (analyzing economic trends).

Whatever your purpose, at times, the strategy of analysis will dominate the text, qualifying it as an analytical genre. (You'll learn more about analytical genres in Chapters 12 through 15.) At other times, you'll engage in analysis to support the primary objectives of a different genre. For example, in a film review, you might choose to analyze the screenplay, cinematography, acting, and so on, in order to provide an evaluation of the overall quality of that production. In a literacy narrative—the ultimate goal being to tell the story of your development as a language user—you would analyze specific events in your life to establish their significance in a larger account of how you learned to read and write. However you deploy it—as a genre or as a strategy—it's certain that you will call on analysis again and again in your college courses and eventually in the workplace.

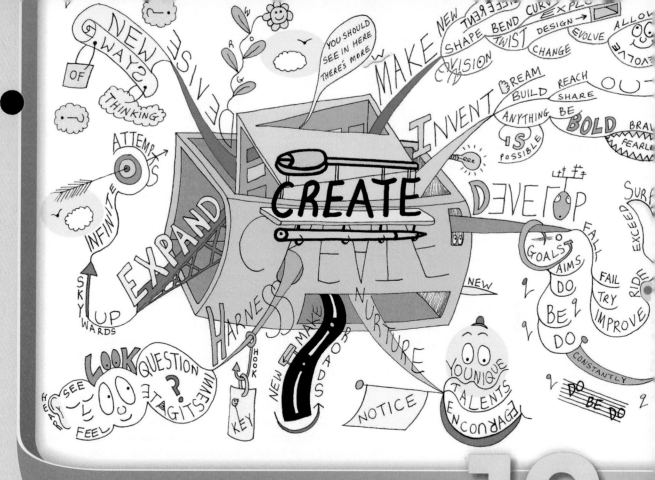

Writing-Process Analysis

This complex and colorful diagram is referred to as a "mind map." This particular mind map captures specific aspects of an individual's creative processes. The reflective activity involved in fashioning this mind map is representative of the kind of thinking you will engage in when preparing to compose a writing-process analysis, the genre highlighted in this chapter.

Think about the last time you struggled with some activity. Maybe you were learning to high-jump in a P.E. class or trying to change a tire on your car. Or maybe you were attempting to perfect Grandma's blueberry pancake recipe. Whatever the case, to adjust your approach, you probably had to reflect carefully on the specific **processes** involved. In particular, you had to think about which procedures were working well, which you might perform more effectively, and how you could improve upon those that were causing problems. Such reflection, as discussed in Chapters 1 and 2, is essential to all problem-solving activities, including writing.

To be sure, those who succeed at writing tend to be highly reflective; in fact, it is probably

The purpose of reflective analyses is to highlight your difficulties as well as your successes. Most teachers would be suspicious of someone who claimed to experience no difficulties when writing. In fact, readers of a reflective analysis want to see a candid and detailed portrayal of your processes because they know that honest, deep reflection is key to improvement. Therefore, you shouldn't worry about revealing your weaknesses; you should worry about *not* doing so. After all, if you don't confront your difficulties, you sidestep a valuable learning opportunity.

safe to assume that they succeed at it *because* they are highly reflective. For this reason, most composition courses will require you to reflect on your **writing processes,** or the specific behaviors and practices you engage in whenever you are faced with a composing challenge. Often, teachers will ask you to discuss your reflections in an essay referred to as a **writing-process analysis.** This genre requires you to break down your larger writing processes into smaller "parts" and to consider how those parts relate to each other and to the whole.

Teachers assign writing-process analyses to increase students' awareness of their own composing processes so that they can manage them more effectively. In fact, if your composition class requires you to submit a portfolio of your best work at the end of the semester, you'll find that a writing-process analysis will be helpful in crafting the introduction to that collection. (You can read more about portfolios and reflective introductions in Chapter 25.)

Because its main goal is to help you assess your successes and challenges as a writer, a writing-process analysis assumes the self as its primary audience. Another audience, of course, is your teacher, who will read your analysis for clues as to how he or she can help you refine your abilities. Peers in your writing course may also be among your readers for this assignment. When peers respond to each other's process analyses, they can share advice about composing strategies, as well as learn about some techniques for improving their own writing processes. (Chapter 24 discusses peer review in detail.) Read the following sections to learn about the essential components of a writing-process analysis and specific strategies for composing in this genre.

Distinguishing Features of a Writing-Process Analysis

Some process-based assignments call for a simple chronological run-through of the steps you follow whenever you are engaged in that activity. However, when you are composing a process *analysis* you need to identify an angle of inquiry—or **interpretive lens**—that will help you make sense of relationships between the whole of that process and its parts. (This is true of all analyses, as discussed in Chapter 11.) Figure 12.1 illustrates how components essential to focusing a writing-process analysis might combine to help you learn more about your own writing processes and how they are working together.

As Figure 12.1 suggests, the thesis for your writing-process analysis should reach beyond a mundane statement like "These are the steps I follow whenever

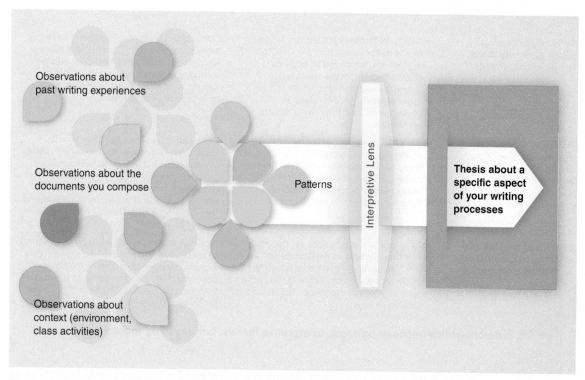

Figure 12.1 Schematic for focusing a writing-process analysis. You can begin to determine the focus of your writing-process analysis by collecting observations about past writing experiences, the documents you have composed, and the context in which they were written. Considered together, these details will help you to better understand the patterns that lead you to think and write the way you do. Next, by choosing an interpretive lens through which to view your work, you will formulate a thesis about a specific aspect of your writing processes.

I write a paper." Instead, it should interpret patterns you observe in your thoughts and actions when composing. It also might connect those patterns to features of your written products. Once you identify the patterns in your writing processes, you can determine what they imply about your tendencies as a writer by viewing them through an appropriate interpretive lens.

The examples in Figure 12.2 clarify how relationships between the components in Figure 12.1 provide focus for a writing-process analysis. Reading Figure 12.2 from left to right, you can see how a pattern in observations about a given student's writing processes—when read through a particular interpretive lens—will lead to a thesis that comments on the larger act of composing as that student has experienced it.

The theses in Figure 12.2 set up essays that, respectively, analyze the difficulties of convincingly supporting claims, the frustrations of writer's block, and the power of journal writing to facilitate thinking. As those theses suggest, writing-process analyses don't necessarily lend themselves to chronological organization

Pattern	Interpretive Lens	Thesis
Difficulty in developing ideas, especially in the context of arguments	• A specific strategy (called the *Toulmin method*) for evaluating the structure of arguments, which led to body paragraphs that discussed the relative strengths and weaknesses of arguments the author made in certain texts and their likely impact on readers	"One of the biggest difficulties I have to work on as a writer is providing sufficient support for my claims. Without valid reasoning, my arguments won't hold any weight with my readers, and I can't hope to influence their thinking."
Difficulty with achieving and maintaining "flow" at various points in the writing process	• Research on causes of writer's block and strategies for overcoming it, which led to body paragraphs that projected the causes of blocks relevant to the author's own composing experiences and clarified how he worked through such episodes	"After all I've accomplished as a writer, I still run into problems with writer's block. I've realized that I need to take breaks (which I now recognize as incubation) and come back only after I am renewed and feel up to creating again. New ideas therefore develop (insight) and I wind up flowing until the end."
Benefits of keeping and referring to a journal to facilitate the composing processes	• Readings and discussions on the power of informal writing to generate and "work out" ideas for formal texts, which led to body paragraphs that connected certain journal entries with successful sections of finished essays	"Journal writing is crucial to my composing process. Journal entries allow me to freely express my own ideas and 'think through' concepts that I need to come to terms with. Such writing has helped me become a better thinker."

Figure 12.2 Relationships between patterns, interpretive lenses, and resulting theses

(an arrangement that systematically traces an act of composing from beginning to end). However, chronological organization might be viable as long as it supports a given interpretive lens.

For example, consider the essay excerpted in the following Look Inside box. In this essay, the author employs a **metaphor** (a comparison between dissimilar objects) as an interpretive lens to analyze the smaller processes she typically engages in during the larger act of composing. By thinking about how an unfamiliar process (e.g., composing) resembles a more familiar process (e.g., cooking), the former is usually illuminated in some way. In addition to revealing benefits of certain practices that the author typically engages in, this essay also leads to the enlightened conclusion that, while viewing an introduction as a recipe can be helpful for some writers, for others, any sort of step-by-step prescription can stifle spontaneity and experimentation.

Processes for Composing a Writing-Process Analysis

Whether your teacher assigns this genre as an informal or a formal assignment, your confidence level should be high in the respect that you are writing about yourself. But remember that you can increase your potential for success in this genre by reviewing Chapters 1 and 2. They address numerous concepts relevant to composing and creative processes that can guide your search for patterns and suggest possible interpretive lenses, as well as theses based on those lenses.

From "My Writing Is Cookin'"

by an Undergraduate Student

Writing involves a process that is extremely personal. Anyone who writes must struggle with this process until it develops into a method for organizing thought, which allows for the creation of a piece of writing. This process will naturally vary for every writer as he or she becomes proficient at a personal writing process. My own technique for producing writing has developed over time from haphazard efforts involving a great deal of guesswork and frustration to a more systematic process that allows for effective organization of thought and material. In reflecting on my own writing process, I realize that it is much like how I go about preparing a meal for guests. Both involve decisions about content, preparation, creation, final clean-up, and an understanding of who the preparation is for. These elements hold important factors in common that illuminate the ways in which my writing process has proved to be helpful and effective.

The first phase in making a meal or writing involves a decision about content. In order to begin preparing the product, be it cuisine or composition, choices must be made about theme, ingredients, and size. Will the meal be Chinese or Cajun, high fat or low fat, small portions or smorgasbord? Will the paper be informative or critical, formal or informal, two pages or fifteen pages? These decisions are based in large part on the guests who will eat the meal or on the audience who will read the writing. I would not prepare steaks for vegetarians and, similarly, I would not fill a paper with technical language for an audience of lay people. These are crucial decisions to be made before actual work begins on a meal for guests or a piece of writing for an audience.

Preparation is the second phase in cooking and writing. Once the choices have been made regarding content, the ingredients must be gathered. In order to begin cooking, I must have the necessary ingredients. Similarly, the "ingredients" of writing consist of whatever information is required to produce the piece being worked on. This may involve information for a research paper or the details of a story for a narrative. When preparing a meal, I always follow recipes because it enables me to be organized and to avoid making major mistakes. When writing a paper, my

A LOOK INSIDE:
WRITING-PROCESS ANALYSIS

The author opens with context that establishes a reason for reading the piece—to see how a struggling writer might hone his or her process.

The thesis identifies the interpretive lens (the metaphor) and notes why it's helpful.

The author transitions into the first point of comparison, which clarifies how writing, like other processes, requires substantial up-front decision making.

The author transitions to a second point of comparison in her journey through these processes, which involves gathering and organizing materials. (Note that the point about introductions becomes crucial to her conclusion.)

recipe is the introduction because it provides me with directions for the body of the paper and I can refer back to it
whenever I feel unsure about the course of the paper. This
aids my organization of material and helps me avoid making major errors in paper construction. When the preparation is in place, I can move on to the creation phase.

   I do not wait until after the meal has been consumed to
do my clean-up. I prefer cleaning everything possible after
the cooking is done, which doesn't take long if I have tried to
clean a little as I have been cooking. Of course there will
always be clean-up to do after the meal has been eaten. The
clean-up phase of writing is the proofreading. I try to proofread as I write to a minimal degree but do most of it after
I have completed the creation phase; just as with a meal,
however, there is usually clean-up which has to be done
after the writing has been read and the reader spots some
"dirty dishes" that I didn't notice. That final aspect of
guest or audience reaction to my product, be it meal or
paper, is the most unnerving aspect of both processes.

> After a paragraph on "creation," or drafting, the author moves to the final phase of the processes she's comparing, asserting that response, perhaps taken for granted in other processes, is a crucial part of editing processes in writing.

   I can see some useful application for this metaphor . . .
particularly [that it is] helpful when looking at the individual
parts of a paper because it can clarify the purpose of a part in
relation to the whole. One part which is critical to a paper's
overall success is the introduction. . . . If writers hear the
example of the introduction as a recipe, it may help them to
understand that it guides the rest of the paper. The paper and
its introduction should be directly related to one another, and
if the paper does not build upon the introduction, it may not
be well organized and developed. One caution with this
approach should be that not all writers will depend upon
the introduction to organize and develop their papers, and
so this should not be considered the only way to develop
a writing process.

> The author ends with observations about the potential relevance of her analysis, even complicating it by noting that her approach to introductions might prove limiting for some writers.

Invention toward First Insight

Because this genre requires deep reflection on your composing processes, you'll
probably want to begin planning for it by searching your memory for information
about past writing experiences. To do so, you might complete multiple brainstorming or clustering exercises (see Chapter 4), with each investigating a different aspect

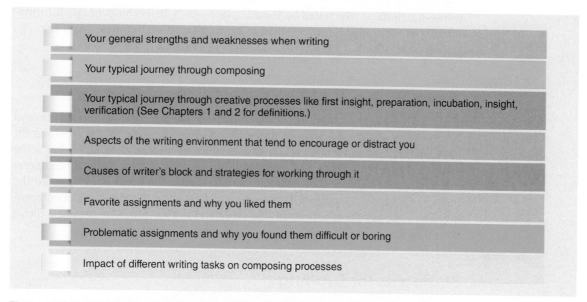

Figure 12.3 **Possible sources of content for a writing-process analysis**

of composing. Figure 12.3 offers ideas for jump-starting these exercises—it lists several different vantage points from which to reflect on your writing processes. Whatever your points of departure, the goal of early invention efforts is to generate as many "mini-insights" about your writing processes as you can to ensure that you have plenty of raw material to consider when you begin thinking about a focus for your paper.

Preparation through Research

While you scratched the surface of your memory during initial bouts with invention, research activities for this assignment should push your memory even further. In addition to the material you produced through prewriting exercises, you might want to learn more about some popular analytical tools that writing teachers and scholars use to understand certain aspects of composing. Examples include those listed in Figure 12.4. Taking any or all of these

Tool	Description
Personality test (Jensen and DiTiberio)	Reveals your tendencies toward being extroverted, intuitive, quick to make decisions, etc., and the manner in which those tendencies can influence your writing practices
Writing apprehension test (Daly-Miller)	Gauges the extent to which you experience writing anxiety and ways in which it may affect your composing processes
Multiple intelligence test (Gardner)	Points to areas of special skill and interest that suggest why you gravitate toward certain composing strategies and how you can capitalize on those skills and interests to improve your writing

Figure 12.4 **Tools for analyzing writing processes**

tests—versions of which can be found online—may help you generate information about your writing processes that wouldn't necessarily arise from prewriting exercises alone.

Invention toward More Focused Insight

Your early invention and research activities should have generated several
observations about your writing processes. Now is the time to start looking for
patterns that lead to insights about your composing processes at large. For some
examples, return to Figure 12.2. Again, notice how the patterns identified suggest
interpretive lenses that will help the authors understand and communicate the
impact of a specific aspect of their writing processes on the larger act of composing. Their theses, then, articulate that realization. Your progress toward a thesis
should follow a similar path.

Strategies for Drafting

As indicated previously, the body of your writing-process analysis might be organized in various ways (by example, in chronological order, etc.). Regardless, this
genre usually asserts a thesis fairly early. That thesis will reveal your interpretive
lens and will be followed by paragraphs filled with detailed support and illustration. Simply *telling* readers what happens when you write will not make for the
most convincing analysis. Instead, you should strive to *show* them what happens by
building the essay's body paragraphs around specific anecdotes, sensory impressions of your writing experiences, excerpts from previously written documents, and
so on—whatever evidence you can muster to help readers experience what you
experience when you write.

Figure 12.5 contrasts a "telling" passage with a "showing" passage from
writing-process analyses written by first-year composition students. While the
passage on the right in Figure 12.5 could go even further in supporting its analytical claim, it clearly surpasses the one on the left. More specifically, the one
on the right shows readers what the author means when she states that she faces
a "challenge with clearly illustrating [her] ideas" by citing a specific example of
the problem from a text she has composed. In contrast, the passage on the left
doesn't offer any examples of instructor comments (the focus of analysis) that
reportedly led to improvement, nor does it offer any examples of the improvements themselves.

Keep in mind that a writing-process analysis is an instructional text of sorts.
Put another way, its primary purposes are to teach you about the intricacies of your
own writing processes and to teach others by example. Your conclusion, then, might
highlight what you've learned. Of course, your discoveries don't need to rise to the
level of some earth-shattering epiphany to be noteworthy. In fact, overstating the
case (e.g., "This analysis has changed my entire outlook on writing!" or "These
reflections are sure to solve all my future writing dilemmas!") can seem insincere,
negatively affecting your credibility.

An Example of Telling

While in high school, I frequently used my first draft as my final paper. I did this because it was usually more than adequate for the assignments we were given and the standards by which they were graded. I have since discovered that I can no longer slide by with that kind of minimal work and effort. Since entering college, I've begun to revise more. One thing that has aided me most in this area is the interaction between instructor and student. Through this kind of interaction, I have discovered what it is specifically that I need to improve on and what problems seem to be part of my writing in general rather than in just one case.

An Example of Showing

An example of my challenge with clearly illustrating my ideas comes from a paper I wrote about the dangers of breast implants. In the opening paragraph, I stated, "Although plastic surgery can be a costly procedure, many people are making the decision to have plastic surgery because of the pressure they feel from society to be physically attractive. This pressure is clearly illustrated by the fact that breast implantation has become fashionable." I claim that breast implantation has become fashionable but give no evidence that what I say is true. The reader could think that I have decided on my own that it is fashionable to have breast implants, and I lose all credibility when my readers think I am just making up facts as I go along. Instead, I might have made the case that so many actresses and models are having implants, and what these high-profile people do often dictates fashion.

Figure 12.5 A supporting passage that tells versus one that shows

Revision and Editing

Questions for Revising

- Is my analysis appropriately geared toward the target audience?
- Do the introductory paragraphs clearly establish an analytical focus that promises to show relationships between writing processes and larger composing acts?
- Does my thesis or controlling idea clearly pinpoint my analytical focus?
- Are the descriptions, anecdotes, or textual details that I selected to support my claims appropriate to the purpose?
- Does the organization follow a logical sequence and employ transitions to effectively connect ideas?
- In places where my analysis employs chronology, is a step-by-step flow of events clearly conveyed?
- Does my conclusion emphasize a sense of discovery or increased understanding?

Questions for Editing

- Are any sources that I used to inform the analysis properly cited?
- Is my finished analysis free of spelling, punctuation, and usage errors?

Transfer to Other Writing Situations

The potential for transferring knowledge you acquire from practicing a writing-process analysis is significant—particularly the knowledge gained about yourself as a writer. This assignment immerses you in reflection on habits, strategies, and skills applicable to composing in different academic and professional contexts. Although written products will vary across disciplines, many of the processes you engage in when generating those products can be transferred across disciplinary boundaries.

In addition, the knowledge you gain in writing about composing processes will help you analyze and depict processes involved in other activities, including those in your career. To be sure, process analyses feed the work of most every field. Figure 12.6 presents some examples.

Even if the processes indicated in Figure 12.6 weren't treated as essay topics in and of themselves, they might be incorporated into larger documents. For example, an engineer's process analysis might be part of a larger analysis of the industry's overall operations; a future P.E. teacher's analysis might be included in a case study of a student's overall performance in a specific class during a given semester; and a nurse's analysis might appear in a training manual for health care workers newly assigned to a particular floor in the hospital. In any case, you can infer from these examples that process analyses are crucial to a variety of professions.

ACTIVITY

Composing Instructions for a Process   Think of a process that you could describe for your peers, and compose a set of instructions to lead them through that process. For the next class period, bring any materials necessary to complete the process you've described. In a group with three or four of your peers, take turns reading your respective instructions aloud while at least one person attempts to follow them exactly as stated. Whether or not that person succeeds is a good indication of how effectively the writer represented the process. For instructions that fall short, work together as a group to determine their insufficiencies.

Discipline	Task	Purpose
Industrial engineering	Compose an analysis of the processes involved in manufacturing a given product.	To determine how procedures might be revised for safety and efficiency
Physical education	Compose an analysis of the processes a student engages in when hitting a baseball.	To determine how aspects of the student's swing influence the length and direction of the ball's flight
Nursing	Compose an analysis of the procedures followed in caring for patients after surgery.	To ensure that patients receive the best care possible and that procedures aren't missed or repeated

Figure 12.6 Process analysis in fields other than composition

IDEA FOR EXTENDED WRITING

Analyzing Your Own Writing Processes For this assignment, analyze some aspect of your composing processes through an interpretive lens arising from the terms, concepts, and theories about writing introduced in your composition course. Feel free to focus on your typical writing processes or your processes as you remember them in the context of a particular writing task. Although the primary purpose of this activity is to help you learn more about your own composing habits, an important secondary purpose is to educate your classmates and teacher (who constitute your audience for this essay) about your composing practices so that they will be prepared to assist you with writing challenges you may face in the future.

The Watcher at the Gates

by Gail Godwin

I first realized I was not the only writer who had a restraining critic who lived inside me and sapped the juice from green inspirations when I was leafing through Freud's "Interpretation of Dreams" a few years ago. Ironically, it was my "inner critic" who had sent me to Freud. I was writing a novel, and my heroine was in the middle of a dream, and then I lost faith in my own invention and rushed to "an authority" to check whether she could have such a dream. In the chapter on dream interpretation, I came upon the following passage that has helped me free myself, in some measure, from my critic and has led to many pleasant and interesting exchanges with other writers.

Freud quotes Schiller, who is writing a letter to a friend. The friend complains of his lack of creative power. Schiller replies with an allegory. He says it is not good if the intellect examines too closely the ideas pouring in at the gates. "In isolation, an idea may be quite insignificant, and venturesome in the extreme, but it may acquire importance from an idea which follows it. . . . In the case of a creative mind, it seems to me, the intellect has withdrawn its watchers from the gates, and the ideas rush in pell-mell, and only then does it review and inspect the multitude. You are ashamed or afraid of the momentary and passing madness which is found in all real creators, the longer or shorter duration of which distinguishes the thinking artist from the dreamer. . . . You reject too soon and discriminate too severely."

So that's what I had: a Watcher at the Gates. I decided to get to know him better. I discussed him with other writers, who told me some of the quirks and habits of their Watchers, each of whom was as individual as his host, and all of whom seemed passionately dedicated to one goal: rejecting too soon and discriminating too severely.

It is amazing the lengths a Watcher will go to keep you from pursuing the flow of your imagination. Watchers are notorious pencil sharpeners, ribbon changers, plant waterers, home repairers and abhorrers of messy rooms or messy pages. They are compulsive looker-uppers. They are superstitious scaredy-cats. They cultivate self-important eccentricities they think are suitable for "writers." And they'd rather die (and kill your inspiration with them) than risk making a fool of themselves.

My Watcher has a wasteful penchant for 20 pound bond paper above and below the carbon of the first draft. "What's the good of writing out a whole page," he whispers begrudgingly, "if you just have to write it over again later? Get it perfect the first time!" My Watcher adores stopping in the middle of a morning's work to drive down to the library to check on the name of a flower or a World War II battle or a line of metaphysical poetry. "You can't possibly go on till you've got this right!" he admonishes. I go and get the car keys.

Other Watchers have informed their writers that:

"Whenever you get a really good sentence you should stop in the middle of it and go on tomorrow. Otherwise you might run dry."

"Don't try and continue with your book till your dental appointment is over. When you're worried about your teeth, you can't think about art."

Another Watcher makes his owner pin his finished pages to a clothesline and read them through binoculars "to see how they look from a distance." Countless other Watchers demand "bribes" for taking the day off: lethal doses of caffeine, alcoholic doses of Scotch or vodka or wine.

There are various ways to outsmart, pacify, or coexist with your Watcher. Here are some I have tried, or my writer friends have tried, with success:

Look for situations when he's likely to be off-guard. Write too fast for him in an unexpected place, at an unexpected time. (Virginia Woolf captured the "diamonds in the dust heap" by writing at a "rapid haphazard gallop" in her diary.) Write when very tired. Write in purple ink on the back of a Master Charge statement. Write whatever comes into your mind while the kettle is boiling and make the steam whistle your deadline. (Deadlines are a great way to outdistance the Watcher.)

Disguise what you are writing. If your Watcher refuses to let you get on with your story or novel, write a "letter" instead, telling your "correspondent" what you are going to write in your story or chapter. Dash off a "review" of your own unfinished opus. It will stand up like a bully to your Watcher the next time he throws obstacles in your path. If you write yourself a good one.

Get to know your Watcher. He's yours. Do a drawing of him (or her). Pin it to the wall of your study and turn it gently to the wall when necessary. Let your Watcher feel needed. Watchers are excellent critics after inspiration has been captured; they are dependable, sharp-eyed readers of things already set down. Keep your Watcher in shape and he'll have less time to keep you from shaping. If he's really ruining your whole working day, sit down, as Jung did with his personal demons, and write him a letter. "Dear Watcher," I wrote, "What is it you're so afraid I'll do?" Then I held his pen for him, and he replied instantly with a candor that has kept me from truly despising him.

"Fail," he wrote back.

Source: Gail Godwin, "The Watcher at the Gates," *The New York Times,* January 9, 1977. Copyright (1995/2001) Gail Godwin. Reprinted by permission of John Hawkins & Associates, Inc.

A Way of Writing

by William Stafford

A writer is not so much someone who has something to say as he is someone who has found a process that will bring about new things he would not have thought of if he had not started to say them. That is, he does not draw on a reservoir; instead, he engages in an activity that brings to him a whole succession of unforeseen stories, poems, essays, plays, laws, philosophies, religions, or—but wait!

Back in school, from the first when I began to try to write things, I felt this richness. One thing would lead to another; the world would give and give. Now, after twenty years or so of trying, I live by that certain richness, an idea hard to pin, difficult to say, and perhaps offensive to some. For there are strange implications in it.

One implication is the importance of just plain receptivity. When I write, I like to have an interval before me when I am not likely to be interrupted. For me, this means usually the early morning, before others are awake. I get pen and paper, take a glance out of the window (often it is dark out there), and wait. It is like fishing. But I do not wait very long, for there is always a nibble—and this is where receptivity comes in. To get started I will accept anything that occurs to me. Something always occurs, of course, to any of us. We can't keep from thinking. Maybe I have to settle for an immediate impression: it's cold, or hot, or dark, or bright, or in between! Or well, the possibilities are endless. If I put down something, that thing will help the next thing come, and I'm off. If I let the process go on, things will occur to me that were not at all in my mind when I started. These things, odd or trivial as they may be, are somehow connected. And if I let them string out, surprising things will happen.

If I let them string out . . . Along with initial receptivity, then, there is another readiness: I must be willing to fail. If I am to keep on writing, I cannot bother to insist on high standards. I must get into action and not let anything stop me, or even slow me much. By "standards" I do not mean "correctness," spelling, punctuation, and so on. These details become mechanical for anyone who writes for a while. I am thinking about such matters as social significance, positive values, consistency, etc. . . . I resolutely disregard these. Something better, greater, is happening! I am following a process that leads so wildly and originally into new territory that no judgment can at the moment be made about values, significance, and so on. I am making something new, something that has not been judged before. Later others—and maybe I myself—will make judgments. Now, I am headlong to discover. Any distraction may harm the creating.

So, receptive, careless of failure, I spin out things on the page. And a wonderful freedom comes. If something occurs to me, it is all right to accept it. It has one justification: it occurs to me. No one else can guide me. I must follow my own weak, wandering, diffident impulses.

A strange bonus happens. At times, without my insisting on it, my writings become coherent; the successive elements that occur to me are clearly related. They lead by themselves to new connections. Sometimes the language, even the syllables that happen along, may start a trend. Sometimes the materials alert me to something waiting in my mind, ready for sustained attention. At such times, I allow myself to be eloquent, or intentional, or for great swoops (Treacherous! Not to be trusted!) reasonable. But I do not insist on any of that; for I know that back of my activity there will be the coherence of my self, and that indulgence of my impulses will bring recurrent patterns and meanings again.

This attitude toward the process of writing creatively suggests a problem for me, in terms of what others say. They talk about "skills" in writing. Without denying that I do have experience, wide reading, automatic orthodoxies and maneuvers of various kinds, I still must insist that I am often baffled about what "skill" has to do with the precious little area of confusion when I do not know what I am going to say and then I find out what I am going to say. That precious interval I am unable to bridge by skill. What can I witness about it? It remains mysterious, just as all of us must feel puzzled about how we are so inventive as to be able to talk along through complexities with our friends, not needing to plan what we are going to say, but never stalled for long in our confident forward progress. Skill? If so, it is the skill we all have, something we must have learned before the age of three or four.

A writer is one who has become accustomed to trusting that grace, or luck, or—skill.

Yet another attitude I find necessary: most of what I write, like most of what I say in casual conversation, will not amount to much. Even I will realize, and even at the time, that it is not negotiable. It will be like practice. In conversation I allow myself random remarks—in fact, as I recall, that is the way I learned to talk—so in writing I launch many expendable efforts. A result of this free way of writing is that I am not writing for others, mostly; they will not see the product at all unless the activity eventuates in something that later appears to be worthy. My guide is the self, and its adventuring in the language brings about communication.

Source: William Stafford, "A Way of Writing" from *Field: Contemporary Poetry and Poetics* #2 (Spring 1970). Copyright © 1970 by Oberlin College. Reprinted with the permission of Oberlin College Press.

READINGS

FOR DISCUSSION

1. What is the interpretive lens for each of the above writing-process analyses? What is the thesis of each piece?
2. What kinds of support do the authors use to illustrate their theses?
3. What similarities and differences do you note between these authors' composing processes?
4. What revelations from these reflections might be helpful in managing your own processes?
5. Which of these process analyses does the better job of showing versus telling? What passages stand out in this regard?

WORKS CITED

Daly, John, and Michael Miller. "The Empirical Development of an Instrument to Measure Writing Apprehension." *Research in the Teaching of English*, vol. 12, 1975, pp. 242–49.

Gardner, Howard. *Frames of Mind: The Theory of Multiple Intelligences.* Basic Books, 1993.

Jensen, George, and John K. DiTiberio. "Personality and Individual Writing Processes." *College Composition and Communication*, vol. 35, 1984, pp. 285–300.

LOUIS VUITTON

Visual Analysis

13

Take a look at this photograph. What story does it seem to be telling? What message is it communicating? How do its specific elements—color, light, shadow, the nature and position of the subjects, and so on— contribute to that message? These are just some of the questions that drive a visual analysis, the genre introduced in this chapter.

Imagine yourself in the picture that opens this chapter. There you are, out on a safari with one of your close friends. As you walk through the golden grass, with a trio of giraffes and hazy purple mountains in the background, you suddenly realize that you're in the midst of an adventure that most only dream about. And what's more . . . you're experiencing it in some

great-looking clothes and accessories by the French fashion house Louis Vuitton.

This ad embodies a sales approach that has become increasingly popular in recent years—using visuals instead of words to convince consumers of a product's desirability. Ads like this draw readers in, not only by means of their striking images but also by means of a riddle they pose—that is, the question of what exactly is being sold. For example, unless you immediately spot (and recognize) Vuitton's name in small print in the lower right-hand corner, you might assume that the ad is making a pitch for anything from travel packages to funding for wildlife preservation. On further reflection, however, you would likely conclude from the foregrounding of clothing and accessories that this is a fashion advertisement. Whatever the case, since no explanation accompanies the photograph, you must study its elements to infer which product it is promoting.

If you are an especially critical reader, you might not be satisfied with merely identifying what Vuitton is trying to sell. Struck by the unique quality of this marketing strategy, you might be compelled to think about how the ad works to persuade consumers through its visual appeal. Whether figuring out what is being sold or how it is being sold, you are **analyzing** a visual text; in other words, you are breaking the picture down into parts to determine how those parts relate to each other and to the whole (see Chapter 11 for an overview of analysis).

The strategies you apply when analyzing images in advertisements are relevant when analyzing other types of visual texts, such as paintings, sculptures, graphs, diagrams, body language, clothing, and even video games. In an increasingly graphic-savvy culture, knowing how to sort through and make sense of components constituting the various images you are bombarded with on a daily basis is crucial to your personal and professional life. For this reason, **visual analysis** is a commonly assigned genre in composition courses.

Distinguishing Features of a Visual Analysis

A visual analysis interprets an image by drawing meaning from its elements, including shapes, colors, sizes, shadows, and positions. In exploring the nature of these elements, their relative emphasis, and the relationships between them, a visual analysis comments on the image's presumed message or the way it communicates to the target audience. Figuring out the message requires that you understand the rhetorical situation (as defined in Chapter 3); the rhetorical situation provides an interpretive lens that will guide your reading of the image in question.

Consider, for example, the photograph in Figure 13.1. Pretend for a moment that this is a snapshot of a close family friend taken after your little brother's piano recital. In that case, the empty and dark status of the room, the uneven rows of chairs, and the woman's seemingly frustrated expression might lead you to interpret the photo as

Figure 13.1 Woman sitting in an empty room

depicting a moment of feigned annoyance over having to wait too long for you. On the other hand, upon learning the actual rhetorical situation—a *Boston Globe Magazine* article in which the author profiles obscure 2008 presidential candidates—you would interpret the significance of the elements just mentioned differently, perhaps as emphasizing the struggle, sense of isolation, and lack of support experienced by aspiring leaders like Ruth Bryant-White (pictured) who fight for recognition in the vast and complex American political system.

The focus for a visual analysis, then, stems from the elements of the image as filtered through an interpretive lens suggested by the rhetorical situation (see Figure 13.2). To see how these components might converge in a visual analysis, consult the following Look Inside excerpt from an article that appeared in *Slate* magazine, an online forum that focuses on politics and culture. Note how author Witold Rybczynski "reads" his subject, the 9/11 Memorial, through an interpretive lens informed by aspects of the rhetorical situation, particularly his awareness of target readers' interest in politics and culture, as well as his knowledge of the controversy surrounding the memorial's design.

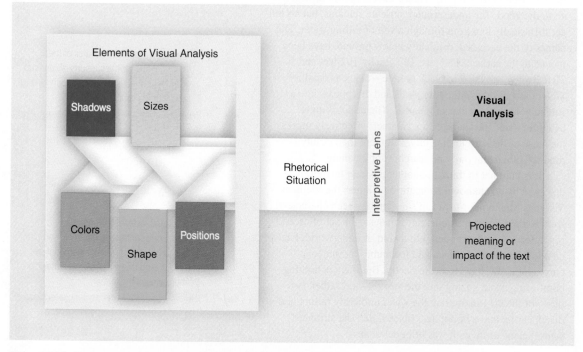

Figure 13.2 Schematic for conceiving a visual analysis. Conceiving a focus for a visual analysis calls for filtering the various elements of an image through an interpretive lens. These elements might include the image's shape, its size, and the colors it uses. The rhetorical situation will help determine which interpretive lens is appropriate for understanding the image's meaning or impact.

From "Black Holes: There Is Nothing Comforting about the 9/11 Memorial"

by Witold Rybczynski

Architect Michael Arad and landscape architect Peter Walker are credited with the design of the 9/11 memorial in New York City, which will be opened to the public on Sept. 12, but an unintentional third designer is Rudolph Giuliani, who as mayor supported the idea that the World Trade Center site was "hallowed ground" on which nothing should be built. By 2003, when a competition was held for the design of the memorial, the idea that the one-acre footprints of the twin towers should be preserved had hardened into a requirement. And that is what people will see on Sept. 12: two vast water-filled pits where the towers once stood.

The design of what has turned into a $700 million memorial has been much simplified since the competition, which is all to the good. The underground museum remains, but no longer theatrically looks out through a veil of falling water. The names of the deceased, originally below ground, have been moved to the surface. The pits, 192 feet by 192 feet and 30 feet deep, are lined in black granite—black as death. Water cascades down the four walls and disappears into a square hole in the center of the pool. The effect is quite beautiful—and the sound of the cataracts effectively masks the noise of the surrounding city. But more than beauty is required of a memorial; one searches for meaning.

It is hard not to think of another abstract memorial designed by an unknown competition winner: the Vietnam Veterans Memorial. Maya Lin's design has been characterized as a gloomy tombstone; nevertheless, the act of ascending, after having descended into a kind of underworld, has an oddly comforting effect, and the names, arranged chronologically, have a severe poetry. But there is nothing comforting about gazing into the vast pit—or, rather, two pits—of the 9/11 memorial, the water endlessly falling and disappearing into a bottomless black hole. The strongest sense I came away with was of hopelessness.

. . .

Although next week's 10th anniversary is billed as the opening of the memorial, the truth is that it will be years before the World Trade Center site is complete. Since the two water features are part of an eight-acre park, until that is finished, it is too

A LOOK INSIDE:
VISUAL ANALYSIS

The introduction notes the controversy central to the author's analysis and offers a glimpse of the memorial that hints at his attitude about it (as previewed in the title).

The author describes features of the memorial and further supports his critique as he begins focusing on the meaning and impact of the structure.

The author extends his analysis by comparing and contrasting the 9/11 memorial with another controversial memorial and then offers a thesis that clearly states his impression of the former.

early to make a final judgment on the memorial. The park will be approached at street level from any of the surrounding four streets, and this intimate connection to the life of the city—at the moment the memorial is isolated from its surroundings—will hopefully counteract the nihilism of the black pits.

The conclusion reasserts a negative interpretation of the 9/11 memorial while recognizing that full integration into the cityscape may alter its impact.

Ultimately, the success of your visual analysis will hinge on your ability to "read" an image critically. Therefore, as Rybczynski does relevant to the 9/11 Memorial (pictured in Figure 13.3), you will need to look not only for what seems obvious on the surface but also for what might be hidden to the undiscerning eye. Understanding aspects of the rhetorical situation can enrich your field of vision, bringing to light features of the image that you otherwise might not have noticed. Articulating a thesis statement about the message or impact you attribute to the visual text and then helping your audience view that text as you see it are fundamental goals of a visual analysis.

Processes for Composing a Visual Analysis

As the Rybczynski piece in the Look Inside box demonstrates, a visual analysis can sustain an entire article. At times, though, it might be used as a support strategy for other genres. For example, reviews of children's books often analyze the artwork while also commenting on the nature of the story, the writing, and so on (see Figure 13.6 for more examples). You will find that most of the strategies discussed in the following paragraphs are applicable to either circumstance.

Figure 13.3 The 9/11 Memorial

Invention toward First Insight

In many classroom situations, you will be asked to select a subject for analysis that has made a special impression on you because of its unique composition, a message it sends, or its capacity to ignite passion. That impression is a wellspring of "first insight," and you'll want to exploit that reaction in search of an angle for analyzing the image. Of course, a subject that is assigned by your teacher might also provoke a strong reaction in you. Even if it does not, you can jump-start your invention processes by thinking about the nature of the visual text and the impact it might have on its intended audience as you search for an interpretive lens. The examples in Figure 13.4 illustrate how this might occur.

Preparation through Research

Whether the subject of your visual analysis is assigned or self-selected, you should make efforts to learn all you can about it through library and Internet research. The information you gather might assist in focusing your analysis by clarifying why the image is considered controversial or significant. It might also supply you with specific observations about the image that could be cited as building blocks for your own analysis. To extend your research, you might want to create a profile of the target audience for the visual text in question. This type of research can deepen your understanding of how the photographer, graphic designer, or artist may have intended the elements of that text to function in achieving a given objective with a particular group of readers.

Invention toward More Focused Insight

As a means of focusing your analysis, you will need to zoom in on the subject to determine if the angle you're considering might be productively narrowed and to probe that image for specific details that will back your "reading" of it. Your interpretive lens will suggest methods appropriate to your specific purposes. For example, if gender is your lens for analyzing a predominantly visual advertisement, you'll want to scrutinize its elements by applying what you know about stereotypes of femininity and masculinity. Figure 13.5 illustrates how such a lens applied to certain elements produces specific avenues for analysis.

Rigorous application of your interpretive lens will reveal aspects of the image that you might not have noticed at first glance. It will also help you sort through your observations in the interest of rejecting those that are irrelevant to your lens so you can move in the direction of a tight, coherent analytical thesis. Ultimately, you will be concentrating your interpretive lens on *how* the image uses elements of composition to portray its subject matter in order to communicate a specific message. The answer to that "how" question will provide the substance of your thesis statement.

University Recruitment Photo

Knowing this photo is intended to entice students to attend a given university, you decide to study how it uses persuasive appeals to grab their attention and fuel their interest.

Famous Model's Publicity Photo

Noticing the contrast between the skin colors of the hands and face in this photo, you decide to explore its attitude about race relations.

Disaster Photo

Viewing this photo of a tornado's aftermath, you are impressed by its capacity for invoking feelings of despair and desolation, and you decide to analyze how it does so.

Figure 13.4 **Photos with possible angles or interpretive lenses**

Strategies for Drafting

The introduction or early paragraphs for your visual analysis should serve several purposes. In addition to establishing your interpretive lens and thesis, somewhere in this section you will need to characterize the image you are analyzing. If you have reproduced that image in your analysis, your description won't need to be as detailed

Element	Observation	Avenues for Analysis
Colors	The women are portrayed in pinks and other pastels, while the men are portrayed in bold, vibrant hues.	What do the colors suggest about the nature or personalities of men and women?
Shapes	The female models are tall and very slim.	What does the appearance of the models suggest about portrayals of "ideal femininity"?
Positions	The women are in the background or standing with a man's arm around them.	What does the placement of women in the scene suggest about submission or dominance and passivity or aggression relevant to gender roles?

Figure 13.5 **Possible points of inquiry for a gender-based analysis**

as it would need to be if your readers did not have immediate access to it. Still, you will need to provide an overview that highlights features of the visual text that are key to your analysis.

The body of your analysis will typically fall into a back-and-forth movement between analytical claims intended to support your thesis and references to specific features of the image that serve as evidence for those claims. In other words, for every interpretive claim about how an element is functioning or what it might mean, you need to offer a direct reference to the visual text so you can show readers that you are not just fabricating your remarks or pulling your observations out of thin air. The body of the analysis, then, gives readers the knowledge and the tools to see that text in the way that you do.

If the body of the document you are writing is especially lengthy or complex, you may want to briefly return in the conclusion to some of the high points of your analysis while avoiding too much redundancy. The conclusion might also emphasize why you went to all the trouble of drawing attention to the image you've been discussing. In other words, you may wish to return to your purpose or reason for writing while hammering home the significance of the analysis in the context of the rhetorical situation that prompted it.

Revision and Editing

Questions for Revising

- Have I appropriately geared the analysis toward my target audience?
- Do I describe the visual in detail fairly early in the essay?
- Do the introductory paragraphs clearly establish my analytical focus?
- Does that focus point to relationships between elements of the visual as they communicate a given message or effect?
- Does my thesis clearly articulate the analytical focus?
- Do I establish tight connections between analytical claims and elements of the visual?
- Does the organization follow a seemingly logical sequence and employ transitions to effectively connect ideas?
- Does the conclusion leave readers with a sense of how parts of the visual work together in carrying an overriding message or effect?

Questions for Editing

- Are the visual and any other sources cited in the analysis properly documented?
- Is the finished analysis free of spelling, punctuation, and usage errors?

Transfer to Other Writing Situations

Visual texts begging for analysis pervade news media, academia, the workplace, recreational activities, and personal interactions. If you want to succeed when reading, writing, or speaking in these various contexts, you will need to watch for indications that there might be more to what you're looking at than a passive glance reveals. To ignore or somehow miss these indications is to settle for incomplete or inaccurate communication.

Practicing visual analysis in your composition course will make you more aware of the diverse forms of nonverbal communication all around you. It will also prepare you for reading and writing visual analyses in other academic and professional contexts. The types of visual texts that you might want or be asked to analyze in school or the workplace are virtually limitless, as are the documents you might want or be asked to compose. Figure 13.6 lists a few possibilities.

Of course, visually oriented fields (e.g., architecture, landscape design, and art history) take for granted the importance of knowing how to analyze images. But, as the examples in Figure 13.6 suggest, individuals studying and working in all fields depend on the ability to analyze visual texts to better understand the ideas of others and to effectively communicate their own thoughts.

Discipline	Genre	Role of Visual Analysis
Business	A report	An accountant might clarify a complex chart that contrasts earnings and expenditures across several years so executives can make projections about their company's future.
Fashion	A fashion editorial	A fashion editor, to ground discussion of the season's runway trends, might analyze a garment or two from a hot designer's new line.
Engineering	A project proposal	A city planner, in forwarding a vision for rejuvenating a dilapidated town square, might analyze the architecture of nearby buildings to establish that projected improvements will not conflict aesthetically with their immediate surroundings.
Journalism	A newspaper article	A journalist might analyze a photograph of a particular occurrence as part of a larger story about a newsworthy event, such as a war or a weather catastrophe.

Figure 13.6 **Genres across disciplines that employ visual analysis**

ACTIVITY

Isolating Elements of a Photograph   Select a photograph from your phone, camera, or photo album that you feel captures the essence of your family or of a special friendship. Study specific elements of that image to discover what, in particular, caused you to select it as representative of your relationship. List your observations and be prepared to share them—and your photo—with your peers.

IDEA FOR EXTENDED WRITING

Analyzing a Magazine Ad   Scan some magazines or the Internet for an advertisement that depends predominantly (if not entirely) on visual appeals to market its product. Identify what appears to be the central message of this ad—that is, what it communicates about consumers who purchase, or don't purchase, the product. Then note how the marketers and graphic designers seem to have employed visual elements to persuade readers to this way of thinking about the product. The more knowledge you have about target readers for the source of this ad, the more effectively you'll be able to conjecture about the strategies employed to sell the product. Assume that you will share this analysis in an essay targeted for *Marketing Today* magazine.

Is Team USA's Militaristic Uniform a Problem?

by Paul Achter

When people across the world tune in to the opening ceremony of the 2012 Olympics on Friday, regular TV programming will be set aside for pageantry and pomp.

Amid all the attention to the "Made in China" controversy about Team USA's uniforms, little has been written about their design. But if numerous online slide shows ranking the best and worst of the opening ceremonies uniforms are any indication, the design is what we're most interested in.

Nations did not always wear uniforms in the Olympic Games, and the United States did not adopt a cohesive look until about 1920. Today, however, with huge world-wide audiences and markets at stake, the uniform is a calculated part of each nation's global image. The colors, patterns, silhouettes, lines and shapes of each nation's uniform form a statement about its identity. U.S. designers, for example, have frequently used white cowboy hats in their ensembles.

Team USA's uniforms designed by Ralph Lauren for the opening ceremony of the 2012 Olympics

Designed by Ralph Lauren, Team USA's 2012 opening ceremony uniforms feature berets and navy, brass-buttoned, double-breasted blazers for the men that—even without chevrons, medals or epaulettes—draw clear inspiration from the dress uniforms of the U.S. Army and Navy.

Should the appropriation of military style concern us?

Almost all Olympic uniforms we see today derive from religious or military forms of apparel. Military apparel migrated to civilian life centuries ago, when veterans realized uniforms invited attributions of reliability, discipline and heroism and when various civil institutions used them as a means of regulating groups of people. Men's clothing strongly has been influenced by military looks, and the fashion industry markets "military chic" to women as well.

America's love affair with military looks is especially intense and enduring. And unlike the Vietnam War, when military uniforms were appropriated in anti-war protests, today's military looks are part of a sartorial status quo that subtly affirms a pro-soldier, pro-military message. We know the athletes are not real warriors, of course, but clothing sends powerful messages. Fashion critics long have charged that military fashions are a problem because they aestheticize war and divorce clothes from their true functions and origins. We ought to be wary of efforts to make any aspect of war desirable.

Considering that the U.S. spends more on defense than the next 10 nations combined, some would argue that dressing the Olympians like members of the armed forces during the biggest television event of the year is an arrogant or impolitic choice.

Skeptics might counter that Jamaica's opening ceremony outfits are militaristic, too. But Jamaica's are more clearly sportswear, and in color, pattern and tone, their look is joyful and lighthearted. And Jamaica isn't a global military power.

For most Americans, however, the military style of the 2012 uniforms will raise little concern because we have been encouraged to ignore the countless ways in which military culture is integrated into our society.

Fashion designers promote military styles as cutting edge, but usually refute the notion that the military aesthetic has anything to do with real war. Glitzy Pentagon marketing campaigns, military-backed Hollywood films and first-person shooter video games elevate the cultural status of uniformed troops and encourage us to identify with them. All of these things help maintain a pro-military citizenry.

The 2012 Olympics uniforms are another in a long series of salutes to and affirmations of the American military. They are a product of an inherited, imperial history of clothing, of our particular war-fighting history and of the "support the troops" trope so common in 21st century war rhetoric.

Whether we're comfortable with it or not, the military uniform of Team USA is at least as American as white cowboy hats.

But there are other choices. Historically, roughly half of the U.S. opening ceremonies uniforms have been inspired by sportswear, including the excellent styles in the 2004 and 2008 Summer Games. Maybe it's time to get more creative.

In the next Olympics, how about getting Betsey Johnson to design a uniform that is radically different?

Source: Paul Achter, "Is Team USA's Militaristic Uniform a Problem?"
© Paul Achter. Reprinted by permission.

The Heritage of Berlin Street Art and Graffiti Scene

by Simon Arms

Art critic Emilie Trice has called Berlin "the graffiti Mecca of the urban art world." While few people would argue with her, the Berlin street scene is not as radical as her statement suggests. Street art in Berlin is a big industry. It's not exactly legal, but the city's title of UNESCO's City of Design has kept local authorities from doing much to change what observers call the most "bombed" city in Europe. From the authorities' point of view, the graffiti attracts tourists, and the tourists bring money to a city deep in debt.

This article looks at the development of the Berlin street art scene, from its beginnings as a minor West Berlin movement in the late '70s to its current status: the heritage of a now unified city.

THE DEVELOPMENT OF THE BERLIN GRAFFITI SCENE

After the few East Germans who crossed the Berlin Wall in the '80s blinked and pinched themselves, what do you think was the first thing they saw?

They saw big bubbly letters, spelling out words in German, English and French. They saw political slogans, either carved indelibly into the concrete or sprayed temporarily onto surfaces, commenting not only on the situation in Germany, but on the whole political world: "God Bless," "Concrete Makes You Happy," "Death to Tyrants." As far as they could see, covering every inch of wall, was layer upon layer of zest, life and color.

If they'd crossed in the '60s, however, they'd have been tempted to jump straight back. Abandoned buildings, derelict streets, piles of rubble—the immediate areas around the wall were reminiscent of World War II, and it would take another 10 years for the first communities to settle there.

Even then, those early settlers weren't "real" Berliners, but outsiders: draft resisters, anarchist punks and Turkish migrants. They either opened businesses or formed squats and, with no resistance from the West German government, began turning walls into monuments to their own thoughts and beliefs.

By the end of the '70s, a new wave of graffiti artists, arriving with innovations such as stencils and spray cans, were contributing genuine works of art. Our East German friends would have been staring not just at the defacement of Communist property, but at what graffiti artists had by then claimed as their Mecca.

AFTER THE WALL

After the collapse of the Berlin Wall, the graffiti artists marched straight into East Germany. Mitte, Friedrichshain, Prenzlauer Berg—all of the areas that the military had occupied became a new playground for the Western artists and became a new world for the Eastern artists who joined them. Few doubted that the East Germans' work was weightier. It wasn't that they were better artists, but that they could express—with authority—the one concept close to the hearts of all people now living in the city: what it meant to be free.

One East Berliner to make an impact during this period was "Tower." With his name printed in a variety of colors and fonts on what looked like car stickers, people must have initially mistaken his work for advertising. But the more they saw it—on lamp posts, on post boxes, on trash cans, on fences—the more they understood what he was trying to communicate: Tower, as in the Communist TV tower; Tower, as in the skyscrapers that dominated the skyline of almost every major city—built not for the people who lived there, but for the egos of the people who ran them. Tower's aim was to reclaim the word as a symbol of strength and, in doing so, proclaim that the majority, not the minority, should be shaping the public space.

. . . The critiques below examine the artwork of three Berlin street artists working today—maybe at this very moment. . . . XOOOOX, Alias and Mein Lieber Prost make certain that their work remains in the public eye, constantly.

XOOOOX

"Berlin has the typical street art spots . . . but I like more the classical writing scene, with the huge street bombings and the masses of tags." – XOOOOX

To most people, the letters xoooox represent hugs and kisses. To XOOOOX, they represent symmetry and strength, for no matter how much he rearranges them, they remain a powerful signature that could belong to no one but him.

This tells XOOOOX's public as much about him as they need to know: what you see is what you get. For instance, many people would like to believe that his black and white stencils are an ironic, anti-capitalist statement. But as the artist claims himself, they are a straight homage to the fashion world.

His fascination with fashion began when he discovered a pile of his parents' old fashion magazines in the cellar. He would cut out parts of the pictures, mix them up and stick them on the walls of his room.

Collage still fascinates him, but he says that on the street, stencils are far more practical. At home, he creates a stencil from one of his fashion magazines—including everything from *Harper's* to *Vogue*—and then, armed with his spray paint and stencil, he replicates the image on the streets.

Analysis of XOOOOX's Work

People enjoy XOOOOX's approach because of his objective treatment of his subjects, presenting each model as neither happy nor sad, neither warm nor cold. He even draws one model urinating on the ground; while some might interpret the piece as a sign of arrogance, XOOOOX's signature, flowing from her head like a thought bubble, persuades sensitive observers to judge her on a more humane level. She is, he suggests, just like everyone else.

What sets her apart is her beauty. The artist highlights this by always spraying her image on the grayest and ugliest of concrete walls, amidst the most innocuous of graffiti scrawls. Like the pretty girl sitting alone in a bar, passersby rarely walk past without giving her a second glance.

Overall, XOOOOX's images show an artist with a genuine appreciation of conventional beauty. In a scene that likes to subvert conventions, this must make XOOOOX the most unconventional artist working on Berlin's streets today.

Sample of XOOOOX's work

ALIAS

"My motives are often introverted and emotional, but . . . they brand . . . themselves on the memory of people passing. They are supposed to inspire people to interpret the motives on their own." – Alias

Judging from the number of his pieces, Alias must rarely sleep. His artwork certainly suggests someone at odds with society: black and white pictures of hooded skater types staring at the ground, and young kids unknowingly sitting on live bombs. One senses that something is very wrong with Alias' world.

Alias left school early and moved to Hamburg, a city with its own impressive array of street artists. Developing his skill there to an advanced level, he moved on to Berlin, where people soon recognized his work as among the best in the city.

Analysis of Alias' Work

Alias' dark and somber images make him the city's most serious artist. He stencils each of his pictures with great care, and always places them in a spot that best communicates his message. His picture of a man asking people to keep his identity a

Sample of Alias' work

secret is stuck not on the wall of a busy thoroughfare, but at the bottom edge of a staircase. It gives the impression that, beyond the playfulness, he genuinely wants to keep his identity a secret.

Alias' signature then is essential to understanding his work. The picture of a hooded teenager with a blank face communicates a need to give outsiders a voice. The irony is that the one person humane enough to give them that voice, a street artist, has to remain anonymous. That, Alias suggests, is his reward for daring to question society.

MEIN LIEBER PROST

"All that's come out is a result of my happiness, my courage, my fantasies or my disappointments. All great artists are great *not* for their technique, but their passion." – Mein Lieber Prost

Most people will walk by graffiti without even noticing it. It hides in the corners of doorways and blends in with its surroundings. Prost's characters, however, point and laugh directly at passersby. The characters are often a simple black outline. On occasion, Prost takes the time to fill the characters in with red, white and black. Whatever the method, he places his artwork in just about any free spot he can find: side streets, high streets, advertisements, doorways, signs. Nowhere in the city is safe.

And yet the public knows little about the artist himself. For legal reasons, he safeguards his identity. At a more artistic level, the anonymity enables him to present the smiley faces, and not himself, as the essence of his work.

Analysis of Mein Lieber Prost's Work

It's easy to miss the point of Prost's smiley faces. On the surface, they look like the simple one-minute doodles of a high-school student. And the artist probably drew them in half that time. But that simplicity is what makes Prost's faces so interesting, for two reasons.

First, it allows Prost to put his images in places that few other artists would dare to go. Alias, for example, needs time to place and

Sample of Mein Lieber Prost's work

spray his images and, therefore, works in more secluded spots to decrease the chances of getting caught. Prost has only to draw a quick outline, and then he's finished. In fact, he has now drawn so many that he no longer needs to leave his signature: his work, rather than his name, has become his identity.

Secondly, the artist positions his characters to look like they are taking in their surroundings, laughing aloud at something happening right at that moment. It is natural, then, on seeing Prost's characters pointing at them, for people to wonder what the joke is, asking themselves: is it me? Each character forces passersby to question their surroundings and (hopefully, if they don't want to leave paranoid) to find a satisfactory answer.

MOVING INTO THE MAINSTREAM

Visitors to Berlin tend to ask the same question: is the street art legal? It is a difficult question for Berliners to answer. In central parts of the city at least, there is variously so much and so little criticism directed at it that no one quite knows. Head of the anti-graffiti team, Chief Detective Marko Moritz, insists, however, that the city views graffiti as a crime.

In an interview with the local newspaper, he states that his team's main goal is to catch the tagging crews whose work has its roots not in art, but in gang culture. In what he calls bombings, crews will spray whole trains and sometimes buildings with their signatures and colors. But Moritz is concerned not only with the defacement of public property; some crews, he claims, are starting to carry firearms.

Their behavior, while disturbing, is a byproduct of the authorities' attempt to turn the street art scene into an industry. When UNESCO named Berlin as a City of Design, few people doubted that the thriving street art scene was partly responsible. Local businesses and even local authorities hired artists to paint murals on the fronts of their buildings. Most famously, on a wall in Kreuzberg, the artist Blu painted two men trying to rip each other's masks off—symbolizing, he claims, Berlin's struggles during its first few years of reunification.

Today, such work has made the street art a tourist attraction. Kunsthaus Tacheles, once an artists' squat and still a focal point of the scene, holds disco nights downstairs and sells urban art books upstairs—its bar is as expensive as anywhere in the city. Artists such as XOOOOX, Mein Lieber Prost and Alias have started to exhibit and sell in galleries. They still work on the street, but they are no longer impoverished artists—if they ever were. They can afford to travel and work in countries across the world.

While these artists believe that street art needs to appeal to a wider audience, the local, more traditional artists, such as the tagging crews, disagree. They argue that street art derives its power from being on the margins of society; only from the outside can they address problems within it. That difference of opinion is opening a space in the scene that can be filled only by the mainstream. In the next few years, street art has the potential to become a social movement as inclusive as anything from the '50s and '60s.

Source: Simon Arms, "The Heritage of Berlin Street Art and Graffiti Scene," *Smashing Magazine,* July 13, 2011. Copyright © 2011. Reprinted by permission of Simon Arms and *Smashing Magazine.*

FOR DISCUSSION

1. What is the thesis for each of the visual analyses included at the end of this chapter?
2. What is the interpretive lens employed in each article, and what passages speak directly to the act of interpreting the image(s) under consideration?
3. Which of these articles is most effective at helping you "see" the object being analyzed through the language it uses? Why?
4. Think about the most striking image that you've come across lately. Why was it so striking? How might strategies in the above visual analyses help you make sense of that image?
5. In what ways and to what communicative advantage does your major field of study (or one you're thinking about pursuing) employ visual texts? How would communication in that field be hindered without them?

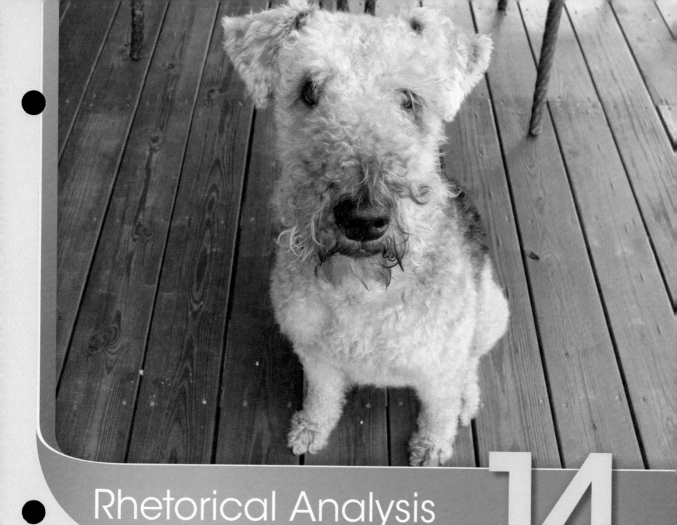

Rhetorical Analysis

14

Few people can look at images of sweet and cuddly animals without feeling a tug at their heartstrings. Of course, the tug feels more like a rip if the pictured animals have been abused. The American Society for the Prevention of Cruelty to Animals (ASPCA) depends on such common emotional reactions when seeking donations for their cause—as is apparent in their long-running public service announcement (PSA) featuring singer Sarah McLachlan. If you haven't seen this PSA, view it on YouTube, and consider the following questions: Who is the primary audience? What specific appeals does it employ? How effective would those appeals be in light of the target audience and purpose and why? What other persuasive strategies does it employ? Questions such as these—which explore how and to what effect a text communicates a given message to its intended audience—are the driving force of a genre referred to as *rhetorical analysis,* the focus of this chapter.

"It's not just *what* you say; it's *how* you say it." As this common adage suggests, the content of a message and the manner in which that message is presented are tightly interlinked. For example, personal criticism is always a bit hard to take, but it stings all the more when it's delivered in a sarcastic tone. On the other hand, a bit of bad news may sit a little easier if it comes sandwiched between bits of good news. Such relationships between content and presentation provide the subject matter for **rhetorical analysis,** a genre that interprets what another author has to say in a given text and how he or she goes about saying it. More specifically, a rhetorical analysis characterizes various elements of a composition and the manner in which they work together to convey the author's purpose to his or her audience.

Rhetorical analyses are popular assignments in composition courses because they reveal *how* successful writers communicate. The benefits of studying and practicing this genre should be obvious, then, when considering that, to a large extent, the ability to communicate effectively defines success in almost every discipline. Whether you want to be a politician, a teacher, a rock star, or a business CEO, being alert to the subtleties of language, its capacity to be manipulated, and the ways it can influence the thinking and behavior of others will increase your potential for success. This heightened awareness can help you communicate to your best advantage, protect you against communications that could *dis*advantage you, and prepare you to judge the validity of claims made in various rhetorical situations you'll encounter.

Distinguishing Features of a Rhetorical Analysis

MYTH

"Rhetoric implies deception."

Thanks largely to modern political discourse, you may associate the term *rhetoric* with the use of fancy words that are empty of any substance or with attempts to deliberately mislead people. In specialized contexts (such as writing courses, where language is the object of study), the term *rhetoric* is regarded as neutral. It simply describes how discourse works and how it goes about pursuing its goals. Adopting this neutral perspective presents opportunities for thought and discussion about uses of language that might escape you if you are concentrating only on finding fault with a text.

REALITY

Any text can be analyzed rhetorically, even those in media other than words, such as paintings, body language, and clothing. Nevertheless, because *rhetoric* is so closely identified with the act of observing all "the available means of persuasion" (Aristotle 37), a rhetorical analysis is particularly revealing in response to texts that attempt to sway readers' feelings, convince them to think a certain way, or move them to action.

As is typical of any analysis, a rhetorical analysis accomplishes its objective by applying an interpretive lens—in particular, the components of a rhetorical situation (defined in Chapter 3). Applying this lens might be compared to viewing light that's been filtered through a prism, with each color cast by the prism representing a different element of the rhetorical situation (see Figure 14.1).

In Figure 14.1, the various cells constituting the interpretive lens represent elements of the rhetorical situation and, therefore, potential angles for your analysis. You'll note that the central elements of a rhetorical analysis are topic, purpose, and audience. After all, it's difficult to gauge the effect of a text on a particular

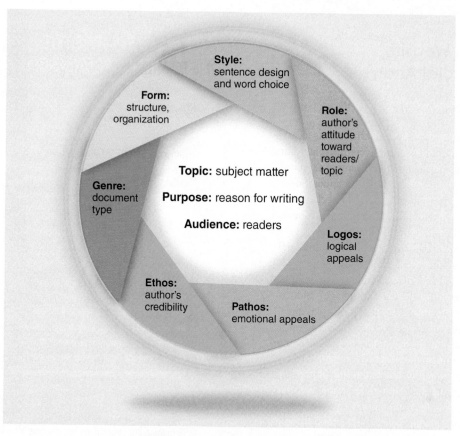

Figure 14.1 **Interpretive lens for a rhetorical analysis.** Applying an interpretive lens for a rhetorical analysis might be compared to viewing light that's been filtered through a prism. Each of the colored sections in the lens pictured here constitutes a different element of the rhetorical situation and a potential angle for your analysis.

audience if you don't have some specific information about its members and if you don't understand the author's purpose in writing to them. While these three elements are essential to rhetorical analysis, the importance of the remaining elements (the outer cells in Figure 14.1) will vary from text to text depending on the extent to which the author emphasizes them.

Consider the rhetorical analysis in the Look Inside box on the next page. In this student essay written for a first-year composition course, the author comments on the public service announcement (PSA) discussed at the beginning of this chapter. After an introduction that describes the purpose of the ASPCA and a few body paragraphs analyzing its website, the author provides an analysis of the organization's most famous ad, focusing on its appeals to credibility (ethos), emotion (pathos), and reason or logic (logos). The Look Inside excerpt preserves large portions of that ad analysis.

From "ASPCA Website and Commercial Analysis"

by a First-Year Composition Student

. . . The ASPCA also runs television advertisements to promote its cause; the most famous of these commercials stars Sarah McLachlan. This particular advertisement exercises ethos through the use of a celebrity as the organization's spokesperson. Because viewers tend to react to celebrities' words more than they react to those of an unknown speaker, they may be more willing to donate to the ASPCA if a famous person encourages them to do so. The commercial also features the famous and melancholy song by McLachlan, "Angel." This heart-wrenching song contains lyrics such as "you are pulled from the wreckage" and "you're in the arms of the angel." As the song is playing, the viewer sees pictures and videos of animals being rescued and hurt pets that may or may not recover. The combination of the song and the pictures appeals to pathos and makes viewers feel emotionally attached to the animals on the screen. After watching the commercial, many feel that donating to the ASPCA is their obligation.

Some of Sarah McLachlan's words contribute to the use of emotions to encourage people to join the ASPCA's cause. After listing a statistic stating the number of animals that had been rescued in the previous year, McLachlan says, "For hundreds of others, help came too late." When viewers hear this statement and simultaneously view pictures of hurt animals, they realize the devastating effects of animal abuse. McLachlan then challenges the audience to "be an angel" for an animal in need. The commercial has tugged on viewers' emotions so much by this point that many people now feel absolutely obligated to make a donation.

This commercial also employs logos to encourage people to join the fight against animal cruelty. The commercial intersperses facts and statistics about animal cruelty among the pictures and videos of abused animals. One statistic states "every single hour, an animal is violently abused." These facts make the existence of animal abuse more of a reality for some viewers. After viewing the statistics, the audience may think that donating to the ASPCA is more logical. . . . The advertisement does not include any extra, unnecessary

A LOOK INSIDE:
RHETORICAL ANALYSIS

The author begins her analysis of the PSA with a discussion of ethos, which is rooted in the spokesperson's status as a celebrity.

The author brings plenty of textual evidence to support her claim about the pathos of the ad, with a focus on Sarah McLachlan's haunting song "Angel," which plays in the background as photos of abused animals flash across the screen.

Here the author transitions into analysis of the PSA's overt appeal to emotion (pathos). A direct statement of the focus occurs near the end of the paragraph.

In this paragraph, the author concentrates on logos, noting the manner and impact of the PSA's appeals to reason through numbers.

information—only the information necessary for the viewer to join the cause. Sarah McLachlan's statement that "just sixty cents a day can save the life of an animal" also appeals to the listener's logos by explaining the relative ease of saving an animal's life.

The conclusion of the piece featured above reasserts the purpose of the analysis—to demonstrate how specific elements of the PSA combine to evoke sympathy for the animals and to encourage donations to help save them. In keeping with the emotional nature of the ad (which some have criticized for being over-wrought), this rhetorical analysis emphasizes pathos. Additionally, it appeals to readers' sense of credibility (ethos) as it considers the influence of McLachlan's celebrity, and it appeals to their sense of reason with reference to statistics about the extent of animal abuse and the ASPCA's success at rescuing mistreated and abandoned pets.

Processes for Composing a Rhetorical Analysis

It's easy to become derailed when composing a rhetorical analysis because of the temptation to react to the values and opinions expressed by the author of the piece you're analyzing. Remember, though, that your purpose is to comment on *how* that document attempts to meet its apparent goals—not to express agreement or dis-agreement with its thesis. To make certain you stay on track, you'll probably want to check yourself on this point multiple times as you move through the processes discussed in the next several paragraphs.

Invention toward First Insight

In the context of rhetorical analysis, invention begins with your very first reading of the text you'll be analyzing. During your early encounters with that text, you'll need to identify the author's controlling idea, purpose, and target audience, as well as compelling communicative strategies that seem ripe for analysis. Marking these observations directly in the text by underlining, highlighting, or writing in the mar-gins (also known as **annotating**) will prove helpful later when you are trying to decide on a focus for your analysis.

Preparation through Research

After reading the article for initial insights about its rhetorical strategies, you'll probably need to conduct some additional research that can add depth to your analysis. For example, this would be a good time to follow up on any texts the article cites so you can gain a specific sense of what they said and can better judge the article's treatment of them. At this point you will also want to pay more attention to the target audience for the text about which you're writing. The greater the understanding you have of the target audience's values and expectations, the greater your potential is for analyzing the text's capacity for reaching that audience. You can increase this understanding by studying the forum in which the speech is delivered or the article is published. Reviews and product descriptions like the one in Figure 14.2 (many of which are available online) are good places to start.

You can see in Figure 14.2 that even this brief excerpt not only pinpoints the age range of *Rolling Stone*'s target readers but also provides insight regarding their special interests and the kinds of activities they enjoy. By thinking critically about this information and further investigating the content, presentation, and political leanings of *Rolling Stone,* you could infer specific qualities of its readers and be able to project how rhetorical elements in one or more of its articles would likely affect them.

Rolling Stone Product Description

Rolling Stone magazine is a cultural icon. It's the number one pop culture reference point for 13 million young adults. In addition to its authoritative position in music, *Rolling Stone*'s sphere of influence reaches into entertainment, movies, television, technology, and national affairs. *Rolling Stone* covers everything that's important, trend-setting, and newsworthy to the thought leaders among young adults.

What You Can Expect in Each Issue:

Rock & Roll: The latest music news on those who continue to rock us

Smoking Section: In-depth, exclusive looks at the rock star lifestyle

Random Notes: A photo collage of who's who in the music biz, and what they're up to

Breaking: A look at the hottest new artists, or old artists with something new

Charts: Billboard's top ten, iTunes top ten, local favorites, and the top 40 albums at issue release

Reviews: Star-rated reviews of new releases, across all media

Rolling Stone Product Description. Advertisement. *Charity Buzz,* 27 Apr. 2010, www.charitybuzz.com/catalog_items/206809.

Figure 14.2 **Detailed profile of *Rolling Stone* magazine**

Invention toward More Focused Insight

Once you have read the article you are analyzing several times and annotated it with an eye toward specifics of the rhetorical situation, you will be prepared to focus your analysis. Your primary objective is to highlight the rhetorical elements that you've determined to be crucial to the author's agenda, particularly those that tend to dominate the text or those that seem somehow closely related to one another. Consider Figure 14.3, which outlines strategies for focusing two different rhetorical analyses, each addressing a different hypothetical article on drunk-driving legislation and therefore emphasizing different rhetorical elements. As Figure 14.3 clarifies, thinking about dominant rhetorical elements, or about relationships between interdependent elements, will help lead you toward a thesis for your analysis.

Strategies for Drafting

When composing the introductory section of your rhetorical analysis (which might consist of several paragraphs), you should keep several objectives in mind. At some point, you need to familiarize readers with the text you're analyzing, ordinarily through a brief summary of it (for a discussion of summarizing, see Chapter 21). This is a crucial component of the introductory section since those who will be reading your analysis may not be familiar with the document being analyzed or may not have recently read it. Also relatively early in your analysis, you'll want to identify why the author is writing and to whom. If you don't, readers will have difficulty understanding your later interpretive claims. Whatever rhetorical elements the author is capitalizing on and however he or she does so, your claims about them will center on a pattern or theme (e.g., the use of vivid narratives to evoke emotion, strategies used to establish a conversational style) that will lead to a thesis for your analysis.

As for the body of your essay, the pattern(s) or theme(s) identified in your thesis will guide the flow of your analysis. Remember that, as you were preparing for that analysis, reading the text over and over, you were "breaking it down," identifying

Strategy	Rhetorical Analysis 1	Rhetorical Analysis 2
Locate the purpose of the text being analyzed.	To argue for stricter DUI laws	To argue for stricter DUI laws
Note dominant patterns of rhetorical appeals and strategies.	• Statistics regarding the number of deaths caused annually in the United States by drunk drivers • Case studies about repeat offenders • Results of experiments showing the extent to which even relatively low blood alcohol content affects physical and mental ability	• A lengthy narrative, consuming the introductory and body paragraphs of the document, that vividly re-creates the pain and suffering of the victims in a drunk-driving accident • A single concluding paragraph that suggests more severe consequences for those who drink and drive
Compose a thesis for your analysis.	"The author argues on the basis of facts and figures from numerous reliable sources, rendering the call for stricter DUI laws difficult to deny."	"The primary vehicle for the author's argument is a detailed, heart-wrenching narrative that is certain to move readers toward support of stricter drunk-driving legislation."

Figure 14.3 Strategies for focusing a rhetorical analysis

parts of the whole and thinking about how they contributed to that whole. Now is the time to explain the relationships you discovered to your intended readers. To convince readers that your interpretive claims are reasonable, you will need to illustrate them with concrete examples from the text and with sound reasoning about why you believe those examples will have the effect you anticipate.

When you turn to the conclusion of your rhetorical analysis, you'll want to reflect on the patterns or themes demonstrated in the body of your paper and reemphasize how the author's most significant rhetorical moves combined to achieve the objectives that you claimed they did. In addition, if your research for this project gave you a sense of the text's role in the larger conversation about its subject matter, or if the text has become famous or infamous for some reason, you may want to share that information. However you shape your conclusion, remember that a rhetorical analysis does not require you to agree or disagree with the author's thesis; your purpose is to analyze how the text works from a rhetorical perspective.

Revision and Editing

Questions for Revising

- Does my analysis portray the text being analyzed in a fair manner?
- Is my analysis appropriately geared toward my target audience?
- Do my introductory paragraphs establish an analytical focus that speaks to relationships between rhetorical elements in the text I'm analyzing?
- Have I provided a brief summary of the text somewhere in the introductory section?
- Have I illustrated my analytical claims with textual features appropriate to those claims?
- Does my essay follow some logical sequence aided by transitions that connect my ideas?
- Does my conclusion leave readers with a global sense of how the text functions in carrying the author's purpose to the intended readers?

Questions for Editing

- Are all documents I've referenced in my analysis properly cited?
- Is my analysis free of spelling, punctuation, and usage errors?

Transfer to Other Writing Situations

The benefits of engaging in formal rhetorical analysis are cyclical—that is, the more you read with an analytical eye, the better writer you will become, and the more you write about rhetorical strategies, the more incisive your critical-reading skills will become. For this reason, probably more than any other genre you'll write for your composition class, a rhetorical analysis helps develop capabilities that you will use in every other course you take and in any profession you might be planning to pursue. For some specifics, consider Figure 14.4, which indicates how rhetorical analysis might be applied in the context of different careers. Even if the diverse purposes for rhetorical analysis don't lead to formal essays, the skills required for each represent a type of critical thinking that is crucial to various methods of communication.

Academia	Public Relations	Politics
Professors weigh in on other professors' publications to advance scholarship (e.g., suggesting that certain claims are not appropriately qualified or that placing emphasis on certain observations over others skews impressions of a study's results).	Public relations personnel comb articles about the people or companies they represent with the intent of countering negative press.	Politicians analyze their opponents' rhetoric for gaps in logic, inconsistencies, and misstatements so they can respond in ways that elevate their own image or that of their political party.

Figure 14.4 Uses for rhetorical analysis in different disciplines

ACTIVITY

Considering the Rhetoric of Fashion Human beings communicate through various media, many of them visual in nature, such as clothing. Locate a picture (like the one of Lady Gaga in Figure 14.5) that depicts someone who is clearly sending a message through his or her fashion choices. Using whatever rhetorical elements or appeals seem most applicable, analyze this person's fashion statement.

IDEA FOR EXTENDED WRITING

Figure 14.5 Lady Gaga using fashion to make a "statement"

Rhetorically Analyzing a Published Essay Think of a document you recently read that really frustrated you, angered you, made you want to cry, excited you, motivated you to take action, made you proud to be a part of something, caused you to admire somebody or some institution, or caused you to view something differently than you viewed it before. (If you can't remember an article that had a strong impact on you, search for one relevant to an issue that really interests you.) Once you have a copy of that article in hand, read it again (and again), paying attention not only to what the author said about the topic but also to the way he or she said it. Apply the tools of rhetorical analysis to help you understand how the author appears to use rhetorical elements and appeals to influence his or her intended audience. Share your conclusions in a formal rhetorical analysis targeted for members of that audience.

A More Perfect Union

Delivered by Senator Barack Obama on March 18, 2008

"We the people, in order to form a more perfect union."

Two hundred and twenty one years ago, in a hall that still stands across the street, a group of men gathered and, with these simple words, launched America's improbable experiment in democracy. Farmers and scholars; statesmen and patriots who had traveled across an ocean to escape tyranny and persecution finally made real their declaration of independence at a Philadelphia convention that lasted through the spring of 1787.

The document they produced was eventually signed but ultimately unfinished. It was stained by this nation's original sin of slavery, a question that divided the colonies and brought the convention to a stalemate until the founders chose to allow the slave trade to continue for at least twenty more years, and to leave any final resolution to future generations. . . .

And yet words on a parchment would not be enough to deliver slaves from bondage, or provide men and women of every color and creed their full rights and obligations as citizens of the United States. What would be needed were Americans in successive generations who were willing to do their part—through protests and struggle, on the streets and in the courts, through a civil war and civil disobedience and always at great risk—to narrow that gap between the promise of our ideals and the reality of their time.

This was one of the tasks we set forth at the beginning of this campaign—to continue the long march of those who came before us, a march for a more just, more equal, more free, more caring and more prosperous America. I chose to run for the presidency at this moment in history because I believe deeply that we cannot solve the challenges of our time unless we solve them together—unless we perfect our union by understanding that we may have different stories, but we hold common hopes; that we may not look the same and we may not have come from the same place, but we all want to move in the same direction—towards a better future for our children and our grandchildren.

This belief comes from my unyielding faith in the decency and generosity of the American people. But it also comes from my own American story.

I am the son of a black man from Kenya and a white woman from Kansas. I was raised with the help of a white grandfather who survived a Depression to serve in Patton's Army during World War II and a white grandmother who worked on a bomber assembly line at Fort Leavenworth while he was overseas. I've gone to some of the best schools in America and lived in one of the world's poorest nations. I am married to a black American who carries within her the blood of slaves and slaveowners—an inheritance we pass on to our two precious daughters. I have brothers, sisters, nieces, nephews, uncles and cousins, of every race and every hue, scattered across three continents, and for as long as I live, I will never forget that in no other country on Earth is my story even possible.

It's a story that hasn't made me the most conventional candidate. But it is a story that has seared into my genetic makeup the idea that this nation is more than the sum of its parts—that out of many, we are truly one. . . .

This is not to say that race has not been an issue in the campaign. At various stages in the campaign, some commentators have deemed me either "too black" or "not black enough." We saw racial tensions bubble to the surface during the week before the South Carolina primary. The press has scoured every exit poll for the latest evidence of racial polarization, not just in terms of white and black, but black and brown as well.

And yet, it has only been in the last couple of weeks that the discussion of race in this campaign has taken a particularly divisive turn.

On one end of the spectrum, we've heard the implication that my candidacy is somehow an exercise in affirmative action; that it's based solely on the desire of wide-eyed liberals to purchase racial reconciliation on the cheap. On the other end, we've heard my former pastor, Reverend Jeremiah Wright, use incendiary language to express views that have the potential not only to widen the racial divide, but views that denigrate both the greatness and the goodness of our nation; that rightly offend white and black alike. . . .

Reverend Wright's comments were not only wrong but divisive, divisive at a time when we need unity; racially charged at a time when we need to come together to solve a set of monumental problems. . . .

And I confess that if all that I knew of Reverend Wright were the snippets of those sermons that have run in an endless loop on the television and YouTube, or if Trinity United Church of Christ conformed to the caricatures being peddled by some commentators, there is no doubt that I would react in much the same way.

But the truth is, that isn't all that I know of the man. The man I met more than twenty years ago is a man who helped introduce me to my Christian faith, a man who spoke to me about our obligations to love one another; to care for the sick and lift up the poor.

He is a man who served his country as a U.S. Marine; who has studied and lectured at some of the finest universities and seminaries in the country, and who for over thirty years led a church that serves the community by doing God's work here on Earth—by housing the homeless, ministering to the needy, providing day care services and scholarships and prison ministries, and reaching out to those suffering from HIV/AIDS. . . .

Like other predominantly black churches across the country, Trinity embodies the black community in its entirety—the doctor and the welfare mom, the model student and the former gang-banger. Like other black churches, Trinity's services are full of raucous laughter and sometimes bawdy humor. They are full of dancing, clapping, screaming and shouting that may seem jarring to the untrained ear. The church contains in full the kindness and cruelty, the fierce intelligence and the shocking ignorance, the struggles and successes, the love and yes, the bitterness and bias that make up the black experience in America.

And this helps explain, perhaps, my relationship with Reverend Wright. As imperfect as he may be, he has been like family to me. . . .

I can no more disown him than I can disown the black community. I can no more disown him than I can my white grandmother—a woman who helped raise me, a woman who sacrificed again and again for me, a woman who loves me as much as she loves anything in this world, but a woman who once confessed her fear of black men who passed by her on the street, and who on more than one occasion has uttered racial or ethnic stereotypes that made me cringe.

These people are a part of me. And they are a part of America, this country that I love. . . .

But race is an issue that I believe this nation cannot afford to ignore right now. . . .

The fact is that the comments that have been made and the issues that have surfaced over the last few weeks reflect the complexities of race in this country that we've never really worked through—a part of our union that we have yet to perfect. . . .

Understanding this reality requires a reminder of how we arrived at this point. As William Faulkner once wrote, "The past isn't dead and buried. In fact, it isn't even past." We do not need to recite here the history of racial injustice in this country. But we do need to remind ourselves that so many of the disparities that exist in the African-American community today can be directly traced to inequalities passed on from an earlier generation that suffered under the brutal legacy of slavery and Jim Crow.

Segregated schools were, and are, inferior schools; we still haven't fixed them, fifty years after Brown v. Board of Education, and the inferior education they provided, then and now, helps explain the pervasive achievement gap between today's black and white students.

Legalized discrimination—where blacks were prevented, often through violence, from owning property, or loans were not granted to African-American business owners, or black homeowners could not access FHA mortgages, or blacks were excluded from unions, or the police force, or fire departments—meant that black families could not amass any meaningful wealth to bequeath to future generations. That history helps explain the wealth and income gap between black and white, and the concentrated pockets of poverty that persist in so many of today's urban and rural communities.

A lack of economic opportunity among black men, and the shame and frustration that came from not being able to provide for one's family, contributed to the erosion of black families—a problem that welfare policies for many years may have worsened. And the lack of basic services in so many urban black neighborhoods—parks for kids to play in, police walking the beat, regular garbage pick-up and building code enforcement—all helped create a cycle of violence, blight and neglect that continue to haunt us.

This is the reality in which Reverend Wright and other African-Americans of his generation grew up. They came of age in the late fifties and early sixties, a time when segregation was still the law of the land and opportunity was systematically constricted. What's remarkable is not how many failed in the face of discrimination, but rather how many men and women overcame the odds; how many were able to make a way out of no way for those like me who would come after them.

But for all those who scratched and clawed their way to get a piece of the American Dream, there were many who didn't make it—those who were ultimately defeated, in one way or another, by discrimination. That legacy of defeat was passed on to future generations—those young men and increasingly young women who we see standing on street corners or languishing in our prisons, without hope or prospects for the future. Even for those blacks who did make it, questions of race, and racism, continue to define their worldview in fundamental ways. For the men and women of Reverend Wright's generation, the memories of humiliation and doubt and fear have not gone away; nor has the anger and the bitterness of those years. That anger may not get expressed in public, in front of white co-workers or white friends. But it does find voice in the barbershop or around the kitchen table. At times, that anger is exploited by politicians, to gin up votes along racial lines, or to make up for a politician's own failings. . . .

In fact, a similar anger exists within segments of the white community. Most working and middle-class white Americans don't feel that they have been particularly privileged by their race. Their experience is the immigrant experience—as far as they're concerned, no one's handed them anything, they've built it from scratch. They've worked hard all their lives, many times only to see their jobs shipped overseas or their pension dumped after a lifetime of labor. They are anxious about their futures, and feel their dreams slipping away; in an era of stagnant wages and global competition, opportunity comes to be seen as a zero sum game, in which your dreams come at my expense. So when they are told to bus their children to a school across town; when they hear that an African American is getting an advantage in landing a good job or a spot in a good college because of an injustice that they themselves never committed; when they're told that their fears about crime in urban neighborhoods are somehow prejudiced, resentment builds over time.

Like the anger within the black community, these resentments aren't always expressed in polite company. But they have helped shape the political landscape for at least a generation. Anger over welfare and affirmative action helped forge the Reagan Coalition. Politicians routinely exploited fears of crime for their own electoral ends. Talk show hosts and conservative commentators built entire careers unmasking bogus claims of racism while dismissing legitimate discussions of racial injustice and inequality as mere political correctness or reverse racism.

Just as black anger often proved counterproductive, so have these white resentments distracted attention from the real culprits of the middle-class squeeze—a corporate culture rife with inside dealing, questionable accounting practices, and short-term greed; a Washington dominated by lobbyists and special interests; economic policies that favor the few over the many. And yet, to wish away the resentments of white Americans, to label them as misguided or even racist, without recognizing they are grounded in legitimate concerns—this too widens the racial divide, and blocks the path to understanding.

This is where we are right now. It's a racial stalemate we've been stuck in for years. Contrary to the claims of some of my critics, black and white, I have never been so naïve as to believe that we can get beyond our racial divisions in a single election cycle, or with a single candidacy—particularly a candidacy as imperfect as my own.

But I have asserted a firm conviction—a conviction rooted in my faith in God and my faith in the American people—that working together we can move beyond some of our old racial wounds, and that in fact we have no choice if we are to continue on the path of a more perfect union.

For the African-American community, that path means embracing the burdens of our past without becoming victims of our past. It means continuing to insist on a full measure of justice in every aspect of American life. But it also means binding our particular grievances—for better health care, and better schools, and better jobs—to the larger aspirations of all Americans—the white woman struggling to break the glass ceiling, the white man who's been laid off, the immigrant trying to feed his family. And it means taking full responsibility for own lives—by demanding more from our fathers, and spending more time with our children, and reading to them, and teaching them that while they may face challenges and discrimination in their own lives, they must never succumb to despair or cynicism; they must always believe that they can write their own destiny. . . .

The profound mistake of Reverend Wright's sermons is not that he spoke about racism in our society. It's that he spoke as if our society was static; as if no progress has been made; as if this country—a country that has made it possible for one of his own members to run for the highest office in the land and build a coalition of white and black, Latino and Asian, rich and poor, young and old—is still irrevocably bound to a tragic past. But what we know—what we have seen—is that America can change. That is the true genius of this nation. What we have already achieved gives us hope—the audacity to hope—for what we can and must achieve tomorrow.

In the white community, the path to a more perfect union means acknowledging that what ails the African-American community does not just exist in the minds of black people; that the legacy of discrimination—and current incidents of discrimination, while less overt than in the past—are real and must be addressed. . . . It requires all Americans to realize that your dreams do not have to come at the expense of my dreams; that investing in the health, welfare, and education of black and brown and white children will ultimately help all of America prosper.

In the end, then, what is called for is nothing more, and nothing less, than what all the world's great religions demand—that we do unto others as we would have them do unto us. Let us be our brother's keeper, Scripture tells us. Let us be our sister's keeper. Let us find that common stake we all have in one another, and let our politics reflect that spirit as well. . . .

READINGS

There is one story in particular that I'd like to leave you with today—a story I told when I had the great honor of speaking on Dr. King's birthday at his home church, Ebenezer Baptist, in Atlanta.

There is a young, twenty-three year old white woman named Ashley Baia who organized for our campaign in Florence, South Carolina. She had been working to organize a mostly African-American community since the beginning of this campaign, and one day she was at a roundtable discussion where everyone went around telling their story and why they were there.

And Ashley said that when she was nine years old, her mother got cancer. And because she had to miss days of work, she was let go and lost her health care. They had to file for bankruptcy, and that's when Ashley decided that she had to do something to help her mom.

She knew that food was one of their most expensive costs, and so Ashley convinced her mother that what she really liked and really wanted to eat more than anything else was mustard and relish sandwiches. Because that was the cheapest way to eat.

She did this for a year until her mom got better, and she told everyone at the roundtable that the reason she joined our campaign was so that she could help the millions of other children in the country who want and need to help their parents too.

Now Ashley might have made a different choice. Perhaps somebody told her along the way that the source of her mother's problems were blacks who were on welfare and too lazy to work, or Hispanics who were coming into the country illegally. But she didn't. She sought out allies in her fight against injustice.

Anyway, Ashley finishes her story and then goes around the room and asks everyone else why they're supporting the campaign. They all have different stories and reasons. Many bring up a specific issue. And finally they come to this elderly black man who's been sitting there quietly the entire time. And Ashley asks him why he's there. And he does not bring up a specific issue. He does not say health care or the economy. He does not say education or the war. He does not say that he was there because of Barack Obama. He simply says to everyone in the room, "I am here because of Ashley."

"I'm here because of Ashley." By itself, that single moment of recognition between that young white girl and that old black man is not enough. It is not enough to give health care to the sick, or jobs to the jobless, or education to our children.

But it is where we start. It is where our union grows stronger. And as so many generations have come to realize over the course of the two-hundred and twenty one years since a band of patriots signed that document in Philadelphia, that is where the perfection begins.

Source: Sen. Barack Obama, "A More Perfect Union" (speech, Philadelphia, PA, March 18, 2008).

Why It Worked: A Rhetorical Analysis of Obama's Speech on Race

by Roy Peter Clark

More than a century ago, scholar and journalist W. E. B. DuBois wrote a single paragraph about how race is experienced in America. I have learned more from those 112 words than from most book-length studies of the subject:

> After the Egyptian and Indian, the Greek and Roman, the Teuton and Mongolian, the Negro is a sort of seventh son, born with a veil, and gifted with second-sight in this American world, a world which yields him no true self-consciousness, but only lets him see himself through the revelation of the other world. It is a peculiar sensation, this double-consciousness, this sense of always looking at one's self through the eyes of others, of measuring one's soul by the tape of a world that looks on in amused contempt and pity. One ever feels his two-ness—an American, a Negro; two souls, two thoughts, two unreconciled strivings; two warring ideals in one dark body, whose dogged strength alone keeps it from being torn asunder.

Much has been said about the power and brilliance of Barack Obama's March 18 speech on race, even by some of his detractors. The focus has been on the orator's willingness to say things in public about race that are rarely spoken at all, even in private, and his expressed desire to move the country to a new and better place. There has also been attention to the immediate purpose of the speech, which was to reassure white voters that they had nothing to fear from the congregant of a fiery African-American pastor, the Rev. Jeremiah Wright.

Amid all the commentary, I have yet to see an X-Ray reading of the text that would make visible the rhetorical strategies that the orator and authors used so effectively. When received in the ear, these effects breeze through us like a harmonious song. When inspected with the eye, these moves become more apparent, like reading a piece of sheet music for a difficult song and finally recognizing the chord changes.

Such analysis, while interesting in itself, might be little more than a scholarly curiosity if we were not so concerned with the language issues of political discourse. The popular opinion is that our current president, though plain spoken, is clumsy with language. Fair or not, this perception has produced a hope that our next president will be a more powerful communicator, a Kennedy or Reagan, perhaps, who can use language less as a way to signal ideology and more as a means to bring the disparate parts of the

READINGS

nation together. Journalists need to pay closer attention to political language than ever before.

Like most memorable pieces of oratory, Obama's speech sounds better than it reads. We have no way of knowing if that was true of Lincoln's Gettysburg Address, but it is certainly true of Dr. King's "I Have a Dream" speech. If you doubt this assertion, test it out. Read the speech and then experience it in its original setting recited by his soulful voice.

The effectiveness of Obama's speech rests upon four related rhetorical strategies:

1. The power of allusion and its patriotic associations.
2. The oratorical resonance of parallel constructions.
3. The "two-ness" of the texture, to use DuBois's useful term.
4. His ability to include himself as a character in a narrative about race.

ALLUSION

Part of what made Dr. King's speech resonate, not just for black people, but for some whites, was its framing of racial equality in familiar patriotic terms: "This will be the day when all of God's children will be able to sing with new meaning, 'My country 'tis of thee, sweet land of liberty of thee I sing. Land where my fathers died, land of the pilgrim's pride, from every mountainside, let freedom ring.'" What follows, of course, is King's great litany of iconic topography that carries listeners across the American landscape: "Let freedom ring from the snowcapped Rockies of Colorado! . . ."

In this tradition, Obama begins with "We the people, in order to form a more perfect union," a quote from the Constitution that becomes a recurring refrain linking the parts of the speech. What comes next is "Two hundred and twenty one years ago," an opening that places him in the tradition of Lincoln at Gettysburg and Dr. King at the Lincoln Memorial: "Five score years ago."

On the first page, Obama mentions the words democracy, Declaration of Independence, Philadelphia convention, 1787, the colonies, the founders, the Constitution, liberty, justice, citizenship under the law, parchment, equal, free, prosperous, and the presidency. It is not as well known as it should be that many black leaders, including Dr. King, use two different modes of discourse when addressing white vs. black audiences, an ignorance that has led to some of the hysteria over some of Rev. Wright's comments.

Obama's patriotic lexicon is meant to comfort white ears and soothe white fears. What keeps the speech from falling into a pandering sea of slogans is language that reveals, not the ideals, but the failures of the American experiment: "It was stained by this nation's original sin of slavery, a question that divided the colonies and brought the convention to a stalemate until the founders chose to allow the slave trade to continue for at least twenty more years, and to leave any final resolution to future generations." And "what would be needed were Americans in successive generations who were willing to do their part . . . to narrow that gap between the promise of our ideals and the reality of their time."

Lest a dark vision of America disillusion potential voters, Obama returns to familiar evocations of national history, ideals, and language:

–"Out of many, we are truly one"

–"survived a Depression"

–"a man who served his country"

–"on a path of a more perfect union"

–"a full measure of justice"

–"the immigrant trying to feed his family"

–"where our union grows stronger"

–"a band of patriots signed that document"

PARALLELISM

At the risk of calling to mind the worst memories of grammar class, I invoke the wisdom that parallel constructions help authors and orators make meaning memorable. To remember how parallelism works, think of equal terms to express equal ideas. So Dr. King dreamed that one day his four children "will not be judged by the color of their skin but by the content of their character." (*By the content of their character* is parallel to *by the color of their skin*.)

Back to Obama: "This was one of the tasks we set forth at the beginning of this campaign—to continue the long march of those who came before us, a march for a more just, more equal, more free, more caring and more prosperous America." If you are counting, that's five parallel phrases among 43 words.

And there are many more:

". . . we may not have come from the same place, but we all want to move in the same direction."

"So when they are told to bus their children to a school across town; when they hear that an African American is getting an advantage in landing a good job or a spot in a good college because of an injustice that they themselves never committed; when they're told that their fears about crime in urban neighborhoods are somehow prejudiced, resentment builds over time."

". . . embracing the burdens of our past without becoming victims of our past."

TWO-NESS

I could argue that Obama's speech is a meditation upon DuBois's theory of a dual experience of race in America. There is no mention of DuBois or two-ness, but it is all there in the texture. In fact, once you begin the search, it is remarkable how many examples of two-ness shine through:

–"through protests and struggles"

–"on the streets and in the courts"

–"through civil war and civil disobedience"

–"I am the son of a black man from Kenya and a white woman from Kansas"

–"white and black"

–"black and brown"

–"best schools . . . poorest nations"

–"too black or not black enough"

–"the doctor and the welfare mom"

–"the model student and the former gang-banger"

–"raucous laughter and sometimes bawdy humor"

–"political correctness or reverse racism"

–"your dreams do not have to come at the expense of my dreams"

Such language manages to create both tension and balance and, without being excessively messianic, permits Obama to present himself as the bridge builder, the reconciler of America's racial divide.

AUTOBIOGRAPHY

There is an obnoxious tendency among political candidates to frame their life story as a struggle against poverty or hard circumstances. As satirist Stephen Colbert once noted of presidential candidates, it is not enough to be an average millionaire. To appeal to populist instincts it becomes de rigueur to be descended from "goat turd farmers" in France.

Without dwelling on it, Obama reminds us that his father was black and his mother white, that he came from Kenya, but she came from Kansas: "I am married to a black American who carries within her the blood of slaves and slave owners—an inheritance we pass on to our two precious daughters. I have brothers, sisters, nieces, nephews, uncles, and cousins, of every race and every hue, scattered across three continents, and for as long as I live, I will never forget that in no other country on Earth is my story even possible."

The word "story" is a revealing one, for it is always the candidate's job (as both responsibility and ploy) to describe himself or herself as a character in a story of his or her own making. In speeches, as in homilies, stories almost always carry the weight of parable, with moral lessons to be drawn.

Most memorable, of course, is the story at the end of the speech—which is why it appears at the end. It is the story of Ashley Baia, a young, white, Obama volunteer from South Carolina, whose family was so poor she convinced her mother that her favorite meal was a mustard and relish sandwich.

> "Anyway, Ashley finishes her story and then goes around the room and asks everyone else why they're supporting the campaign. They all have different stories and reasons. Many bring up a specific issue. And finally they come to this elderly black man who's been sitting there quietly the entire time. . . . He simply says to everyone in the room, 'I am here because of Ashley.'"

During most of the 20th century, demagogues, especially in the South, gained political traction by pitting working class whites and blacks against each other. How fitting, then, that Obama's story points in the opposite direction through an old black man who feels a young white woman's pain.

Source: Roy Peter Clark, "Why It Worked: A Rhetorical Analysis of Obama's Speech on Race," *Poynter* 4/1/08. Copyright © 2008. Reprinted by permission of the author.

FOR DISCUSSION

1. How would you characterize Roy Peter Clark's overriding impression of President Obama's 2008 speech on race?

2. What do you think Clark means when he writes that, like Dr. King's "I Have a Dream" speech, Obama's speech

"sounds better than it reads"? What features of the speech might qualify it for that description and why?

3. Clark spends considerable time reviewing the use of language in Obama's speech. What role does that language play in his analysis?

4. What additional evidence from Obama's speech might Clark have offered to support his analytical claims?

5. Imagine that you were analyzing Obama's speech for a different discourse community—e.g., one that is ultra-conservative. Would your analysis differ from Clark's? Why?

WORKS CITED

Aristotle. *On Rhetoric*. Translated by George A. Kennedy. Oxford UP, 2007.

Literary Analysis

15

In the fairy tale "Snow White," a jealous queen entices her beautiful stepdaughter with a poisonous apple that, when bitten, places her in a deep sleep from which she will awaken only if kissed by her one true love. But what if the apple had been an avocado? Does it matter that the fruit is red or shaped like a heart? What if you view the apple through an interpretive lens informed by

Christianity—does the Garden of Eden come to mind? What might a feminist lens reveal about the portrayal of Snow White, the stepmother, or the huntsman? These are questions that literary analyses of this fairy tale might attempt to answer. Read on to learn about strategies for communicating interpretations of fictional works in your own literary analyses.

Short stories, novels, and plays—these forms of fiction probably dominated the content of your past English courses, maybe to your excitement or maybe to your frustration. But even if you didn't enjoy studying literature in high school (perhaps the subject matter bored you, the time period seemed too far removed, or your teacher directed your thinking), you've likely reflected at one

"Literary analysis is about figuring out the author's intention."

While many scholars writing in past decades placed emphasis on what an author intended to communicate, contemporary scholars celebrate *readers' transactions* with literature, which can be influenced by their cultural background, class, gender, and so on. Of course, this does not mean "anything goes"; you have to be able to justify your reading with evidence from the text. But it does acknowledge that discovering what the author meant to say is not the only worthy approach to literary analysis. After all, in many cases, the author's intention cannot be verified. What's more, the value of a literary work may rest in effects the author did not anticipate.

time or another on the entertainment value that good literature provides. After all, literature inspires many of the films you rush to see at first opening, and, if you are a *Harry Potter, Twilight,* or *Hunger Games* fan, you may have been one of the many people of all ages who couldn't wait to get their hands on the next installment of these popular series.

O.K.—it's true: some people don't view the books in these series as "literature," but this chapter embraces a broad definition of the term, referring to all fictional works that inspire people to read. Moreover, this chapter adopts the notion that strategies involved in **literary analysis** can support and enrich any reading experience, including that of "reading" a movie or TV show. Of course, following such activities, you typically don't jump up to write papers about them. Nevertheless, practicing strategies and skills involved in literary analysis will prepare you not only for future courses that require writing about literature but also for many other rhetorical situations across academic, professional, and personal contexts.

Distinguishing Features of a Literary Analysis

Understanding the features of a literary analysis depends on familiarity with the elements of fiction, which are briefly reviewed in Figure 15.1 (see also Chapter 7). No doubt you recognize these constructs as the building blocks of short stories, novels, and plays. As such, they are central to the acts of writing literature and of learning how to analyze it. In fact, the first two elements listed in Figure 15.1 are helpful in distinguishing literary analysis from genres that are sometimes confused with it: character sketches and plot summaries. Although these descriptive approaches to a text can assist in developing an interpretation, literary analysis extends beyond a simple portrait of a key personality or a play-by-play account of the story's action. Its goal is to provide insights about a literary work that are not apparent from an initial or superficial reading.

Element of Fiction	Definition
Characters	The people or creatures the story is about
Plot	The actions of the characters; the events constituting the story
Setting	The place and time in which the story occurs
Theme	A message or point the story conveys
Style	The way the story is delivered through voice, sentence structure, vocabulary, and imagery

Figure 15.1 **The elements of fiction defined**

Literary insights often arise from **gaps** in the story—that is, features of it that are perplexing or that aren't explicitly addressed (Iser 8-9). A literary analysis offers a plausible response to a question (or questions) sparked by a gap, leading readers to entertain aspects of the work that they may have failed to notice on their own. Think, for example, of a time when you read a story that left you wondering about the motives behind a character's actions; the story's silence in responding to your questions created a gap in understanding. In the interest of filling this gap, a literary analysis would present a thesis statement conveying a possible explanation for the character's behavior.

Consider, for example, the following thesis from Heidi Nielson's analysis of the main character in J. K. Rowling's *Harry Potter* series (you can find the complete article at the end of this chapter):

> Like Shakespeare's character Hamlet, the revenge tragedy genre's most well-known face, Harry is reluctant to adopt this role for most of the seven-volume series. Ultimately, though, Harry not only acts as a revenger, but also struggles with the same complex dilemmas central to Renaissance drama—the loss of family, the loss of self, and the struggle for agency.

This thesis puts forth an interpretive claim intended to help readers understand Harry's actions and feelings. After identifying the gap she will fill, Nielson illustrates her thesis through means that are typical of literary analysis: evidence from the literature itself and citations from published scholarship. The scholarship she cites focuses on the nature of revenge tragedies, which helps explain Harry's motives as a form of retaliation. Other types of scholarship you might incorporate in a literary analysis include history of the period in which the work is set, biographical information about the author, other peoples' interpretations of the same text, and so forth.

The scholarship Nielson cites relevant to the *Harry Potter* series helps define her interpretive lens—that is, knowledge about revenge tragedies, including Shakespeare's *Hamlet*. Indeed, literary analysis, like other analytical genres, depends on an interpretive lens to guide the author's and readers' interpretations. In the case of literature, the lens is often a claim about how certain elements of fiction are functioning within the larger framework of the short story, novel, or drama. While one analysis might emphasize **character** (as Nielson's does), another might focus on **setting** as it displays qualities undergirding a given **theme** (e.g., the barren plains depicted in the opening paragraph of *The Grapes of Wrath* as they mirror the emotional desolation of people who suffered through the Great Depression). An interpretive lens might also be informed by an established theory or school of thought from the field of English studies or another discipline. Nielson's analysis of the *Harry Potter* series invokes **genre theory,** which applies knowledge about the conventions of a given type of literature (in her case, revenge tragedies) as a means of categorizing the work in question and explaining its inner workings. Figure 15.2 lists other theories and the types of analyses they tend to produce.

Whether based on the elements of fiction, a particular theory, or both, the interpretive lens for a literary analysis will be closely tied to your thesis statement. Sometimes the lens precedes the thesis, as in the case of feminists who devote their careers to studying gender issues and, therefore, may automatically apply this lens to whatever they read. At other times, the thesis suggests what sort of lens would be most instructive—for example, a reader who is not necessarily tuned in to gender issues wants to comment on the ways women and men interact in a given work and, therefore,

Lens	Purpose
Cultural	To clarify aspects of a literary work by applying knowledge about the society or culture in which the tale was written or set
Linguistic	To apply specific knowledge about the way language works as a means of understanding how dialogue, metaphor, etc., function within the text
Psychoanalytical	To apply theories of the subconscious in relation to the conscious as a way of understanding characters' (or sometimes authors') motives
Feminist	To apply understanding of gender roles or norms within a given culture as a means of clarifying and questioning them
Marxist	To apply theories of class relations to reveal the characters' or authors' attitudes about them

Figure 15.2 **Interpretive lenses commonly applied to literary works**

turns to feminist theory for help. Whatever the case, Figure 15.3 illustrates how the interpretive lens and other components of a literary analysis relate to one another.

You can see many of the components in Figure 15.3 at work in the Look Inside excerpt from an article about Edgar Allan Poe's short story "The Black Cat" (which is included, in full, at the end of this chapter). Originally published in the academic journal *Studies in Short Fiction*, this analysis by Susan Amper seeks to unravel some peculiarities of **plot** by examining the narrator's (and main **character**'s) account of the action.

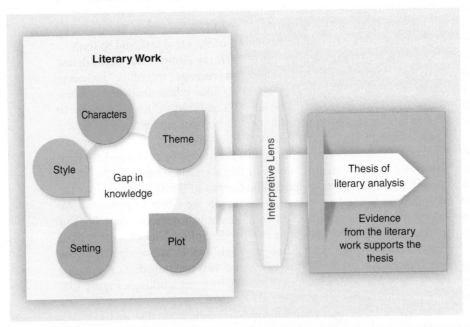

Figure 15.3 **Elements of a literary analysis.** When setting out to compose a literary analysis, begin by considering any potential gaps in your audience's knowledge about the work in question. What specifically about the characters, theme, style, setting, or plot could you analyze to further their understanding of the literary work and, in doing so, fill those gaps? When viewed through a particular interpretive lens, your answer to this question will lead you to a strong thesis. You will support your thesis using evidence from the literary work under analysis.

From "Untold Story: The Lying Narrator in 'The Black Cat'"

by Susan Amper

On the eve of his execution for the murder of his wife, a con-demned man tells a far-fetched tale about how the murder occurred. In it he expresses little remorse, denies responsibility, and blames the murder on an extraordinary sequence of events beyond his control. He tells us that, debilitated by alcoholism and driven by an uncontrollable urge, he merely killed his cat; that an "apparition" of this cat then miraculously appeared on his bedroom wall, tormenting him further; that subsequently a second cat, virtually identical to the first, appeared under curious circumstances and domesticated itself in his home, gradually driving him to frenzy; and that finally in attempting to kill the second cat, he more or less accidentally killed his wife instead.

Obviously the man is lying.

Such would be the reaction of any adult in real life hear-ing the man's self-serving story, and such is the previously unrecognized but ultimately inescapable truth about the nar-rator of "The Black Cat." His tale is a fabrication, by which he seeks to conceal the true nature of his crime, exactly as he sought in walling up his wife's body to conceal the fact of the crime. And just as his subconscious drives him against his will to reveal the hiding place, so does it cause him to plant in his story telltale clues that disclose his guilty secret.

When understood as part fact and part misrepresentation designed to minimize the narrator's guilt, the story gains an important virtue it otherwise lacks: intelligibility. Critics, indeed, have yet to put forth any reasonable interpretation of the actual events of the story. James Gargano concedes as much when he says that the tale, "if read unimaginatively . . . is so mystifying that the narrator seems for once reasonable when he declares that he 'neither expects nor solicits belief' in it" (173). Until now, the foremost analyses of the stories have come from those, including Marie Bonaparte, Daniel Hoffman, and William Crisman, who have abandoned any attempt to address the literal meaning of events, dealing with them exclusively as psychological phenomena.

. . .

The key to [answering questions posed by the plot] is to be found in the fact that the narrator is lying, a fact that he himself suggests in his very first breath. "For the most wild

A LOOK INSIDE: LITERARY ANALYSIS

The author opens with a brief plot summary, sketching a bare outline of events, the finer points of which she hopes to clarify.

Here, the author exercises her creativity, isolating a single line to grab readers' attention and impress upon them that the narrator's account of the action as just summarized is unreliable.

After elaborating on the unreliability of the narrator, the author delivers her thesis.

This paragraph notes the gap the author hopes to fill and the significance of her analysis. It also cites published scholarship that underscores the significance.

yet most homely narrative which I am about to pen," he begins, "I neither expect nor solicit belief. Mad indeed would I be to expect it, in a case where my very senses reject their own evidence. Yet, mad am I not—and very surely do I not dream" (849). If the man is neither mad nor mistaken, and yet is not to be believed, it can only be that he is lying. In effect, the narrator defies the reader to find him out, just as he recklessly defies the police by calling attention to the very wall that conceals his wife's body.

At this point, the author cites evidence from the story and then explains how it can be viewed in support of her analysis.

The knowledge that the narrator is lying, and of his motive in doing so—denial of guilt for the murder of his wife—gives us the vantage point from which we are able to discover the truth. What emerges is this: the narrator murdered his wife, not impulsively on the cellar stairs as he asserts, but willfully and with malice aforethought at the very time he claims to have killed his cat; the supposed cat-killing is a fiction he invents in order to assuage his guilt and, more immediately, to explain away the mysterious "apparition" on the bedroom wall that threatens to expose his crime; the alleged appearance of a second cat is also a fiction, cooked up to explain the continued existence of the supposedly dead cat; it is actually Pluto that is discovered in the basement wall with the wife's body. These conclusions seem at first astonishing; but such is the genius of Poe's story that what proves more astonishing is how confidently they may be deduced from a careful examination of the evidence.

Once it's understood that the narrator is lying, as the author explains, the story can be read as other than a madman's raving or a supernatural occurrence. Further, she claims that the evidence for this reading can be found in the story itself.

The first task, as every armchair detective knows, is to determine the time of death. The narrator wants us to believe that his wife died on the cellar stairs three days before the body was found (858). This idea is belied, however, by a succession of clues the narrator lets slip, culminating in a final fatal slip in his last paragraph.

. . .

This paragraph adds an interpretive lens that takes the analysis beyond a plot or character study, as the author suggests that "The Black Cat" is a specific genre of short fiction—i.e., a detective story.

"The Black Cat" emerges from this analysis as far less mystifying than has been thought. In fact it proves to be one of Poe's least mystifying, and most satisfying, stories: a masterful pre-Dostoevsky, pre-Freud profile of the psychology of crime and punishment, and at the same time a first-rate detective story. Indeed, it is surely Poe's best detective story, with the ideal detective story solution: one that is simplicity itself in explaining all the facts, yet so elusive it has taken a century and a half to be discovered.

The article's conclusion reasserts the thesis (that the plot of "The Black Cat" reveals an intentional crime) as well as the interpretive lens comparing Poe's fiction to a detective story.

In the portion omitted from the Look Inside excerpt, preceding the article's conclusion, the author breaks down the narrator's account of his wife's death and explains how it "proves" that he is lying about the chain of events. In laying out these clues embedded in the plot, the author not only supports her thesis but also adopts the persona of a detective, reinforcing her interpretive lens.

Processes for Composing a Literary Analysis

The literary analyst in action does have much in common with a detective. Faced with a mystery presented by the interplay of fictional elements, he or she generates possible explanations and then combs the work for evidence to back them. Fortunately, in your college courses, you will probably feel less like a lone detective and more like part of an investigative team, as you will have the opportunity to discuss your impressions of a work with teachers and classmates before you begin researching and drafting your analysis.

Invention toward First Insight

Invention for a literary analysis begins with your first pass through a text if, in fact, you are reading actively. Put another way, consciously striving to understand relationships between the story's components will lead to questions about it. Usually, your desire to answer a question or learn more about a particular issue (i.e., to fill a gap) will gain intensity as you continue reflecting on the work. In an attempt to relieve the confusion, it is natural to speculate about possible solutions to puzzles the text introduces. If you didn't begin reading from a particular theoretical vantage point, any ideas you have for answering questions the text poses will point you toward an interpretive lens. Consult Figure 15.4 for illustrations of how these thinking processes might play out relevant to examples discussed earlier in the chapter.

Preparation through Research

Whatever interpretive lens you apply, any hypothesis you entertain about the work during your initial encounters with it can be tested through two activities that are vital to literary analysis. The first, **close reading,** unearths evidence in the literary work that supports your interpretation. This activity involves reengaging the text so you can dig deeper for key passages. The second activity, researching academic databases, will lead you to published scholarship relevant to your line of inquiry. The Modern Language Association (MLA) bibliography and JSTOR are just two examples of databases that compile literary analyses; check with your instructor or librarian for others. You can mine the books or articles housed by these databases for observations you can cite to support your analysis.

Before starting either of these activities, you will want to devise a system for keeping track of and organizing your findings. When preparing for most literary

Literary Work	Sample Questions	Interpretive Lens
"Snow White"	Why did the Queen give Snow White an apple (as opposed to something else)? Is the apple significant to the theme of the story?	Knowledge about apple and color **symbolism** (the study of certain objects as representing other objects, emotions, or principles)
The Grapes of Wrath	Why is the opening so detailed in creating such a bleak setting?	Understanding drawn from other fiction—as well as films—that setting often predicts or reinforces a theme
The Harry Potter series	What motivates Harry through the hardships he faces?	Knowledge about characters in other stories of revenge
"The Black Cat"	The narrator's account of what happened to his wife doesn't ring true—what really happened?	Knowledge about psychology, specifically the fact that guilty parties often reveal themselves

Figure 15.4 Sample questions and interpretive lenses to help clarify them

analyses, it won't be enough to simply underline or highlight sentences in your primary and secondary sources. Because you will probably be marking any and all passages that could contribute to your paper, the results will prove difficult to sort if you don't also indicate their substance and anticipated function, either in the margins of the texts or on separate sheets of paper. By doing so, when you are ready to focus your investigation, you will be able to quickly locate and evaluate findings that are most crucial to it.

Invention toward More Focused Insight

If you find through close reading and research that sufficient support for your interpretation exists, you can articulate it in a working thesis. Given the length requirements for your paper, the focus must be tight enough to allow for thorough development of your claims. You will also need to allow room for background information—either from the literary work or secondary sources—that will help readers follow your analysis. For example, you might need to offer a brief sketch of the plot or a character, or you might need to provide an overview of historical data or a particular theory you are applying.

Managing the complexities of a literary analysis may require you to create a skeletal outline or diagram to help you visualize relationships between all the components you want to address. Will you introduce the plot in your introduction, or will you intersperse excerpts throughout the analysis where they are directly relevant? Where will you cite particular secondary sources? Even if you typically don't map your organization before drafting an essay, you may find it necessary to do so when negotiating the sometimes winding terrain of a literary analysis.

Strategies for Drafting

When composing the introduction of your literary analysis, you have a number of options. As mentioned earlier, you may need to cover background information essential to establishing your interpretive lens. Or, you might want to situate your analysis in comparison or contrast to the interpretations of other scholars. And, of course, at some point, you'll have to decide how to identify the work you're analyzing—by title, author, genre, date of publication, time period in which it is set, and so on. Your thesis should follow not long after these introductory remarks. Readers need to understand the gist of your interpretation up front so they can weigh the significance of the evidence you share in the body of the text.

Perhaps the greatest challenge in drafting a literary analysis is simultaneously weaving all the textual evidence and supporting scholarship together with explanations sufficient to help the audience understand your reasoning. For example, imagine you are writing about setting through the interpretive lens of psychology. After stating your thesis about the meaning of a symbol within that setting as illuminated by the interpretive lens (e.g., a lake as representing the main character's subconscious), you comment on its initial appearance with a brief reference to the plot. From there, as you move to later occurrences of that symbol, you would need to show readers how it is working in conjunction with previous occurrences (e.g., when the character is calm, the surface of the lake is smooth; when the character is troubled, the surface of the lake is turbulent). In other words, you cannot simply drop a piece of textual evidence into your analysis and assume that its significance will be obvious. Rather, you must explicitly address the significance of that evidence as it demonstrates your thesis.

The same holds true for citations and paraphrases from secondary sources. As you place them within your analysis, you need to introduce them through transitions that tie them to the discussion and forecast their relevance. Sometimes, you will introduce them by mentioning the author's name and the place of publication; at other times, you will record the source information in an in-text parenthetical reference. Either approach will take readers to the appropriate entry on a Works Cited or References page (for detailed information about integrating and citing sources, see Chapter 21). After presenting the source material, you need to indicate how it pertains to your analysis. Again, just as you cannot assume that other readers will take the same meaning from a fictional work that you do, you cannot assume that they will accept that a given quote validates your analysis.

Another principle to keep in mind when you are citing sources is to do so judiciously. That is, you don't want to drown your own voice by depending too heavily on what others have to say about the piece you are analyzing. Put another way, your insights and observations about the literary work should dominate the text, and the words of published scholars should surface only intermittently to support or clarify a point you want to make.

Your conclusion should address how your interpretation enriches understanding of the literary work. It might emphasize how your analysis fills the gap you found, reveal a feature that might easily go unnoticed, or introduce a fresh perspective on the piece. If you've had an opportunity to thoroughly research prior scholarship on the work in question, you might want to explain how your analysis advances that larger conversation.

Revision and Editing

Questions for Revising

- Have I effectively geared the analysis toward my target audience?
- Does my thesis address a gap in the literature, or an issue that isn't answered by a superficial reading of the story?
- Does my thesis clearly articulate the analytical focus?
- Do I clearly establish my interpretive lens and explain it well enough for readers to understand how I'm applying it?
- Do I offer enough—and the right kind—of evidence from the literary work to demonstrate that my interpretation is reasonable?
- Do I introduce and explain textual evidence and secondary source material in a way that clarifies how they serve my analytical claims?
- Does the organization follow some seemingly logical sequence and employ transitions to express clear relationships between ideas?
- Does the conclusion leave readers with a sense of how the analysis increases understanding of the literary work?

Questions for Editing

- Are the literary work and any secondary sources cited in the analysis properly documented?
- Is the finished analysis free of spelling, punctuation, and usage errors?

Transfer to Other Writing Situations

Of course, individuals who regularly write literary analyses are those who study literature for a living, but potential writers and readers of this brand of scholarship are not limited to high school and college English teachers. Because so much can be learned about a culture from analyzing its literature, the genre also holds great value for sociologists, anthropologists, and historians. Even some health care professionals are required to take courses in literary analysis as a means of studying empathy, response to tragedy, and other aspects of human psychology.

Outside academic circles, the strategies and skills you apply when interpreting and writing about fiction can help you read and compose nonfictional works such as poetry, biographies, memoirs, newspaper articles—virtually any genre that portrays life events. And to view the relevance of literary analysis even more broadly, you can think about the benefits earned from practicing any type of analysis (visual, rhetorical, etc.). In fact, the call to think deeply and critically about a topic—to understand how its components relate to each other and to the whole—is critical to success in most every academic, professional, or personal endeavor. Contemplating how characters, plot, setting, theme, and style intertwine to make meaning in a work of fiction exercises your mind in ways that promote all other analytical pursuits.

ACTIVITY

Turning Elements of a Picture into Elements of a Story   Examine the photo in Figure 15.5. Write a page-long story about the characters pictured. Share your story with your classmates, comparing and contrasting the fiction you've created. Then reflect together on the reasons for the similarities and differences by focusing on specific elements of the photo that prompted your interpretive leaps.

IDEA FOR EXTENDED WRITING

Figure 15.5 **Photo prompt for a story**

Analyzing a Piece of Short Fiction   Reflect on the short fiction you have previously read for school or for your own pleasure. Which work stands out for raising questions that you would like to have answered? Now is your opportunity to explore those perplexing issues further. Of course, if it has been a while since you read the text, you will need to refresh your memory of it, looking for the gaps that intrigued you before and maybe even some new ones. Select one you'd like to focus on and make it the subject of a literary analysis built on your additional close readings of the story as well as published scholarship that comments on your topic. Be sure to appropriately cite the quotes from the short story and any published scholarship contributing to your analysis, both internally and in a Works Cited or References page. Imagine your audience to be readers of an undergraduate literary journal.

"Neither Can Live While the Other Survives": The Driving Force of Revenge in Harry Potter

by Heidi Nielson, University of Arizona Law School

1. "THE BOY WHO LIVED": AN UNLIKELY REVENGER

Since the 1990s, J. K. Rowling's *Harry Potter* series has grown from a scribble on a napkin to a world-wide cultural phenomenon. The books have caused people to line up outside of bookstores hours, even days, before their release, and have led to a billion-dollar movie franchise. But what makes the story so enticing? What made the series grow from yet another Young Adult fantasy series to a world-wide phenomenon, even, some would say, an obsession? Some will argue that it is Rowling's creativity, her incredible talent for world-building. Others claim that it is the archetypal struggle between good and evil. While I don't discount either of these arguments, I argue that the real driving force behind the series, and its success, is revenge. There are few less likely revengers than Harry Potter—a shy, quiet eleven-year-old boy who, when we first meet him, wants nothing more than a friend. However, just as the books move from childhood to reluctant adulthood, and the plot becomes more twisted, Harry changes from innocent to revenger. Like Shakespeare's character Hamlet, the revenge tragedy genre's most well-known face, Harry is reluctant to adopt this role for most of the seven-volume series. Ultimately, though, Harry not only acts as a revenger, but also struggles with the same complex dilemmas central to Renaissance drama—the loss of family, the loss of self, and the struggle for agency.

2. ROWLING AND THE REVENGE TRAGEDY GENRE

Revenge is the driving force of the *Harry Potter* series. Like every revenge tragedy in the genre's canon, the series is framed by two defining events: the initial crime and the final, bloody battle. The series begins on the night that Harry's parents are murdered, and ends sixteen years later with the "Battle of Hogwarts" (*DH* p. 608). The initial murder is characteristic of revenge tragedies as it involves a close family member. For instance, in *Hamlet,* the revenger's father is also killed. Hamlet is literally haunted by his father's death and, throughout the play, is torn between wanting to revenge his father and simply wanting to remember him. Harry, whose parents and loved ones are all killed, struggles with the same decision throughout the novels.

Early on in the series, Rowling characterizes Harry in a way that predisposes him to become a revenger. A highlight among nearly all revengers in the genre's canon is a value system that places a high premium on family honor, chivalry, and heroism. It is a societal value, but also a personality trait that revengers share, and seems to predispose them to become revengers. For instance, in *The Spanish Tragedy,* the play's main revenger Hieronimo feels honor-bound to revenge the murder of his son Horatio. When he is slow to take revenge, he berates himself: "see, see, oh, see thy shame, Hieronimo . . . to neglect the swift revenge of thy Horatio."[1] The shame that Hieronimo feels for neglecting revenge reveals a personal and societal value system laden with familial honor, duty, and heroism. Though young, Harry shares this value system, and this predisposes him to become a revenger. During the Hogwarts sorting ceremony, the Sorting Hat debates between putting Harry into Slytherin, whose members are described as "cunning" people who will "use any means to achieve their ends," or Gryffindor, whose "daring, nerve, and chivalry set [them] apart" (*SS* p. 118). Against the Sorting Hat's advice, Harry chooses to be in Gryffindor and reveals his heroic moral code (*SS* p. 125). As the series progresses, Harry is further revealed to have a "weakness for heroics," which Voldemort eventually exploits (*OotP* p. 782). The importance that Harry places on heroism, honor, and chivalry causes him to feel honor-bound to revenge his parents' deaths, and thus predisposes him to become a revenger.

Like the most famous revenger, Hamlet, Harry is slow to accept the path of revenge. The first five books of the saga seem to lead to this choice. Like a typical revenger, Harry feels frustrated that redress through the established legal system is impossible because the perpetrator, Voldemort, is in a position of overwhelming power. In *Order of the Phoenix,* Harry is unable to go through the traditional legal channels at the Ministry of Magic, because the Ministry represses the knowledge that Voldemort has returned, and even terrorizes Harry for saying otherwise (*OotP* p. 245). Once the Ministry admits the fact of Voldemort's return, it is a short time before the Ministry itself is taken over by Voldemort and his followers (*DH* p. 159). Voldemort's power, combined with the Ministry's lack of cooperation and then corruption, make it impossible for Harry to go through the established legal system, leaving "lawless" revenge as his only option for redress.

Meanwhile, there is tremendous psychological and social pressure on Harry to take revenge. Harry collects mementos, which remind him of his need for revenge, most prominently "the locket with the note signed R.A.B.," which reminds him of Dumbledore's

---

[1] Thomas Kyd, "The Spanish Tragedy." *Four Revenge Tragedies,* edited by Katharine Eisaman Maus, Oxford UP, 1995, p. 65.

death, and the shard of a mirror that was once Sirius Black's (his late godfather) (*DH* p. 15). John Kerrigan discusses such mementos in *Revenge Tragedy,* describing how revengers, specifically Hieronimo of *The Spanish Tragedy,* "[set] out to secure retribution by equipping [themselves] with objects charged with remembrance."[2] These *memento mori* remind the revenger and the audience of the crime, and constantly prompt the revenger toward vengeance. In addition to the psychological pressure to seek revenge created by the *memento mori,* Harry also faces extreme social pressure, most notably in the last two books. The wizarding community comes to think that Harry is "'The Chosen One,' . . . the only one who will be able to rid [them] of He-Who-Must-Not-Be-Named" (*HBP* p. 39). Because of this belief, the entire wizarding community pressures Harry into action. Harry is faced with the revenger's most common dilemma: a feeling of being honor-bound to seek revenge, but knowing that doing so will go against society's established rules.

Though all of the books are driven by revenge, Harry doesn't become a revenger until the end of the sixth book, *Half-Blood Prince.* Kerrigan describes how "the revenger . . . suspends his own identity" when he decides to seek revenge.[3] Harry, likewise, suspends his identity when he finally accepts the role of the revenger. The first step on this path is Harry's conscious choice to remain in the Wizarding World. After Sirius Black's death, Harry tells himself that he "can't shut [himself] away or—or crack up" (*HBP* p. 77). He realizes he can't escape his duty to revenge by living with the Dursleys in the Muggle World. Harry seems to be aware that, in order to become a revenger, he can no longer be "normal"; he can no longer be himself. At Dumbledore's funeral, Harry makes the final decision to begin "hunting Voldemort" alone, and becomes a true revenger (*HBP* p. 647). He decides to end his relationship with Ginny Weasley, referring to their brief relationship as "something out of someone else's life" because of its normalcy (*HBP* p. 646). He realizes that, once he takes on the role of revenger, he can no longer lead a normal, teenage life, and can no longer totally be himself.

Once Harry accepts this role, he also fulfills a traditional characteristic of the revenger: he loses his moral code. In the *Harry Potter* series, there are three Unforgivable Curses, outlined in *Goblet of Fire:* the Imperius Curse, used to control an individual against his or her will, the Cruciatus Curse, used to torture, and Avada Kedavra, the killing curse. After taking on the role of the revenger, Harry uses both the Imperius and the Cruciatus Curses,

---

[2] John Kerrigan, *Revenge Tragedy.* Oxford UP, 1996, p. 174.

[3] Ibid., p. 8.

reluctantly at first, but eventually to great effect. In *Order of the Phoenix,* Harry first attempts to use the Cruciatus Curse on Bellatrix Lestrange after she kills his godfather, Sirius. However, he is unable to, because, as Bellatrix points out to him mockingly, "[the user needs] to *mean* them, . . . to really want to cause pain— to enjoy it" (*OotP* p. 810). His "righteous anger" is ineffective; he has not yet lost his moral code and become a revenger, and thus cannot properly perform the Unforgivable spells (*OotP* p. 810). After becoming a true revenger, however, he uses both the Imperius Curse and the Cruciatus Curse in *Deathly Hallows*. Harry uses the Imperius Curse first, putting two individuals under the curse while he, Ron, Hermione, and Griphook infiltrate Gringotts Bank. Upon realizing that the goblins know that Hermione is an imposter, Harry puts a goblin under the Imperius Curse. Harry is hesitant to perform the spell and only does so when he knows that they are in imminent danger. The second time, however, Harry "[acts] without thinking," and places Travers under the Imperius Curse as well (*DH* p. 531). This reveals that Harry begins to lose his moral code after performing an Unforgivable Curse. At first, he is hesitant to perform the curse and listens to multiple warnings from Griphook before acting. After first using the Imperius Curse, it becomes easier for Harry to perform the Unforgivable Curse, and he can even place an individual under this spell without thinking. After performing the Imperius Curse, Harry soon becomes able to perform the Cruciatus Curse, further revealing the loss of his moral code. In the *Deathly Hallows* chapter "The Sacking of Severus Snape," Harry uses the Cruciatus Curse on Amycus Carrow after Carrow spits on Professor McGonagall. He uses the curse so effectively that Carrow is "lifted off his feet . . . , smashed into the front of a bookcase and crumple[s], insensible, to the floor" (*DH* p. 593). Harry's ability to use the Unforgivable Curses effectively reveals the loss of his moral code.

3. "ALL THE DIFFERENCE IN THE WORLD": HARRY'S STRUGGLE FOR AGENCY

The central conflict of many of the revenge tragedies in the literary canon is the revenger's struggle to attain agency. The revenger is faced with a fundamental paradox. Because of the initial crime, and the fact that there is no course of redress through typical legal channels, the revenger is forced into a difficult position. While he gains agency by choosing to take revenge and redress the wrong inflicted on him by the perpetrator, in doing so he loses agency by falling into a role that is prescribed for him by others (that is, society, the personification of Revenge, etc.). Kerrigan discusses this paradox in relation to *The Spanish Tragedy:* "In one way,

[Hieronimo] is compelled to travel towards Revenge, for the goddess of his play, Proserpine, has granted Andrea a providential as well as a judgmental 'doom,' and Hieronimo is the instrument of her will. But in another sense he actively chooses to make the journey."[4] Here, Kerrigan highlights the central struggle for agency that revengers face. *The Spanish Tragedy*'s revenger, Hieronimo, is a brilliant illustration of this paradox. Throughout the play, the personification of Revenge controls the events that take place.[5] From the beginning of the play when the ghost of Don Andrea, whose death begins the chain of events that leads Hieronimo to revenge, meets Hades's wife Proserpine to assign Andrea his "doom" and subsequently summons Revenge, there is a strong sense that Hieronimo's revenge is fated by the gods.[6] Even when he chooses to revenge his son's death, his actions are scripted by the personification of Revenge, which strips Hieronimo of agency, and thus reveals the unique and maddening struggle of all revengers: while he seems to gain agency by choosing to revenge, he also loses agency by falling into the scripted role of a revenger.

This paradox is also central to the *Harry Potter* series. Like Hieronimo, Harry's fate to become a revenger and to kill Voldemort seems to be destined in Sybill Trelawney's prophecy: "The one with the power to vanquish the Dark Lord approaches. . . . Born to those who have thrice defied him, born as the seventh month dies . . . and the Dark Lord will mark him as his equal, but he will have power the Dark Lord knows not . . . and either must die at the hand of the other for neither can live while the other survives" (*OotP* p. 841). Because of the prophecy, Harry seems fated to become a revenger. Because Voldemort chose to "mark" Harry as his equal by attempting to kill him, Harry is inextricably tied to Voldemort. There is a strong sense in the final three books that Harry is doomed to face Voldemort, that he is "The Chosen One." This stems both from the prophecy and from Harry's own personification of Revenge, which comes to script his actions. At the same time, however, Harry is also able to "choose" to become a revenger, to pursue Voldemort. In a pivotal discussion with Harry, Dumbledore struggles to make Harry understand the fundamental paradox that he faces—that Harry can simultaneously choose to become a revenger and be destined to revenge. When Harry protests, saying "it all comes to the same thing," that Harry has "got to try and kill him" either way, Dumbledore breaks in: "Got to? . . . Of course you've got to! But not because of the

---

[4] Ibid., p. 175.

[5] Kyd, "The Spanish Tragedy." *Four Revenge Tragedies*, edited by Eisaman Maus, p. 5.

[6] Ibid.

prophecy! Because you, yourself, will never rest until you've tried! We both know it!" (*HBP* p. 511). Here, Rowling introduces the revenger's struggle for agency, the central paradox that revengers face, and tries to help the reader come to terms with it. Perhaps more than other revenge tragedies, Rowling attempts to solve this paradox, allowing Harry both to choose and to be destined to revenge.

But Harry's struggle for agency doesn't end with his choice to become a revenger; once Harry makes his choice, he struggles against the scripted role that Dumbledore, who acts as the personification of Revenge in the *Harry Potter* series, creates for him. Harry's revenge and eventual killing of Voldemort is planned and controlled. In *The Spanish Tragedy,* the personification of Revenge is the one pulling the strings. As the play progresses, Revenge and the ghost of Don Andrea sit on the sidelines and watch the events that lead to the revenge of Don Andrea's death. At one point, Revenge falls asleep, and Don Andrea forces him awake, worried that nothing is being done to avenge his death because of Revenge's lack of attention. However, Revenge replies that "though I sleep, yet is my mood soliciting their souls."[7] After this, he shows Andrea a "dumb show," which reveals the events to come: a bloody wedding and the completion of Andrea's revenge.[8] The personification of Revenge controls all of the events of the play, even while he is not present in the action, or even conscious.

In *Harry Potter,* the figure of Dumbledore acts in a similar way. Particularly after his death in *Half-Blood Prince,* Dumbledore scripts all of Harry's actions. Much of *Deathly Hallows* involves Harry attempting to puzzle out the clues Dumbledore has left for him, Ron, and Hermione in order to defeat Voldemort. Though Dumbledore appears to be absent, Harry finds that Dumbledore has carefully planned the death of Voldemort. After Dumbledore's physical death, "the portrait of Dumbledore" is able to continue to orchestrate Harry's revenge with the help of Severus Snape (*DH* p. 689). In Snape's memories, Dumbledore instructs Snape in each step of Harry's revenge, telling him how and when to hide the sword, scripting Harry's actions so that he constantly feels as if he is unraveling a code, a riddle left for him by Dumbledore (*DH* p. 689). Similar to other revengers, Harry goes back and forth between accepting the scripted role created for him by Dumbledore and wanting to rebel against it. As he watches Ron and Hermione on one occasion, Harry realizes that they "could walk away if they wanted to [while Harry] could not" (*DH* 278). He feels especially resentful

---

[7]Ibid., p. 73.

[8]Ibid.

toward, and even betrayed by, Dumbledore when he discovers in *Deathly Hallows* that Dumbledore's plan for Harry's revenge inevitably leads to Harry's death (*DH* chap. 34). Still, however, Harry accepts his fate. Harry knows that he must not only move toward Voldemort's end, but also to "*his* [own] end" (*DH* p. 693).

4. "A POWER BEYOND THE REACH OF ANY MAGIC": THE SUBVERSION OF THE REVENGE TRAGEDY GENRE

Until this point, Rowling follows the model of a revenge tragedy closely, allowing young readers to grapple with the complex themes of agency and morality. However, in "The Forest Again" chapter of *Deathly Hallows,* Rowling begins ever so slightly to subvert the genre. Like many revengers, Harry accepts his own death as part of the cycle of revenge. Both the revenger and the perpetrator must die in order to expunge society of the chaos and disorder that their conflict causes. Harry resigns himself to this fact after realizing that he is the last Horcrux, meaning that part of Voldemort's fragmented soul resides within Harry's body. He must die in order for Voldemort ever to be killed and revenge to be achieved. After resigning himself to this fact, he walks to meet his death—a kind of suicide—and Voldemort "kills" him.

However, all Voldemort manages to kill is the fragmented piece of Voldemort's soul which resides within Harry, making Harry's soul "whole, and completely [his] own" (*DH* p. 708). Therefore, Voldemort expunges the chaotic and disorderly part of Harry's soul, allowing the "complete," non-revenger Harry to continue to live without disturbing society. Voldemort, however, is not so lucky. Following the tradition of the revenge tragedy, Voldemort is killed. However, he is not killed by the new, "complete" Harry, but by Voldemort's "own rebounding curse" (*DH* p. 744).

Rowling's subversion of the genre here is jarring. She modifies the revenge tragedy genre to allow her revenger to live normally in society. Harry achieves his revenge and manages to eliminate Voldemort, but only through a willingness to engage in self-sacrifice. By deviating from the genre at the final moment, allowing Harry to survive through love, Rowling suggests that love and revenge—two seemingly polar forces—may be intertwined to eliminate evil.

At the end of the saga, the reader is relieved that Voldemort has been killed and that society has been expunged. But at the same time, Rowling's jarring subversion of the revenge tragedy genre leaves the reader somewhat stunned and dissatisfied. The series ends with an epilogue, showing the main characters nineteen years later. Without Voldemort, normalcy has returned; however, Harry is no longer an exciting character. His characteristic scar has "not pained

[him] for nineteen years" (*DH* p. 759). The reader's dissatisfaction with the normalcy of the ending connects *Harry Potter* even more to the revenge tragedy genre, because it reveals the mixed repulsion and intense attraction that humans feel toward revenge.

5. CONCLUSION

Harry not only operates as a revenger, but deals with the complex dilemma of agency and identity that troubled playwrights during the Renaissance. The fact that the series operates as a revenge tragedy raises the uncomfortable question: why a revenge tragedy for children? In the *Harry Potter* series, Rowling doesn't shy away from the ugly, the hateful, and the painful. By making revenge a driving force in the series for both Harry and Voldemort, two opposing characters, Rowling powerfully illustrates to her young readers that people, and life, are imperfect. Furthermore, the fact that children are so wholly invested in the series, and compelled to continue reading until the final revenge is achieved, suggests that revenge is an innate, even involuntary, part of human nature. In the *Harry Potter* series, Rowling highlights an uncomfortable truth about human nature: that humans, of all ages, are at once horrified and enticed by revenge.

Untold Story: The Lying Narrator in "The Black Cat"

by Susan Amper

On the eve of his execution for the murder of his wife, a condemned man tells a far-fetched tale about how the murder occurred. In it he expresses little remorse, denies responsibility, and blames the murder on an extraordinary sequence of events beyond his control. He tells us that, debilitated by alcoholism and driven by an uncontrollable urge, he merely killed his cat; that an "apparition" of this cat then miraculously appeared on his bedroom wall, tormenting him further; that subsequently a second cat, virtually identical to the first, appeared under curious circumstances and domesticated itself in his home, gradually driving him to frenzy; and that finally in attempting to kill the second cat, he more or less accidentally killed his wife instead.

Obviously the man is lying.

Such would be the reaction of any adult in real life hearing the man's self-serving story, and such is the previously unrecognized but ultimately inescapable truth about the narrator of "The Black Cat." His tale is a fabrication, by which he seeks to conceal the true nature of his crime, exactly as he sought in walling up his wife's body to conceal the fact of the crime. And just as his subconscious drives him against his will to reveal the hiding place, so does it cause him to plant in his story telltale clues that disclose his guilty secret.

When understood as part fact and part misrepresentation designed to minimize the narrator's guilt, the story gains an important virtue it otherwise lacks: intelligibility. Critics, indeed, have yet to put forth any reasonable interpretation of the actual events of the story. James Gargano concedes as much when he says that the tale, "if read unimaginatively . . . is so mystifying that the narrator seems for once reasonable when he declares that he 'neither expects nor solicits belief' in it" (173). Until now the foremost analyses of the stories have come from those, including Marie Bonaparte, Daniel Hoffman, and William Crisman, who have abandoned any attempt to address the literal meaning of events, dealing with them exclusively as psychological phenomena.

But the story should make sense, and the narrator himself, in his very first paragraph, implies that it does:

> Hereafter, perhaps, some intellect may be found which will reduce my phantasm to the commonplace—some intellect more calm, more logical, and far less excitable than my own, which will perceive, in the circumstances I detail with awe, nothing more than an ordinary succession of very natural causes and effects. (850)

I think it fair to assume that the narrator has indeed killed his wife and is about to be executed for it. Everything, therefore, is not in his mind, and it is our role as readers to try to separate the real from the imagined. Was there a fire, and if so was it just an accident? Did a figure appear on the bedroom wall, and if so what caused it? Did a second almost identical cat appear? Where did it come from? Did it really have markings in the shape of a gallows? These questions deserve answers, which so far have not been forthcoming, but which I believe the story supplies.

The key to these answers is to be found in the fact that the narrator is lying, a fact that he himself suggests in his very first breath. "For the most wild yet most homely narrative which I am about to pen," he begins, "I neither expect nor solicit belief. Mad indeed would I be to expect it, in a case where my very senses reject their own evidence. Yet, mad am I not—and very surely do I not dream" (849). If the man is neither mad nor mistaken, and yet is not to be believed, it can only be that he is lying. In effect, the narrator defies the reader to find him out, just as he recklessly defies the police by calling attention to the very wall that conceals his wife's body.

The knowledge that the narrator is lying, and of his motive in doing so—denial of guilt for the murder of his wife—gives us the vantage point from which we are able to discover the truth. What emerges is this: the narrator murdered his wife, not impulsively on the cellar stairs as he asserts, but willfully and with malice afore-thought at the very time he claims to have killed his cat; the sup-posed cat-killing is a fiction he invents in order to assuage his guilt and, more immediately, to explain away the mysterious "appari-tion" on the bedroom wall that threatens to expose his crime; the alleged appearance of a second cat is also a fiction, cooked up to explain the continued existence of the supposedly dead cat; it is actually Pluto that is discovered in the basement wall with the wife's body. These conclusions seem at first astonishing; but such is the genius of Poe's story that what proves more astonishing is how confidently they may be deduced from a careful examination of the evidence.

The first task, as every armchair detective knows, is to deter-mine the time of death. The narrator wants us to believe that his wife died on the cellar stairs three days before the body was found (858). This idea is belied, however, by a succession of clues the narrator lets slip, culminating in a final fatal slip in his last paragraph. First, immediately after describing the incident on the cellar stairs, the narrator details his ruminations on how to hide his wife's body:

> I knew that I could not remove it from the house, either by day or by night, without the risk of being observed by the neighbors. Many projects entered my mind. At one period I thought of cutting the corpse into minute fragments, and destroying them by fire. At another, I resolved to dig a grave for it in the floor of the cellar. Again, I deliberated about casting it in the well in the yard—about packing it in a box, as if merchandise, with the usual arrangements, and so getting a porter to take it from the house. Finally I hit upon what I considered a far better expedient than either of these. I deter-mined to wall it up in the cellar. . . . (856–57)

This description, and particularly the references to "one period" and "another," suggest that considerable time passes between the murder and the entombment in the basement wall. The reader is therefore surprised to discover that the entombment is in fact con-cluded on the same day as the incident on the stairs (858). If we questioned the narrator, he would doubtless quickly recover and tell us he meant different periods of a single morning; still our suspicions should at least be aroused.

READINGS

They can only be heightened by the active involvement of the police, which would seem odd if the murder had been committed when the narrator suggests it was. "Some few inquiries" had been made, he tells us, and not one but two "rigorous" searches conducted (858). Is it likely that this level of suspicion and investigation would result from the wife's absence for just three days?

Having raised our doubts, the narrator delivers the clincher in his final paragraph. There he tells us that the body, when found, was "already greatly decayed and clotted with gore" (859). It is inconceivable that a body, walled up immediately upon death in a cool basement, should become "greatly decayed" in the short space of three days. On the contrary, protected from the heat and insects that promote decay, and preserved even from dehydration in the damp cellar, the corpse would have remained in excellent condition, not just for days, but weeks. Unless we are prepared to make the apparently groundless supposition that the narrator is either mistaken or lying about the condition of the corpse, we can only conclude that the murder must have been committed much earlier than he admits.

That there is extensive additional evidence pointing to this conclusion will be seen shortly. It will be asked, however, and it must be considered, how we are to judge the truth of the various assertions the narrator makes. Since we rely on him for all our information, it may seem hopeless for us to determine with any assurance when he is speaking the truth and when he is lying. This problem, however, proves more difficult in theory than in practice. Knowing his situation and his purpose in deceiving us takes us a long way. In weighing the statements of someone accused of a crime, our common sense leads us to the following guidelines: (1) We accept incriminating information as likely to be true, since the suspect would have no reason to invent it; (2) We give less credence to exculpatory details; (3) We do, however, give credence to statements that can be corroborated by other witnesses; (4) We make careful distinction between the suspect's statements of fact and his interpretation of those facts; (5) We are alert to "weasel wording," the practice, perfected by schoolchildren and Congressional witnesses, of devising statements that leave a false impression, but are literally true. (A child accused of breaking an object, for example, may protest, "I never touched it." His statement is true: he did not touch it, the hammer did.)

Pursuing our inference that the narrator is misleading us about the time of his wife's death, let us examine his version of events to see whether we find ourselves at a loss in attempting to separate truth from falsehood (or imagining), or whether our common sense guides us quite easily to a clear and sensible interpretation. A significant point that other critics of the story have ignored is that a jury must have already made a similar attempt at sorting out the facts. They obviously rejected the narrator's explanation of the crime, or they could not have convicted him of premeditated murder. We shall arrive at a similar conclusion.

If we ask, for example, when the murder did occur, only one answer seems likely: the narrator must have killed his wife at the time he says he killed Pluto. We are drawn to this supposition, at first, simply because no other point in the story has sufficient prominence or weight; the moment we entertain the idea, however, we find powerful evidence to support it. To begin with, it clears up one very troublesome passage, the narrator's overwrought description of the cat hanging:

> One morning, in cold blood, I slipped a noose about its neck and hung it to the limb of a tree;—hung it with the tears streaming from my eyes, and with the bitterest remorse at my heart;—hung it *because* I felt it had given me no reason of offence;—hung it *because* I knew that in so doing I was committing a sin—a deadly sin that would so jeopardize my immortal soul as to place it—if such a thing were possible—even beyond the reach of the infinite mercy of the Most Merciful and Most Terrible God. (852)

Such gaudy sentiments, as Gargano points out, constitute "outrageous excess" (173) if applied merely to the killing of a cat. As a reaction to the murder of one's wife, they seem far more appropriate. By contrast, the narrator's reaction at the time of the incident on the stairs seems wholly inadequate to the enormity of the deed. "This hideous murder accomplished," he blithely reports, "I set myself forthwith, and with entire deliberation, to the task of concealing the body" (856). The reactions are misplaced: some reversal has occurred.

This reversal is the substitution of cat for wife and wife for cat, first described by Daniel Hoffman and now widely accepted. There is no doubt that the narrator projects his feelings for his wife onto his cat, but the substitution is even more complete than Hoffman suggests. It is not merely that the wife was always the intended victim; she was the original, in fact the only victim. Moreover, this inference provides a much more compelling reason for the narrator's substitution of cat for wife—or rather twin reasons, for his pretense that he has only killed his cat serves both to ease his own sense of guilt, and to shield him from, prosecution for murder.

Most important, the idea that the narrator has killed his wife rather than Pluto will now provide what all previous analyses of the tale have failed to produce: a clear, logical explanation for the ensuing events of the story.[1] Consider, for example, the matter of the fire and the strange "apparition" that appears on the bedroom wall. What are we to make of this figure? We could call it imaginary, the product of the narrator's guilty conscience. But the figure seems the most real thing in the story, one of the few that we are told has been observed by others. Calling this imaginary, then, is tantamount to dismissing the whole story as a dream. On the other hand, if the figure was really there, where did it come from? There would seem to be two possibilities: natural causes or supernatural. The narrator favors the former, yet he offers an explanation so preposterous that it ranks among American literature's all-time whoppers. First, he tells us that some unidentified neighbor, "probably" in order to awaken the narrator when the fire broke out, "must have" thrown the cat's body through an open window of his bedroom (853). This concerned neighbor, we must assume, in that he rejected the obvious expedient of hurling a stone at and shattering the bedroom window, was one of that large group of people who believe that the best sound for waking people is a dull thud. Next we are asked to believe that the cat's body somehow got moved, through the action of collapsing walls and in defiance of gravity, from the floor on which it presumably fell up onto and into the wet plaster of the wall (or else we must suppose that the flung cat hit the wet plaster in the first place—and stuck). And finally the narrator says that the lime from the plaster, ammonia from the dead cat and the heat of the fire combined to do, um, something that in some unexplained manner completely covered the cat's body with fresh plaster.

The spuriousness of this account is, without doubt, its most conspicuous characteristic. To try to explain away that spuriousness, as at least one critic has done (Halliburton 341), or to kindly

---

[1] One interesting passage is the narrator's assertion that "with great difficulty . . . my wife, a servant, and myself, made our escape from the conflagration" (852). I assume, of course, that it is actually Pluto, not the wife, that has escaped, the narrator continuing to interchange wife and cat. More provocative is the reference to the servant. Clearly if anyone saw the narrator's wife alive, either escaping from the fire or at any time after the supposed cat hanging, my interpretation would be undermined. It is noteworthy, then, that the narrator makes no such claim, except in the person of the servant. Significantly, this character is probably the story's most conspicuously mysterious, on any reading of the tale. The reference to him or her immediately surprises and perplexes us: we had never before heard mention of this character, or for that matter of any servants, and we never do again. In short, we find in this character another of Poe's contributions to the detective genre: the "mystery man"—the witness nobody else saw, who may or may not exist, who the suspect swears can clear him, but who cannot be located. Referred to merely as "a servant," this anonymous

overlook it, as most do, is to adopt the untenable position that Poe did not intend the effect he created. A further reason for rejecting the narrator's account is that, if true, it undercuts the theme of the story. For if the figure really did appear in the incredible manner described, then the narrator is by no means a victim of his own conscience, but of a sequence of occurrences so extraordinary it could make anyone homicidal.

The only alternative is the supernatural interpretation. This view, which Gargano at times appears to adopt, posits that intelligent unseen forces are at work in the story, actively cooperating to restore the moral order that the narrator's crime has disturbed (178). Such an interpretation, while offering logical consistency, is far from satisfying. It seems entirely out of keeping with the psychological tenor of the tale and with the body of Poe's work.

The sensible conclusion is that something has indeed appeared on the standing wall and that there is some rational explanation for this appearance, but for reasons of his own the narrator is not telling us the truth about it. Separating fact from fiction would seem impossible, but only if we assume that it is Pluto who has been killed. Once we realize that it is the narrator's wife who is dead, the logical explanation immediately presents itself. It is *her* body that appears like a bas-relief in the plaster, protruding as it does from *inside the wall, where the narrator has hidden it.* This conclusion accounts, first, for the fresh plaster in the room (853), the presence of which remains otherwise unexplained.[2] Moreover, the narrator supplies direct evidence that he has walled his wife up in his bedroom, thanks to another remark he lets slip at the end of his story. Having completed the entombment in the cellar, he tells us, "I looked around triumphantly, and said to myself: 'Here, at least, then, my labor has not been in vain'" (857). Aside from

---

figure simply disappears from view. The newly impoverished narrator has doubtless let this servant go, and his or her whereabouts remain forever unknown. (It is possible, as I speculate in the following note, that the servant, having seen what he or she was not supposed to see, is actually another of the narrator's victims. Such an interpretation provides an alternative explanation for the aura of mystery that surrounds this character.)

[2] The narrator subsequently tells us that the cellar "had lately been plastered throughout" (857). Does this suggest the existence of additional bodies there? The narrator has acknowledged following the reappearance of the cat that his "usual temper increased to hatred of all things and of all mankind" (856). That statement, combined with the curious absence in the latter part of the tale of any references to the narrator's other pets, or his servant, invites our suspicion. Direct evidence is scant, however, and it is possible to interpret this plastering as the result of the narrator's having established living quarters in the cellar following the fire.

the casual reference to Milton's Satan, this remark makes no sense unless the narrator has previously performed similar work elsewhere.

That work is the first entombment of his wife's body in the bedroom wall. What renders the work vain is the appearance of the figure in the plaster, which excites the "minute and eager attention" (843) of the neighbors, forcing the murderer to invent his absurd explanation. The suspicious nature of that explanation is thus accounted for as the consequence of its being a fabrication, invented on the spur of the moment. The narrator insists, for obvious reasons, that the figure is that of his cat, but it should be noticed that he alone identifies it as such; the neighbors are quoted only as saying, "singular" and "strange" (853). His assertion is belied by his use of the word "gigantic" (853). Pluto has been described as "remarkably large" (850), a far cry from "gigantic." The word makes perfect sense, however, if it is a woman's body being passed off as a cat's. Even the extreme terror that seizes the narrator at the sight of the figure (853) makes better sense when the figure is recognized to be his wife's. It is not just the specter of the victim that frightens him; it is the threat of exposure.

The same kind of analysis can be applied to the supposed appearance of the second cat. The doubtful nature of the narrator's account begins with the sheer improbability of his discovering a second cat virtually identical to Pluto, right down to the missing eye. The circumstances of the discovery confirm our suspicions, for the supposedly new cat makes its appearance, atop a cask of liquor in a barroom, literally out of nowhere. "I had been looking steadily at the top of this hogshead for some minutes," the narrator reports, "and what now caused me surprise was the fact that I had not sooner perceived the object thereupon" (854). In addition, this supposedly strange cat treats the narrator like a long lost friend, responding immediately to his touch, accompanying him home, and domesticating itself at once (854).

Here again we seem surrounded by unacceptable interpretations. We cannot dismiss this cat as an hallucination, since it appears to the police at the end of the story. We are therefore forced once more either to shrug our shoulders at extraordinary coincidence and strangeness, or to accept that the hand of divine retribution is indeed at work in the story, magically delivering duplicate pussies to cat-killers in need of comeuppance. Again, however, a far more reasonable explanation presents itself. The second cat is a fiction: a predictable, indeed necessary, lie that follows directly from the narrator's previous lie. Having explained the figure on the wall by saying that he killed Pluto, he is now compelled to explain the continuing presence of the supposedly dead cat. The only possible way is to try to pass this cat off as a new one. The title of the story tells us the truth. There are not two black cats; there is only Pluto: *the* black cat.

And what of the white splotch on the supposedly new cat's breast: is this evidence that there really is a second cat? But this simply raises the same unanswered questions. Is the splotch real and does it really change its appearance "by slow degrees" (855) as the narrator says? Answer "No," and we give up the story as imagined; answer "Yes," and we are at a loss to account for such a change, except by supernatural forces. If the cat is Pluto, on the other hand, a likely answer offers itself at once: the cat was caught in the recent house fire and was burned; the splotch is simply the grayish-white muscle tissue that would lie exposed where the flesh has burned away; this area changes in outline over the ensuing weeks, as is normal in such cases, as new skin and perhaps hair grow in (Defeis). In this way the facts that the narrator relates are well accounted for. The statement that the splotch resembled a gallows, on the other hand, is not a fact, but the narrator's own interpretation, which we should not hesitate to ascribe to his guilt and fear.

While I have been at pains thus far to explain the "succession of very natural causes and effects" (849) in the tale, my analysis also clarifies the story's psychological lines, for once the narrator's deceitful cover story is revealed, the remaining phenomena emerge quite clearly as the products of his guilty conscience. The splotch on Pluto's breast is a good example. To protect himself from the law and from his own conscience, he has denied his crime by insisting that the victim was only his cat. Pluto's existence is a constant reminder of the falsity of that claim. It is this that makes him dread the cat and associate it with the gallows. He admits as much when he tells us that it was his wife who "called [his] attention" to the shape of the splotch (855). The image of the gallows at all at this point, it should be noted, makes sense only if the wife was the victim; surely the narrator does not fear execution for having hanged a cat.

The continued existence of the cat, filling him with fear and guilt, now drives him mad:

> Alas! neither by day nor by night knew I the blessing of rest any more! During the former the creature left me no moment alone, and in the latter I started hourly from dreams of unutterable fear to find the hot breath of *the thing* upon my face, and its vast weight—an incarnate nightmare that I had no power to shake off—incumbent eternally upon my *heart!* (856)

The struggle to maintain the fiction that his wife is alive threatens to destroy him, and now follows the incident on the stairs, in which he attempts a new strategy, admitting that he has killed his wife, but recasting the act as an accident (or at worst a negligent homicide). This pivotal incident warrants scrutiny. It occurred, he says, when his wife "accompanied [him], upon some household errand, into the cellar . . ." (856). That "errand" was most likely the removal of the wife's body to a more secure hiding place. On the stairs to the cellar, the cat, he tells us, tripped him up. His description proceeds as follows:

> Uplifting an axe . . . I aimed a blow at the animal, which, of course, would have proved instantly fatal had it descended as I wished. But this blow was arrested by the hand of my wife. Goaded by the interference into a rage more than demoniacal, I withdrew my arm from her grasp and buried the axe in her brain. She fell dead upon the spot without a groan. (856)

This passage, with its seemingly empty rhetorical flourishes, appears at first to be bad writing. But when we read it knowing that the wife is already dead, it appears as something quite different and far more amusing: a clever attempt to convey the idea that the wife is alive, while speaking only the literal truth. The seemingly awkward passive, "this blow was arrested by the hand of my wife," slyly suggests volition—and even life—without expressing any. The gruesome, "I . . . buried the axe in her brain" neatly avoids claiming that this blow actually killed the woman. And the statement that she fell dead "without a groan," turns out to be not a cliché, but a black joke. (The narrator offers another version of the same joke in the preceding paragraph, when, referring to his increasingly violent behavior, he observes that his "uncomplaining wife, alas, was the most usual and the most patient of sufferers" [856].)

The narrator is a man at war with himself, consciously trying to hide his crime, while subconsciously seeking to reveal it. The fatal blunders of walling up the cat and subsequently rapping on the cellar wall with his cane are parapraxes, subconsciously designed to expose his guilt. The fire that breaks out in his house the night of the murder is similarly intended to expose his crime, as it nearly does. This occurrence, I might add, is yet another phenomenon that most critics do not even attempt to explain. It will be noticed that this analysis posits neither supernatural forces nor extraordinary coincidences. Everything that occurs is within the capabilities of the narrator, driven by what is today a familiar psychological force; it is this force, not divine intervention, that operates to restore the moral order. The battle between the murderer's conscious and unconscious wills that we see in his actions is mirrored in his narration. From his first paragraph, in which he warns us of his own untrustworthiness and suggests that his story has a logical explanation, he drops hints of the truth he is consciously trying to conceal. His comment on the fire is a good example: "I am above the weakness of seeking to establish a sequence of cause and effect," he says, "between the disaster and the atrocity" (853). In so saying, he alerts us to the very connection that explicitly he denies.

Significantly, his damaging admissions multiply at the end of the narrative. It is here, for example, that he reveals the extent of police involvement and that he makes the remark about his labor not being in vain. The pattern of his narrative thus parallels that of his behavior. The climax of the story's action, and the height of the murderer's guilt-induced folly, occur when, just as the police are about to leave, he raps on the wall within which his wife's body is entombed. In the very same way, readers are but three sentences from finishing the story, largely accepting of the narrator's version of events, when he reveals gratuitously the greatly decayed state of the corpse, providing the crucial evidence that exposes his true crime.

"The Black Cat" emerges from this analysis as far less mystifying than has been thought. In fact it proves to be one of Poe's least mystifying, and most satisfying, stories: a masterful pre-Dostoevsky, pre-Freud profile of the psychology of crime and punishment, and at the same time a first-rate detective story. Indeed, it is surely Poe's best detective story, with the ideal detective story solution: one that is simplicity itself in explaining all the facts, yet so elusive it has taken a century and a half to be discovered.

Souce: Susan Amper, "Untold Story: The Lying Narrator in 'The Black Cat.'" Copyright © 1992. Reprinted by permission of the author.

WORKS CITED

Bonaparte, Marie. "The Black Cat." *Partisan Review*, vol. 17, 1950, pp. 834–60.

Crisman, William. "'Mere Household Events' in Poe's 'The Black Cat.'" *Studies in American Fiction*, vol. 12, 1984, pp. 87–90.

Defeis, Frank, DVM. Personal interview. 15 Mar. 1992.

Gargano, James. "'The Black Cat': Perverseness Reconsidered." *Texas Studies in Language and Literature*, vol. 2, 1960, pp. 172–78.

Halliburton, David. *Edgar Allan Poe: A Phenomenological View.* Princeton UP, 1973.

Hoffman, Daniel. *Poe Poe Poe Poe Poe Poe Poe.* Doubleday, 1972.

Poe, Edgar Allan. "The Black Cat." *Collected Works of Edgar Allan Poe*, edited by Thomas Olive Mabbott. Belknap, 1978, pp. 849–60.

READINGS

FOR DISCUSSION

1. What specific gap in understanding is each of these literary analyses presuming to fill?
2. What "background knowledge" about the literary work did each author provide to help readers follow her analysis?
3. What knowledge about the work being analyzed does each author take for granted?
4. What types of evidence does each author provide in support of her interpretation?
5. Have you read in full either of the literary works being analyzed? If so, did you find the model analysis to be valid? Why or why not?

WORKS CITED

Iser, Wolfgang. *Prospecting: From Reader Response to Literary Anthropology.* Johns Hopkins UP, 1989.

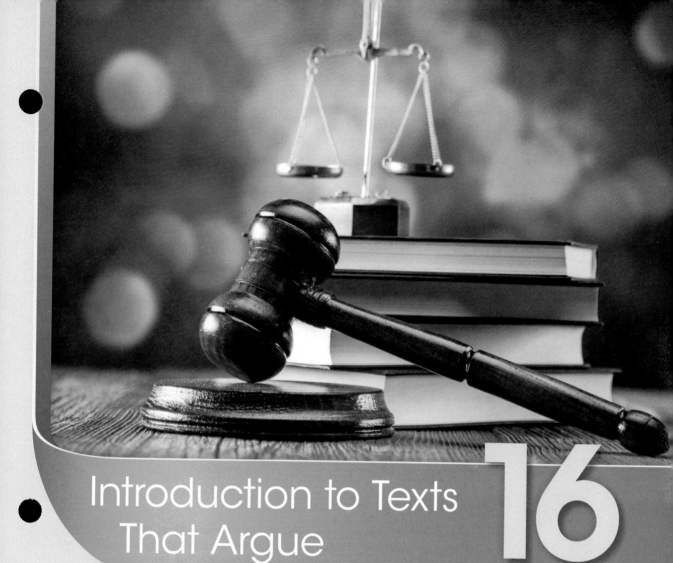

Introduction to Texts That Argue 16

Scales and gavel are symbols of the courtroom, site of some of the most innovative, effective, and certainly most controversial arguments in history. What high profile cases can you recall? That which ended in the removal of Terri Schiavo's feeding tube at her husband's request despite the objections of her parents? That which sentenced actress Lindsay Lohan to mandatory rehabilitation for crimes surrounding a reckless driving offense? Whether or not you agree with the outcomes of these proceedings, the lawyers involved were charged with providing the best case possible for their clients—that is, providing arguments to convince judge and jury to side with them. The following chapter introduces several tools for helping you tip the scales in your favor—in other words, for helping you craft an effective argument.

In the American court system, any individual accused of a crime is entitled to a fair trial, even if the evidence against him or her seems overwhelming. But the fact is, in many cases, the verdict is not about some irrefutable Truth with a capital "T" (even DNA evidence and confessions are not 100 percent reliable); rather, it's about the credibility attributed to competing versions of events. In other words, most courtroom dramas play out in the realm of the probable, as they are subject to the relative believability of witnesses and exhibits that the lawyers present.

In fact, probability, or degree of likelihood, is the measure that guides the creation and analysis of arguments in most every area of communication—including the political, corporate, academic, and even personal. After all, there is no need to argue a claim or assertion if involved parties accept that it is true (e.g., the claim that the Grand Canyon hosts a variety of wildlife or that Miley Cyrus videos have sparked a hotbed of controversy). But, of course, in a society as diverse as America, disagreement abounds over many topics that have significantly impacted (or will impact) your life. For example, legislators rigorously debate health care reform; business leaders wrangle over strategies for increasing profits on their top-selling products; education professors challenge each other's opinions about standards-based school curricula; and parents squabble with their children over the amount of technology they should have access to.

Throughout your college career, you will be asked to "make your case" in response to various unsettled issues (maybe even one or more of those mentioned above), and your ability to argue effectively will influence teachers' assessments of your writing ability. Many of the strategies addressed in previous chapters are central to the processes involved in crafting successful arguments. The paragraphs that follow expand on information in those earlier chapters, with particular attention to the structure of arguments.

Purposes of and Strategies for Arguing

The main reason for engaging in argument is to convince others that your perspective on an issue that you're passionate about is the one that they should adopt. Whether the implications are global or personal, the objective is to marshal as much evidence as you can to persuade your audience that the position you are advancing is the "right one"—or at least worthy of careful consideration. Be aware, though, that evidence is not limited to well-established facts; sometimes, your only support may be in the nature of your own logic or reasoning **(logos).** Moreover, your logic or reasoning can be enhanced by other rhetorical appeals—that is, appeals to emotion **(pathos),** as well as appeals based on your own and your sources' credibility **(ethos).** (See Chapter 3 for a specific discussion and examples of logos, pathos, and ethos.). All of these appeals can be strengthened by attention to tone, the structure of your argument, and resistance to logical fallacies.

Tone

As you consider how to invoke logos, pathos, and ethos in service of your own arguments, you should remember that **tone**—or the attitude you project—is crucial. In other words, even though arguing is sometimes associated with verbal attacks, it by no means requires you to be exceedingly aggressive, overbearing, or critical. In fact, if you come off as degrading or insulting, readers are sure to doubt your integrity. On the contrary, in most academic and professional venues, the most persuasive arguments are those that are sincerely motivated, fair in their treatment of the subject matter, and respectful of those who may believe differently.

Another principle to consider when you are evaluating the tone of your arguments is the intensity of your claims. Given that arguments occur in the realm of the probable, you'll want to be careful about phrasing your assertions as absolutes. To contend that a particular observation is *always,* in *all* situations, and for *all* time an accurate portrayal of the issue at stake is to occupy an extreme position that probably won't hold up to scrutiny. In the realm of the probable, it's more rhetorically astute to temper your claims, indicating your recognition that what readers accept as "truth" at a particular point in time is subject to change or elaboration. As such, most of your claims will employ qualifying language that protects you from charges that you are exaggerating the "rightness" of your views. So, for example, instead of *always,* you might opt for *usually* or *ordinarily;* instead of *all,* you might opt for *most* or *the majority;* and so on. (You can learn more about qualifying claims in the next section.)

MYTH

"If you want to win an argument, you shouldn't even mention ideas in support of the opposition."

You may fear that mentioning others' viewpoints will bring to light some information that's so compelling it could weaken your own position. On the contrary, anticipating, addressing, and possibly even conceding potential counterarguments demonstrate that you have been conscientious in researching the issue. Relevant to tone, specifically, these moves indicate that you are fair-minded in considering multiple perspectives. Both attributes contribute to a strong ethos. (You can read more about counterarguments later in this chapter.)

REALITY

Structure

Because you engage in arguments virtually every day, the processes you use to **structure** them, or put them together, have likely become automatic; therefore, the separate parts may be difficult to uncover and isolate. Various scholars have articulated methods for helping readers and writers analyze and build arguments, but one of the most widely employed methods is attributed to philosopher Stephen Toulmin. The popularity of his approach rests in its specificity, as he clearly identifies six elements that constitute a well-formed argument. These elements and their definitions are provided in Figure 16.1.

While most of the concepts in Toulmin's taxonomy are likely familiar to you, an example, like that in Figure 16.2, can clarify the relationships between them. More specifically, that example breaks down an argument based on a recent controversy in college athletics. The controversy spawned a lawsuit that drew considerable media attention.

Although Figure 16.2 exemplifies all the elements involved in a Toulmin analysis, you should know that published arguments will not necessarily follow the order portrayed. Indeed, confining components of an argument to some rigid pattern might interfere with your ability to express relationships between them. In addition, certain elements, namely the warrant, might be implied as opposed to explicitly

Element	Definition
Claim	An assertion you want to uphold
Data	Reasons you provide in support of your claim
Warrant	A sometimes unexpressed assumption that underlies the relationship between your claim and data
Backing	Evidence that supports your warrant
Qualifier	Words, phrases, or sentences that establish the extent to which or conditions under which your argument is reasonable
Point of rebuttal	Your reference and response to potential counterarguments

Figure 16.1 Toulmin's system for analyzing an argument's structure

Element	Example
Claim	Famous college athletes should earn salaries for playing their sports.
Data	A good portion of athletic department revenues can be tied to these athletes' popularity.
Warrant	Individuals responsible for helping generate profit deserve compensation proportionate to their contribution.
Backing	Several former college athletes support a change in NCAA regulations on this issue, noting the sacrifices athletes make—especially with regard to injury—to play well enough to draw the big crowds.
Qualifier	Of course, scholarship dollars should be taken into account when calculating appropriate additional compensation.
Point of rebuttal	These athletes are on full-ride scholarships the way it is; the university shouldn't have to shell out even more considering its overhead. (*Response:* Yet scholarship money doesn't cover all needs; moreover, the profit margin for universities is so great they would hardly feel the additional payout.)

Figure 16.2 Example of Toulmin analysis

stated. And, finally, most books and articles will contain multiple claims, with the thesis serving as the primary claim. Put another way, most documents of even moderate length will contain arguments within arguments. See Figure 16.3 for an indication of how a thesis (primary claim), supporting claims, and other elements identified by Toulmin might be plotted in the context of an argumentative essay.

Having reviewed some key concepts involved in analyzing and building successful arguments, consider how several of them are applied in the Look Inside excerpt on page 282 from an argument on the topic of biotechnology. In this piece, author David Steele cautions readers about a world in which biotechnology forges ahead unchecked by government regulations. This excerpt illustrates Steele's use of various rhetorical appeals and reveals several elements of the Toulmin system. Beyond this excerpt, Steele provides more evidence for his claim that regulation of biotech research is limited by referencing a report from the Royal Society of Canada, a body of scientists and other academics who advise the government on various matters.

Together, Steele's claims, data, warrants, and backing build toward a fuller articulation of the thesis near the end of the piece: Even though biotech research

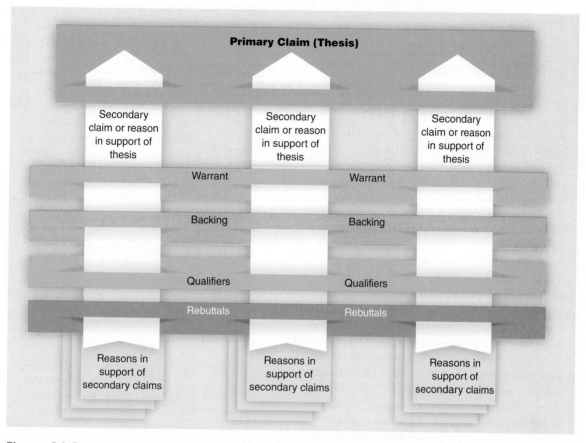

Figure 16.3 **Elements of the Toulmin system plotted in an argumentative essay.** To have a well-supported thesis, an author will need to think through all components of the Toulmin system, deciding how to arrange and stress them in relation to each other. Warrants may go unstated if it's certain the audience will accept them.

produces great benefits, the very real dangers it presents must not go unchecked; thus, public scrutiny of what have been largely privately funded activities must intensify. Steele's strategy of revisiting his thesis in a more forceful, specific way as the article ends is not uncommon, especially since it involves a call to action and readers need to be clear about what they will be acting on and why before they can be convinced to do so.

Logical Fallacies

Your success at convincing others to take action or adopt a particular viewpoint will depend in part on your ability to avoid **logical fallacies**—types of reasoning that, although they may look solid on the surface, are actually flawed. Learning to

From "Danger Lurks in a Biotech World"

by David Steele

I'm a molecular biologist. I've used molecular techniques to study heredity, evolution, gene expression, and even components of heart function (strangely enough using yeast as the model organism). I know how powerful molecular technology can be and how vast its contribution has been to our understanding of life's basic processes and to our medical well-being.

But I'm worried. Very Worried.

Molecular biology, like most sciences, arose from intellectual curiosity. Academic scientists wondered how life works; what kind of information we could cull from manipulating its basic building blocks, what we could learn from shuffling those building blocks around.

The approach proved wildly productive. We've gained unprecedented insights. We've learned what underlies countless diseases, how the basic machinery of our cells operates, and, to varying extents, how to manipulate those operations for our own purposes. We've learned so much that we think we know what we are doing. But all that knowledge cannot compare to what we do not know. And it is in our unrecognized ignorance that the greatest danger lies.

A few years ago, researchers at the Australian National University demonstrated just how appallingly dangerous our ignorance is.

These scientists were trying to make a contraceptive vaccine for mice—a vaccine that would make the animals sterile. To that end, they constructed an artificial virus genetically coded to express (produce) a normal mouse protein. Ordinarily, the protein increases antibody production. Since the Australian group was trying to get the mice to make antibodies to their own

A LOOK INSIDE: ARGUING FOR INCREASED GOVERNMENT REGULATION OF SCIENCE

The author establishes ethos up front by stating his credentials—a smart move given that they clearly qualify him as an expert on the topic and suggest he would be likely to argue the opposite of the position he adopts.

Here, the author delivers part of his thesis, which he elaborates near the end of the piece.

The author strengthens his ethos by considering other viewpoints and noting their benefits. (These could also serve as points of rebuttal in the Toulmin scheme.)

At this point, the author provides reasoning for his thesis (primary claim), which resurfaces near the end of the piece—that there needs to be greater regulation of biotech science. (The warrant is that lax regulation leaves society vulnerable to unwelcome consequences.)

eggs, the approach seemed reasonable enough. But the experiment went terribly wrong.

Instead of making sterile mice, the technique made dead mice. And the deaths were not by a mechanism that the scientists would have predicted. They thought they knew what they were doing. But they couldn't have been more wrong. Instead of boosting the effectiveness of the mouse immune system, the virus effectively shut the system down and killed the animals.

> This paragraph offers backing for the warrant about unwelcome consequences. The backing also serves as an emotional appeal (pathos) to proponents of animal rights.

The virus was contained in the lab and it apparently poses no danger to humans, but that's not the point. The fact is that every day, in labs around the world, scientists are constructing artificial viruses that can infect humans. Many are designed to do precisely that. Some are made for pure research purposes, others to be used, potentially, for "gene therapy"—a hoped for means to cure genetic diseases in living humans. Should one of these viruses go hopelessly wrong, like the Australian mouse virus did, watch out!

> The following paragraphs extend and reinforce the backing, illustrating society's vulnerability, while also noting that intentions are often well-meaning.

What the Australian researchers have demonstrated is that viral experiments are dangerous. Very dangerous. Even when we truly believe that we understand what we're doing, even when our goals are laudable—like curing disease and ameliorating suffering—the results of our experiments can be disastrous. Fortunately, the Australian virus was (very likely) limited to the confines of their lab. A very great deal of biotech research has no such limitations.

> The last line of this paragraph offers another reason to accept the author's primary argument for greater regulation. This datum serves as a subclaim (to the thesis) that in itself calls for support.

Genetically engineered food organisms, for example, are cropping up all around us. Successive Canadian governments have bent over backwards to help the biotech giants bring these "products" to market. In the United States, as the *New York Times* has reported, Monsanto [an agriculture company] essentially wrote its own regulations. Not surprisingly, they're extremely lax. In both the U.S. and Canada, there is very little government oversight.

> Here, the author cites evidence to support the subclaim that regulation is lacking by pointing to examples of rampant genetically engineered crop growth.

recognize logical fallacies will make you a more astute reader of others' arguments, helping you pinpoint and respond to weaknesses in positions you don't agree with. This level of critical awareness will also help you evaluate the quality of sources you may want to cite in your own texts, as well as avoid faulty logic in constructing your own arguments. To get started, consult Figure 16.4, which lists some common fallacies, as well as definitions and examples that clarify their nature.

Of course, in some cases, logical fallacies are employed purposefully when the ends are believed to justify the means. For example, in his argument for tighter regulations on biotech research, David Steele might be accused of intentionally **exaggerating danger** with his warnings about escaped viruses and super-plants running wild. Ordinarily, though, authors try to avoid fallacies because they can undermine perceptions about the quality of the argument on the whole. Moreover, fallacies may call the author's ethos or credibility into question, as some of them are downright misleading (can you think of some advertisements that might fit this description?).

Fallacy	Definition	Example
Red herring	A distraction or side argument that draws attention from the central issue	Residents of Smithsville don't need to be worried about tornado preparedness; given its location, the town is more likely to suffer an earthquake.
Bandwagon	A call to jump on board because everyone else has	Refusing to participate in social media these days is, essentially, declaring yourself a hermit.
Slippery slope	An assertion that one small event will set off a barrage of others	If medical marijuana becomes more readily available, recreational smoking will increase, illegal sales of harder drugs will rise exponentially, and crime rates will soar.
False dichotomy	An approach to an issue that suggests that there are only two choices	We must hold all first-year composition courses in computer labs—either that, or send students into the workforce without the writing skills they will need for success.
Faulty analogy	An argument that rests on an unfair or incomplete comparison	To take the supplement melatonin is dangerous because it is a hormone, as is estrogen or testosterone.
Ad hominem (personal attack)	A criticism of persons associated with a position as opposed to tenets of the position itself	Principal Miller's disciplinary tactics are too strict, which is not surprising since he doesn't have any children of his own.
False authority	An appeal to take the word of someone who lacks the proper credentials or experience	Concern about the safety of high-energy drinks is overblown; after all, a number of famous athletes have endorsed them as part of their training regimens.
Questionable causality	An assertion that because a certain event occurred *after* another it happened *because* of the other	Clearly, the driver of the red car is at fault; witnesses saw him arguing with his girlfriend directly preceding the collision.
Hasty generalization	A conclusion drawn from insufficient information	Airedale terriers are excellent family pets. My friend has one and the dog loves playing with her little sister.
Exaggerated danger	An assertion based on scare tactics	To willingly board a plane these days is an invitation for disaster considering all the reported malfunctions, not to mention the threat of terrorism.

Figure 16.4 Definitions and examples of common logical fallacies

Application in College and the Workplace

Chances are that you are highly conscious of the role argument plays in your everyday interactions with family and friends. And you've probably spent some time analyzing arguments relevant to your status as a citizen—for instance, arguments made by politicians seeking your vote based on their convictions about matters that will affect the society you live in. But how much time have you spent thinking about the role of argument in school and in your future career?

Many, if not all, of your teachers at the college level will expect you to defend your viewpoints on subject matter relevant to their courses. After all, argument is an effective vehicle for exhibiting, developing, and assessing critical-thinking skills. It is also an effective vehicle for expanding perspectives, advancing knowledge, and encouraging productive change. Even if you pursue a field that seems to operate on established fact, such as the hard sciences or math, reflecting on the biotechnology article excerpted earlier—or on the efforts of mathematicians who spent years working to convince others that their theorems were viable—will remind you that argument is crucial to success in these disciplines. Arguments, then, pervade every field of study and emerge in the context of various documents. Figure 16.5 lists genres that tend to be argumentative in nature, along with their purposes.

Composing effective arguments is challenging in the respect that all your rhetorical sensibilities must be on high alert. This reality grows from the fact that debatable issues and controversies can ignite strong feelings in those who are moved to read, write, and speak about them. To be more specific, while readers would probably find little to become offended by in an informative discussion about flight patterns of the great blue heron, they probably *would* become offended—and tune out your assertions—if you argued for full-body scans in airport security lines without being sensitive to the implications of your statements and the emotions they might provoke. The next few chapters (17 to 20) are devoted to helping you develop such sensitivities, as well as your reasoning abilities, in the context of argument-based genres frequently encountered in college coursework.

Genre	Purpose
Cover letter	To convince prospective employers that you are the right person for a job
Safety instruction	To convince others to take specific precautions when using a given product or operating machinery
Review	To convince others about the relative quality of a good, service, activity, or performance
Letter of complaint	To convince others that you deserve compensation for a substandard product or service
Advertisement	To convince others to purchase a certain product or service
Research proposal	To convince others that a project you plan to conduct will yield significant benefits
Position paper	To convince others to think as you do about a given issue
Response or rebuttal	To systematically dismantle a specific argument articulated by another author and provide counterarguments
Problem-solution paper	To convince others that a serious problem exists and that it should be addressed in a particular manner

Figure 16.5 **Common argumentative genres and their purposes**

WORKS CITED

Toulmin, Stephen. *The Uses of Argument*. 1958. Cambridge UP, 2003.

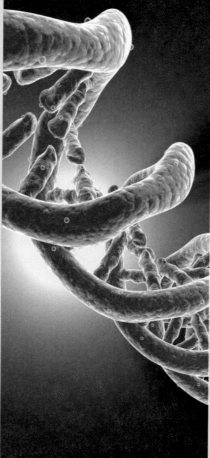

Research Proposal

17

Look closely at these images. What do they have in common? One answer to this question is that they represent research projects that are famous for expanding the knowledge base in their respective fields. The snapshot on the left recalls primatologist Jane Goodall's groundbreaking studies of chimpanzees' social behavior. In the middle lies a photograph of the double helix, the discovery of which revolutionized understanding of human genetics. The figure on the right is a cast of King Tutankhamun, whose tomb, once unearthed, yielded never-before-seen Egyptian artifacts. Although these exciting advancements emerged from different disciplines, they all began with research proposals—the subject of this chapter.

Well-conceived and effectively executed research projects are essential to progress in every field of study. Of course, many research projects depend on independent study and reflection—as in the case of a literature professor poring over early drafts of a novel to trace its development. Other projects, such as those represented by the images that open this chapter, may require additional person power for collecting and analyzing data, as well as travel money for funding on-site observations. To secure

"Undergraduates don't need to practice writing research proposals; this genre is specialized for the needs of professionals."

First-year writing teachers commonly assign research proposals to help students plan and organize large writing projects, but their relevance does not end there. In fact, many institutions have active undergraduate research programs that provide support for young scholars. Moreover, professors will sometimes involve undergraduates in their own research as a way of mentoring them. In both cases, understanding the purposes and special qualities of research proposals is essential or, at the very least, advantageous.

this kind of support, a researcher needs to compose a **research proposal** that argues for the project's significance and justifies a plan for completing it.

Although you probably can't expect financial backing to conduct research for your undergraduate coursework, it's not unusual for a teacher to assign a proposal as the first step in completing a major research project. Teachers who do so believe that proposal writing will help you manage complex assignments by asking you to define the purposes and procedures for an investigation up front. Toward that end, this chapter will introduce you to formal conventions and composing strategies associated with research proposals.

Distinguishing Features of a Research Proposal

To fully grasp the nature of a research proposal, you need to understand its role in the larger enterprise of conceiving and conducting research. Figure 17.1 clarifies where and how a research proposal can inform and propel your own research projects. As that figure indicates, a **research proposal** arises from a gap in knowledge regarding an issue that intrigues you. The proposal should explain your reasons for further educating yourself and others about that issue and should detail the methods by which you will do so. When the proposal is approved—validating the purpose and nature of the research study itself—you will feel prepared to carry out the investigation. Once the investigation is complete, you'll probably want to share your findings, perhaps in a research report. (You can read more about research reports in Chapter 9.)

Regarding the focus of this chapter—the proposal—you'll learn that its most obvious feature is its unique structure; that is, it unfolds in sections, each with its own subheading and purpose. Although, across disciplines, proposals will vary in the way they are arranged or in the way their subheadings are phrased, you'll discover that they do exhibit quite a bit of overlap with respect to elements considered essential for justifying projects and seeing them through. Figure 17.2 serves as a quick reference guide to a research proposal's typical contents.

In your composition course, your approach to grouping and elaborating the components described in Figure 17.2 will depend on your instructor's sense of where the emphasis should lie given the nature of the assigned research project. Whatever the emphasis, additional information about the proposal's components will help you understand their function in relationship to each other and within the full document. This information is provided in the sections that follow.

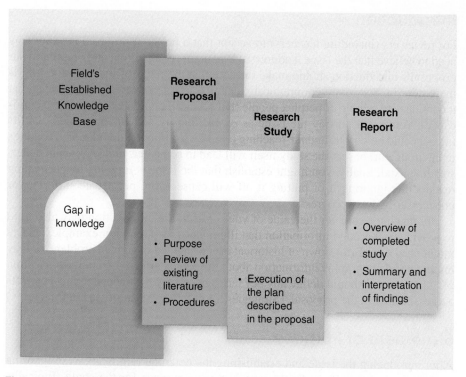

Figure 17.1 Role of a research proposal in the research process. A research proposal explains how you will fill a knowledge gap in a particular field by pinpointing that gap, synthesizing scholarship that helps reveal it, and reviewing steps you plan to follow in conducting your study.

Essential Component	Description
Introduction	Characterizes the issue that your research project will clarify
Statement of purpose	Explains your reasons for pursuing the study
Projected contributions	Identifies the anticipated outcomes of your study, emphasizing its significance in advancing knowledge or applying it
Literature review	Provides an overview of the conversation that has already taken place about the issue in published scholarship and identifies the gap in knowledge that your proposed study will fill
Research methods	Explains in detail the procedures you will follow in executing the proposed investigation
Conclusion	Highlights key points of the proposal, stressing the anticipated benefits of the study
Works cited or references	Records publication information for all resources you cited in preparing the proposal

Figure 17.2 Common components of research proposals

Introduction

For reviewers (including teachers) to accept that a research proposal is valid, they need to believe that the issue it addresses is genuine, compelling, and pressing. Your proposal's introduction should make the case that the focus of investigation fulfills these criteria. You might communicate that an issue is *genuine* by establishing that it continues to trouble or perplex people (but be careful not to exaggerate its significance). You might portray the issue as *compelling* by convincing readers that its impact could be serious and far-reaching (e.g., for a particular population, economy, or environment) or that the study itself will lead to some new and significant understanding. And, finally, you might establish that the issue is *pressing* by persuading readers that ignoring it or putting it off will cause harm, perpetuate suffering, or unnecessarily delay progress.

In making a case for the value of your project, the introduction may also need to provide background information that illuminates the topic. For example, readers might need a brief run-down of historical events that led to a given problem, or they might need demographic information about the people affected. Finally, this section of your proposal should define any key terms necessary for understanding concepts addressed later in the proposal. (Strategies for defining are addressed in Chapter 9.)

Statement of Purpose

After introducing the issue and establishing the potential ramifications of ignoring it, the proposal should explicitly articulate your purpose for the study. Typically, this section will define the scope of an investigation. In addition, it will identify what you hope to accomplish in the proposed study and, generally, how you will go about achieving those goals. An important word in the previous sentence is "generally," as this section should not be confused with the much more detailed discussion of procedures in the research methods section, which appears closer to the end of the proposal.

Projected Contributions

A sure way to convince readers that your project is worthy is to emphasize the "takeaways" you are counting on. Therefore, the projected contributions section of the proposal should explain exactly what you hope to gain by studying the problem you have identified in the particular way you intend to study it. Your expectations for how the project might contribute will grow from a sense of how existing scholarship is lacking—that is, from a gap you have noticed in the current knowledge base.

Gaps assume many forms, some of which are:

- Questions that have never been answered or even broached
- Types of studies that need to be conducted and haven't been
- Weaknesses in the research strategies employed in previous studies
- Discoveries that have not yet been connected with others

Do remember, though, that even small contributions can be valuable. In most cases, you can't presume to solve a complex problem in a single study—especially one confined by a semester-long class. However, you can expect to provide insights that will, at the very least, stimulate further conversation about your topic.

Literature Review

A literature review contextualizes your study by revealing the gist of the scholarly conversation that has already taken place about the issue. In fact, a literature review might be considered a distinct genre in and of itself. For instance, a thesis or dissertation, the capstone achievement in earning a master's or doctoral degree, devotes an entire chapter to surveying previously published scholarship. But since a research proposal devotes only one of several sections to a literature review, you must limit it to the works that *speak most directly* to the issue you are exploring. Indications that someone else's research is important to your project include recognition from another author working in the same area and/or citations of that scholarship in a number of sources addressing the topic.

In addition to highlighting important publications on the topic being investigated, a literature review also details gaps in that research. More specifically, a literature review reveals what the existing scholarship establishes, but it also stresses what remains to be confirmed, clarified, or elaborated. This requires discussing key articles and other resources *in relationship to* one another, or **synthesizing.** Synthesizing involves pinning down points of agreement and disagreement among sources, the former translating to principles you can take for granted (at least for now) and the latter isolating issues in need of further inquiry. By indicating where points of agreement and disagreement exist, a literature review helps readers recognize the gap and understand how the proposed study will attempt to fill it. (For more on synthesizing, see Chapter 21.)

Research Methods

The research methods section of the proposal identifies the questions your study will attempt to answer (based on the gaps exposed by your literature review) and explains the procedures you will follow in hopes of answering them. The length and complexity of this discussion will depend in part on the type of research you are conducting. If, for example, your research will depend primarily on reading library and Internet documents, the methods section will note the databases you consulted, the search terms you employed to locate sources, your guidelines for keeping or discarding certain sources, and your approach to analyzing those resources (e.g., whether you will concentrate on broad themes or mark specific textual features).

If, on the other hand, your study involves observations, surveys, or interviews (see Chapter 5), your methods section will need to provide other kinds of information. In particular, it should identify observation sites or the population of individuals you wish to question, as well as your reasons for selecting them. Furthermore, for interviews and surveys, this section should characterize your strategies for recruiting subjects (if, in fact, the population is too large to consult in its entirety) and the types of questions you will ask them.

Of course, you are not limited to one approach or the other; your study might involve analysis of print artifacts *and* observations, surveys, or interviews. Regardless, the methods section of your proposal should also specify procedures for compiling and interpreting your findings. After attending to that information, this section of the proposal typically ends with a paragraph or table presenting a timeline for completing the study, with each separate stage accounted for.

Conclusion

The conclusion of a research proposal should emphasize key points articulated earlier (without, of course, simply repeating them). Remember that this final paragraph or two is the last chance to impress upon readers the necessity of an investigation and the promise that it will yield valuable results. This part of the proposal-writing process is often referred to as addressing the "so what?" question, which involves convincing readers that the project matters. With this objective in mind, you can imagine that the statement of purpose and projected contributions sections of the proposal will suggest the most suitable content for the conclusion.

Works Cited or References

The persuasive appeal of any research proposal derives in part from its use of existing scholarship to demonstrate the breadth and depth of preparation in conceiving the project. As in other research-based documents, the Works Cited or References page for a research proposal conveniently pulls together all of the publication information for the sources you cite.

You should be aware that research proposals are often accompanied by annotated bibliographies in place of Works Cited or References pages. While similar in purpose and breadth, an annotated bibliography expands on the publication information by offering a summary and, potentially, an evaluation of the source. An annotated bibliography may also include an introduction that previews the concepts that your sources collectively cover. (For more on annotated bibliographies, see Chapter 10.)

The Parts as a Whole

Again, research proposals will differ somewhat with regard to required sections or the arrangement of those sections. But to consider how several of these commonly incorporated elements interact in a finished proposal, you can consult the example in the following Look Inside box. This proposal was written by a student seeking an undergraduate research grant to support a research project intended to isolate and apply the most effective techniques in teaching stage combat to theater students. You can read the full text of this proposal at the end of this chapter.

From "Exploring and Developing Stage Combat Methodologies"

by Whitney Elmore, an Undergraduate Student

Introduction and Significance

Stage combat has been used in theater for over seven-hundred years. Stage combat is the armed or unarmed stage effect of violence without any of the actors harming themselves or each other (Katz 19). Today, it is hard to find a play or movie that does not require training for a fall, slap, or other means of combat. An actor needs to be trained by skilled professionals to successfully and safely execute stage combat (Penrod 109). Serious injuries could result from the lack of proper training.

. . . Developing these skills will enable me to assist . . . faculty and student directors with improved and safer methods of conducting fight choreography for Black Theater Workshop, directed by Lisa Bandele, as well as additional campus shows. . . .

Literature Review

A common saying in many stage combat books is "Safety first, safety last, safety always" (Suddeth 18). This is a basic principle of stage combat. In the Middle Ages, the combat was hardly realistic (Hobbs 7), but now, with film special effects, people won't accept anything that doesn't look genuine. Audiences want the fight scene from Hamlet to look real without anyone actually being hurt. Choreographing a fight ahead of time will ensure that no one inflicts serious injury on themselves or each other (Oxenford 71). James Penrod is quoted as saying, "These are specialized skills that require training under the watchful eye of an instructor or director" (Penrod 109).

. . .

In the Middle Ages, in mummer and pageant plays, such as *Robin Hood* and *St. George and the Dragon,* directors trained actors to use the quarter staff, two-handed sword, and sword and bucklers (shields) so that they could keep their actors around for more than one performance. They even learned wrestling techniques that we now call unarmed or hand-to-hand combat (Gordon 30-32). During the Renaissance, Shakespeare and his contemporaries used an

---

A LOOK INSIDE:
RESEARCH PROPOSAL

In her opening lines, the author defines a key term before establishing the wide relevance and seriousness of the issue she will investigate. In doing so, she levels an emotional appeal (pathos) by noting the dangers of ignoring the problem.

This paragraph indicates the purpose of the research, a specific application of the knowledge base the author will study. It also echoes the above appeal to pathos.

The literature review summarizes approaches to stage combat across history, ending with a transition to the modern period.

assortment of different types of stage combat, such as fencing, broad sword, quarter staff, sword and buckler, point rapier, rapier and dagger, and short sword, to increase the amount of spectacle (Gordon 59-83). Because the emphasis on spectacle grew, the fights lost the illusion of being realistic, but the audience was in awe of the magnificent presentation (Hobbs 7).

. . .

In the modern day theater, training in stage combat helps actors control their body and improve trust among fellow actors. The illusion work is also invaluable. Now instead of just swords and knives, guns are more often used and are included in stage combat. The Society of American Fight Directors (SAFD) and the Society of British Fight Directors (SBFD) are prominent and established organizations dedicated to teaching people stage combat. Chuck Coyl, Drew Fracher, J. Allen Suddeth, David Boushey, and David Leong are renowned masters of SAFD. David Boushey and J. Allen Suddeth also belong to SBFD.

. . .

Many untrained actors do the combat needed in the play in order to get the part, or, in some cases, an untrained director will try to do the choreography himself. This usually results in many bumps and bruises, such as [in our] recent production of *Fool for Love*. The female lead only had to perform a fall, but it resulted in bruises all over the side of her leg and hip. This example is a low-risk scenario. In the production of the movie *The Crow*, the main actor, Brandon Lee, was killed from a gunshot wound after the proper gun combat safety methods were not used (Bird).

> Here, the author indicates a need for further research, pointing to a gap in understanding regarding current practices as illustrated by a couple of anecdotes. These anecdotes support her argument about the dangers of stage combat while generating additional emotional appeal.

Research Questions

1. What are the best practices for ensuring original yet safe combat methods?
2. How can we enact these practices at our university to ensure the safety of actors involved in our campus productions?

> In the original proposal, the author embeds her research questions in a paragraph. Here they are pulled out for easy reference.

Materials and Research Methods

First, I will examine the fight choreography in the special feature section of *Kiss of the Dragon, The Musketeer,* and *The Matrix Revisited* on DVD. Studying these recent works will give me insight into the latest techniques of study. Then I will thoroughly research books that have been written by

> At this point, the author details the procedures she will follow in researching safe stage combat procedures—research that will result in a written product, a curriculum that can be used by theater instructors.

masters of SAFD and SBFD. . . . In July, I will travel to a stage combat conference at the University of Las Vegas, Nevada, to interview and work under Chuck Coyl, Drew Fracher, J. Allen Suddeth, David Boushey, and David Leong for three weeks in the techniques of unarmed, single sword, broadsword, and film fighting. Upon returning, I will assimilate all of the teaching styles used and modify them to teach [several seminars]. . . . From [these seminars], I will assess what worked and what did not work as teaching methods for people who know relatively little about stage combat. After consulting my mentors, one of which belongs to SAFD, and modifying the teaching methods used, I will cultivate a new curriculum . . . that reflects what I have learned through my literature review, interviews, work with stage combat masters, and application of their methods. . . .

Timeline

> Review Film Choreography May 2002
> Review Books about Stage Combat by Fight Masters June 2002
> Interview and Work with Fight Masters July 2002
> Seminar at Kaskaskia College August 2002

· · ·

The author's timeline for completing this project covers many months, but it is edited here to conserve space.

Works Cited

Bird, Simon. "Accidents When Filming." *The Crow*, 1998, www.thecrow.info/accident.htm.

Gordon, Gilbert. *Stage Fights*. Theatre Arts Books, 1973.

Hobbs, William. *Stage Fight*. Theatre Arts Books, 1967.

Katz, Albert M. *Stage Violence*. Richards Rosen Press, 1976.

Oxenford, Lyn. *Design for Movement*. Theatre Arts Books, 1952.

Penrod, James. *Movement for the Performing Artist*. National P Books, 1974.

Suddeth, J. Allen. *Fight Directing for the Theatre*. Heinemann, 1996.

The original list of sources was edited to reflect only those sources included in this proposal excerpt.

Source: Whitney Elmore, "Exploring and Developing Stage Combat Methodologies" student research proposal, Southern Illinois U Research Academy, 2002, pp. 1–5. Reprinted by permission of the author.

Processes for Composing a Research Proposal

The previous portion of this chapter defines the nature and purpose of a research proposal. From that discussion, you can infer some of the creative and composing processes you will engage in when meeting the expectations of this genre. Building on those inferences about process, the remainder of this chapter provides more specific "how to" advice, with a special focus on solidifying your argument.

Invention toward First Insight

First insights for research proposals reflect genuine interest about the subject matter; after all, preparing for, carrying out, and reporting on a research study requires a strong commitment on the part of the researcher. Therefore, when your teacher presents you with the opportunity to propose a study on any topic that you find intriguing, you should devote concerted attention to idea-generating activities, refusing to commit until you've found a topic that will sustain your motivation. Push to escape ruts in your thinking that might direct you down pathways leading to trite or clichéd topics or that might cause you to bypass what you really want to study for fear that it won't be considered "academic" enough.

Such advice may be even more crucial if your teacher requires you to stay within certain subject-matter boundaries. In such a situation, chances are that those boundaries will be fairly broad, so instead of opting for some slightly narrower version of the larger topic imposed, challenge yourself to be innovative and specific. To illustrate, imagine that your teacher requires a research project—and a research proposal—devoted to exploring some aspect of creativity. The following list demonstrates just a handful of research questions that students in a first-year composition course generated in response to such an assignment:

- How have video games informed the field of robotics?
- What is the relationship between dreams and creativity?
- What innovations in aviation have occurred since 9/11 as a means of deterring terrorist acts?
- Are animals capable of creative thought?
- What personality traits are most supportive of creative thought?
- How do scientists come up with fragrances, colors, and names for cosmetics?
- What are the emotional ramifications of DNA testing that can predict future illness?
- How might traditional cancer treatments be complemented by alternative medicine?
- What underlies the success of nonconventional drug rehabilitation programs?

These examples represent tighter focuses on the broad topic of creativity, but most would need to be narrowed even further for projects carried out in a composition course, which usually lasts only a few months and requires that you also complete other assignments. Advice in the following sections should assist you in rendering your research topic more manageable in the context of a typical under-graduate research assignment.

Preparation through Research

As discussed earlier, research in support of your proposal will help you gauge the current status of knowledge about the issue you're investigating and isolate the gap your study will fill. It also will provide content for your literature review. These objectives will require fairly extensive library or Internet research.

To complete the literature review, you will need to synthesize your sources with an eye toward points of agreement, points of disagreement, and a sense of what they collectively have to say about the topic of investigation. This can be a daunting process unless you have a concrete strategy for keeping track of your observations. Many researchers use worksheets to chart their discoveries. Synthesis worksheets can vary effectively across researchers, but Figure 17.3 offers one pos-sible template. Filling in the cells of a matrix like this can help you remember the content of your sources. More importantly, it can help you see relationships between those sources so you can easily group them with regard to similarities and differ-ences in the way they comment on the issue or problem you're exploring. Pinpointing where your sources stand collectively and in contrast to each other will help you frame a specific area of inquiry that the published scholarship has not yet settled or possibly even addressed.

Importantly, the first column in Figure 17.3 encourages you to record each source's publication information. Although doing so at this point may seem tedious, it is crucial to making certain that you won't confuse sources when drafting, therefore misrepresenting their contents or failing to cite them. The former problem could lead to charges of sloppy research; the latter, to even more serious charges of plagiarism. (For reminders about how to manage and cite sources, refer to Chapters 10 and 21.)

Invention toward More Focused Insight

Having charted points of agreement and disagreement among the sources you've collected, you will be able to see gaps in the existing scholarship. Any of these gaps might offer direction for focusing your project. (Sources of gaps are listed in the earlier section "Projected Contributions.") You need to ask yourself which of these openings are most urgent in terms of helping people, facilitating subsequent research, or engaging you and your intended readers.

Resource and Publication Information	Author's Thesis	Primary Support for Thesis	Counterarguments Addressed	My Notes
Source 1				
Source 2				
Source 3				

Figure 17.3 **A synthesizing template for a literature review**

Finding your focus will pave the way to expressing the need and purpose for your research in the early parts of your proposal and will assist in formulating research questions to guide your study—the questions that you will specify in your proposal's methods section. Chapter 4 discusses several invention activities that will be helpful in articulating your purposes and facilitating insights about possible research questions. See especially the structured prewriting techniques, which are intended to move writers from initial ideas about a topic to a thesis statement (which, in a research proposal, asserts the reason your study is important and thus will appear in the projected contributions section). The prewriting techniques discussed in Chapter 4 can also help generate support for your thesis and for other parts of the proposal.

Strategies for Drafting

As with other genres that prescribe a particular format (e.g., annotated bibliographies, business memos), once you have a solid sense of your research plan, you can regard certain sections of the document as mini-essays, each with its own purpose and conventions. Some writers find it necessary when drafting any document to start at the beginning and progress in order line by line; however, because the separate sections of a research proposal are self-contained to some degree, you may find it beneficial to write them out of order. For example, because planning for the literature review—that is, locating the gaps in scholarship—must take place before you can offer your statement of purpose, you may find that writing the literature review first facilitates drafting of the other sections.

Even if you do draft the sections out of order, you need to keep sight of the document's holistic coherence. In other words, the statement of topic must create the reason for conducting the study (the gap), which is further elaborated in the projected contributions section. In turn, the literature review should clearly display the gap in scholarship, which you explain how to address in the research methods section. Ultimately—although they accomplish various tasks—all parts of the proposal work together in justifying the study you plan to pursue.

Finally, when drafting your research proposal, you don't want to lose sight of its status as an argument designed to convince readers of your study's significance and the viability of your research plan. Therefore, you should be vigilant about opportunities for leveraging persuasive appeals (i.e., ethos, pathos, logos—as discussed in Chapter 3), and you should pay close attention to the structure of your reasoning, making sure that you adequately support all your claims. (For guidance in this regard, refer to Chapter 16.)

Revision and Editing

Questions for Revising

- Do the early paragraphs provide essential context, including definitions of key terms?
- Does my proposal clearly establish the purpose and significance of the research I plan to conduct?

- Are my research questions easy to understand?
- Does my literature review provide a balanced portrait of scholarship on my topic and provide a sense of needed additional research (i.e., a gap)?
- Do my research procedures promise to elicit the kind of data that are specifically relevant to answering my research questions?
- Does my proposal effectively target a general academic audience—for example, the reviewers of a college undergraduate research board?
- Have I capitalized on opportunities to persuade readers through appeals to emotion and author credibility?
- Are all of my claims adequately reasoned and supported?
- Do the separate sections follow a logical pattern of organization?

Questions for Editing

- Are my sources properly cited?
- Is the finished proposal free of spelling, punctuation, and usage errors?

Transfer to Other Writing Situations

Potentially any course you take during your undergraduate career might require you to compose a research proposal. After all, this genre guides activity at the very heart of academic life—that is, advancing knowledge. To successfully apply what you learn in this chapter, remember that you will need to do far more than simply plug different content into the form this chapter introduced. On the contrary, you will need to pay close attention to the variations in this structure as imposed by certain fields of study. Such variations aren't arbitrary; rather, they reflect distinct ways of approaching research that are conventional to a given field.

Despite these variations, remember that all research proposals seek to characterize the reasons for conducting a study, the methods for conducting it, and the benefits to be gained from it. As you continue in your college career and become further immersed in your major, your professors will sharpen your abilities as a scholar by teaching you more about the research methods best suited to answering the types of questions that occupy your discipline. And if you learn these strategies and polish the skills involved sooner rather than later, you might even win funding or other types of support for your own undergraduate research projects.

ACTIVITY

Sketching a Research Proposal   Return to some of the Internet sites you regularly visit, and reflect on the documents or images they contain. Why do you find them engaging? What more would you like to know about their subject matter? Based on one of your responses to the previous questions, sketch a preliminary outline for a research proposal that includes the following: an overview of the issue you want to explore; the purpose of your study; the benefits of increasing knowledge about this issue; and the types of sources and research strategies that would be helpful in answering your question. Share your outline with others in your class and have them share theirs with you. Assist one another in more specifically articulating elements of your respective proposals.

IDEA FOR EXTENDED WRITING

Developing a Research Proposal   What motivates you to read, to talk with others, to take action, or to study? In other words, what excites you enough that you are willing to dedicate time and effort, even without a grade at stake, to learn more about it? Identify an issue or problem that fits this description (perhaps the one you identified in the above activity), and, after narrowing it to a question or two that you could study in a few weeks' time, imagine how you might go about finding answers to your question(s). With this study in mind, compose a research proposal that exemplifies essential components of the genre as introduced in this chapter. Of course, you will need to incorporate library and Internet research into this document, but that research needs to be completed before you begin writing as a way of focusing your ideas and gauging the current status of knowledge about your topic. Imagine that your audience for this proposal is academic in nature but not necessarily constituted of experts on your subject matter (e.g., members of your composition class).

Exploring and Developing Stage Combat Methodologies

by Whitney Elmore, an Undergraduate Student

INTRODUCTION AND SIGNIFICANCE

Stage combat has been used in theater for over seven-hundred years. Stage combat is the armed or unarmed stage effect of violence without any of the actors harming themselves or each other (Katz 19). Today, it is hard to find a play or movie that does not require training for a fall, slap, or other means of combat. An actor needs to be trained by skilled professionals to successfully and safely execute stage combat (Penrod 109). Serious injuries could result from the lack of proper training.

. . . Developing these skills will enable me to assist . . . faculty and student directors with improved and safer methods of conducting fight choreography for Black Theater Workshop, directed by Lisa Bandele, as well as additional campus shows. . . .

LITERATURE REVIEW

A common saying in many stage combat books is "Safety first, safety last, safety always" (Suddeth 18). This is a basic principle of stage combat. In the Middle Ages, the combat was hardly realistic (Hobbs 7), but now, with film special effects, people won't accept anything that doesn't look genuine. Audiences want the fight scene from Hamlet to look real without anyone actually being hurt. Choreographing a fight ahead of time will ensure that no one inflicts serious injury on themselves or each other (Oxenford 71). James Penrod is quoted as saying, "These are specialized skills that require training under the watchful eye of an instructor or director" (Penrod 109).

The Romans used combat in their theaters, but instead of using trained professionals in the *naumachiae,* or sea battles, they used prisoners or slaves. Then when the final battle scene came, the loss of life looked realistic and the victims were not missed (Brockett 60). In the Middle Ages, in mummer and pageant plays, such as *Robin Hood* and *St. George and the Dragon,* directors trained actors to use the quarter staff, two-handed sword, and sword and bucklers (shields) so that they could keep their actors around for more than one performance. They even learned wrestling techniques that we now call unarmed or hand-to-hand combat (Gordon 30-32). During the Renaissance, Shakespeare and his contemporaries used an assortment of different types of stage combat, such as fencing, broad sword, quarter staff, sword and buckler, point rapier, rapier and dagger, and short sword, to increase the amount of spectacle (Gordon 59-83). Because the emphasis on spectacle grew, the fights lost the illusion of being realistic, but the audience was in awe of the magnificent presentation (Hobbs 7). During the Restoration period, theater was known for its comedy of manners (Brockett 238). Although plays were known more for their battles of wits than their battles of might, some more subtle uses of stage combat, such as slaps, trips, and falls, were used. At the same time in Asia, Beijing Opera and Kabuki theater were using the quarter staff and swords (Brockett 604-621).

In the modern day theater, training in stage combat helps actors control their body and improve trust among fellow actors. The illusion work is also invaluable. Now, instead of just swords and knives, guns are more often used and are included in stage combat. The Society of American Fight Directors (SAFD) and the Society of British Fight Directors (SBFD) are prominent and established organizations dedicated to teaching people stage combat. Chuck Coyl, Drew Fracher, J. Allen Suddeth, David Boushey, and David Leong are renowned masters of SAFD. David Boushey and J. Allen Suddeth also belong to SBFD. J. Allen Suddeth is the author of the book on fight directing that we currently use in stage combat class. Also, David Boushey, founder of SAFD, owns and conducts a stunt school from which many of Hollywood's stuntmen come (McCollum).

Many untrained actors do the combat needed in the play in order to get the part, or, in some cases, an untrained director will try to do the choreography himself. This usually results in many bumps and bruises, such as SIUE's recent production of *Fool for Love*. The female lead only had to perform a fall, but it resulted in bruises all over the side of her leg and hip. This example is a low-risk scenario. In the production of the movie *The Crow*, the main actor, Brandon Lee, was killed from a gunshot wound after the proper gun combat safety mentods were not used (Bird). . . .

RESEARCH QUESTIONS

1. What are the best practices for ensuring original yet safe combat methods?
2. How can we enact these practices at our university to ensure the safety of actors involved in our campus productions?

MATERIALS AND RESEARCH METHODS

First, I will examine the fight choreography, special feature section of *Kiss of the Dragon, The Musketeer,* and *The Matrix Revisited* on DVD. Studying these recent works will give me an insight to the latest techniques of study. Then I will thoroughly research books that have been written by masters of SAFD and SBFD. . . . In July, I will travel to a stage combat conference at the University of Las Vegas, Nevada, to interview and work under Chuck Coyl, Drew Fracher, J. Allen Suddeth, David Boushey, and David Leong for three weeks in the techniques of unarmed, single sword, broadsword, and film fighting. Upon returning, I will assimilate all of the teaching styles used and modify them to teach a seminar on unarmed combat and quarter staff combat at Kaskaskia College in Centralia, Illinois. For this and other seminars, I will need ten quarter staffs for the participants. From this seminar, I will assess what worked and what did not work as teaching methods for people who know relatively little about stage combat. After consulting my mentors, one of which belongs to SAFD, and modifying the teaching methods used, I will cultivate a new curriculum . . . that reflects . . . what I have learned through my literature review, interviews, work with stage combat masters, and application of their methods. . . .

TIMELINE

Review Film Choreography	May 2002
Review Books about Stage Combat by Fight Masters	June 2002
Interview and Work with Fight Masters	July 2002
Seminar at Kaskaskia College	August 2002
Review Seminar and Modify Teaching Methods	September 2002
Seminar at University	October 2002
Prepare Lesson Plan for Seminar at High School Theater Festival	December 2002
Prepare Demonstration for College Theater Festival	January 9-11, 2003
Seminar at High School Theater Festival	January 2003
Demonstration at College Theater Festival	January 2003
Review Seminar and Demonstration	February 2003
Prepare Demonstration for Final Presentation	March 2003
Final Presentation	April 2003

WORKS CITED

Bird, Simon. "Accidents When Filming." *The Crow*, 1998, www.thecrow.info/accident.htm.

Brockett, Oscar G. *History of the Theatre*. 8th ed. Allyn and Bacon, 1999.

Gordon, Gilbert. *Stage Fights*. Theatre Arts Books, 1973.

Hobbs, William. *Stage Fight*. Theatre Arts Books, 1967.

Katz, Albert M. *Stage Violence*. Richards Rosen P, 1976.

McCollum, Linda. *The Society for American Fight Directors*, 2014, www.safd.org.

READINGS

Oxenford, Lyn. *Design for Movement*. Theatre Arts Books, 1952.
Penrod, James. *Movement for the Performing Artist*. National P Books, 1974.
Suddeth, J. Allen. *Fight Directing for the Theatre*. Heinemann, 1996.

The Evolution of Ethics

by Matt Warren, an Undergraduate Student

I. INTRODUCTION AND STATEMENT OF PURPOSE

Are our morals objective facts or are they only relative to each society? This question is the focal point of an area of philosophy known as meta-ethics, and there are two groups that have opposing answers to it. One group, the objectivists, generally believe that our morals are objective facts; the other group, the relativists, believe that moral values are relative from person to person and from society to society. Take, for example, the moral value of monogamy. An objectivist would claim that monogamy is right or wrong independent of any person's mind. On the contrary, a relativist would believe that the value of monogamy is relative to each person and society. In addition, the objectivist believes there is one absolute answer to whether or not monogamy is right or wrong while the relativist believes there is no answer. If one culture believes in monogamy and another believes in polygamy, then the objectivist would claim that one society is wrong; the relativist would claim that they are both right in respect to their own beliefs.

Both theories of morality have their problems. The main problem facing objectivists is explaining why different societies have different moral values. The objectivist has trouble explaining, for example, why American society believes that killing is wrong while many cannibalistic tribes believe that it is not wrong. The main problem facing the relativists is explaining why we (society) act as if our moral values are objective if they are not so. For example, the relativist has trouble explaining why people engage in moral argument if there is no answer that is to be reached. The relativist also has trouble explaining why we have laws that are sometimes based on our morals if our morals are simply relative.

My aim is to answer the problems facing relativism in a way that has not extensively been explored. To accomplish this I will present our moral development in a much different way than is typical among relativists. I will suggest that our moral values have evolved along with human society. I will also suggest that our morals are based upon the success of societies that at some point made choices (perhaps arbitrarily) on how to run their communities. The fact that some societies have different moral values will be explained by their development in isolation. Why it is that we act as if morals are objective will be explained by showing that people within a society have incredible difficulty in viewing morality without doing so with the eyes of the society in which they have been raised. I will also address problems that may arise as the result of my claim.

The aim of my project, then, is to answer the problems of relativism and provide a new theory of relativism that explains these problems. I plan to give my paper at the Rocky Mountain Student Philosophy Conference at the University of Colorado at Boulder. The conference is usually held in early March and is a unique combination of graduate school students and undergraduate students. This will give me the opportunity to receive feedback on my theory that will be crucial to a final revision of it. After I revise the paper, to take into account objections from the conference, I will submit it for publication in an undergraduate philosophical journal (hopefully the *Student Philosophical Journal* or the *Harvard Review of Philosophy)* or possibly a professional journal.

Contributions

As said above, the problem at hand is the focal point of the discipline in philosophy known as meta-ethics. The problem has been addressed by many of the most famous philosophers throughout history. Plato, Aristotle, Mackie, Kant, Nietzsche, and St. Aquinas are just a few of those who have struggled to explain morality. I feel that my view of relativism is different than those that have been displayed in the past, and that it may have a significant impact on how morality is viewed by philosophers and others. If relativism can explain why people sometimes act as if their morals are objective (and I believe my view will do this), then I believe it will be in a superior position to objectivism.

II. LITERATURE REVIEW

The amount of work on the conflict of moral relativism/moral objectivity is enormous. J. L. Mackie is often looked upon as a founder of moral skepticism and wrote an impressive work called *Ethics: Inventing Right and Wrong* (1). Moral objectivity is oftentimes argued for by those involved with a religion (usually Christianity), but this is by far not always the case.

Different accounts of relativism are given by Gilbert Harman (2), David Hume, and Friedrich Nietzsche (3) among others. However, I have had difficulty finding other authors who have written on the exact resolution that I would like to pursue. I have found three articles [written by Alfred Benn (4), Frederick Pollock (5), and Norman Wilde (6)] that are similar to the topic that I propose, and all three are from the very early 20th century. I will go through all three of these articles extensively and identify why they have failed to become main ideas. I have also found four books, all written within the last five years, that seem to be moving in the direction that I desire to go, but do not explain things in the same way as I would like to. The books are written by Paul Farber, Leonard Katz, Michael Bradie, and Matthew Nitecki. In my work I will attempt to solve the problems that these views faced.

Also, since my work will be based somewhat on a type of evolution theory, it will draw on some of the ideas brought about by Darwin (as does nearly all talk involving evolution). Yet, it will not be on human physical evolution, but instead on human moral evolution. For this I will need to consult a great number of history books and anthropologies in order to find accounts of morality over the course of history.

III. HYPOTHESIS

Why do we act as if our moral values are true if they are relative? This question is the beginning and the focal point of my investigation. I hypothesize that our morals are the result of an "evolution." Hopefully, the explanation I propose will answer the question above. I will suggest that because of the evolution of our morals we are unable to see outside of our own moral schemas/beliefs. We look at them through a window tinted by survival needs and therefore cannot see them for what they truly are. This is the reason why it seems to many people that our morals are objective and that it is right to argue about them and have laws based upon them. In the end, my theory will hopefully show that moral relativism is a much more plausible theory than objectivism and that it has far fewer problems. I find relativism to be a very plausible and likely position (much more so than objectivism), and I would like to dispel some of the problems that face it. I also find my idea, the evolutionary concept of ethics, to be an even more plausible version of moral relativism.

IV. MATERIALS, TIMELINE, AND RESEARCH METHODS

The materials needed for my research project are available at the Lovejoy Library or on inter-library loan. I may also use the journal article system JSTOR (provided by the Lovejoy Library) for some of the research. I will spend September and October of 2003 doing extensive research and reading of all articles and books relevant to my topic. During November and December I plan to write my rough draft and submit it to the Rocky Mountain Student Philosophy Conference. I will then revise my work and prepare to discuss and present it at the Rocky Mountain Student Philosophy Conference in March of 2004. After the conference I will add any needed revision to my paper and submit it for publication in an undergraduate or professional journal by May of 2004.

Since my work is a philosophical theory, it will not be testable by empirical methods. Unlike biology, psychology, archeology, and other disciplines, philosophical developments are usually not tested empirically. Rather, philosophical theories are "tested" by publishing them or giving them at a conference and then receiving feedback. The philosophical theories are usually then revised until they can meet the objections, or the theories are given up on because they cannot answer certain objections. This is exactly the procedure I will use to "test" my theory. I will give the paper at the conference in March and receive feedback; then I will revise my paper for publication and hopefully receive more feedback from other philosophy students or philosophers. Also, when my work is finished, there will not be a final result like there might be in empirical sciences. Instead, my finished work will be a paper that contains the meta-ethical theory that I suggest.

V. REFERENCES

(1) Mackie, J. L. *Ethics: Inventing Right and Wrong.* Penguin, 1977.

(2) Harman, Gilbert, and Judith Jarvis Thomson. *Moral Relativism and Moral Objectivity.* Blackwell, 1996.

(3) Nietzsche, Friedrich. *The Genealogy of Morals.* Translated by Francis Golffing, Anchor Books, 1956.

(3) Nietzsche, Friedrich. *Thus Spake Zarathustra.* Translated by Thomas Common, Dover Publications, 1999.

(4) Benn, Alfred. *International Journal of Ethics*, vol. 11, no. 1, 1900, pp. 60–70.

(5) Pollock, Frederick. *Mind*, vol. 1, no. 3, 1876, pp. 334–345.

(6) Wilde, Norman. *International Journal of Ethics*, vol. 19, no. 3, 1909, pp. 265–283.

FOR DISCUSSION

1. In each of the above proposals, locate the essential elements outlined in Figure 17.1. How do these proposals differ in their placement and treatment of these elements?

2. What is the impact of these various ways of addressing the elements?

3. Which of the proposals is more impressive and why?

4. What rhetorical appeals does each proposal employ, and where do they appear?

5. In each proposal, identify the parts that are clearly arguing for the significance of the proposed study. Subject these sections to a Toulmin analysis as discussed in Chapter 16. Where are the argumentative claims? What reasons serve to support those claims? What are the warrants?

READINGS

Review

18

Your friends are visiting for the weekend, and they want to go out for pizza. How do you decide where to go? Do you choose the place with the greatest variety of fresh toppings? Is the thickness of the crust your guiding principle? Maybe it's the flavor of the sauce—is it spicy enough? Is it too sweet? Of course, your decision might be based on more than the pizza itself. To ensure that your friends

enjoy a satisfying dining experience, you might also consider the cost of the pizza, the restaurant's atmosphere, the quality of service, and so on. In arriving at your final decision, you are engaging in evaluation—that is, you are leveling a judgment based on standards associated with quality restaurants. At times, you may want to share such evaluations, helping to advise others. You can do so in

a review, the genre defined in this chapter.

On any given day, much of your mental energy is devoted to **evaluating**—from selecting which clothes to wear, to determining the most efficient route to your next class, to arguing with your roommate about which reality TV show is the most entertaining. In fact, evaluations are crucial for negotiating the overwhelming

MYTH

"Reading reviews is pointless, as opposing opinions essentially seem to cancel each other out."

Disagreement in reviewing is inevitable to some extent, given personal preferences and differences in standards of evaluation. Nevertheless, sound reviews can be distinguished from questionable ones in accordance with author credibility (ethos)—built on credentials, rigor in applying standards, depth of knowledge, rationality, and the like. Moreover, when several respected reviewers are in agreement, the presumed reliability of their reviews increases.

REALITY

possibilities that surround you and for deciding how you want to spend your money and your time. Many people publish their evaluations in **reviews,** which argue for the relative value or deficiency of various goods, services, activities, and performances. Most anything can be the subject of a review, and the resulting document provides an important service: It offers insights from those who are familiar with a given product to less informed consumers who want to know more about it.

One of the most widely read examples of this genre is the film review, which alerts readers to the strengths and weaknesses of a movie they are thinking about seeing. While film reviews can protect you from the frustrating and costly experience of sitting through a bad movie, other types of reviews may yield even greater benefits. Many appliances and technological devices that you might buy are not only expensive but also essential to managing your life at home and at work. Determining which of the numerous possibilities will best suit your needs can be a mind-boggling experience without some advice from those who've used the appliances or devices, tested their capabilities, and taken time to write about them. The significance of thoughtful reviews becomes even more evident when you think about matters such as choosing schools, health care providers, or financial institutions. All are subject to public evaluations, sometimes in formal reviews.

Distinguishing Features of a Review

As you consider the benefits of reading reviews, think also about how you might assist others by *writing* reviews—by endorsing or critiquing goods and services that you know well. Thanks to the Internet, reviews are widely available and easily published, allowing you to join conversations that evaluate various products and thereby save people from having to act on vague impressions or insufficient information.

Of course, reviews published on the Internet vary in their level of formality, as is illustrated in Figure 18.1, which compares an excerpt from an informal review of a hotel on TripAdvisor.com with an excerpt from a relatively formal review of a book in a literary magazine, *Salamander.* While both of the reviews presented in Figure 18.1 assert an argument (about a vacation spot and a work of nonfiction, respectively), they differ in tone (or attitude). The one from TripAdvisor.com expresses a less serious tone, disregards certain conventions for punctuating and capitalizing, and reads more like a checklist of observations than a cohesive evaluation. This lack of formality, while appropriate for certain forums, would be unsuitable for an essay assignment in

Review on the Internet: Hilton Singer Island Hotel and Resort

The hotel is small (8 stories), newly refurbished, clean, pleasant, and the staff are wonderful. We got an upgrade to a higher floor right away. We had Room 713 with a queen bed (comfortable), small stand up balcony (the sliding glass doors wouldn't unlock) and a beautiful new walk-in shower. Superb! It was quiet and VERY comfy. The hotel is IN THE SAND, on the beach! White sand, shells galore, turquoise water—it doesn't get any better! The umbrella and chairs are $30 per day!!! But the pool is lovely, with a roomy deck and lots of FREE umbrellas and lounge chairs. . . . The breakfast buffets (hot or cold) are very good, and you can eat out on the covered deck practically in the sand! FRESH squeezed orange juice!! Parking is $10 per day. So even if you get a great rate on the room (as we did), it adds up with the beach chair and umbrella charge and the parking charge. . . .

Source: ggirlNewnan. "A Sparkling Little Gem of a Hotel." *TripAdvisor,* 16 Sept. 2013, www.tripadvisor.com/ ShowUserReviews-g1079181-d213861-r177457528-Hilton_Singer_Island_Oceanfront_ Palm_Beaches_Resort-Singer_Island_Florida.html.

Review in a Literary Journal: *Had Slaves* **by Catherine Sasanov**

Catherine Sasanov's poetry collection *Had Slaves* is based on her discovery of the personal and legal papers of her Missouri ancestors. The resulting poems are imaginative articulations of a thorough investigation into her family's complicity in the American slave trade. Sasanov explores deeply personal realms with an attempt at scholarly distance: the volume contains six pages of endnotes detailing the poet's research. For this reader, the notes are not necessary. The poems are documents in themselves. . . .

"How Long It Takes . . ." speaks to the overarching motivation of the collection: burying the dead by first resurrecting them. The poor miller in the poem tends to his land after the Civil War battles have taken place there. Encountering the dead, his "plow's tongue snags on their ribs." . . . At their best, Sasanov's poems address her theme more generally, go beyond her family line. *Had Slaves* offers a portrait of an historic period through a national lens as well as through the lens of a family crisis.

Source: Elizabeth Murphy, "Dispatches: Review of *Had Slaves* by Catherine Sasanov." *Salamander,* vol. 16, no. 1, Winter 2010/11.

Figure 18.1 **An informal versus a formal online review**

your composition course or other academic and professional situations. Rather, such assignments would aim at least for the level of formality demonstrated in a literary journal and other popular magazines and newspapers.

In putting forward their arguments, some formal reviews pass firm judgment, boldly endorsing or disapproving of their subjects, as in the following example: "This is a delightful movie that all parents will want their children to see." Others, however, adopt a more subtle tone, presenting the evidence in ways that suggest rather than announce the assessment (e.g., the author might simply characterize weaknesses and strengths but, in emphasizing the latter, provide validation). Whatever the case, most formal reviews have several features in common. First, they develop theses that state whether you should or should not buy or experience something—or that indicate you should be aware of certain aspects of the product before making a decision.

Second, reviews typically provide some background information about their topics so readers will be better prepared to understand the features being evaluated. After all, people often seek out reviews to learn more about a product or service simply because they've heard others raving about it. But off-the-cuff praise from a friend paints a spotty picture at best, and, therefore, a review needs to be thorough. If the object under consideration is a device or gadget, the review might describe qualities that distinguish it from previous models. If the object is a book, TV show, or film, the review might at some point introduce main characters or briefly summarize the plot (while avoiding spoilers, of course). Without this context, readers might not be able to follow or judge the validity of the reviewer's feedback.

A third distinguishing feature of reviews is that they ground their feedback in **criteria,** or standards appropriate to the product being assessed. For example, in the discussion opening this chapter, several criteria were offered for selecting a pizza place: (1) the quality of the pizza—including variety of toppings, nature of the crust, flavor of the sauce; (2) the price of a meal; (3) the restaurant's atmosphere; and (4) the quality of service. Criteria are the foundation of an evaluation; to be sure, it is impossible to endorse or critique anything if you don't have in mind a clear set of standards to guide your judgments. Each of those standards or criteria, then, can prompt any number of positive or negative claims of varying intensity.

For another illustration, consider Figure 18.2, which elaborates on the example of a film review. The column on the left lists common criteria by which to evaluate a film, and the column on the right offers specific claims relevant to those criteria that would indicate a positive evaluation.

Evaluative Criterion	Evaluative Claims
Storyline	• The opening minutes draw you in and leave you wanting more. • It's full of exciting twists and turns. • The ending brings a satisfying sense of closure to the central plot and all subplots. • It communicates an appealing message.
Acting	• The actors memorably portray a range of emotions. • The actors demonstrate believable chemistry in their relationships. • Their accents are believable for the setting and time period. • Their dramatic timing in delivering lines is impeccable.
Cinematography	• The close-ups are perfectly in sync with the most intense moments experienced by the characters. • The panoramic shots reveal breathtaking landscapes. • The lighting perfectly portrays the mood of each scene. • The filming of the actors on horseback makes you feel as if you're riding along with the characters.
Special effects	• The makeup and prosthetics graphically depict the aging process of the characters. • The simulation of being caught in a horrific storm is exceptionally realistic. • The ancient city appears to be actual—not a mere model or set. • The graphic nature of the battle scenes helps you live the trauma of war along with the characters.

Figure 18.2 **Standards for reviewing a film, with evaluative claims**

Of course, the criteria for reviewing a film identified in Figure 18.2 are by no means comprehensive. You could also consider the quality of the writing, the precision of the sound editing, the insight of the director, the innovation of the musical score, and so on. Moreover, the criteria might change across genres of films. For example, the number of laugh-out-loud moments might be relevant to assessing a romantic comedy but probably would not inform your assessment of a disaster movie (unless it depended on some form of dark humor). In addition, regarding the specific claims in Figure 18.2, you could easily imagine a not-so-rave review by recasting them in language that portrayed noted features as negative or mediocre—for example, "The ending was unsatisfying, leaving a couple of pressing questions unanswered" or "Viewers may find it difficult to empathize with the main character as the lead actor's emotions remain flat through the highs and lows of his experience." Figure 18.3 depicts the prominent role that criteria and claims assume in the context of writing a review, as they create a lens through which to view your subject.

The criteria driving your review will stem in part from your knowledge of your target audience or forum. Although this statement applies to many items or activities you might evaluate, consider again the example of a film review. Certainly, you should be cautious about overgeneralizing, but you are probably safe in assuming, for example, that science fiction fans will be especially interested in the quality of special effects. And religious audiences may be more sensitive than others about certain themes and storylines. Such knowledge can help you predict the types of films that particular audiences might want to learn more about, as well as which aspects of a film to emphasize.

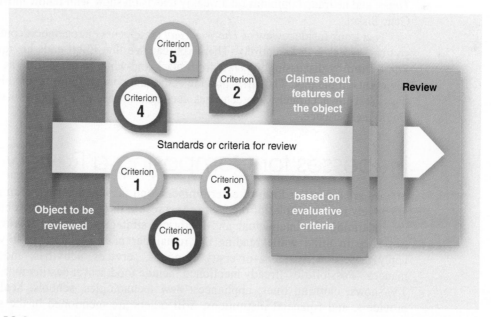

Figure 18.3 Elements of a review. In a review, the evaluative criteria, and the claims made based on that criteria, create a lens through which an audience will consider your subject.

Identifying appropriate criteria for evaluation and assessing how the object of review lives up to those standards are activities most closely associated with the rhetorical appeal referred to as **logos,** or reasoning. But you might also want to capitalize on the other rhetorical appeals—namely, **ethos** and **pathos.** (For more information about these appeals, see Chapter 3). When reviewing a film, for example, you might arouse pathos or emotion by foregrounding a certain character's tragic loss, arguing that potential viewers should see the movie if they are inclined toward tearjerkers. Or you could highlight the film's capacity to inspire, arguing that watching it will dramatically change your readers' worldview or their positions about certain political issues.

Ethos (or your credibility as an author) will arise from the impression that you have specific knowledge of the film and that you can offer detail and insight when developing your observations about it. Ethos also arises from the sense that you have presented the movie in a fair and balanced manner, perhaps by acknowledging contrasting opinions of it. For example, if you are ultimately endorsing the movie, you might want to mention aspects of it that could be construed as weaknesses. On the other hand, if your overriding impression is negative, you might give a nod to qualities that could salvage the film in some people's minds.

These examples point to the fact that reviews do not need to be entirely positive or negative—although sometimes they may be. Such is the case in the overtly favorable review excerpted in the following Look Inside box; the review is focused on one of the most beloved films of all time—*The Wizard of Oz*—and was written by one of the most renowned film reviewers in history—Roger Ebert. For years, Ebert shared his insights about classic and popular films with readers of the *Chicago Sun-Times,* and he traded opinions on a weekly television show with fellow movie critic Gene Siskel.

That Look Inside review of *The Wizard of Oz* appears on rogerebert.com, where you can access it in its entirety. There you can see that Ebert ends his review of *The Wizard* by discussing the shift from black-and-white to color film, as well as key events in the plot. The latter provide additional context illuminating his thesis that the film accurately characterizes feelings, hopes, and dreams that many children experience.

Processes for Composing a Review

Movies are a popular form of entertainment, and (as noted earlier) film reviews are widely read examples of the genre. As a result, they are effective vehicles for demonstrating the intellectual and rhetorical strategies involved in reviewing. But keep in mind while reading the remainder of this chapter that you can apply these concepts to a diversity of goods, services, activities, and performances. (Possibilities already mentioned include food, travel destinations, books, TV shows, clothing lines, appliances, new technologies, schools, health care providers, and financial institutions. Still others are mentioned in the sections that follow.)

From a Review of *The Wizard of Oz*

by Roger Ebert

As a child I simply did not notice whether a movie was in color or not. The movies themselves were such an overwhelming mystery that if they wanted to be in black and white, that was their business. It was not until I saw *The Wizard of Oz* for the first time that I consciously noticed B&W versus color, as Dorothy was blown out of Kansas and into Oz. What did I think? It made good sense to me.

The switch from black and white to color would have had a special resonance in 1939, when the movie was made. Almost all films were still being made in black and white, and the cumbersome new color cameras came with a "Technicolor consultant" from the factory, who stood next to the cinematographer and officiously suggested higher light levels. . . .

If *Wizard* began in one way and continued in another, that was also the history of the production. . . .

We study all of these details, I think, because *The Wizard of Oz* fills such a large space in our imagination. It somehow seems real and important in a way most movies don't. Is that because we see it first when we're young? Or simply because it is a wonderful movie? Or because it sounds some buried universal note, some archetype or deeply felt myth?

I lean toward the third possibility, that the elements in *The Wizard of Oz* powerfully fill a void that exists inside many children. For kids of a certain age, home is everything, the center of the world. But over the rainbow, dimly guessed at, is the wide earth, fascinating and terrifying. There is a deep fundamental fear that events might conspire to transport the child from the safety of home and strand him far away in a strange land. And what would he hope to find there? Why, new friends, to advise and protect him. And Toto, of course, because children have such a strong symbiotic relationship with their pets that they assume they would get lost together.

This deep universal appeal explains why so many different people from many backgrounds have a compartment of their memory reserved for *The Wizard of Oz*. Salman Rushdie, growing up in Bombay, remembers that seeing the film at 10 "made a writer of me." Terry McMillan, as an African-American child in northern Michigan, "completely

A LOOK INSIDE: REVIEW

The author opens with an enticing hook—nostalgic for older readers and intriguing for those who can't remember a time when movies were filmed only in black and white.

By asking questions, this paragraph invites readers to entertain possible reasons behind the enduring appeal of *The Wizard*—one criterion or standard for judging a film's success.

This line introduces the author's thesis, followed by examples that help support and elaborate his claim about the primary reason for the movie's appeal.

Here the author asserts that the film's wide appeal—rooted in common childhood feelings or observations—spans both time and cultures. He then cites literary authorities in support of this claim.

identified when no one had time to listen to Dorothy."
Rushdie wrote that the film's "driving force is the inadequacy
of adults, even of good adults, and how the weakness of
grownups forces children to take control of their own desti-
nies." McMillan learned about courage, about "being afraid
but doing whatever it was you set out to do anyway."

They're touching on the key lesson of childhood, which
is that someday the child will not be a child, that home will
no longer exist, that adults will be no help because now the
child is an adult and must face the challenges of life alone.
But that you can ask friends to help you. And that even the
Wizard of Oz is only human, and has problems of his own.

The Wizard of Oz has a wonderful surface of comedy
and music, special effects and excitement, but we still watch
it six decades later because its underlying story penetrates
straight to the deepest insecurities of childhood, stirs them
and then reassures them. As adults, we love it because it
reminds us of a journey we have taken. That is why any adult
in control of a child is sooner or later going to suggest a
viewing of *The Wizard of Oz*.

Judy Garland had, I gather, an unhappy childhood . . . ,
but she was a luminous performer, already almost 17 when
she played young Dorothy. She was important to the movie
because she projected vulnerability and a certain sadness in
every tone of her voice. . . . Garland's whole persona projected a tremulous uncertainty, a wistfulness. When she
hoped that troubles would melt like lemon drops, you
believed she had troubles.

Her friends on the Yellow Brick Road (the Tin Man, the
Scarecrow, the Cowardly Lion) were projections of every
child's secret fears. Are we real? Are we ugly and silly? Are
we brave enough? In helping them, Dorothy was helping herself, just as an older child will overcome fears by acting brave
before a younger one.

. . .

The movie's storytelling device of a dream is just precisely obvious enough to appeal to younger viewers. Dorothy,
faced with a crisis (the loss of Toto), meets the intriguing
Professor Marvel (Frank Morgan) on the road. She is
befriended by three farm hands (Bolger, Haley and Lahr).
Soon comes the fearsome tornado. . . . Then, after the magical transition to color, Dorothy meets the same characters
again, so we know it's all a dream, but not really. . . .

Source: Reprinted by permission of The Ebert Company.

> These paragraphs expound on the cited authorities' remarks, pinpointing more specific messages about childhood that the film delivers.

> This paragraph addresses another common criterion for reviewing films—the quality of the acting. Note how this standard is connected to the theme about childhood feelings and experiences.

> Near the end of the review, the author provides information about the film's plot as he further develops his thesis.

Invention toward First Insight

A review originates with an urge to convince others that they should or should not purchase or experience something or that they should be aware of its disadvantages or benefits. Maybe you are a faithful follower of a certain TV show and you want others to share in its entertainment value and the sense of community that comes from interacting with individuals who watch the program on a regular basis. Or maybe you contribute to a particular charity engaged in work that you believe is crucial for the betterment of your community and you want others to participate. Conversely, you may have adopted a pet that you feel doesn't make for an especially good indoor companion, or maybe you purchased a phone app that did not function in the manner promised. In most cases, then, the desire to advise others is what motivates you to compose a review. Even when teachers or employers assign a topic, you can draw motivation from an interest in helping readers understand aspects of it that they otherwise may not have considered.

Preparation through Research

In most cases, the research for a review begins with a memory search for the specific qualities of a product that impressed, perplexed, disappointed, or maybe even offended you. And surely you can add depth to your evaluation by studying that product again. One benefit of being *assigned* to review some phenomenon by a teacher or employer is that you will be prepared to take notes on it before, rather than after, the fact. In either case, deep, sustained reflection is essential for identifying features that may deserve commentary.

In addition to searching your memory and taking notes, you may want to locate published reviews as resources for offering other perspectives on your subject or for backing your own assessment of it. In fact, locating an expert's opinion on the product you are reviewing can help validate your assessment. You can reference published reviews in your own review by following guidelines for integrating and citing sources in other types of documents (see Chapter 21 for specifics). And, of course, various library and Internet sources might be useful in providing background information and describing particular aspects of the product.

Invention toward More Focused Insight

Once you have researched the object of your review, you will have an increased understanding not only of the criteria you want to apply in judging that product but also of the specific focus or thesis you want to argue. Certainly, you won't be addressing every aspect of that entity; rather, you'll be formulating an overriding perception based on how well the product fulfills key standards associated with achievement in that realm. For example, in the film review you read earlier in this chapter, Roger Ebert asserts that *The Wizard of Oz*'s theme, plot devices, and acting have delighted millions of viewers across decades and cultures because these features of the movie access universal childhood feelings. In the book review excerpted in Figure 18.1, the reviewer contends that the author sensitively portrays an especially painful period in American history by investigating her subject from both a personal and scholarly perspective.

In other words, if you settle in your review for a laundry list of unconnected claims, you will fall short of expectations. Instead, you need to purposefully select which criteria to focus on, as they help you articulate your main reaction (positive, negative, or neutral) to the product you are evaluating.

Strategies for Drafting

Although reviews composed in response to college or workplace writing assignments ordinarily assume essay form, the genre tends to be more playful than, for example, a business memo, a lab report, or a literary analysis. A review is, to a large extent, an expression of your personality, specifically your values, priorities, and artistic and practical sensibilities. As such, when drafting a review, your voice should dominate as you forward a judgment, not merely a detached description or overview of other people's opinions.

You may want to introduce your review with a creative **hook,** a unique opening that intrigues your readers, enticing them further into the piece. For example, consider the hook in Figure 18.4, which presents the opening to a film review written by *Time Out* critic Trevor Johnston about the 2006 restoration of *The Wizard of Oz.* The opening paragraph's abbreviated, shotgunlike statements about Garland's performance of the opening musical number trail off in an ellipsis, breaking the convention of beginning an essay with a cohesive paragraph. In addition, the emphasis on the emotional impact of the song immediately grounds readers in an iconic feature of the film and previews what will be a primary observation of Johnston's review—that perhaps only by revisiting this classic film as adults can we appreciate the coming-of-age story so memorably characterized by Garland's performance.

In the review excerpted in Figure 18.4, the thesis immediately follows the hook, noting that despite its visual spectacles and nods to childhood fantasy, the film's real power resides in its emotional pull, a power perhaps best appreciated by adult viewers. While your thesis doesn't necessarily have to emerge as early as that in Johnston's review, it should appear fairly early in the piece, at the culmination of whatever

It's like a Pavlovian reaction. I know it's coming but I can do nothing about it. The strings swell for the introduction to "Over the Rainbow" and already I'm wavering. Judy Garland gets a few lines into the song and I'm emotional wreckage. Every single time...

Oh, but this is supposed to be some creaky old kids' movie, a charming relic of vintage MGM showmanship, full of chirpy songs [...] and a wee dog. Not to be taken to heart, surely? Well, intellectually that may be so, but this is one instance where the vagaries of cinematic fashion simply don't apply.

Source: Trevor Johnston, "Review of *Wizard of Oz,*" *Time Out,* 12 Dec. 2006.

Figure 18.4 **Hook for a review of *The Wizard of Oz***

introductory information you wish to provide. Regarding general background information, it can make sense either to place it all before you launch into the specifics of your evaluation *or* to parse it out as it becomes relevant to the specific issues you raise.

The body paragraphs of reviews usually center on the criteria at the heart of your evaluation. This doesn't mean you have to provide one paragraph per criterion; in practice, a single standard might call for multiple paragraphs of commentary, whereas another might be addressed in a few lines. The time you devote to each criterion will hinge on the complexity of the concept you're addressing, as well as the nature of the feedback you want to offer for each. In other words, you will have much to say about certain features of the product and maybe only a single point to make about another.

As with any essay, the conclusion of a review should highlight key points made in the body of the text. In addition, you may want to offer readers an overt recommendation about whether or not they should purchase or experience the entity you have just evaluated. Your decision will depend on the extent to which they may have inferred your advice from the earlier paragraphs. Again, many reviews do not set up an either-or scenario—that is, they don't argue that the product under review is *all* good or *all* bad. If your review fits this description, you may feel the need to clarify your ultimate position near the end.

Revision and Editing

Questions for Revision

- Is my review appropriately geared toward my target audience?
- Does my introduction draw readers into my review?
- Does the review center around a clear thesis that forwards an evaluation of the good, service, activity, or performance under review?
- Are the standards or criteria by which I arrived at that overall evaluation evident in the body of the review?
- Do I provide claims that clarify the extent to which the object of my review excelled, satisfied, underwhelmed, or failed with regard to the standards or criteria?
- Are all my claims backed with sufficient and convincing evidence?
- Does the review provide essential background information—for example, description, plot summary—so that readers can understand and weigh my evaluative claims?
- Have I capitalized on opportunities to persuade readers through appeals to emotion (pathos) and author credibility (ethos)?
- Does my conclusion forward a recommendation consistent with my evaluation?

Questions for Editing

- Are any sources I referred to properly cited?
- Is the finished review free of spelling, punctuation, and usage errors?

Discipline	Objects of Review
Consumer sciences	Food, diets, fashion
Architecture/civil engineering	Buildings, city layouts
Physical education	Exercise programs, sports teams, famous athletes, draft choices, golf courses
Recreation and leisure	Travel destinations, resorts, annual events
Political science	Politicians, current legislation, proposed legislation, polling data
Literature	Novels, poetry, drama, nonfiction, an author's body of work
Medicine	Doctors, hospitals, drugs, treatments
Veterinary science	Vets, clinics, feed, flea and tick powders

Figure 18.5 **Possible review topics across disciplines**

Transfer to Other Writing Situations

As mentioned earlier, the strategies applied in evaluating a film are readily applied in reviewing a variety of goods, services, activities, and performances. In fact, many college courses address the genre to help students better understand and judge the nature and quality of products and practices that define their respective fields. For some examples, see Figure 18.5, which lists several areas of study and the types of reviews they elicit.

The list in Figure 18.5 is by no means exhaustive, but it gives you some indication of how widely the strategies addressed in this chapter might be applied across academic disciplines. In each case, the building blocks of a review discussed earlier are relevant, including a thesis that carries an evaluation, a set of criteria by which to judge the object under review, plenty of support for claims that argue for the subject's relative worth, and an ultimate recommendation about whether to experience or purchase it.

ACTIVITY

Generating Criteria for a Review   Following this paragraph is a list of categories that encompass some rather expensive products about which people would likely consult reviews. Adopting a consumer's mindset relevant to each of these categories, generate a list of criteria that would be crucial in determining how you would select a certain product or model from each category.

- Video game
- Hybrid car
- Cell phone
- Concert
- Tennis shoes
- College education

IDEA FOR EXTENDED WRITING

Reviewing a Creative Performance or Event For this assignment, you will be reviewing a creative product or performance—that is, any product or performance that you consider innovative in some respect. Examples include a ground-breaking film, a cutting-edge video game, a bold new fashion line, an experimental theater production, a sporting event in which the athletes' moves exceeded expectations, and so on. Whatever your focus, remember that a review is built on criteria associated with success. In other words, it requires you to establish what specifically accounts for achievement in a given realm of production or performance. In establishing these criteria, you may want or need to conduct some research, either to provide background information on the object of your review or to survey other people's reactions to it as a means of building on or countering them. Imagine that your review is set to appear in a special back-to-school issue of a newspaper or magazine targeted for peers at your university.

"Gris Grimly's Frankenstein" Revisits, Enhances Shelley's Famous Tale

by Karen Sandstrom

So you say you once tried to read Mary Shelley's *Frankenstein* but quit early and never went back? Welcome to the club.

Even horror master Stephen King admits he bailed on *Frankenstein* as a kid. In a foreword to artist Bernie Wrightson's 1983 illustrated edition of the novel, King admits he returned to it only to teach it in a literature class.

The adult King persevered through florid language (*Frankenstein* was first published in 1818) and an old-fashioned construct to become a big fan. I predict you will, too, if you pick up the latest version of this archetypal tale, done in graphic-novel form by one of my favorite illustrators.

With "Gris Grimly's *Frankenstein*," the mysteriously named Grimly uses ink and watercolor to enliven a respectfully abridged version of Shelley's original text. There's no dumbing down here. Within this 200-page volume, Grimly retains Shelley's ornate language and evokes new imagery for an audience whose expectations may have been shaped by old movies.

You know the story, or at least some of it. Bitten by the bug of scientific curiosity, the young Victor Frankenstein heads off to university and throws himself into his work. His studies lead him to the big questions until, "after days and nights of incredible labor and fatigue, I succeeded in discovering the cause and generation of life; nay, more, I became myself capable of bestowing animation upon lifeless matter."

But years of toil never prepare Victor for the revulsion of seeing his creature, stitched from the scraps of graveyards and charnel houses, come to life. He flees, leaving his newborn wretch to fend for itself. The monster, finding neither home nor companionship, seeks to exact revenge— then extract a favor—from the god who made him.

That's the set-up, though the plot grows complex as innocents begin paying for Frankenstein's scientific folly. The story might be one of the earlier, best illustrations of the law of unintended consequences. Our young scientist was, after all, simply trying to solve a great mystery. Where did it go wrong?

Grimly omits many of Shelley's words to make his *Frankenstein* work. How can I say this politely? I didn't miss them. With the exception of a few abrupt transitions, the novel proceeds seamlessly, propelled by a plot that finally gets past its framing device

(*Frankenstein* contains a story inside a story inside a story) and by Grimly's art.

In an afterword, the illustrator notes that when asked to do this project, "I wanted to set the tale in a world that could only be visited through my imagination." Thus his "Frankenstein" takes place in a wonderfully weird world of steam punk machinery and Goth hairstyles.

A veteran of children's illustration, Grimly draws highly stylized figures that teeter between the grotesque and the cute. His version of Frankenstein's monster is a more revolting thing, with too little skin stretched over bone, its maw gaping in agony. Grimly plays with levels of detail, giving us lots of almost-realistic rendering in one panel and abstracted shapes in the next.

And it all happens against a limited palette of ochers and queasy greens, punctuated by the occasional spot of pink to emphasize skin tone or denote a moment of cheer in a prevailingly gloomy series of events.

Grimly also wisely departs from the lockstep of traditional comics panel illustration. Every spread is beautifully organized, with Grimly controlling the pace by interspersing large and small, wide and narrow, full pages of art and full pages of text.

This illustration pays loving homage to its source, persuading us to wander past a 200-year-old narrative style. There, we find what Shelley herself wanted us to see: ourselves. The empathetic and the ego-bound. The lonely and the loving. The monsters and the monster makers.

Source: Karen Sandstrom, "'Gris Grimly's *Frankenstein*' Revisits, Enhances Shelley's Famous Tale," Special to the *Plain Dealer*, 9/11/13. Copyright © 2013. Reprinted by permission of the author.

Old "Cosmos" vs. New "Cosmos": Who's the King of the Universe?

by Chris Taylor

There were two times in my life when I was literally brought to my knees by the beauty of the night sky. Once was on a camping trip in the Nevada desert in my late 20s, when I looked up, caught the Milky Way shining brighter and clearer than ever I'd seen, like a river of a billion diamonds. My legs started to buckle, apparently realizing their insignificance in the scheme of things. I sat down rather rapidly on the desert floor.

The other time was when I was a child and first watched the late Carl Sagan's 1980 PBS series, *Cosmos,* and had the exact same reaction standing in front of a TV set. Sagan's "ship of the imagination" and the galaxies it span through—well, they weren't quite state of the art special effects, even in 1980, the year of *Empire Strikes Back*. But it was enough, with Sagan's hypnotically confident narration, to send millions of minds spinning into the stars. Mouth agape, head shaking, barely able to stand: this was how we watched *Cosmos*.

Now we have a pretender to Sagan's scientific throne in *Cosmos: A Spacetime Odyssey,* starring the ever-engrossing Neil deGrasse Tyson. It is bold and brassy where Sagan's show was soft and understated; it has up-to-the-minute CGI and has moved to the Fox network, with a budget to match.

This is a beautiful thing for the cause of science education, of course, but you'll forgive us old-time Sagan fans for being wary of the interloper—as wary as *Doctor Who* fans are every time that show replaces the lead actor they've become comfortable with.

To allay these doubts, I decided to watch both first episodes—the 1980 version and the 2014 version—back to back. Had the original aged well? Did Tyson pack more of a punch than his predecessor? How much had the science changed? Does a big budget really make *that* much of a difference when conveying the splendor and mysteries of the universe? Here's what I found.

SAGAN vs. TYSON

Really, it's impossible to choose between these two top-notch communicators. Both knock it out of the park, employing very different styles. You might almost call it a West Coast vs. East Coast battle, since Tyson is from the Bronx and Sagan seems the epitome of the laid-back tanned California professor, but (as we discover later in the series) he actually hails from Brooklyn and spent most of his life at northeastern universities.

Sagan is more lyrical, and his slow, deliberate speech pattern was as satirized as it was beloved (I'll never forget my father imitating his "billions and billions.") Tyson seems more like he's speaking off the cuff; even though he's more muted here than we're used to seeing, he still displays a fondness for the cool flourish (who else could get away with putting on sunglasses in the face of the Big Bang?).

If anything, Tyson is too deferential to his predecessor. He spends ten precious minutes of the show reminding us what a great man Sagan was, and recounting the (admittedly touching) story of the day in his childhood when Sagan invited him to visit him at Cornell, as if assuring us old-school fans that the torch has been passed to the appropriate guy. But we knew that the moment he started talking.

Winner: a tie

SPECIAL EFFECTS

The original *Cosmos* . . . still holds up surprisingly well. It makes do with its PBS budget, and seems quieter and more meditative than its successor (as reflected in the original's subtitle, *A Personal Journey*). There's a beautiful moment where Sagan fakes us out and zooms in on a planet we think is Earth, but turns out to be a speculative alien world criss-crossed with lights; that still gives me chills.

The new *Cosmos,* reflecting its times, seems terrified that you might change the channel at any time, and packs each second with wow-inducing space scenes. There's not a whole lot of room to breathe and contemplate what we're seeing. I didn't quite feel my legs buckling, but I did keep remarking that young kids watching this must be having their minds blown. . . .

Winner: 2014

SHIP OF THE IMAGINATION

Carl Sagan cavorted around the *Cosmos* in a craft that deliberately looked like a dandelion seed: his "ship of the imagination" was light, dreamlike, halfway between real and not. The new *Cosmos* gives us something that could not be anything but a heavy-duty spaceship, one rather reminiscent of Boba Fett's Slave I. That's perhaps not surprising, given that it was created by Ryan Church, concept designer on Star Wars Episodes II and III. Very flashy, but also a little distracting—this is rather too concrete to be an imaginary vessel.

Winner: 1980

MUSIC

I see what the 2014 show's producer, Seth MacFarlane, has done here: he went for a big Hollywood-style orchestral score in order to anchor us in something familiar while watching those mind-blowing images. But it's almost impossible to top the haunting grandeur of the original *Cosmos* theme, taken from the album *Heaven and Hell* by Vangelis.

Winner: 1980

HISTORY

There's no way around it: *Cosmos* is designed to sneak a little history of science in with its universal wonderment. It was, unfortunately, the least compelling part of the 1980 series. In his opening episode, Sagan offered the story of Eratosthenes, the ancient Greek who first calculated the circumference of the Earth, then meanders into a lament for the loss of the Great Library of Alexandria.

Tyson, with writing help from Sagan's last wife Ann Druyan, gives us the far more powerful and appropriate tale of Giordano Bruno, the 16th century Dominican friar who first proposed that the universe was infinite. Here's where MacFarlane's experience as an animator comes into full effect. Bruno's story is far more powerfully rendered as anime than it ever would be as live-action costume drama.

If the rest of the series offers anything as compelling as the scene of Bruno soaring into the heavens in his dreams, my guess is kids won't lose focus during the history segments the way I once did. For some, they may become the main attraction.

Winner: 2014

IN vs. OUT

The major difference between the first episodes: old *Cosmos* took us from the outside in, with Sagan's ship moving from the edge of the universe to our small blue dot of a planet, which we see with new eyes. New *Cosmos* goes in the opposite direction, with the idea of finding our "cosmic address" line by line.

Both are utterly compelling conceits, with surprises along the way—Sagan offered a pulsar and the populated alien planet, while Tyson flies by a completely dark ice planet, floating in interstellar space with no sun to light it. But Tyson just about has the edge here, as he's able to use more effective bells and whistles (the universe in infra-red is much more densely populated) and more up-to-date science (sorry, Pluto).

Pulling all the way out also allowed Tyson to end on an image of the multiverse: universe upon universe, jostling like bubbles in soda. It was at this point in the show that my wife exclaimed something that sounded like "clucking bell."

Winner: 2014

The 2014 *Cosmos* beats its predecessor by the slimmest of margins, 4 to 3. Which is, after all, pretty much what Sagan (who died in 1996) would have expected: that the daisy-chain of scientists across the years, each building on the knowledge that came before, will make slow but steady progress towards the stars. Naturally, it should also produce a cooler Cosmic Calendar and a shinier Ship of the Imagination.

Not all of this is progress, and my enthusiasm for the original series has only been increased by re-watching its first episode.

Still, if every generation's *Cosmos* is a little better than the one before, and buckles more knees in its contemplation of the universe, we must be doing something right.

Source: Chris Taylor, "Old 'Cosmos' vs. New 'Cosmos': Who's the King of the Universe?" *Mashable,* 11 Mar. 2014.

FOR DISCUSSION

1. What is the thesis for each of these reviews?
2. What are the criteria upon which the object of review is being evaluated?
3. Does the introduction encourage you to read the review? Why or why not?
4. Is the reasoning in support of the evaluative claims persuasive? Why or why not?
5. How does the author of each review appeal to pathos and ethos?

Position Paper

19

What if your parents had been able to select your gender? Skin color? Eye color? Hair color? Strength? Intelligence? Does that thought bother you? What about being able to determine these traits for your own children? As technology advances to a point where such characteristics can be controlled through genetic engineering, many people are entering the debate over "designer babies." To learn strategies for debating this—or any other—controversial issue, read this chapter, which will familiarize you with a genre known as the *position paper.*

The question of whether would-be parents should be allowed to choose a child's physical and intellectual qualities incites strong feelings. Some people condemn any move to reduce the mystery of human conception to an act that compares with catalog shopping. They also worry that providing such options will encourage stereotypical thinking and discrimination. Arguing from the other end of the spectrum, some people insist that parents deserve the right to dictate qualities that could predispose future children to fit their family—that is, to look like them, share their interests, excel in ways that they have excelled. And still others believe in allowing for certain options but not others. For example, while they sympathize with couples who would like to guarantee that they have a child of each gender, they have trouble extending the selection process to superficial features that privilege a certain appearance.

In other words, the controversy over the prospect of genetically engineered children is highly complex, as are most issues that sustain ongoing debate. This complexity gives life to multiple positions, as demonstrated in the previous paragraph. The goal of a **position paper** is to carve out your own position in the midst of this complexity. You can improve your ability to argue a firm stance on this and other issues that provoke an intense reaction from you by recognizing the conventions of position papers described in the following section.

Distinguishing Features of a Position Paper

Of course, all argumentative genres involve taking a position; consider, for example, the other argumentative genres addressed in this textbook, as listed in Figure 19.1. All of these documents—research proposals, reviews, and problem-solution papers—could be referred to as "position papers" since they do assert positions relevant to their subject matter. However, they result in outcomes that are distinct from arguing a stance on a controversial issue—that is, they argue, respectively, for the benefits of a study, the quality of particular goods or services, and a solution to an enduring problem. In short, then, you could say that these genres are types of position papers.

An essential characteristic of position papers is that they address issues that are genuinely debatable, issues about which intelligent people might reasonably disagree. In short, some issues just aren't worth arguing about—especially in academic contexts. Such issues include those that are easily subject to verification, that most people already agree on, that are obviously matters of opinion, or that are rooted in faith. Consider the examples in Figure 19.2. As these examples suggest, a position paper argues a stance in response to an issue that people disagree over and that holds the possibility of charting common ground on which various camps might move closer together through open-minded give-and-take. (Refer again to the discussion of designer babies at the beginning of this chapter. Although some people hold diametrically opposed positions, others have paved routes for compromise.)

Genre	Position
Research proposal	That the investigation you are pursuing is valuable and the methods by which you will conduct the study are valid
Review	That the product you are reviewing is positive or negative, admirable or not admirable, advantageous or not advantageous, etc.
Problem-solution paper	That a significant problem exists and that the solution you are proposing is viable or is the best of several possibilities

Figure 19.1 **Positions related to other argumentative genres**

Issue/Position	Debatability?	Reason It's Not Debatable
"People who can't tolerate humid weather should not live in Lake Charles, Louisiana."	Although it may sound like an argument, this is basically an informative statement since a check on the humidity level in Lake Charles is only a Google search away.	This claim is easily subject to verification.
"The U.S. Congress needs to develop a new way of doing business in light of stalemate after stalemate regarding important issues affecting the country."	This may be an argumentative claim, but it doesn't rise to the level of debatability that is ideal for a position paper since a good majority of people—as indicated by poll after poll—already agree with this sentiment.	This claim is widely agreed upon.
"Yorkies aren't as cute as border terriers."	This argumentative claim is clearly a matter of opinion or taste. There are no absolute criteria for cuteness that differentiate dogs from one another, especially those that are similar in size, coat, facial structure, etc.	This claim is a matter of opinion.
"Women should not be ministers because the Bible says so."	This is an assertion in the Bible. Some people believe the Bible is literally true, others believe it is subject to interpretation, and others don't believe it has any truth value at all. People are unlikely to budge much on matters of religion.	This claim is rooted in faith.

Figure 19.2 **Issues that are not genuinely debatable**

Most position papers begin with a "hook" or some sort of provocative opening (see Chapter 8 for more on hooks). They then proceed to an overview of the controversy, which makes clear that the issue is, indeed, debatable. In most cases, the author demonstrates debatability by briefly representing differing positions. Doing so educates readers about various stances that have already been articulated; it also strengthens the author's ethos or credibility by demonstrating that he or she fully understands the nuances of the debate. That credibility further depends on the reader's sense that the author has represented all viewpoints fairly.

After presenting an overview of the controversy, the author clearly states his or her position on it. This claim is the paper's thesis, and all discourse that comes after it is focused on supporting that claim—that is, making the author's case that the best position to occupy in this debate is the one that he or she is arguing. Various subclaims—or reasons on which the thesis is based—are presented in the essay's body paragraphs, along with the evidence and/or logical reasoning intended to support them.

As in all argumentative genres, building the most thorough and credible case for the thesis in a position paper depends on acknowledging and addressing counterarguments. Any given issue might pose a number of viable positions (seldom are there only two!), so attending to counterarguments usually involves isolating the principles that underlie several competing claims. Some of them might be quickly dismissed by pointing out that they are fallacies (see Chapter 16). Others may be more compelling, and, to those, the author will offer a more measured, comprehensive response.

In keeping with the neutral tone applied when overviewing the controversy near the beginning of the paper, the tone for addressing counterarguments in the body of the paper is ordinarily respectful, demonstrating that the author wanted to understand other points of view before responding. This sense of fairness is especially important when considering potential audiences for position papers. Frequently, they appear in forums geared toward a diverse readership of the general public (e.g., many newspapers and magazines). They also appear in more specialized venues such as scholarly journals. Whatever the place of publication, there is bound to be disagreement on the issue at stake, hence its status as a controversy. Most people read position papers to learn more about these controversies, not to simply find others who endorse their own way of thinking. If an author hopes to sway readers, demonstrating respect for where they currently stand goes a long way in persuading them to listen to a different perspective.

The respectful and fair treatment of other perspectives and counterarguments, however, should not cloud the fact that position papers put forward *arguments* designed to convince readers to change their thinking. Figure 19.3 displays the elements that work toward this goal. In addition to the elements discussed in previous paragraphs, Figure 19.3 includes a conclusion, which typically reemphasizes the thesis on the heels of all the supporting paragraphs. Of special note is the placement of the counterarguments. As the figure suggests, they may surface in the overview of the controversy, near the beginning of the paper, but they also might appear later in the text in direct response to the thesis, particular subclaims, or evidence.

You can find all the elements of a position paper in the Look Inside article, which addresses the controversial issue opening this chapter—genetic engineering

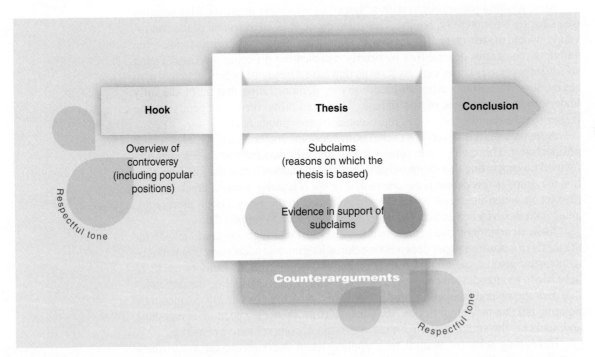

Figure 19.3 Elements of a position paper. Following a hook and an overview of the controversy, present your position in the form of a thesis. Keep in mind that counterarguments often appear at the beginning of a paper, but they might also appear later, in your body paragraphs, where your subclaims, and evidence in support of those subclaims, will be addressed. Remember to maintain a respectful tone throughout your position paper.

Against Designer Babies

by Sheldon Krimsky

You may remember a short period in the 1990s when a broad consensus emerged among biologists about the ethics of human genetic engineering. Somatic cell gene therapy was considered an acceptable biomedical research program, whereas germ line genetic modification was treated as unethical. By the new millennium, that moral boundary had eroded.

A recent debate in New York City in which I was a participant highlighted the cultural change. Our topic: "Babies Should Not Be Genetically Engineered." I argued in support of the proposition to prohibit the genetic modification of human reproductive cells prior to gestation in the womb.

Two compelling reasons to genetically alter human reproductive cells in preparation for childbirth, I argued, are for curing or preventing a disease or for the "enhancement" of a child. With respect to the former, there are safer and more dependable methods for preventing the birth of a child with a severe genetic abnormality than by genetic modification of the germ cells. The use of prenatal screening or pre-implantation embryo diagnosis will suffice in most cases to prevent the birth of a genetically abnormal embryo.

Accordingly, the only remaining rationale for engaging in the genetic modification of human reproductive cells is to enhance the child—to bestow such traits as heightened intelligence, resistance to disease, muscle strength, appealing personality or longevity, to cite a few common examples. I believe that pursuit of this goal represents the greatest scientific folly and moral failure.

First, for whatever enhancement is sought, the only method for determining efficacy is to engage in a clinical trial with a few dozen fertilized human eggs or embryos, where half would be genetically modified, all would be carried to term, and the development of the children would be followed throughout their lives to determine whether the genetic modification worked and worked safely. No animal studies can answer these questions.

It is unimaginable that any humane society would permit such a trial, where the potential risks so outweigh the social benefits.

A LOOK INSIDE: POSITION PAPER

As part of the overview, the author grounds the issue historically. (*Somatic therapy* refers to that which affects a single individual. *Germ line therapy* enables changes to be passed on via altered DNA.)

This paragraph establishes context for more recent discussion and asserts the author's thesis.

In this paragraph, the author raises two counterarguments that respond to his thesis at large. Note how he demonstrates a respectful tone by admitting that they are "compelling." He then directly rebuts the initial counter.

At this point, the author focuses his piece on building his argument against the more controversial reason for engineering children.

His first reason is emotionally charged (as stressed in the isolated sentence).

The second reason to shun genetic enhancement is that it makes no sense from a biological and developmental perspective. The human traits typically cited for enhancement, such as intelligence, personality or musicianship, are complex and not only involve dozens if not hundreds of genes, but are the result of a complex mix of determinants, including nutrition, social and environmental factors, gene-to-gene interactions and epigenetic switches that are outside the reductive chemistry of the DNA code.

Even for height, one of the most heritable traits known, scientists have discovered at least 50 genes that can account for 2 to 3 percent of the variance in the samples. There could be hundreds of genes associated with height. If you want a tall child, then marry tall.

Finally, the idea of genetic enhancement grows out of a eugenics ideology that human perfection can be directed by genetics. I am all for human enhancement, but it must start after an egg is fertilized beginning in utero—by protecting the fetus from neurotoxins and other endocrine-disrupting substances and continuing after birth with nutritional and cognitive enrichment and moral education, for example.

The greatest danger of a belief in genetic engineering lies in its likely social impact. Eugenics will inevitably be used by those with wealth and power to make others believe that prenatal genetic modification makes people better. This would be as much a myth as believing that the sperm from Nobel Laureates will produce a genius child.

Source: Sheldon Krimsky, "Genetic enhancement of human embryos is not a practice for civil societies, argues a bioethicist." Copyright © 2013. Reprinted by permission of the author.

> The second reason, addressed here, is ultimately rooted in numbers (see the following paragraph).

> Here the author levels another powerful emotional argument—powerful because it brings to mind a terrifying moment in world history, the discovery of Nazi Germany's wish to propagate a master race.

> The article ends with further emphasis on the social implications of designing babies and reiterates an earlier point that the technology doesn't offer sure results.

of children. This article was written in response to a 2013 congressional debate about regulation of the technologies that could lead to designer babies. It originally appeared in *Tufts Medicine* magazine.

Author Sheldon Krimsky argues a pretty hard line in this piece, treating the issue as an all-or-nothing prospect. Of course, as discussed in the introduction to this chapter, this issue does lend itself to arguments that are more moderate than those calling for either no regulation at all or, on the other hand, a complete ban on new applications for this technology.

Processes for Composing a Position Paper

The end results of position papers may point toward solutions—for example, the United States needs to regulate genetic engineering. However, because their topics tend to be abstract, their solutions are often theoretical or aimed at changing opinion as opposed to recommending a specific or physical action (in contrast, for example, to problem-solution papers, discussed in Chapter 20). Regardless of where your position paper ultimately takes readers, you can facilitate your composing processes by drawing on strategies discussed in the following sections.

MYTH

"A great topic for a position paper is one of the big three: abortion, capital punishment, or gun control."

These topics *are* controversial, and they *have* sparked considerable debate. Part of the problem is that they have sparked so much debate that the arguments for various positions on these issues have reached the status of clichés. While presenting a fresh perspective on them is not impossible, doing so is especially challenging. In addition, the first two topics often become mired in standoffs about the truth value of the Bible. These are the primary reasons that some teachers will place these topics (and possibly certain others) off limits.

REALITY

Invention toward First Insight

Initial ideas for formal position papers typically arise from awareness about conversations that are taking place across the globe, in your country, and in the communities to which you belong. What are the "hot topics" in the news? What are politicians currently arguing about? What current issues have your friends talking? Of course, some of these matters will not engage you, and you should avoid them if they do not ignite your passion.

The element of passion helps sustain motivation with respect to all writing, but it is essential with regard to position papers, through which you are trying to change people's minds. That is the goal here: As opposed to simply sharing information or offering an interpretation, you are influencing readers' attitudes about important issues that carry significant ramifications. Of course, it's difficult to alter others' thinking if you cannot convey a genuine enthusiasm for the topic and your position on it.

Be this as it may, in some college courses, teachers will place at least a few limits on the topics you can pursue. This is frequently the case in composition classes, where teachers will attempt to steer students away from writing about issues that are not genuinely debatable or that are overdone. (See Figure 19.2, as well as the Myth and Reality box at the top of this page.)

Sometimes in school or the workplace, you will be asked to write about topics that you would not naturally gravitate toward. In such cases, you need to search for angles that spark your interest. While at first a given issue may not seem that stimulating, by reflecting deeply on its significance or potential consequences, you will probably be able to discover some aspect of it that you feel strongly about. (Consult Chapter 4 for strategies that can guide such reflection.)

Preparation through Research

Whatever issue motivates you to write, you will need to research it widely. Doing so will help you develop a fresh perspective on the topic. After all, it makes no sense to rehash the exact same argument that another author has made (unless it's used as a stepping-stone for helping readers comprehend your position). Thorough research will also help ensure your credibility, allowing you to understand the issue inside and out—not only so you can fairly represent other points of view and identify compelling counterarguments, but also so you can make certain that the logic supporting your position is sound.

To be more specific, you need to gather as much background information as possible about the issues adding up to the controversy or debate you have chosen to enter. For example, to counter the positions of others and argue your own position on the topic of designer babies, you would need to know something about the fundamentals of genetic engineering. You might find this information in research reports or other informative documents, or you might turn to other position papers. While you need to be conscientious in documenting any and all sources, you should take special care when consulting other position papers so that you do not mistakenly present their original arguments as your own.

Invention toward More Focused Insight

As you are reading about the debate you are planning to enter, you should look for ways to help your readers consider it from a different vantage point. This doesn't mean that you can't mention any reasons provided by others in upholding the position you favor, but it does mean that you need to tweak or extend the argument in some way. In other words, you need to offer your audience something new to think about, something that just might tip the scales in favor of the position that you are arguing. Often this insight derives from relationships you discover as you combine the ideas of one or more authors. At other times, it grows from applying your own personal experiences and the insights gained from them. To be sure, unique happenings in your life may provide a perspective on the matter that those unfamiliar with such experiences would be unable to anticipate on their own. (Read more about insight in Chapter 2.)

Your contribution to the debate may be attached to your thesis statement, where you not only mention your general position regarding the controversy but also state your primary reason for thinking that way. On the other hand, you might limit your thesis to a broad statement of your position, reserving your contribution as one line of reasoning (along with some others) in support of that thesis. Sheldon Krimsky, the author of the article on designer babies appearing earlier in this chapter, chose the latter tactic. After articulating his broad position—that he is against applying genetic engineering technology in the selection of superficial characteristics—he reviews a number of reasons supporting his stance. The eugenics argument (i.e., allowing for designer babies will lead to a "master race" mentality) is pretty typical in exchanges about this controversy. However, Krimsky contributes to the conversation by presenting statistics about the uncertainty regarding engineered outcomes and by pointing out the inhumane manner in which these technologies would need to be tested (i.e., using control and experimental groups of human subjects). Certainly, these observations are not common fare in the debate about designer children.

Strategies for Drafting

Most articles and essays begin with hooks (see Chapter 8) that entice readers to engage the text, and position papers are no exception. When an issue is controversial, you can probably imagine any number of strategies for capturing readers' attention. For example, you might set up a brief scenario that illustrates why taking a position other than yours might prove harmful. Or you might share some little-known fact about the controversy that you discovered while researching it. After the hook comes the overview—that is, any background information needed for the reader to make sense of the position you will ultimately argue. Generally speaking, that background comes before your thesis, though you might distribute the less fundamental background information throughout the piece. Regardless, in the early part of your draft, you will need to characterize the controversy and stake out your position within it.

Once you have stated your thesis, Toulmin's method for analyzing and structuring arguments will become a valuable tool in deciding what you need to do to convince others that they should consider your position. (For specifics about the Toulmin method, see Chapter 16.) Of course, as discussed in the early part of this chapter, your thesis is a debatable claim; therefore, you will need to back it up with reasons. In turn, the reasons you supply to back your thesis may also need to be supported, perhaps by evidence in the form of facts and figures or by further reasoning or illustrations.

See Figure 19.4, which sketches one line of argument in the Krimsky article that you read earlier in this chapter. Krimsky could have offered evidence to add credence to his reasoning—perhaps examples of genetic experiments gone awry. But, apparently, he presumed that readers would acknowledge the likelihood of such problems, and so he concentrated the remainder of the article on additional reasons and support for his position.

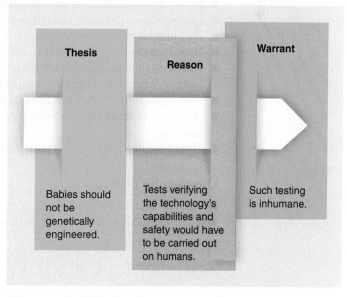

Figure 19.4 **Toulmin analysis of an argument in Krimsky's article**

Thesis: Babies should not be genetically engineered.

Reason: Tests verifying the technology's capabilities and safety would have to be carried out on humans.

Warrant: Such testing is inhumane.

Remember that a crucial element of a position paper is the recognition of counterarguments. Responding to a counterargument that could detract from your position might involve simply walking through a different argument that throws the counterargument into question. At times, though, it might involve uncovering fallacies. Of course, you will need to bring the same critical eye you have focused on your opponents' arguments to your own arguments; in other words, you need to also check your own position for faulty reasoning. After all, the quality of your position paper will lie largely in the tightness of your logic (logos) and the persuasive impact of the evidence you provide. These are qualities that you can emphasize as you reassert your position in the paper's conclusion.

To complement these aspects of your piece, consider whether you have ethically stimulated the emotions of your readers through rhetorical strategies (pathos) that bring them in touch with their own concerns about the issue in question. Also, make sure that you have clearly established your own credibility (ethos) by demonstrating that you have thoughtfully and thoroughly researched the debate and that you can maintain a respectful attitude toward those who believe differently. That level of civility is a hallmark of effective argumentation in academic and professional contexts (with the exception, unfortunately, of some political rhetoric).

Revision and Editing

Questions for Revising

- Have I provided enough background information about the controversy for readers to follow my argument?
- Does my thesis clearly articulate a position within the debate?
- Do I provide convincing reasons in support of my thesis?
- Do I provide enough evidence to back my claims?
- Have I acknowledged and responded to likely counterarguments?
- Have I established my own credibility (ethos) and employed emotional appeals (pathos) where they might be beneficial to my case?
- Is my treatment of other positions respectful and fair?
- Are my language choices and sentence structures appropriate to the target audience?
- Have I employed transitions to effectively connect ideas?

Questions for Editing

- Are any sources I referred to properly cited?
- Is the finished position paper free of spelling, punctuation, and usage errors?

Transfer to Other Writing Situations

People are constantly taking positions relevant to their daily existence. Think, for example, of positions you may have taken in the past when trying to convince individuals to see things your way—that a parent should grant you more freedom to

Field	Issues That Invite Strong Positions
Politics	• A candidate's qualifications for public office • Proposed legislation • A community's or nation's priorities
Business	• Access to a new market • A potential investment
Higher education	• Increases in tuition and fees • Curricular changes
Women's studies	• Contributions of women in a particular context • The status of women in today's job market
Environmental studies	• Effects of industry on air, soil, and water • Stripping of the environment for material products • The impact of fracking

Figure 19.5 **Issues that tend to spark debate in various disciplines**

make your own decisions, that a sibling should lend you some money, that a teacher should assign you a higher grade. To persuade them, you had to bring reasoning and evidence to the table—for example, instances of your responsible behavior, a copy of a bill you needed to pay, reminders about how much your work improved over the semester. Also, you had to think about your credibility, as well as the way you might pull at readers' emotional strings so they would view the situation from your perspective.

Although these personal tugs-of-war seldom find expression in formal documents, they can help sharpen skills that are essential to composing position papers. Formal position papers are common in popular, professional, and academic forums. Indeed, some of the most important writing people do in any of these contexts is trying to convince others of the "right" way of thinking about something. It is through such exchanges that human beings refine understanding and possibly make progress toward productive compromise. Figure 19.5 lists reasons for which you might want or need to take a position in a variety of fields or disciplines. While some of the issues listed in Figure 19.5 might seem a bit specialized, you should be able to assert some type of position about all of them on the basis of your being an engaged citizen.

ACTIVITY

Performing a Toulmin Analysis of a Position Paper   Search the Internet for a position paper on a local, national, or global controversy that concerns you. On a sheet of paper or in a word processing file, first identify the elements of that text that would classify it as a position paper. Then, using the example in Chapter 16 (Figure 16.2), map out the elements of Toulmin's system as they appear in the article you found. Next, trade your article with a peer, and have him or her analyze it in accordance with the Toulmin method; do the same for your peer's article. When both of you are finished, compare your respective analyses and discuss the reasons behind any differences in your readings of these texts.

IDEA FOR EXTENDED WRITING

Taking a Position on an Issue That Irks You   Think about the last time somebody said something that frustrated or annoyed you. Was it a parent lecturing you about dangers lurking on your college campus? Was it a pundit on TV who made a flippant comment about poverty in U.S. society? Was it a world leader who blamed victims of some catastrophe for their own devastating circumstances? Once you decide on some such topic, apply the guidelines presented in this chapter to compose the most convincing position paper you can. Even if your audience is your parents (to whom you might present the paper as a letter), employ your best reasoning and convincing evidence from outside sources to make your case (e.g., if you want to argue that your campus is safe, you might cite statistics about crime on campus or official publications covering campus safety measures).

Homeschooling's Liberalism

by David Mills

The other day someone asked about our children, and my answer worried him, or at least he claimed to be concerned. When they hear the answer to their question, many people get a look on their faces similar, I imagine, to the look they'd get if I said we refused to have our children vaccinated or let them keep rattlesnakes as pets. We homeschool our two youngest, and have done so since they were in kindergarten, with the exception of two years early on at our parochial school.

The response varies. A few people say something nice, with some of them telling you how they'd wished they had done so, or wished they could have done so, some of those explaining a little defensively why they couldn't. Most people suddenly furrow their brows and purse their lips and declare their concerns about home-schooling, which seem always to be less often about the quality of the education as about the children's "socialization." Although the people who say something nice are almost always religious and conservative, the people with the quickly furrowed brows are either religious or secular, and I've been surprised to find out how many seriously religious and politically very conservative people dislike homeschooling and jump to tell you so.

It's a little disconcerting, their apparent concern for making sure our children fit into the society as it is. There is something both aggressive and unctuous in their alleged concern for my children that really annoys me. My wife, who is much more charitable than I am in dealing with annoying people, answers them politely, and sets about to reassure them by telling them about the home-schooling groups to which our children go several days a week and all the other activities they are involved in. Some seem satisfied, others clearly aren't. I have so far resisted the temptation to put my hand on their shoulder, look them in the eye, and ask, "Why is it so important to you that my children be squeezed into the same mold as everyone else?"

I didn't come to this feeling the usual way. I first heard of homeschooling as a child growing up in a college town in New England, when the only people who homeschooled their children were hippies living on communes in the country or academics and political activists protesting against the regimented and regimenting education "the system" provided for its own repressive purposes.

No one I knew ever blinked at the idea of raising children outside the public school system, and indeed it had the romantic appeal such countercultural endeavors enjoyed in those days. It was a little odd, perhaps, but if asked to express an opinion most people would have shrugged and said that it takes all types to make a world, and many would have said something supportive. If some people wanted to opt out of the system and do things their own way, bully for them. If they wanted to raise their fist against the establishment, three cheers. Thomas Jefferson, by consensus I think our favorite founding father, would have approved. Let, as we heard from time to time, a thousand flowers bloom.

Indeed the desire of the countercultural types to take charge of the education of their own children seemed a reasonable extension of the kind of liberty we were being taught, in the public school, that America had been founded to protect, and a rational response to the kind of oppressive social control some of the cooler teachers taught (this was a college town, as I said) capitalist society imposed.

One of my social studies teachers expounded Herbert Marcuse's idea of "repressive tolerance," telling us that we were not free even though we seemed to be, and in fact that the system itself controlled us through what we thought were free choices. I'm not sure we completely got our minds around that idea, but it reinforced the feeling that the good life was found in opposition to the establishment.

Even then, I think, I and others recognized the importance of what Burke called the "little platoons" and others later called "mediating institutions," though the only terms we had for such things were drawn from anarchism. We had a vision of social difference and diversity, which we were taught was threatened by the homogenizing effects of late industrial capitalism, symbolized even then by white bread and processed cheese. The good life, the good society, was one in which all sorts of groups—families, clubs, co-operative societies, small towns run by boards of elders—lived the lives they wanted to live in a creative interaction governed by the spirit of living and letting live.

Those thousand flowers were—this is an image that would never have occurred to me then, but captures our idea of spontaneous order and beauty—wild flowers, whose beauty resulted from their blooming together as they grew up in nature. They would not have been so beautiful, or not beautiful in the same way, had they been chosen (not all would have been) and planted in rows.

This is the way even then, if only vaguely, I thought about the family. The family is a good thing in itself, but a vulnerable thing that needs to have a life apart from the state, and forms a great part of the institutions needed to resist its always expanding desire to control and direct more and more of society. It was a different world then, I realize: The Marxists I knew were happily married to their first wives, gave their kids curfews and chores, and a few even went to church or synagogue.

Thus I was surprised some years later to find the kind of people with whom I'd grown up—the leftists, the intellectuals, the activists, the public-spirited—suddenly alarmed at the growth of homeschooling. (And I first experienced this surprise when we still expected to send our children to the public schools.)

The critics treated it as a threat to the social order and a source of sectarian divisions. Some expressed concern that homeschooled children would find themselves unable to function in a pluralistic society. Many also argued that they would get an inferior education, but that always seemed to be a secondary concern, and grimly amusing coming from advocates of the near-monopoly of a public school system whose failures were beginning to be lamented even by liberal observers.

The critics found themselves so alarmed, of course, because now politically, culturally, and religiously conservative parents were educating their children at home and rejecting the influence of a system in which the critics—so many of them former countercultural types themselves—were heavily invested, and from which, as a Marxist would note, so many of them drew their salaries.

The homeschoolers were no longer a few hippies and leftists, whose numbers were always going to be small and their influence marginal, and who were reliably leftist anyway. Now the homeschoolers were a growing number of average parents, whose countercultural commitments were of the conservative and not the leftist sort, whose numbers might well increase and their influence grow stronger, particularly if the establishment lost its control over the education of children, which happened to be its primary way of reducing parental influence in, to borrow a famous phrase from my youth, the battle for their hearts and minds.

People who have no obvious stake in the matter, like most of the people who have expressed dismay at my wife's and my decision to homeschool our children, tend to side with the establishment against the parents. They've somehow absorbed the key elements of the ideology, like the concern for "socialization," which is either a faux concern for the children's well-being or a real concern for their being educated outside of and probably against the ideas public schools (with exceptions, of course) inculcate and impose.

Before someone remarks that some homeschooling parents are very odd or inept or (in a very few cases) dangerous: Yes, of course, it is not a perfect system. But that doesn't answer the question of who should educate children.

And it's not an argument for the public school monopoly. For one thing, these failures and problems describe the public schools as well, especially if you think some of the ideological commitments that animate a great deal of the educational establishment are dangerous in themselves. I was taught, for example, the Enlightenment mythology of the dark, anti-intellectual ages dominated by the Church and the growth of human knowledge and freedom brought by those who rejected religion and discovered science. Which is, simply as an historical matter, wrong, and inculcates a religious commitment that is far from neutral.

In any event, the widespread presumption against homeschooling that I have encountered among self-styled liberals is, to someone like me, a very strange reversal. Educating your own children is an act of the kind of freedom I was taught our country provided, a freedom of self-determination that is one of its great glories.

Even leaving out the idea I was also taught, that removing oneself from the system was a laudable act of countercultural liberation, with which I still have some sympathy, to teach one's children oneself, being able to choose curricula and readings and customize the teaching to every child's needs and gifts, is the kind of thing I was taught, by teachers of impeccable liberalism, to praise. It is an expression of liberalism and liberality in public affairs. It is one way of planting some of those thousand flowers.

What I learned then, I believe strongly now: that if mass production is bad in the creation of bread or cheese, it is much worse for the formation of vulnerable human beings. The work should be entrusted only to the craftsman who loves his materials and will have his name on the thing he creates.

As the twig is bent, I can't help but think that homeschooling's unctuous critics have betrayed the American vision of freedom with which I grew up, and rationalized the extension of social control in a way my peers and I learned to see and resist. It can only do our nation good to have parents so invested in their children's education, and it certainly won't hurt the cause of liberty to have the monopoly of the public schools so concretely challenged. Down with the gardeners. Let the flowers bloom.

Source: David Mills, "Homeschooling's Liberalism." *First Things: A Monthly Journal of Religion & Public Life,* Jan. 2012.

Educating Girls Is a Good Investment

by Becky Smith Conover

Many of us are inspired by Malala Yousafzai, the 15-year-old Pakistani girl who has become a leading advocate of educational opportunity for girls. We are familiar with the horrific story of Malala riding the bus home from school when a Taliban gunman climbed aboard and shot her in the head, almost killing her. Her "crime" was speaking out about the simple right of girls to go to school.

As we observe International Women's Day today, we need to support a renewed U.S. commitment to improving access to primary education worldwide. In Malala's words, "We cannot succeed when half of us are held back."

Many of us are surprised to learn that less than 2 percent (specifically, 1.4 percent) of the U.S. budget is spent on foreign aid. The total amount of dollars to be used for foreign aid in 2015 has already been approved by our lawmakers. What remains to be decided is how these funds will be allocated to particular foreign aid programs. Let's encourage our policymakers to channel some of these funds to promoting access to quality, primary education through The Global Partnership for Education (GPE). The GPE is the only international organization exclusively dedicated to quality education for all.

Worldwide, roughly 57 million primary school-aged girls and boys are not attending school. In Africa, one in four girls is not receiving a basic education. A young woman in South Sudan is more likely to die in childbirth than she is to finish 8th grade. Even more staggering, 40 percent of children of primary school age worldwide (250 million) cannot read. And those with access to classrooms sometimes fail to obtain basic skills due to the shortage of trained teachers and educational supports.

Why should we channel foreign aid funds to the GPE? Education is known to foster economic growth, promote health and encourage a more stable, secure world. In their 2012 "Education for All Global Monitoring Report," UNESCO noted that people of voting age with a primary education are 1.5 times more likely to support democracy than people with no education. The World Bank publication, Education and Development, observed that countries with higher primary schooling rates and a smaller gap between rates of boys' and girls' schooling tend to enjoy greater democracy and stability.

The GPE mobilizes the resources of developing countries toward their own educational systems, uniting their ministries of education with international donors, the private sector and community groups. It complements U.S. bilateral efforts in global education, extending the reach of taxpayer money.

The GPE reaches those in greatest need, implementing education plans in nearly 60 of the poorest countries in the world. Since 2002, the GPE has enrolled 22 million children in school, constructed 53,000 classrooms and trained 300,000 teachers in challenging places like Somalia, Afghanistan and Haiti.

A better-educated world will be a safer, healthier, more stable and more prosperous world. To help developing countries implement quality basic education is a vitally important use of our foreign aid funds.

FOR DISCUSSION

1. How would you characterize the strategies that the authors use to open their articles?
2. What is the specific thesis in each of these position papers?
3. What particular reasons do the authors assign in support of their theses?
4. What counterarguments do the authors acknowledge? Can you think of others?
5. What fresh contributions do the authors make to the ongoing debates about the controversies in question?

NEW CONGRESSIONAL SCHOOL LUNCH FOOD PYRAMID

Mike Peters © 2011. Distributed by King Features Syndicate, World Rights Reserved.

©2011 DAYTON DAILY NEWS KING FEATURES SYNDICATE grimmy.com

Problem-Solution Paper

20

The cartoon above comments on an enduring problem in U.S. society, one that seems to have been growing in recent years. Take a few minutes to interpret the image and articulate that problem in your own words.

Now, spend some time thinking about possible solutions to that problem. Which of those solutions would have the most immediate impact? Which is the most feasible? The most fair? How might you convince others that this solution is promising? What might be the drawbacks of your solution? By answering these questions, you've practiced some of the fundamental processes underlying the genre addressed in this chapter—that is, the problem-solution paper.

Concern about children's nutrition has intensified in the United States in recent years, with a focus on the ill effects of regularly consuming junk foods. These effects include obesity, hyperactivity, and even decreased mental function. In addition, poor eating habits in children tend to establish patterns that continue into adulthood, setting the stage for debilitating or potentially life-threatening illness. These medical epidemics have shown little sign of letting up in the face of constant media exposure to fat- and sugar-packed foods, the marketing tactics designed to promote them, and their convenience in a fast-paced society.

One initiative to counter the extensive influence of junk food in American society is to regulate the types of snacks and meals to which children have access (as occurred in 2014, when the government placed strictures on the kinds of food available at elementary and secondary schools). While many people applaud such measures, others complain that they infringe on students' rights to enjoy a sweet treat now and then. Of course, this problem invites several viable solutions between unqualified freedom and tight restrictions (such as regulating meals but not snacks, requiring attention to nutrition in school curricula, implementing more physical fitness incentives in educational environments, and offering support for parents in modeling healthy eating habits).

To be sure, few complex problems that surround you—on your campus, in your community, in your country, in the world at large—lend themselves to easy or obvious solutions. What's more, the search for solutions can spark heated debate. This reality provides motivation for learning how to compose problem-solution papers, in which you can argue for the advantages of what you predict will be the most effective responses to problems that concern you. As discussed in Chapter 19, advocating a particular course of action involves assuming a position, so a problem-solution paper can be viewed as a type of position paper. Nevertheless, as you will learn in the following discussion, a problem-solution paper can be distinguished by a number of qualities beyond the position it argues.

Distinguishing Features of a Problem-Solution Paper

Since virtually every area of human activity involves wrangling over problems and solutions, audiences for this genre are potentially diverse. You will get a sense of this diversity in your college courses as you write for teachers across the curriculum. Teachers assign this genre not only to familiarize you with issues that define various fields of study but also to develop your critical-thinking skills in generating and justifying solutions that individuals working in those disciplines would find convincing.

When communicating the results of these activities in formal problem-solution papers, you can expect that your teachers will require you to fulfill many (if not all) of the objectives that are common to the genre as listed in Figure 20.1. This figure reflects the fairly conventional substance and order of problem-solution papers; however, you should not consider it an outline or formula. Indeed, your own thinking about the relationships between the parts and the whole relevant to the situation you're writing about may suggest different ways of arranging your problem-solution paper, particularly the elements between the hook and the call to action.

Figure 20.2 offers a diagram that can help you visualize how the objectives in Figure 20.1 might fit into essay form: that is, introduction, body, and conclusion. As Figure 20.2 suggests, between the hook and the call to action, problem-solution papers tend to group certain objectives together. However, within those sections—as implied by the nonlinear organization—you should feel free to experiment with organization, since the unique features of various problems and solutions may require different strategies for expressing them.

For example, the hook itself may be sufficient for defining the problem, thus satisfying both objectives. And even in the later portion of the body, where logic might seem to dictate that you lay out all the evidence before addressing counterarguments, you might find it more effective to weave in counterarguments intermittently as they apply to particular lines of reasoning. In short, even with its many essential elements, a problem-solution paper affords considerable room for creativity in organizing your paper, as well as in determining how much space you might need to devote to each component.

MYTH

"A call to action is an overt request for readers to make some bold move."

Certainly, a call to action can be an overt appeal for making a bold move. But it can also take a more subtle form, such as a suggestion to think or behave differently or to consider certain options. The nature of the problem, the solution, and the audience all impact how blatant and emphatic your call to action needs to be.

REALITY

Creating a "hook" or unique opening as a way of introducing the problem

Defining the specific nature of the problem and its impact

Making readers aware of the ramifications of ignoring the problem or accepting the status quo

Familiarizing readers with the specific causes of the problem

Indicating how the problem is currently being addressed

Presenting a claim that argues for what you believe to be the most effective solution

Providing evidence and reasoning to persuade readers of the "rightness" of your proposal

Acknowledging any possibly undesirable outcomes of your solution

Countering reservations about the solution

Calling your readers to action with regard to becoming more aware of the problem and supporting the solution you propose

Figure 20.1 **Objectives of a problem-solution paper**

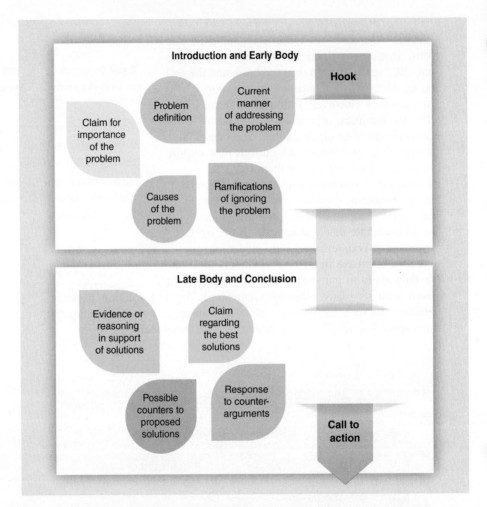

Introduction and Early Body

Hook

Claim for importance of the problem

Problem definition

Current manner of addressing the problem

Causes of the problem

Ramifications of ignoring the problem

Late Body and Conclusion

Evidence or reasoning in support of solutions

Claim regarding the best solutions

Possible counters to proposed solutions

Response to counter-arguments

Call to action

Figure 20.2 **Relationships between elements in a problem-solution paper.**
Though there is no formula for arranging a problem-solution paper, the relationships between its elements might be visualized this way. Following a compelling hook, your introduction or early body paragraphs should define the problem and explain its causes. These first paragraphs might also make claims for the importance of addressing the problem. Your later body paragraphs should lay out the arguments for a particular solution and provide evidence in support of it. At this point, or in the conclusion, you will also want to acknowledge and respond to anticipated arguments against your proposed solution. Calls to action are effectively placed in your paper's conclusion.

To see how one author dealt with the creative challenges of organizing his problem-solution paper, consider the example in the Look Inside box. This blog post for a city newspaper asserts a unique solution to the problem of childhood obesity, demonstrating, even in its brevity, many of the qualities of a problem-solution paper.

Club Sport Participation Could Solve Childhood Obesity Epidemic

by Bill Cullins

SAN ANGELO, Texas — Childhood obesity is a serious health problem, with some reports predicting that today's children may be the first generation to have a shorter life span than their parents.

The obesity crisis is a direct result of too little physical activity and poor nutrition.

Although numerous programs at the local, state and national levels are targeted at healthy diet and exercise, some people believe part of the problem may be the way that sports are organized and enjoyed here in the United States.

Unlike many other countries, our system of sports has evolved as something where a small percentage participate with a much larger percentage of the population watching the action at games or on television.

Michael Hagen, an elite triathlete and former commander of the Army's World Class Athlete program, noted in a 2006 interview that "Sports are the reason so many people in America are overweight—they watch them on TV."

"The American sport media's focus on spectator sports and near disregard of lifetime fitness sports like running leads to so many Americans playing team sports until they finish school/college and then becoming mere spectators thereafter," said Hagen. "The European community-based sport system is far superior in encouraging lifetime fitness."

European schools have very few organized sports teams that are associated with the schools. Instead, participation in sports such as cycling, running, soccer, swimming, triathlon and other activities is structured around sports clubs that are independent of schools.

Members get involved with club activities at an early age and continue into adulthood, with athletically-talented members moving on to compete as members of elite teams and other participants simply continuing the sport for exercise and fun.

Germany is a good example of where club sports enjoy widespread participation.

Annette Hofmann, professor of sports studies at the Ludwigsburg University of Education, notes that "We have

---

A LOOK INSIDE: PROBLEM-SOLUTION PAPER

The article's hook is a shocking fact that would concern parents, as well as others who care about the country's future.

The author quickly moves to major causes of the problem.

Here, the author acknowledges current solutions but then suggests that a different solution may be warranted—one directed at physical inactivity as a cause of obesity.

At this juncture the author names the solution as participation in club sports.

In several body paragraphs, the author shares specifics regarding another country's approach to encouraging physical activity through club sports.

84 million Germans, and 24 million are registered with the club system. We have these clubs everywhere; they are affordable and if the parents are unemployed, they can get support for the annual fees for their children."

If we contrast the German example with what exists in the United States, we end up with a vastly different picture.

Texas requires 135 minutes per week of in-school exercise for elementary students, four semesters of physical education for middle and high school students and one high school physical education (P.E.) credit to graduate.

A 2012 CDC survey of high school students across the nation found that almost 50 percent had no P.E. classes during an average week.

> The author provides statistics to make a case for considering a shift to the European sensibility regarding sports and exercise.

By comparison, the Center for Disease Control's (CDC) minimum exercise recommendation for children and adolescents is 60 minutes or more of aerobic physical activity every day. That also includes muscle and bone strengthening exercises.

A small percentage of students in junior high and high school who are athletically gifted will exceed the CDC recommendations while doing the workouts for their sport, but—in many cases—this activity stops when the student leaves the school.

Given the popularity (and revenue generation) of high school and collegiate sports, a widespread shift to a club sport system such as that in Europe isn't likely to happen in the U.S.

> This section notes potential counterarguments to the proposed solution.

With the continuing addition of increased academic requirements in public schools, it's also doubtful that expanded physical education requirements (especially those that lead to a culture of lifetime fitness) will be added in schools.

The key to solving the childhood obesity problem may be family participation in club sport activities with a decreased emphasis on watching sports on television.

> In response to the counterarguments, the author offers a twist on the broad solution.

Club sports such as (but not limited to) boxing, cycling, golf, gymnastics, martial arts, running, tennis and similar activities that provide healthy aerobic exercise can be started at a young age and continued through adulthood.

. . .

> The omitted paragraphs describe sports (esp. running and cycling) in the author's community.

Ride On, San Angelo, and remember—family participation in club sports activities may be one key to reducing childhood obesity.

> The article ends with a call to action that should resonate with parents, in particular.

Source: Bill Cullins, "Club sport participation could solve childhood obesity epidemic." GO *San Angelo*, 1/14/13. Copyright © 2013. Reprinted by permission of Scripps Media, Inc.

Journalistic venues—such as the one targeted in the Look Inside article—tend to limit the number of words or characters. It seems safe to assume that if Bill Cullins had had more space, he would have elaborated on the causes of obesity. Still, if a component needed to be relatively short in the interest of space, it would be better in this instance to slight the causes as opposed to the solution since the former are already widely acknowledged and the latter represents a contribution that few have probably considered at length.

Processes for Composing a Problem-Solution Paper

As the previous sections have established, a problem-solution paper is, at its core, an argument. Not only do you have to convince others that a problem exists, and that it is serious, but also you have to convince them that the solution you are proposing is the best one possible. The following sections of this chapter offer specific advice for making your case when composing in this genre.

Invention toward First Insight

Earlier, this chapter noted that teachers in your general education and major courses will assign problems for you to write about as a means of engaging you with specific issues at the heart of the discipline you are studying. Even if, on occasion, you do not find these problems compelling, you can draw motivation from the creativity involved in coming up with unique solutions to them.

In many cases, though, you will enjoy the freedom to write about any problem that has caught your attention. For example, you may be asked to identify and respond to a circumstance that is negatively affecting your relationships with friends or family or that is disrupting life on your college campus. However broad the range of choices, you might begin by reflecting on matters that incite strong emotions in you, especially those associated with problems that threaten the security or well-being of others and/or their surroundings. What situations anger you? What situations stir your compassion? What situations do you fear? And why? Answers to these questions point to serious problems that can sustain your motivation and bring about changes that significantly affect your life and the lives of others.

Preparation through Research

Once you have identified the problem you will address in your paper, you will want to learn as much as you can about its nature, its causes, its impact, any responses it has already inspired, and the actual or potential weaknesses in those responses. To begin, you might record what you already know about the problem, perhaps in a journal entry, a cluster diagram, or a Burke's Pentad exercise. The Pentad exercise is particularly instructive for problem-solution papers, as its questions isolate causes, perpetrators, victims, and so on (see Chapter 4 for instructions).

Once you have a handle on the extent of your knowledge about the problem, you can work on filling any gaps in your understanding. While library and Internet research will provide you with relevant and valuable information, some of your best insights will likely come from people who are directly involved with or affected by the situation you are investigating. For this reason, you might consider interviews and surveys as two of your most effective research tools. (See Chapter 5 for discussion of these research strategies.)

While you are conducting research to define your problem, possible solutions will inevitably come to mind. As you prepare for drafting, or even while revising your paper, you will probably need to circle back and conduct additional research to further gauge the viability of the solution you are proposing.

Invention toward More Focused Insight

Through your initial research, you will probably zero in on the crux of the problem you set out to resolve. For example, although at first you may have associated the situation with certain causes or agents, you may discover later that they are different from what you originally assumed. Accuracy in representing such aspects of the situation is crucial to your credibility, for readers will quickly disregard your proposed solution if you have misrepresented the problem in some way.

Narrowing and accurately defining your problem, though, are only a couple of the invention processes involved in conceiving a problem-solution paper. You will also need to spend time generating and critiquing any solutions that you can think of. Even if you don't have much room to maneuver in defining the problem when a teacher (or, down the road, an employer) has assigned it, when conceiving solutions, you will be expected to think outside the box. That's one key to effective problem solving: You must resist the urge to shut down the flow of ideas about possible solutions too quickly.

On the contrary, you should brainstorm radically, being careful not to reject any possibility before you have had ample time to reflect on it. And remember that you don't have to confine yourself to a single or original remedy. Indeed, problem-solution papers might offer multiple solutions, multifaceted solutions, or even tweaks to or combinations of current solutions. Ultimately, your goal is to advance the conversation about solving the problem.

When you finally have a list of plausible answers to the problem you're wrestling with, you need to subject them to close scrutiny, searching for any weaknesses in their logic or feasibility and imagining any counterarguments that naysayers might level against your ideas. As mentioned in the previous section, at this point, you may need to engage in additional research to make certain your proposal is valid. Are the essential resources available? Will the solution be cost-prohibitive? Will it cause different problems that could prove just as serious? These are some of the issues you need to be learning more about through additional research as you prepare yourself for drafting.

Strategies for Drafting

You'll recall that the second section of this chapter introduced you to typical components of a problem-solution paper. While there is no lockstep order to presenting these components, you can categorize them as tending to occur in either the earlier or latter parts of the text. Regarding the earlier parts, this genre typically opens with an engaging hook that references the problem and entices the audience to read further. Just as you tapped feelings of compassion, anger, and fear to identify problems that motivated you to write, you can tap these same emotions in your readers to draw them into your essay. Anecdotes or imaginary scenarios that depict victims of an adverse situation are one source of compelling hooks; so are astonishing facts and figures that communicate the extent of the problem's reach. As such, hooks can also establish the importance of addressing the problem and the consequences of ignoring it. If not, you can always incorporate a direct statement to these effects.

Note also that, depending on its nature, the hook might adequately define the problem. If not, you will need to do so in more explicit terms—perhaps directly following the hook, but definitely somewhere early in the essay. This may involve describing the situation in rich detail, explaining relevant terminology, offering analogies to other, perhaps already well-established, problems, and so on.

Determining where the hook or introduction ends and the body begins is by no means an exact science, but at some point in the initial paragraphs of the paper, you will need to discuss the conditions that gave rise to this problem. After all, the causes themselves may recommend promising responses to a problem; thus, identifying those causes is crucial to building your argument for a solution (see Figure 20.3). When articulating your solution, you can urge readers to consider it by acknowledging what solutions (if any) have already been tried and why they have proved inadequate.

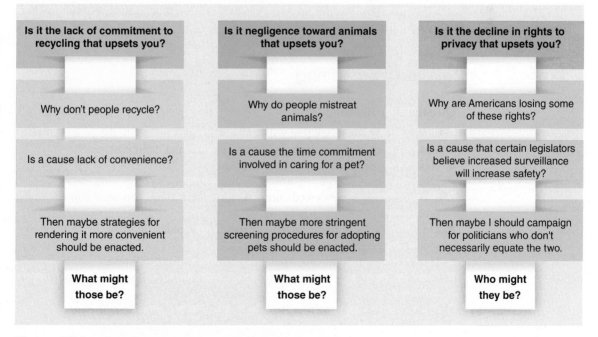

Figure 20.3 **Relationships between causes and solutions**

The features of the genre discussed to this point all work toward setting up the central argument of your paper (or your thesis): that the problem you have identified can be effectively, or more effectively, addressed by the solution you are proposing. Of course, you'll want to characterize the solution before moving on to the reasons for its viability or superiority when contrasted with other responses. As you work to support your reasons, refer to the Toulmin method for structuring and analyzing arguments, explained in Chapter 16.

The focus at this point is on the "whys" of what you are suggesting. Importantly, when you are arguing why readers should accept a certain approach to tackling a situation that troubles them, you should keep in mind that they will have criteria by which they judge the effectiveness of a solution. These criteria may vary with different types of problems, but common criteria include the degree of its impact, the certainty of the effects, their probable endurance, the cost involved, and potential harm or side effects. (The application of such criteria in evaluating a solution mirrors the application of criteria in evaluating other phenomena, as discussed in Chapter 18.) As you build the argument for your solution on sound reasoning and evidence, remember that you can strengthen your credibility by anticipating and responding to potential counterarguments.

The conclusion of a problem-solution paper calls people to action. As the Myth and Reality box earlier in this chapter suggests, the call may seek only subtle change—that is, to become more aware of the problem or open-minded about strategies for approaching it. Of course, the requested action is often more concrete—an invitation to alter behaviors or to support a cause monetarily or through volunteer work. If readers are convinced that your solution makes sense, you'll stand a good chance of moving them to action by appealing to their values: a desire to help others, to protect the environment, to ensure a healthy government, to improve the quality of education, and so on.

Revision and Editing

Questions for Revising

- Have I provided a hook that will engage target readers with the problem?
- Have I clearly defined the problem and established its importance?
- Have I clarified the causes of the problem?
- Does my thesis adequately articulate the solution I'm proposing?
- Have I effectively reviewed current solutions in contrast to what I'm proposing?
- Do I provide sufficient evidence to encourage readers to view my solution as viable and possibly superior to others?
- Have I noted and addressed potential critiques of my solution?
- Does the paper end with a call to action appropriate to the problem and target audience?
- Have I employed transitions to effectively connect ideas?

Questions for Editing

- Are any sources I referred to properly cited?
- Is the finished problem-solution paper free of spelling, punctuation, and usage errors?

Transfer to Other Writing Situations

Despite their possible lack of familiarity, many writing assignments you will encounter in college and the workplace draw on thinking and communication strategies that are so common they have become automatic. Surely, that's the case with problem-solution papers. Just reflect for a moment on the number of times per day that you must reason your way through a problem: How can I unfreeze the locks on my door? How can I turn the few ingredients I have on hand into a meal? How am I going to juggle my work responsibilities with the classes I need to take this semester?

So, whether as a citizen, an employee, or a student, you'll frequently face problems that are serious, complex, and open to multiple responses—and you'll regularly be moved, directed, or assigned to address them in written form. As a citizen, you may want to make the general public aware of a problem and urge a move toward a given solution in a blog, newspaper, or magazine article. As an employee, your supervisor may ask you to explore a company problem and recommend an approach for solving it in a business report. As an academic, you may test a hypothesized solution to a given problem and report your results in a scholarly article. Figure 20.4 lists problems that occupy theorists and practitioners in several disciplines.

Of course, any discipline could be plugged in to Figure 20.4 as a means of establishing the prevalence of problem-solving activity—as could many situations you'll face in your everyday life. This realization makes the examples in Figure 20.4 seem somewhat random. Nevertheless, recognizing how problem-solving activity cuts broadly across all areas of your life should boost your confidence for applying concepts discussed in this chapter in many different contexts.

Discipline	Problem
Microbiology	How to prevent and cure superbugs
Theater	How to stage a flamboyant production in a small venue
Social work	How to shelter the growing number of homeless
Linguistics	How to most accurately represent the meaning of a text written in a different era
Industrial engineering	How to increase efficiency on a given production line
Business management	How to instill a spirit of teamwork among employees

Figure 20.4 **Sample problems in various disciplines**

ACTIVITY

Taking Inventory of Problems That Concern You   On a sheet of paper or on your computer, create a document divided into four columns. Label them in order as follows: Personal Life, Campus, Community, and World. Spend several minutes reflecting on each category, as represented by the labels, and record as many problems as you can think of for each. Share these lists with some of your peers, and see if any of your concerns overlap theirs. For those that do, discuss what you already know about those problems—the specific nature of their impact, current ways of addressing them, and other possible solutions.

IDEA FOR EXTENDED WRITING

Arguing for a Solution to a Problem That Troubles You   Looking over the list of problems you generated and discussed in the brainstorming activity above, select the one that you feel most driven to solve and address it in a problem-solution paper. If the problem happens to be one that you discussed at length with your small-group members during the brainstorming activity, you already have a list of particulars to spark additional thinking about this topic. If you select a problem that is personal, you'll want to broaden your thinking about it to make it relevant to other individuals who may find themselves in similar circumstances. Whatever area of activity you choose, imagine an audience that would have a special interest in the problem (e.g., environmentalists if the problem is deforestation, teachers if the problem is standardized testing, college administrators if the problem is campus safety).

The Creativity Crisis

by Po Bronson and Ashley Merryman

Back in 1958, Ted Schwarzrock was an 8-year-old third grader when he became one of the "Torrance kids," a group of nearly 400 Minneapolis children who completed a series of creativity tasks newly designed by professor E. Paul Torrance. Schwarzrock still vividly remembers the moment when a psychologist handed him a fire truck and asked, "How could you improve this toy to make it better and more fun to play with?" He recalls the psychologist being excited by his answers. In fact, the psychologist's session notes indicate Schwarzrock rattled off 25 improvements, such as adding a removable ladder and springs to the wheels. That wasn't the only time he impressed the scholars, who judged Schwarzrock to have "unusual visual perspective" and "an ability to synthesize diverse elements into meaningful products."

The accepted definition of creativity is production of something original and useful, and that's what's reflected in the tests. There is never one right answer. To be creative requires divergent thinking (generating many unique ideas) and then convergent thinking (combining those ideas into the best result).

In the 50 years since Schwarzrock and the others took their tests, scholars—first led by Torrance, now his colleague, Garnet Millar—have been tracking the children, recording every patent earned, every business founded, every research paper published, and every grant awarded. They tallied the books, dances, radio shows, art exhibitions, software programs, advertising campaigns, hardware innovations, music compositions, public policies (written or implemented), leadership positions, invited lectures, and buildings designed.

Nobody would argue that Torrance's tasks, which have become the gold standard in creativity assessment, measure creativity perfectly. What's shocking is how incredibly well Torrance's creativity index predicted those kids' creative accomplishments as adults. Those who came up with more good ideas on Torrance's tasks grew up to be entrepreneurs, inventors, college presidents, authors, doctors, diplomats, and software developers. Jonathan Plucker of Indiana University recently reanalyzed Torrance's data. The correlation to lifetime creative accomplishment was more than three times stronger for childhood creativity than childhood IQ.

Like intelligence tests, Torrance's test—a 90-minute series of discrete tasks, administered by a psychologist—has been taken by millions worldwide in 50 languages. Yet there is one crucial difference between IQ and CQ scores. With intelligence, there is a phenomenon called the Flynn effect—each generation, scores go up about 10 points. Enriched environments are making kids smarter. With creativity, a reverse trend has just been identified and is being reported for the first time here: American creativity scores are falling.

Kyung Hee Kim at the College of William & Mary discovered this in May, after analyzing almost 300,000 Torrance scores of children and adults. Kim found creativity scores had been steadily rising, just like IQ scores, until 1990. Since then, creativity scores have consistently inched downward. "It's very clear, and the decrease is very significant," Kim says. It is the scores of younger children in America—from kindergarten through sixth grade—for whom the decline is "most serious."

The potential consequences are sweeping. The necessity of human ingenuity is undisputed. A recent IBM poll of 1,500 CEOs identified creativity as the No. 1 "leadership competency" of the future. Yet it's not just about sustaining our nation's economic growth. All around us are matters of national and international importance that are crying out for creative solutions, from saving the Gulf of Mexico to bringing peace to Afghanistan to delivering health care. Such solutions emerge from a healthy marketplace of ideas, sustained by a populace constantly contributing original ideas and receptive to the ideas of others.

It's too early to determine conclusively why U.S. creativity scores are declining. One likely culprit is the number of hours kids now spend in front of the TV and playing videogames rather than engaging in creative activities. Another is the lack of creativity development in our schools. In effect, it's left to the luck of the draw who becomes creative: there's no concerted effort to nurture the creativity of all children.

Around the world, though, other countries are making creativity development a national priority. In 2008 British secondary-school curricula—from science to foreign language—was revamped to emphasize idea generation, and pilot programs have begun using Torrance's test to assess their progress. The European Union designated 2009 as the European Year of Creativity and Innovation, holding conferences on the neuroscience of creativity, financing teacher training, and instituting problem-based learning programs—curricula driven by real-world inquiry—for both children and adults. In China there has been widespread education reform to extinguish the drill-and-kill teaching style. Instead, Chinese schools are also adopting a problem-based learning approach.

Plucker recently toured a number of such schools in Shanghai and Beijing. He was amazed by a boy who, for a class science project, rigged a tracking device for his moped with parts from a cell phone. When faculty of a major Chinese university asked Plucker to identify trends in American education, he described our focus on standardized curriculum, rote memorization, and nationalized testing. "After my answer was translated, they just started laughing out loud," Plucker says. "They said, 'You're racing toward our old model. But we're racing toward your model, as fast as we can.'"

Overwhelmed by curriculum standards, American teachers warn there's no room in the day for a creativity class. Kids are fortunate if they get an art class once or twice a week. But to scientists, this is a non sequitur, borne out of what University of Georgia's Mark Runco calls "art bias." The age-old belief that the arts have a special claim to creativity is unfounded. When scholars gave creativity tasks to both engineering majors and music majors, their scores laid down on an identical spectrum, with the same high averages and standard deviations. Inside their brains, the same thing was happening—ideas were being generated and evaluated on the fly.

Researchers say creativity should be taken out of the art room and put into homeroom. The argument that we can't teach creativity because kids already have too much to learn is a false trade-off. Creativity isn't about freedom from concrete facts. Rather, fact-finding and deep research are vital stages in the creative process. Scholars argue that current curriculum standards can still be met, if taught in a different way.

To understand exactly what should be done requires first understanding the new story emerging from neuroscience. The lore of pop psychology is that creativity occurs on the right side of the brain. But we now know that if you tried to be creative using only the right side of your brain, it'd be like living with ideas perpetually at the tip of your tongue, just beyond reach.

When you try to solve a problem, you begin by concentrating on obvious facts and familiar solutions, to see if the answer lies there. This is a mostly left-brain stage of attack. If the answer doesn't come, the right and left hemispheres of the brain activate together. Neural networks on the right side scan remote memories that could be vaguely relevant. A wide range of distant information that is normally tuned out becomes available to the left hemisphere, which searches for unseen patterns, alternative meanings, and high-level abstractions.

Having glimpsed such a connection, the left brain must quickly lock in on it before it escapes. The attention system must radically reverse gears, going from defocused attention to extremely focused attention. In a flash, the brain pulls together these disparate shreds of thought and binds them into a new single idea that enters consciousness. This is the "aha!" moment of insight, often followed by a spark of pleasure as the brain recognizes the novelty of what it's come up with.

Now the brain must evaluate the idea it just generated. Is it worth pursuing? Creativity requires constant shifting, blender pulses of both divergent thinking and convergent thinking, to combine new information with old and forgotten ideas. Highly creative people are very good at marshaling their brains into bilateral mode, and the more creative they are, the more they dual-activate.

Is this learnable? Well, think of it like basketball. Being tall does help to be a pro basketball player, but the rest of us can still get quite good at the sport through practice. In the same way, there are certain innate features of the brain that make some people naturally prone to divergent thinking. But convergent thinking and focused attention are necessary, too, and those require different neural gifts. Crucially, rapidly shifting between these modes is a top-down function under your mental control. University of New Mexico neuroscientist Rex Jung has concluded that those who diligently practice creative activities learn to recruit their brains' creative networks quicker and better. A lifetime of consistent habits gradually changes the neurological pattern.

A fine example of this emerged in January of this year, with release of a study by University of Western Ontario neuroscientist Daniel Ansari and Harvard's Aaron Berkowitz, who studies music cognition. They put Dartmouth music majors and nonmusicians in an MRI scanner, giving participants a one-handed fiber-optic keyboard to play melodies on. Sometimes melodies were rehearsed; other times they were creatively improvised. During improvisation, the highly trained music majors used their brains in a way the nonmusicians could not: they deactivated their right-temporoparietal junction. Normally, the r-TPJ reads incoming stimuli, sorting the stream for relevance. By turning that off, the musicians blocked out all distraction. They hit an extra gear of concentration, allowing them to work with the notes and create music spontaneously.

Charles Limb of Johns Hopkins has found a similar pattern with jazz musicians, and Austrian researchers observed it with professional dancers visualizing an improvised dance. Ansari and Berkowitz now believe the same is true for orators, comedians, and athletes improvising in games.

The good news is that creativity training that aligns with the new science works surprisingly well. The University of Oklahoma, the University of Georgia, and Taiwan's National Chengchi University each independently conducted a large-scale analysis of such programs. All three teams of scholars concluded that creativity training can have a strong effect. "Creativity can be taught," says James C. Kaufman, professor at California State University, San Bernardino.

What's common about successful programs is they alternate maximum divergent thinking with bouts of intense convergent thinking, through several stages. Real improvement doesn't happen in a weekend workshop. But when applied to the everyday process of work or school, brain function improves.

So what does this mean for America's standards-obsessed schools? The key is in how kids work through the vast catalog of information. Consider the National Inventors Hall of Fame School, a new public middle school in Akron, Ohio. Mindful of Ohio's curriculum requirements, the school's teachers came up with a project for the fifth graders: figure out how to reduce the noise in the library. Its windows faced a public space and, even when closed, let through too much noise. The students had four weeks to design proposals.

Working in small teams, the fifth graders first engaged in what creativity theorist Donald Treffinger describes as fact-finding. How does sound travel through materials? What materials reduce noise the most? Then, problem-finding—anticipating all potential pitfalls so their designs are more likely to work. Next, idea-finding: generate as many ideas as possible. Drapes, plants, or large kites hung from the ceiling would all baffle sound. Or, instead of reducing the sound, maybe mask it by playing the sound of a gentle waterfall? A proposal for double-paned glass evolved into an idea to fill the space between panes with water. Next, solution-finding: which ideas were the most effective, cheapest, and aesthetically pleasing? Fiberglass absorbed sound the best but wouldn't be safe. Would an aquarium with fish be easier than water-filled panes?

Then teams developed a plan of action. They built scale models and chose fabric samples. They realized they'd need to persuade a janitor to care for the plants and fish during vacation. Teams persuaded others to support them—sometimes so well, teams decided to combine projects. Finally, they presented designs to teachers, parents, and Jim West, inventor of the electric microphone.

Along the way, kids demonstrated the very definition of creativity: alternating between divergent and convergent thinking, they arrived at original and useful ideas. And they'd unwittingly mastered Ohio's required fifth-grade curriculum—from understanding sound waves to per-unit cost calculations to the art of persuasive writing. "You never see our kids saying, 'I'll never use this so I don't need to learn it,'" says school administrator Maryann Wolowiec. "Instead, kids ask, 'Do we have to leave school now?'" Two weeks ago, when the school received its results on the state's achievement test, principal Traci Buckner was moved to tears. The raw scores indicate that, in its first year, the school has already become one of the top three schools in Akron, despite having open enrollment by lottery and 42 percent of its students living in poverty.

With as much as three fourths of each day spent in project-based learning, principal Buckner and her team actually work through required curricula, carefully figuring out how kids can learn it through the steps of Treffinger's Creative Problem-Solving method and other creativity pedagogies. "The creative problem-solving program has the highest success in increasing children's creativity," observed William & Mary's Kim.

The home-game version of this means no longer encouraging kids to spring straight ahead to the right answer. When UGA's Runco was driving through California one day with his family, his son asked why Sacramento was the state's capital—why not San Francisco or Los Angeles? Runco turned the question back on him, encouraging him to come up with as many explanations as he could think of.

Preschool children, on average, ask their parents about 100 questions a day. Why, why, why—sometimes parents just wish it'd stop. Tragically, it does stop. By middle school they've pretty much stopped asking. It's no coincidence that this same time is when student motivation and engagement plummet. They didn't stop asking questions because they lost interest: it's the other way around. They lost interest because they stopped asking questions.

Having studied the childhoods of highly creative people for decades, Claremont Graduate University's Mihaly Csikszentmihalyi and University of Northern Iowa's Gary G. Gute found highly creative adults tended to grow up in families embodying opposites. Parents encouraged uniqueness, yet provided stability. They were highly responsive to kids' needs, yet challenged kids to develop skills. This resulted in a sort of adaptability: in times of anxiousness, clear rules could reduce chaos—yet when kids were bored, they could seek change, too. In the space between anxiety and boredom was where creativity flourished.

It's also true that highly creative adults frequently grew up with hardship. Hardship by itself doesn't lead to creativity, but it does force kids to become more flexible—and flexibility helps with creativity.

In early childhood, distinct types of free play are associated with high creativity. Preschoolers who spend more time in role-play (acting out characters) have higher measures of creativity: voicing someone else's point of view helps develop their ability to analyze situations from different perspectives. When playing alone, highly creative first graders may act out strong negative emotions: they'll be angry, hostile, anguished. The hypothesis is that play is a safe harbor to work through forbidden thoughts and emotions.

In middle childhood, kids sometimes create paracosms—fantasies of entire alternative worlds. Kids revisit their paracosms repeatedly, sometimes for months, and even create languages spoken there. This type of play peaks at age 9 or 10, and it's a very strong sign of future creativity. A Michigan State University study of MacArthur "genius award" winners found a remarkably high rate of paracosm creation in their childhoods.

From fourth grade on, creativity no longer occurs in a vacuum; researching and studying become an integral part of coming up with useful solutions. But this transition isn't easy. As school stuffs more complex information into their heads, kids get overloaded, and creativity suffers. When creative children have a supportive teacher—someone tolerant of unconventional answers, occasional disruptions, or detours of curiosity—they tend to excel. When they don't, they tend to underperform and drop out of high school or don't finish college at high rates.

They're quitting because they're discouraged and bored, not because they're dark, depressed, anxious, or neurotic. It's a myth that creative people have these traits. (Those traits actually shut down creativity; they make people less open to experience and less interested in novelty.) Rather, creative people, for the most part, exhibit active moods and positive affect. They're not particularly happy—contentment is a kind of complacency creative people rarely have. But they're engaged, motivated, and open to the world.

The new view is that creativity is part of normal brain function. Some scholars go further, arguing that lack of creativity—not having loads of it—is the real risk factor. In his research, Runco asks college students, "Think of all the things that could interfere with graduating from college." Then he instructs them to pick one of those items and to come up with as many solutions for that problem as possible. This is a classic divergent-convergent creativity challenge. A subset of respondents, like the proverbial Murphy, quickly list every imaginable way things can go wrong. But they demonstrate a complete lack of flexibility in finding creative solutions. It's this inability to conceive of alternative approaches that leads to despair. Runco's two questions predict suicide ideation—even when controlling for preexisting levels of depression and anxiety.

In Runco's subsequent research, those who do better in both problem-finding and problem-solving have better relationships. They are more able to handle stress and overcome the bumps life throws in their way. A similar study of 1,500 middle schoolers found that those high in creative self-efficacy had more confidence about their future and ability to succeed. They were sure that their ability to come up with alternatives would aid them, no matter what problems would arise.

When he was 30 years old, Ted Schwarzrock was looking for an alternative. He was hardly on track to becoming the prototype of Torrance's longitudinal study. He wasn't artistic when young, and his family didn't recognize his creativity or nurture it. The son of a dentist and a speech pathologist, he had been pushed into medical school, where he felt stifled and commonly had run-ins with professors and bosses. But eventually, he found a way to combine his creativity and medical expertise: inventing new medical technologies.

Today, Schwarzrock is independently wealthy—he founded and sold three medical-products companies and was a partner in three more. His innovations in health care have been wide ranging, from a portable respiratory oxygen device to skin-absorbing anti-inflammatories to insights into how bacteria become antibiotic-resistant. His latest project could bring down the cost of spine-surgery implants 50 percent. "As a child, I never had an identity as a 'creative person,'" Schwarzrock recalls. "But now that I know, it helps explain a lot of what I felt and went through."

Creativity has always been prized in American society, but it's never really been understood. While our creativity scores decline unchecked, the current national strategy for creativity consists of little more than praying for a Greek muse to drop by our houses. The problems we face now, and in the future, simply demand that we do more than just hope for inspiration to strike. Fortunately, the science can help: we know the steps to lead that elusive muse right to our doors.

It Can't Happen Here: Why Is There So Little Coverage of Americans Who Are Struggling with Poverty?

by Dan Froomkin

Poverty is hardly a new phenomenon in the hardscrabble highlands of Missouri's Ozarks. But to David Stoeffler, freshly arrived at the helm of the region's main paper, the Springfield News-Leader, the fact that two out of five families in the area with children under 18 lived below the poverty line seemed like a huge story. "We certainly had covered these issues," says Stoeffler, who became executive editor in May 2010, "but I would say it was more episodically, and not in any coordinated way."

Stoeffler decided the paper needed to do more: "My sense was the community needed a little crusading."

After conversations with community groups and among staffers, the newsroom embarked on a major public service project called "Every Child" examining the range of challenges facing children in the region. There was still a problem, though, the one that plagues all poverty reporting: "What we were trying to do is figure out how could we paint this big broad picture and at the same time not bore everybody to death," Stoeffler says. "The goal was to try to raise awareness and get people to say, 'We need to do something about this.'"

So for five consecutive days last September, Stoeffler published stories across the entire front page of the print edition and the homepage of the paper's website. Each day focused on a specific problem: "No home," "No shoes," "No food," "No car," and "No peace." Many readers were shocked, saying they had no idea so many area families were living in such desperate circumstances. Some reached out to families that had been featured. Members of the community the News-Leader had initially brought together as an advisory group formed the Every Child Initiative to push for long-term policy changes. "There seems to be momentum toward wanting to do something sustainable and lasting," Stoeffler says. "We feel like we succeeded in getting the attention of the community."

Sadly, the News-Leader's success is an anomaly in the news business. Nearly 50 million people—about one in six Americans—live in poverty, defined as income below $23,021 a year for a family of four. And yet most news organizations largely ignore the issue. The Pew Research Center's Project for Excellence in Journalism indexed stories in 52 major mainstream news outlets from 2007 through the first half of 2012 and, according to Mark Jurkowitz, the project's associate director, "in no year did poverty coverage even come close to accounting for as little as one percent of the news hole. It's fair to say that when you look at that particular topic, it's negligible."

Instead, as Tampa Bay Times media critic Eric Deggans notes, at most news organizations poverty comes up sporadically. "Poverty becomes a sort of 'very special episode' of journalism that we sort of roll out every so often," he says.

The reasons for the lack of coverage are familiar. Journalists are drawn more to people making things happen than those struggling to pay bills; poverty is not considered a beat; neither advertisers nor readers are likely to demand more coverage, so neither will editors; and poverty stories are almost always enterprise work, requiring extra time and commitment. Yet persistent poverty is in some ways the ultimate accountability story—because, often, poverty happens by design.

"Poverty exists in a wealthy country largely as a result of political choices, not as a result of pure economics," argues Sasha Abramsky, a journalist whose upcoming book is called "The American Way of Poverty." "The U.S. poverty rate is higher than most other developed nations, and the only way you can square that is there are political choices being made—or not being made—that accept a level of poverty that most wealthy democracies have said is unacceptable. We make these policy choices that perpetuate poverty, and then because poverty is so extreme, it becomes impolite to talk about."

The media could try to force the issue but it doesn't—at least not anymore, according to Philip Bennett, managing editor of PBS's Frontline public affairs series: "There are basic questions about the way the country is today that aren't being addressed by the journalistic institutions that used to address them."

The rise (and fall) of the Occupy movement, along with data about the increasingly skewed distribution of wealth and income in the United States, have led to greater interest in inequality. "There's been lots of really good stuff written about inequality, probably more in the last few years than in the previous 20," says Jason DeParle, who's covered poverty policy for The New York Times for 23 years. But much of the debate over inequality has focused on the excesses of the rich rather than the deprivations of the poor.

DeParle also notes that one frequent excuse for ignoring poverty is increasingly anachronistic. "We have tended to congratulate ourselves as a country that 'OK, there's more poverty, but that's because there's also more fluidity in our society,'" he says. But that's just not true anymore. Recent surveys show that Americans now have less economic mobility than Western Europeans. For instance, one study found that 42 percent of Americans raised in the bottom quintile of family income remain stuck there as adults, compared to 30 percent in the historically class-bound United Kingdom. For Bennett, the key unaddressed question is: Has America become a less fair society? "This is a major question of American life," he says. "It's part of our political divide in a really important way. [And yet it] is not receiving the kind of sustained, imaginative, aggressive coverage that it deserves. Shouldn't journalists—and not just one or two—be organizing themselves en masse to ask that question?"

One way to address the question is to confront pernicious myths about poverty. "The reason why people believe that

'47 percent nonsense' [Republican presidential candidate Mitt Romney's leaked comment characterizing 47 percent of the population as "dependent upon the government"] that Romney was swinging is because they don't know the working poor," says Deggans, who is also author of "Race-Baiter: How the Media Wields Dangerous Words to Divide a Nation."

Despite stereotypes of "the lazy poor," for example, more than a third of adults in poverty have jobs; they just don't earn enough to support their families. According to the Economic Policy Institute, 28 percent of workers nationally earn less than $11 an hour. Even working full time year-round, that still leaves a family of four below the poverty line.

Modern low-wage workplaces can make for gripping stories. Noting Wal-Mart's promise to hire any recent honorably discharged veteran, Columbia University journalism professor Dale Maharidge suggests reporters follow one of those soldiers around for a few days. Half of Wal-Mart's more than one million U.S. workers make less than $10 an hour. "See how they cope on $8 or $9 an hour," says Maharidge, author of "Someplace Like America: Tales From the New Great Depression." Then consider the Walton family fortune, estimated to be more than $80 billion. "Look at how much money they're making versus how much their workers are making, through this soldier," Maharidge suggests.

There are also opportunities for business reporters to broaden questions beyond stock prices and acquisitions. Mimi Corcoran, director of the Special Fund for Poverty Alleviation at the liberal Open Society Foundations, urges journalists to grill CEOs about their companies' compensation plans and the ratio between what their employees make and their own income. "What are you doing to provide livable wages? What's the appropriate balance between return on income versus what you're doing to support your workforce?" Corcoran suggests as model questions.

Gary Rivlin, author of "Broke, USA: From Pawnshops to Poverty, Inc.—How the Working Poor Became Big Business," points reporters to the businesses (payday lenders, pawnshops and check cashers) that profit from poverty. "Poor people don't just necessarily happen. The poor have a lot of help staying poor," he says. Rivlin and Barbara Ehrenreich, another writer with a long history of covering poverty, recently helped found a nonprofit group, the Economic Hardship Reporting Project, to encourage precisely that kind of coverage.

There's also a wealth of stories in anti-poverty programs. "You always hear, 'We waged a war on poverty and poverty won,'" says Greg Kaufmann, who covers poverty for The Nation. But the safety net has caught a lot of people who otherwise would have fallen much further, he points out: "It's like saying the Clean Water Act didn't work because there's still water pollution."

Indeed, one of the most overlooked stories of the decade may be the effects of anti-poverty measures that were part of the 2009 Recovery Act. "They had huge effects; they got virtually no attention," says Michael Grunwald, a Time reporter and author of "The New New Deal: The Hidden Story of Change in the Obama Era." The provisions in the stimulus represent the biggest anti-poverty effort since President Johnson's Great Society in the 1960s.

In addition to expanding anti-poverty programs, the White House and Democrats in Congress made a concerted effort "to really do some innovative—and ultimately, in some areas, remarkably effective—things," Grunwald says. A $1.5 billion homelessness prevention fund allowed local governments to assist at-risk people with things like emergency rent payments, utility bills, and moving expenses. "During the worst economic crisis in 90 years, the homeless population actually decreased," Grunwald notes.

Mark Rank, a social welfare professor at Washington University in St. Louis, argues that poverty reporters also sometimes fall into a trap familiar to political reporters: giving both sides of the issue equal weight.

There's the conservative argument that poverty is largely a function of "people just screwing up, just not having the motivation," Rank says. The other argument, which Rank says is supported by the preponderance of research, is that poverty is the result of structural failings, most commonly, not enough jobs.

The most traditional kind of poverty coverage—the sob story—can actually backfire. A 1990 study by political scientist Shanto Iyengar found that "episodic" television news stories that focused on specific victims of poverty, especially black mothers, actually led white middle class viewers to blame the individuals more than social or government institutions. "In a capitalist society where success is judged in part by how much money you make, there's a strong impulse to want to attach personal choices and deliberate action to whether you are poor," says the Tampa Bay Times's Deggans.

Context is key. Put individual stories in their wider context, look at the social factors at play, and examine possible solutions, says Calvin Sims, a former New York Times reporter who now manages the Ford Foundation's portfolio of news media and journalism grants: "Many readers walk away from stories about poverty thinking, 'Well, the poor, they'll always be with us. What can we do?' That's not something that we, as journalists, should leave people with."

News organizations need to "find ways for the work to have resonance in other spaces," according to Sims. That could mean convening follow-up conversations through panel discussions, on video, or through social media, with a particular focus on solutions. He also thinks there's great potential in traditional news organizations for sharing information with others, including the fast-growing ethnic media sector.

At the Springfield News-Leader, Stoeffler feels a sense of satisfaction. Like other newspapers, his has been retrenching; the newsroom is 20 percent smaller today than it was just three years ago. But Stoeffler argues that going after chronic community problems like poverty is more crucial now than ever. "From a journalistic standpoint, we become less and less relevant if we don't go after some of these bigger issues," he says. "It's the way we can distinguish ourselves from other media."

Source: Dan Froomkin, "It Can't Happen Here: Why Is There So Little Coverage of Americans Who Are Struggling with Poverty?" *Nieman Reports,* Winter 2013. Copyright © 2013. Reprinted with permission.

FOR DISCUSSION

1. To what extent are you convinced that the problems these authors describe are worthy of their intended readers' attention? On what do you base your evaluation?
2. What specific elements presented in Figures 20.1 and 20.2 can you locate in these example problem-solution papers?
3. What appeals to credibility and emotion do the authors depend on in establishing the gravity of their problems?
4. What criteria do the authors apparently apply in presuming their solutions will be well-received?
5. Are the calls to action in these pieces subtle or overt? How, specifically, are they geared toward the target audiences?

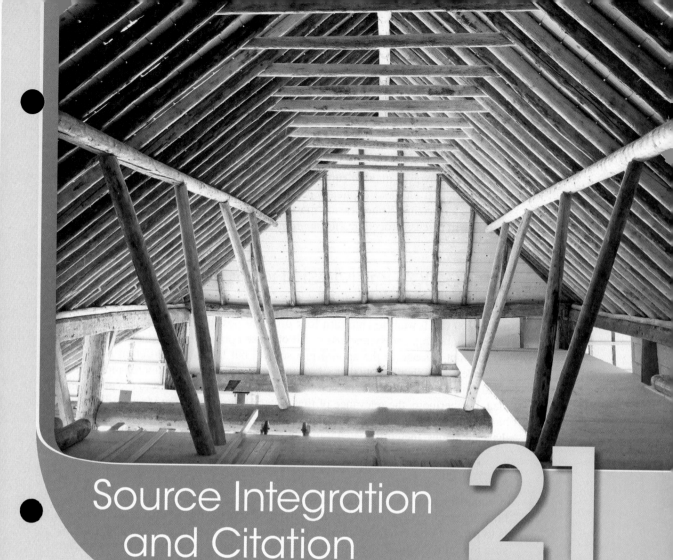

Source Integration and Citation 21

Study the intricate structure in the photo above—the ceiling of a building with exposed beams. Imagine what would happen if you were to remove one of the crosspieces. If the roof didn't immediately cave in, it would probably begin to weaken, causing inhabitants to question its stability. The relationship between a roof and its beams is similar to that between a document and the illustrations or evidence used to construct it. If this kind of support is insufficient, readers will doubt the reliability of your thesis statement and other assertions. Whether writing to inform, analyze, or argue, you often will draw support from published sources, excerpts from which must be tightly integrated with surrounding text and properly credited to the authors who wrote them. This chapter explains aspects of both these processes.

As you learned in earlier chapters, research methods can range from combing your memory (as for a memoir), to interviewing people or observing events (as for a profile), to gathering and studying published documents from the library or Internet (as for a research report). (See Chapter 5 to review strategies for conducting different kinds of research.) Although you wouldn't cite your own memories or observations in the texts you compose, you would, of course, be required to cite interviews and published documents.

Understanding citation practices is crucial to your credibility as a writer, an idea that this chapter will expand on later. But effectively integrating sources involves more than making sure you have recognized others' contributions to your work. It also involves making sure that you thoroughly explain the significance of the sources you cite and explicitly connect them to the surrounding discussion. After characterizing strategies for meshing sources with your own writing, this chapter will discuss procedures for appropriately documenting them.

Strategies for Meshing Sources

When representing the content of personal interviews or published sources in your own texts, you'll want to entertain four different possibilities: summarizing, paraphrasing, quoting, and synthesizing. All of these options require that you attribute the relevant passage to the appropriate source, but they serve different purposes. Regardless, you should note that all summarized, paraphrased, quoted, and synthesized material should be introduced by a transition that connects it to the preceding idea. Furthermore, the relevance of that material to surrounding ideas will need to be explained. In the next several paragraphs, you will learn more about each of these strategies, including when it makes sense to opt for one over the others.

Summary

A summary provides a broad overview of a resource, either an entire text (e.g., book, chapter, article, interview transcript) or at least a large part of it. The goal is to pare a fairly extensive chunk of material down to some key elements, being sure to highlight those that are essential to building your own text. For example, you might determine that the thesis of a particular book establishes knowledge that readers will need to know before they can understand your own thesis. You cannot incorporate an entire book into your own text, so you will need to condense it substantially.

Depending on the length of your source and your purposes for citing it, your summary could consume a few sentences or as much as a few paragraphs, but, typically, it won't exceed such boundaries. Figure 21.1 presents an excerpt from an article that condenses a book of over 400 pages to a few short passages. The purpose of the summary is to provide an overview of a psychological theory detailed in that book so the author of the article can use it to achieve his ultimate purpose: to apply that theory specifically to education. Preceding this excerpt, the author relates an anecdote from his days as a public school teacher that illustrates what he believes is the usefulness of the theory he is about to explain. He then moves directly to the excerpt in Figure 21.1. Note that the summary begins with mention of the source's author and title; no pages are cited because the summary refers to the book as a whole. (You can find more sample summaries in Chapter 10.)

The best place to start when preparing a summary is with a sketch of key points. Creating such a sketch ordinarily will require you to engage the piece more than once, and you should do so with your reasons for citing it clearly in mind. To be more specific, first, you will want to read the source for its gist or main point, making note of it at the top of the page where you are compiling your sketch. Then you will need to read through the source again (or at least through relevant sections in the case of a lengthy document), looking for observations that directly support the main point. During additional readings, you should keep your eyes open for any secondary elements that speak to your composing agenda. For example, an anecdote is usually not considered of primary importance when summarizing, but if it connects perfectly to your own focus, it might be worth mentioning.

When you have drawn out the gist of the source, the primary supporting observations, and maybe a fitting secondary element, you are ready to link them together in your own words in the interest of creating an abbreviated version of the material you wish to cover. The need for radical condensing—for representing concepts addressed across many pages in a small space—tips you off as to when you should be summarizing as opposed to paraphrasing or quoting, as discussed below.

Paraphrase

In contrast to a summary, a paraphrase covers considerably less ground, usually representing only a few sentences of a source or a paragraph at most. A paraphrase is much more focused than a summary, and, therefore, it tends to preserve more of the original content, including examples and other supporting details. Like a summary, however, a paraphrase couches that material *in your own words;* that is, it requires you to take the other author's ideas and present them in completely different vocabulary and sentence structures. Figure 21.2 contains a brief excerpt from a print source alongside a paraphrase of that excerpt so that you can easily contrast the two. Because it is an extreme rewrite, a paraphrase, like a summary, doesn't need to be enclosed in quotation marks. However—also like a summary—the ideas in a paraphrase must be credited to the author by means of procedures discussed later in this chapter.

MYTH

"When in need of a summary, you can simply consult one that's already been written."

First, if you did consult or employ someone else's summary, you would need to cite it like any other source; otherwise, you would be plagiarizing. Second, if you rely on someone else's summary, chances are it won't be as relevant to your own purposes for writing. In other words, at least to some degree, your reasons for writing will determine what issues will be highlighted in your summary.

REALITY

MYTH

"A paraphrase involves simply identifying a passage you like, plugging in a synonym here and there, and then weaving it into your essay."

Changing only a few words in a passage expressed by someone else—even if you cite it—can lead to charges of plagiarism. When you treat something as a paraphrase, you are expected to significantly alter the langauge *and* sentence structures.

REALITY

From "An Educator's Journey toward Multiple Intelligences"
by Scott Seider

Rethinking IQ

What has become a powerful force in the world of education all started in 1983, when Harvard University professor Howard Gardner began his book *Frames of Mind: The Theory of Multiple Intelligences* with some simple but powerful questions: Are talented chess players, violinists, and athletes "intelligent" in their respective disciplines? Why are these and other abilities not accounted for on traditional IQ tests? Why is the term intelligence limited to such a narrow range of human endeavors?

From these questions emerged multiple-intelligences theory. Stated simply, it challenges psychology's definition of intelligence as a general ability that can be measured by a single IQ score. Instead, MI theory describes eight intelligences (see Howard Gardner's Eight Intelligences) that people use to solve problems and create products relevant to the societies in which they live.

MI theory asserts that individuals who have a high level of aptitude in one intelligence do not necessarily have a similar aptitude in another intelligence. For example, a young person who demonstrates an impressive level of musical intelligence may be far less skilled when it comes to bodily-kinesthetic or logical-mathematical intelligence. Perhaps that seems obvious. But it's important to recognize that this notion stands in sharp contrast to the traditional (and still dominant) view of intelligence as a general ability that can be measured along a single scale and summarized by a single number.

> Rather than diving abruptly into the content of the book, the author integrates his summary by linking it explicitly to his larger discussion of education and by specifically introducing the book's author (including credentials).

> Starting with the word "perhaps," the author clarifies the significance of the ideas he's just summarized relevant to his thesis—that is, although MI theory may seem commonsensical, it represents a departure from a strong tradition and, therefore, has not been implemented as widely as it should be.

Source: Scott Seider, "An Educator's Journey toward Multiple Intelligences," originally published in *Edutopia*, 1 Apr. 2009. © Edutopia.org, George Lucas Educational Foundation. Reprinted with permission.

Figure 21.1 A summary

Extending the comparison further, a paraphrase must also be integrated with surrounding text. See Figure 21.3 for an example of how the paraphrase in Figure 21.2 could be tied directly to a larger discussion. As this example illustrates, effective

Excerpt from Source

More than half of the country's schools have some form of dress code, according to a survey of school principals conducted by the National Center for Education Statistics. However, those policies vary drastically between schools, districts, and states. . . . To complicate matters, there is no gold standard for what is acceptable attire in school.

Paraphrase of Excerpt

While many American schools have dress codes, those codes range widely, demonstrating little overlap with regard to what's considered appropriate (Swan).

Source: Noelle Swan, "High School Dress Code: The Battle for Keeping Up Appearances," *The Christian Science Monitor,* 11 Sept. 2013.

Figure 21.2 **Sample excerpt and a paraphrase of it**

When considering the many complex issues that the nation's public school administrators grapple with on a daily basis, you'd think that the question of what students should be allowed to wear would present an easy answer. But, in fact, **while many American schools have dress codes, those codes range widely, demonstrating little overlap with regard to what's considered appropriate (Swan).** To illustrate just how widely ranging these codes can be, the following analysis contrasts policies at three public high schools in various regions across the country.

Following a statement of the primary reason for bringing this issue to light, the author introduces the paraphrase with the *transition* "But, in fact," which signals that its purpose is to offer a view that contrasts with the previous observation.

To directly tie the paraphrase to the discussion that follows, the author repeats words, or forms of them, to make sure readers grasp the relevance of the passage to the following discussion.

Figure 21.3 **A paraphrase integrated into surrounding text**

source integration involves introducing the cited passage by noting its relationship to a previous observation and then following it with commentary on its significance or purpose in the context of the larger discussion.

At this point you might be asking yourself why you would ever choose to paraphrase when you could simply copy the passage word for word, place quotes around it, and be finished. The answer to that question is twofold. Most importantly, you'll find that, at times, the concepts you want to cite are communicated in language structures that are too difficult for your intended readers to process. In such cases, you'll want to present the content of the passage in structures you know your audience will more readily comprehend. Another reason for paraphrasing—as opposed to directly quoting—is that it allows you to put more of yourself into your writing. In other words, you want your texts to sound like you. If you "pad" them with too many passages copied directly from your sources, you end up squeezing out your own views and channeling the style of other writers instead of remaining true to your own voice.

When attempting to paraphrase, it is helpful to look at the passage you want to cite sentence by sentence, recording the topic or point of each one in order. Then, next to the point of each sentence, record details that the author supplied in making that point. Leaving the original passage behind for a few moments, take the information you have recorded and explain the material as it makes sense to you. Finally, return to the passage to check what you have written against the original to ensure that you have accurately captured the meaning you took from it and that you have avoided inadvertently repeating the author's phrasing. Of course, there will be times when you want to keep that phrasing; those are the times when you will opt for a direct quote, as discussed in the following section.

Direct Quote

A direct quote is just what it sounds like—an exact copy of the original passage with quotation marks around it. In fact, the quotation marks communicate to readers that you have incorporated the sentence or paragraph word for word. If you are quoting a passage that is over four lines long, you will need to "block" the quote, which means you will indent each line ½ inch (regular paragraphs are indented ½ inch) and leave off the quotation marks, as the indentation is the signal to readers that you are quoting. You can see how this works in Figure 21.4, which presents an excerpt from an article entitled "How Scholars Read" by John Guillory. Preceding this excerpt, the author discusses the relative speed of different types of reading.

As illustrated in Figure 21.4, if you simply drop a quote into your own text without explaining it, readers may miss its significance. As the author makes clear, Bacon's quote is often misinterpreted. For this reason—and also because your audience can't read your mind regarding the relevance of a given quote to your purposes—you need to carefully tie each quote to the discussion of which it will become a part. You can do so by alerting your audience to the fact that a quote is coming and by explaining the role that it assumes in that part of your text.

In Figure 21.5, you can see how one student author, Kris Washington, accomplishes this in two passages from an essay on blogging and new media. Washington introduces direct quotes by naming their authors, and in the first example also includes the title of the source from which she took the quote. The introductions themselves clearly link their respective quotes to the commentary preceding them. You'll also want to note the differing tactics Washington

The distinctions I make here are clearer in retrospect than perhaps they were to readers in the early modern period. Francis Bacon famously remarks on the implied difference in speed of reading in a passage often quoted out of context:

> Some books are to be tasted, others to be swallowed, and some few to be chewed and digested: that is, some books are to be read only in parts; others to be read, but not curiously; and some few to be read wholly and with diligence and attention. (209)

This passage seems to point to reading practice as determined by the quality of the book. But the context is Bacon's essay, "Of Studies," and the reader here is assumed to be a scholar, presumptively literate in the classical and modern languages. In setting out his typology of fast and slow reading, Bacon is not necessarily anticipating the kind of reading solicited by the novel or by newspapers.

After a transition from the previous discussion, the author introduces the direct quote by naming the person who wrote it.

Though this direct quote may not seem especially lengthy, it took up over four lines of a column in the journal that originally published the article. The general rule of thumb is to block any passage over four lines. (Notice that the quote extends all the way to the right margin and that the period precedes the parentheses.)

Pay attention here to how the author comments on the quote, linking it directly to his thesis that even scholarly writing demands different kinds of reading at different times.

Source: John Guillory, "How Scholars Read," *ADE Bulletin*, Modern Language Association, 2009. Reprinted by permission of the author.

Figure 21.4 **A blocked quote**

employs to mesh the quotes with her own prose: In the first, she preserves a complete sentence from the original source, while in the second she uses only phrases. Finally, in each case the author follows the direct quote not only with the page number on which it is found, but also with a line that ties the quote explicitly to the discourse that follows.

Indeed, when incorporating a direct quote, you don't want to take a chance that your readers will miss the meaning you want them to take from it. To explain it so fully may feel as if you are stating the obvious, perhaps even insulting readers. But you have to remember that they aren't inside your head; they haven't been immersed in the documents that you've been immersed in, and they haven't yet worked through the connections that you've made. You have to show them the way to those connections if you want to ensure that they can follow your line of reasoning.

Incorporating a directly quoted sentence

In his book, *Here Comes Everybody: The Power of Organizing without Organizations*, New York University professor and media consultant Clay Shirky explains how the proliferation of blogs is affecting news: "The change isn't a shift from one kind of news institution to another, but rather in the definition of news" (65-66). Blogging has ushered in a new set of consumer expectations for immediate news coverage distributed widely on a broad range of topics. Bloggers are able to decide what is newsworthy and they have the ability to spread that information globally at very little cost.

Incorporating a directly quoted phrase

Newspapers have been slow to make their content available on mobile devices, and advertising revenue has also been slow to follow. Without that revenue, traditional news companies will be limited in their abilities to print and distribute news and hire staff. Anderson, Bell, and Shirky suggest that news organizations "should master working with amateurs, crowds, machines or other partners to keep cost low and leverage high" and "should assume that cost control is the central discipline" (116). Clearly, a partnership between traditional and new media is essential to the future of journalism.

Blogs are a fast and convenient way to publicize current issues and events, but it's questionable if blogs can offer information as reliable as that of traditional news organizations.

Source: Kris Washington, "Breaking News: Blogging's Impact on Traditional and New Media." *A Writer's Resource*, 5th edition, by Elaine Maimon, et al., McGraw-Hill, 2016.

Figure 21.5 Direct quotes with introductions

Synthesis

Usually when you summarize, paraphrase, or quote, you are working to integrate information from a single source into your writing. Sometimes, though, you'll want to address multiple sources simultaneously, a strategy referred to as **synthesizing.** More specifically (as discussed in Chapter 9), synthesizing involves putting sources in conversation with each other to establish how they agree, disagree, and connect with your own work.

In some cases when synthesizing, you will weave together sources relevant to a particular point you are making by using transitions that indicate how they relate to each other. This approach is useful when sources disagree or when, for some other reason, you need or want to preserve some of the sources' original language. Figure 21.6 illustrates this approach in an excerpt from a student paper on the role of criticism in creative achievement.

Another approach to synthesizing groups sources that agree with each other in a single parenthetical citation. This method is demonstrated in Figure 21.7, which shares a passage from a student paper on the nature of incubation. The strategy depicted in Figure 21.7 is vital to the work of integrating sources because it helps prevent redundancy. In other words, it allows you to collectively attribute a concept

Some creators actually enjoy criticism. They use it as a way to improve their work. Influential jazz musician Wynton Marsalis likes being critiqued. He does note, however, that to deal with critics effectively "you have to assess criticism and then make your own decisions" (167). Unlike Marsalis, who openly welcomes criticism, steel sculptor Richard Serra adopts a somewhat tentative approach to criticism. He says that "if the criticism is structural or intellectual in nature, and it makes sense . . . then you listen to it. If it's personal . . . then you become very, very skeptical" (179).

Here the author indicates that one creative individual she read about is open to criticism—even appreciates it for how it might inform his work.

Figure 21.6 **Example of synthesizing through transitions**

The incubation period also has another highly useful function. It allows the information to rest in one's subconscious; the subconscious then takes the information and applies it to the new idea or creation in different ways than the waking or conscious mind could have (Begley, 2013; Eisner, 2000; Szegedy-Maszak, 2006).

This in-text citation contains three sources. The presumption when reading it is that all of them make the same point, noted prior to the citation.

Figure 21.7 **Example of synthesizing through a collective citation**

to several different sources in a single in-text citation—this as opposed to summarizing, in turn, numerous works that forward essentially the same message. Most importantly, both of the synthesizing moves discussed in this section reveal critical thought about the sources you're citing, particularly how they relate to each other in supporting or refining your claims.

Strategies for Citing Sources

As noted in the previous sections, whether you are summarizing, paraphrasing, quoting, or synthesizing, any time you reference another individual's original material, you must give that individual credit in ways that are conventional within the community or the publication you are targeting. When you are writing for your college courses, you are targeting academic communities whose citation practices are governed by manuals sanctioned by the field. Two of the most commonly used manuals, especially in general education courses, are those published by the Modern Language Association (MLA) and the American Psychological Association (APA). MLA guidelines inform disciplines categorized as humanities; APA guidelines are a popular choice for many of the social sciences.

Given the prevalence of MLA and APA guidelines across the curriculum, the remainder of this chapter concentrates on some of the fundamentals involved in citing sources by either method. Space limitations prevent the inclusion of all the information relevant to these citation styles. Be advised, then, that if you can't find the specifics you need in the following sections, you should consult the original manuals or one of many online writing labs that provide more extensive summaries of the manuals' contents. In addition, you should realize that if your major lies outside the humanities or the social sciences, it might require you to learn a different method of citing sources. Remember, though, that much of the logic behind MLA and APA citation practices will carry over to those contexts.

Logic of Citation in MLA and APA

Both MLA and APA guidelines call for internal or parenthetical citations of the sources you reference. These citations are woven into your own prose following your mention of the source, and they commonly look like this: (Jones 15) for MLA, and (Jones, 2014) for APA. These in-text citations lead a reader from the source to its publication information detailed on the **Works Cited** (MLA) or **References** (APA) page at the end of your paper (see Chapter 10 for examples). The specific mechanism by which they do so is, in most cases, the author's last name (Jones in the above instances). Once readers see that identifying word, they know exactly where to look on the alphabetically organized Works Cited or References page to find numerous details about that source, which will help them evaluate its quality (see Chapter 5 for evaluation criteria) and locate it if needed.

This is the basic logic guiding MLA and APA citation practices. Of course, the general format of an internal citation might vary slightly, depending on the nature of the source. Such variations are sorted out in the remaining sections of this chapter. These sections also cover the various formats for creating entries on Works Cited or References pages for different types of sources that you'll likely consult for your college coursework.

MLA Internal Citations

As noted above, the basic in-text citation in MLA contains the author's last name and the page number on which the cited material appears in the original source. This format applies to a source written by a single author and a passage taken from a single page, but, of course, this example doesn't fit all potentialities. Figure 21.8 lists alternatives to this basic configuration as they reflect different types of authorship, as well as the amount and placement of cited material.

Making sure your internal citation is formatted in accordance with the guidelines in Figure 21.8 requires paying close attention to the punctuation within. You also need to pay attention to the punctuation surrounding the citation. A rule

Citation Form	Explanation	Example
Basic form—alternative	If you name the author when introducing the cited material, simply place the page number in end-of-sentence parentheses, with the end punctuation outside the parentheses.	In his recent travel narrative, Ed Gerke notes that Boundary Peak, Nevada, poses a harrowing challenge, even for experienced climbers (14).
Sources written by three or more authors	When creating a parenthetical citation for a source with three or more authors, name only the first, followed by *et al.,* a phrase which means "and others."	(Carrington et al. 37)
Two or more authors with the same last name	If you are using sources written by different individuals with the same last name, you will need to use their first initials within the parenthetical citation to help readers distinguish between them on the Works Cited page.	(K. Jansen 74) [for Kent Jansen in the case where *another* author you plan to cite is named Mary Jansen]
No author	When the source lists no author, you can either mention the title in full when you introduce the cited material, or you can place the first word of the title in the parenthetical reference, where the author's name would ordinarily be. Punctuate the title as it would appear in text.	("Recommendations" 52)
A source quoted in the text you're citing	If you want to directly quote a passage that is directly quoted in the source you are consulting, you need to indicate as much through the abbreviated phrase *qtd. in.* (The source you are actually working with is the only source to be included on the Works Cited page.)	(qtd. in Knox 9)
One idea, multiple sources	When you are citing an idea that is addressed in more than one of the sources you consulted, you should attribute that idea to all of those sources.	(Foster 65; Jenkins 3; Carrington 44)

Figure 21.8 **Variations on MLA internal citation format**

you can depend on—with the exception of a blocked quote, as noted earlier—is that the parenthetical citation comes *before* the end punctuation.

Verifying that your internal citations contain the correct information and follow punctuation guidelines is only part of your responsibility in accurately documenting the sources you integrate into your own texts. You must also attend to procedures for representing every source that you cite internally on the Works Cited page.

MLA Works Cited Page Entries

The following is a catalog of commonly cited source types and the format designated for each in the MLA manual.

Sample Works Cited Entries

■ **Book by a Single Author:**

West, Elizabeth J. *African Spirituality in Black Women's Fiction: Threaded Visions of Memory, Community, Nature and Being.* Lexington, 2012.

■ **Book by Two Authors:**

Gaiman, Neil, and Terry Pratchett. *Good Omens: The Nice and Accurate Prophecies of Agnes Nutter, Witch.* Harper Collins, 2006.

- **Book by Three or More Authors:**

  Grainger, Teresa, et al. *Creativity and Writing: Developing Voice and Verve in the Classroom.* Routledge, 2005.

- **Two or More Books by the Same Author (i.e., on the same Works Cited list):**

  Johnson, Steven. *The Invention of Air: A Story of Science, Faith, Revolution, and the Birth of America.* Riverhead, 2008.

  ———. *Where Good Ideas Come From: The Natural History of Innovation.* Riverhead, 2010.

- **Book by a Corporate Author:**

  Office for Intellectual Freedom of the American Library Association. *Intellectual Freedom Manual.* 8th ed. American Library Association, 2010.

- **Work in a Collection:**

  Journet, Debra. "Narrative Turns in Writing Studies Research." *Writing Studies Research in Practice: Methods and Methodologies*, edited by Lee Nickoson and Mary P. Sheridan, Southern Illinois UP, 2012, pp. 13–24.

- **Short Story or Poem in an Anthology:**

  Hawthorne, Nathanial. "The Artist of the Beautiful." *Nathanial Hawthorne's Tales: A Norton Critical Edition.* 2nd ed., edited by James McIntosh, Norton, 2012, pp. 198–217.

- **Article in an Encyclopedia:**

  Kim, Kyung Hee, and Robert A. Pierce. "Adaptive Creativity and Innovative Creativity." *Encyclopedia of Creativity, Invention, Innovation and Entrepreneurship*, edited by Elias G. Carayannis, Springer, 2013, pp. 35–40.

- **Article in a Magazine:**

  Dobbs, David. "Beautiful Brains." *National Geographic*, Oct. 2011, pp. 36–59.

- **Article in a Newspaper:**

  Weisman, Jonathan. "Stories of Struggle and Creativity as Sequestration Cuts Hit Home." *The New York Times*, 5 June 2013, national ed. pp. A1+.

- **Article without an Author Listed:**

  "Trouble at the Lab." *The Economist*, Oct. 2013, pp. 23–28.

- **Article in an Academic Journal:**

  Hesse, Douglas. "The Place of Creative Writing in Composition Studies." *College Composition and Communication*, vol. 62, no. 1, 2010, pp. 31–52.

- **Academic Article Retrieved from an Online Database:**

  Hesse, Douglas. "The Place of Creative Writing in Composition Studies." *College Composition and Communication*, vol. 62, no. 1, 2010, pp. 31–52. ERIC, eric. ed.gov/?id=EJ896578.

- **Article in an Online Scholarly Journal:**

  Perry, Kathryn. "The Movement of Composition: Dance and Writing." *Kairos*, vol. 17, no. 1, 2012, kairos.technorhetoric.net/17.1/disputatio/perry/.

■ **Website:**

McFedries, Paul, editor. *Word Spy: The Word Lover's Guide to New Words,* 2016, wordspy.com.

■ **Blog Post:**

Dryden, Emma D. "Procrastination." *Our Stories, Ourselves,* 11 July 2013, emmaddryden. blogspot.com/2013/07/procrastination_11.html.

■ **Article in an Online Reference Work:**

Rise, Brian Edward. "Arthurian Legend." *Encyclopedia Mythica,* 2005, www.pantheon. com/areas/folklore/arthurian/arthurian_intro.html.

■ **Online Visual:**

"Former American Idol Contestant Constantine Maroulis Stars in Rock of Ages." *Washingtonian,* 14 July 2011, www.washingtonian.com/2011/07/14/ theater-review-rock-of-ages-at-the-national-theatre/.

■ **Personal Interview:**

Masters, Ursula Renee. Personal Interview. 18 Jan. 2016.

■ **Published Interview:**

Tharp, Twyla. "Creativity Step by Step: A Conversation with Choreographer Twyla Tharp." Interview by Diane L. Coutu, *Harvard Business Review,* vol. 86, no. 4, 2008, pp. 47–51.

■ **Painting or Photograph:**

Adams, Ansel. *Juniper.* 1930. Ansel Adams Gallery, Yosemite National Park.

■ **Movie:**

The Words. Directed by Brian Klugman and Lee Sternthal, performances by Bradley Cooper and Jeremy Irons. Benaroya, 2012.

■ **Television Show:**

"Flapper Fashion Face-Off." *Project Runway All Stars,* directed by Gary Shaffer, performances by Carolyn Murphy and Joanna Coles, season 2, episode 8, Lifetime, 21 Dec. 2012.

APA Internal Citations

In-text citations in APA work in much the same fashion as those in MLA—that is, they direct readers, by means of the author's last name or first word in the source's title, to an entry at the end of the text that records detailed publication information for the source in question. Despite this similarity in function, the information contained in the internal citation, as well as the way it is presented, differs from that provided in an MLA internal citation. The most noticeable difference is that instead of indicating the page number after the name or title as in MLA format, an APA citation offers the date and only sometimes the page number. Additionally, a comma is used to separate the name and date. Figure 21.9 illustrates various APA in-text citation forms, along with explanations of when they should be employed, and clarifies the unique

Citation Form	Explanation	Example
Basic forms	*When you include the author's name in the introduction to the cited material,* you should follow the name with the source's date of publication in parentheses.	According to Ivan Smith (2014), all constituencies readily agreed . . .
	When you don't include the author's name in the introduction, place both the name and the date in a parenthetical citation at the end of the sentence. Separate the name and date with a comma.	The decision represents a joint effort on the part of all constituencies (Smith, 2014).
	When you are paraphrasing, quoting, or synthesizing and, therefore, can cite a specific page number, you should include that number after the date (pay close attention to the punctuation). If the author and date are used to introduce the material, the page number appears alone in the parenthetical citation.	The decision represents a joint effort on the part of all constituencies (Smith, 2014, p. 81). The decision rendered by Smith (2014) recalled a joint effort on the part of all constituencies (p. 81).
Sources written by multiple authors	*For a source with two to five authors,* cite all of them in the initial citation, and name only the first author, followed by *et al.,* in all subsequent citations (see the example for the citation form directly below).	(Glenn, Klein, Royster, & Howard, 2011, p. 13)
	If the source has more than five authors, provide only the first author's name, followed by *et al.*	(Stoltz et al., 2013, p. 81)
Two or more authors with the same last name	If your References page contains works by authors with the same last name, you should differentiate them by including the authors' first initials along with their last names.	(P. Morton, 2013) [for Penelope Morton in the case where another author you plan to cite is named Frank Morton]
No author	If the source doesn't credit an author, you can introduce the material you cite with a sentence naming its title. Your other option is to place the first word or two of the title (discounting *A, An,* or *The*) in the parenthetical citation, where the author's name would ordinarily be. Don't forget to properly punctuate the titles.	("Adventures," 2014, p. 219)
A source quoted in the text you are citing	When directly quoting material that is directly quoted in the source you are citing, you need to establish that in the internal citation. (The only source to be listed on the References page is the one you have actually read.)	(as cited in Snyder, 2011, p. 33)
One idea, multiple sources	If you find that a given concept you wish to cite appears in more than one of the sources you are working with, you should cite all those sources together in a parenthetical citation at the end of the sentence.	(Bates, 2014, p. 11; Cox, 2012, p. 4)

Figure 21.9 **Variations on APA internal citation format**

properties of APA internal citations in contrast with MLA citation practices. As you might expect, then, the formatting for entries on a References page will differ from that for entries on an MLA Works Cited page. Read on to learn more about these differences and other particulars of APA guidelines.

APA References Page Entries

One obvious difference between an MLA Works Cited page entry and an APA References page entry is that, after naming the author, instead of moving immediately to the title of a piece as MLA would have you do, APA requires that you foreground the date of the publication. This makes sense given the fact that research findings in the social sciences—education, sociology, psychology—can quickly become obsolete in contrast to an interpretation of a poem, for example. Another point of contrast with MLA is that an APA References page subverts conventions for capitalizing titles that you would follow when naming them *within* a document.

Below are examples of properly formatted APA References page entries for types of sources that are commonly cited.

Sample References Entries

- **Book by a Single Author:**

    West, E. J. (2012). *African spirituality in Black women's fiction: Threaded visions of memory, community, nature and being.* New York, NY: Lexington Books.

- **Book by Two or Three Authors:**

    Grainger, T., Goouch, K., & Lambirth, A. (2005). *Creativity and writing: Developing voice and verve in the classroom.* New York, NY: Routledge, 2005.

- **Two or More Books by the Same Author (i.e., on the same References list):**

    Johnson, S. (2008). *The invention of air: A story of science, faith, revolution, and the birth of America.* New York, NY: Riverhead Books.

    Johnson, S. (2010). *Where good ideas come from: The natural history of innovation.* New York, NY: Riverhead Books.

- **Book by a Corporate Author:**

    Office for Intellectual Freedom of the American Library Association. (2010). *Intellectual freedom manual* (8th ed.). Chicago, IL: Author.

- **Work in a Collection:**

    Journet, D. (2012). Narrative turns in writing studies research. In Nickoson, L. & Sheridan, M. P. (Eds.), *Writing studies research in practice: Methods and methodologies* (pp. 13–24). Carbondale, IL: Southern Illinois University Press.

- **Short Story or Poem in an Anthology:**

    Hawthorne, N. (2012). The artist of the beautiful. In McIntosh, J. (Ed.), *Nathaniel Hawthorne's tales: A Norton critical edition* (2nd ed., pp. 198–217). New York, NY: W. W. Norton & Company, Inc. (Original work published in 1844).

- **Article in an Encyclopedia:**

    Kim, K. H., & Pierce, R. A. (2013). Adaptive creativity and innovative creativity. In E. G. Carayannis (Ed.), *Encyclopedia of creativity, invention, innovation and entrepreneurship* (pp. 35–40). New York, NY: Springer.

- **Article in a Magazine:**

    Dobbs, D. (2011, October). Beautiful brains. *National Geographic, 220*(4), 36–59.

- **Article in a Newspaper:**

    Weisman, J. (2013, June 5). Stories of struggle and creativity as sequestration cuts hit home. *The New York Times,* pp. A1–A13.

■ **Article without an Author Listed:**

Trouble at the lab. (2013, October). *The Economist, 409*(8858). 23–28.

■ **Article in an Academic Journal:**

Hesse, D. (2010). The place of creative writing in composition studies. *College Composition and Communication, 62*(1), 31–52.

■ **Academic Article Retrieved from an Online Database:**

Hesse, D. (2010). The place of creative writing in composition studies. *College Composition and Communication, 62*(1), 31–52. Retrieved from JSTOR database: http://www.jstor.org

■ **Article in an Online Scholarly Journal:**

Almjeld, J., Rybas, N., & Rybas, S. (2003). Virtual teaming: Faculty collaboration in online spaces. *Kairos, 17*(2). Retrieved from http://kairos.technorhetoric.net/17.1/disputatio/Perry/

■ **Document on a Website:**

McFedries, Paul. (2014). *Tweetstorm*. Retrieved from http://www.wordspy.com/words/tweetstorm.asp

■ **Blog Post:**

Dryden, E. D. (2013, July 11). Procrastination [Web log post]. Retrieved from Our Stories, Ourselves website: http://emmaddryden.blogspot.com/

■ **Article in an Online Reference Work:**

Rise, B. E. (2005). Arthurian legend: Cadbury. In *Encyclopedia Mythica*. Retrieved from http://www.pantheon.org/articles/c/cadbury.html

■ **Online Visual:**

Former American Idol contestant Constantine Maroulis stars in Rock of Ages [Image]. (2011). Retrieved from http://www.washingtonian.com/blogs/afterhours/theater/theater-review-rock-of-ages-at-the-national-theatre.php

■ **Personal Interview:**

[An APA list of References does not include personal communications. Instead, it requires that the pertinent information be delivered internally: "According to musician U. R. Masters (personal communication, January 18, 2014), creative insight involves . . ."]

■ **Published Interview:**

Coutu, D. (2008). Creativity step by step: A conversation with choreographer Twyla Tharp. *Harvard Business Review 86*(4), 47–51.

■ **Painting or Photograph:**

Adams, A. (1930). Juniper [Photograph]. Yosemite National Park, CA: Ansel Adams Gallery.

■ **Movie:**

Klugman, B., & Sternthal L. (Writers and Directors), & Benaroya, M., Elwes, C., Kelly, T., Rister, L., Young, J. (Producers). (2012). *The words* [Motion picture]. Montreal, Canada: Benaroya Pictures.

■ **Television Show:**

Harrington, S. (Writer), & Shaffer, G. (Director). (2012). Flapper fashion face-off [Television series episode]. In R. Bagshaw (Producer), *Project runway all stars: Season 2.* New York, NY: Lifetime.

Transfer across Writing Situations

Regardless of your major, you will be writing papers that require you to integrate and cite materials you find helpful in fulfilling the objectives of those assignments. Even if you end up in a discipline that uses a formatting style different from MLA or APA, you can still depend on the basic logic informing the relationship between in-text citations and a list of sources you summarized, paraphrased, quoted, or synthesized. Building on that knowledge, you can rely on your teachers to familiarize you with the unique guidelines of any unfamiliar methods for documenting sources. Of course, you can also consult the official style manuals, as well as condensed versions of them in textbooks or online.

Figure 21.10 catalogs the titles of several different manuals—other than MLA and APA—and the disciplines they typically serve, starting with those known for serving multiple disciplines. If the discipline you will be studying doesn't appear on this list, don't assume that it doesn't have its own style manual. Teachers in your major, or a little research, will help to verify. Possibly, you'll find that your discipline honors more than one manual.

While strategies employed for citing sources may vary somewhat from field to field, the strategies for meshing them with your own discourse—summarizing, paraphrasing, quoting, and synthesizing—are widely applicable. Indeed, these methods for *representing the content* of your sources will transfer across disciplines and across documents within those disciplines. Above all, it's crucial to remember that, ultimately, the purpose of all this information on source integration is to make certain that the authors whose work helped you build and support your own assertions about a topic are properly acknowledged for the contributions they've made.

Style Manual	Disciplines Served
Chicago Manual of Style	Multiple, especially those in the humanities
Turabian's *Manual for Writers of Research Papers, Theses, and Dissertations*	Multiple, especially physical and natural sciences
Associated Press Stylebook	Journalism
American Management Association Style Guide	Business management
American Medical Association Manual of Style	Medicine
The Bluebook: A Uniform System of Citation	Legal studies

Figure 21.10 **Prevalent documentation styles and disciplines that use them**

ACTIVITY

Practicing Citation with Various Sources   Team up with one of your peers and, first, independently search the Internet for five different types of sources, listing the web addresses (URLs) for each. When you've located five sources, exchange your lists of URLs. Locate each item on the list that you received, and create a Works Cited or References page that properly documents the publication information for each. Trade your finished Works Cited or References page with your partner, and evaluate each other's page using the resources in this chapter or in an online writing lab.

Document Design 22

Road signs are so common that you probably take them for granted. But where would you be if they disappeared? Unprepared for the nature of the terrain? Wandering around aimlessly? Perhaps even lost? This likely would be the case if you were traveling to a destination you'd never visited before.

Now . . . imagine you're trying to understand a document you've never read before. How do you navigate that terrain without losing your way? Most writers will offer some explicit guidance, employing textual signs—or various design elements, including graphics—to help you follow their ideas. In this chapter, you will learn about a number of design elements you can employ to assist readers in making sense of your compositions.

In many cases when readers have difficulty following a document, the culprits are unfamiliar subject matter or stylistic issues, such as jargon or convoluted sentence structures that obscure meaning. In other cases, however, the difficulty lies in the appearance of the document: the fact that it is dense, heavy with print, undifferentiated by sections—all of which make for writing that is uninviting and difficult to penetrate. Focusing on the latter scenario, you'll want to keep in mind, when composing both print and online documents, that readers appreciate a writer who actively assists them in processing text efficiently and effectively.

You can work toward this goal through various means. For example, you might use visual signals to indicate how a certain word or phrase should be read. In addition, you could play with the impact of white space in breaking up your prose or provide graphics to visually represent or underscore ideas. These strategies are ripe with creative possibility, inviting you to experiment with means for guiding readers through your texts.

Emphasis

Frequently, when drafting or revising a document, you will realize that you want readers to pause over a certain word or phrase—that is, to take particular note of it. You can communicate this intention by changing the nature of the font or by using special punctuation marks. Whatever the case, elements in this design category indicate that, to correctly interpret your meaning, readers will need to **emphasize** a given word or phrase in their minds while processing the text around it. The next several paragraphs address strategies for prompting them to do so.

Bold Print

The features that distinguish **bold print** from surrounding text are, of course, its larger size and more intense color. Bold print is commonly employed to mark the importance of a particular word (or words). Put another way, when you employ bold print, it is as if you are telling readers that they need to mentally "pronounce" that word or phrase with greater inflection (or in a more exaggerated fashion) than they otherwise would be inclined to do.

In addition to suggesting that the word or phrase is significant in a general sense, bold print can help ensure clarity when you fear that your audience might misread a passage by confusing similar words. The following passage offers an example of bold print used for this purpose:

> When it comes to responding to error in student writing, most composition teachers will delay attention to non-stigmatizing errors, such as those having to do with punctuation and mechanics. Instead, they advocate prioritizing **stigmatizing** errors, such as those having to do with standard usage and sentence-boundary confusion, which are more likely to cast the author in a negative light and more difficult to eliminate.

The emphasis here represents the author's attempt to ensure that readers catch the difference between the two categories of error she refers to since their labels are distinguished only by a single prefix (i.e., "non-"). Even if the passage didn't employ bold print, readers might still interpret the passage as intended, but the emphasis increases the odds that they will, without having to backtrack. The point is that when there is a good chance that readers will pass over a word too quickly, you'll want to offer a sign that it requires extra attention.

Along these lines, bold print is often applied to highlight key terms. While this gesture may not be essential for helping readers process the text, it will alert them to information the author deems particularly important. Sometimes, authors will denote key concepts in subheadings (discussed later in this chapter), especially if their documents are lengthy and they want to plot their organization around those concepts. In such cases, they may bold the subheadings for easy identification.

Italics (or Underlining)

While bolding is the act of darkening and slightly enlarging the font, the use of **italics** involves simply changing the shape of the letters, almost as if, when composing by hand, you changed from printing to writing in cursive. You probably know that italics are used to indicate titles of books, magazines, and newspapers. These and other ways italics can be used as punctuation are addressed in Chapter 23 of this textbook. In keeping with the goals of this chapter, though, the following discussion of italics focuses on their capacity for calling attention to words or phrases that will assist readers in navigating your text in the way you intend.

To be more specific, when you want to stress a word or to highlight a concept that you've been discussing along with others, you can use italics in the same manner that you would use bold print. The question of whether to use bold print or italics, according to most experts, can be answered by considering whether the emphasis should be strong (bold print) or subtle (italics). Obviously, the line here is rather fine, but it may help to imagine the decibel level you want readers to apply to the word or phrase when reading it. In other words, bold print might suggest you are speaking loudly enough to be heard by someone at the other end of the house while italics might require speaking only as loudly as you'd need to when summoning someone in the next room.

Another common use of italics for signaling emphasis is to flag a word that you are treating *as a word*. For example:

- *Therefore,* it should be noted, is a transition indicating cause and effect.
- It didn't take me long after arriving in London to figure out that *flat* means to the British what *apartment* means to Americans.

As with the earlier passage on errors in writing, even if the author had not emphasized the words in these examples, readers would still probably grasp the meaning. Chances are, though, that they would struggle more if the italics were not there. In this instance, as well as when considering the use of italics to indicate importance, you should ask yourself not whether your readers will get your meaning but, rather, whether they will have to work extra hard to get it.

MYTH

"Whenever a term calls for italics, it's acceptable to underline instead."

This was technically true before computers became so widely accessible. Now, because word processing software enables writers to italicize with ease, and because underlining is more cumbersome, most publication venues and teachers prefer italics, as they make for a cleaner appearance.

REALITY

Figure 22.1 Air quotes

In short, you don't want to disrupt readers' "flow" by causing them to stop and reread a passage.

Scare Quotes

In oral communication these days, it's not unusual to see someone employing air quotes, or drawing quotes in the air with their hands (see Figure 22.1). Air quotes alert your audience to the fact that you regard the word or phrase you attached the gesture to as meaning something different from what might be assumed. To be more specific, they suggest that the particular way a word or phrase is used in a given context is actually misleading or inaccurate.

If you want to call this kind of attention to a word or phrase in a *written* text, you would simply place it in quotation marks—referred to as "scare quotes" when used for this specific purpose. Indeed, it's important to distinguish this use of quotes as a technique for emphasizing how readers should interpret certain words, as opposed to indicating titles of short works or presenting another person's words verbatim. (See Chapter 21 in this textbook for more on direct quotes.)

The following examples demonstrate how an author might use scare quotes to indicate he or she is subverting common associations for a given term:

- After waiting several weeks for notification of how to proceed with our claim, we thanked the insurance agent for his "timely" assistance.
- Running again on the Republican ballot, this "conservative" politician consistently voted to allocate tax dollars for environmental causes.

The first example suggests that the author is being sarcastic in her use of the word *timely,* which usually signifies that something has occurred in a reasonable time frame. The second example indicates that the author is questioning whether or not a given label applied to a certain individual fits the popular application of that term. In both examples, failure to emphasize the term as questionable could confuse, if not mislead, the audience.

White Space

It can be discouraging, even exhausting, to encounter a piece of writing that is covered from top to bottom and from margin to margin with nothing but letters. Imagine how the negative impact of those tightly packed words and sentences might be compounded across a number of pages. Of course, too much white space can be as disconcerting for readers as a lack of it, but for a different reason—namely, the appearance that the document does not have enough substance to satisfy length requirements. Several strategies exist for introducing white space into your texts. The discussion that follows will help you do so effectively.

Paragraphs

Writers break their prose into paragraphs for a couple of reasons. First, they want to offer their readers a visual and psychological rest. Indeed, the point where one paragraph ends and the next begins is a chance for readers to pause and collect their thoughts before proceeding. A second reason that writers engage in paragraphing is to signal a change in topic, sometimes only a very slight change.

This second point warrants special attention because a topic change may be hard to define. For that reason, some inexperienced writers will interpret the topic-change guideline very rigidly, assuming that if the sentences they are weaving together in any way reference the same issue, they must be bound into a single paragraph.

> **MYTH**
>
> **"A paragraph should be *at least* three sentences long."**
>
> This is a "rule of thumb" but by no means a hard-and-fast rule. While it is true that most paragraphs will be several sentences long, paragraphing is an interpretive exercise, wherein length will be determined by the author's needs in effectively communicating. So, if you have a clear reason for writing a paragraph shorter than three sentences—for example, isolating a sentence or two to accentuate them in making a point—you should feel free to do so.
>
> **REALITY**

But writers should be wary of any paragraph that approaches a page in length for its failure to provide readers that all-important mental rest mentioned previously. The bottom line is that breaking documents into paragraphs is an interpretive exercise, dictated by the author's sense of where his or her prose naturally gives way to a pause.

Illustrating this point, Figure 22.2 contains an excerpt from an article relating the findings of a survey that investigated sources and strategies by which people stay current with the news. Notice that this article contains several paragraph breaks. The first paragraph addresses the frequency with which people consult news reports in any form, while the second focuses on the tendency of people to follow up on those reports with more in-depth study. The third paragraph cites percentages of people who indicate that they pursue more in-depth investigation, and the fourth elaborates on the nature of those individuals.

Because the second, third, and fourth paragraphs in Figure 22.2 all refer to the practice of following up on a news report by seeking more in-depth coverage, they could have been combined under the "same-topic, one-paragraph" guideline. But it is perfectly acceptable to break this passage along the lines that the author did— that is, into smaller topics within the larger topic.

Subheadings

Like paragraph breaks, **subheadings,** or titles of sections within a text, offer readers a rest and signal changes in topic. However, they tend to be reserved for significant shifts in the focus of discussion. In fact, subheadings enable authors to move smoothly between a number of disparate issues within a single document—issues that might prove difficult to unite through simple transitions. As follows, these

Almost all Americans report that they pay attention to the news on a daily or weekly basis. Fully 76 percent of Americans report watching, reading, or hearing the news on a daily basis; another 14 percent report watching, reading, or hearing the news several times per week; and only 10 percent say weekly or less.

Fewer Americans invest additional time into following the news more in-depth. The survey asked people about going in-depth for news two different ways. It asked whether people generally tried to get news in-depth on any subject in the last week. It also asked, when they recalled a breaking news story they followed in the last week, whether they had tried to find out more about it after initially learning of it.

Overall, 41 percent of Americans report that they watched, read, or heard any in-depth news

stories, beyond the headlines, in the last week. Slightly more people, 49 percent, report that they invested additional time to delve deeper and follow up on the last breaking news story they followed.

Interestingly, the people who delve deeper on general news are not the same as those who do more in-depth follow-up of breaking news. Among those who say they generally attend to news beyond the headlines, only just over half (54 percent) say they did so to learn more about the last breaking news story they followed (while 46 percent did not). And as described in Section 5 of this report, age is a significant predictor of the type of news people attend to in-depth. Yet contrary to what some might expect, younger adults are more likely to recall specifically going in-depth on breaking news than older adults. Older adults are more likely to say they follow up on news in general.

Source: "The Personal News Cycle: How Americans Choose to Get Their News." *American Press Institute,* www.americanpressinstitute.org/publications/reports/survey-research/personal-news-cycle/. Reprinted with permission.

Figure 22.2 Paragraphing based on subtopics

section titles help readers to determine, at a glance, the content of the various parts of a document and to quickly perceive possible relationships between them.

Subheadings can occur at different levels of specificity; in other words, it is possible to create subheadings within subheadings. Those at the first level start at the text's left margin and are typically set off from the paragraphs they introduce, occupying their own line and sometimes appearing in a different font, often bold print. As titles, subheadings are usually brief, either a word or a phrase. Whatever the case, all subheadings of the same level of specificity should be the same grammatical unit (e.g., all nouns, all verb phrases). Subheadings at different levels of specificity may or may not be distinguished from one another grammatically, but they should be distinguished visually. You might accomplish this, for example, by representing the first level in all-capital letters, the second in lowercase letters, the third through indention, and so on. (The subheadings in this chapter demonstrate some of these practices. Note also that they employ color to denote level of specificity.)

Bulleted and Numbered Lists

When numerous items in a list are run together in a paragraph, readers may find them difficult to keep track of, especially if the list is lengthy. **Bulleting** and **numbering** are ways of setting lists apart from surrounding prose so that readers can easily grasp the collection of items in their totality, as well as the relationships among them. In the case of bulleting, each item in the list is preceded by a symbol, ordinarily a small circle or square, whereas, in the case of numbering, items are preceded by numerals, starting with 1 and continuing in order.

To consider how bulleted or numbered lists might affect reading processes, refer to Figure 22.3, which presents two versions of a paragraph drawn from an article about motivations for posting on social media. The version on the left, preserving the author's original design, contains a bulleted list. The version on the right is a revision that extracts the bullets and integrates the list with the rest of the paragraph.

It is probably safe to assume that most readers would find the presentation on the left in Figure 22.3 easier to process. First, it renders the beginning and end of the list—as well as all items in between—easy to spot if you need to review. In addition, it provides a rest for the eyes and mind, as paragraphs and subheadings do, visually inviting you to stop for a moment and reflect. As for the question of whether you

---

Original Version: Bulleted List

To achieve this goal, I've been digging into psychology literature for inspirations. Overjoyed, I've discovered some theories and findings that are portable to the social media environment:

- Two modes of thinking, fast and slow, attract different types of attention.
- Sharing on social media is
  - Charged with emotions,
  - Bounded by self-image management, and also
  - By concerns over relationship with others.

Again, this report is based on the three key metrics featured by Facebook Insights: reach, engaged users, and talking about this. According to Facebook, *reach* is defined as "the number of unique people who have seen your post"; *engaged users* as "the number of unique people who have clicked on your post"; and *talking about this* as "the number of unique people who have created a story from your Page post."

Rewritten Version: Integrated List

To achieve this goal, I've been digging into psychology literature for inspirations. Overjoyed, I've discovered some theories and findings that are portable to the social media environment: Two modes of thinking, fast and slow, attract different types of attention; sharing on social media is charged with emotions, bounded by self-image management, and also by concerns over relationship with others. Again, this report is based on the three key metrics featured by Facebook Insights: reach, engaged users, and talking about this. According to Facebook, *reach* is defined as "the number of unique people who have seen your post"; *engaged users* as "the number of unique people who have clicked on your post"; and *talking about this* as "the number of unique people who have created a story from your Page post."

Source: Sonya Song, "Sharing Fast and Slow: The Psychological Connection between How We Think and How We Spread News on Social Media." *NeimanLab,* 14 Nov. 2014. Reprinted by permission of the author.

Figure 22.3 **Contrasting bulleted and nonbulleted lists**

should bullet or number a list in a given circumstance, you might take into account whether you will need to refer to individual items as you continue to draft. In that case, it might be important to number them for quick and easy identification.

Alignment

As you can imagine, relevant to all the design elements addressed in this section—paragraphs, subheadings, and lists—proper **alignment** is key. That is, you want to make sure that parts of the text with similar functions or on the same level of specificity are indented the same number of spaces from the left margin (think of the rules for indenting in the context of a formal outline if you've ever composed one). For example, the first lines of all paragraphs should begin ½ inch from that margin. All lines of a numbered or bulleted list should be indented the same amount, ½ inch, and if the bulleted information spills over to additional lines, those subsequent lines should be indented 1 inch from the left margin. While subheadings and sub-subheadings may all begin at the left margin and be differentiated instead by font changes, when sub-subheadings are indented, they should all line up with each other ½ inch from the margin, and so on.

You can see at a glance how some of these alignment principles work in Figure 22.4, a screenshot of a page from a website offering advice for effectively implementing new initiatives within corporations. The screenshot displays how the

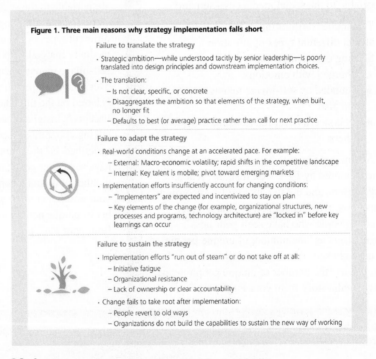

Figure 22.4 **Alignment principles applied to a website**

website's designers align levels of information to assist readers in processing the page's content. For example, you can immediately detect three degrees of indentation, indicating different levels of specificity:

■ First, the line in bold print at the very top, which announces that this section of the document is a three-point list.
■ Second, the lines listing the three types of failure, each followed by bulleted lists of causes.
■ Third, the lines preceded by dashes, which break down each of the causes.

Aided by the faint horizontal lines, the images lined up on the far left and equally spaced from each other clearly distinguish the three parts of this excerpt.

Images and Tables

Chapter 13 of this textbook reveals that images and other visuals are powerful vehicles for communicating knowledge and clarifying difficult concepts. This statement rings truer day by day as the image-rich nature of the Internet and other widely employed digital technologies inevitably heighten users' visual literacy. Taking these observations for granted, this section focuses on certain types of visuals that you might want to incorporate in your own texts. Further, it articulates guidelines for when and how you might do so.

Images

Photographs, charcoal drawings, animated figures, and the like, can all be categorized as images. Writers like to use them, at least in part, because they pack a lot of information into a small amount of space. Writers also like to use them for their attention-grabbing power. More specifically, in a single moment, they can draw readers in, wielding a degree of immediacy that the written word simply can't muster. Of course, images can improve the quality of any written product, but they are crucial in digital environments where every document competes for readers' attention among an onslaught of visually stimulating web pages. In addition, the unique navigational properties of online venues—particularly the capacity for layering text through hotlinks—invites you to experiment with strategies for visually representing relationships among parts of your text through icons that supply those connections for readers with the click of a mouse.

Regardless of whether you are writing in a print or digital environment, at least on an initial encounter, readers typically can grasp the surface message of an image more quickly than they can similar concepts expressed in words and sentences. This capacity of images can serve you when you simply want to provide an example of something you've just described, as well as when you actually need the visual to carry the weight in conveying an idea.

For a demonstration of the latter scenario, consider Figure 22.5, a screenshot from the film *Batman: The Dark Knight*. Looking at that image, you can grasp in a few seconds the nature of the actor's makeup, his expression, his costume, the fire in

Figure 22.5 **Conveying an idea through a visual: Screenshot from a film**

the background, the relationship between the character and the set, and the contrast between his dark appearance and the bright flames. Now imagine that you decided to describe Figure 22.5 instead of providing the screenshot. How long might it take a reader to reproduce the image in his or her mind? It would probably take quite some time. And even then, the risk that the reader's projection might not exactly match the image in your own mind's eye is substantial. Of course, sometimes an exact match isn't necessary or even desirable. Then again, sometimes it is—for example, when analyzing a movie depends on readers' seeing a given scene in the same way you do. In that case, providing the actual screenshot would be a wise move.

When selecting an image that effectively supports your intentions, you might take into account the following criteria:

- *Writer's purpose.* Will the image provide information that won't be written out, or will it simply illustrate something you've just written? (Detail is an important consideration here, especially when the image alone carries the load.)
- *Rhetorical impact.* Does the image need to wield a strong emotional punch—for example, a totaled car in a piece intended to convince others to take action in support of a cause such as tightening drunk-driving laws?
- *Image quality.* Is the image clear, and are the colors vibrant? (If a picture isn't clear, it can't be thoroughly analyzed. Color may also impact analysis, but it is also a powerful attention-grabbing feature.)

Figure 22.6 illustrates these criteria in action. Appearing on the official website of the Vancouver Aquarium, this photograph is the initial image viewers see on the pull-down menu listing what patrons can experience while visiting this renowned attraction. Judging it against the criteria listed above, this picture seems to support the website author's **purpose** by illustrating just one of the sights (an unusual sea creature in close proximity) that might cause a visitor to "be inspired," as promised in the paragraph to the left of the image. It also portrays the wonder and excitement associated with viewing sea creatures in such detail—indeed, the jellyfish in the photograph seems to be swimming right by you! The **rhetorical impact** (i.e., the likelihood that potential visitors would be *persuaded* to buy tickets to the aquarium) rests in no little part on the **image's quality,** namely its clarity and bright blue and white hues set against a black background—a contrast that excites your vision.

Of course, beyond these three criteria, there is much more to be said about the effective use of images

Be Inspired

As Canada's largest aquarium, the Vancouver Aquarium connects hundreds of thousands of Aquarium visitors with the natural world. With over 50,000 animals and unique opportunities to come up close with some of the world's most elusive creatures, every visit is an unforgettable one. Find everything you need to plan your visit to the Aquarium here, including special notices, general facility and accessibility information, and operating hours.

If you can't find what you need, **contact us**.

Figure 22.6 Effective website visual

in the context of writing. In fact, entire books have been written on the subject. Hopefully, though, this brief overview establishes a useful foundation that will jump-start your thinking about how to use photographs, paintings, and so on, to your best rhetorical advantage. And, again, you can learn more about the nature of images and the manner in which they communicate or can support written communication in Chapter 13.

Tables, Charts, and Graphs

Images of any kind might be imported from the Internet or scanned from a print document. However, writers frequently must design their own tables, charts, and graphs to depict data that were gathered specifically for a given project and/or that need to be uniquely presented given the author's purposes. **Tables,** in particular, function similarly to bullets in the respect that they isolate items in a list for quick and easy processing. However, tables are the better choice for lists containing items that require considerable explanation. You can understand why by imagining a bulleted list with each item followed by a paragraph of elaboration: The primary items in the list can become lost in the interrupting text.

In contrast to bulleted or numbered lists, tables clearly separate pieces of information across the page as well as down. This allows writers to fashion an uninterrupted vertical list in a series of cells arranged on the left and to lay out corresponding definitions or illustrations of the listed items in separate cells on the right (see Figure 22.7). Of course, if your explanatory text involves definitions *and*

Listed Items ↓	Explanatory Text ↓

Figure 22.7 Basic table

illustrations, you could designate three columns instead of two. In fact, word processing programs enable you to create with ease as many rows and columns as you might need to effectively display information. What's more, they offer an array of possibilities for making a basic table more visually appealing, and they allow you to apply a color scheme of your choosing. Examples are scattered throughout this textbook.

Tables can be used to present both verbal and numerical data, but most technical writers would agree that data that are largely numerical are more effectively displayed in the form of **charts** or **graphs.** The latter tend to be more efficient than tables in establishing relationships among items since they rely primarily on visual processing. Although certain sources insist on some complex and finely drawn distinctions between charts and graphs, for purposes of this brief overview, they will be treated as similar in function—that is, both of them enhance or support ideas communicated verbally.

As is the case with tables, word processing programs provide ready-made templates for charts and graphs that you can simply insert into your documents and then fill with the numerical data or brief text that you wish to share. Figure 22.8 displays templates for some of these commonly used visuals. By following the instructions provided by your word processing program and experimenting a bit with the design elements characterizing the templates (such as those displayed in Figure 22.8), you will be able to manipulate any of the options in ways that best fit your purposes. Such practice is time well spent when you consider the capacity of charts and graphs—as well as tables—to help readers better understand the ideas addressed in your documents. In addition, these templates, when effectively applied, lend a pleasing and professional appearance to your work.

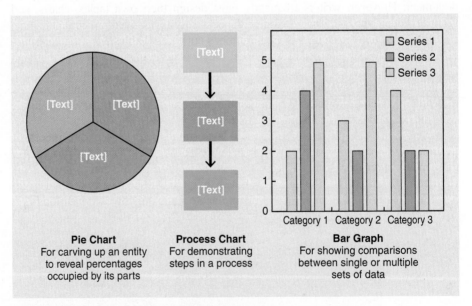

Figure 22.8 Microsoft Word templates for charts and graphs

In regard to the specific features of tables, graphs, and charts, even though the templates offer ready-made designs and color combinations, you can alter them according to your needs and tastes. Colors can be altered with a few clicks of your mouse, and size can be increased or decreased by simply dragging the sides of the template. Regarding color, you might consult one of many Internet sources that cover the interesting field of color psychology. Those sources summarize theories about hues that are presumably the most and least likely to attract attention and the most likely to stimulate a certain mood. As to the size of the graphic, you'll want to make sure it's large enough so that all lettering and numerals are clearly visible but small enough so that it doesn't overtake the main text, imposing a disruption that forces readers to flip back and forth between pages to connect the graphic to the written text that refers to it.

This observation raises the importance of appropriately placing and labeling your visuals—including photographs and other images. As suggested in the previous paragraph, you'll want to situate visual elements as closely as possible to the ideas they support or illustrate. In addition, you'll want to title those visuals and devise a numbering system so that when readers come across a reference to a certain visual they will be able to easily locate it and not confuse it with another.

Having read this section on incorporating visuals, you can understand how writers might regard them as valuable tools in their composing inventories. But don't forget (as noted in Chapter 13) that any graphic imported from a print or Internet source must be properly cited with credit to the artist. Moreover, if you intend to publish your work in some fashion, you may need to acquire permission from the copyright holder.

Transfer across Writing Situations

Much of the information compiled in this chapter is at the heart of technical writing courses, which focus on designing documents for optimum precision and clarity of communication. Many college majors—particularly business-oriented fields—require their students to take at least one technical writing course, and some institutions offer concentrations in technical writing through their English departments. Technical writing and other design-oriented courses—such as those in the graphic arts—are particularly relevant to individuals wishing to pursue careers that involve some form of online communication or publishing. To imagine the significance of such courses for interacting in web-based environments, you need only reflect for a moment on the flood of visually engaging websites saturating the Internet.

That being said, the principles of technical writing highlighted in this chapter will apply in most any composing context. In other words, no matter what your academic discipline or profession, you should be concerned with doing all you can to help readers move through your documents effectively and efficiently. Whether emphasizing certain words or phrases to ensure understanding, introducing white space to provide visual and mental breaks, or incorporating graphics to support or illustrate your ideas, taking the time to think about design elements will increase the likelihood that your message will be well received.

ACTIVITY

Considering the Impact of Design Elements   The chapter you've just finished reading employs many of the design elements that it introduces. Peruse the chapter again, thinking about the impact of those elements and taking notes about how they may have affected your reading experience. (It might help to project what the experience would have been like without them.) Once you've collected your thoughts, team up with a classmate and search the Internet for a site that you find to be especially effective or ineffective in the way it employs design elements. Analyze that site in light of the notes you took about the elements addressed in this chapter. Be prepared to present your findings to the rest of your class.

Revision and Editing

23

When was the last time you found yourself multitasking? Given this fast-moving world, it was probably not too long ago. Maybe you ate your morning cereal *while* watching a news video on your laptop *and* jotting down a shopping list. Maybe you were studying for an exam *while* putting in a few miles on the treadmill *and* listening to that song you just downloaded.

Multitasking can increase your efficiency with regard to simple activities. However, when activities requiring concentrated attention are involved, it can be dangerous (e.g., texting while driving)—or, at the very least, counterproductive.

Such is the case when you're reworking the draft of a document you're composing for final evaluation. Read on to find out

how you can avoid the hazards of trying to do too much at one time as submission dates draw near.

It can be tempting to combine **revision,** or making global changes, with **editing,** or correcting surface errors, since both of these processes are associated with the act of "fixing" a document or making it better. In other words, in an effort to be efficient as you work to improve a text, you resort to multitasking. This might include, for example, scanning for missing apostrophes (editing) *while* you are trying to rearrange paragraphs (revising)—or making sure all your subjects and verbs are in agreement (editing) *while* you are structuring an argument (revising). Of course, in some cases, doing so might save a little time, and the fact is that, to some degree, these processes can't help but occur simultaneously. After all, you are probably not going to ignore an obvious misspelling (editing) if it jumps out at you while you're extensively rewriting your paper's conclusion (revising).

Nevertheless, most experienced writers will tell you that attempts to revise and edit a text simultaneously can lead to a state of mind referred to as **cognitive overload,** wherein the quality of your work may be compromised because you are trying to attend to more concepts and procedures than your brain can effectively handle at one time. Knowing this, it makes good sense to consciously separate the revising and editing processes so that you can "divide and conquer"—that is, so that you can split the work of finalizing a paper into two different sets of activities, each of which will place different kinds of demands on you. This chapter offers advice for keeping these two categories of composing processes distinct from each other and for addressing concerns specifically associated with each.

Revision

In Chapter 2, **revision** is defined as "evaluating and changing global features of a text, such as focus, development, and organization." Strategies associated with revision require more elaborate instruction than this chapter alone can accommodate, not only because they are relatively complex but also because they aren't governed by "rules" or even definitive guidelines. In other words, they are largely dependent on the specific nature of the document you're composing. The paragraphs on revision that follow, then, will serve primarily as a resource, providing suggestions for engaging in productive revision, as well as indicating where in this text you can find additional instruction.

Criteria for Productive Revision

The features of a text that you should prioritize during revision include focus, development, and organization. These features rely on the following composing strategies:

- Appropriately narrowing the scope of your topic given page constraints
- Effectively targeting intended readers
- Offering adequate support for any and all claims
- Presenting information in a manner that readers can easily follow
- Drawing readers in with an engaging introduction
- Ending with paragraphs that provide a sense of closure

In contrast to surface-oriented *editing* processes, which focus attention at the word or sentence level, the revision processes listed at the bottom of the previous page require you to rework a document at the whole-text level. You can find explanations and examples of criteria to keep in mind when addressing these larger concerns in various parts of this textbook:

- *Focus*—in Chapter 4 on invention
- *Audience awareness*—in Chapter 3 on rhetorical situations
- *Support*—in Chapter 16 on structuring arguments

You also can consult Chapters 6 through 20, each of which discusses—in the context of a given genre—how you might address these global features of a text when drafting. By thinking about criteria that guide writers in crafting these features, you can infer what you would need to do to revise them in ways that might improve your own attempts at the genre. In addition, you might consider the "Questions for Revising" near the end of each genre chapter, which focus your attention on specific aspects of the assignment on which you're working.

Processes for Revising

The key to effective revision is a willingness to let go of what you've already written. You won't necessarily *have* to, but you must be *willing* to if you are serious about improving the quality of your draft. Of course, letting go can be painful because of the time and effort typically involved in generating the initial version of a document. To be sure, in many cases, the changes that seem warranted are radical in nature, requiring significant alterations. For example, one revision strategy that expert writers report is turning the conclusion of a draft into its introduction; what becomes the introduction, then, usually calls for entirely new body paragraphs. Another revision strategy—this one having to do with organization as opposed to development—involves physically or electronically cutting a draft into pieces and shifting large portions of it to create a different arrangement.

Both of these revision techniques cause you to re*envision* the text, to apply a fresh perspective on it that can lead to improvement and, therefore, a stronger response to the composing challenge. In particular, turning your conclusion into your introduction allows you to explore insights that you may have gradually written yourself into but don't have room to address in additional pages given the assignment boundaries. Cutting your text apart and testing out different arrangements can forge connections you didn't see before or lead to an organization that carries greater rhetorical impact. Indeed, experienced writers know that remaining open to the possibility of significantly reworking a text can make the difference between a final product that is just good enough and one that might really engage and impress your readers.

Figure 23.1 illustrates this level of revision with an excerpt from a first-year student's paper on animal therapy. While this student didn't completely reorganize her draft or turn its ending into its beginning, she did—among other significant changes—completely rewrite her opening paragraphs. As you can see, the initial

Initial Draft

Stress, depression, trauma, anxiety, mood disorders, fatigue, along with other physical and psychological problems, are common throughout all stages of life and can sometimes lead to severe consequences. Dealing with these problems can be puzzling. People often don't know where to go for help, and sometimes talking to a psychologist is not enough. This is where Animal Assisted Activity (AAA) and Animal Assisted Therapy (AAT) come in. Both of these are great ways of treating these physical and psychological problems.

In the article "Animal Magic," Daniel Allen takes note of very important research based on animal therapy. This research proves how being in the presence of animals helps build up or restore inner confidence in patients with mental illnesses, trauma, or depression.

Revised Draft

Anyone who has pets will know how they have special ways of lightening your day, even just by welcoming you home. Coming home after a stressful day and having your dog greet you wagging his tail brings a relaxed feeling. Adult life can be stressful. This stress occasionally develops into other conditions such as depression, anxiety, and other diseases. Stress levels in adults have increased significantly due to this fast-paced life we all seem to be living, and we are not always aware of the consequences stress can bring. Some adults who have suffered from trauma have to deal with post-traumatic stress. Others who have experienced surgery have high levels of pain, which can cause stress as well. Some have trouble controlling their anger and may have trouble communicating as a result.

Dealing with these problems can be puzzling. People often don't know where to go for help, and sometimes talking to a psychologist is not enough. This is where Animal Assisted Activity (AAA) and Animal Assisted Therapy (AAT) come in. Both of these are great ways of treating these physical and psychological problems. The difference between the two is that AAA involves a more informal exercise, such as observing or petting animals. AAT is when the animal works for a particular goal, as do guide/service dogs.

Source: By Natalie Gulson, a first-year composition student.

Figure 23.1 **Revision of a student paper**

draft and the final draft are quite different from each other, the latter preserving only a portion of the original (i.e., the thesis), which is highlighted.

With this revision, the author increases context for the thesis, helping readers connect personally to the subject matter, especially those who have had positive experiences with animals. In the original introduction, movement to the thesis is abrupt and the author provides little background information (definitions, for example) to help the audience understand central concepts. Certainly the original has a more specialized and detached feel, whereas the revision adopts a more conversational and, therefore, inviting tone—even using first person ("we") and second person ("your") pronouns to communicate a sense of familiarity with readers. Doing so is appropriate in this rhetorical situation since the intended audience is not constituted of scholars but, rather, members of the general public who have an interest in science.

Substantial revisions such as those discussed in the previous paragraphs require a strong commitment to making your work the best it can be. That commitment derives in part from a sense of confidence that the additional effort you are about to put in will strengthen the quality of the final product. As you become a more experienced writer, that confidence will grow as your knowledge about effective writing expands. You can hasten that process by taking advantage of assistance provided by both teachers and peers in pinpointing areas of your drafts that might benefit from revision. (See Chapter 24 in this textbook for a discussion of peer review strategies.) You can also turn to your school's writing center, which offers tutoring services to support students in first-year composition courses; advanced composition courses; and discipline-specific, writing-intensive courses across the curriculum.

Regarding feedback, in composition courses, when it's time to begin thinking about submitting work for evaluation, your teachers will typically provide response exercises that focus you and your peers on the global features of a paper, as discussed in previous paragraphs. However, in writing centers or writing-intensive courses in your major, feedback may be more open-ended, depending on the tutor or instructor. Whatever the case, as you engage in such processes across many learning situations, receiving feedback from a variety of individuals, you'll gain a sense of your tendencies as a writer. For example, you may come to realize that your critical-thinking skills are top-notch but you have difficulty transitioning smoothly between ideas. Or you may discover that you have a talent for capturing readers' attention with provocative introductions but you often struggle to figure out what information you should highlight in a conclusion.

In any case, you can support your own revision practices by reflecting on your experiences with response and revision, keeping track of your challenges, and recording patterns that will serve as points of departure when you revise subsequent projects (as you will be encouraged to do in the end-of-chapter activity). All this makes good sense for reasons mentioned at the beginning of this chapter. Trying to attend to everything at once—even issues associated with revision alone—will dilute your concentration on any one feature of a text and possibly overwhelm you, as all features might seem to be potentially and equally valid starting points for your revision processes. Adding editing concerns to this mix can confound the situation even further, as should become clear in the next section.

MYTH

"If revision advice from different readers conflicts, I should ignore all of it since there's not a clear path for improving the document."

Readers often do not agree on the quality of a text or a plan for making it better. This is because there is no single "right way" to compose any text. When instructors and peers review your work, they are offering possibilities to consider, not surefire cures for perceived weaknesses. You need to weigh that advice against your intentions, your knowledge of the rhetorical situation, and your judgment regarding whether or not a given suggestion will solve the problem at hand. Even if you decide that it will not, the advice could spark another idea about how to proceed.

REALITY

MYTH

"In contrast to revision, editing will be a breeze. After all, the teacher will locate errors for me so I can fix them before the final draft is due."

It's not a teacher's job to find and correct all your errors; rather, it's to help you become more able to find and correct your own. Toward this goal, your teacher may mark a couple of instances of an error to alert you of a pattern and may even offer a solution or two for addressing the problem. In the end, though, if you don't learn to locate and address your own errors, you'll be at a disadvantage in courses that don't focus on writing and in most on-the-job writing situations since they seldom provide in-house editing services.

REALITY

Editing

Chapter 2 defines **editing** as "evaluating and changing surface features of a text, such as usage, spelling, and mechanics." Although editing processes don't usually result in radical changes to a text, they do cover a wide range of issues, from simple typographical errors to awkward sentence structures. In fact, editing covers so many surface features that handbooks devoted to such issues typically total hundreds of pages. Since the remainder of this chapter can offer only a limited amount of guidance in this regard, it focuses on issues that frequently appear in papers written for first-year composition courses.

Common Surface Errors

This section introduces some common surface errors relevant to Standard Written English and demonstrates possible solutions to those errors. It also explores a few composing myths associated with editing processes. But this discussion must be considered merely the beginning of your inquiry into matters of surface correctness. To further that inquiry, you'll need to become proficient in consulting grammar handbooks or online writing labs (OWLs). These resources address errors that this chapter doesn't have space to cover. Do remember, though, when studying *any* grammar resource, that many issues relevant to editing are not to be considered "rules." Rather, they are stylistic choices that you consciously apply as you strive to make your meaning clear to readers.

Handling Homonyms   Homonyms are words that sound alike but are spelled differently and have distinct meanings. Because they are pronounced in the same way, they are easily confused when you are writing. Therefore, you need to develop a heightened sensitivity when using any of them so that you are sure to catch careless substitutions. Figure 23.2 lists some commonly used homonyms and their respective definitions.

Applying Apostrophes   Several of the homonyms listed in Figure 23.2 are contractions (e.g., *it's, they're, you're, who's*). As you can see in that figure, a contraction is a word made up by combining two other words and replacing missing letters with an apostrophe (the punctuation mark that looks like a raised comma). But standing in for missing letters in a contraction is only one of an apostrophe's functions. The other is to denote possession or ownership.

Of course, you know that you can indicate that someone you are writing about possesses or owns something by placing an apostrophe after his or her name or title and then adding the letter "s" to it, like so: **Mike's toothbrush, Laura's new job,**

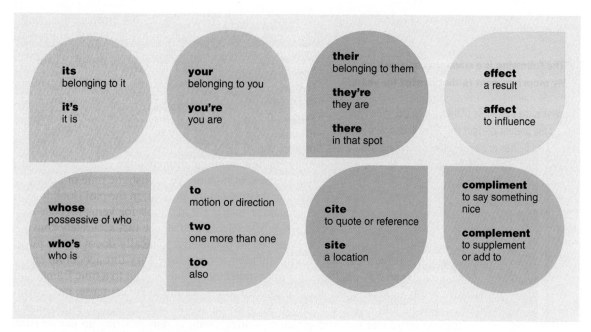

Figure 23.2 **Common homonyms**

and **the teacher's excitement**. But showing possession becomes a little trickier when you are referring to more than one "possessor" or owner at a time—in other words, when you want to use the plural form of a noun. In most cases, you can turn a noun into a plural by simply adding the letter "s" to it: **books**, **jet skis**, and **siblings**. To show possession in such instances, you would place the apostrophe at the end of the word—for example, my **siblings'** birthdays.

An exception to this rule occurs when the plural form of a word involves more than simply adding an "s"—that is, when the plural actually brings about a change in the word's form. Such is the case with the word **children** (for *child*) or **women** (for *woman*). The possessive of *children* is **children's**, with the apostrophe before the "s," and the possessive of **women** is **women's**. Consult a more comprehensive resource to learn of other nouns whose singular and plural forms differ in similar ways.

Controlling Verbs   A frequent mistake involving **verbs** (action or state-of-being words) is the failure to make them agree with the **nouns** (persons, places, or things) to which they are attached. Put another way, when you employ a verb to communicate a noun's action or state of being, you need to make sure that you choose the *singular* form of the verb if the noun is *singular* and the *plural* form of the verb if the noun is *plural*. Many singular action verbs are formed by adding an "s" to the verb's plural status (i.e., several clocks *tick* but a single clock *ticks*). As for state-of-being verbs, an entirely different word may be indicated to designate number. Figure 23.3 provides sentences illustrating these basic lessons in subject-verb agreement (with the verbs in orange and the nouns they correspond with in blue).

MYTH

"The following is a standard construction: 'My mom has went to that dentist for years.'"

Went is the past tense of the verb *to go.* When you need the present *perfect* tense (in which a verb is preceded by *has* or *have*), you need to use *gone* instead of *went* (i.e., "My mom has gone to that dentist for years.").

REALITY

As alluded to earlier, subject-verb agreement is a complex area of study in Standard Written English. In fact, you should know that there are numerous irregular verbs that don't behave in quite the same way as the first two examples in Figure 23.3; for example, **crows fly** but the **crow flies**. Moreover, there exist numerous helping verbs and state-of-being verbs beyond those addressed in Figure 23.3. Again, you'll need to consult a handbook or OWL for specifics.

Another common problem with verbs has to do with their **tenses,** or how they establish the time of an action or state of being (in the present; in the past [look for *-ed* endings]; or in the future [look for verbs preceded by *will*]). While selecting the tense that accurately conveys the time of an occurrence typically doesn't pose much difficulty for writers, maintaining that tense when necessary throughout an entire document can be a challenge. Simply stated, once you commit to a time frame, you want to make certain that all your verb forms assume the same tense, unless you have a logical reason for changing. For example, if you are narrating an event in present tense and the person you're writing about is remembering an earlier time (i.e., engaging in a **flashback**), you might invoke past tense to signal that reflection. Figure 23.4 contains three brief paragraphs: one demonstrating tense consistency, one violating consistency without clear intention, and one violating consistency with a clear intention.

Nonstandard Verb Usage	Usage for Standard Written English	Explanation
Marcus want to go tubing on Kincaid lake.	Marcus wants to go tubing on Kincaid Lake.	The name "Marcus" refers to *one* man; thus, the noun takes the *singular* form of the verb "want"—that with an "s" on the end.
The chipmunks scatters whenever we let the dog out.	The chipmunks scatter whenever we let the dog out.	The noun "chipmunks" is *plural*, indicating *more than one* creature. Therefore, it takes the plural verb, which does not have an "s" on the end.
The children was following close behind us.	The children were following close behind us.	"Was" and "were" are helping verbs in this instance as they assist the verb "following" by indicating when the action occurred (in the past). Children is a plural noun requiring the plural helping verb "were" ("was" is the singular form).
Ali don't like garlic mashed potatoes.	Ali doesn't like garlic and mashed potatoes.	In these examples, the contraction "don't" stands for "do not," and the contraction "doesn't" stands for "does not." "Do" and "Does" are helping verbs for the verb "like" ("not" is an adverb indicating negation). As in the example above, the helping verb, not the main verb, is the one that changes to indicate number. Ali is the name of one woman; thus, she takes the singular "doesn't."
Chris and Kaleb is engaged.	Chris and Kaleb are engaged.	Although they are names of *individuals*, the phrase "Chris and Kaleb" functions as a **compound** (by means of the word "and" linking their names). Two individuals together form a plural. "Is" is a singular state-of-being verb, while "are" is the plural form.

Figure 23.3 **Nonstandard verb usage revised into Standard Written English**

Tense Consistency	Inadvertent Violation of Consistency	Purposeful Violation of Consistency
Aunt Cora was a profound force in my childhood. On a daily basis, she contributed time and energy to raising me. In those days, each of my parents was working two jobs. Sometimes, they worked late into the night. On those occasions, Aunt Cora left her own children with my uncle and came over to spend that time with me. Even though I was in middle school and argued about taking care of myself, I secretly felt much more secure when she was there. A few years ago, she had to go to a nursing home.	When you were a child, you probably didn't fully understand how important certain people were to your life. I was one of those children. My parents depended on Aunt Cora to help raise me. Since they work late at night, they need someone to stay with me, to make sure I had my dinner and go to bed on time. Since she was willing to help us, our lives were much easier than they might have been. A few years ago, she becomes ill and had to go to a nursing home. My whole family has visited her regularly.	Whenever I feel especially busy and consider not visiting Aunt Cora in the nursing home, I think about all her sacrifices in raising me. When my parents worked late at night, she came over to the house and cooked my dinner. She even took me to the hospital when I sprained my ankle playing soccer and waited with me until my parents arrived. So, even though I can always use a few extra hours to devote to school work or my job, I realize that if I don't spend time with Aunt Cora, I'll regret it. I want her to know that I appreciate her.
• This paragraph is written entirely in the past tense, reflecting that the action occurred at an earlier date. Past-tense verbs are printed in red.	• This paragraph randomly mixes present-tense verbs into a paragraph that is predominantly past tense. The present-tense verbs are printed in red.	• This paragraph begins in present tense; purposefully shifts to past tense, indicating a flashback; and then shifts back to present tense. The flashback is printed in red.

Figure 23.4 **Tense consistency and inconsistency**

Avoiding Sentence-Boundary Errors   Sentence-boundary errors are widely considered serious blemishes on the quality of a document. Such errors take three forms: **fragments, comma splices,** and **run-ons** (or fused sentences). They are referred to as *sentence-boundary errors* because they suggest that the writer is uncertain about the essential components or essential confines of a sentence in Standard Written English.

To understand sentence-boundary errors, you first need to know what a **clause** is, and you need to be able to tell the difference between two types of clauses: **independent** and **dependent.** First, a clause can be defined simply as a group of words that contains a **subject** and a **verb.** A subject is the primary agent in the clause—that which performs the action or whose state of being is described. For some examples, see Figure 23.5, which denotes subjects in blue and their verbs in orange.

All the examples in Figure 23.5 contain subjects and verbs—that is, they contain actors who are performing actions or whose state of being is indicated. However, only the first clause can stand alone as a sentence, as it communicates a complete thought. In contrast, the second example doesn't reveal *what happened* as a result of Liam's failure to cancel, and the third doesn't explain who exactly was in the corner. Clauses that can stand alone as complete sentences, like the first example, are referred

Jackson Avenue Coffee Shop sells the best baked goods in town.

Because Liam didn't cancel the order by midnight on the 25th

who was in the corner by the front door

Figure 23.5 **Examples of clauses**

"I should never begin a sentence with *because*."

Some teachers may offer this advice to help students avoid writing fragments, but you should know that it is not an error to begin a sentence with *because*. In fact, this structure enables sophisticated sentences that help you make cause-and-effect claims. For example, consider the result of adding "he was required to pay for it" to the because clause in Figure 23.5.

to as *independent* clauses (i.e., they don't need anything else to complete them). Clauses that can't stand alone, like the second and third examples, are referred to as *dependent* clauses (i.e., they depend on or need something else to complete them).

Dependent clauses are a type of **fragment.** In other words, whenever you capitalize the first letter of a dependent clause and end it with a period—thus, treating it as a sentence—you have written a fragment. But fragments do come in other shapes and sizes, including single words and phrases, or groups of words without *both* a subject and a verb (e.g., "mowing the lawn" and "the dark clouds overhead").

Fragments can be difficult to recognize because people regularly speak in fragments for the sake of efficiency. For example, if a peer in your composition course asks you why you missed the last class meeting, you probably wouldn't respond, "I missed the last class meeting because I went home for my sister's wedding." Rather, you'd probably reply in an abbreviated manner: "because I went home for my sister's wedding" or simply "my sister's wedding." Unfortunately, this shorthand doesn't transfer well to the written page because context necessary for understanding the content of the fragment is addressed in prior sentences, making the line of discussion difficult to follow. On a related point, fragments disrupt the flow of your prose, creating a choppy feel. Of course, sometimes you may *want* to interject a fragment to create a certain effect, such as isolating a few words to draw special attention to them. But remember that intentional or **stylistic fragments** gain power through their rarity, so you'll want to use them sparingly.

Another sentence-boundary error, the **comma splice,** occurs when you take two independent clauses—in other words, two complete sentences—and shove them together with only a comma separating them. You can determine whether you have composed a comma splice if you can see that on *both* sides of a comma you've implemented you have an independent clause or a complete sentence. Consider the following example of this error:

The traffic was backed up for miles, we decided to take an alternative route.

After locating the comma in this example, you'll see that on either side there is a complete sentence. In this instance, the comma is considered insufficient punctuation. Fortunately, once you locate a comma splice, you can easily correct it in one of four ways, as demonstrated in Figure 23.6.

Comma splices can be somewhat difficult to locate because they tend to blend into a document, hidden in a sense by commas used for other purposes. Consequently, if you know you have a tendency to write comma splices, you may want to devote at least one round of editing to reviewing nothing but comma usage. You can follow the thought processes mentioned above; that is, locate each comma and consider if—on both sides of it—you have an independent clause. If you do, you'll know you need

Method for Correcting a Comma Splice	Correction of Comma-Splice Example
Replace the comma with a period and capitalize the first word of the second clause, creating two sentences.	The traffic was backed up for miles. We decided to take an alternative route.
Replace the comma with a semicolon.	The traffic was backed up for miles; we decided to take an alternative route.
Add a conjunction (*and, but, or, for, nor, yet,*) after the comma.	The traffic was backed up for miles, and so we decided to take an alternative route.
Rewrite one of the independent clauses, turning it into a dependent clause.	Because the traffic was backed up for miles, we decided to take an alternative route.

Figure 23.6 **Strategies for correcting comma splices**

to apply one of the strategies listed in Figure 23.6. (You can read more about commas later in this chapter.)

The third type of sentence-boundary error is called a **run-on** or **fused sentence.** This error is similar to a comma splice, but instead of separating the independent clauses or sentences with a comma, you shove them together with *nothing* in between. Using the example in Figure 23.6, a run-on would look something like this:

The traffic was backed up for miles we decided to take an alternative route.

Because there is no comma to tip you off, run-ons may be even more difficult to identify than comma splices. When you edit for run-ons, then, you will need to be especially tuned in to the nature of independent clauses or complete sentences. If you find two *independent* clauses jammed together without any punctuation (i.e., a run-on), you can correct the error by means of the same strategies used for correcting comma splices: separating the clauses with a period, a semicolon, or a conjunction preceded by a comma—or turning one of the independent clauses into a dependent clause (see Figure 23.6).

Employing Commas   Comma placement can be confusing business, mainly because it's difficult to separate the rules from **stylistic preferences**—or what certain individuals like to see, even if that practice isn't absolutely required. Figure 23.7 presents several instances in which you might find yourself wrestling with the question of whether or not you need a comma. Alongside examples of those instances, you'll find advice that will help you make a decision.

Managing Pronouns   A **pronoun** is a word that refers to a noun you've previously mentioned. Pronouns can confuse readers if you fail to make clear which particular noun a given pronoun is intended to represent (this would be an **ambiguous pronoun**). They can also cause confusion if you are inconsistent in matching the number of a pronoun—that is, its singular versus plural form—with that of its **antecedent,** or the noun to which it refers (this would be an error in **pronoun-antecedent agreement**).

Examples of ambiguous pronouns are provided in Figure 23.8. The sentences in that figure are vulnerable to misinterpretation because the pronouns (printed in green) could be read as applying to more than one of the preceding

Instance	Explanation	Examples
Between components in a list	Generally speaking, you'll want to separate items in a list with commas. Whether or not you use a comma after the next-to-last item and before the conjunction *and* prior to the last item is a stylistic preference. Some teachers and publication sites will require it.	To prepare for the marathon, I bought some new shoes, joined a gym, and made some changes in my diet.
	Others will claim that using a comma after the next-to-last item and before the conjunction *and* isn't necessary. (Whatever the case, you need to be consistent on this within a document.)	When Micah and I stopped at the flea market today, I picked up an antique lamp, a walnut end table and a brass umbrella stand.
After an introductory element in a sentence	Following a short introductory element the decision is up to you.	At times, it seems as if the rules for punctuation are stated more complexly than they need to be.
	Following a lengthy element or a dependent clause, you'll need the comma.	Because the wind had picked up over the morning hours, Steve delayed plans to burn leaves until tomorrow.
In a compound sentence	A compound sentence is formed by taking two independent clauses and joining them with a conjunction. Unless the clauses are very short, this structure requires a comma before the conjunction.	Max took Spanish as an undergraduate to prepare for graduate school, but his friend Kevin decided not to pursue a second language.
In a compound-complex sentence	The same is true for compound-complex sentences (the "complex" designation means that at least one of the independent clauses is accompanied by a dependent clause).	Whenever Francesca practices for a recital, she likes to perform at least once in front of her roommates, for they are her most helpful critics.
With a nonessential clause	A nonessential clause modifies a noun in a way that is not required for understanding the sentence. In other words, you could simply remove that clause (in bold in the example at the right), and the sentence would still make perfect sense. To indicate their easy removal, nonessential clauses should be set off with commas from the rest of the sentence.	Bert McDougal, **who recently received the Citizen of the Year Award,** has volunteered to design a new playground to make Morton Park more child-friendly.
	In contrast, essential clauses are not set off by commas (i.e., they can't be "cut out" from the rest of the sentence). For example, try lifting out the dependent clause (in bold) in the sentence at the right. Assuming more than one man is attending the ballgame, without the clause, readers wouldn't be sure which man caught the ball.	The man **who is wearing the striped green shirt** just caught a foul ball.

Figure 23.7 **Various uses of commas**

nouns. Does *it* refer to the carpet or drywall? Does *she* refer to Shawna, Ashley, or Deandra? Does *they* refer to multiple-choice, fill-in-the-blank, or true-false questions? In any of these cases, you might clear up potential confusion by restating the appropriate noun (e.g., "When assessing flood damage to the carpet and drywall, we discovered that the **carpet** was in worse shape"). Or you could

When assessing flood damage to the carpet and drywall, we discovered that it was in worse shape.

Shawna, Ashley, and Deandra play in the brass section of the university's marching band, but she plays the trumpet while the others play the trombone.

The test included multiple-choice, fill-in-the-blank, and true-false questions; of the three, they proved to be the most challenging.

Figure 23.8 **Ambiguous pronouns**

designate the final item with the phrase "the latter" (e.g., "The test included multiple-choice, fill-in-the-blank, and true-false questions; of the three, **the latter** proved to be the most challenging").

As noted previously, another key to accurately employing pronouns is to make sure they *agree* with their respective nouns. Take a look at Figure 23.9, which contrasts a few pronoun-antecedent pairs that disagree with those that do agree. The key to "fixing" the problems on the left in this figure is to make sure that the pronoun in question is the same number as the noun it refers to. *Contestant* is singular; therefore it requires the singular pronoun *his* or *her* as opposed to the plural *their*. As for the second example, even though the collective reference implies several firemen working together, the phrase *each fireman* is singular. The singular calls for the singular pronoun *his*.

Of course, women can also fight fires. If the example in Figure 23.9 had invoked the word *firefighter* instead of *fireman,* you would want to indicate your realization that women *and* men are included under this label. It would be important, then, to communicate that through your pronoun selection, as in the following example: "Each firefighter needed **his or her** oxygen mask to battle the five-alarm blaze." The other option would be to change the noun to a plural, as in **"All firefighters** needed **their** oxygen masks to battle the five-alarm blaze." In both of these examples, the constructions demonstrate how you can avoid gender-biased language, which is an expectation for contemporary rhetorical situations.

Indicating Titles   The guidelines for signaling that a word or phrase in a paragraph is actually a title can be kept straight in large part by remembering that works large enough to contain other works are placed in italics (or underlined) while the smaller works that the larger works contain should be placed in quotation marks. See Figure 23.10 for some examples.

Pronouns and Antecedents That Disagree	Pronouns and Antecedents That Agree
Once the winning number is called, the raffle contestant must present their ticket.	Once the winning number is called, the raffle contestant must present his or her ticket.
Each fireman needed their oxygen mask to battle the five-alarm blaze.	Each fireman needed his oxygen mask to battle the five-alarm blaze.

Figure 23.9 **Pronoun disagreement and agreement with antecedents**

Larger Work	Title	Work within Larger Work	Title
Book	*Mindfulness*	Book chapter	"Creative Uncertainty"
Academic journal	*ADE Bulletin*	Journal article	"Research Is Teaching"
Newspaper	*The Decatur Herald*	Newspaper article	"State Pursuing Highway Safety Initiatives"
Magazine	*Vogue*	Magazine article	"Is the Fashion World Finally Embracing Diversity?"
TV show	*Game of Thrones*	Episode of TV show	"A Golden Crown"
Website	*DIY Network*	Website article	"Building a Retaining Wall"

Figure 23.10 **Conventions for indicating titles**

MYTH

"My word processor's spell- and grammar-checker will catch all my errors."

While spell- and grammar-checkers can alert you to possible errors, they are not foolproof. Often, they will mark as incorrect structures that are perfectly acceptable; they'll also miss certain problems. This is because the computer can't fully understand the context surrounding the supposed mistake, context that is essential for making editing decisions. In short, you should always double-check the machine, applying what you've learned about errors that you tend to commit.

REALITY

Figure 23.10 does not address every possibility you might encounter, but it does offer guidelines that will assist you in many common composing situations for school and the workplace. It also does not cover all the special guidelines for various documentation styles. Consult Chapter 21 or another resource to double-check such conventions.

Processes for Editing

While by no means comprehensive, the previous section on editing does alert you to several errors with which first-year students typically struggle. You might treat it, then, as an editing checklist of sorts, heightening your consciousness about the surface quality of your writing. Of course, some errors will cause more trouble for you than others will. For that reason, you'll want to personalize your editing strategies, just as you were advised to do earlier in this chapter with regard to revision strategies. Doing so will require keeping track of the problems that tend to recur time and again across drafts of the documents you've written. These are your **error patterns,** the issues you'll want to be particularly aware of when you set out to edit your compositions.

In addition to keeping track of your error patterns, you should reserve plenty of time for locating and correcting mistakes before your papers are due for assessment. This point is worth emphasizing because procrastination too often interferes with best intentions and may cause you to rush your editing processes. In anticipation of this potentiality, strive to complete your final draft a few days before it's due so that you can set it aside for a while—try for at least a day. When you return to it, you'll do so with fresh eyes, which are less likely to "read over" any mistakes (reading the text aloud can also help in this respect). Ideally, you'll be able to proofread the text several times, perhaps concentrating your attention on a particular error—and only that error—during each pass. This practice will help stave off the cognitive overload associated with multitasking, as discussed at the beginning of this chapter.

Transfer across Writing Situations

The information addressed in this chapter is potentially applicable in all writing situations that adhere to Standard Written English—that is, in most academic and professional contexts. Even so, it's inevitable that you will encounter at least some disparity across disciplines of study, publication forums, and genres. For example, newspapers and popular magazines tend to be more laid back about pronoun-antecedent agreement when working around gender-biased language (e.g., "It can be upsetting for an educational community when a popular teacher announces **their** retirement"). In contrast, some academic forums may require a more formal register (e.g., "It can be upsetting for an educational community when a popular teacher announces **his or her** retirement"). They will also establish strict requirements with regard to formatting and documentation (see Chapter 21). As for genre, regarding pieces that are heavy on narrative and description (such as memoirs and profiles), readers and editors tend to be more tolerant of sentence-boundary violations that create a certain stylistic impact.

In light of these variations, it's not practical to view "surface correctness" as a matter of memorizing every guideline or convention. Rather, it's a matter of becoming a student of the genre, forum, or field in which you're writing, locating differences from other rhetorical contexts, and learning what you need to do to help satisfy those rhetorical expectations.

ACTIVITY

Developing a Revision and Editing Notebook   Open a computer file or locate a notebook that you can devote specifically to reflecting on and keeping track of your writing challenges. Title the first half of the file or notebook "Revision," and title the second half "Editing." To fill the pages, you'll be creating subheadings (e.g., "Transitions" and "Fragments") that represent special challenges you wish to identify and then elaborating each section with the following:

- Examples of the problem
- Advice from a teacher, tutor, textbook, or OWL that might help you address the issues
- Examples of different strategies for solving the problem

Your initial entries in this notebook might record problems with writing that you've encountered in previous courses. As the semester progresses, you can expand on these issues and add new ones if and when they present themselves.

Peer and Instructor Review

24

How would you translate the equation pictured above into words? A lightbulb is commonly regarded as a symbol for insight, or a solution to a creative problem. As such, the image above points to the idea that a significant insight (the larger lightbulb) is usually the result of smaller, diverse insights coming together. This process occurs through various means, but perhaps the most fruitful and efficient route to insight is interacting with others, or collaborating.

Exposing yourself to many and varied opinions, beliefs, and perspectives will expand your gaze and prompt you to look at problems you are working on from multiple angles, opening fresh possibilities for moving forward. Collaboration in composition courses assumes a number of forms, but the most common are forms of peer and instructor review, both of which are discussed in this chapter.

The familiar saying "Two heads are better than one" captures the essence of **collaboration**—the idea that the potential for solving a problem quickly and effectively increases with the number of minds that are working on it. This is true in all fields, including those whose creations seem to arise primarily from an individual

421

working alone. For example, the pop star, faced with the challenge of recording a new hit that will keep fans interested in his music, relies on an entourage of people, from lyricists, to video producers, to publicists. The Olympic backstroke champion, vying for another gold in a sport where seconds define the difference between medals, depends on trainers, nutritionists, and swimsuit designers to ensure she performs at optimum levels.

Writing is another activity that, more often than not, results in products that are credited to a single person. Nevertheless, like the examples mentioned in the previous paragraph, writers often depend on other people, whether in the act of conceiving, researching, revising, or editing their work. More specifically, they might talk with friends or family members to clarify a task or identify an engaging approach to a project. In addition, they may turn to librarians for suggestions about research strategies or specific resources they can consult. Reading, itself, is a form of collaboration, as it merges the readers' ideas with the ideas of published authors. Finally, successful writers know they should seek feedback from a variety of individuals on drafts of a project, as such response typically reveals avenues for improvement.

Recognizing the vital role of collaboration in composing, many teachers assign in- and out-of-class activities that encourage students to share plans for and drafts of their writing. This chapter characterizes the most common of these activities—**peer review** and **instructor review.** It also offers advice for contributing to and taking advantage of these valuable opportunities for improving your writing.

Invention Workshops

Some of the most challenging work you'll do in your composition courses, as well as in other courses that require writing, is generating ideas and focusing them appropriately to match the expectations for a given assignment. These processes fall under the label invention and can be supported by prewriting exercises, such as brainstorming, freewriting, clustering, and so on (see Chapter 4). In addition to assigning prewriting exercises—and often in conjunction with them—teachers will ask you to discuss your initial plans for composing with some or all of your classmates, and your classmates will share ideas for their own papers. This is the nature of an **invention workshop.**

Invention workshops hold promise for helping you and your peers refine the direction and scope of a document as a result of the cross-pollination of backgrounds, experiences, worldviews, and so on that these exchanges tend to stimulate. As responses to your original idea (as well as responses to those responses) intermingle, they create a complex matrix of possibility that you can draw from in thinking further about your project. This back-and-forth flow of diverse opinions and perspectives spins a web of critical thought that is unique to that moment (see Figure 24.1). A simple change in any of the ingredients—a single person, a memory, the way the memory is articulated, and so forth—would change the outcome of the event. Most importantly, the richness and complexity of such a matrix

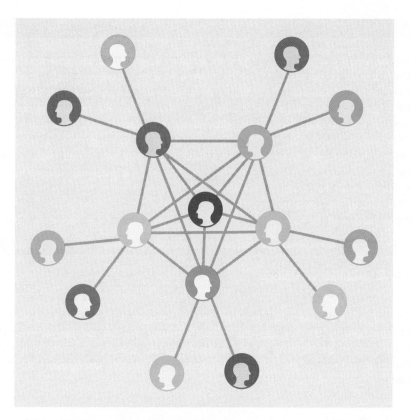

Figure 24.1 **A matrix or web of critical thought**

could not be reproduced outside the interaction of so many minds (i.e., by a writer working alone, talking with a friend, or conferencing with a teacher).

Just *hearing* such a flow of ideas is valuable, typically leading to multiple insights of varied significance. In addition, the opportunity to ask follow-up questions enables you to clarify points of confusion and elicit concrete advice surrounding your most pressing concerns about the piece you are preparing to write. But the benefits don't stop when you are finished explaining plans and hearing advice for your paper; on the contrary, by listening to the plans of others and responses to those plans—as well as asking questions and offering comments about them—additional models and strategies for addressing your own topic will come to light. In fact, many students report that they learn as much from interacting over their classmates' ideas as they do from receiving feedback about their own ideas. See Figure 24.2—an excerpt from an end-of-semester reflective essay—for the thoughts of a first-year composition student on the value of invention workshops.

If, in your own composition course, your teacher prioritizes other elements of composing over invention workshops, it would be well worth your while to organize such an opportunity on your own. Talking with your classmates for a few minutes before and after class, organizing small-group meetings in the evenings or on the weekends to help one another hone ideas, speaking with friends in your

I never wanted to show anyone what I was working on . . . so when [my teacher] announced that we were going to have to sit in a circle and announce our first idea for our paper to the class, I was not a happy camper. If there was ever a day to skip class, that would have been it. But, since I couldn't rationalize it well enough to myself, I showed up. And you know what? I loved it!

As it turned out, the discussion we had about everyone's papers was the best thing that could have happened. . . . Discussing my ideas with the group gave me a chance to get a fresh perspective on some of the subjects I'd been considering, and it really helped me solidify my own ideas and test their feasibility. . . . I also really enjoyed sharing my own thoughts on my classmates' topics; even if they never listened to any of my suggestions, it still got my own mind thinking of how I could improve my own writing to be more original and creative and cohesive.

Source: By Erin Anderson, a first-year composition student.

Figure 24.2 **Student praise for invention workshops**

dorm—all are ways that you can enjoy the advantages of invention workshops in a less formal setting. Even if the individuals assisting you are not part of your class, you can quickly get them up to speed regarding the demands of your assignment. Articulating aspects of the composing challenge will only strengthen your understanding of and response to it.

Peer Review

Talking with peers can also prove helpful later in your composing processes, after you've begun drafting. At this juncture, when you and your peers actually have documents in progress and have already made some important composing decisions, your exchanges will typically be referred to as **peer review.** Peer review activities are typically more **evaluative** in nature than invention workshops, and they can take several forms.

Perhaps the most common form involves exchanging papers with a partner so that each of you can respond to various qualities of the other's draft. At times, your teacher will ask you to provide feedback during the early stages of drafting, when your attention will be concentrated on global issues such as development and organization. At other times, he or she will ask you to help edit or **proofread,** with an eye toward finding mistakes in usage, punctuation, mechanics, and spelling. Whatever the case, in this type of peer review exercise, you ordinarily will be presented with specific questions or tasks posed by your teacher (although you may also have the option of supplementing these prompts with some that reflect your own special concerns). Figure 24.3 presents example peer review questions appropriate for responding to an early draft.

Notice how the prompts in Figure 24.3 require the reviewer to offer more than a yes or no response, as they call for specific commentary on the nature of a problem, advice for improving on a weakness, or description of effective textual features.

- *Does this essay seem appropriate for the target audience?* If so, indicate features of the text that make it so; if not, explain how it might be improved in this regard.
- *Is this draft adequately focused given the limitations of the assignment?* If so, paraphrase what you believe to be the author's main point or thesis. If not, offer suggestions for tightening the scope.
- *Does the essay provide enough support for the claims it makes?* Make note of any claims that leave you wanting more evidence or a different kind. Suggest some resources for locating that evidence.
- *What might the author do to more logically or smoothly organize the paper?* If you feel it is already well organized, identify what you believe is the principle on which the author ordered his or her material and mark effective transitions between ideas.

Figure 24.3 **Peer review questions**

These elaborated goals are intended to guide you and your peers in communicating the kind and range of detailed feedback that writers need if they are going to significantly improve their texts.

After you and your partner have finished responding to the peer review prompts, you should take some time to read over each other's comments before the class ends and you part ways. Doing so is important so that you can discuss any questions the feedback might have raised and test out some revision ideas. If after concluding your conversation with that partner there is any time left in the class period, you may want to exchange papers with a different partner in the interest of gaining another perspective on your draft.

Peer review does not have to be delivered in writing to be effective, nor does it have to be limited to partnerships. Some teachers prefer to conduct peer review activities by arranging classes into small groups of three or four students and having them take turns reading their papers aloud while others take notes on the papers and then react to them orally. As with written peer review exercises, these small-group interactions are usually guided by prompts provided by the teacher; however, you should come prepared with a few of your own questions about your draft in case time allows you to address issues that the teacher's prompts didn't cover. Small-group peer review offers many of the advantages provided by invention workshops, addressed in the previous section. In particular, you have time to receive the opinions of several classmates simultaneously, a situation that can intensify the level of critical thought as members of your group endorse or challenge one another's judgments of a text's qualities.

Many students resist peer review, and they may do so for a variety of reasons. If you are one of these students, you may feel that because students are not writing experts, they are not able to offer especially helpful feedback. What's more, you may fear they might steer one another in directions that will diminish the quality of a draft. On another note, you may be skeptical of peer review for a reason that is often associated with collaborative activities in general: You anticipate that your partner or small group won't devote as much time and effort to the exercise as you will and, therefore, that you'll end up with only a few vague and overly positive comments.

As for the first matter of concern, you should remember that students are not expected to respond as experts or teachers. Rather, they are being asked to respond as *readers.* By virtue of the fact that you and your peers have read and continue to read

MYTH

"If I criticize a classmate's paper, I may offend him or her."

Experienced teachers will tell you that students report they *want* critical feedback. To be sure, simply telling a peer that his or her paper is "great" or that there's nothing wrong with it will do nothing to move the project forward. That being said, whenever reviewing others' work, you should maintain a respectful tone and should offer praise where it is specifically warranted.

REALITY

a variety of documents on a daily basis (probably most of them online), you have considerable insight to offer other developing writers. For example, you do not have to be a teacher to know what strategies or kinds of information might engage a particular audience, what types of evidence might lead to a more convincing argument, or what it feels like when an author fails to transition carefully between ideas. And by no means do these observations (as well as many others you might make) depend on specialized terminology. Again, the primary responsibility of a peer reviewer is to respond as another reader, noting where and how the text succeeds or falters in communicating.

Regarding the other common source of resistance to peer review—the worry that peers won't work as hard as you will—it may help to know that most teachers assess peer review in some fashion, by assigning either a letter grade or a pass or fail mark for participation. When they do so, they usually spend time clarifying what counts as ineffective and effective response, with the latter being defined as detailed and constructively critical. If they do not provide specific guidance, or if that sort of preparation does not seem to help, work proactively with your partners to make sure they are giving you the type and extent of feedback that you want. Granting your permission for them to be honest in their critique or offering some examples of the types of comments that you find most helpful may be all that they need to improve their response.

Instructor Feedback

In addition to peer review, you will likely receive plenty of instructor feedback in the context of your college composition course. Writing teachers may offer advice at various junctures in your composing processes for a given assignment. Sometimes they will intervene as you are generating ideas or drafting. At these times, the feedback will be **formative** in nature, its goal being to help you make productive revisions. Feedback that comes near the end of the road, when your paper (or a portfolio) has been submitted for final evaluation, is referred to as **summative;** its purposes are to forward an evaluation of the document's overall quality and to explain the reasoning behind your grade.

Summative comments can be helpful in grasping the rationale behind the assessment of your performance in a course and can isolate areas that you need to continue working on as you advance to other courses. But the focus of concentration in your first-year composition course will be on formative commentary since it will be the most immediately helpful as you are trying to address weak elements of your compositions and improve subsequent versions of them.

Typically, formative comments are phrased as one of the following:

- Questions designed to spark additional thinking
- Descriptive remarks intended to convey how a passage is affecting the reader
- Suggestions posed in the interest of helping you alter the text

In most cases, your teacher will not mark every problem he or she comes across. Rather, in early drafts, he or she will focus on those that are most serious, leaving those that are less serious for later rounds of response (if, in fact, those other problems still remain after you revise). Even so, formative commentary can, at times, seem overwhelming. Consequently, teachers will usually identify themes in their commentary—noting especially the most serious issues or patterns they observe—to help you understand where you should concentrate your revision efforts.

As soon as your teacher returns formative comments, it makes good sense to read them carefully and to study the parts of your draft that they refer to. Whatever questions you have about their meaning, or about strategies for addressing any problems they identify, should be addressed as soon as possible—while the writing and the feedback are still fresh in your mind, as well as in your teacher's. If the course syllabus doesn't include in-class opportunities for this type of reflection, you should arrange a conference with your teacher outside class during his or her office hours.

A teacher's office hours are always open to students to discuss their papers, whether they have just been assigned or are nearly due. In fact, some teachers prefer to give on-the-spot feedback during conferences when students are able to immediately clear up any uncertainties about the response. Whether your teacher always operates in this manner, cancels a class or two per term for mandatory conferences with each student, or invites students to come by his or her office at their leisure, you should be prepared on your end to make the conference as productive as possible. This means that you need to have specific questions in mind and that you should bring any materials you might want to refer to (the assignment handout, sources you're working with, etc.) in making sense of the conversation.

MYTH

"If a teacher suggests changing something, I better do it, or I will be penalized come grading time."

When responding to papers, most (if not all) teachers wish to avoid the appearance of dictating what their students should do with the next draft. Rather, their goal is to model critical-thinking skills about effective writing and strategies for crafting it. As such, they typically will admire the student who follows his or her own path—a path that may result in a better match with the writer's intentions. Exceptions might include paths that clearly worsen the quality of the text or preserve grammatical mistakes that are governed by conventions of Standard Written English.

REALITY

Writing Center Visits

As suggested in the previous sections, most composition courses present students with many opportunities for receiving feedback from their teacher and peers. But you may find that this amount or manner of assistance is just not enough for you. The good news is that many colleges and universities have **writing centers,**

MYTH

"Only writers who are really struggling in their courses visit writing centers."

Students achieving at all levels—even graduate students—take advantage of the valuable services that writing centers provide. Accomplished writers know that talking with others about their drafts, even when those drafts seem to be in pretty good shape, opens fresh possibilities for improving them. No matter what your unique talents and challenges as a writer, the tutors will welcome your attendance. It is a sign that you take writing seriously and understand what professional writers believe: that feedback from many and diverse readers will only make their writing better.

REALITY

which exist primarily for the purpose of providing tutoring services. Ordinarily, the tutors are undergraduate or graduate students enrolled at that institution who have been trained in effective one-on-one writing instruction. Moreover, these tutors are familiar with the standard curriculum or kinds of assignments that characterize the first-year composition program, and they often have experience teaching within that program. In other words, writing center tutors have specialized knowledge and experience that can prove helpful in moving your projects forward. The potential benefit of their services becomes clear when considering an observation made in the first section of this chapter: The greater the amount and diversity of response to your writing, the more material you have to work with when you are trying to solve a composing problem.

Writing centers are so highly regarded as a student-support service that some composition teachers may *require* students to attend tutoring sessions. If visits are required, the teacher may request a report of work completed during the tutoring session as a means of tracking what has been covered and where he or she might pick up when next interacting with a given student. Doing so increases the efficiency of the feedback-revision loop. If you are not required to visit your school's writing center, you should keep in mind the prospect of visiting it on your own. Along these lines, if and when you do visit, it is important to remember that tutors are not merely proofreaders. While they will assist you in learning how to spot your own surface-level errors, they will not find and correct those problems for you without your active involvement.

If you decide you would like to meet with a writing center tutor, you will probably be able to arrange for an appointment online. You can do this through the center's website, which will, of course, post additional contact information, as well as its location on campus (some institutions will have a main center as well as satellite centers for students' convenience). The website may also provide access to an online writing lab, or OWL, through which you can arrange for online tutoring appointments and access numerous resources that offer guidance pertaining to many different aspects of your writing. These resources explain and illustrate a wide range of concepts, from focusing a topic, to correcting comma splices, to citing sources. And often they are accompanied by exercises through which you can test your growing knowledge. Such resources offer guidance and practice beyond materials in your composition course, providing options for jump-starting your work until you can meet with a tutor. If your writing center hasn't launched its own OWL—or if your own school doesn't have a writing center—you should know that many institutions have opened access to their OWLs by means of the Internet.

Transfer across Writing Situations

The early sections of this chapter emphasize the promise of peer and instructor response to help you improve the quality of papers that may be assigned in your college composition courses. Transferring the motivation to seek response from peers and teachers is one avenue for applying lessons in this chapter to other contexts. Indeed, willingness to work with others in reaction to what you've composed is a disposition that is essential in most academic and professional contexts. In both settings, you may need to garner approval from a supervisor before distributing a document; even if you aren't directed to do so, it may be wise to have others check the accuracy and tone of the documents you compose, especially if they address controversial or sensitive information.

Furthermore, writing on the job will frequently involve you in *drafting* documents collaboratively—that is, in producing multiauthored documents. In light of this reality, your composition course may require you to try your hand at this kind of writing. For multiauthored documents you must work closely with other individuals on conceiving and executing every aspect of a piece. This might involve sitting down at a computer and crafting sentences together, or it might involve drafting sections of the document separately and then merging and revising them as a team. Writing in these circumstances poses special challenges, including those that follow:

- Recognizing one another's strengths and figuring out how best to use them
- Accommodating one another's unique drafting styles
- Compromising about preferences for the final document
- Splitting the workload in a fair manner
- Conducting meetings at mutually convenient times
- Working respectfully through disagreements for the good of the project

Of course, some of these skills are essential to other sorts of collaborative projects, such as general problem solving in the classroom or workplace, oral presentations, and design of visual artifacts. Regardless of the environment, whether a composition classroom or the setting of your future career, success in today's world is defined in part by your willingness to share ideas with, accept the help of, and work in tandem with others.

ACTIVITY

Analyzing Feedback   Reflect on a time when you received some especially helpful feedback on a piece of writing or some other creative project. This can be feedback from anyone: a teacher, a classmate, a parent, a sibling, or a friend. Freewrite for at least 10 minutes about what made this feedback so helpful. Be as specific as you can. Share this freewriting with a small group of peers as all of you prepare to be as helpful as possible in reviewing one another's drafts for an upcoming project. If you can't remember an instance of helpful feedback, write instead about feedback that was not helpful and how that feedback might have been improved.

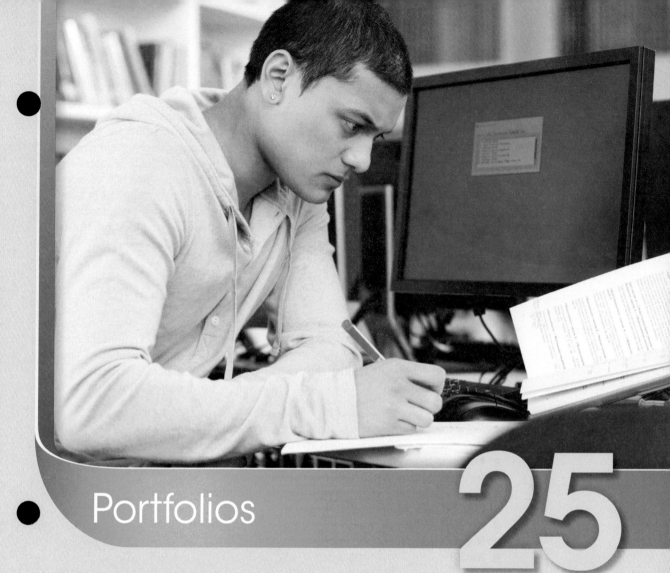

Portfolios

25

You have just been called for a final interview, and it's your last chance to impress. What information about the company do you need to review? What qualities about yourself will you want to emphasize? What will you wear? Of course, your goal is to present yourself in the best way possible to convince employers of your qualifications for the position.

Your goal will be similar when preparing an end-of-semester portfolio for your composition course—that is, you'll want to present your best "writing self" to convince your teacher that you have the qualifications for a passing grade in the course. As in preparing for a job interview, preparing a writing portfolio involves choices. Learn about those choices and other matters relevant to portfolio assembly in this chapter.

How many times have you turned in a paper thinking, "If only I had a little more time"? Of course, for many professional writers, time constraints aren't flexible. News reporters, for example, are constantly racing to meet deadlines for their publications' next editions. Technical writers realize they may lose clients if they cannot deliver projects by the dates designated on contracts they have signed. Even students in a diversity of high school and college-level courses become accustomed to submitting papers for final evaluation every few weeks.

While tight and rigid deadlines are realities in certain professional and academic contexts, many composition teachers believe that, while students are learning to write, they need extended periods of time to absorb and apply concepts and strategies before they are graded on the quality of their work. This attitude is rooted in the observation that writing develops slowly, through repeated practice of new skills—as well as review of skills already mastered when they are applied in new and more demanding situations. To support these needs, many composition teachers organize their classes to allow for an instructional approach referred to as **portfolio assessment,** which is specifically characterized in the sections that follow.

Portfolio-Based Composition Courses

Simply put, a course based on portfolio assessment invites you to work on, and *rework,* every paper you are assigned from the moment it is introduced until the end of the semester. At that point you will submit a collection of documents that you have produced to be graded **holistically** (which means "on the whole"). The extended time before submission will allow you to take your writing projects through many processes essential to composing, such as:

■ *Reflecting* on writing tasks after they are introduced
■ *Reflecting* on writing processes and products as they are completed
■ Engaging in *invention* activities
■ *Incubating* ideas that invention activities generate
■ *Planning* content and global structure for a document
■ Communicating *initial plans* in a draft
■ Receiving *feedback from peers*
■ Receiving *feedback from instructors*
■ *Revising*
■ *Proofreading*

Preceding chapters (especially Chapters 2, 4, 5, 12, 23, and 24) discuss these processes more fully while also acknowledging that they will differ across individuals and assignments. Regardless of the order and extent of these activities, writers cannot reach their full potential when forced to generate substantial documents in a few hours, a few days, or even a few weeks. Because portfolio courses hold off *final* due dates for major writing projects until the end of the course, they allow composing processes to play out in a more realistic and productive manner.

In some portfolio classes, teachers will provide all major assignments up front. In others, you will receive a new essay assignment every few weeks. Whatever the case, you will turn over early drafts of these documents at various points in the semester so that your peers or teacher can offer suggestions for revising them. As this emphasis on response and revision suggests, students in portfolio-based writing courses participate in many of the same activities and exercises that characterize almost any writing course. Besides peer response, these include:

- Assigned readings about composing strategies
- Assigned readings that provide content for your papers
- Teacher-led discussions
- Small-group work
- Postwrites (or reflections on assignments as you complete them)

In addition, some class meetings will be partially or entirely turned over to **writing workshops,** during which you will address some aspect of a major writing project, whether that be formulating ideas, conducting research, drafting, exchanging feedback with peers, or conferencing with your instructor. Workshops are crucial to your success because they enable you to make progress on your assignments in the presence of others who can immediately respond to questions and offer advice.

Near the end of the course—usually with one or two weeks left—your teacher will devote the remaining class periods to an ongoing **portfolio revision workshop,** which will allow you to concentrate on fine-tuning the collection of best work that you will submit for evaluation. To prepare for the revision workshop, you'll need to intensify your reflective efforts, reading through your papers again, considering the feedback of peers and instructors, and looking for patterns in your postwrites and other informal exercises as they reflect your experiences with each assignment. All these materials are vital to helping you determine the best approach to compiling your portfolio and to composing your portfolio introduction (discussed later in this chapter). Relevant to these goals, you need to save *everything* you write during the semester, as well as all the feedback you receive. Doing so will provide you a comprehensive view of your efforts in the course and the progress you've made from beginning to end; it will also guarantee that you have a rich pool of possibilities to draw from in compiling your portfolio.

As the revision workshop draws near, your teacher may schedule an out-of-class conference to discuss your plans for compiling your portfolio. To prepare for this conference, you should take notes so that you can make efficient use of time during the meeting. During the conference, your teacher will listen to your choices for what to include in the portfolio, ask questions about those choices, and maybe even suggest other options. This will also be the time to discuss the shape these projects are in, priorities for revision, specific plans for revising, and a focus for the portfolio introduction. A conference of this nature is intended to help you solidify your intentions for the final push to portfolio submission day.

Portfolio Content

A portfolio is intended to represent your status as a writer at the end of a composition course. To gauge that status, different teachers may prioritize different kinds of written materials that you have prepared throughout the semester. Possible points of variation in portfolio content, across courses, include:

- *Formality.* Will you submit only major essay assignments, or will you include informal exercises as well?
- *Number of papers.* Will you submit all of the formal essays you composed or only a select few?

- *Range of papers.* Will you have total freedom in making your choices, or will certain types of papers be required?
- *Evidence of early work.* Will you include rough drafts of formal essays? Will you include peer reviews that helped you revise?

In line with his or her particular objectives for the portfolio, your teacher will provide directions for assembling and submitting it stemming from the questions raised in the list above. Regardless of how he or she approaches these issues, you can safely assume that most any portfolio compiled for a composition course will contain the following: (1) a few papers representing your very best writing and (2) a **reflective introduction,** or overview of your collected work. The following sections explore these components in greater depth.

Document Selection

In addition to receiving polished essays, some teachers like to see evidence of the processes you engaged in while completing those assignments. If your teacher falls into this category, he or she will want you to supplement your polished work with marked-up preliminary drafts, examples of helpful feedback, and representative invention exercises that led to productive ideas for writing.

Even when your teacher expects your portfolio to contain *only* polished drafts of major writing projects, it is likely that you will enjoy at least some level of choice with regard to what you include. One common scenario for this type of portfolio would permit you to discard your worst paper or two, with no attention to the kinds of assignments that generated them. Another scenario might require you to demonstrate ability across a range of genres (e.g., memoir, rhetorical analysis, and position paper) but allow you to choose your strongest work relevant to any additional assignments. In some cases, along with your most impressive pieces, a teacher will want to see a paper that posed special challenges you were able to improve on since it could more strikingly display your development than papers that came more easily for you.

If your teacher does provide you some leeway in compiling your portfolio, the goal is to select pieces that collectively communicate some message about who you are as a writer. Sure, that message might be, "See what a great writer I am!" And, at first consideration, this would seem like a smart move since a good portion of your grade for the course will be based on your portfolio. But most teachers will hope that you set your sights a little more narrowly, perhaps selecting documents that, together, reveal a certain strength, a way you have improved in the course, or a persistent challenge that you were able to overcome. See Figure 25.1 for some specific ideas.

Of course, the material you include in your portfolio will display more than a single characteristic of your writing, and certainly it might demonstrate how aspects of or changes in your writing processes affected your final products. (See Chapter 12 for specifics on analyzing writing processes.) The point is that, as with an essay, a portfolio needs a focus, and one factor on which you should base your decision about a focus is your ability to identify sufficient evidence from your papers to illustrate it. Being able to identify a focus or theme, as well as to illustrate or support it, will become important to another significant component of your portfolio—its **reflective introduction,** which is explained in the next section.

Reflective Introduction

The reflective introduction is a brief essay (usually three to five pages) that previews the contents of your portfolio. Its thesis will communicate a focus or theme that unifies the collection of documents you have chosen to submit. This focus—examples of which you reviewed in Figure 25.1—should assert what the portfolio communicates about you as a writer and, as relevant, the nature of your experience in the course. Ensuring that it does so requires concentrated reflection, as the title of this genre suggests. (Read more about the significance of reflection for writing development in Chapters 1 and 2.)

Ultimately, the reflective introduction can be categorized as an *analysis* (a composing strategy detailed in Chapter 11). An analysis reads its subject matter through an interpretive lens, which, in the case of a reflective introduction, is typically the concept (or concepts) that helped you arrive at a focus or theme for your portfolio. Put another way, the interpretive lens is tightly connected to your focus or theme and points you to the elements of the portfolio documents that you will discuss in supporting your analysis.

To consider how these elements might coordinate in a reflective introduction, consult the flowchart in Figure 25.2. This flowchart walks you through the thinking and reading processes that a hypothetical writer might engage in when planning a focus for his portfolio and initial strategies for developing his reflective introduction. As the last box in the flowchart indicates, you should feel free to cite early drafts or peer review exercises in your reflective introduction, even if you aren't asked to include those preliminary exercises in the portfolio.

To see how an *actual* writer cites preliminary exercises in this manner, study the Look Inside excerpt on page 437 from a reflective introduction that was written for a first-year composition course. Students in this course were asked to submit

MYTH

"If I want an A on my portfolio, my reflective introduction should hide any weaknesses in my texts and should include lots of praise for the course."

Your reflective introduction should be an honest portrayal of your status as a writer and experience in the course as demonstrated by an analysis of your portfolio content. In fact, your teacher might be suspicious of your motives (e.g., flattery for a high grade) if you expend too much space and energy praising the course. Most importantly, he or she will want to know that you can think critically about your writing, noting strengths, as well as challenges, if warranted.

REALITY

Strengths	Improvements	Challenges
• Engaging introductions • Convincingly supported arguments • Unique and specific theses • Use of humor • Variation in sentence structures	• More tightly focused thesis statements • Integration of direct quotes • Use of descriptive language • Use of invention activities to generate and narrow ideas	• Conclusions that don't simply repeat main points • Effective transitions • Properly formatted Works Cited or References pages • Application of feedback to improve specific features of the texts

Figure 25.1 Example focuses or themes for selecting portfolio contents

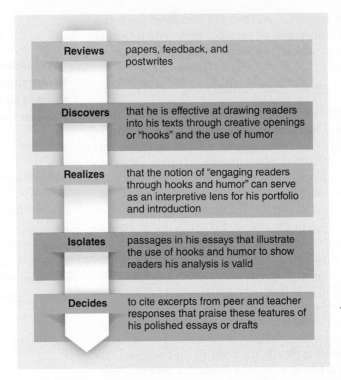

Figure 25.2 Processes for focusing a portfolio and reflective introduction

only polished essays in their portfolios. However, they were able to choose which three of four major essays (drafted prior to the portfolio introduction) they would revise further and present for final evaluation.

Of course, potential focuses or themes for reflective introductions are as numerous as the students asked to compose them. But, again, your own focus should emerge from a careful reading of your portfolio documents in the interest of locating some concept that they collectively demonstrate relevant to your strengths as a writer, improvements you have made, or persistent challenges you have overcome or continue to face.

Up to this point, you've learned about many of the processes involved in conceiving and planning a reflective introduction as it connects to the processes of determining your portfolio's contents. But planning the portfolio introduction is only part of the challenge; you still have to draft, revise, and edit it. Studying the other analytical genres addressed in Chapters 12 to 15 will help in this regard, but a few of these strategies in particular are worth emphasizing.

When drafting your reflective introduction, you want to make certain that the analytical claims you make in the body of your essay are clearly related to the focus or theme articulated in your thesis statement. In addition, you should take care in backing those claims with details from your portfolio documents, as well as from course materials and activities. Finally, don't forget to make time for revising and

From "The Clearer Picture"

by Julia Mosebach, a First-Year Composition Student

My thoughts are and always have been a flurry whenever I sit down to write. But the one thought that was not crossing my mind four months ago as I sat drafting "A Rule-Breaker's Writing Process" is, "Wow, what an obnoxious load of pretention I am." The worst part is, had you asked me if I thought I was pretentious when it came to my writing, I would have said yes. I was not oblivious to my pretenses, but they didn't bother me. I think that, deep down, I thought they were . . . justified. As if [I], a fresh-out-of-high school eighteen-year-old who seldom wrote anything with real zest or appeal, had the right to stick her nose into the air when walking into a college writing course.

The author opens by reflecting on an observation about the first paper she wrote for the course—a writing-process analysis. The self-critique she offers sets up her thesis for the reflective introduction, which surfaces in the second paragraph.

Reading over the five-page portrayal of my writing processes, I can note numerous changes that have been made in the last few months. The most prominent difference, I believe, lies not in the writing process itself, but instead how I view my writing. . . . People had been telling me along the way that there was something I could not see, but I would just shrug those people off. In taking a semester of this writing course, I realized that I needed to enhance my vision. . . .

Here is the author's thesis.

In "A Rule-Breaker's Writing Process," I emphasized that, while I was my own toughest critic, I was quick to reject the criticisms of others. My tone said that their suggestions were pointless, stupid. Not once in that essay did I insinuate that I believed this to be any different in college. This is perhaps why the first peer review session in my English course came to me as such an unpleasant surprise. I had been basking in warm sunlight, and suddenly a bucket of icy water was thrown at my face. I knew that the draft I was giving to my peer was far from perfect, but I didn't think she would notice it too. If she did, I certainly did not think that she would convince me. *I know where my paper is flawed,* I would think. *But other people just don't understand.*

In this paragraph the author supports her thesis with specific reference to the content and tone of her first paper, as well as her reaction to the initial peer review exercise. She even quotes her own thoughts.

This view I held onto for so long, that someone would not notice real faults in my paper where I hadn't already, is a view I let go of almost instantly after just that one peer review session. The peer handed the paper back to me, and I could have sworn she used her little blue pen until it was dry. She then gave me two other pieces of paper, filled front and back with her commentary and suggestions. I remember

The first line of this paragraph echoes the thesis, and the following lines offer additional illustration.

nodding my head as I read over these. She's right, I kept telling myself.

While it might be easy to say that someone is right, it is difficult to acknowledge such as being true. I came to acknowledge this by keeping one thought in mind: if one is to write something, it should be worth reading. Who is more apt to determine this worth than the reader? I had always based the level of what I had written off of how good it felt to write it, not how good it felt for others to read it. So it was through opening up my mind to suggestions from a reader of one of my pieces that I was able to recognize aspects of my writing that I hadn't prior. I was able to see pieces of the picture that before weren't so clear to me.

I am thankful that this change in viewpoint is the first way, because of my English class, that I changed as a writer. I cannot imagine that any other improvements would have been made had I not first learned how to take the opinions of others seriously and recognize that a writer needs a reader in order to really progress.

Class period by class period, my rigidity would crumble. After engaging in a peer review session in which I became open to someone's criticisms besides my own, and seeing that it benefited the overall construction of my paper, I decided to practice this behavior elsewhere. It was through a class discussion that I got my idea of who to interview for my [profile] essay. This led to my participation in the most interesting interview I have ever conducted, which gave me a ton of potential for my paper. Had I shut off the voices in the classroom saying that I should "think outside the box" and "interview someone who wasn't creative in the sense that they created art," then I likely would not have been as successful with the assignment. My narrowed mind would have caused me to write a paper that was probably less interesting. Many class discussions, like the peer review sessions, taught me that it is okay to learn from others. . . .

By the time I began writing the . . . Unit Four assignment, I had been practicing accepting advice and criticisms for a few months, throughout the creation of multiple essays. This last unit essay would call for me to research a topic of my choosing, as long as it related to creativity, and write a ten page paper about it. Sometimes leeway is overwhelming. With such broad criteria, it took me half the period we had to write the essay to even figure out what I was going to write about. I ended up choosing "the appeal behind

> In these paragraphs, the author comments further on the thinking behind her change in attitude and the results of that change.

> At this point the author provides even more support for her thesis by discussing another way that input from potential readers facilitated her writing processes.

Stephen King's work," even though I didn't want to. Several people had talked me into it. Into the construction of the essay, I started to notice where I could incorporate my love for psychology. I also enjoyed learning more about an author I had always been a fan of. This tedious, lengthy paper became something I was passionate in writing, and writing well. . . .

In "A Rule-Breaker's Writing Process," I also emphasized my hope that my tactic of saying "no" would fare as well for me in college as it did in high school. The bottom line is that it will not. If I hope to improve, I must first accept the opinions of others. I must say yes from time to time, because I am not right about everything; I still have plenty to learn. I don't think that I have necessarily improved much as a writer this semester. But I have developed an important attribute, open-mindedness toward others' criticisms, needed for improvement to be possible. This leads me to believe that I will only progress as a writer from here on out.

> The essay's conclusion circles back to the paper mentioned in the first paragraph and hammers home the thesis of the reflective introduction in different terms.

editing. As is explained in Chapter 23, when revising, you will concentrate on global issues such as focus, support, organization, and effective opening and closing strategies. When editing you will concentrate on surface issues, such as usage, punctuation, spelling, mechanics, and formatting.

A Word about Procrastination

As noted earlier, portfolio assessment offers the benefit of ample time to reflect on your writing processes and products for all your major projects so that you have the opportunity to reconsider and revise before your teacher grades them. Unfortunately, when writers have this kind of extended time to write, they don't always take advantage of it. In a portfolio system, the presumption is that you will think *throughout the semester* about papers you have already drafted (*while* you are learning more and more about writing) and that you will gradually make changes to improve their overall quality.

To capitalize on this opportunity, you will have to fight the tendency to **procrastinate,** or to leave all your revisions to the final week or two of the course, when you will also be responsible for generating your reflective introduction. If you do procrastinate, you will magnify your stress level by having to rush the processes associated with revision and portfolio assembly. Additionally, you will deny yourself the benefit of **incubation,** which depends on the intermittent review of problems you're working on as a way of feeding your subconscious mind so that it can make the kinds of creative leaps that lead to better writing. (See Chapter 2 for advice on facilitating productive incubation.)

E-Portfolios

Some composition courses built around portfolios require that they be submitted electronically. If your teacher expects you to compile an e-portfolio as opposed to a paper portfolio, he or she will clarify procedures for doing so that pertain to the course management software adopted by your school. Despite the fact that e-portfolios exist in electronic rather than paper form, a course that requires e-portfolios is based on the same instructional principles discussed in this chapter. The main difference is that digital venues provide unique possibilities for presenting your work. For example, you can create hot links between various papers in the portfolio to help readers process the connections you are making between them—or between a part of your paper and other online documents or images that will illuminate certain features of your texts. This capability allows you to influence the manner in which an audience will process your work.

If your writing class requires an e-portfolio, your teacher will familiarize you with hot-linking and other strategies associated with the software for presenting your essays in ways that emphasize their strengths. And in learning strategies for presenting coursework for your composition course in an e-portfolio, you will be practicing strategies that will help you present all sorts of materials in an e-portfolio that you might someday prepare for a job search. Indeed, many employers today invite e-portfolios from prospective employees as they allow for easy access and representation of a candidate's abilities through various media, including audio and video recordings.

Transfer across Writing Situations

Portfolios are long-standing staples of recognition and advancement within visually oriented fields, including graphic art, architecture, fashion design, interior design, sculpting, painting, and so on. In recent years, more professions (e.g., education, nursing, counseling, and computer science) have advocated that job seekers compile portfolios to supplement the limited information that can appear in a résumé and cover letter. Regardless of your major or the type of position you intend to pursue after graduating, having a portfolio available can enhance your chances of landing a job.

Depending on the discipline, a professional portfolio might contain a variety of visual artifacts. It might also contain a number of written pieces composed by you or by others who can attest to your qualifications. Figure 25.3 lists several types of documents that employers in a diversity of fields suggest that job hunters might want to include in their portfolios.

Documents Written by Portfolio Author	Supplemental Documents
Philosophy of your approach to the position	Evaluations from supervisors or previous employers
Copies of published articles or original presentations	Evidence of special certifications or licenses
Summaries of continuing education and professional development activities	Brochures from continuing education or professional development opportunities
Profiles of organizations or committees you may have served	Copies of agendas and minutes
Instructional materials for classes or seminars you've prepared	Feedback from participants in classes or seminars you've conducted
Applications for grants and summaries of research projects	Any other items documenting experiences that speak to your qualifications

Figure 25.3 **Possible written content for portfolios across professions**

As helpful as knowledge about portfolio assembly can be as you search for a job, it is by no means the only valuable skill that transfers from the experience of preparing a portfolio for your composition course. As mentioned previously, portfolio assessment highlights the role of reflection in composing. Through postwrites, you will regularly reflect on your composing experiences, starting with the first major writing project you tackle. And these postwrites become the cornerstones of a final, more deeply reflective exercise (i.e., your reflective introduction). As is discussed throughout this text, reflection is crucial not only to writing in general or writing across the college curriculum, but to all learning situations. Specifically, it allows you to take stock of what you already know, what you can already do, and how you can improve upon your strengths. When participating in a portfolio-based composition course, then, you enjoy a rich opportunity for refining your writing processes and products while regularly engaging in a vital critical-thinking strategy that will continue to serve you in college, your future career, and even your personal life.

ACTIVITY

Searching Your Course Papers for Themes   Pull out a piece of paper or open a file on your computer and title it "Possible Portfolio Themes." Next, gather all the writing you produced for this course, as well as all the feedback you have received. Begin reading through it—perhaps by units (e.g., all the materials relevant to a given essay assignment) or by type of task (e.g., invention exercises, essays, and peer reviews). Record any patterns you notice relevant to strengths in your writing, improvements you made, or persistent challenges you overcame in this course. Once you finish reading and taking notes, reflect on the list you created, searching for a theme that connects the papers to be submitted in your portfolio and that might become the thesis for your reflective introduction.

Photo Credits

Text and Line Art Credits

CHAPTER 6

Pages 79–80: Elizabeth Bernstein, "Sibling Rivalry Grows Up." Reprinted with permission of *The Wall Street Journal*. Copyright © 2012 Dow Jones & Company, Inc. All Rights Reserved Worldwide.

CHAPTER 7

Pages 89–90, 95: Maya Angelou, excerpts from *I Know Why the Caged Bird Sings* by Maya Angelou. Copyright © 1969 and renewed 1997 by Maya Angelou. Used by permission of Random House, an imprint and division of Random House, LLC. All rights reserved. **pp. 98–102:** Print rights reprinted by permission of the publisher from "Listening" in *One Writer's Beginnings* by Eudora Welty, pp. 5–11, Cambridge, Mass.: Harvard University Press. Copyright © 1983, 1984 by Eudora Welty. Digital rights reprinted by permission of Russell & Volkening as agents for the author. **pp. 102–107:** Richard Rodriguez, "The Hunger of Memory." From *Hunger of Memory: The Education of Richard Rodriguez* by Richard Rodriguez. Reprinted by permission of David R. Godine, Publisher, Inc. Copyright © 1982 by Richard Rodriguez.

CHAPTER 8

Pages 113–114: Sam Jaffe, "Steven Spielberg: The Storyteller." *BusinessWeek*, 7/13/98. Used with permission of Bloomberg, L.P. Copyright © 2014. All rights reserved. **pp. 119–122:** Erin Anderson, "From a Dream to Reality." Reprinted by permission of the author. **pp. 122–130:** Alan Riding, "Reinventing Rio: The dazzling but tarnished Brazilian city gets a makeover as it prepares for the 2014 World Cup and 2016 Olympic Games." *Smithsonian*, September 2010. © 2010. Reprinted by permission of the author.

CHAPTER 9

Pages 135–137: Mandi Jourdan, "The Wizard's Influence." Reprinted by permission of the author. **pp. 143–153:** Amy L. Gonzalez, M.A., and Jeffrey T. Hancock, Ph.D. "Mirror, Mirror on My Facebook Wall: Effects of Exposure to Facebook on Self-Esteem." *Cyberpsychology, Behavior, and Social Networking*, Vol. 14, No. 1–2. Copyright © 2011. Reprinted by permission. **pp. 153–160:** *The History and Psychology of Clowns Being Scary*. Copyright 2013 Smithsonian Institution. Reprinted with permission from Smithsonian Enterprises. All rights reserved. Reproduction in any medium is strictly prohibited without permission from Smithsonian Institution.

CHAPTER 10

Pages 166–167: Jessica Masri Eberhard, "An annotated bibliography of literature on the rhetoric of health and medicine." *Present Tense: A Journal of Rhetoric in Society*. Copyright © 2012. Reprinted by permission of the author. **pp. 173–174:** Nicholas

Kristof, "A Poverty Solution that Starts with a Hug." *The New York Times*, 1/8/2012. Copyright © 2012 The New York Times Company. All rights reserved. Used by permission and protected by the Copyright Laws of the United States. The printing, copying, redistribution, or retransmission of this content without express written permission is prohibited.

CHAPTER 12

Pages 202–203: Gail Godwin, "The Watcher at the Gates." Copyright (1995/2001) Gail Godwin. Reprinted by permission of John Hawkins & Associates, Inc. **pp. 204–205:** William Stafford, "A Way of Writing" from *Field: Contemporary Poetry and Poetics #2* (Spring 1970). Copyright © 1970 by Oberlin College. Reprinted with the permission of Oberlin College Press.

CHAPTER 13

Pages 210–211: "Black Holes: 9/11 Memorial" from *Slate* by Witold Rybczynski. Copyright © 2011 by Witold Rybczynski, originally appeared in *Slate*, used by permission of The Wylie Agency LLC. **pp. 217–218:** Paul Achter, "Is Team USA's Militaristic Uniform a Problem?" © Paul Achter. Reprinted by permission. **pp. 219–224:** Simon Arms, "The heritage of Berlin Street and graffiti scene." *Smashing Magazine*, July 13, 2011. Copyright © 2011. Reprinted by permission of Simon Arms and *Smashing Magazine*.

CHAPTER 14

Pages 241–245: Roy Peter Clark, "Why it worked: A rhetorical analysis of Obama's speech on race." *Poynter*, 4/1/08. Copyright © 2008. Reprinted by permission of the author.

CHAPTER 15

Pages 251–252, 265–275: Susan Amper, "Untold Story: The Lying Narrator in 'The Black Cat'." Copyright © 1992. Reprinted by permission of the author. **pp. 258–265:** Heidi Nielson, "'Neither Can Live While the Other Survives': The Driving Force of Revenge in *Harry Potter*," *Reason Papers*, Vol. 34, No. 1. Copyright © 2012. Reprinted with permission.

CHAPTER 16

Pages 282–283: David Steele, "Danger Lurks in a Biotech World." *The Aquarian Online*, Spring 2004. Copyright © 2004. Reprinted by permission of the author.

CHAPTER 17

Pages 293–295, 301–304: Whitney Elmore, "Exploring and Developing Stage Combat Methods." Reprinted by permission of the author. **pp. 304–307:** Matthew Warren, "Proposal: The Evolution of Ethics." Reprinted by permission of Matthew Warren.

CHAPTER 18

Pages 315–316: Roger Ebert's review of "The Wizard of Oz." Reprinted by permission of The Ebert Company. **p. 318:** Trevor Johnston. 150 word excerpt from review of "The Wizard of Oz." Reprinted by permission of Time Out London. **pp. 322–323:** Karen Sandstrom, "Gris Grimly's Frankenstein revisits, enhances Shelley's famous tale." Special to *The Plain Dealer*, 9/11/13. Copyright © 2013. Reprinted by permission of the author. **pp. 323–327:** Review of "Cosmos" by Chris Taylor. Copyright 2014. Mashable, Inc.

CHAPTER 19

Pages 333–334: Sheldon Krimsky, "Genetic enhancement of human embryos is not a practice for civil societies, argues a bioethicist." Copyright © 2013. Reprinted by permission of the author. **pp. 341–344:** David Mills, "Homeschooling's Liberalism." Institute of Religion and Public Life. © Reprinted by permission of the author. **pp. 344–346:** Becky Smith Conover, "Educating Girls Is Good Investment." *Charlotte Observer*, March 7, 2014. Copyright © 2014. Reprinted by permission of MCT Information Services.

CHAPTER 20

Page 347: Mike Peters © 2011. Distributed by King Features Syndicate, World Rights Reserved. **pp. 351–352:** Bill Cullins, "Club sport participation could solve childhood obesity epidemic." *GO San Angelo*, 1/14/13. Copyright © 2013. Reprinted by permission of Scripps Media, Inc. **pp. 359–366:** Po Bronson and Ashley Merryman, "The Creativity Crisis." First published in *Newsweek*. Copyright © 2010. Reprinted by permission of Curtis Brown, Ltd. **pp. 366–371:** Dan Froomkin, "It Can't Happen Here: Why Is There So Little Coverage of Americans Who Are Struggling with Poverty?" *Nieman Reports*, Winter 2013. Copyright © 2013. Reprinted with permission.

CHAPTER 21

Page 376: Scott Seider, "An educator's journey toward multiple intelligences." Originally published in *Edutopia*, 4/1/09. © Edutopia.org; George Lucas Educational Foundation. Reprinted with permission. **p. 379:** John Guillory, excerpt from "How Scholars Read" is reprinted by permission of the author.

CHAPTER 22

Page 396: "The Personal News Cycle: How Americans Choose to Get Their News." *American Press Institute*. http://www.americanpressinstitute.org/publications/reports/survey-research/personal-news-cycle/. Reprinted with permission. **p. 397:** Sonya Song, "Sharing Fast and Slow." Reprinted by permission of the author. **p. 398:** Screenshot from dupree.com. Reprinted with permission from Deloite Development, LLC. **p. 402:** 3 images from Smart Art. Used with permission of Microsoft.